THE ROUTLEDGE COMPANION
TO MEDIA AND ACTIVISM

The Routledge Companion to Media and Activism is a wide-ranging collection of 42 original and authoritative essays by leading contributors from a variety of academic disciplines.

Introducing and exploring central debates about the diverse relationships between both media and protest, and communication and social change, the book offers readers a reliable and informed guide to understanding how media and activism influence one another. The expert contributors examine the tactics and strategies of protest movements, and how activists organize themselves and each other; they investigate the dilemmas of media coverage and the creation of alternative media spaces and platforms; and they emphasize the importance of creativity and art in social change.

Bringing together case studies and contributors from six continents, the collection is organized around themes that address past, present and future developments from around the world. *The Routledge Companion to Media and Activism* is an essential reference and guide for those who want to understand this vital area.

Graham Meikle is Professor of Communication and Digital Media at the University of Westminster in London. His other books include *Social Media: Communication, Sharing and Visibility* and *Future Active: Media Activism and the Internet*.

THE ROUTLEDGE COMPANION TO MEDIA AND ACTIVISM

Edited by Graham Meikle

LONDON AND NEW YORK

First published 2018
by Routledge
2 Park Square, Milton Park, Abingdon, Oxon OX14 4RN

and by Routledge
711 Third Avenue, New York, NY 10017

Routledge is an imprint of the Taylor & Francis Group, an informa business

British Library Cataloguing-in-Publication Data
A catalogue record for this book is available from the British Library

Library of Congress Cataloguing-in-Publication Data
A catalog record for this book has been requested

ISBN: 978-1-138-20203-0 (hbk)
ISBN: 978-1-315-47505-9 (ebk)

Typeset in Bembo
by Deanta Global Publishing Services, Chennai, India

CONTENTS

v

Contents

CONTRIBUTORS

Miriyam Aouragh is a senior lecturer at the University of Westminster, London. Her PhD focused on the implications of the internet during the Second Intifada (University of Amsterdam) and her postdoctoral work (Oxford Internet Institute) concerned the political role of internet technologies for grassroots activists in Lebanon. A more recent project (Leverhulme) was about digital infrastructures and the Arab uprisings.

Chris Atton is Professor of Media and Culture at Edinburgh Napier University, Scotland. His books include *Alternative Media* (Sage, 2002), *Alternative Journalism* (Sage, 2009) and the *Routledge Companion to Alternative and Community Media* (Routledge, 2015). He is co-founder of the *Journal of Alternative and Community Media*.

Veronica Barassi is a lecturer and the convenor of the BA Anthropology and Media degree in the Department of Media and Communications, Goldsmiths University of London. Her work has appeared in top-ranked international journals and she is the author of *Activism on the Web: Everyday Struggles against Digital Capitalism* (Routledge, 2015).

Red Chidgey is Lecturer in Gender and Media at the Department of Culture, Media and Creative Industries, King's College London. Her research interests lie in the intersection of protest, material culture, gender and memory. Her monograph *Feminist Afterlives: Feminist Memory in Postfeminist Times* is forthcoming with Palgrave Macmillan.

Samantha Close is an assistant professor of Communication at DePaul University, Chicago. Her research proceeds through both writing and the creative production of film and comics. It focuses particularly on transforming models of creative industries, labour and capitalism.

Steve Collins is a senior lecturer in the Department of Media, Music, Communication and Cultural Studies at Macquarie University, Sydney. His research focuses on the music industry and the intersections of copyright law, fair use and creativity.

Sasha Costanza-Chock (pronouns: they/them) is a scholar, activist, and media-maker. They are currently Associate Professor of Civic Media at MIT, Massachusetts. Their work focuses on social movements, media justice and community-led design. More: http://schock.cc.

Donatella della Porta is Dean of the Institute of Humanities and Social Sciences at the Scuola Normale Superiore, Florence, where she directs the Center on Social Movement Studies (Cosmos) and the ERC project Mobilizing for Democracy on civil society participation in democratization processes in Europe, the Middle East, Asia and Latin America.

Lina Dencik (PhD, Goldsmiths) is Senior Lecturer at the School of Journalism, Media and Cultural Studies at Cardiff University, Wales. She is the author of *Media and Global Civil Society* (Palgrave Macmillan, 2012); co-author, with Peter Wilkin, of *Worker Resistance and Media* (Peter Lang, 2015); and co-editor, with Oliver Leistert, of *Critical Perspectives on Social Media and Protest* (Rowman & Littlefield, 2015).

John D. H. Downing is author of *Radical Media* (second edition 2001) and editor of the *Encyclopedia of Social Movement Media* (Sage, 2011). He has taught at universities in Greenwich, Massachusetts, the City of New York, Texas and Southern Illinois, and in China, Denmark, Finland, France, Mexico, Qatar and Turkey.

Jesse Drew, Professor of Cinema and Digital Media at the University of California at Davis, researches working-class alternative and community media. His recent book is *A Social History of Contemporary Democratic Media* (Routledge, 2013).

Ricarda Drüeke is Assistant Professor in the Department of Communication at the University of Salzburg, Austria. Her main areas of research are theories of the public sphere, gender media studies, and social movements and protest.

Stephen Duncombe is an activist and Professor of Media and Culture at New York University. With Steve Lambert, he is co-founder and co-director of the Center for Artistic Activism: http://artisticactivism.org.

Katie Ellis is Senior Research Fellow in Internet Studies at Curtin University, Perth. She has published six books addressing various aspects of disability and the media and is series editor of *Routledge Research in Disability and Media Studies*.

Victoria Esteves is a doctoral researcher at the University of Stirling, Scotland. Her research focuses on the circulation of participatory cultures online, specifically how internet memes are remixed and circulated, and how subsequently they gain social and political meaning.

Anna Feigenbaum is a co-author of *Protest Camps* (Zed, 2013) and author of *Tear Gas* (Verso, 2017). Her writing can be found in a variety of academic and media outlets including *The Guardian*, *The Atlantic* and *Open Democracy*.

Natalie Fenton is Professor of Media and Communications at Goldsmiths, University of London. Her latest publications include *Digital, Political, Radical* (Polity, 2016); *Misunderstanding the Internet* (Routledge, 2012, 2016) (with James Curran and Des Freedman); and *New Media, Old News* (Sage, 2010). She is also an activist and is on the Board of Directors of *Hacked Off* and a founding member of the *Media Reform Coalition*.

Gary Foley, professor, actor, activist and esteemed academic historian, was a key member of the Aboriginal Black Power movement and was a critical figure in establishing the Aboriginal Tent

Embassy of 1972. He has been at the centre of major political activities in Australia for more than 40 years.

Christian Fuchs is a professor at the University of Westminster, London. He is co-editor of the journal *tripleC: Communication, Capitalism & Critique* (http://www.triple-c.at). His research focuses on critical theory and the critical study of the role of media, communication(s) and the internet in society: http://fuchs.uti.at.

Gerard Goggin is Professor of Media and Communications, University of Sydney. Gerard was introduced to disability media activism in the early 1990s, working for an Australian technology and consumer rights NGO. His books include *Digital Disability* (Rowman & Littlefield, 2003), *Disability and the Media* (Palgrave, 2015), *Routledge Companion to Disability and the Media* (Routledge, 2018) and *Voices of Democracy: Listening to Disability* (Routledge, 2018).

Andrew Green is currently Early Career Lecturer at the University of the West of Scotland's School of Media, Culture and Society, having been awarded his doctorate in Ethnomusicology by Royal Holloway, University of London in 2016. His research focuses on music and politics in Mexico, and he has work published and forthcoming in peer-reviewed journals, including *Popular Music, Popular Music and Society*, and *Ethnomusicology Forum*.

Arne Hintz is a senior lecturer at Cardiff University, Wales, where he leads the MA Digital Media and Society, and co-directs the Data Justice Lab. His publications include, among others, *Beyond WikiLeaks* (Palgrave Macmillan, 2013) and *Digital Citizenship in a Datafied World* (Polity, 2018).

Edwina Howell completed her PhD in Anthropology on the activist strategies of the Black Power Movement through the life of Gary Foley in 2013. She has now worked with Professor Foley for over a decade.

Athina Karatzogianni is Associate Professor at the University of Leicester. Her research focuses on the intersections between digital media theory and political economy for the study of the use of digital technologies by social movements, protest and insurgency groups: http://www2.le.ac.uk/departments/media/people/dr-athina-karatzogianni.

Anastasia Kavada is Senior Lecturer in the Westminster School of Media, Arts & Design at the University of Westminster, London. She is co-leader of the MA in Media, Campaigning and Social Change, and Deputy Director of the Communication and Media Research Institute (CAMRI).

Joe F. Khalil is Associate Professor in Residence at Northwestern University in Qatar. He is engaged in researching questions of youth cultures, alternative media and media industries in the Arab world. He authored a policy monograph on Arab satellite entertainment television and public diplomacy and is also a co-author of *Arab Television Industries* (Palgrave Macmillan, 2009).

Steve Lambert is an artist and Associate Professor of New Media at the State University of New York, College at Purchase. With Stephen Duncombe, he is co-founder and co-director of the Center for Artistic Activism: http://artisticactivism.org.

Oliver Leistert works at Leuphana University of Lüneburg. He was awarded a PhD in 2013, and was the winner of the *Surveillance & Society* book award in 2014. His main interests include algorithms, sociality, affect and media. He co-edited (with Lina Dencik) *Critical Perspectives on Social Media and Protest: Between Control and Emancipation* (Rowman & Littlefield, 2015).

Leah A. Lievrouw is a professor in the Department of Information Studies at the University of California, Los Angeles. Her research focuses on the relationship between digital/new media technologies and social change. She is the author of *Alternative and Activist New Media* (Polity, 2011; second edition in preparation).

Geert Lovink is a media theorist, internet critic and author of *Dark Fiber* (MIT Press, 2002), *Zero Comments* (Routledge, 2007), *Networks Without a Cause* (Polity Press, 2012) and *Social Media Abyss* (Polity Press, 2016). He is the founder of the Institute of Network Cultures at the Amsterdam University of Applied Sciences and a professor at the European Graduate School (Saas-Fee/Malta) where he supervises PhD students.

Mark McLelland is Professor of Gender and Sexuality Studies at the University of Wollongong and a former Toyota Visiting Professor of Japanese at the University of Michigan. He is author or editor of over 10 books, most recently *The End of Cool Japan: Ethical, Legal and Cultural Challenges to Japanese Popular Culture* (Routledge, 2016).

André Mesquita, PhD in Social History, is a researcher and the author of *Insurgências poéticas: arte ativista e ação coletiva* (Annablume, 2011) and *Esperar não é saber: arte entre o silêncio e a evidência* (Funarte, 2015), and co-author of *Desinventario: esquirlas de Tucumán Arde en el archivo de Graciela Carnevale* (Ocho Libros, 2015).

Noureddine Miladi is Associate Professor of Media and Communication at Qatar University and former Head of Department of Mass Communication. He is co-author of *Media and Crises: The Art of Manipulation, Misinformation and Propaganda* (Al-Falah Books, ed. 2015, in Arabic) and *Mapping the Al Jazeera Phenomenon 20 Years On* (Al Jazeera Centre for Studies, ed. 2016). He is editor of the *Journal of Arab and Muslim Media Research*.

Toby Miller is Research Professor of the Graduate Division, University of California, Riverside; Sir Walter Murdoch Professor of Cultural Policy Studies, Murdoch University, Perth; Profesor Invitado, Escuela de Comunicación Social, Universidad del Norte, Colombia; Professor of Journalism, Media and Cultural Studies, Cardiff University/Prifysgol Caerdydd, Wales; and Director of the Institute for Media and Creative Industries, Loughborough University London.

Maria Miranda is an artist and, since 2013, an Australian Research Council (DECRA) Research Fellow at Victorian College of the Arts, University of Melbourne. Her publications include *Unsitely Aesthetics: Uncertain Practices in Contemporary Art* (Errant Bodies Press, 2013).

Bruce Mutsvairo is Associate Professor in Journalism Innovation at University of Technology Sydney. He studies citizen participation and digital activism in sub-Saharan Africa. He completed his PhD at Leiden University, the Netherlands.

Norie Neumark is a theorist and artist (www.out-of-sync.com). Her monograph *Voicetracks: Attuning to Voice in Media and the Arts* (MIT Press, 2017) explores voice and new materialism. She is Honorary Professorial Fellow at VCA, Melbourne; Emeritus Professor at La Trobe University, Melbourne; and founding editor of *Unlikely: Journal for Creative Arts* (http://unlikely.net.au).

Zizi Papacharissi, PhD, is Professor and Head of Communication at the University of Illinois at Chicago. She is also editor of the *Journal of Broadcasting and Electronic Media*, and founding and current editor of *Social Media & Society*.

Elena Pavan is Assistant Professor at the Institute of Humanities and Social Sciences of the Scuola Normale Superiore, Florence. Her interdisciplinary work addresses both theoretically and methodologically the nexus between collective action/political participation and digital media.

Camilla Møhring Reestorff is Associate Professor and Leader of Center for Cultural Participation at Aarhus University. She is editor of *Conjunctions:Transdisciplinary Journal of Cultural Participation* and author of *Culture War: Affective Cultural Politics, Tepid Nationalism and Art Activism* (Intellect Ltd, 2017).

Sandra Ristovska is an Assistant Professor in Media Studies at the College for Media, Communication and Information at the University of Colorado Boulder. A scholar and a film-maker, she examines issues about media activism, human rights, visual epistemologies and evidence.

Ned Rossiter is Professor of Communication at Western Sydney University. He is the author of *Organized Networks: Media Theory, Creative Labour, New Institutions* (NAi Publications, 2006) and *Software, Infrastructure, Labor: A Media Theory of Logistical Nightmares* (Routledge, 2016).

Adrienne Russell is Mary Laird Wood Professor of Communication at University of Washington, Seattle. She is author of *Journalism as Activism: Recoding Media Power* (Polity Press, 2016), and co-editor of *Journalism and the NSA Revelations: Privacy, Security and the Press* (I.B. Tauris & Co., 2017).

Sean Scalmer teaches history at the University of Melbourne. He has written several books on the history of social movements and political campaigning, and he is the co-editor of the journal *Moving the Social*.

Frances Shaw (PhD, UNSW) is an honorary associate at the University of Sydney. Her research interests include feminist digital activism, harassment and cyberbullying, the ethics and politics of digital healthcare, and online supportive networks.

Yngvar B. Steinholt, Associate Professor, teaches Russian culture, literature, history and society at Institute of Language and Culture, UiT – Arctic University of Norway. His research spans Soviet and post-Soviet popular music, contemporary Russian art activism and sonic representations of Russia.

John Street is a professor of politics at the University of East Anglia. He is the author of several books, including *Music and Politics* (Polity, 2012) and (with Sanna Inthorn and Martin Scott) *From Entertainment to Citizenship: Politics and Popular Culture* (Manchester University Press, 2013).

Zixue Tai is an associate professor in the College of Communication and Information Media at the University of Kentucky. His primary area of research pertains to the social, political and cultural ramifications of the new media sector in China.

Anamaria Tamayo-Duque is a lecturer in the Institute for Media and Creative Industries, Loughborough University London and Assistant Professor in the Dance and Theater Department, Universidad de Antioquia, Colombia. She has a BA in Anthropology from the Universidad de Antioquia and a PhD in Critical Dance Studies from the University of California, Riverside.

Emiliano Treré is a lecturer at the School of Journalism, Media and Culture at Cardiff University, Wales. He has published extensively on the challenges, the opportunities, and the myths of media technologies for social movements and political parties in Europe and Latin America.

Meggan Taylor Trevey is a PhD candidate in the Department of Political Science at the University of Illinois at Chicago. She studies political communication, political psychology and democracy.

Peter Wilkin (PhD, Southampton) is Reader in the School of Social Sciences at Brunel University London. He is the author of *The Political Economy of Global Communication* (Pluto Press, 2001) and co-editor, with Mark Lacy, of *Global Politics in the Information Age* (Manchester University Press, 2006). He has more recently published *Worker Resistance and Media* with Lina Dencik (Peter Lang, 2015) and *Hungary's Crisis of Democracy* (Lexington Books, 2016).

Elke Zobl is Associate Professor in the Department of Communication and head of the program area Contemporary Arts and Cultural Production, a cooperation for science and art between the University of Salzburg and the Mozarteum University Salzburg.

ACKNOWLEDGEMENTS

Thanks to Chris Atton, Victoria Esteves, Natalie Foster, Athina Karatzogianni and Ana Maria Pineda.

Special thanks to Fin, Rosie and Lola for letting me do another book.

INTRODUCTION
Making meanings and making trouble

Graham Meikle

Let's begin by thinking of an image. You can call up the picture either in your memory or on your screen. It's the photo of Ieshia Evans, a young nurse from Pennsylvania, confronting two armoured policemen at a demonstration in Baton Rouge, Louisiana in July 2016. In the right of the photo, Evans stands serene and still, her summer dress fluttering in the breeze, as upright and undeniable as a stop sign. In the left of the image, standing in front of her, are the two riot police – and behind them in the background scores more – plated with great layers of body armour, helmeted and visored, armed for battle. And yet each of these cops seems off balance, the camera catching them with their feet in motion, as though they are being lifted off the ground and borne back by some unseen force.

Evans had travelled to join the protests against the fatal shooting by police of Alton Sterling, one of the unending line of African American victims of excessive police force, whose death, like so many others, had been captured on mobile phone video and shared across both social media and the established news. The increased visibility of such deaths through social media had led to the emergence of #BlackLivesMatter, a distributed movement with little in the way of formal leadership hierarchy – perhaps more a series of moments than a movement, but moments with a powerful shared name for aggregating outrage and attention, for expressing resistance and unity and for bringing together the personal and the public.

The picture of Ieshia Evans captures the spirit of non-violent protest, of civil disobedience and of the moral force of political resistance. And as a metonymic image of #BlackLivesMatter, it also captures some central dimensions of social movement organization in the early twenty-first century. But note that what caught the attention of so many people in this case was not the participation of one young woman in a street protest, but rather that extraordinary photograph of her participation. What counted was the *mediation* of that moment of activism. Taken by professional photographer Jonathan Bachman and distributed across the planet by Reuters, the picture demonstrates the continued importance of established media for the diffusion of images of activism, and it illustrates the importance of framing and selection in how activist interventions are offered to distant viewers.

Some months after the photo became famous, the moment that it depicts was co-opted by Pepsi for a risible commercial featuring reality TV star Kendall Jenner handing a soft drink to a cop at a demonstration. This recuperation of a protest against police violence in order to sell Pepsi was self-evidently grotesque, and the commercial was quickly withdrawn. But it illustrates the dilemmas of relying on the established media to communicate activist perspectives. Jenner's image was also quickly incorporated into a great many memes by social media users who remixed her into new contexts – marching alongside Martin Luther King, confronting the tanks in Tiananmen Square. These vernacular digital images point to a further dimension of media activism – the uses of everyday creativity for self-expression and political commentary, and the ways in which these activist arts circulate across networks, offering alternative perspectives on the media and political mix of the moment.

The relationships between media and social movements are at the heart of this book, and the image of Ieshia Evans shows just how complex these can be. Here, then, in the image of this young woman staring down the riot squad, are the central themes of this book about media and activism – the strategies and logics of social movements and other kinds of protest organization; the uses and abuses of the media in communicating political contention; the tactics and strategies of activism and civil disobedience; the affordances of digital communication technologies; and the importance of creativity, self-expression and art in activism.

The Routledge Companion to Media and Activism offers 42 chapters that explore and analyze how media and communications are used in campaigns and movements for social and cultural change. Communication is always bound up with such changes. Media always offer – or impose – spaces in which both citizens and governments work out the social structures through which a given society is to be organized. They also provide spaces for the cultural responses that manifest how people feel about those social structures. They make possible both the circulation of information and the formation of movements, the making of meanings and the making of trouble.

This book's approach to definitions of both *media* and *activism* is pragmatic and inclusive. *Media* is taken here to refer to the widest range of communications systems through which meanings are proposed, shared and made visible to others. The book tries not to privilege any one such system, although many contributors do discuss aspects of networked digital media. Alongside these, there is also room for discussion of activist uses of music, craft and graffiti, as well as the more established media repertoires of print and broadcasting. *Activism* is taken here to include the widest range of attempts to effect social or cultural change; this need not exclude work done within established political parties or systems, but the primary emphasis throughout this book is instead on events, campaigns, projects and movements that attempt to influence the sphere of representational politics from outside that sphere's parties and systems.

The themes invoked so far are developed further in this introductory chapter: the next three sections sketch some of the conceptual terrain of the collection; the subsequent sections of the introduction outline the organization and concerns of the book's seven parts. These seven parts should be seen as heuristic rather than as hard and fast divisions. Chapters have been arranged to highlight both common ground and counterpoints, and the different sections do not claim separate domains. Instead, themes and sub-themes travel and echo across the book, and the reader will no doubt make their own connections between ideas as they read.

Movements and moments, tactics and strategies

Social movements are a distinctively modern phenomenon. There have always been crowds, uprisings, insurrections, revolutions – but the social movement as a vehicle for political contention is more recent (Tilly & Tarrow 2015). It emerged at the same time as the beginnings of modern media systems. Anti-slavery abolitionists made use of newspaper ads, pamphlets and the postal service; labour movements established their own newspapers. As photography and telegraphy, then telephony, radio, cinema, television and the internet emerged, social movements found ways to use these. Newsreel footage of Suffragettes can still shock, a century on; audio recording of Martin Luther King can still electrify and galvanize, half a century after his death; and shaky mobile phone video of police violence shared across Facebook can turn disparate individuals into a collective voice.

Mediated communication is central to what Tilly and Tarrow define as a social movement's core activities: 'a sustained campaign of claim making, using repeated performances that advertise the claim, based on organizations, networks, traditions, and solidarities that sustain these activities' (2015: 11). Social movements stage performances – such as demonstrations – of their worthiness, unity, numbers and commitment, or 'WUNC', as some scholars have it (Tilly & Wood 2013). This concept implies the *mediation* of those qualities. Images and stories about the claims and the claimants, the collective identity and the adversary, the demonstrations of WUNC – all need to be mediated in order to influence others. Collective action, as Melucci (1996: 9, my emphasis) observed, 'by the sheer fact of its existence, represents in its very form and models of organization *a message broadcast* to the rest of society'. The connections between media and activism are fundamental.

And yet researchers who write about social movements have not always emphasized this. At times, reading the social movement literature, one is left to wonder how those movements ever got anything done without, apparently, giving much attention to communication. To take just one leading example, the third edition of Tilly and Wood's (2013) major textbook *Social Movements 1768–2012,* grants 'movements and media' a little under five pages. It is, in John Downing's (2001: 26) words, 'on the edge of being weird that there is so little systematic analysis of communication or media in the social movement literature'. So the present collection takes this crucial nexus between media and activism as its starting point.

What tactics and strategies do social movements and other activists, whether individuals, organizations or crowds, use to try to achieve their goals? The ideas available for use in a given place at a given time are, in Tilly's famous phrase, *repertoires of contention* (1986). Gene Sharp (1973) created a landmark taxonomy of no fewer than 198 tactics that appear in such repertoires, from the uses of symbols to various kinds of non-cooperation. Contemporary repertoires comprise often very familiar approaches – demonstrations, boycotts, strikes, occupations – as well as newer tactics that build upon existing concepts: the digital Distributed Denial of Service attack as a variation of a sit-in; social media doxxing as an update of outing; the leaking of massive caches of digital data as a contemporary form of whistleblowing; hashtags and retweets as an extension of the principle of the petition. So contentious politics involve drawing on inherited tactics and strategies as well as devising new ones (Tilly & Tarrow 2015: 7).

A repertoire of tactics is a way of connecting people within and to a movement, and may offer opportunities to publicize, organize and mobilize a constituency. A widely recognized political gesture such as a demonstration can be communicated very simply: as Tilly observes, 'people know the general rules of performance more or less well and vary the performance to meet the purpose at hand' (1986: 390). A tactic may emerge from local experience and be passed down through time, which enables it to suggest symbolic connections to previous social movements (della Porta & Diani 2006: 182). Civil disobedience, for instance – the deliberate breaking of an unjust law – allows a movement to connect back through time to Thoreau, to Gandhi, and to Martin Luther King (King 2000: 433), who paid tribute to Thoreau's 'legacy of creative protest'.

But this invoking of the familiar approach can also close down possibilities for action, as the very familiarity of an existing tactic works to undermine its capacity to bring about real influence (Tilly 1986: 4). In this way, *repertoires* of contention can degrade into *rituals* of contention, in which the known limitations and tacit rules of engagement normalize the protest gesture. Stephen Duncombe describes this phenomenon in reflecting on the ritual elements of a protest demo:

> Leaders organize a 'mass' demonstration. We march. We chant. Speakers are paraded onto the dais to tell us (in screeching voices through bad sound systems) what we already know. Sometimes we sit down and let the police arrest us. We hope the mainstream media puts us on the news for five seconds. Sometimes they do; often they don't.
>
> *Duncombe 2007: 69*

Steve Kurtz of Critical Art Ensemble (1995) has made a similar observation:

> It got to the point in New York in the late 1980s where the cops were just letting ACT UP protesters be as disobedient as they wanted. When a demo appeared, they would close off the street, and just wait for them to go home. The protesters were not even worth arresting any more.
>
> *Interviewed in Meikle 2002: 146*

But repertoires can change. Indeed, they have to, in order to address altered circumstances. In an important historical analysis, Tilly (1986) shows how the protest repertoire of French workers changed with the transition to industrialized capitalism. They developed protest tactics that were more suited to intervention at the national level than at the provincial. So in our own time, what repertoires and what forms of organization do we see emerging that engage at the global level, with transnational corporations, neoliberal governments, supra-national networks, and with planet-spanning digital communication platforms? This question is answered in many different ways in the chapters that follow; the essays in Part 4, in particular, explore different aspects of an emerging repertoire of tactics of mediated visibility for online environments: the inversion of surveillance, the globalization of witnessing, the exposure of data, the seizing of visual attention.

Social movements change, just as their repertoires of action do. Della Porta (2015: 17) offers a useful historical taxonomy of the changing dimensions of social movements: *old social movements,* rooted in class identity; what were once called the *new social movements* of identity politics; the Global Justice Movement of the late 1990s and early 2000s, with its plural identities and class coalitions; and the anti-austerity movements sparked by the global financial crisis of 2008 onwards – waves of collective, grassroots politics rooted in precarious economic and social conditions. These first manifested in citizen mobilizations in Tunisia, and then across the Arab world; in Iceland and then across Europe; and in New York, from where the Occupy movement briefly diffused across the whole US and around many parts of the globe (Castells 2015; Gerbaudo 2017). Anti-austerity impulses would later find dark expression in the electoral politics of countries including the UK, with Brexit, and the US, with Trump.

The uses and abuses of media

If activists and social movements must engage with the media, this means the *news* media above all. James Carey's observation (1989: 87) that reality is 'a scarce resource […] there to be struggled over' retains its force in the digital era. Those news media are in that struggle, in the business of defining reality – of telling their publics those things that the media have decided matter the most; of suggesting the concerns that should be on the minds of their publics; of selecting, framing and interpreting; of turning events into news, which are not the same thing. The symbolic power of the news is about 'making people see and believe' (Bourdieu 1991: 170). Its activities – naming, defining, endorsing, persuading – are attempts to influence others through the exercise of symbolic power (Thompson 1995).

For activists, the media might confer legitimacy or increase the visibility of a message; they might assist in drawing increased numbers to a cause or in bearing witness to an event. But they might also stereotype or demonize, and they offer opportunities, not only for activists to draw new supporters, but also for their opponents and authorities to learn about a movement and perhaps identify its leaders, its participants or its weaknesses. Dealing with the news media means dealing with their preferences for certain types of narrative and story-structure, means dealing with their dependence on visual images and their emphasis on speed and immediacy, means dealing with their reliance on representing authority through official perspectives and interpretations.

These converge in what Scalmer has called 'the dilemmas of the activist' (2002: 41). In Scalmer's analysis, these dilemmas are threefold. First, activists must garner media attention and be reported if their cause is to register with the broader public. Second, such media attention becomes more likely the more disruptive or violent the activist gesture. Third, any coverage in the media of disruptive or violent collective actions will inevitably simplify and perhaps stereotype, meaning that the specifics of a message are unlikely to be communicated through the established media in a way that activists might wish. And yet, trying to avoid these dilemmas risks going unheard: as Castells argues, outside the media sphere, there is, in political terms, nothing but marginality (2004: 370).

One kind of response to these dilemmas is to try to change the media – to influence policy and regulation, to call for access and standards, to affect the media's contexts as well as their contents, through media policy activism, boycotts or lobbying. In the UK, the Stop Funding Hate project (https://stopfundinghate.org.uk) is a powerful example of such approaches: it aims to pressure companies into not advertising their products or services in those national daily newspapers that have run *de facto* campaigns against immigrants for years. A number of the contributions to this collection, particularly those grouped as Part 6, discuss other such approaches to changing the media.

A different kind of response is to create alternative media. There is a long tradition of critical analysis of the social uses of media and of the potentials for different kinds of communication and power relations that could be achieved if audiences became producers or more active participants. These traditions include such figures as Walter Benjamin (1978) [1934], Bertolt Brecht (1993) [1932], Guy Debord (Debord & Wolman 2009) [1956] and Hans Magnus Enzensberger (2003) [1970], each of whom called in different ways and different decades for more participatory engagement in the public spaces of mediated communication. Approaches to this have been conceptualized in various ways that include *radical* media (Downing 2001), *alternative* media (Atton 2002, 2015), *tactical* media (Garcia & Lovink 1997), *citizens'* media (Rodriguez 2001), *community* media (Rennie 2006), *social movement* media (Downing 2011) and *democratic* media (Drew 2013).

The themes and concerns of these different discourses vary – the nature of media content, the organizational strategies, the discourses of professionalism and amateurism, the political economy, the distribution methods, the uses of technologies, the political orientations, and the aesthetics of such media have all been explored (some of this work, such as Downing's *Radical Media,* manages to address all of these). But at the heart of each of these discourses is the question of participation. For Atton (2002: 4), for example, alternative media involve 'offering the means for democratic communication to people who are normally excluded from media production'. Such participation is sometimes argued to be a political outcome in itself, and so should be understood not only in its capacity to effect political change but also 'in terms of the transformative processes [citizens' media] bring about within participants and their communities' (Rodriguez 2002: 79). Such debates animate many of the essays in this collection, especially in Part 5.

Activist arts and everyday creativity

Artists, of course, often engage with politics. We might think of Goya's *The Third of May* 1808, or of the Dadaist photomontages of Hannah Höch or John Heartfield, or of Picasso's *Guernica*, or of Ai Weiwei's curious decision of 2016 to recreate the famous photo of drowned toddler refugee Alan Kurdi with the artist himself posing as the child. But the sphere of activist art is not just that of such global names. Artists often bring political concerns into their creative work, but so too do activists often bring elements of everyday creativity and personal expression into their political concerns (Bradley & Esche 2007; Weibel 2015). The material fabric of political contention is often central to a given campaign. The London V&A museum's 2014–15 exhibition *Disobedient Objects* highlighted this in curating material representations of global protest events – pots and pans repurposed as drums for demonstrations; blockade tripods fashioned from salvaged scaffolding; coins defaced with political slogans to be passed from hand to hand in daily interactions (Flood & Grindon 2014). Haircuts, knitting, dancing and gardening can all constitute media for the communication of contention (Downing 2001; Duncombe 2002). The essays in Part 3 of this book especially engage with different aspects of activist arts and everyday creativity.

An important discourse around the turn of the century was that of *tactical media* (Garcia & Lovink 1997; Meikle 2008). This involved artistic media activism that exploited the possibilities of new communication technologies; that emphasized mobility and transience, impermanence and reinvention; that was often satirical; and that often involved the reworking, reimagining or remixing of found material. Tactical media relations were almost by definition asymmetrical. So these can of course be seen as 'weapons of the weak' (Scott 1985) or as the 'art of the weak' (de Certeau 1984: 37). But there need be nothing weak about those weapons or that art.

The remixing of found material for satirical political ends is often a part of the related discourse of culture jamming (Dery 1993; DeLaure & Fink 2017). Culture jamming is the practice of turning a sign into a question mark, and *jamming* can be understood both as obstruction (as in traffic) and as collaborative improvisation (as in music) (Meikle 2007). Remix strategies for political ends have long artistic pre-histories (Sussman 1989, Evans 2009, McLeod & Kuenzli 2011). But the rise of social media platforms has made the cut-and-paste aesthetics of culture jamming into everyday interaction for many millions of people. Social media are those that allow any user, in principle, to say and make things, and to share the things they have said and made. The daily logic of social media use involves editing and remixing images – through filters and effects – and setting found material – links, images, videos – in new contexts.

And yet those same platforms are by no means an ideal environment for political engagement, operating as they do on a triple logic of surveillance: on the first level, users watch and perform for each other, and at times for unknown others; on the second level, social media firms monitor and archive this behaviour, turning it into commercial data; and on the third level, governments, as confirmed by Edward Snowden, surveil all of this. Zuckerman's (2015) 'cute cat' theory of digital activism argues that a platform developed to let users share cute cat pictures, as can be said more or less seriously of many leading social media, will likely be more robust, user-friendly and impervious to censorship than one developed by activists with fewer resources. But this idea runs into the wall of this triple logic of surveillance (indeed Zuckerman himself was involved in inventing the pop-up web ad, the tracking of which made surveillance into the dominant internet business model). Many of the essays in this collection, especially those in Part 7, assess the limitations, as well as the opportunities, of social media and related contemporary digital developments.

So what does this environment offer activists? One answer to this involves a rethinking of the central social movement concepts of *collective* identity and action (Melucci 1996; Castells 2004; della Porta and Diani 2006, 2015). Bennett and Segerberg (2013) argue that many contemporary political phenomena involve not collective, but *connective* action. This is a more personalized and fluid category than those forms of collective action that were associated with much twentieth-century politics and that involved stable organizations or affiliations such as those around political parties, churches or trade unions. Connective action, they write, 'uses broadly inclusive, easily personalized action frames as a basis for technology-assisted networking' (2013: 2). For example, a personalized frame such as #MeToo enabled a great many people to connect with its underlying concept of sexual harassment. It was also a frame for which *communication* was central, with Twitter and Facebook offering resources for individuals to connect their experiences and perspectives with others in shared networks.

Connective action is above all about the personalization of politics. Social media are characterized by the convergence of public media and personal communication (Meikle 2016), and connective action is a political phenomenon of this communications environment. Connective action, in Bennett and Segerberg's analysis, can be enabled by *organizations*, driving causes and suggesting frames within which individuals are invited to situate themselves; or it can be enabled by *crowds*, as networked individuals coalesce and develop ways of coordinating resources and demands, with little or no formal organization (2013: 47). Of course, these organizations and these crowds can also manifest collective identities at the same time: there is no reason to think that the connective has *replaced* the collective, and the concepts are best understood as complementary. Identity is fluid and multiple, a kind of narrative in that it assigns shape and meaning to behaviour and events, and questions of collective and connective identity animate many of the essays in this book, in particular those in Part 2.

Part I: Themes

Part 1 of the book brings together six chapters that map out much of the ground explored in subsequent sections. These essays lay out central themes and explore these with a shared emphasis on assessing the lessons of history in contemporary perspective. We begin with a chapter by John D. H. Downing, who sets contemporary media activism in historical context, and emphasizes the continuities as well as the transformations that emerge. As in his landmark book *Radical Media,* Downing draws a great diversity of media forms together on a concise canvas, making connections between past and present across print, screen, music and mobile media. His chapter asks how we are to connect pasts and presents, places and sites, and he offers examples that are alert to both historical resonance and contemporary possibilities.

As noted above, mediated communication has not always been given the attention it deserves in social movement studies. This makes the chapter by Donatella della Porta and Elena Pavan especially important, because it synthesizes many of those ways in which media *have* been understood for activist communication; they also discuss the literature on alternative media, noting how these not only provide new forums and information but at the same time enact a critique of the established media. This essay both looks back at how established media and communication systems have been theorized in relation to social movements, and also discusses more contemporary approaches to the relationships between movements and networked digital media. Della Porta and Pavan explore the uses of digital media for social movement organization, for the development of new forms of collective identity, and for the rethinking of protest tactics and repertoires of contentious politics.

A different kind of historical context is brought by Sean Scalmer, who writes here about the relationships between Gandhi's non-violence and the media, and who traces some legacies of the Gandhian tradition of civil disobedience. The core tactics of non-violent action – particularly the many forms of non-cooperation – remain at the heart of many protest repertoires to this day. Scalmer explains Gandhi's complex use of the media of the time, including newsreels, radio and mass-circulation publications, as well as Gandhi's awareness of the dangers of misrepresentation. He describes how Gandhi's tactics influenced subsequent movements in other parts of the world, such as the UK anti-nuclear campaigns of the late 1950s onwards and Martin Luther King's leadership of the US civil rights movements. But Scalmer also explores how the spiritual dimension of Gandhi's philosophy of non-violence was often lost as its surface tactics were diffused through global media. And he observes the trade-off that continues into the twenty-first century for many campaigners, who must weigh up whether being caricatured and attacked by the media is better than being ignored completely.

This dilemma is pursued in our next chapter, in which Anna Feigenbaum writes about both the mainstream media coverage and the alternative media practices of protesters at the women's anti-nuclear peace camp at Greenham Common in the UK in the 1980s. Feigenbaum discusses the gendered politics of media representation, noting how stereotypical coverage of the peace camp by female journalists forced some Greenham women to learn that community requires more than just having something in common. And in an important emphasis, she also pays attention to such everyday creative activities as singing songs, writing letters, or keeping personal scrapbooks. Feigenbaum points to ways in which these can spark new reflections that open up possibilities for thoughts beyond those shaped by the representational practices of the established media.

Stephen Duncombe and Steve Lambert develop this focus in their wide-ranging essay on the nexus between activism and art. Activism, they argue, is about meeting specific goals, about bringing about a particular change, about having some *effect*. Art, on the other hand, is about creating a feeling or a change in perception: about *affect*. And of course, the two are deeply connected, as the political effects of activism provoke affective responses, and as the affect of creative work stimulates political activity. To capture these dynamics, Duncombe and Lambert propose the hybrid term *æffect*. They point out that much of contemporary politics is disconnected from rational argument, and is performed instead on the terrain of the emotions. So those seeking to bring about social change need not just the best evidence and the best arguments, but also the best images and the best stories.

The final chapter in this section on key themes, by Leah A. Lievrouw, provides an overview of *alternative computing*. As communication and media content have converged with computing and information technologies, so those technologies have been contested for political ends. Lievrouw traces the political concerns of early hacker cultures – questions of openness and control, of access and participation – and shows how these find contemporary expressions in three related arenas: in *hacktivism* or electronic civil disobedience; in *design activism,* drawing on computational approaches and a hacker ethos to create alternatives for material cultures and the built environment; and in *data activism*, which engages with the increasing prominence of data and algorithms in daily life. Above all, alternative computing projects, Lievrouw argues, try to change the material basis of contemporary communication itself.

Part II: Organizations and identities

This section of the book brings together seven essays exploring different aspects of how activists organize and how processes of political engagement make possible different senses of identity. In the first chapter, Sasha Costanza-Chock reflects on a decade of work in what they call *transformative media organizing* – an approach that involves developing the capacity for media production within social movements. Costanza-Chock's case studies of transformative media organizing emphasize how developing the media skills of movement activists can help to build community, establish networks and create collaborative visions of social change.

Zizi Papacharissi and Meggan Taylor Trevey concentrate on the affective dimensions of mediated communication for social change. Their chapter explores the ways in which political opportunities emerge through individuals coming together as publics through technological platforms. This has often been approached through the key concepts of collective action, the public sphere and deliberative democracy. But they argue that *collective* action may not be the best way of describing networked political activity, that the *public* sphere may not be the most inclusive way of imagining diverse political behaviour, and that *deliberative* democracy may not capture all the nuances of contemporary mediated politics. Instead, they suggest, publics are motivated by affect and sentiment, find connection and collaborative possibilities through technological networks, and blur the distinctions between the public and the personal.

Zixue Tai provides an overview of social media activism in China, pointing out that the country has a very long history of political resistance. Tai is careful to ground this discussion within the specifics of the Chinese context, with its distinctive mix of authoritarianism and widespread organized contention. He argues that social media offer Chinese people new opportunities for action – often specifically against perceived grievances – but that they also offer the state new opportunities for monitoring and for the routinizing of elements in protest repertoires.

Anastasia Kavada takes up the debate about the distinctions between connective and collective action – between the movements of traditional theory and the crowds of contemporary digital analysis. She argues that these distinctions are not clear, and that the crowds of connective action overlap with the movements of collective action in important ways. Using the example of Occupy, Kavada traces complex relationships between movement dynamics and crowd dynamics. She shows how such fundamentals as leadership structures, administrative responsibilities and decision-making processes can be much more complex for both movement and crowd dynamics than a simple binary between collective and connective implies. And she argues that recognizing the points of intersection and the convergences between these two ways of thinking is vital to understanding each better.

Jesse Drew contributes a historical overview of the uses of communications media by organized labour movements in the US. Drew frames the history of organized labour as 'a struggle over the means of communication'. His chapter traces the media use of unions and guilds from the earliest papers, leaflets and newsletters, through broadcasting and cinema, and up to the uses of networked digital media in a time of increasingly precarious labour. An important emphasis in his essay is that a union is in essence a communication system. Also on the theme of unions, Lina Dencik and Peter Wilkin assess the lessons for organized labour that can be drawn from the uses of digital technologies in networked protest movements. Dencik and Wilkin consider the challenges that face contemporary labour movements, from declining memberships to increasingly precarious employment conditions. In a corporatized employment market that is weighted towards the interests of employers (zero-hours contracts, the 'gig economy'), they suggest that there is a need to find new ways of engaging with digital media that meet the needs of workers.

In a different line from these discussions of collective organization, behaviour and identity, Veronica Barassi's chapter focuses on the individual: she proposes the concept of the activist's 'political biography'. She argues that research on digital media activism has emphasized the uses of personalization and the visibility afforded by social media in order to construct political identities. To complement this, Barassi explores how activists use social media platforms not only to develop a collective identity – a political *we* – but also an individual biography, or political *I*.

Part III: Activist arts

The essays in Part 3 assess a range of approaches to artistic creativity and activism: some involve professional artists, in some cases internationally known ones; others involve everyday, non-professional practices of making and sharing. What links these essays together is their shared emphasis on creative expression for political ends. To introduce this section, Yngvar B. Steinholt writes about a decade of art activism in Russia. He traces the controversies surrounding the punk activist collective Pussy Riot and their contemporaries back to the 1970s. Steinholt describes how often repressive Russian authorities have been unknowingly drawn into contributing to conceptual and performance art pieces that were designed to reveal the state's intolerant or violent characteristics. But he also points to a dilemma, through which provocative art pieces such as Pussy Riot's 'Punk Prayer' may attract the media attention the artists want, but that this can come at the cost of being defined by others rather than self-definition and self-presentation.

Mark McLelland explores the case of Japanese 'vagina artist' Megumi Igarashi, who has used 3D scans of her own vulva as the basis for a number of art works – most famously, as the design for a kayak. She became the first woman to be found guilty under Japan's strict obscenity laws; but McLelland demonstrates how the verdict illustrates the Streisand Effect, through which attempts to suppress information backfire by drawing greater attention than the material in question would otherwise have received. Igarashi – who works under the name *Rokudenashiko* – is not just an artist but an anti-censorship media activist, who argues that Japan's suppression of images of women's genitals has negative consequences for women's health and self-image.

Andrew Green and John Street discuss the often crucial roles of music within activist movements. They offer two ways of thinking about the ways in which music can be part of politics. The first, illustrated by an account of a musical project in support of the Mexican *Zapatistas,* is what they call a *prefigurative* approach, through which musical practices themselves are political and allow participants to enact the kinds of ideal social relations that their movement seeks to achieve more widely. The second, illustrated by a historical case study of the UK's Red Wedge campaign of the 1980s, is what they call a *pragmatic* approach, through which music is bound up with specific and separate political goals: in the case of Red Wedge, this was attempting to secure a Labour government.

Maria Miranda and Norie Neumark explore the political dimensions of work by a range of Australian artists whose creative practices manifest a tension between the political and the aesthetic. Miranda and Neumark call this *political art*, an emphasized 'small-p politics', and discuss how such work can be experienced as an activist intervention even though its makers may operate in quite different registers and with quite different intentions. It is this tension that characterizes the *political*, and that Miranda and Neumark focus on in their chapter. This emphasis on working artists complements the chapter by Ricarda Drüeke and Elke Zobl, which explores the everyday creative relationships between alternative media and the fostering of critical public spheres. They discuss a range of feminist creative practices whose DIY alternative ethos enable the formation of different kinds of critical publics – these include zine-making, collaborative blogging and the uses of hashtags for collective communication and critical action. Their chapter brings together discourses of alternative media and public sphere theory with a range of examples of collaborative, everyday digital creativity.

In the first of two chapters that focus on the remixing and reworking of images, Victoria Esteves discusses the convergence of the political and the personal that can be expressed through the creation and circulation of internet memes. She argues that these practices of remix culture are political in several ways: in the alternative perspectives they provide; in the low barriers to participation they afford; and in their status as contested sites of emerging forms of digital and cultural literacy. Esteves also introduces aspects of *craftivism* – the uses of craft practices, such as embroidery or knitting, in political actions – and argues that such vernacular creativity can be seen as tangible manifestations of local and global politics. Red Chidgey also writes about remix culture in her chapter about the creative and critical reworking and recirculation of iconic images of resistance. She takes the case study of the Rosie the Riveter 'We Can Do It!' image, and traces its circulation, from its origin as a Second World War labour management poster to more contemporary iterations as a commercially available Halloween costume or as a repertoire of motifs adopted by Beyoncé. Chidgey situates her argument within discourses of remix, and the tactics of culture jamming, *détournement,* mash-up, pastiche and sampling. She eschews the discourses of the meme, instead drawing on Deleuze and Guattari's concept of the assemblage as the basis for her own concept of the 'protest assemblage'.

Part IV: Tactics of visibility

The essays in Part 4 all connect with uses of visibility as an activist tactic – they engage with questions of exposure and revelation, of witnessing and visualization, of making visible. Camilla Møhring Reestorff explores the 'sextremist' actions of the radical secularist movement Femen. Her chapter discusses the mediated spectacles of Femen's protest events, in which topless young women subvert the rituals or protocols of organized religions. The exposed body becomes a kind of uniform, even an ironic mask, and enables the expression of a collective identity that operates in part through anonymity; such collaborative anonymities are a strong theme in recent mediated activism, from the collective hacker identity of Anonymous, to the balaclavas of the Zapatistas or Pussy Riot, or the collaborative art pseudonyms of Karen Eliot or Luther Blissett. These tactics of revealing the body, masking the face or adopting a collective name all revolve around visibility in campaigns to effect social change.

Sandra Ristovska, to continue with the theme of visibility, explores practices of bearing witness, in which evidence and emotional affect are bound up with discourses of truth-telling, showing and memory. She explains how witnessing has become a central tactic for human rights activists, in which to bear witness is to take some measure of responsibility for the suffering of others. Ristovska distinguishes between witnessing *of* a human rights violation, for both historical and moral imperatives, and witnessing *for* a specific political goal that can be achieved if sufficient awareness is raised.

Miriyam Aouragh also focuses on questions of visibility and witnessing in her account of digital activism by Palestinians. Aouragh writes about how online Palestinian politics manifest a need to bear witness and to make visible, a need for alternative media perspectives, and a need to enable solidarity and mutual support. Her chapter is careful to set internet tools within the wider Palestinian media context. To the on-going debates about the efficacy of the internet in mediated activism, she adds the crucial point that for Palestinians these media enable the reclaiming of dignity.

Joe F. Khalil addresses a very different use of visibility in his chapter about 'beheading videos'. Khalil analyzes videos that record the execution of hostages, tracing the development of this genre across the Arab world from Beirut hostage videos of the 1980s, through those produced around the Iraq war of the early twenty-first century, and on to more contemporary and more elaborately produced videos associated with so-called Islamic State. The chapter describes how the mediation of these hostage executions has developed from the implicit authenticity of technically crude, user-generated content to more sophisticated productions involving multiple cameras, jib cranes and complex soundtracks. Such videos make visible not just acts of murder, but also the ideology their creators seek to promote, and circulate through social media networks.

As Khalil argues, these videos have become central to the ways in which the established media and their audiences are encouraged to understand their producers, making manifest their ideologies and objectives. The chapter is a powerful example of research into repressive political action by non-state actors, and a striking exploration of political media use whose tactics of visibility are as far removed from discourses of Gandhian non-violence as can be imagined.

Noureddine Miladi writes about the political uses of graffiti, from subcultural expression in 1970s New York, through the circulation of slogans in the Tunisian and Egyptian uprisings of 2011, and on to the siege of Aleppo, whose citizens marked the walls of their city with personal expressions even as they were forced into exile. Miladi argues that we can understand graffiti as a conflict between order and disorder – graffiti makes visible the conflict between the authorities' desire to control public space and the graffiti artists' appropriation of that space as an arena for personal expression and collective communication.

Athina Karatzogianni discusses the phenomenon of *leaktivism* – the politically motivated leaking of often very large databases of classified information. The copying of information from one device to another is intrinsic to digital media, which makes leaks only to be expected. Leaktivism has been a significant tactic – another manifestation of the politics of visibility – since the series of interventions by WikiLeaks in 2010 and their collaborations with established news organizations in disseminating leaked material. Karatzogianni examines a selection of more recent large-scale leaks, and assesses their implications for democracy.

André Mesquita explores the creation and activist uses of alternative maps. A map, he points out, is an instrument of power – a normative representation of political relations that express an ideological view of space and place. His chapter discusses projects that use mapping tools to develop what he calls *counter-cartography* – alternative maps that highlight, question or subvert the relations of power inherent in conventional maps. Mesquita makes a powerful argument for radical mapping to be seen as a central tactic in contemporary repertoires of contention, and he emphasizes how activist mapping projects draw value from their collaborative and creative possibilities.

Part V: Contesting narratives

The essays in Part 5 all engage in different ways with questions of alternative media and alternative narratives – creating alternative media spaces, crafting alternative media narratives, and challenging those of political authorities or the established media. Adrienne Russell examines the repertoire of tactics used by climate justice activists at the United Nations Climate Summit in Paris in 2015. Russell describes these as a project of hacking the media landscape. She identifies a range of complex tactics: using a hashtag to focus media attention on a mock trial of ExxonMobil; creating an alternative media village to create new narratives; and drawing on Paris's rich legacy of creative civil disobedience to stage urban protest games. As with Mesquita's counter-cartography, this last tactic involved developing a map app for coordinating a 'cartography of resistance'. Russell's chapter shows how long traditions continue to inspire digital innovations, with the locative media of the activist gaming app connecting to the Parisian barricades of centuries gone by.

Chris Atton's chapter offers some historical context for the internet use of far-right movements and political parties. He discusses the internet strategies of the UK far-right British National Party in the first decade of the twenty-first century, and how these enabled a discursive production of racist collective identities. Atton's chapter also argues that too much media scholarship assumes activism to be intrinsically progressive (a point also made in the chapter by Christian Fuchs), and he sounds a warning against allowing the distinctions between analysis and activism to be elided.

Bruce Mutsvairo considers the activist uses of social media in Zimbabwe, and how these challenge the state media's control of the news, bringing new spaces for discussion and the possibility of exploring topics banned from the established media. However, he finds that while social media may lead to increased awareness of issues, this awareness is not matched by increased political activity, and self-censorship for fear of government reprisals is common. A more effective medium so far for engaging disaffected publics in this context, Mutsvairo observes, is the much older one of protest music.

Anamaria Tamayo-Duque and Toby Miller recount a case from Colombia, in which a contemporary Twitter mobilization combines with deep resonances from colonial history. They examine an incident in Cartagena in which a plaque commemorating a British-led blockade of the city in 1741 was briefly installed by local authorities. Commemorating the invading forces in a colonial struggle was a strange municipal project, apparently linked to the promotional priorities of the city's tourist industry, and it provoked an immediate outcry on Twitter from citizens who saw it as a betrayal of those who had died defending Cartagena from the British. This social media controversy launched an on-going debate about the contours of local history, and about what a revisionist version of that history might involve.

Gary Foley and Edwina Howell reflect on Foley's experiences as a key figure in the Aboriginal Black Power movement in the 1960s and 70s. Their chapter emphasizes the importance of creating symbols in focusing social change – the creation of the Aboriginal Tent Embassy outside the Australian Parliament, and the invention of the Aboriginal Flag, in which Foley had a hand. The Aboriginal Flag is a powerful symbol that communicates complex meanings and connections through a simple image – indeed, the very creation of a single flag for the many stateless nations of indigenous Australia proved a radical achievement. This indelible image became, as the authors put it, 'a weapon of power in a war of positions'.

Part VI: Changing the media

The essays in this part of the collection all deal with organized attempts to bring about change in the established media, to affect both their contents and their contexts. Arne Hintz's chapter maps some fundamental ways in which campaigners engage with the regulatory and legal contexts in which media are produced and circulated. Media policy and legal frameworks can both enable and constrain activist communication, which makes these a natural arena for activist interventions. Hintz outlines ways that policy activism can intervene in the norms and rules that form the contours of the media environment. He questions the classic binary of *insider* and *outsider* strategies that sees insiders lobbying, advocating and participating within policy debates, and outsiders protesting and disrupting them. Instead, Hintz expands this binary to also allow for repertoires of prefigurative action and for 'policy hacking' approaches.

Natalie Fenton offers an insider account of her involvement in the Hacked Off campaign and the Media Reform Coalition. Fenton reflects on the achievements of these groups in pushing for greater accountability of powerful media organizations. Both were formed in response to revelations of phone hacking by reporters at Rupert Murdoch's *News of the World* newspaper. Fenton notes how the democratic discourse of *freedom of the press* often acts as a cover for *all* activities of the press, including those that may not have any democratic intent. This discourse of press freedom should not allow corporate news media to abuse the public's trust.

A very different set of approaches to influencing the power of the established media is discussed by Samantha Close, who writes about the activist activities of organized groups of fans of popular culture. Fans may lobby TV networks to bring back cancelled shows, or to recognize and respond to the ways in which they interpret those shows. They also often create their own texts in response to their favourite media content, which can bring fans into conflict with copyright owners, leading to further organized responses. She describes how such fan activism offers insights into the self-organizing strategies of networked grassroots groups, but also how such fandoms at times struggle with questions of cultural and ideological diversity.

Steve Collins also discusses how citizens find ways of responding to copyright laws that often feel disconnected from the daily media use of many millions of people – laws that may undermine free expression and creativity. He argues that copyright is a mechanism of cultural regulation, establishing boundaries around how texts and images can be used. This mechanism often seems tilted towards privileging private property at the expense of the public good. Collins shows how, in response, both the Fair Use defence and the Creative Commons platform can be understood as activism, and he explores how file-sharing through BitTorrent can be understood as civil disobedience.

Katie Ellis and Gerard Goggin address media activism by people with disabilities. They point out that, with more than one billion people believed to experience significant disability, this means a very diverse range of approaches to activism. They explain how understandings of disability are both socially and culturally shaped, and how the power relations inherent in these shapings connect to questions of activism (which are in turn themselves both socially and culturally shaped as well). Ellis and Goggin offer a historical overview of disability media activism, as well as its uses of contemporary mobile and social media. Much disability activism is about struggles for access and accessibility, for the capacity to speak and be heard, see and be seen; and so they argue that disability activism demands a reconsideration of what media and communications actually are.

Part VII: Beyond social media

The essays in Part 7 all engage with the networked digital media environment and with versions of the question *what next?* They address the power of algorithms and platforms, the possibilities of developing alternative technologies, and the difficulties of engaging with hostile or repressive ideologies. Emiliano Treré writes about the discourses of algorithms and political power, and about how algorithms can, of course, be deployed both for repressive and for resistant ends. The use of algorithms to drive political bots on Twitter and to disseminate what became known as 'fake news' has been an animating feature of recent electoral politics in a number of countries. Treré examines two case studies: in Mexico, political parties and institutions have used algorithms for propaganda and repression, using bots and exploiting the affordances of platforms such as Twitter to construct consensus positions in the digital public sphere; in Spain, the *Indignados* movement exploited algorithms to maximize their visibility and to carry their narratives into the established media – coordinating activity around a particular hashtag, for example, in order to focus online attention at a chosen moment. Treré makes an important argument for the urgency of developing digital media literacy in an environment where algorithmic strategies are increasingly central.

Oliver Leistert considers potential uses of blockchain technologies – distributed public records of digital participation – for activism. Best known so far for their use in cryptocurrencies such as Bitcoin, blockchain technologies enable far-reaching rethinking of questions of intellectual property, authenticity, labour, trust and control. However, these developments may not be in any way progressive or emancipatory, and instead could enable a new level of control over not only digital transactions but also behaviour, through which the space of the possible is managed into the predictable.

Christian Fuchs discusses the ethics of visibility in social media research, reflecting on the dilemmas of identifiable subjects within qualitative research and arguing that these dilemmas are fundamental to engaging with 'negative' social movements. He asks the reader to imagine the problems of approaching a neo-Nazi user of Twitter to obtain informed consent to quote their tweet in critical research. Fuchs builds this into an important wider discussion of what he sees as the general failure of social movement studies to address movements of the far-right. Also examining the darker sides of the internet, Frances Shaw writes about trolling and harassment on social media, focusing on the development of software tools that enable shared 'block lists' of offensive users as a feminist response to such trolling. She argues that such lists are an example of practical activism against hate speech and online harassment, and that they also enact strong claims for equality of participation in networked digital media.

Geert Lovink and Ned Rossiter challenge assumptions about networks. They begin by observing that the term *network* has been displaced by *platform,* and they then trace trajectories and implications of this shift. They spark connections between the history of industrial music, nineties cybercultures, experimental institutional forms for radical politics, and environmental activism. They question not just *network* and *platform,* but also *movement, crowd* and *party,* asking how political engagement can not only be sparked, but also organized in the current and coming stages of digital media development.

References

Atton, C. (2002) *Alternative Media.* London: Sage.

Atton, C. (ed.) (2015) *The Routledge Companion to Alternative and Community Media.* London: Routledge.

Benjamin, W. (1978) [1934] 'The Author as Producer', in *Reflections.* New York: Harcourt Brace Jovanovich, pp. 220–38.

Bennett, W. L. and Segerberg, A. (2013) *The Logic of Connective Action.* New York: Cambridge University Press.

Bourdieu, P. (1991) *Language and Symbolic Power.* Cambridge: Polity.

Bradley, W. and Esche, C. (eds) (2007) *Art and Social Change: A Critical Reader.* London: Tate.

Brecht, B. (1993) [1932] 'The Radio as an Apparatus of Communication', in N. Strauss (ed.) *Radiotext(e).* New York: Semiotext(e), pp. 15–17.

Carey, J. (1989) *Communication as Culture.* New York: Routledge.

Castells, M. (2004) *The Power of Identity* (second edition). Oxford: Blackwell.

Castells, M. (2015) *Networks of Outrage and Hope* (second edition). Cambridge: Polity.

Critical Art Ensemble (1995) *Electronic Civil Disobedience and Other Unpopular Ideas.* New York: Autonomedia.

Debord, G. and Wolman, G. (2009) [1956] 'Directions for the Use of Détournement', in D. Evans (ed.) *Appropriation.* London: Whitechapel Gallery, pp. 35–9.

De Certeau, M. (1984) *The Practice of Everyday Life.* Berkeley, CA: University of California Press.

della Porta, D. (2015) *Social Movements in Times of Austerity.* Cambridge: Polity.

della Porta, D. and Diani, M. (2006) *Social Movements* (second edition). Malden, MA: Blackwell.

della Porta, D. and Diani, M. (eds) (2015) *The Oxford Handbook of Social Movements.* Oxford: Oxford University Press.

DeLaure, M. and Fink, M. (eds) (2017) *Culture Jamming.* New York: New York University Press.

Dery, M. (1993) *Culture Jamming: Hacking, Slashing and Sniping in the Empire of Signs.* Westfield, NJ: Open Magazine Pamphlet Series no. 25.

Downing, J. D. H. (ed.) (2011) *Encyclopedia of Social Movement Media.* Thousand Oaks, CA: Sage.

Downing, J. with Ford, T.V., Gil, G. and Stein, L. (2001) *Radical Media: Rebellious Communication and Social Movements.* Thousand Oaks, CA: Sage.

Drew, J. (2013) *A Social History of Contemporary Democratic Media.* New York: Routledge.

Duncombe, S. (ed.) (2002) *Cultural Resistance Reader.* London: Verso.

Duncombe, S. (2007) *Dream.* New York: The New Press.

Enzensberger, H. M. (2003) [1970] 'Constituents of a Theory of the Media', in N. Wardrip-Fruin and N. Montfort (eds) *The New Media Reader.* Cambridge, MA: MIT Press, pp. 261–75.

Evans, D. (2009) (ed.) *Appropriation.* London: Whitechapel Gallery.

Flood, C. and Grindon, G. (eds) (2014) *Disobedient Objects.* London: V&A.

Garcia, D. and Lovink, G. (1997) 'The ABC of Tactical Media', 16 May, http://www.nettime.org/Lists-Archives/nettime-l-9705/msg00096.html, accessed 12 September 2017.

Gerbaudo, P. (2017) *The Mask and the Flag*. London: Hurst & Company.

King, M. L. (2000) [1962] 'A Legacy of Creative Protest', in P. Lauter (ed.) *Walden and Civil Disobedience*. Boston, MA: Houghton Mifflin, p. 433.

McLeod, K. and Kuenzli, R. (eds) (2011) *Cutting Across Media: Appropriation Art, Interventionist Collage, and Copyright Law*. Durham, NC: Duke University Press.

Meikle, G. (2002) *Future Active: Media Activism and the Internet*. New York: Routledge.

Meikle, G. (2007) 'Stop Signs: An Introduction to Culture Jamming', in K. Coyer, T. Dowmunt and A. Fountain (eds) *The Alternative Media Handbook*. London: Routledge, pp. 166–79.

Meikle, G. (2008) 'Whacking Bush: Tactical Media As Play', in M. Boler (ed.) *Digital Media and Democracy: Tactics In Hard Times*. Cambridge, MA: MIT Press, pp. 367–82.

Meikle, G. (2016) *Social Media: Communication, Sharing and Visibility*. New York: Routledge.

Melucci, A. (1996) *Challenging Codes: Collective Action in the Information Age*. Cambridge: Cambridge University Press.

Rennie, E. (2006) *Community Media*. Lanham, MD: Rowman and Littlefield.

Rodriguez, C. (2001) *Fissures in the Mediascape: An International Study of Citizens' Media*. Cresskill, NJ: Hampton Press.

Rodriguez, C. (2002) 'Citizens' Media and the Voice of the Angel/Poet', *Media International Australia*, no. 103, pp. 78–87.

Scalmer, S. (2002) *Dissent Events: Protest, the Media and the Political Gimmick in Australia*. Sydney: UNSW Press.

Scott, J. C. (1985) *Weapons of the Weak: Everyday Forms of Peasant Resistance*. New Haven, CT: Yale University Press.

Sharp, G. (1973) *The Politics of Nonviolent Action* (in 3 volumes). Boston, MA: Porter Sargent.

Sussman, E. (ed.) (1989) *On the Passage of a Few People Through a Rather Brief Moment in Time: The Situationist International, 1957–1972*. Cambridge, MA: MIT Press.

Thompson, J. B. (1995) *The Media and Modernity*. Cambridge: Polity.

Tilly, C. (1986) *The Contentious French*. Cambridge, MA: Harvard University Press.

Tilly, C. and Wood, L. J. (2013) *Social Movements 1768–2012* (third edition). New York: Routledge.

Tilly, C. and Tarrow, S. (2015) *Contentious Politics* (second edition). New York: Oxford University Press.

Weibel, P. (ed.) (2015) *Global Activism: Art and Conflict in the 21st Century*. Cambridge, MA: MIT Press.

Zuckerman, E. (2015) 'Cute Cats to the Rescue?', in D. Allen and J. S. Light (eds) *From Voice to Influence: Understanding Citizenship in a Digital Age*. Chicago, IL: University of Chicago Press, pp. 131–54.

PART I

Themes

1

LOOKING BACK, LOOKING AHEAD

What has changed in social movement media since the internet and social media?

John D. H. Downing

Introduction

A spring 2017 exhibition, *Perpetual Revolution*, at New York's International Center of Photography (ICP) pinpointed image wars as a hallmark of our present time. It culled media imagery of six extremely critical current conflicts:

- climate change (e.g. Greenland ice sheet 'calving' – a zone the size of lower Manhattan but several times higher, disintegrating over a few hours – *https://www.youtube.com/watch?v=hC3VTgIPoGU*);
- #BlackLivesMatter and state racism (e.g. photos of Black citizens gunned down by the police or vigilantes);
- LGBTQ movements and gender-bending (e.g. fantasy dress experiments, sharply framed videos, personal statements);
- the global refugee crisis (e.g. concentration camps, rubber dinghies, personal accounts of survival and of those who didn't make it to 'safety');
- White nationalism and the 2016 Trump election (e.g. images of the all-purpose saviour of discarded workers and their families, capitalists yearning for tax breaks, an array of xenophobes, anti-abortion fanatics, panicked masculinists);
- ISIS/ISIL/Daesh recruitment media (e.g. come-and-join-us videos and websites for the Purpose of all Purposes, martyred in purity if so willed, living a meaningful life in the 'caliphate' for the ultimate good of humanity).

These image vectors clash in multiple ways. The first three call for constructive change in the ways we live. The fourth image set attempts to render voices, faces and pasts to voiceless unseen millions. The fifth channels repressive populism, racism, sexism, Islamophobia and anti-Judaism lubricated in the US by shadowy billionaires and 'Christian dominion' fundamentalists. The sixth image vector, drenched in devotional green, redoes imperial masculinist militarism. (The list is rather US-centric, though that country's current weight in world affairs does lend global heft to its domestic dealings.)

The curators proposed in their accompanying exhibition statement that 'an ongoing revolution is taking place politically, socially, and technologically, and that new digital methods of image production, display, and distribution are simultaneously both reporting and producing social change' (International Center of Photography 2017). But whether it's best to talk about a revolution, which implies change is going in a detectable direction, or simply about intense ongoing flux, the deployment of media has unquestionably shifted to far more complex formats than thirty years ago, let alone during prior centuries.

Complex formats: as ever, varying media technologies, cultural shifts and political change are wrapped up in each other. If this essay focused solely on changes in communication technologies as such, it would shrink-wrap the dynamics at work. The ICP exhibition statement is right to glue media technologies and their affordances (potentials for use) to today's often mutually clashing political/cultural movements.

Here, my purpose is to contrast activist media in earlier times with the contemporary scene, so as to see the here-and-now and the maybe-just-round-the-corner in the sharpest possible relief and not to dwell on the past for its own sake. Working conditions, joblessness, women's subordination, climate change, racism, the overweening power of the 1 per cent, state surveillance and lifelong education are among the many issues that demand media activist strategies. But *which* strategies?

A bygone dualistic world?

It is tempting to see earlier eras as much simpler, at least ideologically, than the multi-faceted scenario presented by the ICP exhibition and, correspondingly, media as straightforwardly For or Against. Protestant *Flugblätter* (leaflets/pamphlets) versus Catholic ones in the Reformation in Germany in the 1500s. Pro-independence tracts and books versus pro-British publications in the American Revolution. Anti-royalty versus republican tracts in the French Revolution. The labour press versus the capitalist press. Anti-slavery media versus the racist consensus. Media advancing women's right to vote versus media pooh-poohing the very idea. Anti-colonial media (India, Egypt, Vietnam, Algeria, Ghana, etc.). Antiwar media. Gay and lesbian rights media. Children's rights media, patients' rights media, prisoners' rights media, global anti-*apartheid* media (i.e. the former White-supremacist regime in South Africa).

Correspondingly, the typical activist media narrative of those centuries was indeed a David versus Goliath one with tiny media projects challenging overwhelming state and religious censorship. Most often the media technology deployed was print (flyers, posters, pamphlets, books, newspapers), though political song, satirical jokes, street-plays, graffiti, poems, puppets, cartoons, paintings, dance and dress also played their roles. In the twentieth century, on a very small scale, photos, films and sound recordings made their appearance in social movement hands. Video activism began to make a mark in the 1970s. In many cases, as with the huge and multi-faceted Iranian revolution of 1978-1979, varying media formats were all in play (Sreberny-Mohammadi & Mohammadi 1994) before theocrats ruthlessly hijacked the movement for decades.

But for movement campaigners and demonstrators, first prize was still usually news coverage of any kind in mainstream media, even when hostile in tone. It wasn't that most activists were convinced mainstream media would never speak the truth or would never amplify movement voices, only that expecting, even hoping, for them to do so, was so routinely an exercise in frustration. Michela Ardizzoni, in her *Matrix Activism* (2017), argues that today's conditions are far more fluid, and that now capitalist firms more routinely open up to certain kinds of radical media projects and voices. Huge capitalist firms – Apple, Facebook, Google, Microsoft – currently provide the wherewithal. Her international case studies are absorbing, and maybe she is right. Though conditions at the time of writing in 2017, with autocrats in full cry – in Russia, China, India, the US, Turkey, Egypt, Syria, Saudi Arabia, the Gulf States, Central Asia, Poland, Hungary, the Philippines and Thailand – do not portend well for planetary fluidity.

The principal headache for media activists in the past, even in liberal capitalist regimes, was distribution. Major media firms had capital to expend on delivery vans, newsagent stores and advertising and, in some countries, concessionary postal rates for magazines and newspapers. They equally had capital to allocate to cinema chains for movies, for high-powered transmitters for radio and TV, and later for cable and satellite technology. Virtually none of this was accessible to the contemporary 'pauper press' (the title of Patricia Hollis's landmark 1970 study of the UK's rebellious Chartist movement's print media in the 1830s–1840s).

On the other hand, the pauper press did have one ace in the hole, namely a highly conscious and politically engaged readership – a very different, socially energized audience from mass audiences. Arguably, especially in times of social turmoil, this vector enabled the pauper press to punch well above its weight. Its miniscule readership, compared to mainstream media's, was not the last word on the matter. Plus, its tenaciousness over time was sustained by the ongoing, if intermittently ebbing, energy of social movements. Women's right to vote, the right to contraception, the abolition of chattel slavery in the Americas, colonial freedom, an eight-hour day and paid work-vacations were not won in a year's or a decade's worth of social movement media activism. But they were won.

Let us pause for a moment to illustrate two evocative moments in the saga of pre-digital activist media, namely the US radical movements' press in the first twenty years of the twentieth century, and US radical media in the turbulent 1960s and 1970s. This will hopefully move our discussion closer to the ground (though with further apologies for US-centrism).

Black, White and Red all over

Linda Lumsden's study (2014) examines US activist print media in the period 1900–1920, during the enormous industrial labour migration wave from Eastern and Southern Europe from 1880 to 1920. In a multi-lingual, multi-confessional, multi-national labour force, new in many cases to factory discipline and often vigorously resistant to it, newspapers and magazines of all kinds proliferated, as did a great variety of political trends (not all radical).

Lumsden devotes four chapters to socialist labour newspapers, and then a chapter each to the direct action of the IWW (International Workers of the World, commonly known as the 'Wobblies'), the anarchist press, the leftist intellectuals' press, the Black press and the women's press. A majority were in English, but many were in other languages (Italian, Polish, Yiddish, Russian, Finnish, etc.). Starting with monthly and weekly newspapers, often with local city or state readerships (rural Arkansas alone had fourteen papers), even a daily press emerged, for example the *Call*, based in New York, and the *Milwaukee Leader*. The weekly *Appeal to Reason*, based in mid-western Kansas, sold three-quarters of a million at its height in 1913. Feminist–anarchist Emma Goldman's monthly *Mother Earth*, beginning in 1906, generated social movement ricochets long after she was deported in 1919.

Lumsden (2014: 74) graphically describes reporters' workplace at the *Call*:

> Reporters clambered up a set of rickety stairs to desks lined up in a dimly lit sixth-floor loft littered with old newspapers. Linotype machines rattled and banged louder than the reporters' clacking typewriters amid a foul odor wafting from the stereotyping machine. Everyone worked at least twelve hours a day, some seven days a week.

(Today's term 'to stereotype' was drawn from this now-obsolete mass printing technology.) In the US socialist and radical press of that era, lethal working conditions, harsh pay levels, arbitrary firings, violence against union organizers and strikers, employer lockouts and scab labour were staple news items, though far from the only ones.

In 1960, *New Yorker* journalist A.J. Liebling sardonically wrote that 'the freedom of the press is guaranteed only to those who own one'. The costly distribution issue mentioned above was just one aspect. The ramshackle press technology owned by radical publishers in those days was usually pathetic by standards of the time, let alone the utterly different methods of today. Nonetheless, in their Lilliputian multitude, they succeeded in voicing and sharing the tribulations and sometimes agonies of many millions, and in agitating for organized pushback.

However, as Lumsden also notes (2014: 54), 'the socialist journals' numbers attest to radicals' infinite faith in newspapers to educate and hence convert readers'. Implicitly, if not explicitly, this signaled a very common understanding of the rationale of social movement media as one-way political evangelism. By contrast, the degree of interactivity permitted by internet and social media use, and the educational philosophy of the great Brazilian educator Paulo Freire (1921–1997) – the notion that genuinely educative communication is mutual – were barely visible. We shall return to that issue below, but for the moment let us just note that a huge wave of political repression descended on the US once World War I was over, sometimes referred to as the 'Red Scare', and sometimes as 'the Palmer Raids', after then-Federal Attorney General Palmer. The radical press was not squelched out of existence, but was greatly diminished.

Smoking typewriters

The 1960s and 1970s were indeed turbulent times in the US, and as John McMillian's study (2011) documents, an energetic and highly diverse activist press both lived from and fed the social movements of the period: Black and Latino Civil Rights, the Black Power movement, opposition to the Vietnam war, second-wave feminism, gay and lesbian rights and Native American rights. The Black press was far and away the oldest, with a long and energetic history dating back to the *Freedom's Journal* in the 1820s. It needs to be understood, however, that these 1960s movements, while influencing each other at points, were mostly conducted separately from each other. Indeed, women's negative experiences at the hands of men in both the Civil Rights and the antiwar campaigns (the 'New Left') significantly triggered second-wave feminism's emergence – although some of the most active feminists had family roots in union and socialist households (the 'Old Left').

While some of the 1960s media had Leninist or generally authoritarian hierarchies, anarchist and libertarian editorial models were more strongly evident than in the 1900s and 1910s, giving space to a variety of voices within the same outlet. For instance, SDS (Students for a Democratic Society), the left-libertarian agency of nationwide activism against the Vietnam war, really did practise a strong grassroots democracy for most of its active life.

The same economics of movement newspapers persisted, though, with the stencil duplicating machine, known also as the mimeograph, serving as printing press for many activist publications. McMillian (2011: 13), describing the SDS Chicago main office, writes:

> It scarcely mattered whether it was day or night … Amid the frequently ringing
> phones, the tap-tap-tap of perhaps a dozen typewriters, and the periodic rumble of
> a nearby elevated train, they worked, ate, and talked in dimly lit rooms, perched on

wobbly chairs, surrounded by sheaves of paper and battered desks … One journalist … described it as something between a newsroom and a flophouse, drawing attention to "an unmade cot, several laundry bags, a jar of instant coffee, and a half-eaten chocolate bar" … Taped to one of the walls was a picture of a mimeograph machine. Just beneath it someone had written the words "Our Founder".

Distribution was largely by hand, bicycle, motorbike or personal car and at demonstrations, teach-ins and campus occupations.

Not everything was peachy-keen. In chapter 6 of *Smoking Typewriters*, McMillian gives a blow-by-blow account of ferocious internal squabbles at *Liberation News Service*. Joan Micklin Silver's splendid feature film *Between the Lines* (1977) gives a comparable picture of fraught life in a Boston community newspaper. As though these internal fissures were not enough of a head-ache for activist media projects, the FBI – obsessed with domestic political dissent ever since the Palmer Raids – mounted a major new initiative in November 1968 to squelch the movements and their media. They first assembled a detailed survey of every such project, before proceeding to use undercover agents to inflate existing tensions among activists, or getting the Federal tax authorities to conduct long-drawn-out audits on project finances. They harassed landlords who rented to these media, ransacked media offices, destroyed equipment, even planted incriminat-ing evidence. Pornography was a favourite charge, given the sexual freedoms often trumpeted by media activists. Columbia Records, which advertised pop music in many of these media, withdrew its ads after FBI pressure resulted in the slashing of their budgets.

Print's companion media

Up to this point, print technologies, including the photocopier, clearly dominated the activist scene. In *Adjusted Margin*, her study of photocopier use in the 1970s Global North, Kate Eichhorn (2016: 82) writes:

> urban curbs, gutters, flagstones, trees, posts, poles, bins, bridges, fences, barrels, boxes and signs were all claimed as potential parts of this urban canvas … these constantly shifting, collaboratively produced and spontaneous paper structures were the work not only of artists and musicians but also of community activists and just regular citizens … publicizing events and concerns that would have been otherwise difficult to promote.

Technologies other than print were present, but mostly scarce. Film had been in scattered use since the 1930s, but was extremely expensive to process and practically never found commercial exhibition. The introduction of 16mm and Super 8 film stock reduced shooting costs, but did not dent distribution difficulties. Activist still photos, beginning with the German, Dutch and American worker-photography movements in the 1930s, did not lend themselves to widespread diffusion.

The emergence of portable video cameras (camcorders) in the very late 1960s began to make a mark. Deirdre Boyle (1997: 27), herself a video-activist of this period, writes in her book *Subject to Change: Guerrilla Television Revisited*:

> the video underground shot hundreds of hours of documentaries, tapes on New Left polemics and the drama of political confrontation, as well as lifestyles and video erotica … inventing a distinctive style … handheld fluidity was in … Gritty black-and-white tapes were generally edited in the camera … opposed to conventional

television "reality", with its quick, highly edited scenes, and narration by a typically white male figure.

But so-called 'bicycle-distribution' of videocassettes was still the only way to distribute these products. Alex Juhasz (1995: 216–217), an AIDS activist and video-maker, describes the process in her book *AIDS TV*:

> labor-intensive, pro-active strategies that take the tape to the people that need it … This means phone calls, follow-up, letter campaigns, follow-up, then long train rides to hard-to-find agencies, a small audience, and then, finally, few of the institutionally accepted markers of success … A *successful* screening finds a tape playing to fifteen members of an HIV support group or women's club, the tape introduced by the makers and then discussed afterward.

It was only in the late 1980s that Deep Dish TV started renting cheap transponder time on a satellite to ferry its ongoing video-documentary series to upwards of 300 community TV stations around the US. The series ranged across HIV/AIDS, the 1990-1991 Gulf War, the US prison industry, systemic school failures in US public schools, corporate media, and much more. In due course, Deep Dish switched to streaming, but it was the first to break out of the distribution stranglehold on activist media. It's important to realize, though, that the varying-length documentaries in all Deep Dish's series were produced by *local* groups across the US, then edited together by Deep Dish to uplink them. This was a golden opportunity to realize grassroots localism, as opposed to the swoop-in/swoop-out 'localism' of mainstream TV's typical offerings.

Radio, soon after its broadcast use became established in the early 1920s, was overwhelmingly state-run or commercial around the globe. In Latin America, though, there was an increasingly vigorous activist radio movement from the 1950s onwards, the mining community radio stations of Bolivia being amongst the most renowned. As Canadian researcher Alan O'Connor (2004: i–ii) writes in introducing his translated collection of Latin American essays on the Bolivian stations (*Community Radio in Bolivia*):

> cheap, transportable, functioning independently of literacy, [radio] enjoys tremendous flexibility and accessibility … Talk, drama, music, news, personal messages, the hook-up with phones … all make radio the medium of choice for the world's majority.

Popular music is the other key zone to address (then as now). To do it justice is way beyond the space here, but Michael Kramer's study, *The Republic of Rock: Music and Citizenship in 60s Counterculture*, provides considerable insight. For instance, concerning the antiwar movement that soon developed inside the US military itself, he observes that to lift morale, the top brass began to send electric guitars, saxophones, drum kits and more, especially to high-danger camps, for the 'grunts' to make their own rock music. Thus:

> GIs could … flip a switch between sanctioned broadcasts and sanctuaries of dissent … But this counterpublic was not a coherent one. Rather, it was composed of streaks, eddies, fissures and shards … It was atmospheric, a lurking commons for civic inquiry rather than an open space for outright democratic deliberation … While the music may have improved spirits temporarily, it undermined morale in the long run by importing countercultural dissonance, engagement and civic questioning.
>
> *Kramer 2013: 151, 177*

To sum up, briefly, before moving to current times: the twentieth century social movement and media activism world we have looked at was not especially dualistic (even if some of the mobilization tactics made it out to be so), but just as complex in its own ways as is ours. Nor have we unmoored it and sent it out to drift at sea. Core media technologies may have been upgraded, their distribution processes transformed, but video, TV, film, radio, print, recorded music and photocopiers are very much still with us. So are the issues that dominate us, from working conditions and joblessness to lifelong education, as listed early on.

Here and now, then, what is really different?

Let us address some fundamental points: (1) where do we draw our examples from when we think about digital activist media? (2) how far do we link the past to our grasp of the digital present? (3) where and what are the continuities and ruptures with that past?

Examples from where?

Our focus, inevitably, is on the fresh affordances offered to social activism by computers, the internet, Web 2.0, the blogosphere, smartphones and connective ('social') media. Already in the mid-1980s, the first two of these were already being experimented with in the now-legendary The Well in California, the annual Computers for Social Change conferences at New York City's Hunter College and many other locations across the Global North. Three decades of growing digital activism …

But part of the problem with assessing the Here and Now is that so much of the discussion of the Here has been drawn from examples in the Global North. The Arab region rebellions of 2011 and the years following briefly expanded the geographical focus of attention to social media. But often commentators on the 'Arab Springs' failed to get beyond the short step they anticipated from dizzy technical novelty (Facebook, Twitter, etc.), to magical transition from repressive rule to a liberal democratic nirvana. The modern histories and actual dynamics of Arab countries were a blank sheet to these observers, totally besotted as they were with new communication technologies.

Former journalist Paolo Gerbaudo, in his *Tweets and the Streets* (2012), took the trouble to contrast the uses of connective media in the 2011 Egyptian explosion, and in both Spain's huge nationwide *Indignados* (The Outraged) movement and the Occupy Wall Street movement of the same year. This comparison alone illustrated how unwise it is to leap from what happens at a single time and place with digital media sites to making general conclusions; unmooring, and thus fetishizing, technology.

At that time, perhaps 0.25% of the entire Egyptian population used Twitter for any purpose at all (though that still meant potentially up to 200,000 people nationwide). Facebook had a somewhat larger set of users, but still was a distinctly minority habit. So the frequent vision of half or more of Egypt's public as riveted to these two connective platforms and about to force an instant peaceful shift to Western-style liberal democracy was wildly fanciful. In New York's Occupy movement, Twitter was also hardly used in the initial month or two of the campaign and Facebook was woefully under-utilized at first, because no rapid dialogue responses were organized to fresh postings. In Spain, both platforms were used intensively, and indeed the hashtag #15M – 15 May, the date of the initial vast demonstration in Madrid's Puerta del Sol Square – became a movement emblem.

Gerbaudo offers still more than this contrast. He focuses on crucial recent social movement history in the three countries, and underscores the importance of emotion and the irreducible role of interpersonal conversation. He also pokes an especially large hole in the common claim, including by some movement activists, that all these movements were leaderless, spontaneously bubbling up through horizontal digital media. Leadership, he shows, played crucial roles, including the uses of Facebook and Twitter among leaders for coordination and response. His correctives are a crucial starting point for understanding social media.

Is history 'just history'?

The excitingly instantaneous quality of internet and phone connection risks foolishly overestimating them for activist media purposes. In riposte, when political scientist Mohamed Zayani's *Networked Publics and Digital Contention* (2015) analyzes connective media in his native Tunisia's Arab Spring eruption, front and centre are (a) Tunisia's history since independence from French rule in 1956, and (b) the politics of everyday life there. Among the other ingredients of rebellion's emergence were the distinctive role of the legal profession in Tunisia, many of the General Labor Union's local cells, the development of a Tunisian expatriate community in France and beyond, and the emergence of an active – but not insurrectionary – blogosphere in everyday life over the years 2006–2009.

Effectively, the roles of connective media in contributing to the anti-regime explosion were entirely unanticipated, quite slow and obscure in the making. Ironically, they were enabled by the regime's desire to preen itself as a technological modernizer among Arab nations. Thus, its internet capacity was easily highest in the region. (And its police's internet surveillance technologies.) Yet, as Zayani (2015: 182) writes:

> By the time the authorities became alarmed at the mobilizing potential of social media, Internet dynamics took on a life of their own … the fear of government reprisal started to dissipate.

Thus there was *nothing* instantaneous about social media's roles in the Tunisian revolt, except in the upsurge's very last weeks. They meshed with numerous Tunisian specifics, and slowly came into their own affordances in the emerging process. History counts. The excitement of immediacy can be a trap.

On a related tack, long-time labour, media and university militant Jesse Drew (2013: 3) insists we credit the past with the present's media commonsense:

> [Today's] media-from-below shift was fostered by many popular movements that strove for media self-reliance, carried out with a DIY attitude. These creative forces have ranged from video artists and public access advocates to punk and hip-hop artists to radical political … movements.

Continuities and ruptures?

Continuities include the ongoing plethora of movement media formats, from street theatre and demonstrations, and art and blogs to video and popular song. Community radio, for example, continues to flourish in many parts of the world, as witness the Community Radio entries in the *Encyclopedia of Social Movement Media* (Downing, 2011). Connective media are an additive, not a substitute. They may help in many ways to relay and re-process material generated in legacy media formats. ('Earlier' media or 'old' media are stupid terms – the point is utility, not antiquity.)

Among the ruptures, the most obvious of all is the sheer access to making media. The price of computer use in the Global South continues to be very high indeed, but access to simpler mobile phones now is open to the majority of humans. Liebling's printing press costs are evaporating.

The second obvious rupture appears to be distribution, on the face of it a nightmare no longer. Not only is distribution feasible, but – *if* languages, telecoms infrastructure and state censorship *together* permit – it can traverse the planet, if necessary, and at a hitherto unimaginable speed. Images, books, the unfamiliar, voices, debates, counter-hegemonic news and often in one or other form of interactivity. So Paulo Freire's vision of interactive education, the *comunicación horizontal*, which he and many Latin American media activists, with Bolivia in mind, proclaimed as their goal in the 1970s, now have media technologies that permit them to function interactively at distances. The point being, not that the technology itself improves the content or the process, but that it makes them possible at all. Yet there is a large worm in this bud; see below.

The third rupture is the emergence of a meso-level of media communication, in between face-to-face and the 'one-to-many' mass audience, flexibly alternating between the highly personal to sometimes *very* large numbers of people, hyperlinking in every conceivable direction.

The fourth is the portability and ubiquity of multiple uses of 4G phones. Sharing on-the-spot images of police violence or the true size of a demonstration, or a witty movement meme, or connecting among organizers in different locations, are some examples. (No wonder then that, in the name of personal data security from phone theft, or terrorism, police forces from China to Sudan to the US and UK are buying kill-switch mobile phone technologies.)

The fifth is the much greater ease of mobilization for demonstrations, marches, sit-ins, pickets, road blockages, vigils. Yet hand in hand with this advantage goes a caution. Much of the excitement about social media, in particular, focused on rapid mobilization, but the mobilization, aside from clicktivism, was typically tied to old-style public demonstrations and the like. The caution is that social movements also need media to help *debate and hammer out* competing long-term policy-development practicalities, whether for healthcare or climate change, for women's opportunities or prison reform, for control over corporate procedures or labour rights, local, national and international. Rapid mobilizations and marches are only a necessary component of generating such policies. Demos alone cannot. Can Twitter, Instagram or Snapchat directly function in this much longer process? Facebook, already, yes. YouTube, yes, evidently.

And then there are new headaches. Direct political repression of media is hardly new, but its scope has sharply expanded, in the form of internet and phone surveillance technologies, as Edward Snowden's extremely courageous revelations made clearer than ever. Furthermore, the global telecoms infrastructure – ocean cables, cellphone towers, satellites, etc. – is privately owned, or in some cases state-owned, both versions of control giving inordinate power to the owners in terms of policies, access and content. Media ownership grows ever more monopolistic. Thus the distribution headache has moved to a new and in principle far-reaching plane.

The result is that it is no longer sufficient to be a media activist. Now the remit has to stretch all the time to embrace *information* activism and *media reform* activism, the urgent but long-run struggle to push back monopoly ownership of major media firms (Freedman *et al.* 2016).

Nor are 'nanomedia' anything like an undisputed terrain. Authoritarian and racist populist movements have long been using new media technologies. The Ku Klux Klan was one of the first to deploy digital bulletin boards back in the early 1980s. Local extremist talk radio has flourished in the US for decades. Racist rock music is readily available online.

The ICP exhibition from which this essay began nicely characterized our huge contemporary clashes of agendas, melding of legacy and digital media activism. Let us not anticipate any media activism comfort zone.

References

Ardizzoni, M. (2017) *Matrix Activism: Global Practices of Resistance.* New York: Routledge.

Boyle, D. (1997) *Subject to Change: Guerrilla Television Revisited.* New York: Oxford University Press.

Downing, J. D. H. (ed.) (2011) *Encyclopedia of Social Movement Media.* Los Angeles, CA: Sage Publications, Inc.

Drew, J. (2013) *A Social History of Contemporary Democratic Media.* New York: Routledge.

Eichhorn, K. (2016) *Adjusted Margin: Xerography, Art, and Activism in the Late Twentieth Century.* Cambridge, MA: MIT Press.

Freedman, D., Obar, J. A., Martens, C. and McChesney, R.W. (eds.) (2016) *Strategies for Media Reform: International Perspectives.* New York: Fordham University Press.

Gerbaudo, P. (2012) *Tweets and the Streets: Social Media and Contemporary Activism.* London: Pluto Press.

Hollis, P. (1970) *Pauper Press: Study in Working-Class Radicalism of the 1830s.* Oxford: Oxford University Press.

Juhasz, A. (1995) *AIDS TV: Identity, Community and Alternative Video.* Durham, NC: Duke University Press.

Kramer, M. (2013) *The Republic of Rock: Music and Citizenship in the Sixties Counterculture.* New York: Oxford University Press.

Lumsden, L. J. (2014) *Black, White, and Red All Over: A Cultural History of the Radical Press in Its Heyday, 1900–1917.* Kent, OH: Kent State University Press.

McMillian, J. (2011) *Smoking Typewriters: The Sixties Underground Press and the Rise of Alternative Media in America.* New York: Oxford University Press.

O'Connor, A. (ed.) (2004) *Community Radio in Bolivia: The Miners' Radio Stations.* Lewiston, ME and Lampeter, UK: The Edwin Mellen Press.

Sreberny-Mohammadi, A. and Mohammadi, A. (1994) *Small Media, Big Revolution: Communications, Culture, and the Iranian Revolution.* Minneapolis, MN: University of Minnesota Press.

Zayani, M. (2015) *Networked Publics and Digital Contention: The Politics of Everyday Life in Tunisia.* New York: Oxford University Press.

2

THE NEXUS BETWEEN MEDIA, COMMUNICATION AND SOCIAL MOVEMENTS

Looking back and the way forward

Donatella della Porta and Elena Pavan

The widespread adoption of digital media as tools for protest and activism during critical junctures – such as the Arab Springs, or the severe economic crisis in Europe and all over the world – has prompted a highly interdisciplinary reflection on how increased communication possibilities entwine with the organizational and the symbolic dimensions of social movements, but also on media practices as forms of resistance in their own right. Thus, this new strand of research revamps and, at the same time, updates a longer-term discussion on the role of media within contentious politics – one that developed in a mediascape dominated by mass media but that remains particularly relevant to understand the implications of the current 'hybrid media context' (Chadwick 2013). In this chapter, we offer a brief introduction to the study of the 'intricacy of interactions between media and movements' (Mattoni & Treré 2014: 252). We start from traditional approaches developed within social movement studies, then summarizing the current debate on the nexus between digital media and movements by paying specific attention to three main aspects: the modes in which movements organize and act, the formation of collective identities and the hybridization of action repertoires. We conclude by identifying some promising areas of research that can contribute to further developing our knowledge in this domain.

Communication and media within social movement studies

Traditionally, social movement studies have not paid particular attention to the nexus between collective action, media and communication processes, which has remained of secondary importance in comparison to movement organizational and symbolic practices (Mosca 2014). Moreover, the interplay between protest and media has been approached mostly through an 'instrumental-structuralist' perspective (Johnston 2009: 3) for which communication dynamics are not considered as objects of study in their own right but, rather, as functional to understanding movements' features, strategies and consequences. In this context, communication has been conceived as a process mainly directed towards 'the outside' of movements and strategically tailored to gain public 'acceptance' of alternative frames proposed by activists (Gamson 2004), while news coverage about movements and their activities was seen as a sign of their 'discursive presence or influence in the production of culture' (Amenta *et al*. 2009: 636). Along these lines, movements' features and outcomes have been linked (also) with their capability of framing arguments in a way that challenges but, at the same time, resonates with the surrounding cultural milieu (McCammon et al. 2007).

One particularly renowned translation of this epistemological orientation is the concept of 'discursive opportunity structure'. Starting from the idea that the political culture mediates the reception and the acceptance of movements' messages and frames, this concept addresses the cultural conditions that determine 'which ideas are considered "sensible", which constructions of reality are seen as "realistic", and which claims are held as "legitimate" within a certain polity at a specific time' (Koopmans & Statham 1999: 228). Together with institutional opportunities (Tarrow 1994), discursive opportunities incentivize the mobilization of collective endeavours with certain collective identities, goals and strategies, while constraining the organization of other collective endeavours aimed at different demands (Koopmans et al. 2005).

Mass media have been located at the very core of this overall discursive opportunity structure. Scholars indeed defined mass media as a 'master arena' for the development of public discourse (Ferree et al. 2002: 10) as well as for the crystallization of specific 'interpretative packages' constituting the 'public opinion' on relevant issues (Gamson & Modigliani 1989: 3). Thus, mass media have been seen as relevant to social movements' success first of all in light of their capability of shaping a more or less receptive environment for movements and their claims. As noted by Ferree and colleagues (2002: 10) in their study of the public discourse on abortion, 'when a cultural code is being challenged, a change in the media forum both signals and spreads the change'. Moreover, observers noted that the 'mass media public sphere' constitutes a decisive space for the development and the unfolding of contentious dynamics (Koopmans 2004). Also, the space created by mass media is a *learning space* for authorities, which become aware of movements, their actions and aims, but most notably for activists, who 'depend to a considerable degree on the mass media for information on the standpoints of authorities, third parties, and the larger public on the issue that concern them ... and they learn about others' reactions to their action from the news media' (Koopmans 2004: 370).

Nonetheless, interactions between media and movements have been often depicted as conflictual. In general, mass media have been considered as 'communication gatekeepers' able to determine the modes and the extent to which contentious messages are delivered to the broader public (Bennett & Segerberg 2016: 369). In his work, Koopmans proposed to conceptualize movements' discursive opportunities as resulting from the entwinement of three 'selective mechanisms' operated by news media onto movements' messages (Koopmans 2004). The first process is that of *visibility*, for which media condition the extent to which movements' messages are made publicly known. The second process is that of *resonance*, i.e. the extent to which media make movements' message reverberate through third-parties' reactions, whether these are positive or negative. Finally, media confer on movements' messages different degrees of *legitimacy*, depending on how they balance supportive and critical reactions to them. As noted by della Porta (2013), often these selective mechanisms result in rather narrow media opportunities which, together with political opportunities, have been considered as structural constraints to the diffusion of movements' messages.

And yet, in a mediascape in which news media are crucial to mobilize support and validate alternative messages, as well as to enlarge the scope of collective action (Gamson & Wolfsfeld 1992), movements have developed several strategies to attract attention of the media and, consequently, of the public. For example, della Porta and Diani (2006: 170–8) identify three main logics behind protest repertoires, all of which can, to some extent, increase media attention: the *logic of numbers*, that yields to the realization of large-scale and highly participated protest events; the *logic of bearing witness*, through which extremely risky actions are purposively undertaken; and the *logic of material damage*, which privileges the choice of highly disruptive action repertoires over non-conflictual ones. With specific attention to the mass media, Rucht (2004: 36–7) singles out four main strategies: *abstention* from interactions with media, which results in a preference for infra-group communication; *attack*, that is, an open confrontation with and an explicit critique of the media; *adaptation*, the proactive attitude towards marrying media logics to increase the newsworthiness of the movement; and *alternative*, the explicit choice to set up and exploit different communication means than the mainstream ones.

With particular regards to this latter strategy, a parallel strand of research developed at the crossroads between movement and communication studies to inquire how media are appropriated and reconfigured strategically in view of creating alternative and counter-cultural spaces in direct opposition with commercial and élite-oriented mainstream media narratives and for the empowerment of communities and marginalized groups (Mattoni et al. 2010). In Downing's definition (2001: 3), 'radical alternative media constitute the most active form of the active audience and express oppositional strands, overt and covert, within popular cultures'. They are 'media, generally small scale and in many different forms, that express an alternative vision to hegemonic policies, priorities and perspectives' (ibid.: v). Analysis focused on movement-near media – variously defined as alternative, activist, citizens', radical, autonomous (Mattoni 2009: 26–9) – pointed at their particular content and rhetoric, linking them to specific forms of news production. As social movement organizations, these alternative media produce a critique of the established media (Rucht 2004) as well as promoting a 'democratization of information' (Cardon & Granjou 2003). What is more, radical alternative media broaden the range of information and ideas, being more responsive to the excluded (Downing 2001).

In comparison to more canonical claims analysis of mainstream media, alternative media studies put more stress on the agency of social movements and their communicative practices, as well as the integration of (or, at least, overlapping between) different actors and fields of action in media seen as contentious arenas (Gamson 2004). Typical of alternative media, together with their critical, counter-hegemonic contents, is their capacity to involve in news production not only (or mainly) professional journalists, but also normal citizens. Their horizontal links with their audience (Atkinson 2010) allow, at times, overcoming the distinction between audience and producers, readers and writers through co-performance (ibid.: 41). Therefore, alternative media studies helped to clarify that movements do not only operate within institutional and discursive opportunities structures but also within complex *media environments* defined as 'open, unpredictable and controversial spaces of mediatization and communication, made up of different layers which continuously combine with one another due to the information flows circulating within the media environment itself' (Mattoni 2009: 33). In them, different actors intervene and different types of media interact as 'individuals simultaneously play different roles, especially in particular situations of protest, mobilization and claims making' (Mattoni 2009: 34). Additionally, attention has progressively been turned towards media practices as practices of resistance in their own right (Cammaerts 2012; Mattoni & Treré 2014) that go beyond repertoires of interaction with media actors. These include the ways in which 'people exercise their agency in relation to media flows' (Couldry 2006: 27), as 'reading media imagery is an active process in which context, social location, and prior experience can lead to quite different decoding' (Gamson et al. 1992: 375).

Social movements in complex media environments

In a context in which digital media have become ubiquitous, critical reflections developed in the previous mediascape dominated by mass media and their functioning logics have rapidly been complemented by an increasing number of studies aimed at unveiling the consequences of the pervasive diffusion of participatory and networked communication platforms. The transition from a mass-media to a 'spreadable media' communication environment (Jenkins, Ford & Green 2013), where citizens are no longer simply receivers of messages but increasingly act as producers and transmitters of contents (Bennett 2003), irreversibly modified the overall 'field of opportunities and constraints' (Melucci 1996: 4) in which collective endeavours emerge and unfold. Indeed, as noted by Castells (2009: 116), technological developments in the media field transformed the audience into a 'communicative subject increasingly able to redefine the process by which societal communication frames the culture of society'. In this sense, while continuing to reflect on the gatekeeping role played especially by commercial media, observers have begun to address more thoroughly the new ways of consuming, producing and distributing contents allowed by the increased diffusion of digital communications and which challenge established media power (Couldry 2003).

While it is recognized that the potential of digital media to multiply public spaces for deliberation and political action (della Porta & Mosca 2005) as well as to reach out to the general public (Peretti 2004) remains constrained by infrastructural and skill divides (van Dijk 2005), social movement studies have intensified their interest for the interplay between media, communication processes and collective action dynamics. More particularly, digital media are increasingly recognized to generate several impacts in relation to collective endeavours – in particular, in relation to the organization of protest, the construction of collective identities and the enrichment of collective action repertoires (Earl 2016).

Digital media and the organization of social movements

In her recent overview on the impacts of online protest and activism, Earl (2016) argues that a first way in which digital media impact upon the organization of collective endeavours is by supporting offline mobilizations (like rallies or demonstrations). In this respect, she distinguishes related and yet crucially different effects of digital media on social movements. On the one hand, digital media can exert a 'supersize effect' (Earl & Kimport 2011: 13) – that is, they allow the faster, wider and cheaper organization of activism yet without changing it substantially. On the other hand, digital media are a prelude to the realization of 'e-mobilization' (Earl & Kimport 2011: 4–5) – that is, activists use the communicative and networking potential of platforms like Facebook and Twitter to 'turn people out to offline events' (Earl 2016: 368). In turn, digitally-enabled participation contributes to amplifying participation and reaching collective goals, often mobilizing citizens who were not previously engaged in protest – in particular youngsters, women and lower-status citizens (Enjolras, Steen-Johnsen & Wollebæk 2013). In addition, they generate media coverage, which, as seen above, is fundamental to foster changes in the public opinion and to create a more receptive environment for movement messages (Earl 2016).

Not only do digital media assist the organization of offline contentious dynamics, but they also enable the organization of protest activities in the online space that do not substitute but, rather, complement offline collective expressions of dissent (Pavan 2014). Within 'e-movements' (Earl & Kimport 2011: 5–8), digital media platforms become new 'organizational hubs' able to link single individuals within online networks that are true sources of 'social power'

(Castells 2011) to challenge and reform the status quo. What is peculiar about e-movements – such as protests against the US Congress internet piracy and intellectual property legislation (Benkler *et al.* 2015), the networked Occupy! (Bennett & Segerberg 2013), or campaigning efforts to reclaim ICTs to end all forms of gender-based violence (Pavan 2017) – is their capacity to link individuals regardless of their formal affiliation or membership within social movement organizations (SMOs), and rather through a 'connective logic' for which engagement becomes 'relaxed and highly personalized' (Bennett & Segerberg 2013: 11–13). By producing and spreading their own content, and by being exposed to others' experiences and perceptions, individuals find proof that their claims are shared, and connect within fluid online networks of communication that are, by all means, actual components of contemporary collective efforts (Pavan 2014).

Especially in reaction to the emphasis put on social media within recent contentious episodes (including those in the Arab Springs, the spread of Occupy protests, the rise of the *Indignados* and others), some argue that online communication networks are residual or even detrimental for collective action dynamics (e.g. Diani 2011). However, less sceptical observers identify several reasons why online activism should not be dismissed too quickly (see Earl 2016: 378–9). First, although quicker and more ephemeral, levels of online mobilization are larger than those that could be achieved online and, in this sense, amplify the strategic effects that are typical of the above-mentioned *logic of numbers*. Moreover, as we will discuss more at length below, online forms of activism tend to be innovative in the type of repertoires adopted – whereas the newness of the tactics adopted is largely recognized to be a predictor of a movements' success.

Digital media and the construction of collective identities

Although it is less often explored than the organizational dimension of digitally enabled activisms, the construction of collective identities is also affected by the pervasive diffusion of digital media. Broadly speaking, collective identities consist of 'an interactive and shared definition produced by a number of individuals (or groups at a more complex level) concerning the *orientations* of their action and the *field* of opportunities and constraints in which such actions is to take place' (Melucci 1996: 70, emphasis in the original). Whereas in the pre-digital era much of the work to define these opportunities and the field for collective action was carried out by a restricted number of activists and, in any case, within the boundaries of formalized social movement organizations (Bennett & Segerberg 2013, Earl 2016), the diffusion of digital media and their extensive use as tools of protest and activism have enlarged the spaces and enriched the contributions that shape collective identities.

In this respect, observers note that, as much as in previous mediascapes, the construction of collective identities remains an inherently conflictual process that requires the difficult coordination of heterogeneous inputs delivered by a myriad of dispersed participants (Kavada 2015). Nonetheless, the continuous negotiation between perceptions, ideas, knowledge and expertise is carried out today in a dynamic interplay between the 'interactivity' that is typical of social media platforms (for example, the possibility they offer to change our profile pictures, to update our status at any point in time, to react in different ways to others' contributions) and the social need for a 'we' within which individuals can recognize themselves as part of a powerful collective (Gerbaudo & Treré 2015). On the one hand, digital media shape the modes in which individuals can express and propose themselves in public (boyd 2011). On the other hand, individuals are not passively subjected to these material constraints but, rather, purposively create, select, juxtapose and publicly display digital contents of all types (photos, video, texts, animated gifs, etc.) that, altogether, define their public presence (Milan 2015).

In this way, contemporary protest dynamics are characterized by identities that are inevitably fluid (Gerbaudo & Treré 2015), but nonetheless capable of orienting the collective pursuit of social and political change, as they meet citizens' needs to find 'more flexible association with causes, ideas, and political organizations' (Bennett & Segerberg 2013: 5).

Hybrid action repertoires

In the definition developed by Charles Tilly (1986: 2), collective action repertoires include the 'whole set of means [a group] has for making claims of different types on different individuals'. While the first conceptualization of repertoires of action has been criticized for focusing only on public display of disruptive action, in his most recent work Charles Tilly (2008) has talked of broader contentious performances, stressing the constant innovation in the various forms of contentious politics. As a theatrical repertoire, a repertoire of contention is constrained in both time and space because 'far from the image we sometimes hold of mindless crowds, people tend to act within known limits, to innovate at the margins of the existing forms, and to miss many opportunities available to them in principle' (Tilly 1986: 390).

The diffusion of digital media and the related change in the role played by users from receivers to prosumers of information entailed a radical transformation of action possibilities in the hand of activists. Analogously to what we argued above in relation to the consequences of digital media for the organization of social movements, online action repertoires do not replace but, rather, complement, offline tactics. In this respect, for example, Earl and Kimport (2011: 9) speak about the diffusion of 'e-tactics' – i.e. 'numerous instances of collective action with varying degrees of off- and online components and varying degrees of affiliations with social movements and SMOs'. Similarly, Van Laer and Van Aelst (2010) distinguished movement repertoires involving the use of internet along two dimensions. On the one hand, they envisage a dimension that opposes internet-based tactics, such as email bombing or hacktivism, to internet-supported tactics, that is, to more traditional and conventional modes of protesting, such as demonstrations and boycotts, which can be organized more easily and on a larger scale. On the other hand, the authors distinguish between low and higher threshold tactics depending on the levels of risk activists commit to when engaging in action. Thus, contrary to claims according to which online activities are forms of 'nano-activism' or 'slacktivism' (see Morozov 2009) that are 'undertaken only by those that are too lazy to participate in more meaningful ways' (Earl *et al.* 2016: 356), Van Laer and Van Aelst (2010) argue that some online tactics, such as launching a protest website or engaging in DDoS attacks (i.e. Distributed Denial of Service), require a lot of resources and also entail a great risk for activists – for example, of being accused and prosecuted for cyberterrorism or of suffering from personal attacks, not only in the online space but also offline, in their everyday life.

Future perspectives

In only a few years, social movement studies have made great steps forward in understanding the multiple facets of the interplay between media, communication and collective action dynamics. From a research context in which movements were seen mainly as penalized by existing media powers, we have now shifted towards a more nuanced comprehension of how enhanced technological possibilities are *actively*, *creatively*, and *strategically* exploited by activists, SMOs, but also by citizens engaging with collective causes.

Nonetheless, because digital media are tools designed to be in a 'permanently beta' version, that is, to be constantly in evolution, also their interplay with collective endeavours is very likely to remain fluid and ever-evolving. As we have shown in the second part of this chapter, it is increasingly recognized that all possible transformative effects that digital media may exert on social movement dynamics are played out at the crossroads between material and social factors and thus are inherently sociotechnical (Lievrouw 2014). However, in the urge of reclaiming the activeness of movements in relation to media and media power, less attention has been paid to the 'material agency' that is proper of digital media and that conditions the modes and the forms in which online protest and activism occur (Pavan 2014). Not only would a more thorough reflection on material agency help us understand what is truly 'new' about online activism in comparison to offline protest dynamics and already-known alternative media practices, it would also allow us to reflect more systematically on how online and offline activism entwine, how they complement each other and how they jointly concur to achieve social and political change (Earl 2016).

Also, so far, the interplay between media, both traditional and digital, and social movements has been addressed mainly looking at short-term instances of contention such as protest events (e.g. riots, demonstrations and/or occupations) or when digital contents happen to 'go viral'. In this sense, we possess only a partial understanding of how media practices across the online/offline boundary couple with the evolving nature of movement processes, and 'according to the state of the mobilization, the activities sustaining protest as well as the social actors who [are] using them' (della Porta & Mattoni 2015: 41). In turn, this limited perspective has so far hampered the shift toward a more complex view of movements and their media practices – able to grasp simultaneously the variety of uses that activists make of different information and communication tools they are endowed with, their interactions with media professionals, and the ways in which they actively engage in the production and the diffusion of their alternative narratives (Mattoni & Treré 2014).

Finally, while we have paid increasing attention to how social movements exploit digital media affordances to overcome political and cultural obstacles, we have paid admittedly less attention to investigating the contents of the 'alternative political imaginaries and theories about how to actualize these imagined possibilities' (Chesters 2012: 147) that movements elaborate at the crossroads between enlarged participation, inclusivity and material constraints imposed by the technologies they decide to appropriate. Thus, accounting more systematically for the knowledge that movements produce in the current digital mediascape appears to be a necessary step to comprehend how fluid and ever-evolving communication networks can become agents of democratization.

References

Amenta, E., Caren, N., Olasky, S. J. and Stobaugh, J. E. (2009) 'All the Movements Fits to the Print: Who, What, When, Where, and Why SMO Families Appeared in the New York Times in the Twentieth Century', *American Sociological Review*, vol. 74, pp. 636–56.

Atkinson, J. D. (2010) *Alternative Media and Politics of Resistance*. New York: Peter Lang.

Benkler, Y., Roberts, H., Faris, R., Solow-Niederman, A. and Etling, B. (2015) 'Social Mobilization and the Networked Public Sphere: Mapping the SOPA-PIPA Debate', *Political Communication*, vol. 32, no. 4, pp. 594–624.

Bennett, W. L. (2003) 'New Media Power, The Internet and Global Activism', in N. Couldry and J. Curran (eds) *Contesting Media Power. Alternative Media in a Networked World*. Lanham, MD: Rowman & Littlefield, pp. 17–37.

Bennett, W. L. and Segerberg, A. (2013) *The Logic of Connective Action*. New York: Cambridge University Press.

Bennett, W. L. and Segerberg, A. (2016) 'Communication in Movements', in D. della Porta and M. Diani (eds) *The Oxford Handbook of Social Movements*. Oxford: Oxford University Press, pp. 367–82.

boyd, d. (2011) 'Social Network Sites as Networked Publics: Affordances, Dynamics and Implications', in Z. Papacharissi (ed.) *A Networked Self*. New York and London: Routledge, pp. 39–58.

Cammaerts, B. (2012) 'Protest Logics and the Mediation Opportunity Structure', *European Journal of Communication*, vol. 27, no. 2, pp. 117–34.

Cardon, D. and Granjou, F. (2003) 'Puet-on se liberer des formats mediatiques? Le movement alter–monidialisation et l'Internet', *Mouvements*, vol. 25, pp. 67–73.

Castells, M. (2009) *Communication Power*. Oxford: Oxford University Press.

Castells, M. (2011) 'A Network Theory of Power', *International Journal of Communication*, vol. 5, pp. 773–87.

Chadwick, A. (2013) *The Hybrid Media System: Politics and Power*. Oxford: Oxford University Press.

Chesters, G. (2012) 'Social Movements and the Ethics of Knowledge Production', *Social Movement Studies*, vol. 11, no. 2, pp. 145–60.

Couldry, N. (2003) 'Beyond the Hall of Mirrors? Some Theoretical Reflections on the Global Contestation of Media Power', in N. Couldry and J. Curran (eds) *Contesting Media Power. Alternative Media in a Networked World*. Lanham, MD: Rowman & Littlefield, pp. 39–55.

Couldry, N. (2006) *Listening Beyond the Echoes. Media, Ethics and Agency in an Uncertain World*. New York: Paradigm.

della Porta, D. (2013) 'Bridging Research on Democracy, Social Movements and Communication', in B. Cammaerts, A. Mattoni and P. McCurdy (eds) *Mediation and Protest Movements*. Chicago, IL: Intellect, pp. 21–37.

della Porta, D. and Diani, M. (2006) *Social Movements. An Introduction*. Malden, MA: Blackwell Publishing.

della Porta, D. and Mosca, L. (2005) 'Global–Net for Global Movements? A Network of Networks for a Movement of Movements', *Journal of Public Policy*, vol. 25, pp. 165–90.

della Porta, D. and Mattoni, A. (2015) 'Social Networking Sites in Pro-democracy and Anti-austerity Protests: Some Thoughts from a Social Movement Perspective', in D. Trottier and C. Fuchs (eds) *Social Media, Politics and the State: Protests, Revolutions, Riots, Crime and Policing in the Age of Facebook, Twitter and YouTube*. London: London, pp. 39–65.

Diani, M. (2011) 'Networks and Internet into Perspective', *Swiss Political Science Review*, vol. 17, pp. 469–74.

Downing, J. D. H. with Ford, T.V., Gil, G. and Stein, L. (2001) *Radical Media: Rebellious Communication and Social Movements*. Thousand Oaks, CA: Sage.

Earl, J. (2016) 'Protest Online. Theorizing the Consequences of Online Engagement', in L. Bosi, M. Giugni and K. Uba (eds) *The Consequences of Social Movements*. Cambridge: Cambridge University Press, pp. 363–400.

Earl, J. and Kimport, K. (2011) *Digitally Enabled Social Change. Activism in the Internet Age*. Cambridge, MA: MIT Press.

Earl, J., Hunt, J., Garrett, R.K. and Dal, A. (2016) 'New Technologies and Social Movements', in D. della Porta and M. Diani (eds) *The Oxford Handbook of Social Movements*. Oxford: Oxford University Press, pp. 355–364.

Enjolras, B., Steen-Johnsen, K. and Wollebæk, D. (2013) 'Social Media and Mobilization to Offline Demonstrations: Transcending Participatory Divides?', *New Media and Society*, vol. 15, no. 6, pp. 890–908.

Ferree, M. M., Gamson, W.A., Gerhards, J. and Rucht, D. (2002) *Shaping Abortion Discourse. Democracy and the Public Sphere in Germany and the United States*. Cambridge: Cambridge University Press.

Gamson, W. A. (2004) 'Bystanders, Public Opinion, and the Media', in D. Snow, S. A. Soule and H. Kriesi (eds) *The Blackwell Companion to Social Movements*. Malden, MA: Blackwell, pp. 508–30.

Gamson, W. A. and Modigliani, A. (1989) 'Media Discourse and Public Opinion on Nuclear Power: A Constructionist Approach', *American Journal of Sociology*, vol. 95, no. 1, pp. 1–37.

Gamson, W. A. and Wolfsfeld, G. (1993) 'Movements and Media as Interacting Systems', *The Annals of the American Academy of Political and Social Science*, vol. 520, pp. 114–25.

Gamson, W. A., Croteau, D., Hoynes, W. and Sasson, T. (1992) 'Media Images and the Social Construction of Reality', *Annual Review of Sociology*, vol. 18, pp. 373–93.

Gerbaudo, P. and Treré, E. (2015) 'In Search of the "We" of Social Media Activism: Introduction to the Special Issue on Social Media and Protest Identities', *Information, Communication & Society*, vol. 18, no. 8, pp. 865–71.

Jenkins, H., Ford, S. and Green, J. (2013) *Spreadable Media. Creating Value and Meaning in a Networked Culture*. New York: New York University Press.

Johnston, H. (2009) 'Protest Cultures: Performance, Artifacts, and Ideations', in H. Johnston (ed.) *Culture, Social Movement and Protest*. Farnham: Ashgate, pp. 3–32.

Kavada, A. (2015) 'Creating the Collective: Social Media, the Occupy Movement and its Constitution as a Collective Actor', *Information, Communication & Society*, vol. 18, no. 8, pp. 872–86.

Koopmans, R. (2004) 'Movements and Media: Selection Processes and Evolutionary Dynamics in the Public Sphere', *Theory and Society*, vol. 33, pp. 367–91.

Koopmans, R. and Statham, P. (1999) 'Ethnic and Civic Conceptions of Nationhood and the Differential Success of the Extreme Right in Germany and Italy', in D. McAdam, C. Tilly and M. Giugni (eds) *How Social Movements Matter*. Minneapolis, MN: University of Minnesota Press, pp. 225–52.

Koopmans, R., Statham, P., Giugni, M. and Passy, F. (2005) 'Introduction. The Contentious Politics of Immigration and Ethnic Relations', in R. Koopmans, P. Statham, M. Giugni and F. Passy (eds) *Contested Citizenship. Immigration and Cultural Diversity in Europe*. Minneapolis, MN: University of Minnesota Press, pp. 1–30.

Lievrouw, L. (2014) 'Materiality and Media in Communication and Technology Studies: An Unfinished Project', in T. Gillespie, P. J. Boczkowski and K. A. Foot (eds) *Media Technologies. Essays on Communication, Materiality, and Society*. Cambridge, MA: MIT Press, pp. 21–51.

McCammon, H. J., Sanders Muse, C., Newman, H. D. and Terrel, T. M. (2007) 'Movement Framing and Discursive Opportunity Structures: The Political Success of the U.S. Women's Jury Movements', *American Sociological Review*, vol. 72, pp. 725–49.

Mattoni, A. (2009) *Multiple Media Practices in Italian Mobilizations against Precarity of Work*. PhD Thesis, Florence: European University Institute.

Mattoni, A. and Treré, E. (2014) 'Media Practices, Mediation Processes, and Mediatization in the Study of Social Movements', *Communication Theory*, vol. 24, pp. 252–71.

Mattoni, A., Berdnikovs, A., Ardizzoni, M. and Cox, L. (2010) 'Voices of Dissent: Activists' Engagements in the Creation of Alternative, Autonomous, Radical and Independent Media', *Interface: A Journal for and About Social Movements*, vol. 2, no. 2, pp. 1–22.

Melucci, A. (1996) *Challenging Codes. Collective Action in the Information Age*. Cambridge: Cambridge University Press.

Milan, S. (2015) 'From Social Movements to Cloud Protesting: The Evolution of Collective Identity', *Information, Communication & Society*, vol. 18, no. 8, pp. 887–900.

Morozov, E. (2009) 'Why Promoting Democracy via the Internet Is Often Not a Good Idea', *Foreign Policy*, 24 April, http://foreignpolicy.com/2009/04/24/why-promoting-democracy-via-the-internetis-often-not-a-good-idea, accessed 9 May 2017.

Mosca, L. (2014) 'Bringing Communication Back', in C. Padovani and A. Calabrese (eds) *Communication Rights and Social Justice: Historical Accounts of Transnational Mobilizations*. New York: Palgrave Mcmillian.

Pavan, E. (2014) 'Embedding Digital Communications within Collective Action Networks. A Multidimensional Network Perspective', *Mobilization. An International Journal*, vol. 19, no. 4, pp. 441–55.

Pavan, E. (2017). 'The Integrative Power of Online Collective Action Networks beyond Protest. Exploring Social Media Use in the Process of Institutionalization', *Social Movement Studies*, vol. 16, no. 4, pp. 433–46.

Peretti, J. (with M. Micheletti) (2004) 'The Nike Sweatshop Email: Political Consumerism, Internet, and Culture Jamming', in M. Micheletti, A. Follesdal and D. Stolle (eds) *Politics, Products and Markets. Exploring Political Consumerism Past and Present*. New Brunswick, NJ: Transaction Publishers, pp. 127–42.

Rucht, D. (2004) 'The Quadruple "A": Media Strategies of Protest Movements since the 1960s', in W. van de Donk, B. Loader, P. Nixon and D. Rucht (eds) *Cyberprotest: New Media, Citizens and Social Movements*. London: Routledge, pp. 29–56.

Tarrow, S. (1994) *Power in Movement*. Cambridge: Cambridge University Press.

Tilly, C. (1986) *The Contentious French*. Cambridge, MA: Harvard University Press.

Tilly, C. (2008) *Democracy*. New York: Cambridge University Press.

van Dijk, J. A. G. M. (2005) *The Deepening Divide. Inequality in the Information Society*. London: Sage.

Van Laer, J. and Van Aelst, P. (2010) 'Internet and Social Movements Action Repertoires', *Information, Communication & Society*, vol. 13, no. 8, pp. 1146–71.

3

NONVIOLENT ACTIVISM AND THE MEDIA

Gandhi and beyond

Sean Scalmer

In the early years of the twentieth century, the political experiments of Mohandas Karamchand Gandhi helped to refine a new form of political activism. Gandhi called it *satyagraha*, a neologism that combined the Sanskrit words for 'truth' and 'firmness'. Its promulgation signaled a break from earlier practice (for no English term was thought an adequate descriptor of Gandhi's new approach), a connection with Indian traditions and a claim to embody spiritual as well as tactical imperatives. Advanced in efforts to win civil and political rights for Indians in South Africa and then to pursue Indian Home Rule, *satyagraha* impressed even sceptics with its capacity to inspire mass nonviolent sacrifice. But this was never simply a tool of self-assertion, and the Indian leader understood *satyagraha* as a 'message' or 'lesson' for the whole world, a means to secure 'universal nonviolence' across the globe (Gandhi 1964: 262, 1968: 127, 1977: 390–1). His experiments won international interest and then emulation. Gandhian nonviolence became an enduring form of political activism in the West as well as the East (Scalmer 2011). How were these political achievements secured? And what was their relationship to the mass media? In this chapter, I seek to provide answers, explaining how Gandhi created *satyagraha*, and how the media helped to develop, amplify, diffuse and transform it.

Gandhi's political campaigns have been narrated and analyzed in several thousand works (see Pandiri 1995). The product of a fertile and creative mind, they rested also on a combination of political resources. There was an Indian tradition of nonviolent action, and Gandhi was able to invoke this lineage in advocating a practice he originally termed 'passive resistance' or 'soul force' (e.g., Gandhi 1921a). The *Bhagavad Gita* – one of the most sacred of Hindu texts – was widely interpreted as a parable of nonviolence. Gandhi especially cited the *Gita* as a means of justifying his actions to a predominantly Hindu community (Scalmer 2016).

Western political traditions offered additional resources. Jesus Christ could be considered an emissary of nonviolence (Gandhi 1962: 119, 1971: 438). Quakers and celebrated Christian pacifists – among them Count Leo Tolstoy – provided further exemplars of the nonviolent way (Tolstoy 1961). And Henry David Thoreau's advocacy of 'civil disobedience' might be grasped as another significant precedent (Gandhi 1963: 65).

Western politics also provided recent examples of successful collective campaigning. Developing from the early nineteenth century, the modern 'social movement' combined a series of political tools in a new way: a repertoire of predominantly nonviolent political performances (among them the demonstration and the protest march); the building of mass organizations; public displays of worthiness, unity, numbers and commitment (see Tilly & Wood 2015). Over the succeeding decades, these methods were applied by campaigners against slavery, for Catholic emancipation and for democratic rights. Sometimes, they were tied to especially striking and dramatic performances of moral force: the petitions and processions of the Chartists; the passive resistance of English non-conformists; the theatrical militancy of the suffragettes.

Educated as a lawyer in London, Gandhi was exposed to such political techniques. He joined the Vegetarian Society from London and spoke and wrote in support of the cause (Guha 2013). He referenced the writings of Tolstoy and Thoreau. He closely observed the suffragettes, admiring particularly their boldness and commitment (Gandhi 1962: 453, 1963: 65, 189). These were political inspirations. They were also points of identification or commonality, through which Gandhi's original approaches might be legitimated and understood.

Satyagraha and the media

Alongside those many influences, the media was also a significant political resource. The invention of the telegraph in the 1840s had made possible the transmission of news reports across continents with an unaccustomed alacrity (Schudson 1978: 4). The establishment of global news agencies in the years afterward (most notably Reuters, American Associated Press, and United Press International) brought coverage of far-flung events within the reach of vastly greater numbers (Boyd-Barrett 1978: 192, 206–07). The development of photography and then newsreels helped to capture the visual character of political life, and to heighten the interest of the media in spectacular and arresting mass events (Tickner 1987: 58–9).

If Gandhian *satyagraha* was based on many precedents in the East and West, then its political efficacy rested especially on a capacity to exploit the increasingly global and visual character of the media industries. Gandhi's successful nonviolent campaigns were aided by the media in several ways. First and most obviously, nonviolent protest – often encompassing the conscious violation of laws, the deliberate courting of punishment and the mass assembly of the people – precipitated moments of heightened dramatic intensity. This, in turn, elicited the interest of the metropolitan media. And the media could bring the nonviolent challenge of the *satyagrahi* to an audience that straddled the globe.

Gandhi possessed an unusual capacity to anticipate media interest and to choreograph protest campaigns that might win great coverage. Observers likened him to a dramatist, a publicity agent, a playwright, a producer, a stage manager and a star (e.g. Fisher 1932: 47; Wheeler 1944: 200). But if sometimes scorned for an apparent desire for 'keeping up the publicity stunt' (Viceroy 1931), Gandhi's dramatic flair was necessary to the effectiveness of *satyagraha*. Without the interest of metropolitan media, the grievances and moral sacrifices of Indians could not be known. And the success of nonviolent appeal rested on prior knowledge as well as sympathetic understanding.

It was Gandhi's political creativity that helped from the early 1920s to make the case of Indian Home Rule a regular subject of Western debate. At this time, a large metropolitan audience first became aware of a major political movement, 'headed by a leader and conducted by methods which astounded and bewitched Occidental reporters' (Case 1923: 347). Attention waned somewhat over the mid-1920s, but rebounded by 1929. It reached unimagined heights in the first years of the new decade, as Gandhi's 'salt *satyagraha*' campaign mobilized participants across much of India.

Now a new generation of American correspondents joined an already substantial contingent of British reporters. Members of the South Asian community in America also took up the pen, and Gandhi's emissaries (including Sarojini Naidu, Madeleine Slade, and C. F. Andrews) visited the West (Gordon 2002: 347). Gandhi's open civil disobedience came to dominate the news (Seshachari 1969: 58). He was named *Time* magazine's 'Man of the Year' in 1930, and the *New York Times* published more than 500 articles that referenced the Mahatma in that 12-month period alone. In fascinated and sometimes breathless news reports published at this time, an image of 'nonviolence in action' was compressed and shared with the Western world. The correspondence of Webb Miller and Negley Farson, initially censored, proved especially influential (Scalmer 2011: 47). Newspaper coverage of Gandhi in the major broadsheets increased by one-half again over 1931. African American newspapers also evinced considerable interest in the Mahatma at this time, as the early curiosity of the *Crisis* and the *Negro World* was succeeded by a more general enthusiasm for matters Gandhian (Kapur 1992: 25, 45).

Metropolitan interest dulled slightly thereafter, as the Indian campaign subsided. But there was a later (though less elevated) peak of interest in a new nonviolent campaign he led from the middle years of WWII, and then further attention upon the achievement of Indian independence in 1947. Gandhi's assassination in 1948 also served as a focus for reminiscence and argument, unloosening another 'flood of publicity', on the reckoning of noted American pacifist, A. J. Muste (Muste 1948).

While the journalists scribbled, the photographers snapped. One critic of the Mahatma argued that 'his prestige owes much to the press photographer' (Hodson 1941), and it is true that his unmistakable figure graced the pages of the leading journals more frequently than other Indian subjects, whether individual or collective. The craze to represent the Mahatma also crossed from the newspaper to the art gallery, and extended even to consumer items (Scalmer 2011: 28–9). Much more than a conventional leader of a political campaign, the Mahatma was eventually imagined into something of an icon. Whether the collective campaign for 'Home Rule' was relatively mobilized or quiescent, Gandhi – its symbol – maintained newsworthiness. For the adherents of the Indian cause, and for the advocates of peaceful protest, this proved a substantial political resource. Always, the attention of the press could be expected.

However, the Mahatma was not simply the object of media interest. Gandhi was conscious of the dangers of media misreporting, and frequently lamented its ubiquity (Scalmer 2011: 42). He responded with his own media interventions, using the media to support his claims and to share the virtues of the nonviolent way. Challenging media bias, Gandhi composed press releases especially for inquiring journalists, and even for news agencies themselves (Pyarelal and Nayar 1991: 15). He also sent informative cables to expatriate Indians in the metropole. When marching and protesting he employed early forms of the sound bite (Hardiman 2003: 253). The Mahatma edited independent publications that attained an influential circulation in the West (Gandhi's *Collected Works* would eventually sum to around 100 thick volumes). And he eagerly embraced any opportunity to use the radio, or directly to answer his critics in hostile newspapers (Scalmer 2011: 63).

In writings, speeches, interviews and public letters, Gandhi explained his purposes and values. Repeatedly and clearly, he framed the underlying moral and intellectual basis of *satyagraha*: an unwavering commitment to nonviolence, whatever the circumstances (Gandhi 1917: 51, 1930a: 694); the pursuit of truth rather than victory over an antagonist (Gandhi 1921b: 158, 1930b: 70); love for one's enemy (Gandhi cited in Dalton 1996: 40); a willingness to suffer, in the hope that such conscious suffering might convince an opponent to 'see the error of their ways' (Gandhi 1910: 224); the expectation that political conflict would end in conversion of evil-doers, not in a personal triumph (Gandhi 1930a: 698). These were radical and unfamiliar ideas to most Westerners. Gandhi needed to use the media to illuminate the meaning of his actions. His media interventions served both to enhance the effectiveness of his campaigning and to win a broader interest in *satyagraha* as a means of change.

Globalizing satyagraha: the media and other forces

Alongside Gandhi, a cosmopolitan group of supporters emerged to publicize the Indian cause and to explain the intricacies of the Mahatma's approach. All adroitly used the media, especially the print media, publishing pamphlets, books and articles; delivering lectures that were frequently the object of press interest. They included Non-conformist Ministers; Christian women; African American pastors; and Indian expatriates (for details, see Scalmer 2011: 93–103). Their efforts helped to transmit *satyagraha* to the world.

The major Western institutions dedicated to peace – The Fellowship of Reconciliation and the Peace Pledge Union – also acted to publicize and promote *satyagraha* to Western audiences. From the early 1940s, the Fellowship of Reconciliation's 'racial-industrial' department in the US started to organize conferences dedicated to the application of Gandhi's ideas to the problems of racial oppression and conflict (Scalmer 2011: 128). Soon afterward, a fragment of the Fellowship broke away as 'the Congress of Racial Equality', and began to experiment with nonviolent direct action (Meier & Rudwick 1969). A similar dynamic was evident in the United Kingdom. There, the Peace Pledge Union served as a home of vigorous debate around Gandhi's ideas for several decades. After many false starts, those activists most convinced of the merits of *satyagraha* formed a new organization, 'Operation Gandhi', in the early 1950s. This grouping later became the 'Non-Violent Resistance Group', and launched a series of nonviolent campaigns against nuclear weaponry.

Western experiments of these kinds were reliant on the media. The attempt to adapt Gandhian techniques was prefaced by persistent discussion of Gandhi and *satyagraha* within the movements' own alternative media (Scalmer 2002). The pioneering Western acts were framed and justified in special movement publications and newssheets that were frequently the object of intense activist debate and attention (see Scalmer 2011: 140–2). And the novelty and radicalism of these first Western protests self-consciously influenced by Gandhi drew a very broad media coverage that helped to secure notable success.

Building on such experimentation, large-scale nonviolent protests inspired by Gandhi shook the major Western polities some decades after the Mahatma's death. From the later 1950s, movements for civil rights and against nuclear arms perfected *satyagraha* as form of mass politics for the West. In Britain, the campaign to 'ban the bomb' encompassed invasions of rocket sites from 1958 and 'sit-down' demonstrations in central London from 1961. At Easter time that year, 150,000 people joined the 52-mile march from the Aldermaston nuclear reactor to the national capital; later that September, 1,300 were arrested in a knowingly illegal demonstration in central London. In the United States, the movement for African American civil rights mobilized earlier and ranged even further. A boycott of segregated buses in Montgomery, Alabama began in December 1955, when 50,000 residents united under the leadership of a young pastor, a certain Dr Martin Luther King Jr. From February 1960, a 'sit-in' movement spread from Greensboro, North Carolina. Within a month, mass protests had jumped the borders of seven states; nearly 4,000 demonstrators were eventually arrested in more than 100 cities. A 'freedom ride' to desegregate bus terminals across the South left Washington, DC in May 1961. Marchers converged upon Washington two years later, where a quarter of a million listened to Martin Luther King's dreams. Community-wide protest campaigns convulsed Albany in 1961, Birmingham in 1963, and Selma in 1965. In these heroic and thrilling acts, Gandhian non-violence became a powerful and enduring presence in the Western world.

These were nonviolent protests launched in a television age, and they quickly became television news. Gandhian-style acts were at first unusual, and that made them interesting (Gamson 1990: 157). The initial Aldermaston marches, southern sit-ins and urban sit-downs all reached the nightly bulletins. And with generous media coverage came the prospect of powerful political effects. It was a pattern of attention most evident in the struggles of the civil rights movement in America's South. There, the initiation of peaceful protest was answered with a terrible violence; images of martyrdom were broadcast to the world (Garrow 1986: 239–40; Arsenault 2006: 165–66). The brutality of white police dramatized an obvious battle between good and evil (Kertzer 1988: 92). In consequence, a new generation of supporters swept into the movement, and the notice of elites was riveted upon the disorder as well as its deeper cause (Gitlin 1987: 144).

A theorist as well as a practitioner of nonviolent protest, Martin Luther King Jr's 'Letter from a Birmingham Jail' analyzed the workings of this political technique in perhaps the most sophisticated and influential terms. As King explained, nonviolent direct action possessed the capacity to 'create' a 'crisis' and to 'dramatize' an issue, thereby ensuring that it could 'no longer be ignored' (King 1964: 78–9). Through the 'creation of tension', and the attraction of outside interest, social evils would face a new scrutiny. Exposed to debate and to an increasingly aware public, change eventually became possible:

> Like a boil that can never be cured so long as it is covered up but must be opened with all its ugliness to the natural medicines of air and light, injustice must be exposed, with all the tension its exposure creates, to the light of human conscience and the air of national opinion before it can be cured.
>
> *King 1964: 85*

The initial success of King's strategy had implications not just the cause of racial equality, but also for the fact and the utility of nonviolent protest. Television news captured the power and effectiveness of nonviolent display. It thereby served as a means of recruitment to political campaigns. Over a few heady years, nonviolent protests in the West rapidly increased in size and in number. Soon, 'mass direct action' replaced smaller demonstrations (Bell 1968: 17), and nationwide events became regular features of the activist calendar. The process was evident not just in the battle for racial justice, but also in movements for student rights, peace, women's rights, sexual liberation and the environment. Indeed, successful mobilizations led by 'early risers' opened the way for a cluster of later challengers (Tarrow 1998). What came to be called 'new social movements' emerged as potentially transformative political actors (Touraine 1974).

Diffusion, transformation and the media

The attention of the mass media was central to both the efficacy of nonviolent protest and the diffusion of Gandhian nonviolence to new polities and new causes. But if the media aided nonviolence, then it was not simply a means of transmission: it transformed as much as it spread nonviolent activism. For India's Mahatma, *satyagraha* rested on a bedrock of principle: it was not simply a tool of politics, but rather a creedal commitment. Gandhi's initial Western disciples shared these principled attachments, too (Scalmer 2011: 137–48). However, those swept into the mass campaigns of the 1960s typically lacked long-term exposure to Gandhian writings or ideas. For them, nonviolence was a 'tactic' or a 'utilitarian' practice, not a creedal commitment (Sutherland 1965: 30, Ryan 1988: 194). Observing nonviolent protest through the mass media, they largely understood this form of activism as a pragmatic means to win attention to a favoured cause.

This less philosophical attachment to nonviolent activism was increasingly evident on both sides of the Atlantic. April Carter, secretary of the Direct Action Committee (one of the most significant of British organizations at this time), noted even in the early 1960s that the tenor of nonviolent protest was therefore changing. She identified a 'move towards mass civil disobedience by a number of individuals who don't believe in n.v. [non-violence] in Satyagraha terms'. As such, she admitted, 'inevitable risks' were involved: the hegemony of 'nonviolent' activism was increasingly threatened (Carter 1960).

Writing a few years later in the United States, American sociologist Inge Powell Bell discovered a similarly 'shallow' view of non-violence in the civil rights movement, characterized by an emphasis on 'practical techniques' and an absence of 'soul searching' around the 'inner attitudes' of the activist (Bell 1968: 26, 42–3). Eddie Gottlieb, considering the peace movement in the US, also hit upon an equivalent view. Writing in 1968, Gottlieb looked back on what now seemed a too-rapid growth, as participation and expectations inflated unduly over a few exciting years. 'We were too successful for OUR own good,' he now felt:

> The Movement swarmed with newcomers who successively wanted to take off from each new height. They were enticed by the victories of the non-violent Movement but they looked for total success by the short cuts that violence seemed to offer.
>
> *Gottlieb 1968*

This interpretation has been supported by later historical analysis (e.g. Gitlin 1980: 30, 128–9). Untutored or unbelieving, many participants in large protests increasingly rejected the nonviolent faith. And as the size of the campaign grew, so the nature of the problem, and the difficulty of asserting control, expanded to equivalent dimensions. On both sides of the Atlantic, large demonstrations were successively disrupted by the activity of determined opponents of the *satyagraha* way. The sheer size of the developing movement made complete non-violence almost impossible (Goodman 1967: 36).

The tastes of the mass media appeared to intensify this dynamic. While at first highly attuned to the novelty of Gandhian-inspired protests, journalists came with time to regard most peaceful demonstrations as relatively routine and familiar. Episodes of more obvious insurgency and physical conflict increasingly drew a greater share of attention (Bond 2001: 31; Lee 2002: 143–4). This made nonviolence less effective as a form of mediated appeal: it thereby contributed to the adoption of increasingly disruptive and violent protest techniques.

The (always incomplete) rejection of nonviolence by many of the social movements of the 1960s was, of course, driven by forces beyond the media. Peaceful appeals to wrongdoers were met most often with violence rather than conversion (Scalmer 2011: 206–8); the growing conflict between protesters and police polarized radicals and convinced many that violence was now the only way (on polarization: Della Porta 1995: 76–7, 137, 214); early advocates of *satyagraha* were exhausted or dejected by years of repression (Farmer 1968: v); and the increasing rejection of formal authority nurtured an 'anti-disciplinary protest' which made the order and control of Gandhian nonviolence appear restrictive and somewhat old-fashioned (Stephens 1998). But among these many forces, the media's priorities undeniably contributed to a disaffection with nonviolence. Contemporary activists wrestle still with the complicated legacies.

Conclusion

Inspired by Gandhi and drawing strength from the genuine success of other nonviolent campaigns since the 1960s, many activists around the world retain a faith in nonviolent protest. Some of the most successful campaigns of recent decades have encompassed the widespread deployment of nonviolence: human rights advocacy, especially in Latin America and Eastern Europe; the revolutions that overthrew communism in 1989; the environmental direct action of Greenpeace; the anti-austerity mobilizations of the *Indignados* and of the Occupy movement; the Arab revolutions of 2011. Moreover, recent nonviolent campaigns (including explicitly anti-violence campaigns) have sometimes combined peaceful and creative protest with creative use of new information technologies and social media (Bock 2012; Gerbaudo 2012). And the internet itself has increasingly been conceptualized as a space for new forms of nonviolent direct action, including hacking and cryptography (see Assange 2012: 5). Reflecting and sometimes contributing to these developments, many scholars have come to more fully appreciate the efficacy of nonviolence, to refine its tactical basis, and to argue for its adoption (e.g. Ackerman & Duvall 2000; Schock 2005).

None of this is to suggest that the relationship between the media and nonviolent activism is completely harmonious, for it remains beset by tensions. Reflecting these tensions, nonviolent activists continue to adopt various attitudes to the media: there is no consensus. Some activists court the mainstream media with relatively moderate and respectable interventions; others focus attention on developing alternative media; others still choreograph potentially disruptive performances, expecting that their nonviolent acts will be criticized and even caricatured, but believing that hostile coverage is preferable to relative silence or neglect (see Maddison & Scalmer 2006: 215–23).

Gandhi, of course, never promised that the path of nonviolence would be easy, or that he possessed all the answers. On the contrary, he self-consciously presented *satyagraha* as an experimental science, not yet fully understood; his aim was to encourage others to continue to 'experiment' with the method, according to individual 'inclination' and 'capacity' (Gandhi 1927: x). Gandhi's injunction to continued experimentation challenges activists to new nonviolent campaigns. It implies, too, the possibility that these might generate fresh political discoveries, among them unforeseen means of attracting, influencing and deploying the media in the quest for peaceful political change.

References

Ackerman, P. and DuVall, J. (2000) *A Force More Powerful: A Century of Nonviolent Conflict*. New York: Palgrave.

Anderson, J. (1998) *Bayard Rustin: Troubles I've Seen*. Berkeley, CA and London: University of California Press.

Arsenault, R. (2006) *Freedom Riders: 1961 and the Struggle for Racial Justice*. New York: Oxford University Press.

Assange, J. *et al* (2012), *Cypherpunks: Freedom and the Future of the Internet*. London and New York: OR Books.

Bell, I. P. (1968) *CORE and the Strategy of Nonviolence*. New York: Random House.

Bock, J. G. (2012) *The Technology of Nonviolence: Social Media and Violence Prevention*. Cambridge, MA: MIT Press.

Bond, J. (2001) 'The Media and the Movement: Looking Back from the Southern Front', in B. Ward (ed.) *Media, Culture, and the Modern African American Freedom Struggle*. Gainesville, FL: University Press of Florida, pp. 16–40.

Boyd-Barrett, O. (1978) 'Market Control and Wholesale News: The Case of Reuters', in G. Boyce, J. Curran, and P. Wingate (eds) *Newspaper History: From the Seventeenth Century to the Present Day*. London: Constable, pp. 192–204.

Carter, A. (1960) 'Letter to Michael Randle, 28 September'. In *Direct Action Committee Papers*, Commonweal Collection, J. B. Priestley Library, University of Bradford, Box 7, Bay E, Folder: 'Miscellaneous Papers'.

Case, C. M. (1923) *Non-Violent Coercion: A Study in the Methods of Social Pressure*. New York and London: The Century Co.

Dalton, D. (1996) *Mahatma Gandhi: Selected Political Writings*. Indianapolis: Hackett Publishing Company.

Della Porta, D. (1995) *Social Movements, Political Violence, and the State: A Comparative Analysis of Italy and Germany*. Cambridge: Cambridge University Press.

Farmer, J. (1968) 'Foreword', in I. P. Bell *CORE and the Strategy of Nonviolence*. New York: Random House, p. v.

Fisher, F. B. (1932) *That Strange Little Brown Man Gandhi*. New York: Ray Long and Richard B. Smith.

Gamson, W. (1990) *The Strategy of Social Protest*. Belmont: Wadsworth Publishing.

Gandhi, M. K. (1910) 'Price of Freedom', in R. Iyer (ed.) *The Moral and Political Writings of Mahatma Gandhi, Volume III*. Oxford: Clarendon Press, 1987.

Gandhi, M. K. (1917) 'Extract from Letter to Bhaishri Shakaralal', in R. Iyer (ed.) *The Moral and Political Writings of Mahatma Gandhi, Volume III*. Oxford: Clarendon Press, 1987.

Gandhi, M. K. (1921a), *Hind Swaraj, Or, Indian Home Rule*. Madras: S. Ganeson and Co.

Gandhi, M. K. (1921b), 'The Poet's Anxiety', in R. Iyer (ed.) *The Moral and Political Writings of Mahatma Gandhi, Volume III*. Oxford: Clarendon Press, 1987.

Gandhi, M. K. (1927) *An Autobiography, Or, The Story of My Experiments with Truth*. Ahmedabad: Navajivan.

Gandhi, M. K. (1930a) 'Letter to Lord Irwin, Viceroy and Governor-General of India, March 2', in C. Chatfield (ed.) *The Americanization of Gandhi: Images of the Mahatma*. New York and London: Garland Publishing.

Gandhi, M. K. (1930b) 'Some Rules of Satyagraha' in R. Iyer (ed.) *The Moral and Political Writings of Mahatma Gandhi, Volume III*. Oxford: Clarendon Press, 1987.

Gandhi, M. K. (1962) *The Collected Works of Mahatma Gandhi* [henceforth *CWMG*], vol. 7, Delhi: Publications Division, Ministry of Information and Broadcasting.

Gandhi, M. K. (1963) *CWMG*, vol. 10, Delhi: Publications Division, Ministry of Information and Broadcasting.

Gandhi, M. K. (1964) *CWMG*, vol. 13, Delhi: Publications Division, Ministry of Information and Broadcasting.

Gandhi, M. K. (1968) *CWMG*, vol. 28, Delhi: Publications Division, Ministry of Information and Broadcasting.

Gandhi, M. K. (1971) *CWMG*, vol. 48, Delhi: Publications Division, Ministry of Information and Broadcasting.

Gandhi, M. K. (1977) *CWMG*, vol. 68, Delhi: Publications Division, Ministry of Information and Broadcasting.

Garrow, D. J. (1986) *Bearing the Cross: Martin Luther King, Jr., and the Southern Christian Leadership Conference*. New York: William Morrow and Company.

Gerbaudo, P. (2012) *Tweets and the Streets: Social Media and Contemporary Activism*. London: Pluto Press.

Gitlin, T. (1980) *The Whole World is Watching: Mass Media in the Making and Unmaking of the New Left*. Berkeley, CA and London: University of California Press.

Gitlin, T. (1987) *The Sixties: Years of Hope, Days of Rage*. New York: Bantam Books.

Goodman, P. (1967) 'The Duty of Professionals', *Liberation*, vol. 12, no. 8, pp. 36–9.

Gordon, L. A. (2002), 'Mahatma Gandhi's Dialogues with Americans', *Economic and Political Weekly*, 26 January.

Gottlieb. E. (1968) 'Workshop in Nonviolence, Chicago 1968'. In *Fellowship of Reconciliation Papers*, Swarthmore College Peace Collection, DG 13, Series D, Box 72, Folder: 'For Ronald Young Files – Anti-war Movement, Mobilization, Chicago Aug. 1968'.

Guha, R. (2013) *Gandhi Before India*. London: Allen Lane.

Hardiman, D. (2003) *Gandhi in His Time and Ours*. New Delhi: Permanent Black.

Harrison, I. (1956) *Agatha Harrison: An Impression by Her Sister*. London: Allen and Unwin.

Hodson, T. C. (1941) Letter to *The Times*, 24 January.

Kapur, S. (1992) *Raising Up a Prophet: The African-American Encounter with Gandhi*. Boston: Beacon Press.

Kertzer, D. I. (1988) *Ritual, Politics and Power*. New Haven, CT and London: Yale University Press.

King, M. L., Jr. (1964) 'Letter from a Birmingham Jail' (1963) in M. L. King, Jr., *Why We Can't Wait*. New York: New American Library.

Lee, T. (2002) *Mobilizing Public Opinion: Black Insurgency and Racial Attitudes in the Civil Rights Era*. Chicago and London: University of Chicago Press.

Maddison, S. and Scalmer, S. (2006) *Activist Wisdom: Practical Knowledge and Creative Tension in Social Movements*. Sydney: University of New South Wales Press.

Meier, A. and Rudwick, E. (1969) 'How CORE Began', *Social Science Quarterly*, vol. 49, no. 4, pp. 789–99.

Muste, A. J. (1948) 'Observance of Gandhi's Birthday', *Peace News*, 2 July.

Pandiri, A. M. (1995) *A Comprehensive, Annotated Bibliography on Mahatma Gandhi*. Westport, CT: Greenwood Publishing Group.

Pyarelal and Nayar, S. (1991) *In Gandhiji's Mirror*. New Delhi: Oxford University Press.

Ryan, A. (1988) *Bertrand Russell: A Political Life*. New York and Oxford: Oxford University Press.

Scalmer, S. (2002) 'The Labor of Diffusion: the Peace Pledge Union and the Adaptation of the Gandhian Repertoire', *Mobilization*, vol. 7, no. 3, pp. 269–86.

Scalmer, S. (2011) *Gandhi in the West: The Mahatma and the Rise of Radical Protest*. Cambridge and New York: Cambridge University Press.

Scalmer, S. (2016) 'Gandhi and the Humanitarians of Empire: Influence, Resistance and the Invention of Nonviolent Politics', *Journal of Colonialism and Colonial History*, vol. 17, no. 1, https://muse.jhu.edu/article/613285, accessed 18 November 2017.

Schock, K. (2005) *Unarmed Insurrections: People Power Movements in Nondemocracies*. Minneapolis, MN: University of Minnesota Press.

Schudson, M. (1978) *Discovering the News: A Social History of American Newspapers*. New York: Basic Books.

Seshachari, C. (1969) *Gandhi and the American Scene: An Intellectual History and Inquiry*. Bombay: Nachiketa Publications.

Slade, M. (1960) *The Spirit's Pilgrimage*. New York: Coward-McCann.

Stephens, J. (1998) *Anti-disciplinary Protest: Sixties Radicalism and Postmodernism*. New York and Cambridge: Cambridge University Press.

Sutherland, E. (1965) *Letters from Mississippi*. New York: McGraw-Hill Book Company.

Tarrow, S. (1998) *Power in Movement*. New York: Cambridge University Press.

Tickner, L. (1987) *The Spectacle of Women: Imagery of the Suffrage Campaign, 1907–14*. London: Chatto and Windus.

Tilly, C. and Wood, L. J. (2015) *Social Movements 1768–2012*. London and New York: Routledge.

Tolstoy, L. (1961) *The Kingdom of God Is within You*. New York: Farrar, Straus and Giroux.

Touraine, A. (1974) *The Post-Industrial Society*. London: Wildwood.

Viceroy (1931) 'Letter to the Secretary of State for India', 12 October, India Office Library, MSS EUR E 240/5.

Wheeler, P. (1944) *India Against the Storm*. New York: E. P. Dutton and Co.

4

CAN THE WOMEN'S PEACE CAMP BE TELEVISED?

Challenging mainstream media coverage of Greenham Common

Anna Feigenbaum

The curious thing was that no-one knew how to draw a Greenham lesbian.
– Ruth Wallsgrove on the tabloid press

Every note you take
Every tale you make
Every film you fake
Every muck you rake
We'll be watching you
– Greenham Women's Protest Song (to the tune of Sting's 'Every Breath You Take')

On 5 September 1981, a group of women ended their march from Cardiff, Wales outside the Greenham Common United States Air Force base in Newbury, England in protest of the 1979 NATO decision allowing US nuclear cruise missiles to be housed at military bases in Europe. Greenham Common would be the first base to receive missiles, with over 100 warheads scheduled to arrive. The group of around 35 marchers, mostly women, demanded a televised debate with the Ministry of Defense over the decision to site cruise missiles in England. The women's request was not granted, so they refused to leave. As supporters and supplies came in, an encampment soon emerged.

The physical location of the Greenham encampment outside of a military base set to store nuclear cruise missiles directed media attention towards this issue. From living rooms to pubs, political meetings to prison cafeterias, reports of Greenham travelled through newspapers, magazines, television, radio, and often through word of mouth. The onslaught of press coverage the peace camp received between 1982 and 1984 made 'Greenham' a household name. As the peace protest's popularity grew, women at the camp quickly became aware of their public image and began to devise strategies to challenge mainstream media's dominant representations.

The diversity of media coverage Greenham received offers rich material for an analysis of the dynamic interplay between media outlets, media producers and media readers. In this chapter I examine how the mainstream media reported Greenham and some of the strategies women used to subvert and challenge these dominant representations. I use the term 'mainstream media' to include national as well as local television and print media that were produced, generally for profit, by trained journalists. To produce this analysis I draw from a wide range of materials gathered from archives, rare book distributors and women's personal collections. These materials include a large range of national newspapers, movement magazines, anthologies on Greenham, novels and plays, camp newsletters, recorded interviews and personal papers.

Representing Greenham

In the 1984 'Peace Not Quiet' special issue of the British feminist magazine *Spare Rib*, occasional Greenham camper and independent journalist Ruth Wallsgrove (1984: 21) wrote:

> The way the papers have treated Greenham is surprisingly predictable. You could use it as a pocket guide to the British Press – liberal, decent *Guardian* and *Daily Mirror*, pseudo-objective *Times*, snobby *Telegraph* and absurdly reactionary *Sun, Daily Mail* and *Daily Express*.

As Wallsgrove points out in her article, press coverage of Greenham varied quite significantly across Britain's different national publications. While the tabloids ran attention-grabbing stories focused on women's sexuality, their lack of femininity and the muddy conditions at the camp, the *Guardian* often celebrated the 'ordinary housewives' who had left home for peace. In what follows I offer a brief overview of the national papers, as well as some of the local papers that paid particular attention to the Greenham protests.

Alison Young (1990: 56) argues that both the space of the peace camp and the bodies of the peace campers were described as dirty, filthy and mucky in a number of press reports, particularly those written for the *Sun, Daily Mirror* and *Daily Express*. While in the early months of Greenham there was some supportive coverage of protests, those women hailed as noble housewives soon became defiled as 'no good mothers.' Ruth Wallsgrove (1984: 21) commented:

> The *Daily Mirror* … has always stressed the sacrifices for the sake of the children. But the same ideas – of leaving families behind, of weathering the mud – have been consistently used *against* women at Greenham by other papers.

The 'liberal, decent' *Guardian* offered the most national coverage of Greenham, and likewise was perhaps the most frequently discussed media source. While the *Guardian* generally contained articles that were supportive of the peace camp, the paper frequently highlighted the maternal and 'respectable' elements of the protesters, ignoring or overshadowing Greenham's more radical, anarchic and queer dynamics (Roseneil 2000: 156).

The line of communication between Greenham women and the *Guardian*-reading public extended beyond those readers already involved in the Peace and feminist movements. Large-scale symbolic events that were meant to raise awareness of particular issues relied on the liberal press as a vehicle to gain public support. Issues such as the harms of nuclear radiation, the conditions at Holloway prison and the exploitative ventures of uranium mining companies could not reach a broader support base without this press coverage. It was also not unusual for articles, particularly those by columnist Paul Brown, to contain inserts with detailed information on upcoming demonstrations or needed supplies. Jenny Peringer sardonically captured this in a diary entry dated 12 May 1983, 'Bad time for an eviction. Even the *Guardian* is slagging off Greenham at the moment' (Harford & Hopkins 1984: 145).

The Berkshire press and other local papers across the United Kingdom also contained articles on Greenham women. Coverage was especially common in lefty papers such as London's *City Limits*. In addition, reports appeared frequently in papers from places that were the home of many Greenham women such as Cardiff, Wales. In *Greenham Women Everywhere*, Cook and Kirk recognize this local publicity and advised women to contact local papers for coverage of their peace actions as it is often easier to have a 'newsworthy' story in your locality (1983: 99). Local papers often provided a more immediate connection between the camp and women living outside of urban, political centres than the national press could. By connecting issues raised at Greenham – particularly those around women-only spaces, women's empowerment, mother-hood and sexuality – to people's local lives and communities, this press coverage worked to make Greenham more relevant. This was especially significant for those women who were supportive of protests but could not come to the camp.

Additionally, a number of Greenham supporters (and detractors) wrote letters that were published in local papers. Letters sections offer people access to their local newspaper-reading community without demanding the expenditure of much time or resources. Also, as letters sections devote space to a (however limited) range of perspectives, they can serve as a forum of debate. At times they provide a catalyst for reflective thinking about one's own position and foster possibilities beyond those contained or limited by the representational frameworks that shape a newspaper's editorial content.

Newbury Weekly News

While local papers outside of Newbury were often supportive of the peace camp, the content of the *Newbury Weekly News* was almost unilaterally negative and reactionary. This paper had the most extensive and consistent coverage of the Greenham protests, with almost weekly reports throughout 1982–1984. At first the paper was relatively supportive of Greenham. However, the longer the women stayed at the camp, the more hostile coverage of the protests became. A second page article run on 22 October 1981 reported 'the protesters have main-tained friendly relations with both base security men and police' (*Newbury Weekly News*, 22 October 1981).

By 21 January 1982 – nearly a year before the first December mass action – the tone had already begun to shift. The headline of the front page news read, 'PEACE CAMP WOMEN TOLD TO GO.' Mr Cyril Woodwand, chairman of the Newbury recreation and amenities committee, told the paper: 'We have given the women a reasonable amount of time to make their protest, but they are trespassing and they must go' (*Newbury Weekly News*, 21 January 1982).

Viewed over time, the newspaper can be seen to have systematically de-legitimated the Peace Women and rallied residents against them. The paper's editor, Lou Cummings, and man-aging director, Reg Blake, were both prominent figures in the community. They were linked to major businessmen, local politicians, the chief superintendent of the Newbury police and the town's head magistrate through their active membership in the Rotary Club. This, as Lynchcombe (1984) argues, explains the paper's condemnation and increasing frustration with the Greenham protests.

Television coverage

Television coverage of Greenham was less regular but equally ambivalent in its approach to Greenham. Crews came to report on the camp during large-scale events such as the embrace the base demonstrations, the silo action, early court trials and evictions. The sporadic nature of television coverage was due to both the difficulties of 'capturing' Greenham for a news report and women's hesitations to inform the media of every action they planned.

Photographer Ann Snitow wrote that getting good visual footage of Greenham, in industry terms, was a challenge for television crews. She described the difficulties of 'capturing' the peace camp:

> Meetings without podiums, spontaneous acts that can erupt anywhere without notice, a world without hierarchies of space or time – this is the Greenham that has every intention of maddening the media which always demand a controlled orchestration of event.
>
> *Snitow 1985: 45–6*

Nick Couldry makes a similar argument in his media analysis of Greenham's television coverage. He writes that Greenham disrupted the 'specific spatial order implicit in media production' that the 'right place to debate on issues such as nuclear weapons is a place at the "centre"' (Whitehall, Westminster, television studios), rather than the site of the weapons themselves' (Couldry 1999: 339).

Women journalists and Greenham

One way that Greenham women attempted to confront sexist treatment and misogynist representations was by enforcing a women-only media mandate. When this was in effect, reporters and crew members had to be women in order to gain access to the protest campers. In a report on the first December 'Embrace the Base' mass action, Alma (1983) reported in the feminist newspaper *Outwrite:*

> A row [took] place when the women at the main gate refused to talk to the smartly dressed creeps who did not hesitate to put women down: 'shut up you stupid woman – if we had not given you such publicity (when?) you would not have had … this turn out' (piss off you silly git) … the women did not shut up and continued shouting for women reporters (not many around). When women photographers turned up at the gate, the women were pleased to oblige.

As women were significantly underrepresented in these fields, the policy both called attention to women's exclusion and provided opportunities for the few women performing these technical jobs.

However, women-only mandates and investing trust into women journalists was not always a successful strategy. As Gwyn Kirk (1989: 123) notes, 'There was no guarantee that mainstream newspapers would use photos from freelance photographers.' Likewise, most supportive women freelance writers were published in the movement press rather than the mainstream papers. In addition, the tabloid press would often exploit Greenham women's commitment to working with other women by sending in undercover reporters or soliciting women to go to Greenham to produce 'insider stories'.

The inside scoop: exploiting Greenham's women-only mandate

In November 1983, A '*Sun* Special Inside Report' appeared, lambasting Greenham women's separatist politics and sexual expression. Titled in capital letters, 'MEET THE GREENHAM MANHATERS,' the *Sun* special contained a large font pull-quote reading, 'Four in every five are lesbians – all are united in their hatred of men.' Jean Ritchie, who went to Greenham as a visitor in order to garner this story for the *Sun*, writes, 'The younger they are, the more butch they are.' A bit later in the article, an emboldened part of text reads, 'Women openly kiss, cuddle and hold hands at the camp.' Ritchie ends with a lament that these Greenham women have 'turned away genuine peace campaigners' and other women, who like her, 'only half-qualified' because they were committed to their husband and sons at home (Ritchie 1983).

The interspersion of overtly homophobic sentiments with the threat of physical violence evidences the ways in which gender, sex and desire are simultaneously policed. Here, for example, lesbianism is affixed to the culturally intelligible categories of 'man-hater' and 'butch'. This move aligns sexuality (lesbianism) with desire (woman-lover/man-hater) and ascribes these traits through, as well as onto, a gendered body (butch) that is characterized by female masculinity. Normative gender markers including assertiveness, confidence, short hair, baggy clothes, punk insignias, etc. were common to those women classified by the press as 'aggressive,' 'man-hating' or 'butch'.

As Judith Halberstam argues, the refusal to accept ambiguously gendered female bodies points towards a conservative and protectionist effort to keep the power of masculinity attached to men (1998: 15). Such protectionism takes on the form of verbal, discursive and at times physical assault. In this article, the negative or negating associations attached to the butch lesbian perform the normative function of delegitimizing (and hence dehumanizing) the bodies of Greenham protesters. Gender and sexual nonconformity are offered as justification for the soldiers' attitudes. This, in effect, worked to sanction the violence against Greenham women perpetuated by authorities and vigilantes.

Anne Robinson's inside scoop on Greenham, written for the *Daily Mirror,* begins from a very different perspective than this *Sun* exposé. Robinson distances herself from other journalists who deploy dominant representational markers of Greenham women as poorly dressed, dirty, smelly and 'all lesbians'. Yet, while her article is certainly less demeaning than Ritchie's, the position she takes seeks to justify women as 'ordinary' or 'normal' by positioning them as *not* 'lesbian subversives'.

Robinson tells readers that upon arrival at Greenham a soldier shouted to his friend: 'Ah, there's a smelly.' As she approached the camp, Robinson says she felt surprised at the warm welcome she received. She was 'not spat at, mocked, hectored or indeed propositioned'. The next section of text reads in italics: 'I didn't find myself among a group of lesbian subversives. Most of the women I could just as likely have bumped into in a bus queue.' Robinson concludes her article arguing that 'what Greenham women suffer from more than anything else … is a distorted public image'. While the 'stronger women' have been filmed by the media in ways that 'portray them as angry, unpleasant, vicious and violent,' the 'gentler majority are rarely seen' (Robinson 1983).

In Robinson's report there are two very distinct representations of groups mobilized: one, a vocal, strong mass of lesbians; the other a gentle set of ordinary mothers. As linguist Roger Fowler (1991: 94) contends, '"fictitious groups" have conceptual solidarity for the culture, but typically do not display social solidarity; their members do not necessarily associate with one another'. Such categorical group constructions function within the discursive paradigm of news journalism as a means of simplifying and familiarizing readers with social movement participants. Robinson's attempt to position herself as both an objective observer and a movement sympathizer is also a common strategy in press coverage of social movements, employed both to create an 'insider' feel and to politically align a publication for or against a cause. While Robinson's article may help elicit support for Greenham by taking on this perspective, its portrayal of Greenham women bears little resemblance to women campers' personal accounts of life at the camp.

The assumption that women journalists' loyalties would rest with Greenham women over the institutions they worked for was often misguided. The careerist interests of women journalists often superseded the very possibility of a shared feminist politics. Women journalists' homophobia, as well as the homophobic media institutions in which they operate, also prevented them from forging alliances with Greenham women. On some occasions, the disloyalty of women journalists to Greenham women cost protesters their jobs and family support as these exposé reports would name women as lesbians and drug takers (Roseneil 2000: 290).

At the same time, producers and editors intentionally employed women to create intra-gender divisions that delegitimated Greenham protests. The disappointment some campers felt following the publication of journalists' exposé reports exhibits women's broader anxiety around the relationship between gender and (feminist) politics. Many women at Greenham discovered first-hand that 'sisterhood' did not organically emerge from women's gender identity – a reality that the Women's Liberation movement at the time was confronting more broadly.

Undermining the inside scoop

While the defamatory remarks made in articles such as these were often illegal according to the policies of the press board, the cost and resources needed to bring charges of libel against a newspaper (particularly if it was part of a larger media conglomerate) were far more than most campers could incur. In the later years of the camp, long-term camper Katrina Howse, who was fed up with years of media defamation, brought on a libel case. In 1992 Howse won a suit against News Group Newspapers. She filed for damages for libel after an article in the 3 November 1990 issue of the *Sun* called her a 'scrounger' and a parasite, accusing her of not working or paying poll tax.

The judgment for this case ruled that the *Sun*'s remarks were entirely unfounded. Howse was an active mural artist, an unwaged political worker and exempt from poll taxes as she lived at Yellow Gate. Howse described working on the case as requiring tremendous support from others doing 'tireless research' and 'endless writing'. However, as the press release for her successful trial states, this notable case 'broke with the tradition that says only the rich can defend their character (there is no Legal Aid for defamation actions)' (Yellow Gate News 1993).

Live media offered another space for women to resist the misogyny and homophobia perpetuated by the institutional media. Unlike pre-recorded news reports, producers of live programs could not censor or edit women's statements. Carole Harwood (1983: 111), a married woman protester with three children, recounts one occasion on which she took the opportunity of a live broadcast:

> [I made connections] between male violence and war, talking about the media treatment of rape, pornography, Greenham women. The friendly breakfast show personality went paler and I swear his eyes narrowed, just like in the stories. He didn't say goodbye as I left the studio, nor politely stand as he'd done when I arrived.

Harwood's refusal to reaffirm a safe or sanitized sexuality of the Greenham camp expressed her commitment to building a space that could simultaneously cultivate a lesbian community and confront women's homophobia. Harwood's intervention on this radio program signaled for her the work she was engaged in to 'root out' homophobia.

Parody and activist practice

Perhaps the most widely deployed way women collectively articulated their criticism of the press was through the use of humor and parody. Women at Greenham wrote songs, drew cartoons, recounted anecdotes and even wrote a play mocking the way media content represented Greenham women. For example, the second verse of the song 'At the Peace Camp, Newbury, Berkshire', sung to the tune of 'An English Country Garden', relates the repetitive nature of reporters' questions:

> What are the questions the media will ask us
> At the Peace Camp, Newbury, Berkshire?
> I'll tell you now of some that I know,
> And the rest, you'll read them later.
> 'Why did you make this sacrifice?'
> 'Can I talk to someone nice?'
> 'How does it feel now you have failed?'
> 'Can you pose by the gate?'
> 'Hurry up, it's getting late.'
>
> *At the Peace Camp, Newbury, Berkshire; printed in Roseneil 2000: 86*

The use of familiar tunes functioned to create a sense of collectivity and made teaching lyrics easier as many protesters already knew the original song. A dramatized parody of the media is also offered in the Common Ground collective's play *The Fence*. Like the lyrics from 'At The Peace Camp, Newbury, Berkshire', *The Fence* performs the repetition of the media's questions. Scene six, 'The Media', opens with a series of posed headlines:

> MAX *holds kettle over fire.*
> Caption: 'Polly puts the kettle on.'
> WOMEN *hug and leer at each other.*
> Caption: 'Lessies for Peace'
> WOMEN *wave angry fists.*
> Caption: 'Angry women harass male visitors.'
>
> *Common Ground 1985: 121*

In this play, women physically animate spectacularized media scenes, or frames, freezing their bodies to express how journalists can manipulate photographs that capture selected, static moments of time. Juxtaposed with sensationalized captions, this bodily performance of media myths and symbols is deployed as a mode of deconstruction. It reveals how caricatured identities literally get attached to images of women's bodies, which, through repetition and broad circulation, become dominant representations. As a mode of communication, the play exhibits what Margaret Laware terms Greenham's women's 'embodied rhetoric' (2004: 19). Laware argues that in order to understand how Greenham women communicated their resistance, we must conceptualize rhetoric as a material, embodied and collective act (29). Performances like *The Fence* attest to this claim.

Parody – as an activist tactic – was very effective for calming nerves and raising spirits, yet the media critique these parodies produced could only travel so far. Whether planned or spontaneous, these collective performances were practiced primarily in the space of the camp. While geographically confined, it is important that such community practices are understood as far more than cathartic relief. As a localized strategy that functioned primarily for those already involved in the protests, parody can be an essential collective ritual that sustains the energy and passion of social movement communities (Taylor & Rupp 1993).

Scraps of resistance

Even when a news article's content ridiculed Greenham women, it marked the occurrence of a protest event and often functioned to peak women's curiosity. This phenomenon is dramatized in Sarah Daniels's play *The Devil's Gateway*, originally published in 1983. The main character, Betty, is a housewife currently receiving state benefits and living in council housing with her children, mother and emotionally abusive husband. Betty becomes fascinated by Greenham women as she reads news stories and sees short pieces covering protest events on television news programs. Intrigued, Betty begins clipping out articles on Greenham women from newspapers and buying extra newspapers to find out more about the protests. She hides her collection of clippings in an old cereal box to keep it out of sight from her family, and in particular away from her husband who derides the Greenham women's protests (Daniels 1991).

Betty has no access to Greenham except for what she can read from papers and watches on the television news. As Betty clips these articles from newspapers and begins to assemble her own cereal box container for them, the values and labour practices that initially shaped this content shift. While Betty's husband espouses the derogatory content he hears and reads on Greenham women as truth, for Betty such news content generates a passionate curiosity.

By cutting these articles out, Betty is able to move them around. She dumps them out on her kitchen table, piecing together the bits of information they contain in new and unsanctioned ways (Daniels 1991). Freed from their original format, Betty's clippings are stored in a cereal box – an artifact emblemizing her relegation to, as well as her control over, the domestic space of the kitchen. What publication the articles came from or who wrote them is not significant for her purposes. This personal archive, actively created by Betty, becomes another sort of container entirely. One that stores stories, but not in the ways they were intended to be told or heard.

Feminist technology scholar Zoe Sofia argues that media artifacts can be thought of as container technologies that actively shape, as well as carry, the content that they store. Sofia's conception borrows from Donald Winnicott's 'intersubjectivist accounts' that view the 'holding and supply' of space 'as the result of maternal labours' which require 'care' (190–1). Similarly, in her work on the history of scrapbooking, Ellen Gruber Garvey (2003: 221) argues 'the scrapbook absorbed material and labor, processing and transforming them'. Rather than writing, the scrapbooker's labour – or authorship – consists of 'a process of recirculation, in which information is sorted and stockpiled until it can acquire value by being inserted into a new context' (224). The sorting and stockpiling of texts – here, for Betty, via the assistance of a cereal box storage container – detaches meaning from the original source of the texts. Garvey argues that scrapbookers 'literally made new media out of old' (224).

Another group of women who sometimes clipped and stored stories of Greenham from mainstream newspapers were women prisoners. National newspapers have a much greater ability to travel into and around prisons than other media forms, as prison officials carefully censor incoming materials. Thus, although the content of these articles rarely offered an accurate documentation of Greenham women's lives or actions, the very fact that such records circulated served to establish connections between imprisoned women and Greenham protesters.

One Greenham camper, Carmel McConnell, served a short prison sentence for her involvement in the occupation of the base's sentry box (guard booth) at the Main Gate on 27 August 1982. In a diary entry she recorded on prison toilet paper (and smuggled out in her sock), McConnell mentioned her surprise at prisoners' knowledge of Greenham's existence. She wrote: '[The] most important thing is that the women in here know something about us and have been coming up to us with newspaper cuttings about Greenham' (Harford & Hopkins 1984: 83).

The content of these scrapbook archives was then passed between prisoners and imprisoned Greenham women as a mark of recognition. The physical movement of these cuttings shifted the value of this media content as their function was transformed from bearers of (mis)information to a gift or token of affinity. The labour involved in cutting and collecting these scraps contributes to this shift in value. Here, the women prisoners' actions signified to Greenham women that their work was important enough to save or store.

Some Greenham campaigners also strategically collected and circulated press clippings and recordings of television and radio news programs. This enabled them to see patterns in the coverage and develop tactics to challenge recurring misrepresentations. In 1984 camper, Beatrice, wrote:

> During the last 3 years a lot of things have been written about us ... A lot of people collect a lot of stuff about us – but did you realize that it is for us important as well – to be able to look up things – information [about] what happened on certain dates – information about the bases – articles being used as evidence in court – or little things just adding to the history of the camp.
>
> *Green and Common News 1984*

Here Beatrice suggests ways in which Greenham women can use the media's documentation of their activities. Beatrice notes how constant evictions and occasional prison sentences make it difficult for any individual woman living at the camp to collect for the file alone. With the help of other women, Beatrice says she will organize a file for collective use at the camp.

As I discussed earlier in relation to Betty's clippings, Beatrice's file becomes a new kind of archive or container for information on Greenham. While Greenham women might object to the 'factual' content and representations found in official media news and police reports, these materials provide other functions. For example, they can do the work of data recording, logging dates events took place and the names of authorities involved at a protest action or arrest.

Conclusion

While protesters at Greenham were often angry and disappointed about misrepresentative and defamatory mainstream media coverage, many were also keenly aware of how these negative representations were being constructed. They knew that the institutionalized practices of journalists made it impossible for them to control their representation and devised innovative strategies for resisting 'the media frame'. Stories of Greenham travelled outside of the camp, transforming newspaper coverage. This movement of media changes the meaning and significance of representations in relation to where, how and why people engage media texts. Through this movement, negative media coverage can be transformed into objects of inspiration, offering disenfranchised women models of activist subjectivity, despite (or in spite of) the coverage's denigration of the camp.

Over the past decade, digital technologies have become increasingly used as activist tools. Looking back before the tweet storms and Facebook event pages can help us remember that while communication practices and infrastructures are shaped by new technologies, it is the relationships between people that really matter. In creating strategies to manage the media, Greenham women experimented with women-only mandates, trained themselves as what we would today call 'citizen-journalists' and became autonomous media makers. As Hakim Bey wrote in his discussion of the activist 'web' that existed before today's 'network of networks' (Castells 2015):

> Word-of-mouth, mail, the marginal zine network, 'phone trees,' and the like already suffice to construct an information webwork. The key is not the brand or level of tech involved, but the openness and horizontality of the structure.
>
> *Bey 1991: 108*

Greenham women's webs of communication as resistance show how the rituals, conversations and creative production involved in collective living are often the very means through which movements develop media strategies. As one *City Limits* reporter posed the question in the December 16–23, 1983 edition, 'Will protests ever be the same again after Greenham Common?'

References

Alma (1983) 'The Press', *Outwrite Newspaper*. Feminist Archive South.

Bey, H. (1991) *TAZ: The Temporary Autonomous Zone, Ontological Anarchy, Poetic Terrorism*. New York: Autonomedia.

Castells, M. (2015) *Networks of Outrage and Hope: Social Movements in the Internet Age*. Cambridge and Malden, MA: Polity Press.

Common Ground (1985) 'The Fence', in S. Lowe (ed.) *Peace Plays*. London and New York: Methuen, pp. 111–35.

Cook, A. and Kirk, G. (1983) *Greenham Women Everywhere*. London: Pluto Press.

Couldry, N. (1999) 'Disrupting the Media Frame at Greenham Common: A New Chapter in the History of Mediations?' *Media, Culture and Society*, vol. 21, pp. 337–58.

Daniels, S. (1991) 'The Devil's Gateway', in S. Daniels *Plays: One*. London: Methuen Drama.

Fowler, R. (1991) *Language in the News: Discourse and Ideology in the Press*. London and New York: Routledge.

Garvey, E. G. (2003) 'Scissoring and Scrapbooks: Nineteenth-Century Reading, Remaking, and Recirculating', in L. Gitelman and G. B. Pingree (eds) *New Media 1740–1915*. Cambridge, MA and London: MIT Press, pp. 207–27.

Green and Common News, July/August 1984 (London, England, Women's Library, Archive Collection 5GCW/E).

Halberstam, J. (1998) *Female Masculinity*. Durham, NC: Duke University Press.

Harford, B. and Hopkins, S. (1984) *Greenham Common: Women at the Wire*. London: Women's Press.

Kirk, G. (1989), in A. Harris and Y. King (eds), *Rocking the Ship of the State*, Boulder, CO: Westview Press.

Laware, M. L. (2004) 'Circling the Missiles and Staining Them Red: Feminist Rhetorical Invention and Strategies of Resistance at the Women's Peace Camp at Greenham Common'. *NWSA Journal*, vol. 16, no. 3, pp.18–41.

Lynchcombe (1984) At Least Cruise is Clean. UK: Niccolo Press.

Newbury Weekly News, 22 October 1981. *Women's Library Archives.*

Newbury Weekly News. (1982) Women's Library, Greenham Common Press Cuttings, 21 January.

Ritchie, J. (1983) 'Meet the Greenham Manhaters', *Sun*, 7 November. (Women's Library 5GCW/E/2).

Robinson, A. (1983) 'Why the Greenham Women Aren't What They Seem', *Daily Mirror*, 23 November. (London, England, Women's Library, Archive Collection, 'Press Cuttings', 5GCW/E/2).

Roseneil, S. (2000) *Common Women, Uncommon Practices: The Queer Feminisms of Greenham*. London and New York: Cassell.

Snitow, A. (1985) 'Pictures for 10 Million Women'. *Frontiers: A Journal of Women's Studies*, vol. 8, no. 2, pp. 45–9.

Sofia, Z. (2000) 'Container Technologies', *Hypatia*, vol. 15, no. 2, pp. 181–201.

Taylor, V. and Rupp, L. J. (1993) 'Women's Culture and Lesbian Feminist Activism: A Reconsideration of Cultural Feminism'. *Signs*, vol. 19, no. 1, pp. 32–61.

The Greenham Factor (1983) London: Greenham Print Prop.

The New Anti-Nuclear Songbook (n.d.) Nottingham: Mushroom and Peace News.

Wallsgrove, R. (1984) 'The Press'. *Spare Rib*, May.

Yellow Gate News (1993), June (Bristol, England, Feminist Archive South).

Young, A. (1990) *Femininity in Dissent*. London and New York: Routledge.

5

ARTISTIC ACTIVISM

Stephen Duncombe and Steve Lambert

The truth shall not set us free

We are beholden to a powerful story, and imagine ourselves as part of it: it is the story of The Power of The Truth. One variation is 'The Emperor's New Clothes', Hans Christian Anderson's nineteenth-century fairy tale. The story, as you may recall, is about an emperor who is tricked into buying a spectacular suit of non-existent clothing. Eager to show off his new duds, the emperor parades through town in the buff. The crowd, eager to share in the fantasy, exclaims how marvelous the emperor's imaginary attire is. Then, from the sidelines, a young boy exclaims, 'But he has nothing on!' Upon hearing this undeniable fact, the people whisper it mouth to ear, awaken from their illusion, and, of course, live happily ever after. Many activists have imagined themselves as the courageous boy in this kind of story. We simply have to reveal The Truth, The People will hear us, and the scales will fall from their eyes. They will finally see the world as it really is (which, of course, means seeing the world as we see it). Then, *everything changes* and we all live happily ever after.

This is a fairy tale, but like most such stories this one taps into our deep-rooted beliefs, fears and desires. The myth that there is power in simply knowing The Truth is older than Hans Christian Anderson. The Bible says, 'And ye shall know the truth, and the truth shall make you free' (John 8: 32). And how many times have we heard, or said, the maxim: 'Knowledge is power'? At one time this may have been true. Throughout history, powers-that-be have stayed in power by having a monopoly on knowledge. The European medieval church, for example, kept a firm grip on the rules for proper thinking, doing and being in the Christian world by allowing access to the Bible only to sanctioned users, priests and educated readers of an arcane language, Latin. In China, during the same period, access to literacy was only allowed for an elite Mandarin class. Even today, totalitarian governments restrict access to information, ban books and artworks, and repress intellectuals, activists and artists, out of fear of any ideas that might challenge their official Truth. When the economy of information is one of scarcity, knowledge *does* equal power.

But that's not the world in which most of us live in today; quite the opposite: we have a surplus of information. The internet contains terabytes of knowledge which we access with unprecedented ease. In our classrooms, on our blog pages and in discussions amongst friends or arguments with our adversaries we freely ponder, consider and rant. We are retrieving, discussing, forwarding and re-tweeting ideas all the time; we are awash in information. If Knowledge is Power, and knowledge is now so freely available, then why does power still remain firmly in the hands of the few? Something is wrong with the equation.

A great deal of our faith in the liberatory potential of facts and The Truth has to do with how we have been taught politics works. According to political theorists, the model for modern democracy is the seventeenth century European coffee house. In these public places, men of relative privilege and leisure sat around, reading newspapers, discussing and deciding upon the important political topics of the day. They were reasonable, educated men making rational decisions with full and open access to all the facts. Whether we know this history or not, it is often the shape ideal democracy takes in our imaginations.

Coffee house denizens and democratic theorists were on to something. Making rational decisions, based upon reasoned discussions, with access to facts is a worthy ideal we probably should aspire to. Activists need to be trained to think critically about the world as it is and make a cogent case for how it could be different. And a reasoning public supplied with factual information *is* the basis for a thoughtful democracy.

It is also naive.

A nation of considered thinkers or a republic of rationality may be our ideal of politics, but the practice of effective politics resembles little of this. We make sense of our world through things like symbols and stories as much, if not more, than we do through facts and figures. We have emotional attachments to issues, perspectives and politicians more than we have reasoned political positions. What determines our political engagement is less a reasoned evaluation of all possible options and arriving upon a rational decision, and more a felt response: people are *moved* to think and act in certain ways (Duncombe 2007).

The First Rule of Guerrilla Warfare is to know your terrain and use it to your advantage. If contemporary activism is to have discernable impact it must operate on this *real* terrain, not the democratic fantasy of the European coffee house. This means rationally understanding that politics are not only rational; the truth about politics is that it is not about truth. Politics is about people's *perceptions* of the truth, their *feelings* about facts and their visceral *experiences* of the world.

The irrational has been used politically by some pretty unsavory characters; it is stock-in-trade for fascists, bigots and demagogues. But if activists motivated by peace, justice and democracy cannot learn how to tap into people's experiences and feelings, they give up a large part of the political landscape to the other side. Just because the irrational has been (ab)used does not mean it can't be used in a different way. None of this is to say that people's rationality should be ignored, that facts do not matter or that the truth is relative and malleable. Let us be crystal clear about this: facts are important, and truth needs to be the foundation of our analysis, our actions and the worlds we create. But facts and truth don't speak for themselves. They need to be made into symbols and stories that people can make sense of and care about. The truth needs help.

The power of art

Traditional political theory does help activists navigate the terrain of the non-rational, but there is a field and a practice that has long dealt with such concerns: the arts. For over 40,000 years, from cave paintings in Indonesia up to the most cutting-edge conceptual work coming out of art schools today, artists have been using signs and symbols, stories and spectacles to move us.

Art is particularly good at translating objective things – events, facts, ideologies – into stories, images, performances: subjective and poetic forms we can experience, feel … and remember. As the author Jorge Luis Borges (1999) summed up at the end of his life:

The task of art is to transform what is continuously happening to us, to transform all these things into symbols, into music, into something which can last in man's memory.

Art allows us to imagine things that are otherwise unimaginable. Art allows us to say things that can't be said, and give form to abstract feelings and ideas and present them in such ways that they can be communicated with others. In an essay called 'Poetry is Not a Luxury', the radical poet Audre Lorde (1984: 37) writes.

I could name at least ten ideas I would have once found intolerable or incomprehensible and frightening, except as they came after dreams and poems.

And art is a means to conjure up new visions, not just offer a new perspective on what already exists. Again, we turn to Lorde (Lorde 1984: 37) to state this as only a poet can:

Poetry is the way we help give name to the nameless so it can be thought. The farthest external horizons of our hopes and fears are cobbled by our poems, carved from the rock experiences of our daily lives.

Art, if we let it, allows us to take stock of the mundane, imperfect world we live in and transform it with radical, idealistic visions of the future.

There's much, much more that art does. But to get into all the intricacies of exactly how art works would take hundreds of pages and, even then, we couldn't ever offer a complete explanation. But that is really the point: despite tens of thousands of year of art practice, thousands of years of philosophical discussion, hundreds of years of art criticism, and, most recently, brain studies of the neurological effects of exposure to art, the power of art is largely beyond rational explanation.

In the past, philosophers and critics called this the 'sublime' quality of art. The sublime can be beautiful or it can also be horrific; in either case it is beyond direct description, beyond measurement, beyond even comprehension. The philosopher Immanuel Kant (Kant 1952) called this the 'supersensible'. As mystical as the sublime power of art is, or perhaps because it is so mystical, it can be a powerful force in the real world. The ancient Greek philosopher Longinus (Longinus 1964) believed that power of the sublime lay not only in its capacity to provoke awe, but in its ability to persuade. That is why when we are affected by a piece of art we often say it *moves* us.

This sublime power of art to circumvent our rational minds and affect our emotions, our bodies, even our spirit, has been recognized for millennia. And been feared for just as long. The Bible and the Quran are filled with strictures against visual depictions of all manner of things both holy and profane. Witness the jealous God of Exodus when he commands Moses: 'Thou shalt not make unto thee any graven image, or any likeness of any thing that *is* in heaven above, or that is in the earth beneath, or that is in the water under the earth' (Exodus 21:4).

This fear of art is further elaborated in Isaiah. God, we are told, is the creator of all things and for humans to create is an affront to his power. In God's understanding of things, he is the subject and we are but objects. Human creativity – particularly any which might deign to represent God – reverses this relationship, making humans subjects and God a mere object (Isaiah 40–45).

Plato was so frightened by the power of art that he devoted a chapter in *The Republic* to explaining why it should be banished from his ideal society. Plato's objections are many, but his criticisms culminate in his fear that art can move its audience. Watching a play or listening to a poem, the audience experiences the pleasure and pain of the character in the drama. Rationally, the audience knows that these are merely made-up characters, fictive creations of the artist, but emotionally they feel as if the struggles and victories of these fictions are theirs (Plato 1955: book 10). The ability of artists to create worlds and move people, which strikes fear into the hearts of philosophers and gods, is what makes art so powerful as a form of activism.

The problem with art, from an activist perspective, is that all this power is often wasted. A painting hangs on the wall of a museum. It moves us. And then, all too often, we move on. We leave that experience, and its power, behind us on the walls of the museum. We are also taught art is something 'special', and therefore separated from the everyday world. Except, of course, it isn't. The power of art is used to command big ticket prices or boost the cultural capital of institutions and individuals; in our world, the sublime is in the service of capitalism and hierarchy. But what if we could harness the 'supersensible' power of art and apply it to the world-changing potential of activism?

This is the promise of artistic activism.

What is artistic activism?

Artistic activism is as hard to define as the power of art. What it does is equally contestable. In recent years, prominent critics have argued that the function of artistic activism is the 'defunctionalizing [of] the status quo' (Groys 2014), the making of 'agnostic spaces' (Mouffe 2007), the fostering of 'dialogic art' (Kester 2004), or embracing 'antinomy' (Bishop 2006). There is nothing wrong with these explanations, but they don't get us any closer to understanding what artistic activism is, and is not. We believe it is more profitable to reason inductively, starting with a range of actual practices:

I Wish This Was. Hurricane Katrina devastated the city of New Orleans in 2005, leaving in its wake thousands of damaged residences and stores and the massive job of rebuilding the city. It soon became clear that plans for the redevelopment of New Orleans favoured tourist hotels and convention centers, while the needs and desires of residents were ignored. In response the artist Candy Chang did something small and powerful: she made simple fill-in-the-blank stickers that read: 'I wish this was_____.' She posted these stickers on vacant buildings and left them in boxes at local businesses all over the city. And like a participatory poem of the community's dreams, people filled them out and posted them up: 'I wish this was: A Community Garden.' 'I wish this was: A Grocery! Locally Owned!' 'I wish this was: Fixed.' 'I wish this was: Heaven.' By asking people to write their own responses, Chang prompted everyday citizens to imagine what *they* would like for their community, and raised the critical question of whose interests are catered to when urban areas are developed.

Undocubus. In 2012 a group of undocumented immigrant activists bought an old bus, painted 'No Fear' across its side and decorated it with images of brightly coloured monarch butterflies. The Undocubus was taken on a road trip through the Southern United States to protest local anti-immigration laws that had created a climate of fear amongst undocumented immigrants and fueled xenophobia amongst the native-born. Following in the footsteps of Civil Rights 'freedom riders' who made a similar journey to register African American voters a half century previously, the Undocubus activists drew upon the now sanctified mythos of that movement. In addition to adopting and adapting the symbols of previous social movements, they made one of their own: the monarch butterfly, a beautiful creature who annually migrates across North America, from Canada to the US to Mexico and back again. Covering their bus, emblazoned on their shirts, donning butterfly wings at their demonstrations -- the Undocubus activists forged an association of human immigration to a natural and majestic migration, reframing the image of a population unjustly feared and routinely degraded. Who, after all, can be enraged at a butterfly?

Y'en a Marre. Y'en a Marre or 'We're Fed Up' is a youth movement that started in Senegal in 2011 to protest power outages in Dakar and then took on political injustice and social inequality across the country. At first glance there is nothing particularly artistic about this, except that Y'en a Marre was started by artists, a hip-hop group called the Keur Gui Crew, and the core of the movement is a network of artists who articulate their criticisms of the present and ideals for the future through rap. In Senegal, where political language is associated with corruption and the abuse of power, Y'en a Marre uses hip-hop music to speak politically to youth – comprising 60 per cent of the population – who would otherwise never listen to politics. Through rap, Y'en a Marre provides a political voice for young people in a language they feel is their own.

Billionaires for Bush. 'Yes, I'm a Billionaire. And, yes, I'm for George W. Bush', says an earnest young man to a Fox News reporter during the US presidential contest of 2004. Enjoying the crisp New Hampshire autumn at a protest 'against' progressive presidential candidate Howard Dean, the young man – impeccably dressed in a double-breasted suit, bowler hat, walking stick, and monocle – certainly looks like a billionaire, or at least like one in the Monopoly board game. It was all part of a satirical campaign called Billionaires for Bush which, by creating a visible – and visibly absurd – 'People of Wealth' interest group, highlights the hidden power of money in politics. Simple to stage, easy to emulate, and fun to enact, Billionaire chapters sprang up across the United States and, since 2004, have spawned numerous 'Billionaires for …' or 'Billionaires against…' campaigns-cum-media spectacles drawing attention to the outsized, yet often obscured, political influence of individual and corporate wealth.

War on Smog. Chinese cities are notorious for their smog. Chinese authorities, wary of a repeat of the Tiananmen Square protests, are equally notorious for being hostile toward street demonstrations. Cleverly responding to this challenging political terrain, artistic activists in Chongqing city in Southwest China, staged a public performance piece in 2014 called War on Smog (the name borrowed from a public proclamation of the Chinese Premier). Their 'war' was fought by a couple being wed in gas masks, a parade of tutu-clad women, likewise in gas masks, and other 'artistic performers' who brought attention to air quality in the city. Mixing a street protest with an art piece was a stroke of brilliance. Since it didn't look like a political protest to the authorities, no activists were arrested. But the style and creativity of the War on Smog provided arresting images for both local and world media. By riding the line between politics, which is repressed, and art, which is tolerated and even celebrated in China, these artistic activists found the space to safely protest within an authoritarian regime.

Traffic Mimes. Antanas Mockus faced many serious challenges when he became mayor of Bogotá, Colombia in 1995. The city, one of the most violent in the Western Hemisphere, also had a seemingly intractable problem with traffic congestion. Cars and people alike ignored signs and laws, and the result was chaos: gridlock and fatal accidents. Rather than imposing heavier fines, which he knew would be resented, or displaying more traffic signs, which he knew would be ignored, the mayor did something very creative: he hired 420 mimes to direct traffic. These traffic mimes roamed the streets of the capital in brightly coloured clothes and painted faces, mocking and shaming pedestrians and drivers using the centuries old art of pantomime. The shock-value of the mimes' presence, along with their appeal to citizens' sense of humour (and their fear of ridicule) was impressively effective. Due to the mimes, and other creative tactics, traffic fatalities dropped in Bogotá by over 50 per cent. The mimes were so successful that other Latin American cities followed suit, using humour and ridicule to solve their traffic problems.

Zapatista Air Force. New Year's Day 1994 and the day the North American Free Trade Agreement went into effect. Out of the mountains of Southern Mexico walked three thousand indigenous peasants wearing black ski masks, some carrying rifles and machetes, others long sticks, declaring war on the Mexican oligarchy. They were the Zapatista Army of National

Liberation (EZLN). Within days, images of this ragtag rebel army, and the words of its resident poet-in-arms Subcomandante Marcos, spread across the globe. Six years, dozens of campaigns, and hundreds of communiqués later, the Zapatistas unveiled their 'air force' against a Mexican Army encampment. EZLN guerrillas wrote notes to soldiers asking them to put down their weapons, folded these notes into hundreds of paper airplanes, and then flew them over the razor wire encircling the army camp. Pitted in a battle of military force, they had no chance, but with humour and imagination they captured public sympathy and support, creating a potent political force.

Operation First Casualty. Like many US veterans of the Iraq War, Aaron Hughes returned home to discover the war that so many citizens enthusiastically supported was at best an abstraction, if not largely absent from public life. So, in 2007, Aaron and his fellow activists from Iraq Veterans Against the War (IVAW) decided to 'demonstrate' what the war was really like. In full battle dress, with their hands held in front of them as if they were cradling weapons, these veterans carried out the same maneuvers they had done in Iraq on the streets of US cities. They went out on patrol, took sniper fire, and violently broke up a political protest. Staging the spectacle of violence and fear that was part of everyday life for soldiers and civilians in wartime forced passersby in the US to confront the 'reality' of the war their country was waging. The soldiers of IVAW brought the war home.

24hr Museum. Alfredo Jaar is a Chilean-born artist trained in architecture. Fairly well known in the art world, he was invited to Skoghall, Sweden to do an art installation. Skoghall is a company town, where the local paper industry provides jobs, housing and municipal services for everyone. And because it is Sweden, they do a pretty good job. Jaar noticed, however, that the one thing that had not been provided for the citizens was an art museum. So, as his art installation, he built one, constructed of the heavy waxed paper the mill manufactured and the long wooden poles they used as paper spindles. When the museum was done, the people of the town were invited to bring and exhibit their own art work. There was a big celebratory opening, a brass band played and the people of Skoghall were happy. Then, 24 hours later, Jaar removed the art and burned the museum to the ground.

What sort of artistic activism is this? The story goes on …. A few weeks after he left town, Jaar received a telephone call from the mayor of Skoghall. The mayor told him that the citizens of the town, for the first time ever, had petitioned the town government to request something themselves: that a permanent museum be built, and they wanted Jaar to be the architect. Having experienced their museum for a day, the people longed for what they hadn't even known they wanted, and they mobilized themselves to get it.

These are just a *few* case studies of artistic activism. As you may have noticed, some of these examples hew closer to the arts, with an emphasis on immediate creative expression while others are integrated into long-term and more instrumental activist campaigns. Some are the work of individual artists while others are the fruit of activist collectives. (For thousands more examples, from around the world, you can check out our free, user-generated, digital database of artistic activist case studies at Actipedia.org.)

Although artistic activism encompasses many practices, it is also *not* a lot of things people frequently think of when imagining art combined with activism. 'Political art', for instance. Political art has an important place in the art world, and no global biennale would be complete without it, but most political art shown in museums or sold in galleries or celebrated in art textbooks is merely art with political or social injustice as its subject matter or muse; a means to express the artist's opinion or feelings about social problems or injustices. As the art critic Lucy Lippard (1984: 349) puts it, 'political art tends to be socially *concerned* and "activist" art tends to be socially *involved*'. In brief, political art is often art *about* politics, not art that *works* politically.

Art   Activism

Expressive   <===================>   Instrumental

Tactical   <===================>   Strategic

Individual   <===================>   Collective

Cultural Impact   <===================>   Material Change

Esoteric   <===================>   Accessible

Affect   <===================>   Effect

Figure 5.1   Art–activism spectrum

Conversely, artistic activism is not activism which uses art as a window dressing. This is often how art is used by organizations and advocacy groups, who may ask an artist to design a poster or banner on a short deadline, or donate their talents and prestige to raise money or awareness for a shared cause. Artistic techniques may help make a protest more palatable, or profit a cause, but without using creativity in designing tactics, strategies or goals from square one, the potential power of art is relegated to an afterthought.

Artistic activism is not wholly art or activism – it resides somewhere between the two. Working with our colleague Risë Wilson, founder of the artistic activist Laundromat Project, we came up with a series of scales that can help us think about artistic activism on a spectrum between arts and activism (Figure 5.1).

Artistic activism is a shifting point between two fields, each with their own history and traditions, practices and intentions. Each articulation of artistic activism will graph itself differently onto the lines above. But it is the last of these spans, between the poles of Affect and Effect, that is likely the most significant in understanding what artistic activism is and how it works.

Affect, Effect and Æffect

Activism, as the name implies, is the activity of challenging and changing power relations, what the political scientist Harold Lasswell (1936) once defined as 'who gets what, when and how'. Activism does not necessarily mean a mass protest outside a government building to demand more resources; it can just as easily mean organizing a small child care collective amongst parents in a neighborhood, thereby empowering the community to create new resources for itself. There are many ways of doing activism and being an activist, but the common element is an activity targeted toward demonstrable outcomes: changing a policy, mobilizing a population, overthrowing a dictator, or organizing a child care collective. The goal of activism is *Action* to generate an *Effect*.

Art, on the other hand, doesn't have such a clear target. It is hard to say what art is for or against; its value often lies in showing us new perspectives and ways to bring meaning to our lives. Its impact varies from person to person, is often subtle and hard to measure, and even confusing or contradictory messages can be layered into the work. As we suggested above, good art, in our opinion, always contains a surplus of meaning: something we can't quite describe or put our finger on, but moves us nonetheless. Its goal, if we can even use that word, is to stimulate a feeling, move us emotionally, or alter our perception. In short: Art is an *Expression* that generates *Affect*.

Stripped down to essentials the relationships might look like this:

Activism → Effect

and

Art → Affect

At first glance these aims seem at odds with one another. Activism moves the material world, while Art moves the heart, body and soul. The scope of the former is social change, while the latter is individual impression. But effect and affect can be complementary. We're moved by affective experiences to do physical actions that result in concrete effects: Affect leads to Effect. And concrete effects have affective impact, generating personal emotion: Effect leads to Affect. We might call this complementary combination *Affective Effect*, or perhaps *Effective Affect*. But in the great academic tradition of coining new words, we used the grapheme *Æ,* and invented the term *Æffect*.

If we were forced to sum up the defining characteristic of artistic activism, it would be a practice that generates æffect. Art can do all sorts of amazing things: it can inspire, horrify, alter our perspectives, and allow us to imagine things that seem unimaginable. But it's not enough. In order for the emotional affect of art to have political effect, art needs to be combined with activism. Activism can bring people together, harness their power and transform society. But it can only do this if people are moved to participate and can imagine an alternative. In order for the political effect of activism to have an emotional affect, activism needs to be combined with art. Artistic activism is neither art nor activism; it is a dynamic hybrid which exists in the creative space between art *and* activism, and this is its power.

References

The Bible: Authorized King James Version. (1991) Oxford: Oxford University Press.

Bishop, C. (2006) 'The Social Turn: Collaboration and its Discontents', *Artforum*, February, pp. 178–83.

Borges, J. L. (1999) 'Interview with the Filmmaker German Kral', in *Images of the Absence/Buenos Aires, meine Geschichte*, German Kral Filmproduktion/Hochschule für Fernsehen und Film München.

Duncombe, S. (2007) *Dream: Re-imagining Progressive Politics in an Age of Fantasy*. New York: New Press.

Groys, B. (2014) 'On Art Activism', *E-Flux Journal,* vol. 56, no. 6, http://www.e-flux.com/journal/on-art-activism, accessed 10 June 2016.

Kant, I. (1952) *The Critique of Judgement*. Translated by James Creed Meredith. Oxford: Clarendon Press.

Kester, G. (2004) *Conversation Pieces: Community and Communication in Modern Art.* Berkeley, CA: University of California Press.

Lasswell, H. D. (1936) *Politics: Who Gets What, When, How*. New York: McGraw-Hill.

Lippard, L. (1984) 'Trojan Horses: Activist Art and Power', in B. Wallis (ed.) *Art after Modernism*. New York: New Museum of Contemporary Art, pp. 341–58.

Longinus (1964) *On the Sublime*, edited and translated by D. A. Russell. Oxford: Clarendon Press.

Lorde, A. (1984) 'Poetry Is Not a Luxury', in *Sister Outsider*. Berkeley, CA: Crossing Press, pp. 36–9.

Mouffe, C. (2007) 'Artistic Activism and Agonistic Spaces', *Art & Research*, vol. 1, no. 2, http://www.artandresearch.org.uk/v1n2/mouffe.html, accessed 10 June 2016.

Plato (1955) *The Republic*. Translated and edited by Desmond Lee. London: Penguin.

6

ALTERNATIVE COMPUTING

Leah A. Lievrouw

Computation is an integral component of contemporary media logic: mediated communication has become as much a matter of tinkering, reconfiguring, playing, hacking, pranking, coding and jailbreaking as it is of production, representation, signifying, reception or consumption. Computers have been recognized as 'communication devices' at least since the 1960s (Licklider & Taylor 1968). However, the tendency to attribute intelligence and responsiveness to computing machines has been evident ever since Alan Turing (1950) proposed his 'Turing test', and Joseph Weizenbaum (Weizenbaum 1966) and his colleagues, with some dismay, observed the Turing phenomenon at work in their experimental natural-language system ELIZA, designed to mimic the responses of a non-directive therapist. Skeptics have challenged the inflated claims of artificial intelligence (AI) since its earliest days (e.g. Dreyfus 1992, Agre 1997), warning of the ethical hazards of attributing human capacities, including communicative competence, to machines (Weizenbaum 1976).

However, activist engineers, technologists, artists and designers have also embraced computation as a tool to envision, build and defend good societies and cultures, and to resist powerful interests or regimes that restrict open expression and access to information and technological systems. Over time, as computing has diffused into all aspects of everyday culture and interaction – that is, as computers have become media – some of the emancipatory ethos of the early technology activists has also diffused into the wider media culture. Along the way, digital media and information systems have become crucial sites for contestation, mobilization and opposition to established power, and for enacting alternative culture and politics.

This chapter explores *alternative computing*. Originated in the early 2000s by the anthropologist David Hakken in his studies of free/libre open-source software, the term is used here more broadly, to describe a genre of media activism defined by its method of direct action and intervention in computational infrastructures, resources and products, and an ethical and political commitment to information access, open systems and freedom of information and communication as fundamental rights and necessary conditions for political and social/cultural participation (Lievrouw 2011). Like other types of activism, it often embraces contrarian or outsider perspectives or community interests, and takes a small-scale, often *ad hoc* approach (though particular actions may have far-reaching consequences). As activist practice, alternative computing is distinctive not only for using digital systems as channels of activist expression and interaction, but also for treating digital devices, data and algorithms themselves as material forms of cultural, social and political power and participation.

The chapter begins with a brief historical sketch of the ethical questions and values that have influenced activist computer professionals, engineers, designers and hobbyist amateurs, and the signature issues they have defended (intellectual freedom and speech rights, surveillance and privacy/autonomy, and intellectual property/free culture). Several main types of alternative computing projects and interventions that have carried this ethos forward in current media culture are discussed, including the longstanding tradition of hacking and *hacktivism*; *design activism*, which advances computationally-based design alternatives for the built environment and material culture; and *data activism*, which contests the growing role of data and algorithms as sources of legitimate knowledge and value.

From debate to advocacy

Historically, as a class of technology, machine/electronic computation has captured the imagination of experts and the general public alike, evoking comparisons with human brains, intelligence and (when combined with robotics) physical strength, stamina and precision. In popular culture, computers are figures of hope, dread, oppression, companionship, control, liberation and ease. Debates arose at an early point among computer professionals, cultural critics and academics, not only about what machines should be built, how or for what purposes, but *who* should have access to them and why. Given early systems' extraordinary cost, scarcity and technical complexity, these debates mainly involved experts in major research institutions and the handful of private-sector firms that could afford computers and specialists to operate them, along with critics and philosophers concerned with the machines' cultural and social influence.

Mid-twentieth century thinkers moved among conceptions of computing as Turing-style 'symbol manipulation' and programming as analogous to human language, information-theoretic notions of signal and noise so eagerly appropriated by mid-century communication scholars (Peters 1986), and the generalized claims of man–machine studies (*sic*). However, some also doubted the easy parallels drawn between computer systems and human cognition, 'natural language' communication as a model for human–machine information exchange, and computers' likelihood to automate and even replace human thought, skills and judgment. Cyberneticist Norbert Wiener, for example, saw computers as basically emancipatory, with the potential to free people from repetitive, stressful administrative tasks and manual labour—but he also recognized their potential as tools for human oppression and redundancy (Wiener 1950). Philosopher and phenomenologist Hubert Dreyfus (1992) was a persistent, effective critic of the very idea of 'artificial intelligence'.

J. C. R. Licklider (an early proponent of what he called 'man–computer symbiosis' [1960]) and his co-author Robert Taylor (Licklider & Taylor 1968: 28) believed computers had the potential to 'revolutionize communication'. However, they criticized most computing engineers' (and many social scientists') conceptions of communication as simple transmission and switching, dismissing this as 'communication through a computer' (1968: 28) or 'computer-aided communication' (p. 29). This was not communication in the human sense: 'to communicate is more than to send and to receive. Do two tape recorders communicate when they play to each other and record from each other?' (1968: 21). True human–computer communication would require machines with 'an interactive, cooperative modeling facility', i.e. able to generate and adapt 'mental models' much as humans do – though Licklider and Taylor acknowledged that there would be 'powerful legal and administrative obstacles' to any such development (1968: 28). Later, Jerome Bruner (1990), a founder of cognitive psychology, would object strenuously to any suggestion that equated human thought and automated information processing.

These observers focused mainly on the ethical implications of computers for human autonomy, agency, and meaning. But as Fred Turner (2006) shows, the conversation took a new direction in the late 1960s and 1970s with the development of networked computing and telecommunications, miniaturization in electronics, the diffusion of computers beyond a handful of elite labs and institutes and the larger countercultural upheavals in the academy and wider society associated with movements for racial equality and civil rights, feminism, antiwar and student movements and environmentalism, among others. Like their egalitarian, radicalized counterparts in those movements, graduate engineering students, computer hobbyists and technology activists saw no reason to reserve computing for industry, research and the military. They sought the self-sufficiency and independence captured by the motto of the flagship counterculture publication *Whole Earth Review*: 'access to tools.' These new activists tinkered with and built DIY devices and interfaces, tapped into telecommunications networks, wrote and swapped computer code, and organized collectives and start-ups with the kinds of technological competence and social freedom to innovate and interact that they enjoyed in academic or research settings, but were often forbidden in the corporate workplace. In essence, they created 'personal computing'.

Computing visionary Ted Nelson crystallized this sensibility in *Computer Lib / Dream Machines* (1974), two self-published, hand-illustrated, techno-cultural manifestos printed as a single, back-to-back, zine-style volume. *Computer Lib* (urgently subtitled *You Can and Must Understand Computers Now*) and *Dream Machines* became something of a sensation among computing aficionados, self-styled geeks and hackers who saw computers as revolutionary tools for expression, creativity, interaction, alternative lifestyles and community. For them, the ability to use, break down, reverse engineer and reconfigure computers was as essential to a good society as literacy, the printing press, telephone and transportation networks, free-to-air broadcasting or the electrical grid – perhaps all of these rolled into one.

Like other countercultural activists, they agitated for freedom – free speech and expression, free press and access to information, freedom from repressive (and technologically uninformed) social norms and state authority, and resistance to pervasive consumerism, corporate monopolists and economic injustice – a sort of 'digital utopianism' (Turner 2006). But instead of philosophical debates about the nature of human autonomy and dignity, these utopians looked to the collaborative, interventionist and fiercely meritocratic 'hacker culture' that had arisen within top engineering schools like the Massachusetts Institute of Technology (MIT), where risk-taking and elaborate pranking projects were encouraged to cultivate engineering students' creativity and skills for solving intractable technical and design problems (Thomas 2002; Peterson 2003; Nissenbaum 2004). Hacker culture – itself deeply rooted in the norms of science and the academy, plus the determined non-conformism of the counterculture – developed its own ethos of mutual support; personal responsibility; valuing technological mastery and virtuosity over social rank or status; open, rigorous (even ruthless) debate and critique; and using technology to advance the common good.

Indeed, academic computer scientists themselves have often articulated an explicitly progressive approach to systems design. Reflecting on the cultural and intellectual limits of his own training in AI, for example, computer scientist and cultural scholar Philip Agre formulated *critical technical practice* (CTP) (Agre 1997). Rather than positing an ideal, expert, 'best' solution to a given problem, Agre said, programmers and engineers should adopt a more humanistic, reflexive, dialectic approach to design, moving back and forth between design/building and culturally-informed, participatory critique and revision. Turner, in contrast, highlights the alliance among professional and amateur 'techies' and the San Francisco-based counterculture associated with the *Whole Earth Review*, its founder Stewart Brand and its pioneering community computing network, the WELL (Whole Earth 'Lectronic Link) (Turner 2006). Those ties, and others across the computing community beyond the Bay Area, eventually grew into a network of broadly progressive advocacy groups and policy projects.

For example, in 1981 researchers at Stanford University and nearby Xerox PARC (Palo Alto Research Center) formed Computer Professionals for Social Responsibility (CPSR) to oppose President Reagan's 'Star Wars' programme to build space-based offensive weapons incorporating artificial intelligence. CPSR's agenda soon expanded to include various ethical and political controversies related to computing and internet technology. Until 2013, the group gave the Norbert Wiener Award to recognize 'outstanding contributions for social responsibility in computing technology … to share concerns that lead to action in arenas of the power, promise and limitations of computer technology' (http://cpsr.org/about/wiener).

To advance their critical-technology approach, CPSR organized the Directions and Implications in Advanced Computing (DIAC) Conferences, as well as the Participatory Design Conferences, which continue to meet biannually. Participatory design (PD) originated in Scandinavian auto factories in the 1960s and 70s, where unionized line workers joined with management to redesign and fine-tune automated assembly lines (Schuler & Namioka 1993; Gregory 2003). 'User-centred' PD techniques eventually developed into a distinct software/ systems development philosophy, adopted in both private industry and non-profit organizations seeking to counter the dominant decision-making power of management and elite engineers, and to improve the quality of work and workplace conditions.

With respect to law and policy, the Electronic Privacy Information Center (EPIC, https:// www.epic.org) – a CPSR spinoff – has been a key civil-society advocate and litigant in high-profile intellectual property, surveillance, privacy, Fourth Amendment (search-and-seizure) and other online civil liberties cases in the US. The Electronic Frontier Foundation (EFF, https://www.eff.org), a prominent research and advocacy organization, was launched by prominent members of the WELL community in 1990, including software entrepreneur Mitch Kapor and technologist/Grateful Dead lyricist John Perry Barlow. They opposed political restraints on technological innovation, and provided legal defense against increasingly intrusive, but technologically ignorant, law enforcement raids and investigations of presumed software theft. EFF's original roster of supporters, donors and board members included Apple founder Steve Wozniak, USENET and encryption pioneer John Gilmore, *Whole Earth*'s Stewart Brand, and technology journalist and philanthropist Esther Dyson.

Instead of litigation and policy advocacy, the Free Software Foundation (FSF, http://www.fsf. org) promotes free, open-source technology development among programmers, engineers and designers. Former Harvard graduate student and programmer Richard Stallman, founder of FSF and its progenitor, the GNU Project, is passionately committed to the communitarian, free-software ethos he first experienced among academic programmers who openly shared, circulated and modified code, and in the process made unprecedented advances in computing from the 1960s onward. GNU, an early-1980s open-source software collaboration, was intended to rival AT&T's proprietary operating system, UNIX (Stallman's waggish 'recursive acronym' stands for 'GNU's Not UNIX'). But the GNU Project also made two other enduring contributions to the digital media landscape: first, as the basis of the Linux operating system developed by Linus Torvalds and other collaborators; and second, with the development of the GNU Public License (GPL), a legal agreement that inverts the logic of copyright to what Stallman calls 'copyleft'. In exchange for authorship credit, licensees must ensure that the code they produce or adapt remains free and open to anyone to use, study or modify.

Today, Linux's many versions and distributions run most internet servers and supercomputers worldwide. It enjoys a reputation for being reliable, secure and a powerful tool for rapid software prototyping and repair (see https://en.wikipedia.org/wiki/Linux; https://opensource.com/ open-source-way). Open-source pioneer Eric Raymond's famous 'Linus's Law' captures the basic collaborative philosophy and strategy behind Linux's continued resilience: 'given enough eyeballs, all bugs are shallow' (https://en.wikipedia.org/wiki/Linus%27s_Law). Likewise, the GPL was the forebear of today's widely-used Creative Commons licenses (https://creativecom-mons.org). Developed by attorney-activist Lawrence Lessig and his colleagues (including the late programmer, entrepreneur and renowned free-culture activist, Aaron Swartz), Creative Commons licenses limit intrusive, punitive intellectual property restrictions, and protect public domain, fair use, first sale and patent exhaustion as legal principles that safeguard the re-use of creative works and innovation (Lessig 2004).

These organizations and projects only begin to suggest the range of early activist projects that helped make computing a sustainable platform for creativity, communication and culture. Others include the Internet Archive, a digital library founded in the 1990s by software entrepreneur and philanthropist Brewster Kahle to capture and save the World Wide Web, and later the whole corpus of online content and huge collections of media content, in perpetuity to preserve 'universal access to all knowledge' (see https://archive.org; https://en.wikipedia.org/wiki/Internet_Archive). The collaborative Wikipedia project depends on contributions and amendments by tens of thousands of volunteer editors, and is the world's largest and most frequently consulted online reference source on virtually any subject, in dozens of languages.

The activities of these diverse forums, organizations and projects continue to reflect a vision of computing as both a product of culture and an essential creative tool for those who make it. However, from the perspective of social change or movement mobilization, we might observe how that vision and its attendant values have diffused into the larger society along with access to computing power (however unevenly or precariously). Early-1990s browsers and search engines gave non-expert computer users unprecedented search and information retrieval capabilities. In the mid-2000s, the advent of social media and 'smart' phones, touch-screen interfaces and simplified mobile applications ('apps') encouraged users to pursue their minutest niche interests and far-flung social interactions. Today, voice-driven interfaces and the vaunted 'internet of things' (IoT) hold out the promise of automated 'assistants' and mediation for even the most banal, routine activities – while users surrender real-time flows of personal data to unprecedented collection and algorithmic scrutiny in the process.

Yet the rebellious sensibility of early technology visionaries and the original 'hacker ethos' still underpin alternative computing as a distinctive genre of political and cultural activism. It surfaces in formal policy controversies and popular discourse surrounding the digital intrusions of government and the private sector: in the grass-roots resistance of online civil libertarians; in community 'crypto parties' where programmers and designers teach novices how to protect personal data; in open-source software collaborations; in 'hackathons' where local residents build and monitor their own community data; and in opposition to the overreach of intellectual property rights holders, whether among free culture and social justice advocates or individuals who repair their own cars or phones. In the remainder of this chapter, we consider three important types of contemporary alternative computing projects in which the hacker ethos continues to inform dissent and active resistance.

From advocacy to intervention

As the preceding discussion suggests, technology activists have long insisted on their right and responsibility to intervene in systems, devices or code that they view as oppressive, intrusive, unjust, designed to impede communication or creativity, or simply not fit for purpose (e.g. the FSF's 'Defective By Design' campaign, https://www.defectivebydesign.org). Three types of contemporary alternative computing projects embody these commitments: *hacktivism*, *design activism* and *data activism*.

Hacktivism

The origins and ethos of hacker culture in elite engineering schools have already been noted. Programmers in the 1970s and 1980s tinkered, pranked, shared code and built software and devices collaboratively, often outside market demands for profit that appropriated their work and stifled innovation. In this context, professional engineers as well as self-styled 'phone phreaks', 'crypto-anarchists' and 'cypherpunks' explored and exploited system features and flaws as a basic design method (Meikle 2002; Thomas 2002; Jordan & Taylor 2004; Taylor 2005). Later, law enforcement and private-sector interests would attempt to co-opt the word *hacker* – then and now, something of an honorific term among elite programmers – and the hacker ethos as synonyms for criminality, sabotage and subversion of legitimate authority (Nissenbaum 2004).

Nonetheless, despite increasingly punitive legal sanctions on unauthorized access or uses of computing systems, the hacker sensibility remains a touchstone for activist projects seeking to expose and undermine repressive, fraudulent, exploitive or coercive systems and institutions. Although some writers define *hacktivism* loosely as any activism that involves computers, the term was coined in the late 1990s by the Austin, Texas art/technology collective Cult of the Dead Cow (cDc) to denote explicitly political uses of computing tools and techniques, or 'hacks'. (Information security analyst Dorothy Denning [2015] has surveyed the origins, history and current activities of various hacktivist projects in the US and internationally by both non-state and [increasingly] state-supported actors.) Hacktivist techniques have included distributed denial of service (DDoS) attacks, which flood websites with automated queries meant to overload and disable them, and bits of code (so-called worms) that alter log-in screens or public web sites. Hacktivists build 'back doors' into system files and data, and encrypted 'dropbox'-type repositories where whistle-blowers might upload incriminating documents without identifying themselves to authorities.

Hacktivists often act independently or in small, loosely organized groups, and carefully conceal the identities and whereabouts of their members. One of the best known examples is the amorphous, ingeniously self-promotional collective Anonymous, known for using a Guy Fawkes mask (originally designed for the Warner Brothers film *V for Vendetta*) as an impromptu 'brand' in live and online protest actions. Its targets have included the Church of Scientology, military and government security contractors, the Visa and MasterCard banking services, and the government of the People's Republic of China (Coleman 2014).

Design activism

Recent art and design have been notable for an expressly political and activist turn. Certainly, political art is nothing new: modern designers often put their social, cultural and political ideals to work in architecture and urban design, industrial and product design, graphics and so on. However, *design activism* has developed as a distinctive design philosophy and approach that embraces the hacker ethos. Its 'purpose is not to offer immediate solutions to problems, but to spark interest in [social issues] and show, often paradoxically or provocatively, that there are different ways of seeing and resolving them' (Manzini 2015: 46). Or, as designer Anne Thorpe (2014: n.p.) has put it, 'design activists practice a different form of activism … by generating positive alternatives to the status quo. Rather than being resistant, design activism is mostly "generative"'.

Computing plays a special role in design activism, not only as rendering, visualization or illustration tools, but also as a key component of design solutions that engage, contend with and resist an increasingly digitized, mediated material world and social reality. Designer Régine Debatty's website, *We Make Money Not Art* (http://we-make-money-not-art.com) features a range of activist design projects for DIY dissent, such as Ben Grosser's 'Facebook Demetricator', a web browser extension that strips Facebook page/feed metrics and prevents its algorithms from capturing the user's 'likes' as sentiment data (http://bengrosser.com/projects/Facebook-Demetricator). Finn Brunton and Helen Nissenbaum (2015: 78) emphasize the tactics of *obfuscation*, where voluminous, misleading, or mixed-up information conceals users' activities, promotes 'informational justice', and overcomes 'asymmetries of power and knowledge' between individuals and small groups, on one hand, and institutional and corporate/state actors, on the other. Nissenbaum and her colleagues developed *AdNauseam*, an ad blocker/browser extension that automatically clicks on all ads being served to the user to obscure which ads the user actually notices, while advertisers are charged for huge streams of click traffic.

Some designers specialize in data visualization, a persuasive tool for critiquing and rendering in graphical form the essential 'story', unexpected findings or biases in datasets (Lima 2011). (The new specialization of data journalism employs data visualization techniques as a regular part of news gathering and investigative reporting.) The current 'maker' movement also reflects the design-activism perspective. Matt Ratto (2011) and his colleagues have advanced *critical making*, a design method based on Agre's critical technical practice (1997). Here, design, building and critique are inextricably linked as a way to counter the implicit economic, social and political assumptions of typical technology solutions (see also Hertz 2016).

Design activists have also created a recent wave of anti-facial recognition projects. These often take an ironic, fashion-conscious stance, introducing clothing, hairstyles and makeup tips specially designed to defeat facial recognition systems (which their proponents claim are nearly 100% accurate). Projects here include Adam Harvey's Hyperface, StealthWear and CVDazzle projects (https://ahprojects.com), and Simone Niquille's FaceValue accessories – AntiContact lenses that prevent iris scanning; Watermark_Crystals makeup, applied in complex anti-recognition patterns that spoil high-definition flash photography; and the Realface Glamouflage line of T-shirts, printed with remixed images of celebrity faces that defeat surveillance cameras (http://technofle.sh).

Data activism

If hacktivism and design activism are notable for intervening in computing devices and systems, or in the computer-mediated places, objects and activities of everyday life, data activism focuses on the fundamental commodities and products of digital culture and communication: data and algorithms. Data activists recognize that virtually all aspects of routine action, communicative expression, interaction and relations are being reconceived and rendered as data, and subjected to computational analysis using proprietary algorithms. Data flows and algorithms are largely hidden from public scrutiny, built into invisible, smooth-running technological infrastructures (Bowker *et al.* 2010). Thus, to achieve social change activists must also expose data and algorithms as manifestations and consequences of cultural, economic and political power. '[W]e must expand from the study of communication as signs or discourse to include the study of communication as data collection, storage and processing' (Langlois & Elmer 2013: 2). And while critique is necessary, it is not sufficient: 'citizens [should] take a critical approach to big data, *and appropriate and manipulate data for advocacy and social change*' (Milan & Gutiérrez 2015: 11; emphasis added). Like their hacker forebears, data activists must harness, re-craft and re-direct big data and algorithms for themselves and their communities, 'from the bottom up' (Couldry & Powell 2014).

In many ways, the turn to data activism as a specific movement or contention strategy responds to the rise of so-called *big data* over the last decade – a term popularized by technology industries determined to exploit and monetize the dramatic growth of computing power, data storage and processing capacity in global-scale networks. Although the word *data* has been used to denote measurable information since the rise of electronic computing in the mid-twentieth century, the vastly larger scale and commodification of big data is suggested by the proliferation of extractive, resource-based metaphors for computing processes and systems (e.g. mining, silos, warehouses, torrents, clouds, farms). There is no single, agreed-upon definition of big data beyond flip observations that 'if it's too big to copy, it's big data', or 'big data is only big when the amount or complexity takes you out of your comfort zone'. But the term captures the sense that there is simply more information being generated and circulated through global computing systems than ordinary people can reasonably comprehend. Thus automated programs – algorithms – help us manage the 'three v's' of big data (*volume, variety, velocity*; http://www.zdnet.com/article/volume-velocity-and-variety-understanding-the-three-vs-of-big-data), classify and identify patterns in the data, and make automated decisions based on the patterns. Artificial intelligence and 'machine learning' algorithms are trained to perform specialized tasks (facial recognition, language translation, game playing, credit profiling, assessing financial market volatility, operating self-driving vehicles) using enormous data collections and adapt as data changes. Ultimately, algorithms may 'learn' without explicit human programming.

However, many researchers and activists reject the idea that data or algorithms are socially, economically or culturally neutral, or an inevitable, unalloyed social good. *Critical data studies* (Kitchin 2014) and *critical algorithm studies* (https://socialmediacollective.org/reading-lists/critical-algorithm-studies) have emerged as research fronts in their own right, and as important influences for data activists. Like big data itself, there is no single definition of data activism. Researcher Stefania Milan and her colleagues, for example, distinguish between 'reactive' data activism (more defensive practices, e.g. encrypting personal communications or installing ad blockers in web browsers), and the 'proactive' variety, where activists build and modify datasets and algorithms directly (Milan & van der Velden 2016). Helen Kennedy (2016) would include only 'data focused' projects, including Milan's 'proactive' category, but also campaigns for open data policies and laws, communities' and individuals' 'DIY self-production', data visualization and the mobilization of collective expertise via crowdsourcing.

However defined, data activism has developed quickly on several important fronts, notably in academic/research and government open-data movements, and in grassroots efforts among community activists to identify biases or omissions in public data. *Community informatics* helped to lay the groundwork for such projects; its purpose is to make computing technologies and data 'usable and useful to the range of excluded populations and communities' (Gurstein 2007: 11). *Civic hacking* aims to open public data and government data practices to citizen review and participation, 'requesting, digesting, contributing to, modeling, and contesting data' (Schrock 2016: 581). For example, grassroots activists in the New York City area obtained and reinterpreted official statistics about the effects of Hurricane Sandy to 'paint alternative pictures' of the storm and its consequences for the city's poorest (Liboiron 2015: 146).

Closing remarks

This short introduction cannot possibly convey the variety and ingenuity of alternative computing projects today, or their influence on the tenor and quality of dissent online and off. But some basic observations can be made. First, the influence of engineering, design and computing culture on today's media logic and culture deserves a closer look from media historians and critical media scholars. The hands-on, interventionist approach emphasizing creativity and problem-solving, and its ameliorative, and frankly idealist ethos, are modes of communication in their own right, and have helped shape assumptions about computers as communication media, as well as the architectures and affordances of the systems themselves.

A second, related point is the ongoing turn to 'algorithmic media', where the distinctions between channel and content are not only blurred, but largely obliterated: the model of static stocks of content moving through stable distribution networks is giving way to dynamic, recombinant, and even 'learning' data flows and algorithmic modulation where form and meaning change continuously in use. This constitutes a fundamental change in the nature of communication media and thus how they must be studied, with attendant implications at every level of communicative action, from interpersonal relations to civil society.

In sum, the hacker ethos, design activism and data activism seek to change not only the perceptions, opinions, attitudes and action of individuals, but to transform the very material conditions of human communication itself. We might ask, what are the prospects for social change, movement mobilization and action in such conditions of communicative flux?

References

Agre, P. E. (1997) 'Toward a Critical Technical Practice: Lessons Learned in Trying to Reform AI', in G. C. Bowker, S. L. Star, W. Turner and L. Gasser (eds) *Social Science, Technical Systems, and Cooperative Work*. Mahwah, NJ: Lawrence Erlbaum Associates, pp. 131–57.

Bowker, G. C., Baker, K., Millerand, F., and Ribes, D. (2010) 'Toward Information Infrastructure Studies: Ways of Knowing in a Networked Environment', in J. Hunsinger, L. Klastrup and M. Allen (eds), *International Handbook of Internet Research*. Dordrecht: Springer, pp. 97–117.

Bruner, J. S. (1990) *Acts of Meaning*. Cambridge, MA: Harvard University Press.

Brunton, F. and Nissenbaum, H. (2015) *Obfuscation*. Cambridge, MA: MIT Press.

Coleman, G. (2014) *Hacker, Hoaxer, Whistleblower, Spy*. New York: Verso.

Couldry, N. and Powell, A. (2014) 'Big Data from the Bottom Up', *Big Data & Society*, vol. 1, no. 2, pp. 1–5.

Denning, D. (2015) 'The Rise of Hacktivism', *Georgetown Journal of International Affairs*, 8 September, https://www.georgetownjournalofinternationalaffairs.org/online-edition/the-rise-of-hacktivism, accessed 18 November 2017.

Dreyfus, H. L. (1992) *What Computers Still Can't Do*. Cambridge, MA: MIT Press.

Gregory, J. (2003) 'Scandinavian Approaches to Participatory Design', *International Journal of Engineering Education*, vol. 19, no. 1, pp. 62–74.

Gurstein, M. (2007) *What Is Critical Informatics and Why Does It Matter?* Milan: Polimetrica, https://arxiv.org/ftp/arxiv/papers/0712/0712.3220.pdf, accessed 16 August 2017.

Hertz, G. (2016) 'What Is Critical Making?', *Current* 07, http://current.ecuad.ca/what-is-critical-making, accessed 16 August 2017.

Jordan, T. and Taylor, P. A. (2004) *Hacktivism and Cyberwars*. London: Routledge.

Kennedy, H. (2016) *Post, Mine, Repeat*. London: Palgrave Macmillan.

Kitchin, R. (2014) *The Data Revolution*. London: Sage.

Langlois, G. and Elmer, G. (2013) 'The Research Politics of Social Media Platforms', *Culture Machine*, vol. 14, pp. 1–17, https://www.culturemachine.net/index.php/cm/issue/view/25, accessed 16 August 2017.

Lessig, L. (2004) *Free Culture*. New York: Penguin.

Liboiron, M. (2015) 'Disaster Data, Data Activism: Grassroots Responses to Representing Superstorm Sandy', in J. Leyda and D. Negra (eds), *Extreme Weather and Global Media*. New York: Routledge, pp. 144–62.

Licklider, J. C. R. (1960) 'Man–Computer Symbiosis', *IRE Transactions on Human Factors in Electronics*, March, pp. 4–11.

Licklider, J. C. R. and Taylor, R. W. (1968) 'The Computer as Communication Device', *Science & Technology*, vol. 76, pp. 21–41.

Lievrouw, L. A. (2011) *Alternative and Activist New Media*. Cambridge: Polity.

Lima, M. (2011) *Visual Complexity*. New York: Princeton University Press.

Manzini, E. (2015) *Design, When Everybody Designs*. Cambridge, MA: MIT Press.

Meikle, G. (2002) *Future Active*. New York: Routledge.

Milan, S. and Gutiérrez, M. (2015) 'Medios Ciudadanos y Big Data: La Emergencia del Activism de Datos', *Mediaciones*, vol. 14, May-June, pp. 10–26, http://biblioteca.uniminuto.edu/ojs_desa/index.php/med/article/view/1086/1027, accessed 16 August 2017.

Milan, S. and van der Velden, L. (2016) 'The Alternative Epistemologies of Data Activism', *Digital Culture & Society*, vol. 2, issue 2, pp. 57–74.

Nelson, T. H. (1974) *Computer Lib/Dream Machines*. Self-published. ISBN: 0-89347-002-3.

Nissenbaum, H. (2004) 'Hackers and the Contested Ontology of Cyberspace', *New Media & Society*, vol. 6, no. 2, pp. 195–217.

Peters, J. D. (1986) 'Institutional Sources of Intellectual Poverty in Communication Research', *Communication Research*, vol. 13, no. 4, pp. 527–59.

Peterson, T. F. (2003) *Nightwork*. Cambridge, MA: MIT Press.

Ratto, M. (2011) 'Critical Making: Conceptual and Material Studies in Technology and Social Life', *The Information Society*, vol. 27, no. 4, pp. 252–60.

Schrock, A. (2016) 'Civic Hacking as Data Activism and Advocacy: A History from Publicity to Open Government Data', *New Media & Society*, vol. 18, no. 4, pp. 581–99.

Schuler, D. and Namioka, A. (eds) (1993) *Participatory Design*. Hillsdale, NJ: Lawrence Erlbaum.

Taylor, P. A. (2005) 'From Hackers to Hacktivists: Speed Bumps on the Global Superhighway?' *New Media & Society*, vol. 7, no. 5, pp. 625–46.

Thomas, D. (2002) *Hacker Culture*. Minneapolis: University of Minnesota Press.

Thorpe, A. (2014) 'Design as Activism: To Resist or to Generate?' *Current* 05, http://current.ecuad.ca./design-as-activism-to-resist-or-to-generate, accessed 16 August 2017.

Turing, A. (1950) 'Computing Machinery and Intelligence', *Mind*, vol. 59, issue 236, October, pp. 433–60.

Turner, F. (2006) *From Counterculture to Cyberculture*. Chicago: University of Chicago Press.

Weizenbaum, J. (1966) 'ELIZA – A Computer Program for the Study of Natural Language Communication Between Man and Machine', *Communications of the ACM*, vol. 9, no. 1, January, pp. 36–45.

Weizenbaum, J. (1976) *Computer Power and Human Reason*. New York: W. H. Freeman.

Wiener, N. (1950) *The Human Use of Human Beings*. New York: Houghton Mifflin.

PART II

Organizations and identities

7

TRANSFORMATIVE MEDIA ORGANIZING

Key lessons from participatory communications research with the immigrant rights, Occupy, and LGBTQ and Two-Spirit movements

Sasha Costanza-Chock

Introduction: making media and making change

The relationship between the media and social movements is hotly contested by scholars and activists alike. However, relatively few studies are grounded in the deep specificity of social movement media practices, and fewer still employ participatory action research approaches. This chapter summarizes findings from a decade of mixed methods participatory action research with three social movements in the United States: the immigrant rights movement (between 2006 and 2016), the Occupy movement (2011–2012), and Lesbian, Gay, Bisexual, Trans★, Queer (LGBTQ) and Two-Spirit movement(s) (2014–2016) (Costanza-Chock 2012; Costanza-Chock 2014; Costanza-Chock, Schweidler & TMO 2016). Research methods include surveys, interviews, analysis of media archives, data hackathons and participatory data analysis, and community-based media making workshops. Although I played a lead role in each research process, these were Participatory Action Research (PAR) projects (see Fals Borda 2001), and research teams in each case included a diverse group of researchers, activists and community organizers. Across the three movements, we found that despite scarce resources, community organizers often have an intersectional analysis of linked systems of race, class, gender identity, sexual orientation and other axes of identity. Many seek to do media work that develops the critical consciousness and leadership of their communities, create media in ways that are deeply accountable to their social base, use participatory approaches to media making, are strategic and cross-platform in their approach and root their work in community action. We call this combination of characteristics *transformative media organizing*, and we believe it describes an emerging paradigm for social movement media practices in the current media landscape. Before we delve into key findings, a few words about the social movement context are in order.

The immigrant rights movement

The global political economy increasingly allows capital to flow freely across national boundaries, while states militarize their borders against human migration, whether migrants are driven by economic necessity, ecological devastation and climate change or war. Yet closed and militarized borders are a relatively recent invention, and there is nothing inevitable about them. Battles over migration policy are fought in the halls of power, in the streets and in the media system. Over the last decade, immigrant rights activists in the United States gained increasing visibility in mainstream (Anglo) television, Spanish-language commercial newspapers, radio and television and in social media platforms. Despite Obama's dubious distinction as 'Deporter-in-Chief', based on his administration's record-breaking deportation rates, and the 2016 election of Trump on an anti-immigrant platform, the last few years also saw limited gains by the immigrant rights movement. Undocumented youth used direct action to secure Deferred Action for Childhood Arrivals, a programme that (although temporary) provided legal status for about 750,000 people; this provided access to jobs, credit and respite from the threat of deportation. Many gains took place at the municipal and state levels: in California, the movement secured passage of A.B. 60, which provided access to drivers' licenses for more than 1.4 million people; similar bills passed in more than ten states. In many states, undocumented students secured access to in-state tuition for higher education. A growing number of 'sanctuary cities' have refused to cooperate with the federal detention and deportation system, and have taken steps to limit data sharing between local police and immigration officers.

Between 2006 and 2016, I worked closely with immigrant rights activists and organizations in Los Angeles, Boston and Washington, DC. I participated in nearly one hundred media workshops, took part in many protest actions and co-founded immigrant rights media projects such as Mobile Voices (VozMob), Radio Tijeras, the UndocuTech network and more. I also conducted forty semi-structured interviews with movement activists and organizers, focused on media work within the immigrant rights movement. Based on this work, I published *Out of the Shadows, Into the Streets!* (2014), a book about media and community organizing in the immigrant rights movement. Many of the key findings, as we shall see below, closely parallel findings in other social movements.

Occupy research

Inspired by the Arab Spring, Occupy Wall Street began on 17 September 2011 in New York City, and spread rapidly throughout the US and around the globe (Gerbaudo 2012). The Occupy movement focused on social and economic inequalities, particularly the increasing disparity between the wealthiest 1 per cent of the population and 'the 99 per cent'. The movement grew quickly, established protest camps in hundreds of cities, captured a great deal of media attention and attracted support and resources from a diverse range of people. The broad umbrella frame of 'the 99 per cent' encouraged people to link problems faced by their own communities to a larger social movement frame. Yet, who took part in Occupy, and why? Were participants already politicized, or was this their first social movement? How did Occupiers use media to create and share their narratives? To investigate these and other questions, a group of scholars, activists and organizers co-founded Occupy Research: an open activist research network that conducted regular calls, meetups, data hackathons and research sprints. As movement researchers, we were committed to advancing the theory and practice of research justice for movement building. We launched in September of 2011 and grew rapidly: our active mailing list had over 350 participants; we formed project-based working groups and coordinated regular conference calls joined by researchers from across the country and around the world. We shared ideas, research questions, methods, tools and datasets, and worked to gather, analyze, discuss, write, code and otherwise develop theory and practice together. An archive of the activities of the network is available at http://bit.ly/occupyresearcharchive.

One of our key activities was the Occupy Research General Demographic & Participation Survey (ORGS), designed to:

> 1) create better understanding of who participated in Occupy, who did not participate, and why; 2) identify, document and challenge race, class, gender, sexuality, age, disability and other inequalities reproduced within movement spaces; 3) support movement actors to share ideas, strategies and tactics; 4) spread research skills, tools and methods more broadly throughout the 99%; 5) challenge dominant narratives about the movement by creating and sharing data that highlighted the views of Occupiers in their own words.

We designed ORGS through an open, collaborative process that included Occupy participants and researchers from across the globe. We ultimately gathered 5,074 completed surveys (for more on our methodology, see Occupy Research 2012, and see also Kidd 2015). We also analyzed media activism within the Occupy Movement, from the People's Mic to GlobalRevolution.tv. Our findings were published in a number of places, and as we shall argue below, we found that media activism in the Occupy movement demonstrated several characteristics similar to the immigrant rights and LGBTQ movements.

The Transformative Media Organizing project

In the United States, LGBTQ and Two-Spirit movements have won a series of important victories. ('Two-Spirit' is used by many Indigenous North American peoples as an umbrella term for individuals whose spirits are a blending of male and female; many Indigenous cultures recognized more than two genders, and are reclaiming these other genders after centuries of attempts by European settler colonialism to erase and destroy them. For more information, see twospiritjournal.com). LGBTQ youth of colour in NYC and New Orleans recently joined with other community-based organizations to win bans against discriminatory police profiling and stop and frisk; at the federal level, the LGBTQ movement convinced the executive branch to issue orders against workplace discrimination based on sexual orientation or gender identity (SOGI), alongside race, ethnicity, religion, age, disability, HIV status, immigration status and housing status; LGBTQ people are increasingly elected to office. These victories have come in the wake of broader cultural shifts, including greatly increased and diversified representation throughout the media system (film, TV, popular music, advertising, social media, fashion and so on). Yet at the same time, Queer and Trans* People of Colour face oppression and structural inequality, including police harassment and violence, physical attacks, high rates of youth suicide, homelessness, school pushout, incarceration and murder. Most recently, Trump's election signals the arrival of a period of rollbacks and resurgent attacks – political, cultural and physical – against LGBTQ and Two-Spirit people and communities.

Within this broader context, the Transformative Media Organizing project (TMO) is a network that links LGBTQ and Two-Spirit organizers, media makers and tech-activists across the United States. TMO was designed to build stronger intersectional LGBTQ and Two-Spirit movements through a shared approach to media making. From 2013 to 2016, we provided a free monthly media skillshare series (archived at transformativemedia.cc), and we conducted a nationwide strengths and needs assessment of LGBTQ and Two-Spirit organizations, based on mixed methods participatory research. Together, we developed research questions about current media capacity, media organizing strategy, vision for media and social change, barriers, needs, and opportunities and how to strengthen media work. Our goal was to provide groups that work with LGBTQ and Two-Spirit communities, as well as their allies, researchers and funders, with a snapshot of the current challenges and opportunities in media and communications work. Our methods included a nationwide organizational survey with 231 respondents, 19 expert interviews and a series of workshops with partners and advisers. As we shall see, we found that despite scarce resources, LGBTQ and Two-Spirit organizations make powerful media across a wide range of platforms to tell their own intersectional stories, integrate media making as a key component of their service, advocacy, organizing and community building work, and use media to win policy and electoral campaigns, as well as to shift culture at large.

Key findings across movements

Across all three movements, we found that those who produce the most effective social movement media work tend to: 1. have an intersectional analysis of the matrix of domination and the possibilities of resistance; 2. seek to develop critical consciousness and leadership among their base; 3. employ both formal and informal accountability mechanisms to ensure that the narrative of their media work fits the needs of their communities; 4. engage in participatory media practices; 5. produce media across multiple platforms; and 6. root media work in ongoing community organizing processes. We call this combination of characteristics *transformative media organizing*.

Employ intersectional analysis and narratives

The Transformative Media Organizing project, following Crenshaw (1991), defines intersectionality as 'the ways in which structural oppression based on gender identity and sexual orientation is not independent from (but rather intersects with) that based on race, class, immigration status, disability, age, poverty, and other axes of identity' (see transformativemedia.cc). We found that the many LGBTQ and Two-Spirit organizations have an intersectional analysis of oppression and resistance, work with communities at the intersection of multiple forms of oppression, operate across multiple issue areas and use a wide range of strategies (including media activism) to advance the interests of their communities. However, many of our interviewees and survey respondents note that both funders and mass media coverage tend to focus narrowly on 'single issue' strategies and stories. They find this deeply frustrating and work hard to shift the media narrative to better represent the complexity of their communities; for example, by producing media about the lives, needs and policy concerns of Queer People of Colour.

A similar dynamic is at play in the immigrant rights movement, where queer undocumented activists have been at the forefront of many of the most effective campaigns, mobilizations and approaches to organizing. Undocuqueer activists developed a new political identity based on the intersection of immigration status, gender identity, sexual orientation and more. They made this identity visible in part through cross-platform media work including the poster and flyer art of 'artivists' like Julio Salgado, video production and social media campaigns, face to face media workshops and trainings and more. Undocuqueer organizing makes clear the necessity for intersectional narratives, and demands both that the broader immigrant rights movement pay attention to the lived experience and policy needs of queer undocumented folks, even while pushing the mainstream LGBT movement to recognize the importance of immigrant rights to LGBTQ liberation.

Occupy may initially seem like an unlikely place to look for intersectional narratives and practices, since it was widely read through a one-dimensional class-based lens as a response to growing wealth inequality under neoliberal globalization. However, on the ground, many of the protest camps did attempt to develop an intersectional praxis. In NYC, the People of Color Working Group (POC WG), formed by a small group of Women of Color (WOC) who successfully blocked consensus on the Declaration of the Occupation of New York until language about race and gender was included, regularly had more than 200 POC participants. The NYC POC WG inspired similar groups in many other Occupy camps, who developed and widely circulated intersectional analysis of the interlocking systems of class, race and gender. Many General Assemblies and Working Groups adopted 'progressive stack', a technique that prioritizes the voices of women, POC, LGBTQ people and other marginalized folks during meetings. Groups like Occupy the Hood formed in order to develop stronger links between Occupy camps and social movement organizations in communities of colour (Costanza-Chock 2012). In the ORGS survey, the Occupy Research Network found that many of the most active participants were women, POC and/or LGBTQ folks. That said, Occupy did fail in many ways to broaden beyond its majority white initial constituency, and never publicly centred a truly intersectional analysis of power and wealth inequality in the United States. The core movement narrative contained a fundamental tension between universalizing rhetoric that produced shared movement identity based on wealth inequality ('We Are The 99%'), and the lived reality that there is massive wealth and power inequality *within* the 99 per cent, structured specifically by race, gender, immigration status and disability (Occupy Research 2012).

Social movements increasingly operate with an intersectional analysis of power and resistance, but struggle to centre narratives that break the single-issue mould.

Develop critical consciousness and grassroots leadership

There is power in telling our own stories, both for ourselves, and for others.
Research participant, Transformative Media Organizing project

Social movement scholars often emphasize the importance of ICTs as tools for mobilization, visibility, and/or tactical coordination. However, a key finding across all three movements was that the *media-making process itself can be a powerful force for social movement identity creation* and for personal, group and community transformation (see Downing 2001; Rodriguez 2001).

For example, media practices in Occupy were organized to help develop the capabilities of participants: media, communications and technology working groups were (for the most part) open to participation by both seasoned media activists and 'newbies', while physical media tents served as open-air schools and training spaces where Occupiers shared a wide range of media production and tech skills (Costanza-Chock 2012). These ongoing media trainings took place within a self-produced narrative frame of Occupy as a 'leaderful' movement. This claim was supported by our survey findings: of 5,074 ORGS respondents, of those who had physically been to an Occupy protest camp, more than 2/3 attended General Assemblies and participated in street protests at the camps, more than 40 per cent volunteered to provide food or services, 40 per cent took part in workshops, and nearly 40 per cent participated in working groups of some kind (Occupy Research 2012).

In the immigrant rights movement as well, frequent media-making trainings and workshops serve as sites for the development of media skills, stronger movement networks and leadership (Costanza-Chock 2014). Just as in Occupy and the immigrant rights movement, the TMO project found that two-thirds of surveyed LGBTQ and Two-Spirit organizations see media making as a chance for leadership development. Three-quarters also mentioned individual and community growth and healing as one of their 'highest priority' outcomes for media work (the personal healing potential of storytelling is another, deeply understudied, aspect of media activism). At the same time, respondents noted that transformative impacts are hard to measure, and that media impact assessment (often required by funders) tends to ignore both personal and organizational transformation (Costanza-Chock, Schweidler & TMO 2016).

Accountability mechanisms

Effective media activism requires clear accountability mechanisms. Without specific structures for community accountability, mediated representation, stories, frames, narratives, demands and requests for action can too easily slide away from the lived experience, strategic imperatives and real needs of the social movement base.

In the immigrant rights movement, increased professionalization of media activism has sometimes led to narratives and demands that are delinked from movement goals. Immigrant rights organizers have described the tensions they felt with documentary filmmakers who received funding to produce films that were meant to support the movement, but who ended up reproducing harmful 'good immigrant, bad immigrant' narratives and action asks (Costanza-Chock 2014). In the TMO project national organizational survey, we asked about accountability mechanisms and found that three-quarters of LGBTQ and Two-Spirit organizations seek written or verbal consent to use their members' stories, while about half review campaign messages with their membership. One-fifth maintain a community steering committee or similar body that is tasked with developing media messaging and framing. Most feel the need for stronger accountability mechanisms when working with external media producers such as reporters or documentary filmmakers (Costanza-Chock, Schweidler & TMO 2016).

In Occupy, on the one hand, the directly democratic and consensus-based decision-making in General Assemblies and Working Groups, including media, communications and tech WGs, provided very strong internal accountability mechanisms. In other words, the media narratives that were produced and circulated about Occupy by participants in the protest camps largely reflected the ideas, frames and desired messaging of Occupiers, in contrast to the narratives produced by professional journalists. However, at the same time, the media narratives of Occupy lacked connection to and coordination with already existing organizations, especially those led by working-class People of Colour (Occupy Research 2012). This failure to develop accountability to existing movement groups led by the communities most affected by the rise of wealth inequality under neoliberalism, or to centre intersectionality in messaging and framing, as well as in daily community organizing practices, was ultimately a key limiting factor that inhibited Occupy's growth and power.

Participatory media practices

The rise of social media and mobile phones may make it seem like a given that activist media is participatory media. This is largely true; for instance, three-fifths of LGBTQ and Two-Spirit organizations ask their members to create media, and four out of five share their community members' stories as part of their media work (Costanza-Chock, Schweidler & TMO 2016). Similarly, 77 per cent of Occupiers said that they had 'posted about Occupy via Facebook, Twitter, or other social media' (Occupy Research 2012). At the same time, for social movements, 'participatory media' is not synonymous with 'social media'. As social movement scholars have noted, social movement media makers have long deployed a very wide range of 'offline' participatory media, such as signs, banners, flyers, graffiti, protest music, photography, radio and more (Downing 2000). Indeed, movements have always appropriated every available platform and sought to circulate their messages by any media necessary (Dizikes 2014; Jenkins *et al.* 2016). This remains the case even with the rise of digital and social media. Key media forms in Occupy included both the latest digital tools, such as livestreams from smartphones, and long-standing practices, such as the 'people's mic' technique for amplifying a speaker's voice in large crowds (Costanza-Chock 2012). Similarly, when asked to describe highly effective media work, LGBTQ and Two-Spirit organizations mentioned participatory social media campaigns like the #GirlsLikeUs hashtag, launched by trans★ author Janet Mock, but also talked about projects such as Black & Pink's newsletter, a participatory publication that features writing and artwork by incarcerated LGBTQ people and their allies that is physically printed and sent to thousands of people inside the prison system (see blackandpink.org).

Additionally, within the broader shift towards participatory media as the hegemonic mode of activist media making, persistent challenges remain. First, there are tensions between activist organizational structures and the unruly process of participatory narrative production. Professionalized organizations that seek tight message control continue to struggle with the openness of social media messages, memes and frames. Second, access to ICTs and to read-write digital media literacies remains deeply unequal, structured by (and reproducing) broader inequalities of class, age and global geography, including between what Chandra Mohanty calls the '1/3 world' and the '2/3 world' (Mohanty 2003). Third, widespread use of social media by social movement participants enables greatly increased surveillance of activist networks by state, corporate and countermovement actors (Costanza-Chock 2004; Uldam 2016).

Cross-platform production and circulation

Media activists produce media across many platforms, both offline and online. While widespread access to mobile phones and social media do signal a decisive shift in media activist practices, it would be a mistake to focus solely on social media. Journalists writing about Occupy for mass media outlets often emphasized the digital tools used by Occupiers; breathless reporters snapped pictures of protesters with Apple computers and iPhones, then used these images to delegitimize the movement on thinly coded class grounds. In reality, Occupy struggled with internal digital inequality. Digital inequality both shapes, and is shaped by, larger structural inequalities (Hargittai 2008), and many Occupiers recognized this fact. Social media were indeed a critical space, but Occupiers produced and circulated media across every platform they had access to. They created a great deal of analog and 'low-tech' media, even as they worked with cutting-edge technologies and ran hackathons to create new tools and platforms. Media, Press and Tech Working Groups systematically built presence on Twitter and Facebook, shot and edited videos, operated 24-hour livestreams like Globalrevolution.tv, organized print publications like the Occupied Wall Street Journal, built websites like OccupyTogether.org and wikis such as NYCGA.cc and coded autonomous movement media platforms and tech infrastructure (see Occupy.net). Members of these WGs also worked with the press, from independent reporters and bloggers to mainstream journalists. OWS thus engaged in media activism that was cross-platform, participatory, linked directly to action and shaped by a large number of movement participants, rather than by a few spokespeople.

Unsurprisingly, immigrant rights and LGBTQ activists also struggle with digital inequality, and also make media across many platforms. When we asked LGBTQ and Two-Spirit activists to talk about 'media that works', or to describe media projects or campaigns that they consider to be highly successful, they provided an extremely wide range of examples, from trans★ film festivals to Two-Spirit pow-wows featuring dance, music and ceremonial garb; from social media hashtags to face-to-face know-your-rights trainings for queer and trans★ youth of colour who are heavily targeted by police (Costanza-Chock, Schweidler & TMO 2016). Additionally, savvy social movement communicators understand that mass media (print, TV and radio) continue to play a crucial role in movement visibility, reach and, ultimately, power. Commercial Spanish language radio hosts were perhaps the most important promoters of the 2006 immigrant rights mobilizations that brought millions to the streets and defeated the anti-immigrant Sensenbrenner Bill; many immigrant rights organizers continue to work closely with journalists for Spanish language mass media companies such as Univision and Telemundo, who provide regular and often sympathetic coverage of immigrant rights actions (Santa Anna *et al.* 2007; Félix *et al.* 2008; Costanza-Chock 2014).

Ultimately, social movements today use media across platforms, both digital and 'physical', participatory and top-down, based on the context, skillset and the needs of the moment. Relationships with sympathetic journalists continue to be one of the most crucial media strategies for broader social movement visibility, even in the age of social media.

Rooted in community action

'Media work is most powerful and effective when it is deeply rooted in the struggles, narratives and actions of the community' (TMO 2014).

In the wake of the Trump victory, it is tempting to reaffirm the maxim that 'no publicity is bad publicity'. However, for many of the activists and organizers we talked to and worked with, media attention that is delinked from community needs, narratives and demands is all too often useless, at best, and harmful in the worst instances. Media scholars such as Herman Gray have pointed out that misrepresentation can be more destructive than invisibility. Gray argues that Black people have long suffered from a crisis of overrepresentation in the US media ecosystem: excessive but misleading visibility, with constant repetition of particular persistent narratives of criminality and dehumanized sexuality (Gray 2005). Other scholars have found that stories about social movements in the mass media are often deeply misleading. Classic case studies of the civil rights movement (Halloran, Elliott & Murdock 1970) and Students for a Democratic Society (Gitlin 1980) found that protest coverage in the US media since the civil rights movement has increasingly deployed frames of 'violence' and 'conflict with police', and that over time, coverage of the actual demands and arguments of protesters has declined. Mass media continue to trivialize and demonize political protest, even if the situation has grown more complex in an increasingly fragmented media ecology, as Cottle (2008) argues.

Across the three movements we studied, we found that when social movement organizations focus primarily, or only, on media work, they are sometimes able to achieve national visibility. However, without strong connection to community organizing, base building or specific service and/or advocacy work, they typically find it difficult to leverage this visibility to advance concrete gains for their communities. Most feel that media work is best when it responds to and advances other forms of work. For example, among LGBTQ and Two-Spirit organizations, most engage in a wide range of activities to advance their communities' needs: seven in ten conduct social media campaigns, six in ten provide leadership development programmes, and half are involved in policy advocacy. About four in ten provide direct services, and one in four use direct action, among other approaches (Costanza-Chock, Schweidler & TMO 2016).

Similarly, in Occupy, media work was popular among ORGS survey respondents, but was far from the only, or main, form of movement engagement. We have already seen how Occupy was indeed a 'leaderful' movement; at the same time, Occupiers were highly engaged in diverse forms of civic and social movement activity outside of Occupy itself. About 40 per cent said that Occupy was their first social movement, but 60 per cent said they had previously been involved in other movements. Outside of Occupy, more than half belonged to non-profit organizations and political parties; during the past year, about 90 per cent signed petitions, boycotted or buycotted; 80 per cent contacted a civil servant to express their views; and 70 per cent donated money or raised funds for a social or political activity. Most are actively involved in electoral politics: 90 per cent voted in the 2008 presidential elections. These proportions are all extremely high relative to the general population, as measured by the General Social Survey (Occupy Research 2012).

The key point is that across movements, media work may be conducted both by specialists and by the broader movement base, but most organizers feel that it should not be a 'standalone' activity: media work is most effective, they say, when rooted in the life, struggles and diverse tactics of community-led social movement organizations.

Conclusions

Social movements have always been tightly linked with media making. Through media production, circulation and analysis, social movement participants develop their own consciousness, narratives and, more broadly, capabilities. Media making is also an opportunity to build community, identify like-minded individuals, organizations and networks, and construct a shared vision of the possible. Researchers who work closely with social movements, develop engaged scholarship and use participatory research approaches can develop a more grounded theory and practice of social movement media. We have tried to present an analysis of the ways that diverse social movements today employ what we call a transformative media organizing approach. Organizers who use this approach conduct media work that is intersectional, transformative, accountable, participatory, cross-platform and rooted in community action. We hope that our findings are useful to scholars and activists alike, as they strive to make media, make trouble, and change the world.

References

Costanza-Chock, S. (2004) 'The Whole World Is Watching: Online Surveillance of Social Movement Organizations'. in P. N. Thomas and Z. Nain (eds), *Who Owns the Media? Global Trends and Local Resistances.* London: WACC and Penang: Southbound, pp. 271–92.

Costanza-Chock, S. (2012) 'Mic Check! Media Cultures and the Occupy Movement', *Social Movement Studies*, vol. 11, nos. 3–4, pp. 375–85.

Costanza-Chock, S. (2014) *Out of the Shadows, into the Streets!: Transmedia Organizing and the Immigrant Rights Movement.* Cambridge, MA: MIT Press.

Costanza-Chock, S., Schweidler, C., and the Transformative Media Organizing Project (2016) 'Toward Transformative Media Organizing: LGBTQ and Two-Spirit Media Work in the United States', *Media, Culture & Society*, vol. 39, no. 2, pp. 159–84.

Crenshaw, K. (1991) 'Mapping the Margins: Intersectionality, Identity Politics, and Violence Against Women of Color', *Stanford Law Review*, pp. 1241–99.

Dizikes, P. (2014) 'By Any Media Necessary', *MIT News*, http://news.mit.edu/2014/book-social-media-political-movements-1125, accessed 20 January 2017.

Downing, J., with Ford, T., Gil, G. and Stein, L. (2001) *Radical Media: Rebellious Communication and Social Movements.* Thousand Oaks, CA: Sage.

Fals Borda, O. (2001) 'Participatory (Action) Research in Social Theory: Origins and Challenges', in P. Reason and H. Bradbury (eds) *Handbook of Action Research: Participative Inquiry and Practice.* London: Sage, pp. 27–37.

Félix, A., González, C. and Ramírez, R. (2008) 'Political Protest, Ethnic Media, and Latino Naturalization', *American Behavioral Scientist*, vol. 52, no. 4, pp. 618–34.

Gerbaudo, P. (2012) *Tweets and the Streets: Social Media and Contemporary Activism.* London: Pluto Press.

Gray, H. (2005) *Cultural Moves: African Americans and the Politics of Representation.* Berkeley, CA: University of California Press.

Halloran, J. D., Elliott, P. and Murdock, G. (1970) *Demonstrations and Communication: A Case Study.* Harmondsworth: Penguin.

Hargittai, E. (2008) 'The Digital Reproduction of Inequality', in D. Grusky *Social Stratification.* Boulder, CO: Westview Press, pp. 936–44.

Jenkins, H., *et al.* (2016) *By Any Media Necessary: The New Youth Activism.* New York: NYU Press.

Kidd, D. (2015) 'Occupy and Social Movement Communication', in C. Atton, *The Routledge Companion to Alternative and Community Media.* London: Sage, pp. 457–68.

Mohanty, C. T. (2003) *Feminism without Borders: Decolonizing Theory, Practicing Solidarity.* Durham, NC: Duke University Press.

Occupy Research (2012) 'Summary of Findings from the Occupy Research General Survey', in K. Khatib, M. Killjoy, and M. McGuire (eds) *We Are Many: Reflections on Movement Strategy from Occupation to Liberation.* Oakland, CA: AK Press.

Rodriguez, C. (2001) *Fissures in the Mediascape: An International Study of Citizens' Media.* Cresskill, NJ: Hampton Press.

Santa Ana, O., *et al.* (2007) 'A May to Remember', *Du Bois Review: Social Science Research on Race*, vol. 4, no. 1, pp. 207–32.

Uldam, J. (2016) 'Corporate Management of Visibility and the Fantasy of the Post-political: Social Media and Surveillance', *New Media & Society*, vol. 18, no. 2, pp. 201–19.

8

AFFECTIVE PUBLICS AND WINDOWS OF OPPORTUNITY

Social media and the potential for social change

Zizi Papacharissi and Meggan Taylor Trevey

Premise

Think of technology and politics as two uneasy buddies. On the one hand, politicians and the public hope that technology will somehow revive democracies or bring about revolutions in non-democratic regimes. On the other, technology is rarely created to serve political purposes, and doing so frequently undermines its potential (e.g. Papacharissi 2010; Curran, Fenton & Freedman 2012). The relationship between the two naturally conjures up questions about how one impacts the other. Yet decades of political communication and political science scholarship dismiss such claims of technological determinism. Still, people are compelled to ascribe some form of political agency to technology. Do social media make or break movements, enhance or entrap publics, bring about or stall social change? More recently, does the manner of disseminating and sharing information through social media influence our understanding of contemporary questions and, ultimately, how we vote on important referenda and elections? (Here, the authors refer to recent events that include the Brexit referendum, the 2016 Austrian elections and the 2016 US elections.) Political institutions and technological systems are not designed to work together, yet somehow we expect them to. This chapter focuses on the relationship between technology and politics in the contemporary context. That being a broad question, we focus specifically on contemporary social media that have led to a platformization of the web (e.g. van Dijck 2013; Hellmond 2015), and on the current political context. Explicitly, we examine the conditions under which opportunities for change may emerge as people come together and engage with technology and politics.

This chapter synthesizes theory and research on collective action, the policy process and social media to propose a theoretical framework for understanding the role technology can play in politics. As we sharpen our focus, three core constructs emerge out of this synthesis of literature and form the basis of our proposed framework: Affective Publics (Papacharissi 2014), Connective Action (Bennett & Segerberg 2013) and the theory of Punctuated Equilibrium (Baumgartner & Jones 1993). Seeking to move away from a conventional approach that emphasizes collective action, utilizes the concept of the public sphere and places the emphasis on deliberative politics, we argue: a) that the potential for civic action or inaction is misunderstood when examined under the auspices of collective action (and that perhaps collective action, in its pure form, is more of an ideal than an actuality), b) that the multitude and versatility of civic behaviours that count as political is limited when viewed under the analytical lens of the public sphere and c) that the role technology can play is misjudged when measured against theoretical models that value deliberative modes of expression over more nuanced and inclusive modalities of civic engagement.

We suggest that in contemporary societies, affectively motivated and networked publics come into being, connect or disband around bonds of sentiment. These bonds of sentiment are facilitated through modalities of connective action: action mobilized by technology as a conduit of connection, collaboration, yet not collectivization of personally framed expression. Depending on context and according to punctuated equilibrium theory, these modalities permit windows of opportunity for social change to emerge, by affording actors liminal access to power and specific pathways to agency. Before we tackle the specifics of how these windows of opportunity emerge, it is essential we examine certain conditions that give shape to the contemporary political environment.

Contemporary politics and civic engagement

A popular refrain characterizes politics around the globe. It appears that there was, sometime in our collective historical past, an era when politics was pure, politicians not corrupt, and citizens utterly engaged. This appeared to have produced democratic regimes of unparalleled superiority, which have somehow degenerated in our recent history. This refrain is echoed in affectively charged slogans that capture this longing, reflected most recently in President Trump's campaign chant: 'Make America Great Again.' The modern-era citizen is characterized as passive, cynical, out-of-sync and often left behind. Careful historical examination of the evolution of citizenship, however, reveals that these tendencies are not specific to our era (e.g. Schudson 2003; Coleman 2005), and that similar complaints about the state of democracy and decreased citizen engagement are as old as democracy itself. With the understanding that nostalgia is a natural human state, and that these claims should be placed in historical context and fact-checked, rather than imprudently reproduced, we would like to draw your attention to the following conditions that typify regimes that approximate some form of democracy:

1. Societies are grand and massive assemblages of people, institutions, norms and imaginaries. Individuals are increasingly developing a political conscience structure around atomized wants, desires and concerns (e.g. Bauman 2000). We are motivated to act on our personal hopes and fears. This is not a *proactive* conceptualization of political action, but a *reactive* one: we react to politics as they unfold in real time, filtering incoming political information through the lens of our existing beliefs, and our preferences form and evolve endogenously in this process (Lodge & Taber 2013; Druckman 2014). But rarely do these reactions move beyond the personal to identify the core causes of political problems or solutions to them, thus prompting feedback loops of atomized agendas. This plays a part in how we contribute to formal channels of participation in a democracy, such as voting. People pay attention to politics when they believe an issue is relevant to them, and they understand relevance through emotion and personal identity. Citizens want personalized responses and to feel as though they have some say in their own governance, but the prevailing system of democracy is representative; it affords limited opportunities for direct communication with political elites and delivers conflicting messages when imposing enforced structures on responses that are meant to be nuanced, personal and individual. Mass societies are not built for direct democracy, yet that is what the citizens crave, all too often turning to technology for this reason.

2. The model of representative democracy relies on homogeneity and stability of public opinion and emphasis on majority rule, which preclude any possibility of true pluralism (e.g. Mouffe 2000). Representation is thus paradoxical. Acts of representation do not simply correspond to

the preferences or interests of constituencies; rather, they are themselves involved in the creation and evolution of those interests. What legislators *do*, in other words, affects how citizens think and feel about political issues and what they want from politics, thereby creating the 'constituency paradox' of representative democracy (Disch 2012). Further, representative democracy is not about representing individual viewpoints; it is about a compromise dance, often between conflicting viewpoints, so as to arrive at a solution that may not be ideal but is the one the majority agrees on. Thus, the paradox: the promise of democratic representation cannot be met without giving in to some form of compromise.

3. Polls dominate how we have come to measure, understand and 'listen' to public opinion and sentiment. Public opinion is, as Bourdieu (1972) has eloquently argued, an abstraction of convenience that does not literally exist. Public sentiment, also an abstraction, is often misidentified by polls, a technology which has always been flawed, and which, given the recent advances in communication, is now dated with its place firmly located in the previous century. The aggregation of public opinion has often mischaracterized and constrained public sentiment and misled politicians, the media and the public. Polls reduce politics to policy preferences: they ignore emotion and morality and constrain the definition of public opinion to topics of interest to researchers and elites. And the cross-sectional nature of polling assumes stability of opinion, completely missing the process-based, *political* nature of opinion formation. Political scientists and political communication scholars have long made this argument, with Susan Herbst (1993) explaining in great detail how polls trade in individuality, detail and the authenticity of personal opinion on public affairs so as to produce an aggregate concentration of opinions that she termed 'numbered voices'; yes/no responses to standardized questions. Understandably, this tendency not only misinforms, but further distances publics from elites.

4. This distance is reflected in developing cynicism toward political and media systems that turn a listening ear, only to aggregate and distort responses delivered. It should not surprise us that the confluence of these conditions produces a growing reluctance to participate in politics through formal or conventional channels of civic engagement, such as voting, community involvement and volunteering, for a variety of reasons (e.g. Carey 1995; Delli Carpini 2000; Coleman 2013). It is only natural that a public that has been serially misrepresented would look for authenticity in candidates, even though that is not a necessary condition of most job descriptions, in politics and elsewhere. Cynicism and skepticism drives political participation for many (Patterson 1993, 1996; Cappella & Jamieson 1996, 1997; Fallows 1996), as meaningful or impactful avenues for engagement languish, leaving citizens with impressions of powerlessness, distrust and lack of control.

5. The mounting cynicism has resulted in a feeling of continuous insecurity, of a fiscal, political and general existential nature. Amplified by a financial crisis that is taking its time to de-escalate, political instability and global problems, like terrorism, addressed with locally-specific strategies, these politics of insecurity leave citizens further disillusioned, disappointed and confused (Rojecki 2016). These insecure publics consist of people who feel they have lost agency over what happens in their lives. They are susceptible to affectively charged claims, because those are soothing to an insecure civic psyche, and are also possibly people who look for a political messiah to come and instantly fix long-standing problems. People process political information emotionally, through the lens of existing beliefs and attitudes, and because we are motivated to maintain our own existing belief structures, we resist information that contradicts our pre-existing beliefs and readily agree with information that conforms to what we already believe (Lodge & Taber 2013). Media portrayals of political issues as disconnected from each other, black-and-white, with simple either/or policy solutions exacerbate the tendency of insecure publics to latch onto easy fixes. For President Trump, this defined campaign strategy, as he

delivered, in refrain after refrain, repetitive statements aimed at taking control of one's life, almost like a motivational speaker. The media hesitated to completely expose him, because our media are insecure too. They are financially insecure, and they are also politically insecure, concerned of being framed as liberal. The refrains Trump delivered are hollow, and many were reversed following his election. But the connection they awoke is present, intense, affective and, thus, pointedly directionless. This is precisely where the texture of expression and connection across social media and the notion of affective publics become relevant. Let us explain.

Without question, online media augment visibility to issues frequently marginalized by the societal and media mainstream (Berry, Kim & Spigel 2010; Couldry 2012). The past few decades have witnessed the growth of movements that use digital means to connect with broader publics and express their point of view. Prevailing research, however, suggests that the internet pluralizes, but does not inherently democratize (e.g. Bimber 1998; Papacharissi 2010). The path to mobilization may increasingly be becoming digital, yet remains not only digital (Couldry 2010; Howard 2011). Impact is not determined by the technology, but rather by the historically singular interplay of the various socio-cultural, economic and political conditions at work. This does not leave social media platforms outside of the democratic impact equation. Instead, we argue, social media afford a form of impact that is *symbolic*; a type of agency that is *discursive*; and access to power that is *liminal*. While individual actions may be symbolic, the impact they can have en masse may be amplified, via the organizing logic of connective action. We examine how next.

Connective action

Political scientists are used to thinking about mobilization and political action in terms of Mancur Olson's *Logic of Collective Action* (1965), which counter-intuitively suggests that groups should rationally *not* form, even when people share common interests and would all benefit from collective outcomes. According to Olson, individuals who share common interests will only band together to solve collective problems if there are enough incentives to join together to outweigh the costs associated with acting toward the collective goal. Without added incentives, rational individuals in Olson's world should 'free-ride' on the efforts of others (e.g. not act) because they would receive the collective benefits anyway without any costs to themselves, which offered a compelling explanation as to why such collective action is rare. In Olson's world, and in much of the subsequent political science literature, only organized groups with clear political goals and plenty of resources to provide such membership incentives would form at all, and the only avenue for ordinary citizens to impact politics was through these rarely forming groups.

This traditional view of political action assumes that action is only impactful when the cost to individuals is high and the goal is achieved. This line of reasoning is problematic for two reasons: (1) it assumes that the higher the cost of an action is to an individual, the more it matters politically, which is an unsupported claim, and (2) it looks only at goal-oriented action, when in fact, everyday, non-goal-oriented actions could reasonably be considered politically impactful (Puig-i-Abril & Rojas 2007; Bayat 2009). Individuals also engage in non-instrumental and expressive forms of action, such as everyday talk (Mansbridge 1999; Graham 2015) and the public expression of personal opinions and attitudes (Puig-i-Abril & Rojas 2007; Papacharissi 2008), which impact politics, and which resource- and group-based approaches to action fail to recognize.

Bennett and Segerberg (2013: 760) outlined a new logic of action that recognizes that the internet, especially social media, fundamentally restructured the ways in which individuals could act in the political system:

The linchpin of connective action is the formative element of 'sharing': the person-alization that leads actions and content to be distributed widely across social networks. Communication technologies enable the growth and stabilization of network structures across these networks. Together, the technological agents that enable the constitutive role of sharing in these contexts displace the centrality of the free-rider calculus and, with it, by extension, the dynamic that flows from it – most obviously, the logical centrality of the resource-rich organization. In its stead, connective action brings the action dynamics of recombinant networks into focus, a situation in which networks and communication become something more than mere preconditions and information.

In other words, because the internet organizes individuals into networks of actors who share political information without coercion or incentives, the necessity of organizing action through resource-rich hierarchical group structures in order to impact politics is diminished. Organized groups are no longer the only players in the political action game. Instead, networks enabled by digital technologies have become 'core organizations in their own right' and need to be taken seriously as political actors in the political process (Castells 2000).

This means that individual actors responding to political information by sharing personalized reactions online can generate self-organizing, *de facto* political organizations with the capacity to shift attention and thus potentially punctuate the policy equilibrium of a political system. It is important to highlight the different logics that underlie collective and connective action as both are relevant to the study of democratic power. While the logic of *collective* action emphasizes the importance of goal orientation, the high costs of group formation and the organizational power of groups relative to individuals, the logic of *connective* action emphasizes the importance of personal expression, scalability and the organizational power of networks.

Bennett and Segerberg (2013) understand connective action as a normative predisposition for individuals who align with issue publics on the basis of life politics. It is the latest development in a long continuum of changes that have led to individuation, increased self-monitoring and reflexive restructuring of individual narratives. Connective action practices permit people to express inter-est in or allegiance to issues without having to enter the complex negotiation of personal vs. col-lective politics. Online and convergent platforms like Twitter serve as conduits that link together personalized interests, thus enabling people to connect around commonalities without having to compromise their own belief systems or join a hierarchical political organization.

Whereas sustainable collective action requires coordination, goal orientation, consensus building and leadership, the connective model emphasizes network-based, over group-based, forms of mobilization that utilize digital means to sustain prolonged protests of a global scope. Distinct from collective action, connective action develops out of personalized reactions to political issues. These personalized frames on issues turn into broader themes shared via various personal communication technologies. Whereas collective action frequently involves the more formal structures of non-government organizations (NGOs), connective action is encountered in recent protests mobilized by the *Indignados* and Occupy movements, and the various Arab Spring uprisings.

The logic of connective action reflects a contemporary reluctance to associate with formal organizations. Bennett and Segerberg (2013: 748) suggest that these networks 'operate impor-tantly through the organizational processes of social media, and their logic does not require strong organizational control or the symbolic construction of a united "we"'. Because person-alized action frames do not require reframing for attunement with a greater collective, they attain virality easily, as they are shared through informal conversational practices that resemble interpersonal communication.

Affective publics

We understand affective publics as networked public formations that are mobilized and con-nected, or disconnected, through expressions of sentiment. Building on boyd's (2010) definition of networked publics, affective publics are discursively rendered, technologically connected and affectively bound. Networked speaks to the form of the connection. We prefer the term affective publics, which describes both the form of the connection and the texture of expression that it supports. Hashtag publics, another term that is frequently used is similar, but not the same as our term of interest, for is oriented around the issue that has led to a particular public formation.

Affective publics materialize and disband around connective conduits of sentiment every day, and find their voice through the soft structures of feeling sustained by societies. Structures of feeling is a term that describes *social experiences in solution*; different expressions of sentiment that capture the sentiment of a particular moment or era (Williams 1961). Media frequently serve as connective conduits that permit these loose structures to come into being, and Williams had referred to the industrial novel of the 1840s as an example of one structure of feeling that emerged out of the development of industrial capitalism to give form to middle-class con-sciousness. Social media platforms serve as such conduits of interconnected structures of feeling, lending rise to not just sentiment-driven publics, but connecting and redirecting expansive meme-plexes of expression deriving from a variety of media, social and not. Hashtags frequently provide us snapshots of these affective publics in evanescent formation, but they are not the only digital trace these publics deposit as they are rendered. Memes, gifs, slogans, songs, books, podcasts, radio broadcasts, favourite shows, movies and other media artifacts function as conduits that call affective publics into being.

A few points that are essential in understanding the impact of affective publics, and the role of social media in effecting this impact:

1. Affective publics materialize uniquely and leave distinct digital footprints
These publics materialize uniquely and leave distinct digital imprints. The digital texture of mobilized support varies, depending on socio-cultural context and political economy systemic factors. This is an obvious point, yet one worth repeating, for all too often we assume that social media use will have the same results for all types of movements or publics. We detect similarities, but also key differences in affective public formations.

2. Affective publics support connective, yet not necessarily collective action
These publics facilitate collaborative, yet not collectively informed storytelling. This implies that narratives about a movement produced via Twitter or Facebook, for example, will have collabo-rative but also potentially fragmented texture. The cohesiveness of the narrative produced and the story that it tells depends on curation. We tend to notice more cohesive narratives develop out of structures of feeling that have been carefully curated, such as the Twitter activity leading to the resignation of Hosni Mubarak in 2011, but not necessarily the social media noise follow-ing that time period.

3. Affective publics are powered by affective statements of opinion, fact or a blend of both, which in turn pro-duce ambient, always-on feeds further connecting and pluralizing expression in regimes democratic and non
As such, these public formations are energized by a form of expression that blends the phatically informed practices of interpersonal conversation with the conventions of broadcasting, recon-ciling, potentially, what Ong (1982) termed a primary with a secondary orality, thus leading into a genre of expression that is hybrid and can only be described as digital orality.

4. Affective publics typically produce disruptions/interruptions of dominant political narratives by presenting underrepresented viewpoints

They are essential to amplifying voice and enhancing visibility for viewpoints that typically have already been formulated. This point is key in theorizing the impact of such public formations and the structures of feeling that support them.

5. Ambient streams sustain publics convened around affective commonalities: Impact is symbolic, agency claimed semantic, power liminal

All too often we are swayed by the virality with which information spreads online, and we assume that change will follow, at an equally speedy pace. As a result, we entertain certain assumptions, utopian and dystopian, about the impact of social media. When change does not promptly follow, we feel disappointed, but it is not these mediated platforms that have let us down. It is our own expectations. For change *is* gradual and revolutions *are* long (Williams 1961), and they have to be long in order to acquire meaning. Gradual change is also built into governmental institutions in the first place; gradual change is a *feature* of our political system. The impact of these media, and the public formations they support, is not political, socio-cultural, economic or instantaneous. It is, however, symbolic, for it permits forms of expression that semantically renegotiate the meaning and role of institutions in society, and it affords power, even if that power may be of a transitional nature. In order to change our institutions, we must reimagine them first. Punctuated equilibrium theory helps us understand the significance of the historical moment in the *longue durée*, and so we explicate this next.

Punctuated equilibrium theory

It is one thing to recognize that affective publics arise out of the networked dynamics and affordances of social media; it is another to determine how this impacts politics. We argue that political science has already provided a theory to suggest how mass attention to political issues might impact political systems – punctuated equilibrium theory:

> [Punctuated equilibrium theory] emphasizes two related elements of the policy process: issue definition and agenda setting. As issues are defined in public discourse in different ways, and as issues rise and fall on the public agenda, existing policies can be either reinforced or questioned. Reinforcement creates great obstacles to anything but modest change, but the questioning of policies at the most fundamental levels creates opportunities for major reversals in policy outcomes.
>
> *True, Jones & Baumgartner 2007: 156*

How citizens and policymakers respond to information thus determines what policy issues get addressed by government.

The premise is simple: decision makers cannot possibly attend to every single political issue at all times, so they must prioritize. How they decide to prioritize which issues get on the government agenda is a matter of attention (Jones & Baumgartner 2005). Policymakers have limited attention spans and are boundedly rational (i.e. they selectively pay disproportionate attention to some issues at the expense of others), so getting an issue on the governmental agenda requires disruption of the policy subsystem such that policymakers pay attention and react (Baumgartner & Jones 1993; Jones & Baumgartner 2005). Here is how they suggest classic bounded rationality in the policy process works:

> Because of the cognitive and emotional constitutions of decision makers, decision making is cybernetic, continually under adjusting and then overcorrecting in an erratic path. Suddenly decision makers recognize that previously ignored facets of the environment are relevant and scramble to incorporate them. Choice is attention driven because unmonitored aspects of reality must be brought into the choice calculus as it becomes impossible to ignore them.
>
> *Jones & Baumgartner 2005: 334*

Policy conflict is thus fundamentally *attention driven*, so the dynamics of political attention allocation are central to the question of political power in a system.

The concept of punctuated equilibrium explains both apparent policy stability and rapid policy change. First, it is important to understand that governmental power is fragmented into policy subsystems – interest groups, legislators, and bureaucrats who collectively maintain the status quo in a specific policy arena. These subsystems inherently favour the interests of existing subsystem members over outside interests because the actors involved share values. And this institutionalization of favoured interests results in apparent system equilibrium (Baumgartner & Jones 1993). However, equilibrium is fragile. When the scope of conflict expands to include new actors with different values, the balance of power can shift (Schattschneider 1960). In other words, when new actors with different preferences become interested in an issue, the apparent equilibrium in that issue area that has long kept policy stable can be punctuated, which can result in rapid policy change. These 'windows of opportunity' for governmental change open when the scope of political conflict expands beyond the boundaries of a policy subsystem and into the public imagination. We argue that social media affords new ways to shift the dynamics of attention and open windows of opportunity for change – not by instrumental political action through organized groups, but via individually framed political expression that can, via the logic of connective action, raise the salience of issues to the level of decision maker awareness.

A new paradigm for social change

Windows of opportunity occur when new actors realize there is a problem, when viable policy solutions exist to solve the problem and when policymakers are willing and able to do something about it (Kingdon 1984). Further, these windows provide space for issue framing, counterframing and idea competition, which can result in policy change (Baumgartner, Green-Pedersen & Jones 2006). Windows of opportunity, however, do not *guarantee* change. Policy equilibrium is not always punctuated. The dynamics of attention allocation and preference formation in the political realm thus play a pivotal (and inherently disruptive) role in the political process.

Applied together, the constructs of affective publics and connective action help illuminate how punctuated equilibrium theory affords windows of opportunity, through which social change can occur. Connective action helps us reimagine the modalities through which mobilization may occur, by explaining how actors come together in organic, evanescent and non-collective formations. Publics that come into being as a result of connective action are neither crowds, nor are they leaderless. While they employ varying degrees of formal organization, they are not governed by a collectively informed hierarchy. The texture of the connection that calls these publics into being is affective; it takes shape as bonds of sentiment connect, divide and identify people that, for a fleeting moment in time, share a common feeling about an issue, problem or question. These people may reconnect in future political encounters, diverge over other issues or never again cross paths. But in the moment of connective action, their commonly shared sentiment brings an issue to center of attention, and affords that issue an affectively charged frame.

It is the force of the affective refrains, produced and propagated through connective action, that open up windows of opportunity: unique moments in time when change can occur. Windows of opportunity are about the liminal moment when the possibility of gradual change begins to take shape. And it is the logic of connective action, expressed through the shared sentiments of affective publics, that helps visualize the opportunity for change, and imagine, then render, a window of opportunity for it to take place.

References

Bauman, Z. (2000) *Liquid Modernity.* Cambridge: Polity Press.

Baumgartner, F. and Jones, B. (1993) *Agendas and Instability in American Politics.* Chicago, IL: University of Chicago Press.

Baumgartner, F., Green-Pedersen, C. and Jones, B. (2006) 'Comparative Studies of Policy Agendas', *Journal of European Public Policy*, no. 13, pp. 959–74.

Bayat, A. (2009) *Life as Politics: How Ordinary People Change the Middle East.* Stanford, CA: Stanford University Press.

Bennett, W. L. and Segerberg, A. (2013) *The Logic of Connective Action: Digital Media and the Personalization of Contentious Politics.* Cambridge: Cambridge University Press.

Berry, C., Kim, S. and Spigel, L. (2010) *Electronic Elsewheres: Media Technology and the Experience of Social Space.* Minneapolis, MN: University of Minnesota Press.

Bimber, B. (1998) 'The Internet and Political Transformation: Populism, Community, and Accelerated Pluralism', *Polity*, vol. 31, no. 1, pp. 133–60.

Bourdieu, P. (1977) [1972] *Outline of a Theory of Practice.* (R. Nice, trans.). Cambridge: Cambridge University Press.

boyd, d. (2010) 'Social Network Sites as Networked Publics: Affordances, Dynamics, and Implications', in Z. Papacharissi (ed.) *Networked Self: Identity, Community, and Culture on Social Network Sites.* London: Routledge, pp. 39–58.

Cappella, J. and Jamieson, K. H. (1996) 'News Frames, Political Cynicism, and Media Cynicism', *Annals of the American Academy of Political and Social Science*, vol. 546, pp. 71–85.

Cappella, J. and Jamieson, K. H. (1997) *Spiral of Cynicism: The Press and the Public Good.* New York: Oxford University Press.

Carey, J. (1995) 'The Press, Public Opinion, and Public Discourse', in T. Glasser and C. Salmon (eds) *Public Opinion and the Communication of Consent.* New York: Guilford, pp. 373–402.

Castells, M. (2000) *The Rise of the Network Society.* Oxford: Blackwell.

Coleman, S. (2005) 'The Lonely Citizen: Indirect Representation in an Age of Networks', *Political Communication*, vol. 22, no. 2, pp. 197–214.

Coleman, S. (2013) *How Voters Feel.* Cambridge: Cambridge University Press.

Couldry, N. (2010) *Why Voice Matters: Culture and Politics after Neoliberalism.* London: Sage.

Couldry, N. (2012) *Media, Society, World: Social Theory and Digital Media Practice.* Cambridge: Polity Press.

Curran, J., Fenton, N. and Freedman, D. (2012) *Misunderstanding the Internet.* London: Routledge.

Delli Carpini, M. X. (2000) 'Gen.com: Youth, Civic Engagement, and the New Information Environment', *Political Communication*, vol. 17, pp. 341–9.

Disch, L. (2012) 'Democratic Representation and the Constituency Paradox', *Perspectives on Politics*, vol. 10, no. 3, pp. 599–616.

Druckman, J. (2014) 'Pathologies of Studying Public Opinion, Political Communication, and Democratic Responsiveness', *Political Communication*, vol. 31, no. 3, pp. 467–92.

Fallows, J. (1996) 'Why Americans Hate the Media', *The Atlantic Monthly*, vol. 277, no. 2, February, pp. 45–64.

Graham, T. (2015) 'Everyday Political Talk in the Internet-based Public Sphere', in S. Coleman and D. Freelon (eds) *Handbook of Digital Politics.* Cheltenham, UK: Elgar, pp. 247–63.

Hellmond, A. (2015). The Platformization of the Web. *Social Media & Society,* vol. 1, no. 2, https://doi.org/10.1177/2056305115603080.

Herbst, S. (1993) *Numbered Voices: How Opinion Polling Has Shaped American Politics*. Chicago, IL: University of Chicago Press.

Howard, P. N. (2011) *The Digital Origins of Dictatorship and Democracy: Information Technology and Political Islam*. New York: Oxford University Press.

Jones, B. and Baumgartner, F. (2005) 'A Model of Choice for Public Policy', *Journal of Public Administration Research and Theory*, no. 15, pp. 325–351.

Kingdon, J. (1984) Agendas, Alternatives, and Public Policies. London: Longman.

Lodge, M. and Taber, C. (2013) *The Rationalizing Voter*. Cambridge: Cambridge University Press.

Mansbridge, J. (1999) 'Everyday Talk in the Political System', in S. Macedo (ed.) *Deliberative Politics: Essays on Democracy and Disagreement*. Oxford: Oxford University Press.

Mouffe, C. (2000) *The Democratic Paradox*. London: Verso.

Olson, M. (1965) *The Logic of Collective Action*. Cambridge, MA: Harvard University Press.

Ong, W. J. (1982) *Orality and Literacy: The Technologizing the Word*. New York: Methuen.

Papacharissi, Z. (2008) 'The Virtual Sphere 2.0: The Internet, the Public Sphere and Beyond', in A. Chadwick and P. Howard (eds) *The Handbook of Internet Politics*. London: Routledge, pp. 230–45.

Papacharissi, Z. (2010) *A Private Sphere: Democracy in a Digital Age*. Cambridge: Polity Press.

Papacharissi, Z. (2014) *Affective Publics*. New York: Oxford University Press.

Patterson, T. (1993) *Out of Order*. New York: Knopf.

Patterson, T. (1996) 'Bad News, Bad Governance', *Annals of the American Academy of Political and Social Science*, vol. 546, pp. 97–108.

Puig-i-Abril, E. and Rojas, H. (2007) 'Being Early on the Curve: Online Practices and Expressive Political Participation', *International Journal of Internet Science*, vol. 2, no. 1, pp. 28–44.

Rojecki, A. (2016) *America and the Politics of Insecurity*. Baltimore, MD: Johns Hopkins Press.

Schattschneider, E. E. (1960) *The Semi-Sovereign People*. New York: Holt, Rhinehart and Winston.

Schudson, M. (2003) *The Sociology of News*. New York: Norton.

True, J., Jones, B. and Baumgartner, F. (2007) 'Punctuated Equilibrium Theory: Explaining Stability and Change in Public Policymaking' in P. Sabatier *Theories of Policy and Process* (second edition). Boulder, CO: Westview Press.

van Dijck, J. (2013) *The Culture of Connectivity: A Critical History of Social Media*. New York: Oxford University Press.

Williams, R. (1961) *The Long Revolution*. London: Chatto and Windus.

9

SOCIAL MEDIA AND CONTENTIOUS ACTION IN CHINA

Zixue Tai

Introduction

Social media have been spearheading the latest waves of network technology breakthroughs and innovations in the global society. In China, a variety of blossoming social networking sites have elevated grassroots participation to brand-new territories. As a result, the expanding social media space has engendered creative ways of mass collaboration and peer production, and it has ushered in new formations of digital activism through which dispersed individuals and organized groups coordinate efforts to contemplate, mobilize and organize variegated forms of contentious action.

This chapter offers a critical overview of the evolving field of social media activism in China. Situated in China's contemporary state–society relations and highly controlled information environment in the wake of decades of economic reform, the chapter starts with a discussion on the contextual factors that have shaped the field of contentious action in the country, followed by an analysis of the diverse patterns of social media activism in China today. It then goes into depth in examining the important dynamics and particular socio-cultural traits pertaining to social media activism in relation to contentious action from inception to mobilization to actualization.

Contentious action and mass protest in China: continuity and change

China lays claim to one of the most robust legacies of mass resistance, rebellion and revolution in the world from ancient to modern times (Perry 2001). In recent decades, fast-paced economic development in the reform era has accentuated diverse patterns of conflict and grievances, and has disentangled new dynamics in the landscape of popular contention and mass resistance. In particular, contentious activities ranging from environmental protection to property rights to labour relations have been on the rise since the 1990s with the deepening of economic reform and the continuous widening of disparity in terms of material benefits and wealth distribution among individuals in society.

The fertile ground for popular contention has transitioned China into a 'contentious authoritarianism' in which 'a strong authoritarian regime accommodates widespread and routinized collective protests' (Chen 2012: 189). Chen's penetrating analysis of social protest leads him to identify three interrelated factors underpinning the surge of contentious activities in recent years. First, collective protests allow a venue for the ordinary people to lodge complaints and extract state responsiveness amidst the 'contradictions and ambiguities' embedded in the Chinese power structure. Second, economic reform has fundamentally reconfigured state–society relations, and has created divergent, sometimes competing interests among sectors and social groups. Third, protests are a tactical way to strengthen the bargaining power of certain constituents in maximizing gains through negotiating with state agents and interest groups.

The ability of the Chinese regime to reconsolidate itself in the face of rising challenges and hold on to power while maintaining ruling legitimacy is summarized in the perspective of 'authoritarian resilience' (Nathan 2003). A key aspect of this resilience is the establishment of channels of mass participation and appeal which permit citizens to pursue grievances and voice complaints without potential threat to the regime as a whole. Instead of destabilizing regime control, some (e.g. Lorentzen 2013) contend that regularizing protests, narrowly tailored and under circumstances that the central authorities can keep tabs on, actually provides a mechanism for the Chinese government to maintain political stability. In a polity in which reliable sources of information are not readily available about actions by local officials or discontent of individuals and organized groups, tolerating protests provides a viable monitoring device on both.

In their sweeping overview of popular contention in China since the early 1990s, Steinhardt and Wu (2016) pinpoint four defining characteristics encompassing the repertoire of collective action in the landscape of Chinese sociopolitical activism and contentious politics. First, most of the protests have been 'cellular', involving narrow constituencies linked with pre-existing social ties. Second, the mobilizing grievances tend to hinge on factors related to protesters' immediate interests such as monetary compensation and restoration of property and residential rights. Third, victimhood-driven resistance is the norm, with the goal of participants confined to seeking compensation or retrospective justice for acts or harm that already occurred. Fourth, there is a noticeable absence of policy advocacy in most contentious activities. Since the mid-2000s, Steinhardt and Wu note that an emerging repertoire of environmental protest has been setting the new trend departing from these four patterns attracting large numbers of participants unknown to each other in pursuit of goals that revolve around public goods, policy concerns and symbolic values relevant to the community or even the country at large.

One significant factor that has shaped contentious actions in the new context is the rising public awareness and popular consciousness among the ordinary people about their rights and expanding repertoires of options for redress of grievances (Perry 2009; Li 2010). As a result, mounting acts of 'rightful resistance' have been noted in recent years, especially in China's vast rural territories in which protesters invoke the rhetoric and normative language of the powerful in anchoring defiance and mobilizing allies to curb the exercise of power by respective authorities in direct contravention of their rights (O'Brien & Li 2006). In terms of logistics, the Chinese state is often perceived by boundary-pushing activists as sending mixed signals in setting the limits of participation: 'Beyond some well-marked no-go zone, acts of advocacy are treated unpredictably, with suppression, tolerance, and endorsement all possibilities' (Stern & O'Brien 2012: 188). This murkiness may incentivize individuals and groups with unconventional acts of protest in order to extract responsiveness from state agents. Moreover, government authorities are more likely to respond immediately to citizen demands manifested through collective contentious activities, or even the mere threat of staging them, as evidenced in the field experiment by Chen, Pan and Xu (2016).

Social stability is a centrepiece of the ideal-typical society the Chinese Communist Party preaches. Disruption of stability and social order, therefore, is a slap in the face of ruling authorities in the domain/region affected, from the central government to township bureaucrats.

Understandably, hand-in-hand with the relentless pursuit of economic growth is the obsession of the state with stability maintenance (Yang 2017). As Jonathan Benney (2016) demonstrates, *weiwen* (stability maintenance) has functioned as the de facto local-level conflict-resolution mechanism in China, especially when legal and political resources do not produce practical benefits to citizens. As a practice of social control, *weiwen*, of course, works the most effectively as a pre-emptive strategy to stop mass incidents and public protests from happening, or under other circumstances, to prevent them from getting out of control. On the other hand, grassroots activists who resort to collective action often strategically stage public acts of disruption in order to gain leverage in their bargaining power with *weiwen* officials.

Social media activism: China and beyond

Media have been afforded an indispensable role in academic and pragmatic deliberations of social/political activism across national contexts. As Meikle (2002) demonstrates, from culture jammers to dissident Indymedia to pioneer hacktivists, media activism takes variegated forms and shapes. In their explication of media activism via the lens of social movement theory, Carroll and Hackett (2006) identify three concentric circles. At the center are groups within or around the media industries whose affiliation and intimacy with the media establishment allows them the insight of the alienation, constraints and exploitation of the media system; they are also the most proficient in utilizing existing media sources to their advantage in advancing a particular cause. The second circle consists of subordinate groups whose interests may be sidelined by the media machinery and whose access to media is limited, but who are actively seeking rightful media representation. The outermost circle comprises more diffuse groups whose concern over and engagement with the media are tangential, and whose media-related motive is niche and narrow. These different groups vary in their possession of source resources, and differ drastically in their strategies of intervention.

One important hallmark to bear in mind in discussing media activism in China is the tightly controlled nature of the media apparatus. As a direct part of the marketization reform, the media have transitioned from the hitherto state-subsidized model in the pre-reform era to their current advertising-supported financing system. This is not to say, however, that the state has relinquished efforts to control the media. To a great extent, the media have to fulfill the dual role of serving the audience while succumbing to state propaganda mandates. As a result, while the media may perform tasks such as monitoring local officials and promoting information transparency, they are still most likely to stay away from controversial issues and contentious topics (Shirk 2011). With regard to the new media environment, China has been noted to have developed and implemented a multi-tiered and multifaceted networked surveillance system in targeting proscribed content in its vast online networks – aka the 'Great Firewall of China' (Tai 2015a). State regulations stipulate that all internet sites involved in any type of content publishing be licensed by designated state authorities and work in tandem with official censors in real-time monitoring of online activities.

It is no wonder that online communication becomes the target of government cleansing, considering its network size and volume of content. The latest report by the China Internet Network Information Center (CNNIC) reveals, as of December 2016, China's internet users reached 731 million, 695 million of which surf the net via their smart phones (CNNIC 2017). Social media use is led by three types of applications: WeChat and Qzone are regularly used by 85.8 per cent and 67.8 per cent of Chinese netizens respectively, while Sina Weibo (a micro-blogging service) is accessed routinely by 37.1 per cent of the online population. This aligns well with the overall observation I made of the Chinese virtual culture through comparative analysis of longitudinal surveys of internet users in different national settings, which points to an unmistakable pattern of proclivity among Chinese netizens to contribute to and rely on a variety of User-Generated Content (UGC) (Tai 2006). I attribute this deviation to the closely controlled nature of the Chinese information environment in which content propagated by the state media (and often deemed boring by average users) pervades online space, and steers netizens away to popular venues of peer production.

Explosive developments in social media platforms and technologies in the past decade have consolidated this overall pattern of user-centered information production and consumption. This is best illustrated by the recent overnight rise of a particular type of social media platform called 自媒体, meaning 'Self-made Media' or 'We-Media' in Chinese, as a purposeful designation vis-à-vis the mainstream, state-orchestrated media. Many of these We-Media platforms rely on celebrity-type anchors in branding their niche, original content and programmes, and have garnered a humongous base of zealous followers. The ultra-popularization of these services makes them the easy target of state regulation. On 2 May 2017, the State Internet Information Center – the top-most official agency in setting the rules of online information control – announced the Provisions on the Management of Internet Search Services, a complete overhaul of a government direc-tive promulgated in 2005 targeting online information publishing (http://www.cac.gov.cn/2017-05/02/c_1120902760.htm). The Provisions, which became effective on 1 June 2017, detail rules on the qualifications, licensing and boundaries of content publishing for all online entities in China. It comes as no surprise that one focal domain of sanitizing is social media. Immediately following the enforcement of the ordinance, hundreds of We-Media outlets published via WeChat and Weibo accounts were terminated for violations such as 'dissipating low taste,' 'propagating vul-garity' and 'breaking legal statutes' (*International Financial News* 2017, *Zhenzhou Daily* 2017). This latest development serves as a reminder that the Sword of Damocles can fall on practitioners of We-Media at the mercy of state censors at any time if they veer into the unbeaten path.

This does not mean, of course, that the state is always effective in staying on top of the game of networked information control. The distributed, participatory and free-wheeling nature of internetworked communication creates an environment in which variegated forms of digital insurgencies and popular resistance by different constituents and social groups may exist, survive and occasionally burst. As a particular form of grassroots activism on social media in recent years, dispersed individuals in China have been able to masterfully coordinate, collaborate and orches-trate collective action on China's blossoming social media platforms in uncovering, exposing and publicizing outrageous wrongdoings and transgressions committed by government officials and targeted individuals. Through doing this, grassroots activists have achieved a certain level of success in extracting timely government responses in punishing selective corrupt officials and redressing instances of social, economic, environmental and political injustice as brought to light on social media (Tai 2015b).

Sociopolitical activism takes on many forms and shapes. In explicating the term 'activism,' Joss Hands (2011) identifies three distinct elements in terms of their opposition to prevailing power: dissent, resistance and rebellion. Dissent (or protest) 'is the expression of dissatisfaction with a state of affairs' while resistance 'suggests a more active and stubborn approach' and takes place 'when acts readily cross the boundary into defiance of authority or perceived injustice' (2011: 4). Rebellion, on the other hand, moves beyond the above two to embody necessary 'col-lective and cooperative' actions towards a particular goal line. In direct relevance to the case of China, as Hands (2011: 5) points out, dissent 'in an authoritarian society can be resistance when the act of speech itself becomes a direct refusal of power'.

In deliberating on internet activist campaigns, Graham Meikle (2010) pinpoints four dimen-sions of activism: intercreative texts, intercreative tactics, intercreative strategies and intercreative networks. Intercreative texts involve reworking or re-imagining existing media texts or creating new texts to effect social change; intercreative tactics develop new variations on established tactics and subvert existing media formats; interactive strategies employ the creation of brand-new alternative media spaces for the expression of dissonant perspectives; and intercreative networks focus on mobilizing resources through collaborative deployment of information networks. What makes this line of scholarship interesting as well as challenging is that the dynamics vary substantially with the specific conditions of the national context and they constantly change to adapt to an ever-evolving technological environment.

In their discussion of social activism in China, Ching Kwan Lee and You-tien Hsing (2010) propose a spectrum of politics in three strands – namely, the politics of (re)distribution, recognition and representation – based on the goals and the basis of formation of the collective social actors. The politics of (re)distribution 'entails struggles and claims for material interests or between social groups and state actors that spring from their common or differential class locations' (2010: 3). The politics of recognition is concerned with 'the discovery and articulation of needs previously denied or ignored, especially the demand for social recognition of certain groups' moral status, political position and identity' (2010: 4). The third strand, the politics of representation, is related to the expression of ideas and symbols, or 'symbolic contestations'.

With specific regard to online activism, Guobin Yang (2009) makes the distinction among four types of popular contention: cultural, social, political and nationalistic. Cultural activism expresses concern over values, morality, lifestyles and identities; social activism, on the other hand, focuses on issues such as corruption, environmental protection and the rights of disenfranchised groups. Political activism touches upon topics regarding how the country is or should be governed; online nationalism often permeates China's internet, especially during particular moments of dispute with other countries.

Organizing dynamics and mobilizing structures

In our research on the use of QQ groups in organizing collective action from self-organizing travel tours to well-planned property activists (Tai & Liu 2016), we noted a clear pattern of collaborative and participatory dynamics from contemplation to actualization:

1   share and distribute information to relevant individuals and constituencies;
2   deliberate and debate on possible courses of action and consequences of action/inaction;
3   strategize and call for action (e.g. sit-ins, protests and other public acts);
4   engage in and coordinate collective action.

As social networks become increasingly embedded in routines of daily life, social media has empowered grassroots involvement by diversifying and expanding the repertoire of collection action. In what follows, we discuss how social media has enabled digital action networks and revolutionized organizing capabilities in terms of shared awareness, (re)activating potent and existing social connections and mobilization tactics.

Sharing is the linchpin of social media, and digital activism naturally starts with a communal sense of 'shared awareness', which is defined by Clay Shirky (2011: 35–36) as 'the ability of each member of a group to not only understand the situation at hand but also understand that everyone else does, too'. This shared awareness starts with the communication of information, but it moves beyond simply informational sharing. This condition of shared awareness, Shirky (2011: 36) points out, leads to the so-called 'dictator's dilemma' in that 'a state accustomed to having a monopoly on public speech finds itself called to account for anomalies of its view of events and the public's'. This finds echo in Zuckerman's (2015: 132) 'Cute Cats Theory' of digital activism, which argues that 'resilience to censorship may be a less important benefit than the ability to leverage participation, remix and humor to spread activist content to wider audiences'. In other words, activist content that permeates apps on social media works more effectively in inducing change than a few isolated tools (which tend to be the target of censorship and control in China). Individual users, once exposed to the technology, often find creative ways to get the message out and accomplish what they intend on social media. A related idea is 'speech cascade,' which argues that 'public understanding of what constitutes impermissible speech may change abruptly, sparking bandwagons of uncensored speech' (Druzin & Li 2016: 369). As Druzin and Li demonstrate, structural change in the social conditions in the country allow for the potential for China's cyber-censorship regime to unexpectedly collapse alongside spontaneous eruption of open online speech. The accumulation of 'mass incidents' – so called due to their involvement of mass individuals under certain circumstances of social protest – in China over the years offers testimonial to this claim.

Resource mobilization lies at the center of classic social movement theory (Tilly 1978). In his deliberation on the relational aspects of political contention, Tilly refines the core concept of *catnets* by Harrison White (1965) (commonly understood as any set of individuals comprising both a *category* and a *network*) and assigns a central role in the mobilization process. He argues that collective action only materializes to the extent that categorical traits work in tandem with specific relational structures; these catnets convert individual attributes into collective properties and create necessary resources to sustain collective action (Tilly 1978). Traditionally, one of the biggest challenges for the underprivileged and the resource-poor to organize collective action has been the lack of efficient and effective means of mobilization. This, however, has dramatically changed with the mass diffusion of various forms of social media. It is particularly relevant for China, where mobilization resources had been mostly aggregated to the state power apparatus prior to the arrival of the network era.

While the internet has been proclaimed as an empowering tool for media activism (Meikle 2002), and activist-produced information has been made available at an unprecedented scale online, there are still important constraints and barriers with online distribution of activists-centred messages. For one thing, it is still a monumental task to compete with the well-funded and all-pervasive commercial media in churning out and disseminating information to the mass audience. In the case of China, an added barricade for activist-generated information is the state regulation that all information producers must be licensed by the state in order to propagate original information onto the web. As a result, user-generated content in China has been largely limited to BBS-type forums, for which sanctioned platform providers are relegated the responsibility of monitoring and cleansing by following the directives of state censors (Tai 2015a). Social media, however, thrives almost exclusively on mass users, and its culture and technological implementation shift the dynamics of information production and consumption to favour the users.

Our interviews of QQ group users (Tai & Liu 2016) illustrate the power and the draw of soft information via social media to individual users. Although identical information may often be available through online searches or other web-based sources, the circulation of content – even when it is obtained through third-party resources – adds a particular context and human perspective to the otherwise hard information. On prominent social media platforms such as Weibo, QQ or WeChat, it is typical that individuals who pass on third-party information often add their own interpretations, perspectives and comments alongside the repackaged content, which adds a unique appeal for users when reading the messages. The added sense of authenticity, personalization and trust makes social media a special venue for information sharing. Besides repackaging of existing information, social media is also a viable form of distributing highly targeted original messages in the context of collective action, our research reveals, especially with regard to social media groups exclusively established in organizing group actions: insiders' views, backchannel updates, and personal experiences are all well received in these groups.

In their conception of 'the Logic of Connective Action', Bennett and Segerberg (2012: 753) view digital media as core organizing agents through enabling 'the self-motivated (though not necessarily self-centered) sharing of already internalized or personalized ideas, plans, images, and resources with networks of others'. The co-production of personalized expression on social media, of course, goes beyond the sharing of content. What it cultivates is an on-going, regenerative process of conversation – a type of everyday discursive articulation that resembles what James Scott (1990) calls 'hidden transcript'. This is a particular way for the subordinate to stage their 'disguised, low-profile, undeclared resistance' against domination and the hegemonic discourses as exerted in the public transcript, which translates into official doctrines and state-approved rhetorical invocations on China's networked space. As a specific example, Gleiss's analysis of Weibo posts by Love Save Pneumoconiosis (LSP) activists points to prevalent strategies of contestation: first, the activists articulate alternative discourses that constitute subtle forms of critical challenges to the official discourse; second, activists employ polyphonic expressions to (de)politicize their articulations and legitimize the undertaking of the organization.

Chinese netizens have invented ingenious ways to encode counter-hegemonic discourses and dissenting voices in linguistic wordplays and graphic images in order to bypass state censors and yet convey subtle messages to fellow users (Yang 2016). Over the years, the repertoire of common practices includes creative and ironic reappropriation of official language in everyday speech practices both on- and offline to subvert official rhetoric and state propaganda (Nordin & Richaud 2014), online satire by employing easily identifiable symbols of resistance to challenge the policies or malpractices of the Chinese state (Lee 2016), and the prolific culture of *e-gao* (恶搞) which embeds spoof videos and 'narrative dissidence' in a special type of trickster discourse in the construction of counter-official memory in the average users (Li 2016).

Framing processes are considered an important part of collective action in the network era (Garrett 2006). Proliferation of social networking sites means that individual users and groups can offer their competing perspectives, personal action frames and slogans that may resonate among targeted individuals and trigger participation. Tilly (2004: 3–4) mentions three elements that define the success and failure of social movements: a campaign (sustained, public claims-making efforts); social movement repertoire (ensemble of variable public performances); and participants' concerted public representation of WUNC (worthiness, unity, numbers and commitment) on the part of themselves and/or their constituencies. In relevance to China's rights defense movement in recent years, Biao Teng (2012), a famed activist and lawyer for defending citizen rights, noted a clear pattern and strategy by organized civilian groups in inventing and propagating WUNC frames on social media and offline in organizing and coordinating protest activities. Pu and Scanlan (2012) found that concise framing is essential in mobilizing support for successful collective action by aggrieved farmers whose land was expropriated by the local government for economic development.

One particular type of digital activism in China is the Human Flesh Search (HFS) engine, which involves mass collaboration in tracking down the identity of individuals caught in online controversies (Tai 2016). Individuals who are exposed in online acts of public wrath and outrageous transgressions instantaneously make themselves targets of collective denunciation, and dispersed individuals self-mobilize to search, collect, process and share what is often private information in hunting down and punishing individual violators. Gao (2016) conceives this as a special type of political protest, because an HFS tirade often is directed at official misconduct.

In Chinese culture, *guanxi*, or the network of interpersonal connections, carries special weight in one's social life. The role of personal ties has assumed a more prominent role due to the steady decline in social trust in Chinese society in the past decades, leading 'one to trust only these individuals in one's personal networks' (Yan 2009: 286). Jun Liu's research on the use of mobile devices and personal ties for mobilizing protests in China shows that 'The involvement of *guanxi* as the mobilizing agent, and precisely, a strong sense of moral duty and reciprocal obligation from *guanxi*, acted as the driving force for both recruitment and participation in protests' (Liu 2017: 9). Because social media builds primarily on pre-existing social networks, it also is an effective tool to activate personal ties in facilitating recruitment and engagement in contentious action. On the other hand, social ties such as relatives, friends and native-place connections may also be used by local authorities to practice relational suppression as a form of control in demobilizing and defusing contention (Deng & O'Brien 2013).

Classic theory on social movements places significant emphasis on the role of formal organizations and clearly identifiable leadership in the mobilizing process (Tilly 1978). The social media culture, however, introduces drastically different dynamics. As Gerbaudo (2012) has demonstrated through his research on the Arab Spring movement, protest mobilization in the era of social media has become horizontal, decentralized, fluid, self-nurturing and instantaneous. The distributed nature of networked activism allows for 'organizing without organizations' (Shirky 2008), which comes as a blessing for contentious action in China, because the traditional strategy by the state is to go after identifiable leaders and organizations to stop mass movements.

This is not to suggest that social media activism no longer needs or benefits from leadership. Rather, it means that leadership can be rendered anonymous – unidentifiable, faceless and not clearly connected to any individuals. This is summarized aptly by Poell *et al.* (2016: 1009; original emphasis): 'Facilitated by social media, this mode of leadership revolves around *inviting, connecting, steering, and stimulating*, rather than *directing, commanding, and proclaiming*.' This finds confirmation in our research on the use of QQ groups for mobilizing collective action in China (Tai & Liu 2016). Our extensive in-depth interviews of activists indicate a multilayered organization mechanism. Social media groups focusing on collective action typically enforce a stringent certification process in formation, as individuals who intend to join have to show proof of identity and relevance to the mission of the contention, and those who are deemed extraneous or unlikely to participate are excluded. Moreover, members in the group are monitored for their contribution to group conversations, and are constantly reminded to stay on track in the type of content they disseminate. Violators face the risk of being expelled from the group. This is necessitated by the constant practice of government authorities and other targets of grievances (e.g. real estate developers) in trying to infiltrate into contentious activities, especially in the planning stage, in order to defuse or derail them. Another interesting discovery in our findings is that group leaders often resort to a more exclusive, smaller group reserved for reaching consensus on strategizing among core activists, and will then turn to the larger social groups for mobilization and organization.

Conclusion

Despite its sustained efforts to brand the country as a harmonious society, China's high-capacity authoritarian regime has not eliminated or even reduced popular contention and organized protest. Further economic activities in the reform era have unleashed conditions for variegated forms of conflict and contestation. Lack of established institutional and legal recourses to address grievances and resentment has turned the country into a fertile land of collective action by diverse interest groups and organized entities. Amidst rising public awareness and popular consciousness about individual rights and the expanding repertoire of options is the quick routinization of social media tools in the everyday communication of Chinese citizens.

Due to the highly controlled conventional media environment, the distributed and peer-to-peer nature of social media technology has empowered grassroots communication and turned it into a viable venue in planning, coordinating and staging collective action. Besides expanding access to brand-new types of user-produced information, the embedding of social networking applications into routine life cultivates a shared awareness among the vast populace in understanding not only what information is available, but also what can be done as individual members work together. While the government has intensified its efforts in monitoring and censoring networked communication, and it has been largely successful in blocking individual sites and eradicating isolated tools, it is much harder for the regime to control the lifestyle or mentality induced by widespread social media use in society in the wake of permeation of activist messages and dissenting information on social media.

Social media activates relations of catnets (that is, categories of people manifested in different networks), and has transformed ways to communicate, organize and coordinate collective action. This is particularly so in China, where interpersonal networks and personal connections have assumed prominent roles in social life. Individuals are more likely to respond to calls of contentious action via social media, and they are more likely to contribute to causes advocated through trusted entities from social networking groups. As we have seen on numerous occasions in recent years, creative use of social media has introduced new dynamics into the conception and mobilization of contentious action. In this regard, the continuous development of social media into new terrains gives us hope for more optimism in the years to come.

References

Bennett, W. L. and Segerberg, A. (2012) 'The Logic of Connective Action: Digital Media and the Personalization of Contentious Politics', *Information, Communication & Society*, vol. 15, no. 5, pp. 739–68.

Benney, J. (2016) 'Weiwen at the Grassroots: China's Stability Maintenance Apparatus as a Means of Conflict Resolution', *Journal of Contemporary China*, vol. 25, no. 99, pp. 389–405.

Carroll, W. K. and Hackett, R. A. (2006) 'Democratic Media Activism through the Lens of Social Movement Theory', *Media, Culture & Society*, vol. 28, no. 1, pp. 83–104.

Chen, J., Pan, J. and Xu, Y. (2016) 'Sources of Authoritarian Responsiveness: A Field Experiment in China', *American Journal of Political Science*, vol. 60, no. 2, pp. 383–400.

Chen, X. (2012) *Social Protest and Contentious Authoritarianism in China*. New York: Cambridge University Press.

China Internet Network Information Center (CNNIC) (2017) 'China Statistical Report on Internet Development', http://www.cnnic.net.cn/hlwfzyj/hlwxzbg/hlwtjbg/201701/P020170123364672657 408.pdf, accessed 20 June 2017.

Deng, Y. and O'Brien, K. J. (2013) 'Relational Repression in China: Using Social Ties to Demobilize Protesters', *The China Quarterly*, no. 215, pp. 533–52.

Druzin, B. and Li, J. (2016) 'Censorship's Fragile Grip on the Internet: Can Online Speech be Controlled?', *Cornell International Law Journal*, no. 49, pp. 369–414.

Gao, L. (2016) 'The Emergence of the Human Flesh Search Engine and Political Protest in China: Exploring the Internet and Online Collective Action', *Media, Culture & Society*, vol. 38, no. 3, pp. 349–64.

Garrett, R. K. (2006) 'Protest in an Information Society: A Review of Literature on Social Movements and New ICTs', *Information, Communication & Society*, vol. 9, no. 2, pp. 202–24.

Gerbaudo, P. (2012) *Tweets and the Streets: Social Media and Contemporary Activism*. London: Pluto Press.

International Financial News (2017) '85 We-Media Accounts Forced to Close', 10 June, http://finance.sina. com.cn/roll/2017-06-10/doc-ifyfzhpq6534326.shtml, accessed 7 August 2017.

Lee, S.Y. (2016) 'Surviving Online Censorship in China: Three Satirical Tactics and Their Impact', *The China Quarterly*, no. 228, pp. 1061–80.

Li, H. S. (2016) 'Narrative Dissidence, Spoof Videos and Alternative Memory in China', *International Journal of Cultural Studies*, vol. 19, no. 5, pp. 501–517.

Li, L. (2010) 'Rights Consciousness and Rules Consciousness in Contemporary China', *The China Journal*, no. 64, pp. 47–68.

Liu, J. (2016) 'Mobile Phones, Social Ties and Collective Action Mobilization in China', *Acta Sociologica*, vol. 60, no. 3, pp. 213–27.

Lorentzen, P. L. (2013) 'Regularizing Rioting: Permitting Public Protest in an Authoritarian Regime', *Quarterly Journal of Political Science*, vol. 8, no. 2, pp. 127–58.

Meikle, G. (2002) *Future Active: Media Activism and the Internet*. New York: Routledge.

Meikle, G. (2010) 'Intercreativity: Mapping Online Activism', in J. Hunsinger, L. Klastrup and M. Allen (eds), *International Handbook of Internet Research*. Dordrecht: Springer, pp. 363–77.

Nathan, A. J. (2003) 'Authoritarian Resilience', *Journal of Democracy*, vol. 14, no. 1, pp. 6–17.

Nordin, A. and Richaud, L. (2014) 'Subverting Official Language and Discourse in China? Type River Crab for Harmony', *China Information*, vol. 28, no. 1, pp. 47–67.

O'Brien, K. and Li, L. (2006) *Rightful Resistance in Rural China*. New York: Cambridge University Press.

Perry, E. J. (2001) *Challenging the Mandate of Heaven: Social Protest and State Power in China*. New York: M. E. Sharpe.

Perry, E. J. (2009) 'A New Rights Consciousness?', *Journal of Democracy*, vol. 20, no. 3, pp. 17–20.

Poell, T., Abdulla, R., Rieder, B., Woltering, R. and Zack, L. (2016) 'Protest Leadership in the Age of Social Media', *Information, Communication & Society*, vol. 19, no. 7, pp. 994–1014.

Pu, Q. and Scanlan, S. J. (2012) 'Communicating Injustice? Framing and Online Protest against Chinese Government Land Expropriation', *Information, Communication & Society*, vol. 15, no. 4, pp. 572–90.

Scott, J. C. (1990) *Domination and the Arts of Resistance: Hidden Transcripts*. New Haven, CT: Yale University Press.

Shirk, S. L. (2011) 'Changing Media, Changing China', in S. L. Shirk (ed.) *Changing Media, Changing China*. New York: Oxford University Press, pp. 1–37.

Shirky, C. (2008) *Here Comes Everybody: The Power of Organizing without Organizations*. New York: Penguin.

Shirky, C. (2011) 'The Political Power of Social Media: Technology, the Public Sphere, and Political Change', *Foreign Affairs*, vol. 90, no. 1, pp. 28–41.

Steinhardt, H. C. and Wu, F. (2016) 'In the Name of the Public: Environmental Protest and the Changing Landscape of Popular Contention in China', *The China Journal*, vol. 75, no. 1, pp. 61–82.

Stern, R. E. and O'Brien, K. J. (2012) 'Politics at the Boundary: Mixed Signals and the Chinese State', *Modern China*, vol. 38, no. 2, pp. 174–98.

Tai, Z. (2006) *The Internet in China: Cyberspace and Civil Society*. New York: Routledge.

Tai, Z. (2015a) 'The Great Firewall', in A. Esarey and R. Kluver (eds) *The Internet in China: Cultural, Political, and Social Dimensions (1980s–2000s)*. Great Barrington, MA: Berkshire Publishing Group, pp. 64–74.

Tai, Z. (2015b) 'Finger Power and Smart Mob Politics: Social Activism and Mass Dissent in China in the Networked Era', in P. Weibel (ed.) *Global Activism: Art and Conflict in the 21st Century*. Cambridge, MA: MIT Press, pp. 396–407.

Tai, Z. (2016) 'Networked Activism in China', in A. Kurylo and T. Dumova (eds) *Redefining Communication in the Era of Social Networking: Cultural, Social, and Political Perspectives*. Madison, NJ: Fairleigh Dickinson University Press, pp. 145–60.

Tai, Z. and Liu, X. (2016) 'Invisible Ties, Perceptible Reciprocity, and Real-time Gratifications in Online Community Networks: A Study of QQ User Groups in China', in B. Bagio (ed.) *Analyzing Digital Discourse and Human Behavior in Modern Virtual Environments*. Hershey, PA: IGI, pp. 164–80.

Teng, B. (2012) 'Rights Defence (*Weiquan*), Microblogs (*Weibo*), and the Surrounding Gaze (*Weiguan*): The Rights Defence Movement Online and Offline', *China Perspectives*, no. 3, pp. 29–41.

Tilly, C. (1978) *From Mobilization to Revolution*. Reading, MA: Addison-Wesley.

Tilly, C. (2004) *Social Movements, 1768–2004*. London: Paradigm Press.

White, H. C. (1965) *Notes on the Constituents of Social Structure*. Working Paper, Department of Social Relations, Harvard University.

Yan, Y. (2009) *The Individualization of Chinese Society*. Oxford: Berg.

Yang, D. L. (2017) 'China's Troubled Quest for Order: Leadership, Organization and the Contradictions of the Stability Maintenance Regime', *Journal of Contemporary China*, vol. 26, no. 103, pp. 35–53.

Yang, F. (2016) 'Rethinking China's Internet Censorship: The Practice of Recoding and the Politics of Visibility', *New Media & Society*, vol. 18, no. 7, pp. 1364–81.

Zhenzhou Daily (2017) 'We Media Should Stay Above the Legal Bottom Line', 11 June, http://hn.ifeng.com/a/20170611/5737478_0.shtml, accessed 7 August 2017.

Zuckerman, E. (2015) 'Cute Cats to the Rescue?', in D. Allen and J. S. Light (eds) *From Voice to Influence: Understanding Citizenship in a Digital Age*. Chicago, IL: University of Chicago Press, pp. 131–54.

10

CONNECTIVE OR COLLECTIVE?

The intersection between online crowds and social movements in contemporary activism

Anastasia Kavada

Introduction

The rise of more flexible, decentralized and individualized forms of activism has prompted a rethinking of the 'collective' in collective action. Scholars highlight the vital role played by social media in current mobilizations, emphasizing the socio-technical and communicative character of contemporary activism (Bennett & Segerberg 2013; Dolata & Schrape 2016; Flanagin, Stohl & Bimber 2006; Kavada 2016; Mattoni & Treré 2014). However, they seem to disagree on the types of collectives facilitated by social media.

On the one hand, new frameworks like the 'logic of connective action' by Bennett and Segerberg (2013) examine the emergence of diverse online crowds on social media and stress the potential of such platforms for personalized expression and interpersonal networking. Bennett and Segerberg suggest that social media can serve as 'organising agents' of the crowd, enabling the coordination of connective action by performing functions that are traditionally undertaken by activist organizations. On the other hand, research focusing on the perspectives of core activists has demonstrated the persistence of more conventional collective action dynamics in recent mobilizations. Studies have revealed the patterns of leadership characterizing the management of social media accounts, the strategies around the collaborative production of social media content, as well as the efforts to create a common identity for participants in collective action (Coretti & Pica 2015; Gerbaudo 2015; Kavada 2015; Treré 2015).

Yet a closer look at the literature on the topic confirms that what at first glance appears as a disagreement over the collective nature of online mobilizations, is instead a misunderstanding that arises from the diverging concepts and methods of two distinct but overlapping lines of enquiry. While scholars like Bennett and Segerberg (2013) examine the online crowds constituted on social media platforms, other researchers focus on core activists and their social media strategies and experiences. While the study of online crowds mainly involves social network analysis of large datasets of social media content, research concentrating on core activists takes a more qualitative and ethnographic approach that spans different media. Crowds and social movements do have overlaps but they are not one and the same.

These two diverging approaches tend to talk across rather than to each other. Thus, commenting on studies of the 'movements of the squares', Bennett (quoted in Mercea, Iannelli & Loader 2016: 285) notes the analytical gap in researching 'the relationship between core activists who are in the camps, who are running the media operations and the crowd, the periphery who are building a public for these protests' and argues that 'it is time [...] to theorize the relationships all along the way' (ibid.). In this chapter, I take on this task by tracing the differences and intersections between online crowds and social movements as concepts and objects of analysis. The chapter also outlines the role of social media in the constitution of both crowds and movements, and particularly in processes of bonding, collective identity formation and group coordination.

For reasons of brevity, I will focus on studies of the Occupy movement which has been explored from the perspective of both online crowds and social movement activists. Occupy emerged in September 2011 with the occupation of Zuccotti Park in New York. Inspired by the Arab Spring, activists rallied against what they saw as the excesses of Wall Street and the dysfunction of a political system that privileged the richest 1 per cent of the population rather than the 99 per cent. The movement soon spread around the US and other parts of the world, with occupations appearing in the central squares of major cities. Occupy attempted to enact its vision of a better democratic system in its own decision-making practices, with major decisions taken by consensus in open assemblies. Occupy also used social media to disseminate information, attracting online crowds who came together in a variety of Facebook pages and Twitter hashtags like #ows.

Crowds and social movements: conceptual definitions

Crowds and social movements are different analytical concepts. The notion of the crowd most often refers to temporary gatherings of individuals who share the same feelings and grievances. In the nineteenth and twentieth century, crowds tended to be depicted 'as brutal, primitive, even criminal, mobs' (Dean 2016: 7). Le Bon's (1893/2006: 13) famous treatise on the subject argued that the 'conscious personality' of individuals vanished in the crowd as 'sentiments and ideas of all the persons in the gathering take one and the same direction'. Dean (2016: 7) criticises such conceptions of the crowd as reactionary and conservative, stemming from a fear 'of the collective power of the masses' that was strengthened with the emergence of mass democracy and the expansion of the suffrage. Yet with the emergence of digital media, the notion of the crowd has started to assume a different meaning. Rather than primitive and suggestible, crowds have now become 'smart' (Rheingold 2002) and 'wise' (Surowiecki 2004), characterized by collective intelligence and more complex processes of self-organization and knowledge generation.

Focusing on online crowds around political and social issues, Bennett and Segerberg's (2013) analysis of connective action views crowds in this more positive light. Their framework identifies two ideal-types of connective action, an organization-enabled and a crowd-enabled type. In the latter, social media platforms perform the function of activist organizations, serving as an 'organizing agent' that structures crowd coordination. As Bennett and Segerberg (ibid.: 22) put it,

> [t]he second pattern, typified by the *indignados* and the Occupy protests in the United States, entails technology platforms playing the role of virtual political organizations to coordinate the actions of people operating in geographically scattered face-to-face settings, where important but otherwise potentially isolated decisions, plans and actions take place.

Such networks may discourage the involvement of already existing organizations and instead operate with informal and minimal coordination mechanisms (ibid.: 47). Crowd-enabled connective action, at least in its ideal-type, is also based on 'personal expression shared over social networks' (ibid.), while 'communication content centers on emergent inclusive personal action frames' (ibid.). Therefore, in contrast to Le Bon (1893/2006), Bennett and Segerberg (2013) reject the idea that individuals lose their 'conscious personality' in the crowd. Instead, networked crowds arise out of the digital structuring of individual expression which is still present and discernible in connective action.

Other authors approach the same protests from the point of view of social movements, rather than online crowds. Their analysis thus foregrounds different processes as, unlike crowds, social movements are collective actors with a sense of their own agency. They are not simply 'an aggregation of atomized behaviours' (Melucci 1996: 23), but involve solidarity, 'the ability of actors to recognize others, and to be recognized, as belonging to the same social unit' (ibid.). Solidarity develops with the formation of a collective identity, 'an interactive and shared definition produced by a number of individuals (or groups at a more complex level)' (Melucci 1996: 70) concerning the means and ends of their action, as well as the boundaries of the movement and its relationship with its environment. Looking at social movements from a constructivist perspective, the Italian scholar Alberto Melucci urges us to study them as multitudinous entities that are always in the making. The collective identity of a social movement should therefore be perceived as an open-ended process of negotiation among the different actors constituting the movement. This process of 'identization' is both cognitive and emotional, as social movement participants develop feelings of solidarity and invest emotionally in the shared cognitive schemas constructed through this process.

To create a sense of themselves as actors with their own agency, social movements also require 'a network of *active relationships*' that includes forms of organization and leadership, as well as channels of communication (ibid.: 71). Organizing forms may vary, but social movements are considered as more loosely coordinated actors. They are characterized by 'organized informality' (Dolata & Schrape 2016: 4) as they tend to lack legal frameworks, visible hierarchies or official processes of membership and affiliation. However, social movements develop more complex and differentiated structures over time. They devise 'their own, primarily informal, rules, norms and organizational patterns' (ibid.) that stabilize collective action and ensure its durability. Movements may also comprise more formally structured Social Movement Organizations (SMOs) that have a variety of functions, from mobilizing participants and resources to setting aims and goals to sustaining participation in the movement through time (Della Porta & Diani 2006: 137).

Crowds and movements also play a different role within the political system. Social movements express a deeper conflict between actors struggling to appropriate resources that they consider valuable (Melucci 1996: 22). They are not simply a reaction to a crisis but centre on systemic conflicts. Social movements thus constitute a form of collective action that 'entails a breach of the limits of compatibility of the system within which action takes place' (Melucci 1996: 28). The crowd, by contrast, 'does not have politics. It is the opportunity for politics' (Dean 2016: 8). Crowds generate a rupture, an opening, that gives rise to a site of struggle over the meaning and politics of the crowd (ibid.). It is, therefore, the political struggle that follows the emergence of crowds which determines their meaning and subject. This points to the crucial political connection between crowds and social movements, as in the site of struggle activated by crowds, social movements strive to translate, stir, represent and draw legitimacy from the crowds formed around contentious issues.

Although crowds and social movements are different theoretical concepts, they may have overlaps as objects of analysis as, empirically, they may encompass similar sets of actors. For instance, the Twitter accounts posting on the same hashtag may include the individual accounts of core activists, as well as collectively-managed social movement accounts and a variety of bystanders or outsiders, such as journalists and the police. This empirical overlap can be a source of confusion as scholars who focus on the same protests may study them from a different perspective and highlight different aspects of the processes of framing, bonding and organizing. Yet in order to start bridging the analytical gap between these two lines of enquiry, we need to trace not only the differences but also the intersections between online crowds and social movements. The following section attempts to do this by drawing mainly on studies of the Occupy movement and its use of social media.

Social media and the intersections between movements and crowds: organizing and boundaries

The processes through which online crowds and social movements arise, and the key roles played by social media, constitute a first point of intersection in the study of crowds and movements. Social media operate as systems of shared awareness (Dolata & Schrape 2016), bringing together crowds with similar grievances and feelings of discontent. They allow users to monitor the reactions of others towards issues of common concern and to gauge public opinion. Online crowds can be seeding grounds for the emergence of new social movements. However, in many cases online crowds do not rise spontaneously, but through careful planning and dedicated efforts by already existing activist networks and organizations. Activists may set up Facebook event pages or social media accounts in the name of the movement or launch hashtags that serve as focal points around which online crowds gravitate. As Flesher Fominaya (2014) argues, the spontaneity with which social movements seem to emerge is often manufactured and part of a strategy to present movements as an authentic expression of grassroots feeling.

Crowds and social movements also differ in their organizing and coordination practices. Research on the organizational dynamics of online crowds mainly involves the study of social media content. Employing predominantly social network analysis, researchers generate network graphs that show patterns of behaviour in information exchange. Within this perspective, the organizing process of the crowd thus revolves around the peer production and structuring of information around contentious issues. For instance, in their study of three Occupy hashtags, Bennett, Segerberg and Walker (2014) suggest that the online crowd organized itself through the production, curation and dynamic integration of symbolic resources that mainly included hyperlinks. This organizing structure is not intentional or planned, but constitutes a kind of 'emergent order' that arises from the interaction on social media platforms and that is partly shaped by the rules encoded in the software.

By contrast, the organization of social movements is intentional, although often unplanned. Activists decide on what needs to be done, from managing press relations to taking care of logistics, in an ad hoc basis and in response to emergent conditions. The organizing structure is built through processes of internal differentiation between organizing units, as well as mechanisms that join these units and regulate their relationships. Movements develop specific guidelines and codes of conduct, as well as decision-making rules and processes. The way in which a movement organizes, particularly if it is of the prefigurative variety, is intimately linked to its collective identity and its function within the political system. Occupy is exemplary in this regard. Typified by open assemblies and consensus, the movement's process of decision-making became one of its defining characteristics, so much so that activists found it difficult to modify the process once it was deemed too slow and ineffective. The mode of decision-making was also integral to the political function of the movement as it expressed a key conflict between the 99 per cent and the 1 per cent. This was a conflict that breached the limits of the system, since the movement's demand for a process of governance that privileged the many over the few required a complete overhaul of the system of representative democracy.

Yet, the organizing mechanisms of the crowd and the movement intersect in various ways. The most obvious overlap regards the presence of the movement's social media accounts in the online crowd. Although the crowd as a totality does not possess an intentional structure, the movement's accounts are more strategically oriented. In the Occupy movement, some of the collectives tasked with posting messages on social media developed sophisticated editorial guidelines and processes (Kavada 2015). Social media administrators wielded power within the collective as they could play the role of 'digital vanguards' (Gerbaudo 2017) or 'connective leaders' (Poell *et al.* 2016) attempting to influence and stir the online crowd. The administrators of Facebook pages could exclude users from the page and moderate discussions. Activists responsible for social media accounts could also use the platforms to crowdsource organizing tasks by appealing to people who did not form part of the movement's core. However, research on online crowds often disregards the strategies and experiences that may underlie a node's behaviour in the crowd, focusing instead on observable behaviours. They are thus less able to show whether or how the movement's social media accounts influence the 'emergent order' of information exchange on social media. Studies of online crowds also need to consider how specific genres of social media communication affect the organization of the crowd. For instance, the interaction on an #Occupy Twitter hashtag differs from that on an Occupy Facebook page. The latter provides more control to the team managing the page, while the former facilitates the bottom up structuring of crowd interaction. Using the framework of connective action, one can say that the former is more of the crowd-enabled type, while the latter is more organizationally enabled.

Furthermore, the movement's use of digital media is integral to processes of internal differentiation and the organic development of structure. In the Occupy movement, one of the first actions of new organizing units was to set up their own communication spaces, such as email lists or social media accounts, thus informally registering the existence, purpose and boundaries of the unit. Differential access to these spaces shaped the internal hierarchies of the movement. Access to more closed or secret spaces that involved a small number of 'vetted' users distinguished core from peripheral activists (Kavada 2015). There was no organizational diagram that designated an activist's position in the movement's structure, but a flexible process of affiliation and membership that was facilitated by digital media.

However, social media tend to blur the boundaries between the inside and the outside of the movement. The online crowds coming together on social media are temporary formations with more open and vague boundaries. They include both actors that identify with the movement, as well as a variety of bystanders and outsiders. In other words, online crowds both obscure and open up the boundaries of the movement. They can be considered as an in-between space, offering movements with the opportunity to convert bystander publics into movement participants. This was most obvious in the Occupy movement, whose identity centred around the inclusive frame of the 99 per cent versus the 1 per cent. The social media teams of the movement thus attempted to use its social media accounts in ways that emphasized the inclusiveness of the movement by erasing the boundary between inside and outside and by encouraging social media users to take a more active role in the movement (Kavada 2015).

Intersections in processes of framing and bonding

The creation of solidarity and collective identity further require processes of framing, the development of common schemas of interpretation. Within social movements,

> [c]ollective action frames are constructed in part as movement adherents negotiate
> a shared understanding of some problematic condition or situation they define as in

need of change, make attributions regarding who or what is to blame, articulate an alternative set of arrangements, and urge others to act in concert to affect change.

Benford & Snow 2000: 615

Thus, frames can have diagnostic, prognostic and mobilization functions. They may also refer to the identity of the movement and to how it distinguishes itself from its environment. The development of common frames involves difficult negotiations around the demands and principles of the movement. By contrast, online crowds may gather around vague frames of action that can be easily personalized and customized (Bennett & Segerberg 2013). Such personalized communication hinges on 'symbolic inclusiveness […] and the relative absence of cues that signal ideological and definitional unanimity' (ibid.: 58). Frames generated by individuals, rather than collective decision-making, can become popular in the crowd and shared widely on social media. For instance, remarking on processes of framing on the main Occupy hashtags, Papacharissi (2015: 78) notes the 'subjective pluralism that […] sought to connect a number of individual contributions to Occupy'.

However, the framing processes in the online crowd intersect with those in the movement. As mentioned earlier, some of the frames that the online crowd congregates around may be strategically crafted by the social media teams of the movement. The production of social media content by these teams is also guided in part by the collective frames developed by the movement. At the same time, frames that become popular in the online crowd may be de facto adopted by the movement through an informal process of acclamation rather than through the more official decision-making routes. We can view this relationship as a dynamic process, with the online crowd opening up possibilities for personal expression and polysemic framing (Papacharissi 2015), while the movement attempts to strategically curate, select, define (and thus close down) the framing of the movement.

Apart from cognitive schemas, both online crowds and social movements are brought together by shared feelings and emotions. Focusing on what she terms 'affective publics', Papacharissi (2015: 117) argues that social media offer 'soft structures of feeling' that allow strangers to connect to each other in experiences of togetherness. As Papacharissi (2015: 78) notes with regard to Occupy, social media 'permitted individuals approaching the movement through online means to affiliate effectively and to join in and be counted alongside other Occupy supporters, thus adding intensity to the movement'. However, Poell and van Dijck (2015: 532) question 'whether there is a natural progression from "togetherness" to "community"' on social media. While the techno-commercial character of these platforms is conducive to the algorithmic creation of moments of togetherness, their architecture does not necessarily allow these temporary online crowds to develop durable relations, a process that is necessary for the consolidation of social movements.

A closer look at the types of bonding facilitated on social media, the 'network of active relationships', to use Melucci's (1996) phrase, that they tend to foster partly confirms this point. Studies show that social media platforms tend to facilitate interaction between already existing interpersonal networks. They ease the aggregation of individuals, rather than the formation of organizational networks (Juris 2012). Social media genres designed specifically for organizational communication, such as Facebook pages, may stimulate interaction between individual users and the owners of the page but not between individual users who do not already know each other. In their analysis of the use of Facebook by the Italian movement Popolo Viola, Coretti and Pica (2015: 957) show that users of the movement's Facebook page 'seldom discussed among themselves, and thus the potential to build strong ties was scarce'. The design of Facebook entails that users interact with posts on their individual newsfeed, meaning that while they may respond to the posts of page owners, they do not interact as much with users who may be commenting on the same post. Thus, Facebook pages are more suited to the strengthening of affiliative ties (Flanagin, Stohl & Bimber 2006), an abstract sense of connection arising from the common affiliation to the movement (Kavada 2012).

The emphasis on personal and individual expression is also considered to be antithetical to the creation of the collective and to the development of more stable relations of commitment and solidarity. The business model of social media platforms translates into a design that encourages interpersonal networking in an effort to augment the volume of data generated by users (Poell & van Dijck 2015). Social media are thus characterized by a 'logic of self-centered participation' (Fenton & Barassi 2011: 183) that privileges the individual over the collective, the formation of temporary online crowds rather than social movements. This connects with broader sociological trends that have seen the entrepreneurial and networked individual emerging as a key figure in recent mobilizations (Mason 2012). The conditions of late modernity and Western liberal democracy, with the decline of grand narratives and ideologies, as well as the weakening of traditional membership organizations, has provided individuals with greater choice in terms of the social groupings to which they belong (Bennett & Segerberg 2013; Flanagin, Stohl & Bimber 2006). Individuals can now move more fluidly between different collectives in ways that help them build their own individual narrative. Competition within neoliberal markets also places a premium on networking. The neoliberal logic transforms people into 'human capital' whose 'constant and ubiquitous aim [...] is to entrepreneurialize its endeavors, appreciate its value, and increase its rating or ranking' (Brown 2015: 36) in order to survive in a fiercely competitive market. The growing emphasis on networking can thus be considered as part of an individual's effort to 'attract investors' and increase its 'market value'. Social media platforms, with their emphasis on self-expression and interpersonal networking, are uniquely suited to this type of entrepreneurial and self-reflexive citizen.

Thus, while people can come together on social media, the design of these platforms does not facilitate the complex interactions that give rise to social movements (Juris 2012). Instead, it is the rituals and collective processes also developed through face-to-face communication that foster a more concrete sense of the collective, by allowing movement supporters to develop interpersonal relationships, common frames and organizational structures more quickly and easily (Kavada 2015). The study of social movements therefore requires a perspective that spans the communication ecology of the movement (Mercea *et al.* 2016; Treré & Mattoni 2016) and that considers the role of social media in relation to other platforms and communication spaces.

Conclusion

Researchers of online crowds and social movements study the same mobilizations but from a different angle and by employing diverging methods and conceptual frameworks. Attempting to bridge the analytical gap between these lines of enquiry, this chapter defined crowds and movements as two distinct analytical concepts. It then reviewed research on the role of social media in the processes of bonding, organization and framing that characterize both the online crowds and the social movements coalescing around the same protest. The aim was to trace the intersections between crowds and movements: between the emergent order of information that characterizes the organization of online crowds and the organic process of structuring that social movements develop through time; between the individually-generated, inclusive and personal framing arising from the crowd and the collective negotiation and decision-making in social movement framing processes; between the affective elements of online crowds and the development of strong ties and durable emotional investment in the movement. Thus, in this chapter

I argue that it is not a matter of either/or, of connective or collective. Both approaches can be used to study the same phenomenon as long as researchers are explicit about what each perspective highlights and what it obscures. Yet to advance research on the topic, it is important not only to distinguish analytically crowds from movements, but also to understand their confluence and their points of intersection.

I have left for last the most important, but paradoxically least researched, aspect of the debate: the ways in which crowds and movements relate to power and agency. While crowds open up the opportunity for politics (Dean 2016), it falls on social movements, as actors expressing a systemic conflict and aware of their own agency, to capitalize on this opportunity. Movements need to define the politics of the crowd and use this definition in the struggle to impose their own understandings and codes on the rest of society. But are social movements necessary in this process? Dean (2016: 14) argues that '[i]n the complex networks of communicative capitalism' the challenge is 'the generation and circulation of the many in order to produce the one' or, in other words, of how the crowd engenders a collective subject. Authors like Bennett and Segerberg (2013) are more ambivalent about this. They posit that by facilitating more inclusive and personalized participation without commitment, crowd-enabled connective action may still be powerful in terms of swaying public opinion and influencing the agenda. The existence of a formally structured and durable collective in the form of a conventional organization is not always necessary. In more repressive and authoritarian regimes, it may actually be outright dangerous. Such questions of power and agency are the most challenging to answer. They are however the most crucial in evaluating the intersection between online crowds and social movements in the study of contemporary activism.

References

Benford, R. D. and Snow, D. A. (2000) 'Framing Processes and Social Movements: An Overview and Assessment', *Annual Review of Sociology*, no. 26, pp. 611–39.

Bennett, W. L. and Segerberg, A. (2013) *The Logic of Connective Action: Digital Media and the Personalization of Contentious Politics*. New York: Cambridge University Press.

Bennett, W. L., Segerberg, A. and Walker, S. (2014) 'Organization in the Crowd: Peer Production in Large-scale Networked Protests', *Information, Communication & Society*, vol. 17, no. 2, pp. 232–60.

Brown, W. (2015) *Undoing the Demos: Neoliberalism's Stealth Revolution*. New York: Zone Books.

Coretti, L. and Pica, D. (2015) 'The Rise and Fall of Collective Identity in Networked Movements: Communication Protocols, Facebook, and the Anti-Berlusconi Protest', *Information, Communication & Society*, vol. 18, no. 8, pp. 951–67.

Dean, J. (2016) *Crowds and Party*. London: Verso.

della Porta, D. and Diani, M. (2006) *Social Movements: An Introduction* (second edition). Malden, MA: Blackwell.

Dolata, U. and Schrape, J. (2016) 'Masses, Crowds, Communities, Movements: Collective Action in the Internet Age', *Social Movement Studies*, vol. 15, no. 1, pp. 1–18.

Fenton, N. and Barassi, V. (2011) 'Alternative Media and Social Networking Sites: The Politics of Individuation and Political Participation'. *The Communication Review*, vol. 14, no. 3, pp. 179–96.

Flanagin, A. J., Stohl, C. and Bimber, B. (2006) 'Modeling the Structure of Collective Action'. *Communication Monographs*, vol. 73, no. 1, pp. 29–54.

Flesher Fominaya, C. (2014) 'Debunking Spontaneity: Spain's 15-M/*Indignados* as Autonomous Movement', *Social Movement Studies*, vol. 14, no. 2, pp. 149–63.

Gerbaudo, P. (2015) 'Protest Avatars as Memetic Signifiers: Political Profile Pictures and the Construction of Collective Identity on Social Media in the 2011 Protest Wave', *Information, Communication & Society*, vol. 18, no. 8, pp. 916–29.

Gerbaudo, P. (2017) 'Social Media Teams as Digital Vanguards: The Question of Leadership in the Management of Key Facebook and Twitter Accounts of Occupy Wall Street, *Indignados* and UK Uncut', *Information, Communication & Society*, vol. 20, no. 2, pp. 185–202.

Juris, J. S. (2012) 'Reflections on #Occupy Everywhere: Social Media, Public Space, and Emerging Logics of Aggregation' *American Ethnologist*, vol. 39, no. 2, pp. 259–79.

Kavada, A. (2012) 'Engagement, Bonding, and Identity across Multiple Platforms: Avaaz on Facebook, YouTube, and MySpace', *MedieKultur*, vol. 52, pp. 28–48.

Kavada, A. (2015) 'Creating the Collective: Social Media, the Occupy Movement and Its Constitution as a Collective Actor', *Information, Communication & Society*, vol. 18, no. 8, pp. 872–86.

Kavada, A. (2016) 'Social Movements and Political Agency in the Digital Age: A Communication Approach', vol. 4, no. 4, pp. 8–12.

le Bon, G. (1893/2006) *The Crowd: A Study of the Popular Mind*. New York: Cosimo Classics.

Mason, P. (2012) *Why It's Kicking Off Everywhere: The New Global Revolutions*. London: Verso.

Mattoni, A. and Treré, E. (2014) 'Media Practices, Mediation Processes, and Mediatization in the Study of Social Movements', *Communication Theory*, vol. 24, no. 3, pp. 252–71.

Melucci, A. (1996) *Challenging Codes: Collective Action in the Information Age*. Cambridge: Cambridge University Press.

Mercea, D., Iannelli, L. and Loader, B. D. (2016) 'Protest Communication Ecologies', *Information, Communication & Society*, vol. 19, no. 3, pp. 279–89.

Papacharissi, Z. (2015) *Affective Publics: Sentiment, Technology and Politics*. Oxford: Oxford University Press.

Poell, T., Abdulla, R., Rieder, B. and Woltering, R. (2016) 'Protest Leadership in the Age of Social Media', *Information, Communication & Society*, vol. 19, no. 7, pp. 994–1014.

Poell, T., & van Dijck, J. (2015) 'Social Media and Activist Communication', in C. Atton (ed.) *The Routledge Companion to Alternative and Community Media*. New York: Routledge, pp. 527–37.

Rheingold, H. (2002) *Smart Mobs: The Next Social Revolution*. New York: Basic Books.

Surowiecki, J. (2004) *The Wisdom of Crowds: Why the Many Are Smarter Than the Few*. London: Abacus.

Treré, E. (2015) 'Reclaiming, Proclaiming, and Maintaining Collective Identity in the #YoSoy132 Movement in Mexico: An Examination of Digital Frontstage and Backstage Activism through Social Media and Instant Messaging Platforms', *Information, Communication & Society*, vol. 18, no. 8, pp. 901–15.

Treré, E. and Mattoni, A. (2016) 'Media Ecologies and Protest Movements: Main Perspectives and Key Lessons', *Information, Communication & Society*, vol. 19, no. 3, pp. 290–306.

11

THE COMMUNICATIVE CORE OF WORKING CLASS ORGANIZATION

Jesse Drew

Introduction

Media analyses and studies that investigate the role of media in organizations of workers, whether based at the point of production or in other sectors of service labour, have typically presented media practices as extraneous or peripheral to the primary efforts of labour. Labour issues are frequently framed as a conflict over land, labour and capital. I would force a fourth consideration into that triumvirate: communications. The struggle of the working class since its first stirrings has been a struggle over the means of communication. If politics is the conflict over the allocation of scarce resources, then labour politics can be understood as the struggle over who controls the printing press, the microphone and the camera. This would hold true over the entire scale of communications – from interpersonal face-to-face, to traditional broadcast and cable television, to social media platforms such as Facebook and Twitter. The construction of a movement of workers is based as much upon fellow workers' ability to communicate one-on-one with co-workers as it is upon the ability for labour leaders to broadcast to a major television audience.

This essay re-examines labour-based media, particularly in the United States, and places them at the core of labour organization, positioning communications practice in its many different forms as central to the task of uniting workers and building movements, organizations, collective actions and institutions that strengthen the position of wage-earners. This re-evaluation posits four primary developmental stages of labour organization and respective media practices: the early craft and trade union movement; the growth and institutionalization of the industrial union movement; the militant and reform caucuses within the established labour unions; and the current phase of worker organization in the new global, precarious labour system. Regardless of the particular stage of labour organization, communications strategies – one-on-one, face-to-face, small house meetings, limited-run newsletters, mass circulation newspapers, radio broadcasting, video, television, computer and mobile-based social media tools – have played and will continue to play a central and catalytic role in worker organization.

Finding labour's voice

For thousands of years, human communication was linked to transportation, as the technical means of transferring thoughts and ideas depended upon their physical transference, whether it was the delivery of documents or the arrival of spokespeople. The physical proximity of people with shared values, interests and material conditions was essential in creating a public that could debate and take action on grievances or reforms. At the dawn of wage labour, the amassing of the machinery of capital agglomerated masses of human beings into its paid labourers, thus creating the spaces of physical interaction where workers congregated and ideas could be exchanged. The free and independent assembly of workers created the conditions for the beginnings of the self-consciousness of labour and the preliminary steps towards assembling social movements for worker power. Thus, the gathering of workers has been a fundamental and respected manifestation of labour communications. From the beginnings of labour movements unto the present day, the public square, the soapbox, the mass rally and the parade have been integral to workers' fights for economic justice, human dignity and solidarity. From the vibrant Mayday rallies of an earlier era to contemporary Labor Day picnics, the physical gathering of labour to come together to listen to public speakers and talk to one another has been recognized as fundamental to the foundations of the labour movement. As Downing (2001: 105) remarks: 'The most accessible and most fundamental mode of radical expression is speech for public purposes.'

The movement of working people from the beginnings of labour depended to a large degree upon getting their word and platform out to potential members and the public at large. The early trade unions were founded not only upon local proximity of workers who shared skilled trades but, just as importantly, around shared languages. Many of the early trade unions in the US were formed to a large extent from groups of workers who found it essential to create media tools that could reach out to their respective language groups. Thus, beginning union efforts depended to a large degree upon utilizing the print technologies of the day to generate an array of union newspapers in German, Yiddish, Italian, Polish, Russian and many of the other prevalent languages shared by workers. As Dubofsky and Dulles (2004: 33) point out, the 'widespread growth of labour newspapers took place in the early 1830s, with no less than sixty-eight such journals upholding the workingmen's cause and agitating for labour reforms'.

From the early trade union militancy of the National Labor Union and the Knights of Labor following the US Civil War through the end of the Great Depression and the powerful Congress of Industrial Organizations (CIO) organizing drives of the 1930s, workers' organizations have relied upon the printed word to organize and to advocate their cause. Newspapers, broadsides, leaflets, journals and newsletters were valuable communication tools in working class activity during these times, as they were relatively cheap to produce and easy to distribute either publicly or clandestinely. In the early part of the twentieth century, there were at least a dozen daily labour papers and hundreds of weekly publications. One of the largest was the socialist newsweekly *The Appeal to Reason* published in Girard, Kansas. The *Appeal*, whose circulation ranged from 500,000 to 1,000,000 readers, was affiliated with Eugene Debs, president of the American Railway Union and one of the most powerful and popular labour leaders of his time (Morais & Cahn 1948: 86).

The Industrial Workers of the World (IWW) published many newspapers to assist in their organizing drives and strike activities, including *The Industrial Worker* and *Solidarity*. Printed leaflets, flyers and songbooks were integral to IWW campaigns for the free speech and assembly rights of workers. The IWW editors were frequently arrested and their papers shut down, only to spring up again with new editors in other locales (Dubofsky 1969: 178). Newspapers were especially important to the stability of the IWW as many of its members were itinerant workers who worked seasonally picking crops and fruit or logging in northwestern forests, and the printed word kept them in touch with organizing campaigns and direct actions across the US, despite being geographically isolated in rural areas and small towns.

With the industrial expansion of the mid-1800s, technological developments offered new means of media propagation and communication. The steel rails of the train tracks and the telegraph lines that sprouted up alongside them provided rapid communications and travel between far-flung towns and cities and helped create the means for the first national union organizations, and the first nationwide strikes as well. The American Railroad Union took advantage of both rail and wire to build the first nationwide labour strike in 1894, uniting railroad workers across the United States in support of striking Pullman workers at their plant in Illinois.

While the printing press, the railroad and the telegraph were instrumental in building working class unity across geographical regions, labour media innovators were paying attention to newer communications techniques as well. At the turn of the last century it was the silver screen of cinema that enthralled and excited the growing publics. As the working class flocked to the nickelodeons and picture shows, labour saw great potential in the possibilities of celluloid to capture the imagination of fellow workers. There is little written about the cinematic history of labour, as many of the original films have disintegrated over time, but printed evidence shows unions saw in the film industry an exciting opportunity to raise working class consciousness using the cinematic language of both narrative and documentary.

As Steven J. Ross (1998: 7) explains in his illuminating study *Working-Class Hollywood: Silent Film and the Shaping of Class in America*:

> as early as 1907, workers, radicals and labor organizations were making movies that challenged the dominant ideology of individualism and portrayed collective action – whether in the form of unionism or socialist politics – as the most effective way to improve the lives of citizens. Over the next two decades, labor and the left forged an oppositional cinema that used film as a medium of hope to educate, entertain, and mobilize millions of Americans.

The invention and eventual mass production of the vacuum tube in the 1920s and 1930s brought about a dramatic evolution in media technology and ushered in the sound motion picture (the talkies), the audio amplifier and, most importantly, radio. Radio was an inexpensive medium and became widespread in workers' households. Labour saw radio as an ideal medium and a great potential to bring the voice of labour into the household easily and inexpensively. In the early days of radio, its enthusiasts were comprised not of business interests, but community groups, labour groups, church groups, educational institutions and civic organizations. Many labour radio programmes could be heard on the radio dial, from small town community broadcasters to the powerful clear channel station WCFL of the Chicago Federation of Labor. In his study of WCFL, McChesney (1992: 2) states that:

> During the embryonic stage of radio broadcasting in the United States, between 1920 and 1935, before the network-dominated, advertising-supported system became entrenched, elements of organized labor endeavored to establish a national, non-profit, listener-supported, labor broadcasting network to provide a 'working-class perspective' on public affairs and counteract what was regarded as the 'anti-union' bias of the commercial broadcasters.

Labour took the effort to create its own media voice very seriously in the beginning stages of the union movement, as it believed the opinions and interests of labour were not the same as the managerial and employing classes. A significant reason for this media independence was the fact that many of the early trade union movements were linked to the revolutionary strategies of political parties who believed that in order to ameliorate the conditions of workers, they must contend for political power in addition to contractual power over working conditions and wages. In the United States, these political affinities revolved around the Socialist Party, the syndicalist, the IWW or the Communist Party, all of which maintained a strong desire for an independent workers voice and an independent workers culture.

Workers pick up the megaphone

During the Great Depression in the United States, as the craft unions associated with the American Federation of Labor (AFL) began to weaken, the impetus from industrial unions took centre stage with the organizing wave of the Congress of Industrial Organization (CIO). Breakthroughs in steel, auto, glass, rubber and other key industries reinvigorated the union movement through an avalanche of militant and successful strikes. During the organizing drives of the 1930s, hundreds of labour publications flourished, in large cities and small towns, catering to many different trades and in dozens of different languages. The names of these papers reflect the wide regional diversity of labour media: the *Seattle Union Record, Butte Daily Bulletin, Oklahoma Daily Leader, New York Call*. The labour press had its own press bureau, Federated Press, modeled after the Associated Press (De Caux 1970: 123). Federated Press had fulltime labour reporters in New York, Chicago and Washington, DC, and stringers in many other states and internationally as well.

The victory of the industrial labour movement by the end of the 1930s led to widespread recognition of labour unions and the signing of thousands of labour contracts between workers and industries. The hopes for labour prosperity faded quickly with the US entry into World War II, which brought hundreds of thousands of workers out of the plants and to the front, leaving a domestic labour force with wage freezes, shortages of parts and materials, entry into the labour force by lower-paid women and the reorientation of production towards the war effort. The national unity evoked by the war against fascism helped suspend the enmity between the working class and the industrialists in the quest for national unity and patriotism. At the end of World War II, a right-wing coalition of industrialists and politicians initiated the 'Cold' war and the extreme anti-communism and red-baiting that marked the 1950s, which marginalized and expelled many of the militant labour leaders who had fought to build an independent voice for workers.

Labour media initiatives on a mass scale disappeared or were marginalized substantially in the 1950s, due to the combination of McCarthyite repression, a growing consumer culture, and labour's 'great compromise' that relegated labour's role to service and contract enforcement and away from overt political participation. As the movement for labour's political independence began to recede, there was little interest in a strong public voice for the viewpoints of workers. This was especially pertinent in the United States, one of the only modern Western countries to not have a labour-oriented political party. With the class compromise taken by labour to focus solely on labour contracts and avoid direct involvement in the political realm, there was essentially no labour involvement in the extremely influential and rapidly developing medium of television that became the predominant communications medium in the post-war period. Yet, even with the demise of labour's independent media voice, labour's views were still represented in the mass media, with almost every major paper in the US assigned a labour writer focused on labour issues. This was no doubt due to the continuing clout of the labour unions, representing nearly 1 in every 3 workers, that led an unprecedented wave of strikes in the 1950s to increase wages which had fallen behind during the war effort. Today, there are no labour writers left at any major US media outlet even though mainstream newspapers devote a substantial amount of their print to covering the viewpoints and interests of business, which is uniformly hostile to labour unions.

Radicals and reformers grab the mic

During the industrial expansion of the US in the 1950s, labour played a generally conservative role, sharing in the industrial wealth of the US that rose during the post-war consumer economy, the rebuilding of shattered European nations in the aftermath of WWII and cold-war military spending. Beginning with the upheavals of the 1960s, and the rise of the anti-war and civil rights movements, radical groups emerged within the traditional labour movement to challenge an entrenched leadership and to move labour in a more radical direction. Many of these reformers came from the ranks of the anti-war movement, the radical veterans' movement and the black liberation movement. These groups often took as their first step the establishment of newsletters and newspapers by which to reach coworkers receptive to their ideas for independent labour action.

Dissident groups within labour unions have played a substantial role in building labour media. In the 1960s, the Dodge Revolutionary Union Movement, an African American auto workers group and forerunner of the League of Revolutionary Black Workers, developed around a newspaper, the *Inner City Voice*. The newspaper gave Black workers a platform to lead a struggle against the entrenched conservative leadership of the United Automobile Workers Union and the racist policies of the automobile industry in Detroit, Michigan. Reform movements in the Teamsters Union, the United Mine Workers, the Steelworkers and other large unions have at times developed a strong media presence in order to organize members to unite against union corruption or bureaucratic inaction. Independent cross-union voices from within the labour movement, such as *Labor Notes*, an influential labour newsletter based in Michigan, developed as important communications tools for union reformers and labour militants.

Within the mainstream institutions of unions, labour media is primarily relegated to the specific magazines and newsletters of each respective labour organization. In general, labour union media are not geared towards a national, general audience of workers but are internal, directed towards specific union memberships, their retirees and external allies. This is not to say that content is only relevant to the member of that particular labour union. Most labour publications do have a broad appeal, offering analysis on everything from the economy to environmentalism to foreign policy to sports, recipes and crossword puzzles. Labour union activists firmly believe that all working people are natural allies, and thus labour media actively addresses the concerns of all workers, organized or not. The particular role of labour media today though is to act as the official organ of the union leadership, and not to offer independent and wide-ranging opinions that would truly appeal to a wide audience of workers. For this reason, labour media is positioned in the margins of the public consciousness. It is an anomaly that labour media is considered a form of alternative, non-mainstream media in the United States, considering that working people make up the majority of the US population. For this reason, it would make sense that the voices and perspectives of workers would be well represented in media. But this is at present not the case.

The circulation of many union publications is not to be lightly dismissed however, as they often surpass that of large urban newspapers. *AFSCME Works*, for example, with a circulation of 1.7 million, is delivered to more people than the *New York Times*. The National Education Association publication, *NEA Today*, has a circulation of 2.7 million, higher than any US newspaper. *Solidarity*, the journal of the United Auto Workers, reaches over one million people, as do the *Teamster* and several other labour journals.

At times, union publications have taken on wider importance through their leading roles in social movements. *El Macriado*, the newspaper of the United Farm Workers Union under Cesar Chavez, could be seen far beyond the fields of California's central valley. The black eagle emblem built an audience in many urban areas, particularly in places with Spanish-speaking workers. The United Farm Workers Union also relied upon radio broadcasting generated by their sister organization, the National Farm Workers Service Center, which owned radio stations in farmworker towns in the Central Valley of California, Arizona and Washington. The United Electrical Workers (UE) newspaper, *UE News*, became influential during the 1960s, as the UE was one of the first unions to oppose the war in Vietnam. Similarly, the *Dispatcher*, voice of the West Coast International Longshore and Warehouse Union (ILWU), covered the anti-apartheid movement in South Africa closely, and helped US workers take labour action against the injustice of apartheid. The solidarity of the ILWU was praised by Nelson Mandela in a speech before thousands of longshore and other workers in Oakland, California, shortly after he was freed from prison.

Innovative unions do not limit themselves to print publications, and frequently use other forms of expression, including radio, video, posters, buttons, T-shirts and other means. Labour cartoonists such as Fred Wright from the UE and independent artist Gary Honapacki have developed audiences far beyond the labour press. Guerilla theatre, marches, demonstrations, sit-ins, picketing, billboarding, parades and other interventions into public space also serve as part of the arsenal at the disposal of labour. Actions that thrust the views of workers into the public realm have been very successful at breaking the barrier that often stands between mediated text, voice and image and the very real people that unions represent. Public intervention plays a critical role in making visible a workforce that is often invisible to many. Justice for Janitors, for example, brought thousands of custodial workers into downtown financial centers, raising public awareness of the vital role they play in maintaining centres of commerce. The United Farmworkers Union led thousands of strawberry pickers far from the remote agricultural fields and marched through downtown shopping areas to remind the public who picks their food. Typically, these communications interventions are initiated by established labour unions in a bid to secure traditional union recognition and labour contracts. New aggressive anti-labour tactics, however, have forced unions to forge different tactics under new economic and political conditions in the new global economy.

Since the 1970s, the great compromise that led to labour–industry collaboration has been under sustained attack by industry, through tactics as 'the southern strategy', the 'off-shore-ization' of capital or the global assembly line. The deindustrialization and flight of capital was accompanied by virulent attacks on the rights of workers, notably beginning with Ronald Reagan's attack on the Professional Air Traffic Controllers Organization (PATCO) union in 1981. These attacks spurred media initiatives from unions, primarily from union reform groups and social movement advocates that sought to reconnect to a broader working-class audience by adopting electronic media technologies into their communications strategies.

In the 1980s and 1990s, public access television provided labour focused television programmes to home cable audiences, such as *Labor Beat* in Chicago, Illinois, and *Labor Link TV* in San Diego, California. Union media proponents made attempts to extend labour media into the national television audience on more conventional broadcast platforms as well. One of the more successful attempts was *We Do the Work*, a labour television programme syndicated to Public Broadcasting Stations (PBS) nationwide, which was eventually discontinued due to lack of funding. Early internet activity, such as the online bulletin board service *Labournet* based at the Institute for Global Communications (IGC), began as an early form of computer-based social networking among labour activists, years before the popularity of the World Wide Web. Labour computer networks facilitated information sharing and concerted labour action among workers worldwide who were also strategizing against the onslaught of globalization. The growth of community radio and, more recently, low-power FM radio has contributed to radio programmes that cover labour issues, such as the *Workers Independent News Service* based in Wisconsin and *Democracy Now* based in New York City. Despite detractors' claims that unions are 'old-fashioned', technological innovation is not new to labour. Unions rely upon the latest media technologies to maintain memberships, share contract information, organize new workers and agitate for workers' rights. Many labour media advocates see a national media strategy as essential to building workers' political power beyond labour contracts and work conditions to address workers' issues like human rights, arts and culture, universal health care and political change.

The precariat and new media tools

Since the beginnings of the Industrial Revolution, workers have relied upon the concentration of their numbers in physical proximity and their ability to communicate in order to better their conditions of work. Today, many of these conditions have collapsed. The growth of precarious conditions of employment, characterized by part-time work, remote locations, outsourcing and non-standard shift changes, means that workers frequently lack the shared physical environment of earlier generations and the social interchange that went along with it. Added to this difficulty are the profound changes in media that offer far fewer platforms for broad public social interchange that has been so vital for building public consensus and civic conversation. What was once a mass media is now a multitude of splintered, demographically-atomized media, as daily newspapers and local television news have dwindled considerably. Vital communicative links that have been used for reaching a wide public have dissolved, creating a huge challenge for those who want to communicate with a broad spectrum of working people.

These changes have created enormous opportunities as well. New forms of media offer a more direct and unfiltered apparatus for communications. The ubiquity of cell phones and computers means that conversations can occur across borders and time zones, in metropolises as well as remote rural communities. The proliferation of such media can accommodate a greater democratic access to communications tools, allowing many people to be able to be message senders as well as receivers. The speed at which messages can be sent has also been a great boon, allowing instantaneous decision-making and logistic support. Labour organizations have been struggling with these new technologies and the new conditions they create. In many cases labour organizers have used them to great advantage, while others eschew them, considering them gimmicky and of not much use. Many believe that labour should pay greater attention to these tools and devote the necessary resources to share positive experiences, avoid fruitless ones and develop new applications and means of communications in order to combat the challenge labour faces in the new conditions of precarious work. Labour media activists remain convinced that workers' organizations should pool their many resources to create a national and daily source of media content that could bring labour's perspective to the national audience, noting that while the ranks of labour and the strength of labour solidarity have suffered in recent years, new social movements have had great success using communications and social media tools to build new solidarities based upon race and national origin, gender, sexual orientation and environmental concerns. Labour media advocates believe these tools can and should be used to accelerate advances in organizing the next stage of labour organization, not as an alternative to face-to-face organizing, but as a means to enhance the ability to bring workers together to confront the challenges that face them. For, at its heart, a labour organization is a communications system, a bond of solidarity forged by conversation, debate, discussion, commitment and agreement among workers that enable them to take collective action.

References

De Caux, L. (1970) *Labor Radical: From the Wobblies to the CIO*. Boston, MA: Beacon Press.

Downing, J. with Ford, T.V., Gil, G. and Stein, L. (2001) *Radical Media: Rebellious Communication and Social Movements*. London: Sage.

Dubofsky, M. (1969) *We Shall Be All: A History of the IWW*. New York: New York Times Book Company.

Dubofsky, M. and Dulles, F. D. (2004) *Labor in America: A History*. Wheeling, IL: Harlan Davidson.

McChesney, R. W. (1992) 'Labor and the Marketplace of Ideas: WCFL and the Battle for Labor Radio Broadcasting, 1927–1934'. *Journalism Monographs*, vol. 134, pp. 1–40.

Morais, H. M. and Cahn, W. (1948) *Gene Debs: The Story of a Fighting American*. New York: International Publishers.

Ross, S. J. (1998) *Working-Class Hollywood: Silent Film and the Shaping of Class in America*. Princeton, NJ: Princeton University Press.

12

DIGITAL ACTIVISM AND THE FUTURE OF WORKER RESISTANCE

Lina Dencik and Peter Wilkin

Much debate on the relationship between digital media and protest has focused on how digital technologies allow for activists to organize and mobilize in new and easier ways and at lower costs. The power of digital media is seen to lie in the spontaneous and unpredictable ways in which networks of protest and solidarity can emerge and subsequently disappear. These platforms have therefore become integral to how we understand contemporary forms of protest and resistance as activists and campaigners integrate digital media into broader practices of organizing and mobilizing. However, the main focus on digital media and protest has been on popular majoritarian uprisings and the emergence of 'new' protest movements in recent years, such as the Occupy movement, the Arab Spring and Gezi Park, that seem to introduce new dynamics and structures of protest that speak to more spontaneous, horizontal and user-driven forms of political activism that accompany the narratives of digital media platforms.

Much less attention and debate has concerned itself with long-standing institutions and infrastructures of resistance such as organized labour that have engaged with and utilized such digital media platforms for mobilizing and organizing workers in these times of protest. In this chapter, we will look at what we have learnt about digital media and activism from debates on these new protest movements and what this means for unions and the labour movement more broadly in terms of advancing worker resistance. We will start by situating the turn to digital activism in the labour movement in the context of the failures of the corporatist model and a decline in union membership, particularly in Western democracies. We will then move on to consider some of the opportunities and challenges of turning to digital activism for protecting and advancing workers' interests, focusing particularly on issues of hierarchical union structures, the decline of labour power, and the precarity of work and organized political forms. We will end by pointing to some future trajectories that may be increasingly relevant for worker resistance in a digital age.

The decline of the labour movement

In many respects, the twenty-first century represents an important juncture for the labour movement globally as it faces a series of fundamental questions about its future. There is a widespread recognition within the established labour movement that unions are struggling to make themselves relevant, with a decline in membership and influence in many of the core countries in the world-system. At the same time grassroots and worker-led union initiatives are beginning to make themselves heard in significant parts of the semi-periphery including, most important, China (Butollo & ten Brink 2012). In parallel to that, the successes that the labour movement were able to gain in Europe and North America in particular, but also in a number of other states, from the corporatist model with unions building alliances and partnership with political parties and businesses, has been in retreat since the later 1970s with the ascendancy of neoliberalism as a global social and political ideology. Although the embrace of neoliberal ideas has been uneven and complex, the driving principles of liberalized trade, privatization and deregulation of the economy have nonetheless been adopted by national governments and international organizations as a new global common sense (Peck & Tickell 1994). The consequences have been stark, as the economist Michael Hudson trenchantly notes: a redistribution of wealth from the 99 per cent to the 1 per cent (Hudson 2012, 2015).

Digital transformations in the economy, in conjunction with the broad shift to neoliberal ideology across Western democracies and beyond, have seen the rise of a corporatization of politics and a seizing of the state, particularly by the financial sector, which has unsurprisingly led to attacks upon workers' rights and conditions (Hudson 2015). To be clear, the turn to corporatism within the labour movement has to be understood as the expression of class compromises in the world-system, especially, over a particular and limited period of time. It was seen by its proponents as a means of managing the regular crises of growth and depression that capitalism generates. That elite consensus, always contingent and temporary, has now gone, and any gains made by labour, unevenly distributed and insecurely entrenched, have been up for confiscation since the 1980s. One consequence of this can be seen in the recently established Global Rights Index created by the International Trade Union confederation to rank countries in terms of how well they protect employment rights: of the 139 countries surveyed, only Denmark was found to honour all 97 fundamental aspects of employment rights as grounded in international human rights law (Wearing 2014).

The changes within corporations and the state that have, in combination, often come to suppress attempts at organizing workers, have sparked numerous debates within the labour movement about its future and how it can find renewed relevance in the twenty-first century. In many of the post-communist societies, where independent trade unions have struggled to emerge and escape the embrace of the old Communist Party legacy, there has been a hope for forms of 'social partnership' that are often seen as intrinsic to the development of the EU (Ost 2006; Wilkin 2016). As should be clear though, even the strongest states in the EU, such as Germany where workers have various forms of representation on company boards, have retreated from previous corporatist commitments. Similar developments are spreading now across the political discourse of France and other countries that have been more resistant to neoliberal ideas.

So, what are the consequences of this for labour? Some have argued that this is the greatest moment of experimentation in the history of organized labour. We are seeing, for example, a recognition that the nature of work, and what constitutes a worker, has changed to an extent to which making the workplace the primary focus for organizing worker resistance may no longer be the most effective. Rather, unions have had to recognize that global capitalism requires a global labour movement; that meaningful organizing might take place outside of the workplace and within communities; and that unions need to work in solidarity and alongside other pertinent social movements and actors, and be an active voice in articulating an alternative vision for society, a political imaginary, and shaping a social justice agenda (Dencik & Wilkin 2015). This also means potentially moving away from the relationship with established political parties and businesses. Digital media and the changing protest culture plays an important role in all of these debates. The development of new protest cultures evidenced with uprisings around the world in recent years that are said to have a central role for social media in particular are significant for how labour movements have moved forward. One of the most noticeable divisions raised by these digital protests has been how absent or slow the established labour movement has been to recognize that they share similar concerns about establishing a decent quality of life for all. Despite its much vaunted solidarity and internationalism, the labour movement has been far less flexible and dynamic in responding to these movements.

Can digital activism fix it?

Historically, unions have been slow adapters to the internet (Lee 2013). Digital media practices within unions are marked by a long-term and entrenched culture that is not immediately receptive to a digital environment. Indeed, the appropriation of media technologies by unions and worker organizations has been diverse, multi-faceted and certainly not consensual. Attitudes and perceptions of the use of digital media amongst labour activists and union officials are often conflicting and contradictory, partly due to the contradictory nature of these technologies in themselves. The early adaptations to computer-mediated communications by trade unions were primarily concerned with improving communications between trade unionists, creating networks of exchange across borders and boundaries in various incarnations of 'labournets' (Lee 1997). These early adoptions of the internet became increasingly oriented towards establishing new forms of 'internationalism' that developed relatively quickly into discussions about the potential for a 'global labournet' (Lee 1997). Although the technological infrastructure was there, developing a global communications network for the labour movement was never going to be a straightforward process. Waterman (1984, 1992) has written about the failure of unions to advance such a project in those early stages and argues that it had to do with ignorance or hostility towards the new technology, organizational conservatism and a conscious or unconscious strategy of informational deprivation (or limitation) as a membership control device. These themes are still prevalent today and there has been a continued concern with using digital technologies within a framework of centralized control and organizational status quo. This has meant a prevalent focus on the internal dynamics of the labour movement and how to deliver existing services more efficiently without challenging hierarchical structures or threatening union leadership (Fitzgerald, Hardy & Lucio 2012; Drew 2013).

Despite the limited advances in the democratization of unions and the prevalence of centralized control, developments of new communication technologies did from the outset lend themselves to new possibilities for grassroots solidarity and collective activism that frequently by-passed established international trade union bodies and other usual channels of co-ordination. We saw early signs of this in the 'anti-globalization' movement or 'global justice movement' (della Porta 2007) that descended on the streets of Seattle for the World Trade Organization conference in 1999 (Wilkin 2000). These events demonstrated some of the innovative uses that digital media technologies afforded resistance movements. In particular, activists could communicate, collaborate and demonstrate in new ways by aggregating small contributions into a broader movement (Van Aelst & Walgrave 2004). New alliances between labour organizations and new social movements and nongovernmental organizations were built in response to the onslaught of neoliberal restructuring programmes and free trade agreements. It illustrated the possibilities of a reinvigorated movement of workers in solidarity with other progressive sectors of civil society, not historically linked with organized labour.

The problem here has been, as advanced by the more libertarian wing of the labour movement, that there is a fundamental conflict of interest between union leadership and its rank and file or grassroots (Mills and Schneider 1948; Fitch 2006). As unions evolved over the course of the twentieth century they tended to eschew anti-capitalist ideas other than for rhetorical purposes, choosing instead to become elite-led institutions that sought to become a normal part of the political structure of their societies. This generated many important gains for the membership, but at the expense of diminishing grassroots activity and autonomy, de-fanging the union and, worse still, seeing the union become a business whose job was 'representing' its members rather than seeing the union run by its members. This shift to what can be described as more authoritarian union structures is crucial in explaining one aspect of the decline of unionism, alongside the dismantling of union legal rights by states adopting anti-union neoliberal policies. This compromise ultimately served to undermine unions' ability to resist neoliberal policies as they lacked the legitimate support and activity on the part of their members that they needed in order to offer a different vision of a good society.

In recent years there has been a particular focus on the need for the labour movement to engage with broader visions of society as the nature of work and the possibilities for organizing workers have undergone significant transformations. Digital media have come to occupy an important place in this debate in conjunction with the broader structural changes of the economy and labour market. In particular, the move to consider organizing workers outside the workplace and outside of collective bargaining agreements has gained increased significance in light of developments in social media and recent popular uprisings. Initiatives such as US-based unions AFL-CIO's *Working America* and SEIU's *Fight for a Fair Economy* set out to describe a revised, more flexible vision of how to mobilize low-income workers who cannot get union recognition in their workplace. With a significant increase in low-wage insecure labour, unions have actively been considering how to build more flexible types of membership that are focused on community affiliation and communicated at home – online – rather than the workplace. This has meant an increased focus on community organizing and a concerted effort to broaden mobilizing strategies and tactics.

An important caveat here is that both the above initiatives do nothing to transcend the fundamental problems of nationalism and elite-led unionism that have divided workers effectively since the nineteenth century. They are, rather, reassertions of a nationalist form of unionism which, in this case, and following the rhetoric of former SEIU leader Andy Stern, aim to make 'America great again' (Stern 2006). It is difficult to see how a union movement can renew itself by committing to the same strategies that have failed it in times which were far more sympathetic to such appeals. Nationalism remains the greatest dividing factor for leftist social movements, including trade unions, but an adequate response to it cannot be built by simply reasserting its primacy as the basis for a renewed labour movement. Which is why the emergence of new local and global protest movements with much less clearly defined forms of *national* identity is a particularly important development today.

However, the labour movement's engagement with the new protest culture and digital activism is complex and contradictory. New forms of labour organizations that challenge traditional corporatist models of trade unionism are certainly emerging. Social movements such as Occupy have been part of a move towards society-based labour organizations that target broad economic issues, such as income inequality and the call for a living or citizen's wage. We have also seen the rise of occupation-based or immigrant community-centred labour organizations such as worker centers and alliances. In the UK and the US, for example, alliances made up of janitors or cleaners that aim to support low-wage workers mostly from immigrant communities have become a significant force. In the US, we are also increasingly seeing employer-based labour organizations that are formed to deal with individual employers – such as OURWalmart or the Starbucks Workers Union – often seeking to be independent unions, illustrating ways in which workers can exert influence on employers to improve working conditions outside of collective bargaining agreements (Dencik & Wilkin 2015). The labour movement is being shaped by these new forms of organization and is moving in a direction that might increasingly try and take advantage of new forms of communication and digital media at a pivotal moment of social experimentation in worker representation (Freeman 2013).

Digital activism has been said to offer new ways of organizing and practising dissent that can overcome some of the obstacles that have traditionally marked social movements and political organizations. In particular, developments in digital media platforms have been seen to allow for more spontaneous, more horizontal and more majoritarian protests and movements to emerge, which were particularly highlighted in the wave of uprisings that began in early 2011 with the Arab Spring (Bennett & Segerberg 2012; Castells 2012; Mason 2012). The Arab Spring itself was foregrounded by widespread labour protests in Egypt that paved the way for the subsequent overthrow of the Mubarak regime (Del Panta 2016). In some instances, digital activism has also been considered to provide a broader repertoire of resistance to groups who might otherwise lack resources such as precarious and low-wage workers (cf. Mattoni 2012). Scholars like Richard Freeman have argued that the spread of low-cost digital communication tools gives labour activists inexpensive ways to mobilize, organize demonstrations and campaigns, and connect workers outside of the workplace. It also takes power and control away from union hierarchies and places it in the hands of the grassroots workers (2013). Analyses of worker organizations such as OURWalmart, that have actively sought to transform the nature and purpose of the labour movement by stepping outside mainstream union frameworks and tactics with more emphasis on direct action and reputational damage, have given a prominent role to digital media (Wood 2015). Similarly, the Fight for 15 campaign that initially focused on fast food workers in the United States deliberately incorporated tactics often associated with digitally-enabled networks of protest, making use of one-day 'flash-strikes' and rallies that could be amplified and widely distributed via social media, despite a relatively small base of organized fast food workers (Dencik & Wilkin 2015). In this sense, digital activism can exercise forms of symbolic power as a way to advance worker resistance in contexts where industrial and labour power might otherwise be difficult to leverage (Wood 2015).

However, debates on social media and new protest movements have also highlighted some concerns with regards to digital activism that also permeate parts of the labour movement. This is not just about questions of control or keeping hierarchical structures in place, as is often the accusation towards unions and their hesitance towards adopting new technologies. Research has questioned the notion of spontaneous and horizontal protest movements emerging through digital activism, highlighting both the importance of historical and political context (e.g. Porto & Brant 2015; Curran, Fenton & Freedman 2016) as well as the importance of leaders (Gerbaudo 2012) and a rooted sense of collective identity (Treré 2015a). Moreover, the use of digital media platforms might be counter-conducive to forms of activism by placing an onus on visibility as the central tenet of participation and belonging (Milan 2015), speeding up the life-cycle of campaigns and pressuring activists into a rhythm of continuous production of content without the time necessary for democratic and participatory decision-making around a common political project (Barassi 2015; Kaun 2015), and also of putting activists at heightened risk by pushing activity onto easily monitored corporate platforms over which they have no control (Hintz 2015; Leistert 2015). These aspects of much contemporary digital activism can undermine efforts to build long-term sustainable social movements with coherent agendas and can come to create divisions, tensions and paranoia within activist groups as they negotiate the prominent place of digital infrastructures in their practices (Treré 2015b).

Such concerns come to have particular relevance in organized political forms such as labour unions. At the same time as distributed networks of communication, as advanced by digital activism, challenge the hierarchical structures of many mainstream unions and encourage a potentially more democratic form of mobilization, there is simultaneously a question with regards to the sustainability of digitally-enabled protest that thrives on the dismantling of political organization as traditionally understood. Indeed, notions of 'connective action' (Bennett & Segerberg 2012), popular as an alternative to the more common understanding of movement practices in terms of collective action, posit that digital media overcome the shackles of organizational dilemmas, as movements become based on weak-tie networks, do not require strong organizational control or the construction of collective identities, but are nevertheless able to react effectively to given opportunities (Haunss 2015).

For the labour movement, this provides moments of mobilization and pressure that can prove to be very effective; but there are simultaneously concerns about a turn to digital activism and a growing focus on public image and symbolic power at the expense of organization and a sustained base of worker empowerment to advance their own interests (Dencik & Wilkin 2015). The transient nature of 'connective action' is actually very much in keeping with neoliberal ideas about the changing nature of subjectivity, and might generate a temporary and limited form of protest which seems unlikely to generate the transformation of global order that the urgent problems of the twenty-first century (climate change, nuclear war, global poverty) demand. The labour movement, in this context, risks becoming a pressure group like any other. As Taylor (2016) has argued, there has been a turn away from organizing in favour of activism, yet organizing is what the left must cultivate to make its activism more durable and effective, to sustain and advance causes 'when the galvanizing intensity of occupations or street protests subsides'.

The future of worker resistance

How, then, might the labour movement engage with digital media and find renewed relevance? The protest culture of recent years has presented unions with both significant opportunities as well as key challenges. Some unions have been able to engage with an environment more geared towards direct action and straight confrontation by minimizing the 'institutional baggage' of unions and downplaying their presence in campaigns with a stronger emphasis on digital media and the 'spontaneous' uprising of workers (Dencik 2015). However, there has been a continued struggle to overturn the established model of business unionism and to incorporate digital technologies as part of a broader transformation in the hierarchical structures of organization that continue to dominate the labour movement. This has limited the potential for a comprehensive labour engagement with the digital environment. In particular, developments in digital infrastructures have predominantly been approached as communication questions, viewing digital media platforms as an extension of communication and public relations strategies (Dencik & Wilkin 2015). As mentioned above, this has sidelined organization as a key focus in favour of public image and media attention. More broadly, it has stifled a more critical negotiation with the implications of digital technologies from a labour perspective that also engages with the exploitative nature of these technologies in the wider context of the global political economy.

Whilst there has been a recognition that the nature of work is changing, unions, and mainstream unions in particular, have been slow at appreciating the role of digital media in such transformations. The use of these technologies in extending control over workers, extracting labour value and developing business models largely based on suppressed labour costs presents a core challenge to the future of the labour movement and the ability to protect workers' interests long-term.

Digital labour takes on many different forms in the contemporary economy and relates to not only data collection of online users but to algorithmic management structures and the broader growth of a gig economy based on platform capitalism (Scholz 2016). These developments fundamentally defy central tenets of the labour movement that were established during the twentieth century and question the possibilities for labour power to be mobilized through traditional trade unionism, let alone be leveraged through traditional channels whether that be in trade disputes with management or via national legislative frameworks (Graham, Wood & Lehdonvirta 2016).

This speaks to the need for the labour movement to shift engagement with digital media as part of a much broader transformation in how workers' interests should be protected and advanced long-term. No longer based around collective bargaining, securing contracts or partnering with political parties, worker resistance is being advanced through other forms that can find more relevance in an increasingly digitized political economy that overwhelmingly favours corporate interests. Social movement and community unionisms, whilst not new, have found new relevance and strength in their willingness to go beyond the workplace to build powerful alliances with communities, non-governmental organizations and the international labour movement in pursuit of their goals, building new networks of solidarity (Dencik & Wilkin 2015). Moreover, it has been the independent, networked and worker-driven self-organizing unions that have so far sought to rise to the challenge of platform capitalism (e.g. IWGB organizing Deliveroo couriers in the UK) (Woodcock 2017). This has been accompanied by a wider debate on the role of unions in advancing an alternative model to platform capitalism in the form of 'platform cooperativism' that incorporates digital technologies as part of a worker-owned organizational structure (Scholz 2016).

Such initiatives challenge the labour movement to consider its role in society and what part unions can have in articulating alternative social visions as part of a broader alliance. The key for the labour movement is how it can take what is good, useful and democratic about the new digital technologies and use them in ways that help to build a genuinely grassroots and independent union movement. At the same time, there is a need for the labour movement to be wary of the transient nature of many of these activities, to recognize that a *moment* does not in itself become a *movement* for change without something more enduring underpinning it. Clearly there are multiple narratives about a good or post-capitalist society being generated by anti-capitalist movements across the world-system; and for a twenty-first century left to succeed, it needs to be building upon these to create a vision that can both mobilize and win the support of people globally and locally. At present, the labour movement, like the left in general, appears in retreat as we witness far-right and nationalist parties taking power in many parts of the world, from the US to India. For the far-right, the goal is easier: take power, seize the state, impose order upon populations (starting almost inevitably with the labour movement – anyone who thinks that labour movements are irrelevant should have to explain why it is the case that the first thing the right always does is attack them). For the left, the goal is more difficult and the means for achieving it are integral to constructing a better society. Patterns of poverty, inequality, under- and unemployment show that there is a mass of discontent across the world-system for the labour movement to mobilize and engage with as part of a broader social movement. The extent to which this can be achieved will be perhaps the defining moment for the left in the twenty-first century.

References

Barassi, V. (2015) 'Social Media, Immediacy and the Time for Democracy: Critical Reflections on Social Media as "Temporalizing Practices"', in L. Dencik and O. Leistert (eds) *Critical Perspectives on Social Media and Protest: Between Control and Emancipation*. London: Rowman & Littlefield International, pp. 73–88.

Bennett, W. L. and Segerberg, A. (2012) 'The Logic of Connective Action: Digital Media and the Personalization of Contentious Politics', *Information, Communication & Society*, vol. 15, no. 5, pp. 739–68.

Butollo, F. and ten Brink, T. (2012) 'Challenging the Atomization of Discontent: Patterns of Migrant-worker Protest in China during the Series of Strikes in 2010', *Critical Asian Studies*, vol. 44, no. 3, pp. 419–40.

Castells, M. (2012) *Networks of Outrage and Hope: Social Movements in the Internet Age*. Cambridge: Polity Press.

Curran, J., Fenton, N. and Freedman, D. (2016) *Misunderstanding the Internet* (second edition). London and New York: Routledge.

Del Panta, G. (2016) 'Labour Movements and the Arab Uprisings', working paper. http://www.sisp.it/docs/convegno2016/203_sisp2016_partecipazione-movimenti-sociali.pdf, accessed 5 May 2017.

della Porta, D. (2007) *The Global Justice Movement: Cross-national and Transnational Perspectives*. Boulder, CO: Paradigm.

Dencik, L. (2015) 'Social Media and the "New Authenticity" of Protest', in L. Dencik and O. Leistert (eds) *Critical Perspectives on Social Media and Protest: Between Control and Emancipation*. London: Rowman & Littlefield International, pp. 203–18.

Dencik, L. and Wilkin, P. (2015) *Worker Resistance and Media: Challenging Global Corporate Power in the 21st Century*. New York: Peter Lang.

Drew, J. (2013) *A Social History of Contemporary Democratic Media*. New York and London: Routledge.

Fitch, R. (2006) *Solidarity for Sale: How Corruption Destroyed the Labor Movement and Undermined America's Promise*. New York: PublicAffairs.

Fitzgerald, I., Hardy, J., and Lucio, M. (2012) 'The Internet, Employment and Polish Migrant Workers: Communication, Activism and Competition in the New Organisational Spaces', *New Technology, Work and Employment*, vol. 27, no. 2, pp. 93–105.

Freeman, R. B. (2013) 'What, If Anything, Can Labor Do to Rejuvenate Itself and Improve Worker Well-being in an Era of Inequality and Crisis-driven Austerity?', *Perspektiven der Wirtschaftspolitik*, vol. 14, nos. 1–2, pp. 41–56.

Gerbaudo, P. (2012) *Tweets and the Streets: Social Media and Contemporary Activism*. London: Pluto Press.

Graham, M., Wood, A. and Lehdonvirta, V. (2016) 'Digital Labour and Development: New Knowledge Economies or Digital Sweatshops', Paper presented at *Platform Cooperativism: Building the Cooperative Internet*. New School, New York, 11 November.

Haunss, S. (2015) 'Promise and Practice in Studies of Social Media and Movements', in L. Dencik and O. Leistert (eds) *Critical Perspectives on Social Media and Protest: Between Control and Emancipation*. London: Rowman & Littlefield International, pp. 13–33.

Hintz, A. (2015) 'Social Media Censorship, Privatized Regulation and New Restrictions to Protest and Dissent', in L. Dencik and O. Leistert (eds) *Critical Perspectives on Social Media and Protest: Between Control and Emancipation*. London: Rowman & Littlefield International, pp. 109–26.

Hudson, M. (2012) *The Bubble and Beyond: Fictitious Capital, Debt Deflation and the Global Crisis*. Dresden: Islet.

Hudson, M. (2015) *Killing the Host: How Financial Parasites and Debt Destroy the Global Economy*. Petrolia, CA: Counterpunch Books.

Kaun, A. (2015) '"This Space Belongs to Us!": Protest Spaces in Times of Accelerating Capitalism', in L. Dencik and O. Leistert (eds) *Critical Perspectives on Social Media and Protest: Between Control and Emancipation*. London: Rowman & Littlefield International, pp. 89–107.

Lee, E. (1997) *The Labour Movement and the Internet: The New Internationalism*. London: Pluto Press.

Lee, E. (2013) Personal interview. 16 December.

Leistert, O. (2015) 'The Revolution Will Not Be Liked: On the Systemic Constraints of Corporate Social Media Platforms for Protests', in L. Dencik and O. Leistert (eds) *Critical Perspectives on Social Media and Protest: Between Control and Emancipation*. London: Rowman & Littlefield International, pp. 35–52.

Mason, P. (2012) *Why It's Kicking Off Everywhere: The New Global Revolutions*. London and Brooklyn, NY: Verso.

Mattoni, A. (2012) *Media Practices and Protest Politics: How Precarious Workers Mobilise*. Farnham, UK and Burlington, VT: Ashgate.

Milan, S. (2015) 'Mobilizing in Times of Social Media: From a Politics of Identity to a Politics of Visibility', in L. Dencik and O. Leistert (eds) *Critical Perspectives on Social Media and Protest: Between Control and Emancipation*. London: Rowman & Littlefield International, pp. 53–71.

Mills, C. W. and Schneider, H. (1948) *The New Men of Power*. New York: Harcourt, Brace, pp. 6–9.

Ost, D. (2006) *The Defeat of Solidarity: Anger and Politics in Postcommunist Europe*. Ithaca, NY: Cornell University Press.

Peck, J. and Tickell, A. (1994) 'Jungle Law Breaks Out: Neoliberalism and Global-local Disorder', *Area*, vol. 26, no. 4, pp. 317–26.

Porto, M. P. and Brant, J. (2015) 'Social Media and the 2013 Protests in Brazil: The Contradictory Nature of Political Mobilization in the Digital Era', in L. Dencik and O. Leistert (eds) *Critical Perspectives on Social Media and Protest: Between Control and Emancipation*. London: Rowman & Littlefield International, pp. 181–200.

Scholz, T. (2016) *Uberworked and Underpaid: How Workers Are Disrupting the Digital Economy*. Cambridge, UK and Malden, MA: Polity.

Stern, A. (2006) *A Country that Works: Getting America Back on Track*. New York: Simon and Schuster.

Taylor, A. (2016) 'Against Activism', *The Baffler*, no. 30, https://thebaffler.com/salvos/against-activism, accessed 5 May 2017.

Treré, E. (2015a) 'Reclaiming, Proclaiming, and Maintaining Collective Identity in the #YoSoy132 Movement in Mexico: An Examination of Digital Frontstage and Backstage Activism through Social Media and Instant Messaging Platforms', *Information, Communication & Society*, vol. 18, no. 8, pp. 901–915.

Treré, E. (2015b) 'The Struggle Within: Discord, Conflict and Paranoia in Social Media Protest', in L. Dencik and O. Leistert (eds) *Critical Perspectives on Social Media and Protest: Between Control and Emancipation*. London: Rowman & Littlefield International, pp. 163–80.

Van Aelst, P. and Walgrave, S. (2004) 'New Media, New Movements? The Role of the Internet in Shaping the "Anti-globalization" Movement', in W. van de Donk *et al.* (eds) *Cyberprotest: New Media, Citizens, and Social Movements*. New York: Routledge, pp. 97–122.

Waterman, P. (1984) 'Needed: A New Communications Model for a New Working Class Internationalism', in P. Waterman (ed.) *For a New Labour Internationalism: A Set of Reprints and Working Papers*. The Hague, the Netherlands: International Labour, Education, Research and Information Foundation, pp. 233–55.

Waterman, P. (1992) 'International Labour Communication by Computer: The Fifth International?', working paper, no. 129. The Hague, the Netherlands: Institute of Social Studies.

Wearing, D. (2014) 'Where's the Worst Place to be a Worker? Most of the World', *Guardian*, 22 May, http://www.theguardian.com/commentisfree/2014/may/22/worker-world-index-employment-rights-inequality, accessed 5 May 2017.

Wilkin, P. (2000) 'Solidarity in a Global Age – Seattle and Beyond', *Journal of World-Systems Research*, vol. 6, no. 1, pp. 19–64.

Wilkin, P. (2016) *Hungary and the Crisis of Democracy*. Lanham, MD: Lexington Books.

Wood, A. J. (2015) 'Networks of Injustice and Worker Mobilization at Walmart', *Industrial Relations Journal*, vol. 46, no. 4, pp. 259–74.

Woodcock, J. (2017) 'Automate This! Delivering Resistance in the Gig Economy', *Mute*, 10 March, http://www.metamute.org/editorial/articles/automate-delivering-resistance-gig-economy, accessed 5 May 2017.

13

FORMING PUBLICS

Alternative media and activist cultural practices

Ricarda Drüeke and Elke Zobl

Introduction

Media and cultural practices represent a central component of civil society engagement. These practices intervene in the process of meaning production and form publics that can promote social and cultural change. Alternative media and participatory cultural practices are of seminal importance to the production of critical publics. In recent decades, social movement and communication scholars have offered a range of conceptual frameworks to define the different purposes, processes and contents of alternative media. Studies on alternative media have increasingly focused on the use of digital media and the development of new modes of expression, communication and networking. While they mainly examine the micro-level of practices of media production and activism, the focus of our contribution is on the relationship between alternative media and the multiplicity of publics.

In this chapter, we advocate an approach embedding alternative media into public sphere theory. This makes it possible to consider multiplicity, interweaving with daily life, power dynamics, rhizomatic interactions and networks, and civil society. Activist cultural practices, which take place in the context of a do-it-yourself (DIY) culture, play an important role in these processes. These include such diverse practices as zine making, producing blogs and hashtags, community radio and TV, and culture jamming.

In what follows, we carve out an understanding of alternative media and cultural practices that engage in and enable activism within the public sphere. We are interested in investigating the question of what kinds of publics are created in and through alternative media and cultural activism that go beyond a dichotomous understanding of alternative and mainstream media. We demonstrate how publics can be formed by various practices of activism. In what follows, we first consider the theoretical models that attempt to make sense of the specificity and complexity of alternative media production. Secondly, we point to several theoretical references that argue for a diversity of publics to emphasize how the public sphere can be perceived as a site where social meaning is generated, circulated, and contested. Thirdly, we exemplify this through alternative media and cultural production practices in feminist protest articulations and from transnational feminist movements. Finally, we discuss how these forms of activism and protest create and shape various publics.

Understanding the diversity and specificity of alternative media

Alternative media is often seen in a problematic dichotomous and binary opposition to mainstream mass media. Various media theorists have gone beyond such an understanding to consider the context, consequences, processes and relational aspects of alternative media forms (see Gunnarsson Payne 2009). They have developed a range of models, typologies and frameworks to analyze alternative and activist media and cultural practices that take account of their diversity, fluidity, contingency and process-oriented openness (Rodríguez 2001; Atton 2002; Bailey, Cammaerts & Carpentier 2008; Lievrouw 2011; Zobl & Reitsamer 2012).

Clemencia Rodríguez (2001), for example, attempts to break the binary thinking of alternative versus mainstream media by suggesting the concept of 'citizens' media'. She builds on radical democratic theory and links alternative media to civil society. She argues for recognizing the local, small-scale ways that these highly heterogeneous media foster and propagate democracy and social change: 'I suggest redirecting our focus to understanding how citizens' media activate subtle processes of fracture in the social, cultural and power spheres of everyday life' (ibid.: xiv). Rodríguez further argues for paying attention to power relationships within media-producing communities, which are being permanently re-constituted, and maintains that: 'citizens' media are rupturing pre-established power structures, opening spaces that allow for new social identities and new cultural definitions, and, in a word, generating power on the side of the subordinate' (ibid.: 160). While the concept of citizens' media carries with it problematic notions of nation-state-based understandings of citizenship, Rodríguez's concept of citizens' media allows us to pay attention to the constantly renegotiated power relationships and structures interwoven into everyday life that constitute the public sphere.

Similarly, Olga Buedes Bailey, Bart Cammaerts and Nico Carpentier (2008) try to overcome the limitations of mono-theoretical approaches in presenting a panoptic and multi-faceted model of the diversity and specificity of alternative media by laying out and combining four different approaches. They argue: '[A]lternative media should be seen as a multiplicity of public spaces, a [...] myriad of media initiatives as diversified as society itself' (ibid.: 153). Taking Ernesto Laclau and Chantal Mouffe's political identity theory as an overarching framework in order to move away from essentialist approaches, they identify two media-centred approaches to alternative media, namely 'serving the community' and 'an alternative to mainstream', as well as two society-centred approaches, namely 'linking alternative media to civil society' and 'alternative media as rhizome'. While advocating a 'simultaneous application of these approaches' (ibid.: 30), Bailey, Cammaerts and Carpentier see a threefold advantage for using the rhizome metaphor in particular to make sense of alternative media: with its focus on society and democracy, it moves away from many media-centric theories; it strengthens the civil society approach; and it allows the antagonistic positions towards mainstream media as well as towards the market and the state as such to be overcome. We also see the strength of the rhizomatic approach in its focus on the agonistic and interconnecting aspects of media in the public sphere in relation to networks and professional and amateur practices.

The features and functions of alternative media illustrate the role that alternative media can play in the production of the public sphere. What these models do not offer is a deeper understanding of the kind of discursive space alternative media create and negotiate in the public sphere, and the role they play within it, which we would like to explore.

The formation of publics

A growing body of literature is concerned with the processes by which publics are constituted and mobilized for political activism and struggles. Various scholars have pointed out that publics are always and simultaneously constituted through and around political and cultural discourses, and that publics vary in their orientation, intention and scale of address (e.g. Hermes 2006; Couldry 2006; Klaus & Lünenborg 2012).

The prospect of various publics contradicts the original Habermasian idea of a relatively homogeneous public sphere (Habermas 1991). Asen and Brouwer (2001: 6) suggest a reconceptualization of the public sphere as a 'multiplicity of dialectically related public spheres rather than a single, encompassing arena of discourse'. Fraser (1992), in particular, points out that, regardless of their participation in discursive processes, social movements and counterpublics are not included in the liberal model of the public sphere. In contrast to Habermas, she assumes that there is not only a hegemonic public sphere, but also numerous counterpublics or subaltern publics that shape the public sphere. Rather than rational discourse, the articulation of the experiences of various social groups is at the centre of communication processes and can therefore make subject-positions visible in discursive processes (Scott 1991). Klaus (2006) defines the public sphere as a process of social negotiation whereby the norms and values of a society are produced and reproduced. In her view, publics vary in scale and scope based on the complexity of the communication forums that are involved in shaping the social negotiation processes. From there, she differentiates between simple, intermediate and complex publics, each of which has its own communication forms and forums. These three layers are not without crossover, but rather present ideal-typical descriptions of the public process. Negotiations in various publics are not necessarily oriented on consensus. Mouffe (2005) refers to the agonistic character of the public sphere, which also includes conflicts. In this perspective, power relations are recognized as basic components of democratic societies, but the permanent agonism between social positions is stressed. Agonistic forms of communication are thus found between various publics, but also within publics.

All of the aforementioned models draw on the assumption of a co-existence of different publics. Rather, the public sphere is perceived as a site where social meaning is generated, circulated and contested. Just as in the concepts of alternative media, it is important not to think in binaries, that is, not merely to distinguish between a hegemonic public and a counterpublic, but to emphasize the diversity of publics. Simple publics and practices of everyday life are considered political and part of civil society. Alternative media are also a part of publics and can establish connections in and between different publics through their rhizomatic character. Digital publics such as Twitter or blogs can be characterized as everyday publics where individuals are organized in social sub-groups and interact spontaneously. Einspänner-Pflock, Anastasiadis, and Thimm (2016) also discuss so-called mini-publics – which, after Klaus, we call simple or everyday publics – that evolve on media platforms like Facebook or YouTube and are based on the media logics of the digital environment. These everyday publics vary according to their origin and temporality. They offer specific affordances for engagement (such as cross-referencing) and make the distribution of opinions and participation more convenient. They have become an important space not only for the self-understanding of society, but also for political action and power struggles. Taking these considerations as our theoretical basis, we elaborate how alternative media and activist cultural practices are an integral part of social negotiation processes and how they form various publics.

Feminist media and cultural practices in the context of DIY culture

Feminist activists use alternative media and cultural practices to express political positions, to construct identities and to create publics that are strongly interwoven into everyday life. In what follows, we explore the role of feminist zines and online activism in the construction of alternative meanings by drawing on the aforementioned theoretical models. As short case studies, we present feminist activism expressing itself through zines as well as blogs and hashtags. In the context of feminism, a lively cultural activism based on doing-it-yourself (Chidgey 2014) has developed, whereby cultural and media production is fused with activism and the boundaries between organizer, participant and audience are blurred.

Feminist zines

An integral part of a lively DIY culture are zines – ephemeral, self-published magazines (Duncombe 1997). Zines are used for feminist networking and critical reflection by zine makers in different parts of the world, as evidenced by a vibrant transnational network of feminist zinesters and grassroots projects (Schilt & Zobl 2008; Zobl 2009; Zobl & Drüeke 2012; Zobl & Reitsamer 2014). It is important to recognize that feminist zines are embedded in rich histories and are as heterogeneous in form, content and quality as they are in their contexts, producers and motivations. They have emerged out of the alternative press of the feminist movement and stand in interrelation to other artistic, social and political movements. During the 1990s, electronic zines emerged, often serving as resource and network sites, while blogs are predominant today. Although the internet has made zine production and distribution easier and cheaper, many continue to produce paper zines, both to acknowledge the digital divide and out of appreciation for their physical quality and creative possibilities.

Zine makers turn to self-publishing for a variety of reasons, but one of the main reasons is to create an oppositional history and an alternative to the narrow and distorted representation of women, queer and transgender people in the mainstream in order to reflect and resist their cultural devaluation (Schilt 2003). Overall, zines and the transnational network – however dispersed and sometimes contradictory – provide a public forum where people can experiment with ideas, express themselves and describe experiences otherwise suppressed by mainstream society (Duncombe 1997: 176ff).

Zine makers lay open and document their first-hand personal experiences, thoughts and concerns, and cover just about anything that interests them in their daily lives – from personal issues to political discussions, including music, pop culture, politics, sexuality and women's and transgender rights. Often the concerns of many zinesters are still fear and the experiences of sexism, rape, violence, homophobia, racism, human rights abuses and religious pressure. For example, the editors of *Bendita: Latin Women's Initiative Against Violence towards Women* (Brazil) see their zine as a 'big FUCK YOU to a patriarchal society that tells us to shut up when it comes to rape' (Zobl 2001). Such zines gather personal experiences (in this case, of sexual violence) from everyday life while negotiating and critically reflecting upon the norms and values of society. The focus is not on success in terms of the number of zine readers; rather, the heterogeneity and multiplicity of voices that are otherwise not heard is crucial.

Building a supportive feminist community and network is an often-stated goal of zine makers. *Ladyfriend* zine editor Christa Donner (United States) believes that 'one of the primary strengths of the current feminist movement is that there is this global network of young women who are able and eager to help each other succeed, promote each others['] projects' (quoted in Zobl 2002). A rhizomatic network of zine distros, mailing lists, message boards and resource sites, as well as zine archives, festivals, exhibits and workshops, is closely tied to a vivid DIY cultural activism. A number of informal and grassroots-organized feminist collectives use self-publishing alongside artistic strategies (such as culture jamming, street art and public performances) and other activist strategies (such as conducting workshops with marginalized communities). In such grassroots contexts, zines can function as 'a kind of backbone to subcultural feminist activism, allowing zine makers to link personal experiences to larger political activist work' (Schilt & Zobl 2008: 187).

In this way, zines establish public spheres on both an everyday, practical level as well as a networked, activist level. In these, an examination of social norms takes place, courses of action are bolstered or rejected and additional positions in the cultural production of meaning are offered. These publics are local, but can also form transnationally through networking and exchange. They fulfil the function of addressing their own concerns and formulating positions. Through the possibility of raising one's own voice, exchanging ideas and engaging in feminist activism, a wide range of perspectives and marginalized social positions become visible.

Feminist blogs

Feminist blogs are likewise part of feminist media production. In such blogs as the German *Mädchenmannschaft* or the English *the fbomb*, the authors work as collectives of varying composition; the contributions are written individually or by a group. The texts of the aforementioned blogs correspond to no specific genre and cannot be reduced to specific topics. According to Scharff, Smith-Prei and Stehle (2016: 12), this apparent unclassifiability is a strength that can be used to cause trouble.

The bloggers of *the fbomb* also critically claim that their entries are 'created by and for teen and college-aged individuals who care about their rights and want to be heard' (*the fbomb*, n.d.). Opinion forming, as these practices of writing make clear, is the result of a process (Keller 2013). Through the process of group writing and the exchange with other bloggers, these blogs also represent a training ground to test feminisms and to further develop feminist ideas, as the interviews with bloggers from *the fbomb* show (Keller 2013). The current underlying understanding of feminism is a result of these negotiations. This allows the bloggers to build feminist identities and to express them in their texts. These feminist identities retain their constructive character, as they are continually modified and further developed as feminist identities '*in flux*' (Keller 2012: 141). Feminist blogs also aid in the exchange and circulation of ideas and are a part of feminist discourse (cf. Keller 2013: 166). The interpretation of current events creates a common feminist understanding; mutual references and so-called blogrolls – which link to favourite blogs – reinforce this. This production of feminist knowledge and its deployment and visualization for others contributes to the construction of feminist online knowledge archives.

Feminist blogs can thus play an important role in public discourses, as they provide positions and contextualize and bundle topics. Mobilization is also a central concern, as referenced in, for example, campaigns against sexualized violence. Rather than just offering personal descriptions of experiences, the experiences were generalized and the political and social impact was discussed. A critical confrontation with the coverage of this debate in the traditional mass media also occurred. Feminist blogs thereby adopt a translation function in that they gather and generalize themes and positions.

Hashtagged discourses on sexual violence

Hashtags can provide a platform for feminist political action and protest. Using feminist hashtags that discuss sexual violence against women we illustrate how these forms of activism can create publics through protest articulations. Over the past several years, an intense discussion of sexual violence has been among the themes particularly present on Twitter – for example, under the English hashtags #shoutingback and #EverydaySexism, the Turkish hashtag #sendeanlat (meaning 'also talk about it') or, in the German-speaking world, the hashtag #aufschrei. All of these hashtags thematized experiences with everyday sexism and sexual violence. McLean and Maalsen (2015) argue that these hashtags form 'globally linked discursive feminist spaces' which 'allow for distributed feminist networks to converge in online spaces to focus support on contemporary gender issues and create a community around this'.

In these tweets, experiences with sexualized violence are mostly discussed through storytelling. These personal experiences form the central component of the hashtags, as Clark (2016) elaborates in her analysis of #whyIstayed. It is precisely in the embedding of individual experiences within structural contexts that a political potential unfolds. The case of #aufschrei also demonstrates that personal experiences are similarly associated with structural inequalities (Drüeke & Zobl 2016). The tweets show that the collective (unjust) experiences of certain groups become clear beyond the statements made by the individual persons affected. The narrative of one's own history can lead to subjects that are frequently hidden or curtailed in public debates, such as sexualized violence and sexist structures, being taken up and thus made visible. The important features of such negotiation processes are reciprocal references and expressions of solidarity. With #aufschrei, there were many tweets made in the form of mutually supportive and affirmative commentaries, resulting in a kind of solidarity among the users. This means that the communication method is not one-sided; rather, the users form an active audience by means of mutual exchange (see Clark 2016).

Thus, feminist hashtags can serve to trigger a feminist articulation of protest, leading to the development of social demands that disrupt existing value systems and publicly express criticism. On the one hand, Twitter allows the development of personal relationships, but at the same time, it also creates publicity. These articulations of protest thus fulfil an important function within feminist movements. The publics that emerge via Twitter are characterized by shared issues. Through the sharing of experiences and the gathering of themes and positions through hashtags, mobilization can take place at various layers of the public sphere.

Forming publics through alternative media and activist cultural practices

Feminist activism through zines, hashtags and blogs has made itself heard. Through DIY practices and simultaneous or nearly simultaneous digital interfaces, a discursive space of feminist activism and protest at the nexus of the national/international and the grassroots/digital is created that gives momentum to interdependent and rhizomatic online and offline activities. While experiences and negotiations in everyday (and private) life are seldom perceived as being part of the political, such publics gain significance as identities and notions of society are drafted and generated in everyday life.

By drawing on theories on the multiplicity of the public sphere, it becomes clear that the perspective of who is involved and who takes part in the negotiation process of society is shifting. Communication in everyday life becomes as much a part of the public sphere as of social movements and the mass media. These processes of social negotiation occur not in distinct but in mutually permeating spheres of discourse, however. It is necessary to reach different public layers in order to devolve mobilizing power. Alternative media construct a movement public sphere (della Porta 2011). This also includes a movement culture encompassing the networks, spaces and personal relationships of the actors (Wischermann 2003).

As presented earlier, Klaus has differentiated between three layers of the public sphere. Statements made via hashtags in particular assume the function of a simple public in Klaus' model, since they arise in everyday communication and not through highly organized connections. Communication develops mostly spontaneously and, in everyday life, the forms of communication are reciprocal and equal. In these publics, mainly personal experiences are gathered and values and norms are negotiated at a practical, everyday level. Zines and blogs are both part of a simple public sphere, but in interlinked blogs and zines, which are part of the networked process of zine making, topics and positions are already bundled in such a way that they also show the characteristics of an intermediate public. They thereby adopt a translation function in that they gather and generalize themes and positions that are discussed at the simple public layer. Patterns of interpretation are negotiated that grapple with hegemonic political and media discourses. Feminist actors must often compete for political voice, recognition and publicity in online spaces (Fotopoulou 2016), which makes the visibility of this debate crucial.

Conclusion

In this chapter, we have attempted to contextualize the role of alternative media in the public sphere. Alternative media and cultural practices are of central importance for the production of critical publics. Therefore, we argue for an analytical approach that takes into account the elusiveness, specificity, complexity and diversity of these media practices as well as the plurality and simultaneity of publics. Furthermore, by embedding alternative media into public sphere theory, it is possible to consider this multiplicity, as well as its interweaving with daily life, power dynamics, rhizomatic networks and civil society. This allows a perspective that considers the agency of alternative media, cultural expressions and cultural activism in the construction of publics. Understanding alternative media and cultural practices as integral parts of the public sphere permits us to see the abundance of cultural activist practices and to better analyze them as part of the political. As such, we should take them seriously as tools for cultural resistance, political critique and social change. This is well illustrated by Tea Hvala, a blogger, zine maker and co-organizer of the Red Dawns festival in Slovenia: 'Whether you speak about individual acts of resistance, about organised struggles, about art projects, about self-managed social experiments, even about the invisible day and night dreaming that expand the mental space, all these things, in my view, are re-envisioning and transforming society' (quoted in Jiménez & Zobl 2008).

References

Asen, R. and Brouwer D. C. (2001) 'Introduction', in *Counterpublics and the State*. New York: SUNY Press, pp. 1–32.

Atton, C. (2002) *Alternative Media*. London: Sage.

Bailey, O. G., Cammaerts, B. and Carpentier, N. (2008) *Understanding Alternative Media*. Maidenhead, UK: Open University Press.

Chidgey, R. (2014) 'Maker Pedagogies, Do-It-Yourself Feminism and DIY Citizenship', in M. Boler and M. Ratto (eds) *DIY Citizenship: Critical Making and Social Media*. Cambridge, MA: MIT Press, pp. 101–13.

Clark, R. (2016) '"Hope in a Hashtag": The Discursive Activism of #WhyIStayed', *Feminist Media Studies*, vol. 16, no. 5, pp. 788–804.

Couldry, N. (2006) 'Culture and Citizenship. The Missing Link?', *European Journal of Cultural Studies*, vol. 9, no. 3, pp. 321–39.

della Porta, D. (2011) 'Communication in Movement', *Information, Communication & Society*, vol. 14, no. 6, pp. 800–19.

Drüeke, R. and Zobl, E. (2016) 'Online Feminist Protest Movements and Alternative Publics: The Twitter Campaign #aufschrei in Germany', *Feminist Media Studies*, vol. 16, no. 1, pp. 35–54.

Duncombe, S. (1997) *Notes from Underground: Zines and the Politics of Alternative Culture*. London: Verso.

Einspänner-Pflock, J., Anastasiadis, M. and Thimm, C. (2016) 'Ad hoc Mini-publics on Twitter: Citizen Participation or Political Communication? Examples from the German National Election 2013', in A. Frame and G. Brachotte (eds) *Citizen Participation and Political Communication in a Digital World*. New York: Routledge, pp. 42–59.

Fotopoulou, A. (2016) 'Digital and Networked by Default? Women's Organizations and the Social Imaginary of Networked Feminism', *New Media and Society*, vol. 18, no. 6, pp. 989–1005.

Fraser, N. (1992) 'Rethinking the Public Sphere: A Contribution to the Critique of Actually Existing Democracy', in C. Calhoun (ed.) *Habermas and the Public Sphere*. Cambridge, MA: MIT Press, pp. 109–42.

Gunnarsson Payne, J. (2009) 'Feminist Media as Alternative Media? A Literature Review', *Interface: A Journal for and about Social Movements*, vol. 1, no. 2, pp. 190–211.

Gunnarsson Payne, J. (2012) 'Feminist Media as Alternative Media? Theorising Feminist Media from the Perspective of Alternative Media Studies', in E. Zobl and R. Drüeke (eds) *Feminist Media: Participatory Spaces, Networks and Cultural Citizenship*. Bielefeld: transcript, pp. 55–72.

Habermas, J. (1991) *The Structural Transformation of the Public Sphere. An Inquiry into a Category of Bourgeois Society*. Cambridge, MA: MIT Press.

Hermes, J. (2006) 'Citizenship in the Age of the Internet,' *European Journal of Communication*, vol. 21, no. 3, pp. 295–309.

Jiménez, H. and Zobl, E. (2008) 'The Curved / Stripburger / Pssst…: 'Artfully Transforming Society'. Interview with Tea from Ljubljana, Slovenia', Grrrl Zine Network, http://www.grrrlzines.net/interviews/tea_thecurved.htm, accessed 25 February 2017.

Keller, Jessalynn. (2012) '"It's a Hard Job Being an Indian Feminist": Mapping Girls' Feminist Identities and Close Encounters on the Feminist Blogosphere', in: E. Zobl and R. Drüeke (eds) *Feminist Media: Participatory Spaces, Networks and Cultural Citizenship*. Bielefeld: Transcript, pp. 136–45.

Keller, J. (2013) '"Still Alive and Kicking": Girl Bloggers and Feminist Politics in a "Postfeminist" Age'. Dissertation, University of Texas, https://repositories.lib.utexas.edu/handle/2152/21560, accessed 25 February 2017.

Klaus, E. (2006) 'Öffentlichkeit als Selbstverständigungsprozess. Das Beispiel Brent Spar', in U. Röttger (ed.) *PR-Kampagnen. Über die Inszenierung von Öffentlichkeit*, Wiesbaden: VS Verlag, pp. 51–74.

Klaus, E., and Lünenborg, M. (2012) 'Cultural Citizenship. Participation by and through Media', in E. Zobl and R. Drüeke (eds) *Feminist Media. Participatory Spaces, Networks and Cultural Citizenship*, Bielefeld: transcript, pp. 197–212.

Lievrouw, L. (2011) *Alternative and Activist New Media*. Cambridge: Polity Press.

McLean, J. and Maalsen, S. (2015) 'From #destroythejoint to Far Reaching Digital Activism: Feminist Revitalisation Stemming from Social Media and Reaching Beyond', in E. Gordon and P. Mihailidis (eds) *Civic Media Project*, http://civicmediaproject.org/works/civic-media-project/fromdestroythejointtofarreachingdigitalactivismfeministrevitalisation, accessed 25 February 2017.

Mouffe, C. (2005) *On the Political*. London and New York: Routledge.

Rodríguez, C. (2001). *Fissures in the Mediascape: An International Study of Citizens' Media*. Cresskill, NJ: Hampton Press.

Scharff, C., Smith-Prei, C. and Stehle, M. (2016) 'Digital Feminism: Transnational Activism in German Protest Cultures', *Feminist Media Studies*, vol. 16, no. 1, pp. 1–16.

Schilt, K. (2003) '"I'll Resist with Every Inch and Every Breath": Girls and Zine Making as a Form of Resistance', *Youth & Society*, vol. 35, no. 1, pp. 71–97.

Schilt, K. and Zobl, E. (2008) 'Connecting the Dots: Riot Grrrls, Ladyfests, and the International Grrrl Zine Network', in A. Harris (ed.) *Next Wave Cultures: Feminism, Subcultures, Activism*. New York: Routledge, pp. 171–92.

Scott, J. (1991) 'The Evidence of Experience', *Critical Inquiry*, vol. 17, no. 4, pp. 773–97.

Wischermann, U. (2003) *Frauenbewegungen und Öffentlichkeiten um 1900. Netzwerke – Gegenöffentlichkeiten – Protestinszenierungen*. Königstein/Taunus: Ulrike Helmer.

Zobl, E. (2001) '"Zine Making Is a Way to Exist". An Interview with Isabella Gargiulo from *Bendita* (Sao Paolo, Brazil) and Amy Schroeder from *Venus* (Chicago, U.S.)', Grrrl Zine Network, http://www.grrrlzines.net/interviews/bendita_venus.htm, accessed 25 February 2017.

Zobl, E. (2002) '"For Ladies and All Their Friends: *Ladyfriend* Zine." An Interview with Christa Donner', Grrrl Zine Network, http://www.grrrlzines.net/interviews/ladyfriend.htm, accessed 25 February 2017.

Zobl, E. (2009) 'Cultural Production, Transnational Networking, and Critical Reflection in Feminist Zines', *Signs: Journal of Women in Culture and Society*, vol. 35, no. 1, pp. 1–12.

Zobl E. and Drüeke, R. (2012) *Feminist Media: Participatory Spaces, Networks and Cultural Citizenship*. Bielefeld: transcript.

Zobl, E. and Reitsamer, R. (2014) 'Gender and Media Activism: Feminist Alternative Media in Europe', in C. Carter, L. Steiner and L. McLaughlin (eds) *The Routledge Companion to Media and Gender*. New York: Routledge, pp. 233–44.

Zobl, E. and Reitsamer, R. with Grünangerl, S. (2012) 'Feminist Media Production in Europe: A Research Report', in E. Zobl and R. Drüeke (eds) *Feminist Media: Participatory Spaces, Networks and Cultural Citizenship*, Bielefeld: transcript, pp. 21–54.

14

SOCIAL MEDIA ACTIVISM, SELF-REPRESENTATION AND THE CONSTRUCTION OF POLITICAL BIOGRAPHIES

Veronica Barassi

Introduction

Media technologies have been at the heart of the history of social movements and political struggle. Tarrow (1998) applied Anderson's (1991) understanding of imagined community to the analysis of social movements and suggested that the rise of the popular press in Britain and France at the end of the eighteenth century triggered the creation of new associations that developed around the production and exchange of printed materials. Downing (1995: 180–91) traced the roots of dissident publications back to the revolutionary pamphleteers of the American War of Independence and showed how media activism has been a central form of political action from the nineteenth century women's press and the suffragette movement to the civil rights movements of the 1960s.

If media technologies have been at the heart of the history of social movements and activism, the development of the internet has profoundly transformed the way in which media activism was imagined, understood and practised (Meikle 2002; Atton 2004). According to many, internet technologies had enabled a new way of understanding political participation, which was fundamentally different from earlier social movements, and deconstructed older, identity-based forms of political engagement and belonging (Castells 1997; Juris 2008).

In the last decade, however, the rise of social media activism has brought about another important transformation in the field of media activism. Scholars questioned and analyzed the different ways in which political activists were appropriating and using social media technologies to organize and partake in collective actions and mass protests (Castells 2012; Barassi & Treré 2012; Gerbaudo 2012; Postill 2014; Wolfson 2014; Barassi 2015; Kavada 2015). They also investigated the complex relationships between technological affordances and the emergence of new political repertoires of protest (Wolfson 2014; Gerbaudo 2015) and considered collective understandings of online political identity construction (Kavada 2015; Milan 2015; Treré 2015).

Although insightful, what is missing from these analyses is a careful appreciation of a fundamental aspect of social media activism: the relationship between political self-construction, digital storytelling and identity. Whilst some communication scholars in the past have considered the relationship between digital storytelling and 'alternative' publics (Bennett & Toft 2008; Couldry 2008), within the current literature on social media activism the only example of work that tackles the complex relationship between the self-construction of political activists, identity narratives and digital storytelling is the work of Vivienne (2016), which explores everyday activists' use of digital technologies as tools for self-construction through narratives.

The aim of this chapter is to address this gap in the field by introducing the concept of digital 'political biography'. Drawing on the findings of an ethnographic study of activists in Italy, the UK and Spain, the chapter will argue that social media have become a platform where activists construct their political biographies with reference to both civic engagement and family life. The understanding of the interconnection between social media technologies and political biographies amongst activists is particularly important today, because it can enable us to ask questions about the tension between the creative elements of social media practices for political activists, and about the broader political economic implications for activists of data flows on the commercial web.

Social media activism: how does it differ from other forms of media activism?

As argued elsewhere (Barassi 2016) there are two fundamental characteristics that differentiate social media activism from other forms of media activism. In the first place, political participation on social media is heavily personalized (Bennett & Segerberg 2012; Fenton & Barassi 2011). This personalization is expressed by two different processes. On the one hand, the individual relies on personal networks to gather and share information, mobilize and organize. On the other hand, the individual displays one's own identity narrative through the production of political posts, comments and images. In the second place, political participation on social media is based on a new logic of visibility. In her engaging critique of social media, Milan (2015) argued that in the last few years we have witnessed a transition of political repertoires, from a politics of identity to a politics of visibility. Politically engaged citizens and activists today are constantly sharing posts and information about their political experiences and direct actions, and their political practices are often defined by a mediatized understanding of visibility.

In the last few years, a lot of attention has been placed on these different characteristics of social media activism. On the one hand, scholars have challenged techno-optimistic understandings of individual agency on social media (Castells 2009) to argue that the personalization of social protest leads to a series of challenges for protest movements by calling into question the effectiveness and strength of a given protest (Bennett & Segerberg 2012), and by challenging collective discourses and representations (Fenton & Barassi 2011). On the other hand, scholars have mapped the social tensions that emerge within social movements in the collective construction of a 'we' (Barassi 2015; Gerbaudo & Treré 2015; Kavada 2015; Milan 2015).

The question about the personalization and individualization of media activism on social media has inevitably led scholars to critically investigate the complex relationship between social media, protest cultures and processes of collective identity construction. Different scholars, in fact, reached the conclusion that the very notion of collective identity is being re-negotiated on social media platforms. Treré (2015) for instance draws on Goffman's (1990) analysis of self-representation and argues that activists not only construct their identity through 'frontstage' tactics (such as social media posts) but also through 'backstage' practices (such as discussions, private messages, etc.) and that these practices are key to the construction of collective identity.

In the same special issue of the journal *Information, Communication and Society*, Kavada (2015) shows that the process of collective identity construction on social media, or 'identization' as she defines it, is tightly linked to what Melucci (1996) understood as those sets of common practices, codes of conduct, demands and statements that are then codified in shared 'texts'. Both scholars, together with the other scholars who have participated in the special issue, provide us with a critical and thorough understanding of processes of collective identity construction on social media, by arguing that – although these platforms promote forms of media activism that are individualized and personalized – overall they are also crucial to the construction of a common 'we'.

These works are of central importance, as they shed light on the fact that social media platforms, as in other forms of media activism, become the space where collective identity is not only imagined but also practiced. The understanding of collective identity as defined by both imagination and practice can be found within the work of della Porta and Diani (1999: 85–8), who argued that within new social movements the construction of a common 'we' is made possible both by imagination and the constant social participation in collective action. Although insightful, what is missing from this body of literature is a careful exploration of how activists often use these platforms not only to negotiate the construction of a common 'we' but also as tools to construct one's political 'I'.

Within and beyond the collective: the importance of self-representation in social media activism

In the literature discussed above, it is clear that scholars are aware of the fact that social media activism does not only enable processes of identity construction that are linked to the construction of a collective we, but also to intimate and personal processes of self-representation and construction (e.g. Treré 2015). Yet within the literature the discussion about processes of self-construction is somehow overshadowed by broader debates about collective identity.

In this chapter, I wish to focus precisely on these processes of individual identity construction. In contrast to collective identity, which can be understood as a collective process of negotiation in the construction and identification of a common 'we', I want to highlight those individual *processes of negotiation which work towards a self-construction, adaptation and incorporation to a specific common 'we'.* In other words, my intention is to focus on the notion of political identity as related to the self.

The importance of individual processes of self-construction within social movements emerges clearly in della Porta and Diani's (1999) analysis of three different women's collectives. According to these scholars, collective participation was a definer of the individual identification process: the individual was not only empowered by the reference to the collective 'we' but, most importantly, adapted itself to that 'we' in a constant process of self-construction. A key example that they advance is the one of Irma, a member of a women's collective in Milan, who explained:

> For me, being part of a women's group is an essential influence, not only on my way of life, but also on my thinking. It is important to know yourself. The collective has died and been reborn many times over, along with my aspirations. But wherever I go I will always find a women's group.
>
> *Quoted in della Porta & Diani 1999: 84*

It seems to me, therefore, that any understanding of social media activism should take into account not only how these technologies enable the construction of a 'common we', but also how through these technologies activists enact their own sense of political 'self', which moves through time across different political collectives and realities.

In order to understand this process, it might be interesting to look at the anthropological literature on political identity. According to Escobar (2004) and Pratt (2003), political identity is a relational concept, a concept which defines both self-consciousness and participation to communities of imagination and practice. In contrast to other scholars who largely focused on the notion of identity practice, anthropologists were interested in 'political identity' as a complex human process. For them, political identity is not something carried as a definer of the individual, but a process of self-imagination, which is constantly constructed though the everyday practice in the encounter with others (Escobar 2004: 252).

This understanding of political identity is largely influenced by the belief that individuality is shaped by both an internalized cultural perception of the 'person' and a sense of distinctiveness and agency (Morris 1994: 10–14). The difference between these two realms can be found in Mauss's (1985) famous understanding that human beings have a sense of self (*moi*) which is different from the culturally constructed understanding of the moral/collective person (*personne*) (e.g. the good Christian, the good citizen, the good activist), and that both of these levels contribute to the construction of people as persons. The self cannot be understood as an a priori category, but rather as a feeling of individuality and distinctiveness from the group (Cohen 1985).

Anthropological theory is usually disregarded in communication studies, and in understanding self-representation scholars often refer to Goffman (1990) or Foucauldian models of subjectivity. However, the anthropological literature is particularly interesting because, on the one hand, it highlights processes of subjective construction that are not only defined by domination and self-governance, as Foucauldian models suggest, or social interaction and performance on the other, as Goffman would explain. The anthropological literature is interesting because it combines a bit of both by showing that self-construction is an intimate processes of negotiation with past and present personal experiences, as well as with hegemonic meanings and cultural differences. This perspective can be very important in the study of social media activism.

In addition to this, and as we shall see later, the anthropological literature on social movements is particularly relevant to the study of social media activism for its attention to the concept of *identity narrative*, as developed by Pratt (2003). This understanding, as we shall see in the next two parts, sheds light on an important yet underinvestigated dimension of social media activism: the relationship between digital storytelling and the construction of political biographies.

Self-representation on social media: the question about digital storytelling and voice

In the last decade, within communication research, we have seen the emergence of different studies that have focused on digital storytelling. The earliest works in this regard can be found in the volume edited by Lundby (2008). One of the big merits of the book lies in its ability to address both the creative dimension and the structural constraints of digital storytelling online. In fact, on the one hand, some contributions focus on how personal narratives and authenticity have been transformed in the digital age (Hertzberg Kaare & Lundby 2008), and how digital technologies have redefined the relationship between authorship and authority (Friedlander 2008). On the other hand, other contributions explore how all digital stories are immersed within broader processes of mediatization (Couldry 2008; Lundby 2008), and are constrained by the affordances of social media technologies (Brake 2008).

At the heart of these debates about online digital storytelling lies the question about the relationship between 'voice' and democratic emancipation, which as Couldry (2010) has argued is one of the key questions of our times. Within these debates, scholars focused broadly on the relationship between digital storytelling and 'alternative' publics (Couldry 2008; Bennett & Toft 2008), and argued that online storytelling is just one aspect of a broader transformation brought about by digital culture, where the 'need to tell one story' is simultaneously defined by political economic structures in the digital age, as well as by broader emancipatory transformations (Thumim 2012).

All these contributions provide us with important keys of analysis on digital storytelling and the construction of alternative publics. Yet what seems to be missing from this body of literature is an in-depth exploration of the lived experience of political activists. This is thoroughly explored in the work of Vivienne (2011, 2016). Drawing on qualitative interviews, discourse analysis and ethnographic methodologies amongst queer activists, Vivienne makes a powerful claim about the importance of understanding the complex relationship between digital storytelling, activism and processes of identity construction. One of the main merits of her work is represented by the fact that, drawing on philosophical and postmodern thought, she understands identity as a contradictory and messy process, which is tightly linked to performance, and hence storytelling. In this framework, she demonstrates that digital media (and she is broad in her definition) are the spaces for people to carry out – through digital storytelling – the work of constructing one's own 'networked identity' by building bridges between multiple, co-existent, understandings of self, family and community (2016: 132–73).

Vivienne's work is insightful and thought-provoking and, I believe, so far the most important contribution to the analysis of the relationship between social media activism, self-representation and digital storytelling. Her work on 'everyday activists' is crucial because it shows that in the study of social media activism we need to develop an approach that departs from that through which, as Alleyne (2000) has argued, not only life histories are used within political groups as a model of reference, but also political action is often related to a life project. This understanding lies at the very heart of social movement research, which argues that *collective repertoires* are internalized in persons (Tilly 1994: 244). Such an approach would entail that we shed light on the fact that self-imagination and identity construction are tightly interconnected to the process of storytelling on social media.

Social media activism, identity narratives and the everyday construction of political biographies

As it emerges from the above discussion, on the one hand, contemporary debates about digital storytelling lack an in-depth focus on the everyday, ethnographic realities of social movements. On the other hand, debates about social media activism lack a thorough understanding of the relationship between digital storytelling, self-representation and processes of political identity construction. I realized this gap in the literature as I was carrying out my own research. Between 2007 and 2013, I carried out a cross-cultural ethnographic analysis of three different activist groups. After working for a year with a political organization which was involved in the Labour movement in the UK, I carried out research with two other organizations: one embedded with the Italian Autonomous movement and one with the Spanish environmental movement. In the last few years, I also engaged in a digital ethnography of ten activists' Facebook profiles, and analyzed how activists' Facebook timelines enabled practices of self-construction through digital storytelling.

My own research revealed that, through social media, activists constructed a personal narrative which was highly political. On the one hand, they used these platforms to show their participation in collective initiatives and to negotiate collective meanings and codes (Kavada 2015; Treré 2015). On the other hand, they used these platforms to frame their personal experiences in political terms. It was by looking at these two different and messy processes of self-construction, which required the internalization, adaptation and self-imagination (Escobar 2004) of collective political narratives, that I came to the conclusion that, on social media, activists were constructing a political biography through digital storytelling.

The concept of *political biography* is largely influenced by Pratt's concept of *identity narrative*. Pratt (2003) argued that in the study of social movements and political activism, we have much to gain if we approach the understanding of identity as *narrative* and appreciate how this narrative develops on two different, albeit interconnected, axes. On the one hand, identity narratives are constructed through the *hierarchical axis*, which suggests who 'we' are, through opposition and the creation of the *other*. On the other hand, identity narratives are constructed through the *biographical axis*, which establishes who people are through the medium of time and by looking at personal experience (ibid.: 10).

My research revealed that on the Facebook timelines, these two axes interconnected and overlapped. The *hierarchical axis* of the narrative was constructed through an everyday process of association to or disassociation from specific political collectives, issues or events. This finding emerged very well in the Facebook timeline of Dario (a fictional name to protect the participant's anonymity), an activist engaged in environmental politics in Spain, as well as with LGBTQ collectives. Dario's Facebook timeline was constructed through a variety of different – at times incoherent and accidental – posts which highlighted his praise, enthusiasm and support for the multiple activities and events of different political groups. The timeline also included a self-representation of his own participation to specific direct actions, demonstrations and events. What I found particularly interesting of these digital practices is the fact that by posting comments and photos on Facebook, as well as by sharing links and information, Dario effectively constructed his sense of belonging to the different political collectives he was part of. At the same time, he distanced himself from the work of 'other' collectives. This process of inclusion and 'othering' was reinforced by the comments and interactions with other activists who belonged to the groups in question. This discursive dimension of his identity narrative, therefore, speaks directly to Pratt's (2003) understanding of hierarchical axis of political identity, whereby people construct who they are with reference to the collective and to the construction of the 'other'.

Dario's social media use also highlighted that he not only constructed his online selves in relation to the collectives they belonged to (hierarchical axis), but also used these online platforms to reflect upon his daily personal experiences, family life, and early childhood in a political way (biographical axis). This was a common practice shared amongst the other activists as well. There were multiple ways in which activists constructed the *biographical axis* of their identity narratives. As argued elsewhere in greater detail (Barassi 2017), activists used social media platforms to re-think their childhood experiences and everyday family relations in political terms. Hence they either uploaded old images of childhood, and created a textual narrative around these images that was highly political, or they posted images of their family members and discursively constructed these images by presenting their family members as political and moral agents. The construction of the biographical axis of the identity narrative, however, was not only defined by practices of self-construction in relation to one's own childhood and family life but also in relation to everyday personal experiences. Activists discussed how they experienced their everyday, mundane chores, at the post office or at work, in a political way. Alternatively, they reflected on what they witnessed on the streets, in shopping centres or on their own day-to-day consumer habits. All these personal experiences were discursively framed in relation to their sense of political self and as a reinforcement of their political values.

My research revealed that on social media activists brought together different dimensions of their complex political identities. This finding relates well to Vivienne's (2016: 132–73) argument that digital storytelling is often used to do the 'work of network identity', and hence build bridges between multiple, co-existent, understandings of self, family and community. Yet my research, which drew on Pratt's (2003) concept of 'identity narrative', brought Vivienne's (2016) understanding a bit further. In fact, by focusing on the hierarchical versus biographical aspects of identity narrative construction, it showed that the production of one's own networked identity involves two very different processes of digital storytelling and meaning construction; and that through this dynamic interplay, activists constructed their 'political biography' on social media – a digital, and widely public, auto-biographical story of their political self.

The concept of 'political biography' therefore enables us to appreciate the permeability and social impact of online digital storytelling amongst activists. Political biographies, as shown, are largely shaped through the same process as the identity narratives described by Pratt (2003). However, according to Pratt (2003), identity narrative is an internal process of self-construction or self-narration through oral history. This implies that, in the majority of cases, no trace is left behind, and one could constantly re-create his or her own identity narrative. The same cannot be said about the construction of political biographies on social media that become digital artefacts which define activists' political identities. Of course, social media posts can be deleted or edited, but my research revealed that this is seldom the case and that, if one wanted, one could research almost ten years of political posts shared by activists. Part of the reason for keeping this archive, as I was told by Mark, an activist engaged in the Autonomous movement in Milan is: 'this is my story, this is my life'. Hence, when thinking about political biographies on social media, we need to appreciate them for their personal and affective dimension, which is linked to one's own sense of agency and distinctiveness, as well as to the actualization of a sense of creative self. At the same time, we need to perceive these as public narratives that can be shared, analyzed, exploited and remediated, and that are open to public scrutiny and surveillance.

Conclusion

This chapter has argued that there two fundamental characteristics that differentiate social media activism from other forms of media activism: the personalization and visibility of political participation. Research on social media activism has largely focused on the complex ways in which personalization and visibility of political action have transformed collective mobilization and the construction of collective identity. However, as this chapter has argued, within current research on social media activism little attention has been placed on the complex relationship between social media activism, digital storytelling and processes of self-construction. The aim of this chapter was to address this gap.

The chapter brought together the communication literature on digital storytelling and voice with the anthropological literature on the person and political identity. It has shown that, through social media, activists develop a complex personal narrative that is simultaneously shaped by processes of identification and distancing to political groups, as well as by processes of meaning construction of their own biographical experiences. This dynamic interplay of personal data flows enables the construction of their 'political biography', making political beliefs, opinions and actions widely public. Whilst the aim of this chapter was to focus mostly on how political biographies are constructed through social media activism, there are critical questions that emerge on the broader political and social implications of these narratives on the commercial web. As argued elsewhere (Barassi 2016), what is becoming clear is that these personal data flows online are tightly linked to processes of digital profiling (Elmer 2004) and, as Gangadharan (2012, 2015) has argued, digital profiling can have a fundamental and often discriminatory impact on social minorities. Hence, after appreciating the relationship between social media activism and the construction of political biographies as we did in this chapter, we should start tackling critical questions on the impacts these narratives can have on the political profiling and discrimination of activists.

References

Alleyne, B. (2000) *Personal Narrative & Activism: A Bio-ethnography of 'Life Experience with Britain'*. London: Goldsmiths College.

Anderson, B. (1991) *Imagined Communities: Reflections on the Origin and Spread of Nationalism* (second revised edition). London and New York: Verso Books.

Atton, C. (2004) *An Alternative Internet: Radical Media, Politics and Creativity*. Edinburgh: Edinburgh University Press.

Barassi, V. (2015) *Activism on the Web: Everyday Struggles Against Digital Capitalism*. New York: Routledge.

Barassi, V. (2016) 'Datafied Citizens? Social Media Activism, Digital Traces and the Question about Political Profiling', *Communication and the Public*, vol. 1, no. 4, pp. 494–9.

Barassi, V. (2017) 'Digital Citizens? Data Traces and Family Life', *Contemporary Social Science*, vol. vol. 12, nos. 1–2, pp. 84–95.

Barassi, V. and Treré, E. (2012) 'Does Web 3.0 come after Web 2.0? Deconstructing Theoretical Assumptions through Practice', *New Media & Society*, vol. 14, no. 8, pp. 1269–85.

Bennett, W. L. and Segerberg, A. (2012) 'The Logic of Connective Action', *Information, Communication & Society*, vol. 15, no. 5, pp. 739–68.

Bennett, W. L., and Toft, A. (2008) 'Identity, Technologies and Narratives: Transnational Activism and Social Networks', in A. Chadwick and P. N. Howard (eds) *The Routledge Handbook of Internet Politics*, London: Routledge, pp. 246–58.

Brake, D. (2008) 'Shaping the "Me" in MySpace: The Framing of Profiles on a Social Network Site', in K. Lundby (ed.) *Digital Storytelling, Mediatized Stories: Self-Representations in New Media*. New York: Peter Lang, pp. 285–301.

Cammaerts, B., Mattoni, A. and Mccurdy, P. (2013) *Mediation and Protest Movements*. Bristol and Wilmington, NC: Intellect.

Castells, M. (1997) *The Power of Identity*. Malden, MA: Wiley–Blackwell.

Castells, M. (2011) *Communication Power* (2nd edition). Oxford: Oxford University Press.

Castells, M. (2012) *Networks of Outrage and Hope: Social Movements in the Internet Age*. Cambridge: Polity Press.

Cohen, A. (1994) *Self Consciousness: An Alternative Anthropology of Identity*. London and New York: Routledge.

Couldry, N. (2008) 'Digital Storytelling, Media Research and Democracy: Conceptual Choices and Alternative Futures', in K. Lundby (ed.) *Digital Storytelling, Mediatized Stories: Self-Representations in New Media*. New York: Peter Lang, pp. 41–61.

Couldry, N. (2010) *Why Voice Matters: Culture and Politics after Neoliberalism*. London: Sage.

della Porta, D. and Diani, M. (1999) *Social Movements: An Introduction*. Malden, MA: Wiley–Blackwell.

Dencik, L. and Leistert, O. (eds) (2015) *Critical Perspectives on Social Media and Protest: Between Control and Emancipation*. New York: Rowman & Littlefield International.

Downing, J. (1995). 'Alternative Media and the Boston Tea Party', in J. D. H. Downing, A. Mohammadi, and A. Sreberny-Mohammadi (eds) *Questioning the Media: A Critical Introduction* (second edition) Thousand Oaks, CA: Sage, pp. 238–53.

Elmer, G. (2004) *Profiling Machines: Mapping the Personal Information Economy*. Cambridge, MA: MIT Press.

Escobar, A. (2004) 'Identity', in D. Nugent and J. Vincent (eds) *A Companion to the Anthropology of Politics*. Malden, MA: Blackwell, pp. 248–67.

Fenton, N. and Barassi, V. (2011) 'Alternative Media and Social Networking Sites: The Politics of Individuation and Political Participation', *The Communication Review*, vol. 14, no. 3, pp. 179–96.

Friedlander, L. (2008) 'Narrative Strategies in the Digital Age: Authorship and Authority', in K. Lundby (ed.) *Digital Storytelling, Mediatized Stories: Self-Representations in New Media*. New York: Peter Lang, pp. 177–97.

Gangadharan, S. P. (2012) 'Digital Inclusion and Data Profiling', *First Monday*, vol. 17, no. 5, http://firstmonday.org/ojs/index.php/fm/article/view/3821, accessed 6 March 2017.

Gangadharan, S. P. (2015) 'The Downside of Digital Inclusion: Expectations and Experiences of Privacy and Surveillance among Marginal Internet Users', *New Media & Society*, vol. 19, no. 4, pp. 597–615.

Gerbaudo, P. (2012) *Tweets and the Streets: Social Media and Contemporary Activism*. London: Pluto Press.

Gerbaudo, P. and Treré, E. (2015) 'In Search of the 'We' of Social Media Activism: Introduction to the Special Issue on Social Media and Protest Identities', *Information, Communication & Society*, http://www.tandfonline.com/doi/full/10.1080/1369118X.2015.1043319

Goffman, E. (1990) *The Presentation of Self in Everyday Life*. London: Penguin.

Hertzberg Kaare, B. and Lundby, K. (2008) 'Mediatized Lives: Autobiography and Assumed Authenticity in Digital Storytelling', in K. Lundby (ed.) *Digital Storytelling, Mediatized Stories: Self-Representations in New Media*. New York: Peter Lang, pp. 105–23.

Juris, J. S. (2008) *Networking Futures: The Movements against Corporate Globalization*. Durham, NC: Duke University Press.

Kavada, A. (2015) 'Creating the Collective: Social Media, the Occupy Movement and Its Constitution as a Collective Actor, *Information, Communication & Society*, vol. 18, no. 8, pp. 872–86.

Lundby, K. (2008). 'Introduction: Digital Storytelling, Mediatized Stories', in K. Lundby (ed.) *Digital Storytelling, Mediatized Stories: Self-Representations in New Media*. New York: Peter Lang, pp. 1–21.

Mattoni, A. (2012) *Media Practices and Protest Politics How Precarious Workers Mobilis*. Surrey, UK: Ashgate.

Mauss, M. (1985) 'A Category of the Human Mind: The Notion of Person; the Notion of Self', in M. Carrithers, S. Collins and S. Lukes (eds) *The Category of the Person: Anthropology, Philosophy, History*. Cambridge: Cambridge University Press, pp. 1–25.

Meikle, G. (2002) *Future Active: Media Activism and the Internet*. New York: Routledge.

Melucci, A. (1996) *Challenging Codes: Collective Action in the Information Age*. Cambridge: Cambridge University Press.

Milan, S. (2015) 'From Social Movements to Cloud Protesting: The Evolution of Collective Identity', *Information, Communication & Society*, vol. 18, no. 8, pp. 887–900.

Morris, B. (1994) *Anthropology of the Self: The Individual in Cultural Perspective*. London: Pluto Press.

Postill, J. (2014) 'Democracy in an Age of Viral Reality: A Media Epidemiography of Spain's Indignados Movement', *Ethnography*, vol. 15, no. 1, pp. 51–69.

Pratt, J. (2003) *Class, Nation and Identity: The Anthropology of Political Movements*. London: Pluto Press.

Tarrow, S. G. (1998) *Power in Movement: Social Movements and Contentious Politics*. Cambridge: Cambridge University Press.

Thumim, N. (2012) *Self-Representation and Digital Culture*. Basingstoke, UK: Palgrave Macmillan.

Tilly, C. (1994) 'Afterword: Political Memories in Space and Time', in J. Boyarin (ed.) *Remapping Memory: The Politics of TimeSpace*. Minneapolis, MN: University of Minnesota Press, pp. 241–57.

Treré, E. (2015) 'Reclaiming, Proclaiming, and Maintaining Collective Identity in the #YoSoy132 Movement in Mexico: An Examination of Digital Frontstage and Backstage Activism through Social Media and Instant Messaging Platforms', *Information, Communication & Society*, vol. 18, no. 8, pp. 901–15.

Vivienne, S. (2016) *Digital Identity and Everyday Activism: Sharing Private Stories with Networked Publics*. Basingstoke, UK: Palgrave Macmillan.

Wolfson, T. (2014) *Digital Rebellion: The Birth of the Cyber Left*. Urbana, IL: University of Illinois Press.

PART III

Activist arts

15

CATS, PUNK, ARSON AND NEW MEDIA

Art activism in Russia 2007–2015

Yngvar B. Steinholt

On 9 November 2015 Petr Pavlenskii (b. 1984), Russia's perhaps most daring art activist, staged his performance 'Threat'. He poured petrol on the main entrance to the notorious Lubianka building in Moscow, headquarters of the Russian security services FSB and formerly of the Soviet KGB, set the doors on fire and posed in front of them on photo and video images holding the empty jerry can. The action marked a culmination point of roughly seven years of spectacular art activism in Russia, highlighted – at least as far as Western media are concerned – by the feminist/LGBT art activist collective Pussy Riot's February 2012 performance of a 'Punk Prayer' in Moscow's Christ the Saviour Cathedral. The flourishing of art activism during these seven years was facilitated by the expansion of internet-based media. Notably, however, online-disseminated art activism was not simply born out of technological advancements. A whole range of approaches and strategies were already developed, tested and ready for implementation in the quickly expanding internet. Thus, in order to fully appreciate Russian art activism's expansion into the web, its development since the mid-1970s has to be taken into account. Following a brief historical overview, this chapter presents three major exponents of Russian art activism's 'golden age' of 2007–2015 and some of their key performances.

Conceptualist and performance art in Soviet and post-Soviet Russia

In 2014 Andrey Erofeev curated the art exhibition 'Pussy Riot and the Cossacks: Russian Tradition of Art Resistance' (Erofeev 2014) which filled three floors of the spacious gallery Havremegasinet in Boden, Sweden. The exhibition traced the roots of contemporary Russian art activism back to the poet and conceptualist artist Dmitry Prigov (1940–2007). A thorough discussion of Prigov in the context of late- and post-Soviet Culture is found in Rutten (2017). By many held as the father of Russian conceptualism, Prigov began writing poetry in the 1960s. A first milestone in his performance work was the infamous 'bulldozer exhibition' in the Moscow suburb of Belyaevo on 15 September 1974. Prigov and the Moscow conceptualists organized a public exhibition for unsanctioned contemporary art. The authorities responded by levelling the premises with a bulldozer and burning the remaining artworks. For cubists and abstractionists who were arrested, some even forced into emigration, the event was deeply traumatic (Erofeev 2014: 9). However, Erofeev asserts, a minority fronted by the young artists

Vitalii Komar (b. 1943) and Aleksandr Melamid (b. 1945) regarded the razing of artworks by the government as the main artistic performance and a great success. The authorities had been provoked into playing the role assigned to them by the artists, and thus the Soviet regime's inherent violence and intolerance was exposed (Erofeev 2014: 9). This manner of making hostile authorities involuntarily or unknowingly contribute to a performative work of art would become an enduring feature of Russian art activism.

The bulldozer exhibition became the starting point for what Komar and Melamid termed 'Sots-art'. An ironic and deliberately ambiguous blend of Socialist Realism and Western Pop Art, Sots-art played with the parodic and inappropriate representation of authorial signs and language. Its deconstruction of Soviet Utopia generated involuntary laughter in the public, which in turn reflected back on the authorities (Jonson 2015: 25; Erofeev 2014: 12). Initially, dissemination was minimal. Komar's and Melamid's performance 'To eat the Truth' (1976), where articles from the main ideological organ of the Soviet Communist Party, the newspaper *Pravda* (*The Truth*), were ground into mince and consumed by the artists as ideological food in the form of 'meatballs', could reach wider audiences mainly by word of mouth (Erofeev 2014: 17). Enter the post-Soviet 1990s, with artists such as Aleksandr Brener (b. 1957) and Oleg Kulik (b. 1961), and the media gradually came to play a more prominent role as artists turned to ironic self-staging and roleplay. As early as 19 August, during the coup of 1991, Vladislav Mamyshev-Monroe (1969–2013) had photographed himself jubilantly smiling in front of an advancing row of tanks (Erofeev 2014: 21). On 30 December 1995 outside the Kremlin, Brener began a warm-up routine dressed in boxing shorts and gloves, shouting for president Yeltsin to come out and settle their dispute (over the Chechen war) in a fight man to man (Russian Gesture 2012). Impersonations of suffering artist, duped citizen, or both gradually grew more extreme, to the point where Kulik appeared as a wild dog (Smith 1997).

In the 2000s, the steady spread of conceptualist art performances and political direct action initiatives coincided with a significant shift in the media. From 2006 to 2007 file-sharing became increasingly common, and by 2011 the protest movement had become regular users of internet-based networks (Facebook, Vkontakte, LiveJournal) (Gabowitsch 2017: 79). From 2011 to 2012 the number of Russians ranking the internet as their primary source of information doubled to about 15 per cent (Wijermars 2016: 19–20). Now, high resolution video footage spread to tens of thousands of people within hours of an event. Newspapers and TV stations, liable to impose their own agendas, could be by-passed. This enabled the whole arsenal of conceptualist art strategies to return in a new format.

Voiná

Art group Voiná ('War') was formed in Moscow in winter 2007, when Natal'ia Sokol's (b. 1980) and Oleg Vorotnikov's (b. 1978) art group Sokoleg fused with Leonid 'Fucked-Up Lyonya' Nikolaev's (1984–2015) art group Bombily. The founding members were students at the Moscow State University (MGU), the Rodchenko School of Photography and Tartu Univerity. Amongst the 50–60 individuals who contributed to the collective were Nadezhda Tolokonnikova (b. 1989), her partner, lawyer Petr Verzilov (b. 1987), transgender activist Grey Violet (b. 1986), Yekaterina Samutsevich (b. 1982) and Aleksei Plutser-Sarno (b. 1962), whose LiveJournal chronicle remains the primary source on Voiná's activities (Plutser-Sarno 2017). Initially gathering at Oleg Kulik's Moscow workshop and planning a joint performance with Dmitry Prigov, Voiná consciously aligned themselves with the local tradition of conceptualist performance art, whilst repeatedly stating that they were not artists (Jonson 2015: 150).

Voiná's first performance took place on International Labour Day 2007. The activists entered a McDonald's restaurant on Serpukhovskaya Square, armed with starved homeless cats, which were thrown across the counter to attack the burgers. Police intervened and arrested the activists and, as evidence, three of their cats. Shouting 'Death to fast-food!' and 'No to global fascism!' the activists merged quirky animal right activism with alter-globalist denouncement of corporate fast-food. The performance was presented as a gift of art to underpaid workers in boring and meaningless jobs. Last but not least, the activists wished to challenge the lack of rebellious spirit in the general populace of Russia (Plutser-Sarno 2017).

In contrast to political direct actions, Voiná distanced themselves from ideology, regarding rebellion as an end in itself. Their motivation was multilayered, and the cats' dual function as aesthetic objects and agents in their own right enhanced the artistic qualities of the performance. The police were exposed both as oppressors, exercising law and order at the expense of courageous artists, and as comic cat catchers. Coincidentally or not, the meat metaphor in Voiná's statement also echoed that of Komar and Melamid's ideological meatballs.

Voiná's first action suggests a concept of revolution and call for rebellion absent in Sov-art irony, yet deliberately multilayered in contrast to political direct action. Their disruptive agenda retained a strong social message in its call for a change in the general behaviour of the populace, making it more than disruption for its own sake. This is confirmed by the harsh directness with which the activists describe their actions. Whilst the scenarios of flying cats attacking burgers and police chasing cats might be openly comical, the artists take on the role of activist idealists, remaining self-ironic, yet escaping ridicule.

By 2007 the climate of NATO's eastward expansion and what the Kremlin regarded as Western interference in Russia's 'near abroad' was beginning to have a limiting impact on cultural and civic life. The colour revolutions in Ukraine and Georgia in 2003–2004 convinced the Kremlin of the necessity to keep culture on their side and gave the Russian Orthodox Church a prominent role in protecting Russia from harmful Western influences. Thus, Voiná's plan to carry a cupboard containing a poetry-reading Dmitry Prigov up the stairwell of the Moscow State University formed part of a chain of actions marking resistance against state appropriation of the arts. With Prigov's death the performance became a wake on the Moscow metro where, on 25 August a festive table was set in a carriage on the circle line. Passengers were invited to honour the memory of the great artist and poet (Plutser-Sarno 2017).

The Voiná group first made international headlines after 29 February 2008, when five couples of Voiná activists staged a sex orgy in the Biological Museum of Moscow under the banner 'Fuck for the Heir of Little Bear' (Gololobov 2011). Gabowitsch informs that the performance was meant to show how those in power are fucking the people (2017: 181). In typical Voiná-style the connection was achieved through multi-layered references, the 'little bear' ('medved' is the Russian word for 'bear'), suggesting the heir is Medvedev's, and the sexual acts pointing to recent government responses to low birth rates (Jonson 2015: 150).

As Gabowitsch points out, although the church hierarchy preferred to respond to criticism of the church 'in veiled rhetorical form' (2017: 181), low-level clergy and orthodox zealots often responded more resolutely. Avdey Ter-Oganyan's 1999 performance 'Young Atheist', where he took an axe and chopped up reproductions of religious icons inside a church (Erofeev 2014: 26, 28), led to his subsequent exhibition in Marat Gelman's private gallery being vandalized and spray-painted (Gabowitsch 2017: 179). In January 2003, the Moscow exhibition 'Careful! Religion' at the Sakharov Centre was attacked by Orthodox militants and works of art destroyed. On both occasions gallery owners, curators and artists were fined for 'inciting religious hatred' after suing their attackers for compensation (Gabowitsch 2017: 180). Ter-Oganyan was granted political asylum in the Czech Republic in 1999. In March 2007 the scenario repeated itself after curator Andrei Erofeev and former director of the Andrei Sakharov Museum and Human Rights Center, Yuri Samodurov, were taken to court with the same charge for exhibiting 23 previously banned works of art in their exhibition 'Forbidden Art 2006' (HRW 2010). This time, however, art activists struck back.

When court proceedings opened at the Taganskii regional court on 29 May 2009, guitar-carrying Voiná activists stood up on their chairs and performed a punk song entitled 'All Cops Are Bastards'. The activists stated that the action was 'a protest against the repressions of intellectuals supported by the federal government' (Plutser-Sarno 2017). In 2010, Jonson states, Erofeev and Samodurov were found guilty of expressing 'a cynical and contemptuous attitude to the religious feelings of orthodox believers' and fined 150,000 and 200,000 roubles respectively. The prosecution had demanded three years in a penal colony (Jonson 2015: 119). Meanwhile, Voiná continued targeting the political elite and security apparatus. From 15 to 20 May 2010 Leonid Nikolaev protested against blue flashing lights on parliament members' cars to ensure them priority in traffic. Wearing a blue bucket on his head he literally ran over the offending cars (Calvert Journal 2015). His stunt spurred a brief 'blue bucket movement' across the country as other activists followed his example. On 14 June 2010 followed the most famous Voiná action, the painting of a 65-meter high phallus on the Liteynyi drawbridge in St Petersburg (Voiná 2010, Jonson 2015: 153–54). Entitled 'Dick Captured by the FSB', the sketchily drawn erection rose to face the security service building as the bridge was raised. Major controversy, accounted for in detail by Johnson (2013), erupted when the controversial work won Voiná the 2010 Innovation Prize, an award for emerging artists administered by the National Centre for Contemporary Arts and backed by the Ministry of Culture. Ultimately, uneasy with the potential for co-optation, Voiná donated the prize money to the support of political prisoners (Johnson 2013: 593).

Vorotnikov, Sokol and Nikolaev subsequently declared war on the Russian prison system with their action 'If a Friend Is in Jail, or How to Cook a Chicken for a Holiday' on New Year's Eve 2011 (Free Voiná 2015). From the viewpoint of Russian authorities the activists irreversibly crossed the line from art activism to political extremism by torching a prison van. Vorotnikov and Sokol fled Russia and applied for political asylum in the Czech Republic with their young children in 2016 (BBC 2012; Balmforth 2016). Leonid Nikolaev died in a work accident in Moscow in September 2015 (Calvert Journal 2015).

Pussy Riot

Preceding the militant turn of the actions of the St Petersburg-based Voiná wing, the group had in effect split into two factions. The softer approach of the Moscow wing (Samutsevich, Tolokonnikova, Verzilov and others) is demonstrated by their action of late February 2011, in which female Voiná members forcefully kissed policewomen on the capital's metro lines. Slogans accompanying the video posting, including 'Gay policemen and lesbian policewomen are the avant garde of Medvedev's modernisation!' demonstrated the integration of LGBT activism in the agenda of the 'militant-feminist faction of the Voiná group' (Voiná 2011).

In late autumn 2011 Pussy Riot was formed as a direct answer to Vladimir Putin's decision to run for a third presidency. Taking the idea of the 2009 court room punk concert to its logical conclusion, the activists set up an all-female punk band to specialize in preparing and recording public performance for online publication. Rather than merely documenting a given performance, Pussy Riot compiled images from several performances, presenting them in the form of an edited music video. For each performance a pre-recorded soundtrack was prepared and merged with live audio-visual footage from the event, giving the impression of DIY spontaneity, despite meticulous planning and editing. Richly illustrated LiveJournal blogposts accompanied the video postings, documenting the preparation and execution of each performance. Pussy Riot appeared anonymously in colourful home-knitted balaclavas and expressed themselves strictly collectively (until named members were put on trial), implying that in principle anyone could become Pussy Riot.

The initial list of Pussy Riot's key political interests (Pussy Riot 2011d) brings together feminist and LGBT activism, the anarchist rhetoric of the early Voiná group, the agenda of the extra-parliamentary opposition, prominent environmental issues and the National Bolshevik idea of a Russian capital city in the Far East. Five performances staged from December 2011 to February 2012 follow up this agenda to various degrees. Published on Revolution Day (7 November), their first video 'Release the Cobblestone' documented performances in Moscow metro stations and on top of a trolleybus (Pussy Riot 2011a). The song calls the citizens of Russia to revolt against the emerging police state, inciting them with a feminist whiplash. The follow-up, 'Kropotkin vodka' (Pussy Riot 2011b) emerged on parliamentary election day (4 December), compiling performances in favoured meeting places for the elite: a catwalk, a fashion store, a car exhibition and a café. More improvised, the third video documents a single performance on a rooftop facing Moscow's custody facility No. 1, where demonstrators against election fraud were being detained (Pussy Riot 2011c). The videos incorporate audience reactions to demonstrate the effect of each performance, from the enthusiasm of rock celebrities in the metro, via the panic of a male celebrity guest at the fashion show, to incarcerated protesters cheering in response to 'Death to Prison – Freedom to Protest'.

Their next two performances won Pussy Riot the attention of the world media. On 20 January 2012 eight members climbed onto Lobnoe mesto on the Red Square to perform 'Uproar in Russia – Putin Pees His Pants' (Pussy Riot 2012a), making headlines in *The Daily Telegraph* the same day. This built momentum for the famous 21 February 'Punk Prayer' performance in the Yelokhovo and Christ the Saviour Cathedrals (Pussy Riot 2012b). The 'Punk Prayer' became a news item in 87 countries (Kananovich 2016: 407), a major breakthrough for the activists, but simultaneously marking the transition from self-presentation to being defined by others. The rapidly developing Western media narrative presented Pussy Riot reductively as a 'feminist punk band' and was quick to pigeonhole the activists as anti-Putin, effectively downplaying their messages of global relevance (Yusupova 2014; Wiedlack 2016). In Russia as well, Kananovich demonstrates, neither liberal-oppositional nor government-owned newspapers offered informed interpretations of the political message of the activists (2016: 406).

With the Lobnoe mesto performance, Pussy Riot began targeting the church as part of a male-chauvinist power elite (Pussy Riot 2012a; Jonson 2015: 181). When Patriarch Kirill on behalf of the church backed Putin's presidential campaign and described his first term in office as 'a miracle of God' (Bryanski 2012), he made the church a legitimate target in the eyes of the activists. Applying explicit sexual vocabulary to Russian Orthodoxy, the activists challenged conservative religious zealots and the church leadership alike. The 'Punk Prayer' was the next logical step, but as it turned out, the activists had underestimated its effect and were taken aback by the following crackdown and ensuing court case (Verzilov 2013). Their carefully constructed, multilayered and multireferential message was rendered invisible in the court proceedings as well as in the international media coverage. The complex web of references included true faith as represented by the activists' ally Virgin Mary versus the political co-optation of religion and commercial church business; the ambivalence of the Christ the Saviour Cathedral as simultaneously a church and an entertainment venue complete with luxury shops (Christ the Saviour Cathedral 2017); and the tradition of religious laughter during the carnival season (Willems 2015: 414). As core members Tolokonnikova, Samutsevich and Alekhina received their prison sentences, political and judicial pressure on free cultural expression and LGBT rights increased considerably. Correspondingly, after their release, the art activists were met with unprecedented hostility. At the 2014 Sochi Winter Olympics, their performance was halted by cossack police armed with whips (*Daily Telegraph* 2014). In March 2014 Tolokonnikova, Alyokhina, Verzilov and members of their prisoners' rights NGO were attacked by hostile activists while having lunch, pepper sprayed and drenched in green antiseptic (Gogol's Wives 2014). Whilst the core members moved their NGO abroad, several of the remaining 14–20 Pussy Riot activists had by then already left Russia, fearing arrest (Verzilov 2013).

Pavlenskii

On 23 July 2012, in the commotion surrounding the Pussy Riot trial a new art activist made his debut with a performance entitled 'Seam'. Referencing works and actions by Stelarc, Wojnarowicz and Parr, Petr Pavlenskii sewed his lips shut in solidarity with the defendants, whose right to give testimony was severely restricted. He then took up position outside the court building holding a poster stating: 'Pussy Riot's performance was a re-enactment of Christ's famous action. Matthew 21:12–13' (Gabowitsch 2017: 34–35). This marked the beginning of a series of actions in which Pavlenskii, beginning with the freedom of speech, directed attention to a series of crucial social issues. Where Pussy Riot screamed to the public about the vices of an oppressive patriarchal society, Pavlenskii's actions soon forced the authorities into an unwilling dialogue with the artist. Re-inventing the concept of the bulldozer exhibition, Pavlenskii used his naked body to achieve similar effects. On 3 May 2013 Pavlenskii returned, protesting against the passing of a series of laws to limit civic activism with the performance 'Carcass' outside the St Petersburg Legislative Assembly, where he appeared naked, enveloped in a roll of barbed wire (TV Rain 2013). Six months later he performed 'Fixation', nailing his scrotum to the plaster stones of Moscow's Red Square to direct attention towards widespread apathy, political indifference and fatalism amongst Russian citizens (Walker 2014). Unlike Pussy Riot's artistic engagement with web-based media, Pavlenskii's was utilitarian and minimalistic. He made sure that his actions were documented in stills and video and issued very brief statements explaining their meaning, the shock effect of his actions ensuring high media exposure in Russia and beyond.

Each action forced police and emergency services to respond by covering the naked artist and removing him from public space. Having to free the passive and silent body carefully from the barbed wire, to remove the nail fixing his scrotum to the paving stones, highlighted the police officers' vulnerability and awkwardness with a situation requiring care, rather than the demonstration of authority and force. Following each action Pavlenskii was subjected to a psychiatric examination; each time declared sane (Hlebowicz 2015: 70, 75). Unsurprisingly, then, 'Segregation' of 19 October 2014 focused on forced psychiatric treatment of dissidents. Again, Pavlenskii succeeded in exposing the helplessness of authorities faced with a non-violent individual activist. Sitting naked on the wall of the The Serbsky State Scientific Center for Social and Forensic Psychiatry, he cut off his right earlobe with a kitchen knife and remained there awaiting society's inevitable response (Guzeva 2014). That response was delayed because it first had to be established whether he was the responsibility of the Institute (he was technically on its territory yet not, as it turned out, its patient) and whether the police had the authority to remove him. The artist was literally occupying a space between sanity and insanity, outside and inside the asylum (Hlebowicz 2015: 58). The dual reference through action and location to the iconic image of Van Gogh reinforced the action's qualities as a work of art, demonstrating the inadequacies of law, order and medical science in dealing with the creative human spirit.

With his final performance in Russia to date, 'Threat', a live staging of a metaphor from the height of Stalin's terror, comparing the doors of Lyublyanka to the gates of hell, Pavlenskii challenged the Russian judicial system to convict him for committing an act of terrorism (Walker 2016). He was charged and in June 2016 convicted of vandalism, despite a protocol of protest signed by 128 prominent names from the Russian contemporary art community, denouncing the court's reduction of 'Threat' from artistic project to banal vandalism and Pavlenskii from art activist to mere vandal (Civitas 2016). After the verdict Pavlenskii was fined 500,000 roubles and released. In January 2017 he left Russia after allegations of sexual assault (Luhn 2017). Pavlenskii claims the allegations against him and his wife are constructed by the authorities and has applied for political asylum in France (Flynn 2017).

End of an era

Faced with an increasingly active and protesting civic society during 2011–2012, the Kremlin responded by playing the cards of national patriotism and, supported by the Russian Orthodox Church, traditional moral values. A series of laws were passed which restricted the activities of the extra-parliamentary opposition, NGOs, civic initiatives and art activism, critics of the Kremlin increasingly being accused of unpatriotic behaviour and of assisting Western interests in undermining Russia. In addition the Russian internet has become increasingly controlled, monitored and subject to pro-government trolling. The 2014 annexation of Crimea, the civil war in Eastern Ukraine, and the killing of opposition figurehead Boris Nemtsov in February 2015 virtually broke the back of the Russian opposition movement, bringing an end to public mass demonstrations.

With so many influential art activists having left their home country, it appears that the 'golden age' when Russian high-profile art activism took centre stage in social and traditional media has come to an end. At present, the risks involved in attracting too much attention have become too great, yet under the radar a rich and active undergrowth of conceptualist protest art is still simmering with activity. Perhaps what we are observing is a retreat back to the point of origin, to the relatively safe turf of small-scale performances for the devoted few. If that is indeed the case, chances are the retreat is only temporary.

References

Balmforth, T. (2016) 'Fugitive Russian Protest Artist, Now Putin Supporter, Seeks Asylum in Europe', *Radio Free Europe/Radio Liberty,* 23 September, http://www.rferl.org/a/fugitive-russian-protest-artist-putin-supporter-seeks-asylum-europe/28009295.html, accessed 30 January 2017.

BBC (2012) 'Art-gruppa "Voiná" sozhgla avtozak piterskoi policii', *BBC Russian Service,* 2 January, http://www.bbc.com/russian/russia/2012/01/120102_voina_police_truck.shtml, accessed 30 January 2017.

Bryanski, G. (2012) 'Russian Patriarch Calls Putin Era "Miracle of God"', *Reuters,* 8 February, http://uk.reuters.com/article/2012/02/08/uk-russia-putin-religion-idUKTRE81722Y20120208, accessed 30 January 2017.

Calvert Journal (2015) 'Art Activist Leonid Nikolaev Dies', *The Calvert Journal,* 24 September, http://calvert-journal.com/news/show/4737/art-activist-leonid-nikolaev-dies, accessed 30 January 2017.

Christ the Saviour Cathedral (2017) 'Khram Khrista Spasitelia', cathedral webpage, http://www.xxc.ru. See also 'Fond Khrama Khrista Spasitelia', foundation webpage, http://www.fxxc.ru, both accessed 30 January 2017.

Civitas (2016) 'Diplom dlia Petra Pavlenskogo', *Civitas – Vestnik grazhdanskogo obshchestva,* 14 March, http://vestnikcivitas.ru/news/3941, accessed 30 January 2017.

Daily Telegraph (2014) 'Pussy Riot Attacked with Whips by Police at Sochi', *Telegraph.co.uk/video,* 19 February, https://www.youtube.com/watch?v=ivT-I-yxtdY, accessed 30 January 2017.

Erofeev, A. (2014) 'Pussy Riot and the Cossacks: Russian Tradition of Art Resistance', in Havremagasinet länskunsthall Boden, *Pussy Riot and the Cossacks 28 June - 28 September 2014*, exhibition catalogue, https://issuu.com/petersundstrom/docs/pussy_riot, accessed 30 January 2017.

Free Voiná (2015) 'Lenya's Actions. Happy New Year, Prisoners!', *Free Voiná*, 4 October, http://en.free-voina.org/post/130463374476, accessed 30 January 2017.

Flynn, N. (2017) 'Russian Artist Pyotr Pavlensky Is Seeking Asylum in France', *Dazed*, 17 January 2017, http://www.dazeddigital.com/artsandculture/article/34346/1/russian-artist-pyotr-pavlensky-is-seeking-asylum-in-france, accessed 28 January 2017.

Gabowitsch, M. (2017) *Protest in Putin's Russia*. Cambridge: Polity Press.

Gogol's Wives (2014) 'Pussy Riot attacked in Nizhny Novgorod McDonalds', *YouTube*, 5 March, https://www.youtube.com/watch?v=t_Xnf5bDBTg, accessed 30 January 2017.

Gololobov, I. (2011) 'Punk, Law, Resistance … War and Piss', *Critical Legal Thinking*, 8 March, http://criticallegalthinking.com/2011/03/08/punk-law-resistance-war-and-piss/, accessed 30 January 2017.

Guzeva, A. (2014) 'Severed Earlobe Is Merely Latest Scandalous Art Stunt by Pyotr Pavlensky', *Russia Beyond the Headlines*, 21 October, http://rbth.com/society/2014/10/21/severed_earlobe_is_merely_latest_scandalous_art_stunt_by_pyotr_pavlen_40775.html, accessed 30 January 2017.

Hlebowicz, S. (2015) *A Holy Fool for Our Time? Petr Pavlenskii as a Case Study of the Paradigm of Iurodstvo in Modern Russian Art*. MA thesis in Russian Literature, UiT – The Arctic University of Norway.

HRW (2010) 'Russia: Reverse Judgment Against Human Rights Defender; Investigate Misuse of Anti-Extremism Law to Stifle Artistic Expression', *Human Rights Watch*, 12 July, https://www.hrw.org/news/2010/07/12/russia-reverse-judgment-against-human-rights-defender, accessed 25 November 2016.

Johnson, O. (2013) 'War on the Ru-net: Voiná's *Dick Captured by the FSB* as a Networked Performance', *Third Text*, vol. 27, no. 5, pp. 591–606.

Jonson, L. (2015) *Art and Protest in Putin's Russia*. London and New York: Routledge.

Kananovich, V. (2016) 'Progressive Artists, Political Martyrs, or Blasphemous Hussies? A Content Analysis of the Russian Media Coverage of the Pussy Riot Affair', *Popular Music and Society*, vol. 39, no. 4, pp. 396–409.

Luhn, A. (2017) 'Radical Russian Artist in Real-life Drama over Sexual Assault Claims', *The Guardian*, 20 January, https://www.theguardian.com/world/2017/jan/20/russia-artist-pyotr-pavlensky-teatr-sexual-assault-allegations, accessed 30 January 2017.

Plutser-Sarno, A. (2017) 'The VOINA Art-Group ("War"). Actions 2006–2013 – Ironic Notes about VOINA Group, Protest Street Art and Radical Political Artists', LiveJournal, http://plucer.livejournal.com/266853.html, accessed 30 January 2017.

Pussy Riot (2011a) 'Devchonki iz Pussy Riot zakhvativaiut transport', *YouTube*, 6 November, http://www.youtube.com/watch?v=qEiB1RYuYXw, accessed 30 January 2017.

Pussy Riot (2011b) 'Gruppa Pussy Riot zhzhet putinskii glamur', *YouTube*, 30 November, http://www.youtube.com/watch?v=CZUhkWiiv7M, accessed 30 January 2017.

Pussy Riot (2011c) 'Pussy Riot poiut politzekam na kryshe tiur'my', *YouTube*, 14 December, http://www.youtube.com/watch?v=mmyZbJpYV0I, accessed 30 January 2017.

Pussy Riot (2011d) 'Osvobodi brushchatku', *LiveJournal*, 7 November, http://pussy-riot.livejournal.com/5497.html, accessed 30 January 2017.

Pussy Riot (2012a) 'Pussy Riot na Krasnoi ploshchadi s pesnei Putin zassal', *YouTube*, 20 January www.youtube.com/watch?v=yqcmldeC7Ec, accessed 30 January 2017.

Pussy Riot (2012b) 'Pank-moleben "Bogoroditsa, Putina progoni" Pussy Riot v Khrame', *YouTube*, 21 February, http://www.youtube.com/watch?v=GCasuaAczKY&feature=plcp, accessed 30 January 2017.

Russian Gesture (2012) 'Online Russian Performance History: Alexander Brener 1995 "Boxing Champion" (The First Glove)', *Livejournal*, http://ru-performance.livejournal.com/6855.html, accessed 30 January 2017.

Rutten, E. (2017) *Sincerity after Communism*. New Haven, CT and London: Yale University Press.

Smith, R. (1997) 'On Becoming a Dog By Acting Like One', *New York Times*, 18 April, http://www.nytimes.com/1997/04/18/arts/on-becoming-a-dog-by-acting-like-one.html, accessed 30 January 2017.

TV Rain (2013) 'Sadovye nozhnicy i odeialo. Kak piterskie policeiskie vynimali obnazhennogo khudozhnika iz kolochei provoloki', TV Dozhd'Video, 4 May, https://tvrain.ru/teleshow/here_and_now/sadovye_nozhnitsy_i_odejalo_kak_piterskie_politsejskie_vynimali_obnazhennogo_hudozhnika_iz_koljuchej_provoloki_video-342684/, accessed 30 January 2017.

Verzilov, P. (2013) Live video-link interview, *Re-Aligned Art* exhibition opening, Tromsø Kunstforening, Norway, 14 September.

Voiná (2009) 'Khuj v otsjko: Vse menty ubljudki', *YouTube*, 12 June, http://www.youtube.com/watch?v=EUaJLNonytg, accessed 30 January 2017.

Voiná (2010) 'Khui v plenu u FSB', *YouTube*, 19 June 2010, http://www.youtube.com/watch?v=Sw-rx6JqQIE, accessed 30 January 2017.

Voiná (2011) 'Gruppa Voiná zacelivaet mentov', *YouTube*, 28 February, http://www.youtube.com/watch?v=l0A8Qf893cs&feature=plcp, accessed 30 January 2017.

Voronina, O. (2013) 'Pussy Riot's Punk Prayer on Trial Online and in Court.' *Digital Icons*, no. 9, pp. 69–85.

Walker, S. (2014) 'Petr Pavlensky: Why I Nailed My Scrotum to Red Square', *The Guardian*, 5 February, https://www.theguardian.com/artanddesign/2014/feb/05/petr-pavlensky-nailed-scrotum-red-square, accessed 30 January 2017.

Walker, S. (2016) 'Protest Artist Petr Pavlensky in Court after Setting Fire to Lubyanka', *The Guardian*, 28 April, https://www.theguardian.com/world/2016/apr/28/petr-pavlensky-appears-court-russia-setting-fire-to-lubyanka-protest, accessed 30 January 2017.

Wiedlack, K. (2016) 'Pussy Riot and the Western Gaze: Punk Music, Solidarity and the Production of Similarity and Difference', *Popular Music and Society*, vol. 39, no. 4, pp. 410–22.

Wijermars, M. (2016) Memory Politics in Contemporary Russia: Television, Cinema and the State. PhD Thesis, Reichsuniversiteit Groningen.

Willems, J. (2015) 'Why "Punk"? Religion, Anarchism and Feminism in Pussy Riot's Punk Prayer', *Religion, State and Society*, vol. 42, no. 4, pp. 403–19.

Yusupova, M. (2014) 'Pussy Riot: A Feminist Band Lost in History and Translation', *Nationalities Papers: The Journal of Nationalism and Ethnicity*, vol. 42, no. 4, pp. 604–10

16

ART AS ACTIVISM IN JAPAN

The case of a good-for-nothing kid and her pussy

Mark McLelland

Introduction

In July 2014 Japanese 'vagina artist' Megumi Igarashi, who works under the name Rokudenashiko or 'Good-for-nothing kid', was arrested at her home in Tokyo on suspicion of distributing obscene material (Rokudenashiko 2016: 11). The objects in question were a number of art pieces that she had fashioned from silicon moulds as well as a digital 3D scan of her own vulva, or *manko* in Japanese. Although Rokudenashiko was released one week later without charge, she was re-arrested in December that year and held for three weeks, this time being officially charged with obscenity. In the resulting court case her various 'deco-man' (decorative *manko*) were found not to be obscene but she was found guilty of distributing an obscene item – the data from the 3D scan of her vulva.

The use of her vulva as part of her artistic activities was by no means a stunt, since Rokudenashiko had for several years been promoting *manko* art as a vehicle for discussion about the taboos and misunderstandings surrounding the female sex organ in Japan (Rokudenashiko 2016: 31). Her use of the term *manko*, which sits somewhere between the English terms 'pussy' and 'cunt' regarding its impact, was a deliberate strategy to force people to think about the double standard that she claimed surrounds male and female sex organs in Japanese culture. In keeping with the artist's wish that this term should be normalized and used in discussion without shame or dissimulation, I use *manko* in place of vagina/vulva throughout this chapter.

The Japanese police have a long history of using obscenity law to regulate cultural space – having successfully prosecuted artists and translators associated with literature, film, photography and even manga (comic books) (Cather 2012). Rokudenashiko's case is interesting in that it involves a new form of media communication – that of 3D scans – and is also the first time that a female defendant has been charged and found guilty of obscenity. Although a wide range of cultural products have been investigated on obscenity charges, the actual number of cases that reach the courts is few given that most defendants approached by the police avoid court through issuing an apology and withdrawing the work in question. In more serious cases defendants often choose to accept a summary indictment, which means that they can plead guilty and accept a token fine imposed by a judge without suffering the embarrassment of going through a court case. Rokudenashiko, however, refused to apologize or accept any wrongdoing. As she said in her defence during the trial, 'neither my genitals nor my artistic activities are obscene.'

In this chapter I look at the various media discussions surrounding Rokudenashiko and her trial as well as activities that she engaged in to draw attention to her case. I point out how, even though the rationale behind Japan's obscenity law is to restrain and rein in text or representations that are considered injurious to the public good, in Rokudenashiko's case the international publicity she received has had the opposite effect and amplified both her own visibility and that of her message. However, not all recent obscenity charges in Japan have received this kind of international interest and support – and I also look at the conditions that have made Rokudenashiko such a sympathetic figure to her overseas supporters and the role that her media activism has played in this.

Rokudenashiko's artistic activities

Rokudenashiko explains that her interest in using her *manko* as a design motif originally arose from anxieties that her genitalia may not have been 'normal'. She explained how, given the cultural taboos around speaking about or depicting genitalia in Japan, she had no sense of what constituted 'normality' regarding female genitalia. As a result she opted to undergo a labiaplasty procedure which she described in her first published manga (Rokudenashiko 2016: 130).

It is well documented that pornography is not a good source for depictions of regular-looking genitalia, with many female models undergoing plastic surgery to achieve a more streamlined appearance (Iglesia 2012). The situation in Japan is made more complex given that all officially produced and distributed pornography, whether in photographic or video format, must have the genitalia covered by *bokashi*, that is, pixilation (Hambleton 2015: 5). So, unless one searches for overseas porn sites (which Rokudenashiko says she was reluctant to do), there is no means for women to compare their genitalia with that of others. This is not just an issue for women in Japan, as UK artist Jamie McCartney discovered while taking plaster casts of the vulvas of over 100 women for his sculptural project 'The Great Wall of Vagina', completed in 2011. He was surprised how the volunteers 'were looking at the casts of other women's vulvas and were having a similar epiphany. They were saying things like, "Oh my God! I had no idea they looked so different"' (McCartney 2015).

In order to encourage women to think more positively about their *manko* and to encourage discussion of genital variety, Rokudenashiko began to take silicon casts of her own *manko* and use it as a motif in various art objects. These included dioramas where her *manko* was used as part of a landscape, a sculptural installation and a gold pendant chandelier. She also produced pop art items incorporating the motif, such as phone cases and figurines. In addition she created a cute cartoon character named Manko-*chan* and depicted in manga form the discrimination and misrepresentation she faced on a daily basis. None of these items evoked a sexual context, nor did they reference any kind of sexual activity – indeed, Rokudenashiko's intent was to produce items that were 'bright and cheerful' and that showed an everyday body part in a new light in the pop art tradition. As she later said at a press conference at the Foreign Correspondents Club of Japan (FCCJ), 'It may be obscene if you are depicting something actually engaging in sexual activities, but I'm just presenting a part of my body just as it is. I don't think that is obscene' (Pothecary 2014).

These small items had been exhibited and sold at galleries and online for several years without drawing police attention. However, in 2013 Rokudenashiko wanted to make larger *manko* art that would have more impact and conceived the idea to produce a *manko* boat – actually a kayak cover that utilized the *manko* design. For this purpose she needed to scale up the *manko* motif and consequently set up an appeal on the crowdfunding website Camp Fire to raise money for the loan of a digital scanner and 3D printer that could manufacture the *manko* cover. The scheme was successful and in 2014 she created a bright yellow '*man*-boat', which she paddled around the Tama River in Tokyo and later exhibited in a gallery. As a gesture of thanks to her supporters on the crowdfunding site she made the digital data of her *manko* scan available via a URL, encouraging them to make their own *manko* art. Her lawyer speculated that it was this act that prompted police intervention (FCCJ 2014).

After having been detained in a police cell for one week without charge in July 2014, Rokudenashiko was released only to be arrested again in December of the same year. She was arrested along with Minori Kitahara, a feminist and outspoken critic on a range of social issues (Rokudenashiko 2016: 118). Kitahara is also the owner of feminist sex shop Love Piece (Dales 2005: 191–95) where several figurative art pieces based on Rokudenashiko's *manko* design were being exhibited. This time Rokudenashiko was kept in police detention for the full three weeks allowed before finally being charged with the distribution of obscene data and displaying an obscene object. The artist pled not guilty, stating, 'I am engaged in artistic activities; neither the data nor the artefacts are obscene.' Her not-guilty plea precipitated a court case that was resolved at first instance in May 2016, where she was found not guilty of displaying an obscene object (her *manko* figurines) but was found guilty on the charge of transmitting obscene data (NBC News 2016). To understand how this verdict was reached it is necessary to consider the relationship between obscenity and art in Japan.

Obscenity and art

As previous defendants of obscenity charges in Japan have pointed out, obscenity was not a concept that existed in the Japanese legal system prior to the opening to the West that came with the Meiji Restoration in 1868 when Japan's legal code was restructured along European lines. Indeed the previous Edo period (1603–1867) had seen an outpouring of erotic art known as *shunga* or 'spring pictures' that were subsequently deemed offensive and strictly censored by the new regime, with regulations on their reproduction and display not being removed until very recently (*Japan Times* 2015).

The concept of obscenity has historically not been deployed to prosecute sexual acts or practices but has instead been used to restrict depictions of certain acts in words or images – it has been about publication, dissemination and possession of *representations* and not acts or things themselves. To this extent it is an attempt to place limits on the kind of imagery that, were it to be accessed by the general public, might 'deprave and corrupt' the minds of the viewer (Sceats 2002: 133). It is essentially about controlling thought. Thus an obscene image functions in a kind of obverse manner to the purpose of art, at least as art is defined by government institutions that regard its purpose as one of 'moral uplift' (Miller 1994: 268).

When considering issues of freedom of expression, particularly that of the artist, it is pertinent to consider that artistic expression never has been nor can be free from outside influence. Any kind of public expression is not only caught up in the processes of governmentality but is in fact always already constituted by those forces prior to its articulation. As Toby Miller (1994: 264) points out, multiple organizations 'teach, circulate, fund, define and exclude actors and activities that go under the names of artist or artwork'. In Rokudenashiko's case both the police and the local media were implicated in this de-valuation of her work by choosing to refer to her in official reports as a 'self-proclaimed artist' (*jijō geijutsuka*), suggesting that there was no support or validation for her work offered by other artists or the art world itself (Rokudenashiko 2016: 70). Yet, although not trained at any of Japan's elite art institutions, at the time of her arrest, Rokudenashiko was already a published manga artist, her *deco-man* work had been exhibited at independent galleries in Japan, and in addition, the guilty verdict was later protested by the Japan branch of the International Association of Art Critics (*Asahi Shinbun* 2016a).

Rokudenashiko was prosecuted under Article 175 of Japan's Penal Code, first promulgated in 1907, which stipulates that:

A person who *distributes, sells or displays in public* an obscene document, drawing or other objects shall be punished … The same shall apply to a person who possesses the same for the purpose of sale.

My emphasis

Article 175 is one of the main mechanisms whereby the Japanese state maintains some control over the cultural sphere given that Japan's 1947 Constitution contains a robust defence of freedom of expression. Article 21 of the Constitution states that 'no censorship shall be maintained', and it is this article that is invoked in most obscenity trials as the defendants claim that the government's use of Article 175 is nothing other than a form of censorship. Significantly, obscenity is not defined in the legislation and this has made it a very flexible term that has been used, especially in Japan's imperialist period (1868–1945), to limit any discussion or representation of sexuality in the media as well as film, literature and art, of which the government of the day disapproved (McLelland 2015).

There has been some confusion in the Western press reports about the status of censorship in Japan since the general impression given is of a very permissive sexual environment in the realm of popular culture, especially in manga and animation (CNN 2014). This is to do with the particular way in which censorship has been applied since the liberalization of rules governing pornography in the 1970s. Interpretations of obscenity since that time have tended to focus not so much on the general scenario surrounding a sexual act or situation, nor the nature of the acts described, so much as the degree of realism with which the sex organs are depicted (Allison 1996: 149; McLelland 2015). Until 1991 there was a complete ban on the depiction of the genital areas of men and women, including any pubic hair. This required the airbrushing of the pubic areas of actors and models in films and photographs, even in non-sexual contexts. The year 1991, however, saw a further liberalization of these rules due to the 'hair debate' occasioned by the publication of a best-selling photo book of nudes of teen actress and media personality Mie Miyazawa which showed glimpses of her pubic hair in several artfully posed frames. From this time on glimpses of hair have been allowed but there is still a prohibition on sexual organs, both male and female (Allison 1996: 149). All commercially produced and distributed pornography in Japan, including that imported from overseas (covered by Article 21 of the Customs Act), must be pixelated in order to cover genital areas. The specific focus on depiction of genitalia at the expense of overall scenario has actually proven beneficial to women's erotica in Japan, of which there are many examples, including the highly sexualized 'ladies comics' genre as well as the 'boys love' manga and anime popular with girls and young women (McLelland 2016; see also Hambleton 2015; O'Keefe 2016).

That Japanese legislators do move against the unmasked depiction of male as well as female sex organs is clear not only from historical cases such as the prosecution of gay rights activist and magazine editor Ken Tōgō in the 1970s (Helms 2000;, McLelland 2012), but in a recent incident when prominent Japan-based celebrity photographer Leslie Kee was arrested and detained for 48 hours in February 2013 (that is, *prior* to the Rokudenashiko case) for selling copies of his photobook of male nudes. According to the police, 'models' erect genitalia were featured extensively in the 50-page-photobook, some of which also alluded to ejaculation' (*Asahi shinbun* 2014a: 26). Unlike Rokudenashiko, who insisted on her innocence, Kee pleaded guilty to a summary indictment, meaning he paid a fine determined by a judge without having to go through a trial. Kee argued that unlike female nudes, which have been accepted for display for some time, exhibitions of male nudes are rare, and that is one reason why the police regarded his work as obscene (Poole 2013) – precisely the opposite of the argument proffered by Rokudenashiko, who claimed that her *manko* art had been unfairly targeted.

As can be seen from Kee's case, the impression given in the Western media that female sex organs are the specific target of police interest and intervention is not borne out by actual events – in keeping with protocols in place since the 1970s, it is the open and undisguised representation of the genital regions of both sexes that is targeted.

Media response to Rokudenashiko's arrest and trial

Responses to Rokudenashiko's arrest and trial in the local Japanese press were mainly neutral. Most of the major dailies simply reported on the facts of the case, offering little in the way of analysis. The exception was Japan's *Asahi* newspaper, the most 'progressive' of Japan's dailies, which featured several longer articles including commentary by art critics and academics. However, although there was general acceptance that her activities did not constitute obscenity, Rokudenashiko was not without criticism. Feminist academic Chizuko Ueno, for example, thought that Rokudenashiko had been naïve in making the digital data of her *manko* available online since she then lost control of how it would be circulated and reproduced (*Asahi Shinbun* 2016b: 13). Some journalists also questioned the value of her work, arguing that although it was not obscene, it lacked originality and did not qualify as art (*Asahi Shinbun* 2015: 9).

Unlike the case of Lee, mentioned above, which received little or no international media attention, Rokudenashiko's case was well covered in the overseas press and given a great deal of exposure on social media, where support was much more effusive than it had been in Japan. The fact that Rokudenashiko explicitly situated her art work as both feminist and political meant that it was much easier for the overseas press to frame her arrest in terms of the repression of free speech. The cute 'pop' nature of her work also lent itself to being discussed across a wide range of media, despite its supposedly confronting topic matter. As Andrew Pothecary points out, to a foreign audience Rokudenashiko's arrest 'made yet another "weird Japan" story', and was even picked up in a segment of the highly popular US comedy program *The Daily Show with Jon Stewart*. It was Stewart's show that put forward the claim that the *manko* is treated differently from the penis in Japanese culture, his example (one also used by Rokudenashiko) being the Kanamara (Iron Penis) Festival, an annual Shinto event that celebrates the suppression of a demon by an iron penis. The equivalence between the repression of Rokudenashiko's *manko* art versus the celebration of the male sex organ in the festival was, however, questioned in the Japanese press (*Asahi Shinbun* 2014b: 35). Shinto rites have historically been much concerned with fertility and there are festivals that celebrate the *manko* – but these festivals were not reported on in the English-language press, other than one article in the *Japan Times* (O'Keefe 2016).

Major newspaper outlets in North America and Europe also covered Rokudenashiko's story, following the progress of the court case and reporting on its resolution. This mainstream media exposure meant that the topic was picked up in alternative media, blogs and articles concerned with sexuality, feminism and art – resulting in many opportunities for Rokudenashiko to engage with an international audience. This included a 15-minute video interview with the artist as well as local and international commentators featured on Vice channel's Broadly site (Broadly 2015).

The artist's arrest drew particular attention in the Chinese world, with Rokudenashiko receiving an invitation to meet with controversial artist Ai Weiwei in Beijing. An interview with Ai was later published in a Japanese weekly art and subculture magazine *Shūkan dokusho-jin* on 17 April 2015 where he recounted his meeting with Rokudenashiko and supported her views on feminism, the body and freedom of expression. Ai's support of Rokudenashiko's work added further gravitas to her cause given his major profile as an artist also working against state oppression. Rokudenashiko also received an invitation to speak at the Parasite art space in Hong Kong in September 2015. This lecture was timed to coincide with the *Gender, Genitor, Genitalia – Rokudenashiko Tribute* exhibition that was staged at the Woofer Ten gallery, where local artists drew parallels between Rokudenashiko's treatment in Japan and their own struggle to maintain freedom of expression in the face of mainland Chinese pressure in Hong Kong. The event was reported favourably in Hong Kong's *South China Morning Post* with the artist's work being firmly positioned as a feminist response to the 'male gaze' that structures the majority of mainstream sexual depictions (Kwong 2015).

Fuyuki Kurasawa can help us understand the almost unanimous support that Rokudenashiko has received from overseas, including from major artists. Kurasawa (2009: 91) is interested in the globalization of activism against social injustice. He shows how the media, especially social media, help establish audiences who 'bear witness' and respond to distant injustice. Although his focus is more on human rights violations on a mass scale, his analysis is useful for understanding how the media accelerate the 'transnationalization of bearing witness' and help establish solidarity with local causes among a territorially disperse collection of 'concerned citizens around the planet' (ibid.: 93). From the outset, reports in the overseas press positioned Rokudenashiko as a victim of police harassment and endorsed her art as a form of feminist activism against Japan's perceived patriarchal social system. This is despite the fact that some of the evidence brought to bear in this narrative, lacking as it does a nuanced sense of local context, has not been accurate.

Rokudenashiko has played a part in crafting a positive self-image – presenting herself as a single woman, a seemingly easy target for the police, since she was without the support of a gallery or agent and had very limited financial resources. However, the artist turned out to be skilful at using the notoriety brought about by her arrest and court case in order to advance her cause. One of her first activities after her initial arrest was to produce a book of manga, photographs and short essays describing her artistic career to date, her arrest, and her week-long detention in the police cells. The book was published in 2014 and in 2016 was released in an English translation entitled: *What Is Obscenity? The Story of a Good for Nothing Artist and Her Pussy*. The book, presented using the same kind of pop art style that defines much of her work, painted an extremely unflattering picture of the police (ten of whom turned up at her home to arrest her). Although the conditions of her detention were severe, spending many hours handcuffed and not allowed to change clothes or bathe, Rokudenashiko manages to find humour in the situation – mostly at the expense of the police and prosecutors who were clearly made uncomfortable by her constant use of the term *manko*, refusing to use the circumlocution *josei seiki* (female sexual organ) while being questioned, as they demanded. The artist also made several public appearances after her release, sometimes in cos-play guise as a female police officer or wearing a giant *manko* suit or an inflatable *manko* arm-band. Videos were made of some of these appearances, as were videos of comedy skits featuring the artist and her supporters mocking the police actions, which were then distributed via social media. If the police had thought that Rokudenashiko's arrest would give the artist pause for thought and make her terminate her activities – as is usual in these cases – they were mistaken. As Rokudenashiko stated in an interview at the FCCJ: 'If I give up then the regulations will be strengthened'. Through taking this stance the artist broadened her appeal, and was perceived as standing up not only for her own freedom of expression but for the freedom of other artists in Japan.

The international media attention resulted in a number of speaking engagements outside Japan, including an Asian American writer's workshop in New York in May 2015 where Rokudenashiko spoke about the creation of the manga *What Is Obscenity?* At the New York meeting the artist was accompanied by the translator of her manga, Anne Ishii, who is also a director of the online store MASSIVE that offers merchandise from queer and feminist artists in Japan, including Rokudenashiko's 'free *manko*' pins. The support of sites such as MASSIVE, which is represented at comic conventions, book fairs and queer events around North America, underlines the connections between feminist and queer artists: both groups are challenging the codes regulating visual representation of sexuality in Japan, connecting what can seem local issues to larger questions concerning the regulation of sexuality in a global context.

Conclusion

In choosing to fight the obscenity charge, Rokudenashiko proved herself to be a good judge of public opinion, at least outside Japan – perceiving the court case as an excellent means to draw attention to her work and establish connections with overseas activism. She was also able to draw attention to some fundamental contradictions in the notion of obscenity itself. Inherent in obscenity law and underlying the arguments of its prosecutors is the idea that there is something particularly compelling about the nature of sexual imagery and that sex will capture the imagination of the broader population in a more compulsive manner than other kinds of imagery. It is for this reason that, as Sceats (2002: 144) points out, there is 'an awareness amongst more savvy agitators that the audience guaranteed by the strength of these reactions generates important opportunities for communicating political dissent'. Indeed, there is a long tradition going back to the revolutions of the eighteenth century of using pornographic pamphlets to destabilize authority figures. With this point in mind we can situate Rokudenashiko's artistic endeavours as political and not pornographic, given that her art has never been about drawing attention to *manko* as an *object* of sexual arousal but rather has been an attempt to bring *manko* into discourse, an attempt to encourage women to own discussion of and representation of their *manko* as *subjects*.

Rokudenashiko's pop art treatment of the vagina, a body part which well over half the world's population encounters on a daily basis, but which cannot be represented or spoken about directly in Japan's public sphere, is an attempt to use the strength of public reaction to open space for political dissent. Her work is clearly political and arguably, from a feminist perspective at least, about empowerment and the very 'moral uplift' that the state sees as the purpose of art. It is difficult to find an audience that was or could have been depraved and corrupted by the digital data provided by the artist, given that its only recipients were the self-selecting community of supporters who had contributed to her artistic endeavour via the crowdfunding site. Indeed, in the course of the trial it became clear that the only persons who had actually downloaded the data and used a digital printer to make a replica of Rokudenashiko's *manko* were the police involved in the investigation.

Rokudenashiko's art work has nothing at all to do with sexual excitement and yet her arrest and trial do make sense within the Japanese system since she broke the main convention governing obscenity – the unambiguous depiction of a sexual organ. Contrary to the argument staged in overseas media, the *manko* is not unfairly treated – there are several recent examples of male nudity also being prosecuted (see also *Asahi Shinbun* 2014a). However, the perception that she was being unfairly targeted certainly helped her case as it fed into an already well-established script about 'weird Japan' and its patriarchal culture. Any complexity in this description was mostly overlooked, enabling a global 'witnessing' of the injustice waged against Rokudenashiko that afforded her a celebrity-like status. Indeed, due to celebrity support garnered for her cause on social media, in 2014 the artist met folk-rock group The Waterboys' frontman Mike Scott, whom she married in 2016, and the couple recently had a baby. Having moved to Ireland with her new husband, Rokudenashiko is free to explore her artistic pursuits without fear of further intervention from the Japanese police. The international support and attention the artist has received has not however resulted in her conviction being overturned, as Tokyo's High Court confirmed the lower court's decision in April 2017 (Kikuchi 2017). Whether a further appeal to the Supreme Court will see her artistic endeavours vindicated remains to be seen.

References

Allison, A. (1996) *Permitted and Prohibited Desires: Mothers, Comics and Censorship in Japan*. Boulder, CO: Westview Press.

Asahi Shinbun (2014a) '*Bijutsukan tenji shashin, kenkei 'waisetsu' aichi, ichibu oou* [Prefectural Police Demand "Obscene" Parts of Museum Exhibited Artworks Be Covered]', 13 August, p. 26 (morning edition).

Asahi Shinbun (2014b) 'News: seiki wo katadotta sakuhin geijutsu ka waisetsu ka [News: Are Art Works That Are Shaped Like Female Genitals Art or Obscenity?]', 17 December, p. 35.

Asahi Shinbun (2015) '*Yūbae: waisetsu to geijutsu no kyōkaisen* [The Evening Glow: The Borderline Between Art and The Obscene]', 19 October, p. 9 (evening paper).

Asahi Shinbun (2016a) '*Hyōgen no jiyū meguri kikikan hyōronka/gakugei'inra shinpo* [A Sense of Crisis over Freedom of Expression: A Symposium of Critics and Curators]', 2 August, p. 4 (evening paper).

Asahi Shinbun (2016b) '*(Kōron) seihyōgen to hō kisei Hayashi Michio san, Hirano Kei'ichirō san, Ueno Chizuko san* [(A Discussion) Expression of Sexuality and Regulatory Law, with Hayashi Michio, Hirano Kei'ichirō, and Ueno Chizuko]', 27 July, p. 13.

Broadly (2015) 'Who's Afraid of Vagina Art?'. 15 August, https://broadly.vice.com/en_us/video/whos-afraid-of-vagina-art, accessed 25 April 2017.

Cather, K. (2012) *The Art of Censorship in Postwar Japan*. Honolulu, HI: University of Hawai'i Press.

CNN (2014) 'Sexually Explicit Japan Manga Evades New Laws on Child Pornography', 18 June, http://edition.cnn.com/2014/06/18/world/asia/japan-manga-anime-pornography, accessed 25 April 2017.

Dales, L. (2005) 'Feminist Futures in Japan: Exploring the work of Haruka Yōko and Kitahara Minori', in Mark McLelland and Romit Dasgupta (eds) *Genders, Transgenders and Sexualities in Japan*. London: Routledge, pp. 183–99.

Foreign Correspondents' Club of Japan (FCCJ) (2014) 'Megumi Igarashi (Rokudenashiko): "Art and Obscenity: Did the Japanese Police Go Too Far with Her?"', https://www.youtube.com/watch?v=u35rEg_nTV8, accessed 25 April 2017.

Hambleton, A. (2015) 'When Women Watch: The Subversive Potential of Female-Friendly Pornography in Japan', *Porn Studies*, vol. 3, no. 4, pp. 427–42.

Helms, U. (2000) 'Obscenity and Homosexual Depiction in Japan', *Journal of Homosexuality*, vol. 39, nos. 3–4, pp. 127–47.

Iglesia, C. (2012) 'Cosmetic Gynecology and the Elusive Quest for the "Perfect" Vagina', *Obstetrics & Gynecology*, vol. 119, no. 6, pp. 1083–84.

Japan Times (2015) 'Exhibition of Erotic Japanese Art Draws 200,000 Visitors', 25 December, http://www.japantimes.co.jp/culture/2015/12/25/arts/exhibition-erotic-japanese-art-draws-200000-visitors, accessed 25 April 2017.

Kikuchi, D. (2017) '"Vagina Artist" Megumi Igarashi Continues Her Battle with Japan's Definition of Obscenity', *Japan Times*, 18 April, http://www.japantimes.co.jp/news/2017/04/18/national/vagina-artist-megumi-igarashi-continues-her-battle-with-japans-definition-of-obscenity/#.WPfwpfJH5W0, accessed 25 April 2017.

Kurasawa, F. (2009) 'A Message in a Bottle: Bearing Witness as a Mode of Transnational Practice', *Theory, Culture and Society*, vol. 26, no. 10, pp. 92–111.

Kwong, K. (2015) '"Making the Vagina More Pop and Accessible": Japanese Artist Megumi Igarashi Brings Works to Hong Kong', *South China Morning Post*, 25 August, http://www.scmp.com/lifestyle/arts-entertainment/article/1852351/making-vagina-more-pop-and-accessible-japanese-artist, accessed 25 April 2017.

Pothecary, A. (2014) 'Obscenity, Thy Name Is Vagina', *Number 1 Shimbun*, 4 September, http://www.fccj.or.jp/number-1-shimbun/item/450-obscenity-thy-name-is-vagina/450-obscenity-thy-name-is-vagina.html, accessed 25 April 2017.

McCartney, J. (2015) 'The Great Wall of Vagina: An Interview with Artist Jamie McCartney', *beutiful magazine*, http://beutifulmagazine.com/2015/04/14/the-great-wall-of-vagina-an-interview-with-artist-jamie-mccartney, accessed 25 April 2017.

McLelland, M. (2012) 'Death of the Legendary Okama Tōgō Ken: Challenging Commonsense Lifestyles in Postwar Japan', *The Asia-Pacific Journal*, vol. 10, issue 25, no. 5, <http://apjjf.org/2012/10/25/Mark-McLelland/3775/article.html>, accessed 25 April 2017.

McLelland, M. (2015) '"How to Sex?" The Contested Nature of Sexuality in Japan', in J. Baab (ed.) *The Sage Handbook of Modern Japanese Studies*, Thousand Oaks, CA: Sage, pp. 194–209.

McLelland, M. (2016) 'New Media, Censorship and Gender: Using Obscenity Law to Restrict Online Self-Expression in Japan and China', in L. Hjorth and O. Khoo (eds) *The Routledge Handbook of New Media in Asia*, London: Routledge, pp. 118–29.

Miller, T. (1994) 'Culture with Power: The Present Moment in Cultural Policy Studies', *Southeast Asian Journal of Social Science*, vol. 22, pp. 264–80.

NBC News (2016) 'Megumi Igarashi, AKA "Rokudenashiko," Not Guilty of Obscenity', 9 May, http://www.nbcnews.com/news/world/megumi-igarashi-aka-rokudenashiko-not-guilty-obscenity-n570411, accessed 25 April 2017.

O'Keefe, A. (2016) 'Western Media Cherry-pick Facts and Phalli to Fit the "No Vagina" Narrative in Japan", *Japan Times*, 3 July, http://www.japantimes.co.jp/community/2016/07/03/voices/western-media-cherry-pick-facts-phalli-fit-japan-no-vagina-narrative, accessed 25 April 2017.

Poole, R. (2013) 'After His Tokyo Arrest, Full Frontal Photog Leslie Kee Talks Art and Obscenity', *BlouinArtinfo*, 20 February, http://www.blouinartinfo.com/news/story/869614/after-his-tokyo-arrest-full-frontal-photog-leslie-kee-talks, accessed 25 April 2017.

Rokudenashiko (2016) *What Is Obscenity? The Story of a Good for Nothing Artist and Her Pussy*. Tokyo: Koyama Press.

Sceats, S. (2002) 'The Legal Concept of Obscenity – A Genealogy', *The Australian Feminist Law Journal*, vol. 16, pp. 133–45.

Shūkan dokushojin (2015) '*Ai Weiwei intābyū: Rokudenashiko, geijutsu no hyōgen, feminizumu* [Ai Weiwei Interview: Rokudenashiko, Artistic Expression, Feminism]'. 17 April.

17

MUSIC AND ACTIVISM

From prefigurative to pragmatic politics

Andrew Green and John Street

Introduction

Music is a recurring feature of activism, from the iconic status of 'We Shall Overcome' in civil rights and peace movements to the efforts of New Song musicians to foment support for the Communist government of Salvador Allende in Chile (Tumas-Serna 1992; Eyerman & Jamison 1998; Rosenthal & Flacks 2012). The scholarly literature on political activism highlights multiple roles for music. To begin with, music can form a locus of efforts at fundraising for political causes, as in the case of the Live Aid concert that took place in support of famine relief for Ethiopia in 1985 (Widgery 1986; Street, Hague & Savigny 2008; Rachel 2016). However, music is not just a source of cash; musical practice can itself constitute the terrain on which politics is contested, as in the case of the black and white musicians performing together at Rock Against Racism rallies (Love 2006; Goodyer 2009). Music can also serve as a form of political communication and persuasion; a means of transmitting political messages, stories or information. Music can, furthermore, *embody* political action. Live music – whether the singing of a national anthem or the drums accompanying a demonstration – can serve as a means to enact a sense of ritual togetherness, allowing participants to perform a sense of community (Anderson 1983; Mattern 1998). Indeed, in a broader sense, music may provide a platform on which ideal social relationships can be presented, for instance by encouraging participation, egalitarianism and improvisation, or else producing forms of expression perceived as 'authentic' (Higgins 2008; Turino 2008). Finally, musical performances can claim public spaces, or maintain their status as a site in which political organization can legitimately emerge (Green 2016). This was evident in the occupations of Tahrir Square in Egypt and Gezi Park in Turkey, and in the various spaces used by Occupy.

It is perhaps both the complexity of such highly varied social dynamics, alongside a logocentric tendency within academic circles, which has led to music's role within politics being sidelined or ignored in much of the scholarly literature in political science. Yet the recent 'emotional turn' in the social sciences has exposed the limitations of rational choice theory to explain human decision-making in practice. According to this perspective, cultural forms of social activity – containing a rich combination of emotional, affective and bodily expression – ought not to be dismissed as irrelevant to politics; rather, they are key to the way that politics functions (DeNora 2000; McDonald 2006; Shank 2014).

An ongoing challenge within the literature on music and activism, however, is to connect formal, sonic, affective and subjective aspects of musical experience to observable political processes. As some scholars have highlighted, statements of intention to perform this task have often unravelled in practice (Peddie 2012: xiv). Studies connecting 'music' and 'politics' are often constructed around an alienation of lyrics from sound, allowing writers to analyze song as, in effect, a literary category (e.g. Boucher & Browning 2004). Furthermore, studies which have addressed the use of music in activist movements have often either lacked empirical detail or failed to contextualize musical practice within a much larger political and cultural field (thus effectively exaggerating its potency). For example, Eyerman and Jamison's (1998) important study of music and twentieth-century American political movements, while drawing attention to the place of music in activism, devotes most of its attention to the political context and practices, examining musical practice in less detail. A similar criticism might be made of Mark Mattern's (1998) study of the different functions that music can play in political settings.

Where these scholars treat music in somewhat functional terms, we suggest that a richer account can be given if music is not subordinated, from an analytical perspective, to politics. In this chapter, we introduce and contrast two distinct approaches to using music in political activism: 'prefigurative' and 'pragmatic'. The strength of these concepts as analytical frames, we contend, lies in their ability to draw attention to different features of musical practice from the standpoint of politics. While a prefigurative approach understands musical practices to constitute the political during performance through allowing participants to embody ideal social relations, a pragmatic approach ties music to specific, pre-given political goals and thus highlights the ways that different kinds of music can be used to regulate and control human behaviour. Our emphasis is on the role and form of music in these two guises in different activist contexts. This, we suggest, may aid understanding of the ways that music-making is organized and ordered within activist movements, and what is entailed in activist musicianship (that is, forms of musical creativity with which activists seek to effect political change). The contrast between the prefigurative and pragmatic is therefore to be found in music being respectively regarded 'expressively' (as giving form to the end) and 'instrumentally' (as a means to an end).

Our discussion of 'prefigurativism' and 'pragmatism' is not intended as an absolute binary categorization of music-making within activist movements; indeed, we also highlight how these approaches coexist within the same music-oriented activities. Rather, it is intended as a means of structuring the analysis of political movements, which can help to focus attention onto both the ways that musical creativity is incorporated into different activist strategies, and the musical features of this creativity.

Musical prefigurativism and political activism: the case of Rola la Lucha Zapatista

'Prefigurativism' refers to an approach to political activism in which, rather than seeking to achieve external political objectives, members of activist groups seek to foment ideal social relationships in their interactions with one another, thus 'prefiguring' an idealized future in the present. For Boggs – the author of the term – prefigurativism refers to 'the embodiment, within the ongoing political practice of a movement, of those forms of social relations, decision-making, culture, and human experience that are the ultimate goal' (1977: 100). Graeber (2004) points out that the principles of prefigurativism have, in recent years, become dominant across a broad spectrum of activist groups worldwide. Equally, the principles of prefigurativism can be applied to a variety of activities, beyond those explicitly deemed 'political' or 'activist'; and, although it is typically associated with groups with anarchist and leftist tendencies, it can also be used to describe the activities of right-wing groups (Yates 2015).

Within this definition, prefigurative approaches can be perceived in a wide variety of musics, and express many different political stances. Some genres of jazz, for instance, have been held up as a model of egalitarianism and collective empowerment within music (Saul 2003: 15). Equally, classical orchestras are valued by some because of their embodiment of utopian principles of 'order' and 'discipline' (Baker 2014: 111–15). Prefigurativism, then, constitutes an analytical frame that draws us into the details of musical practice, but which may nonetheless frustrate any observer seeking to understand the political impact of musical practices outside of the web of social values in which they are embedded. When we engage with prefigurativism, we are engaging with a set of political ideals which may be expressed musically, but which are most typically expressed in language.

During recent decades, the alternative political Left has canonized a number of social movements, of which the Zapatista movement constitutes a particularly notable example of prefigurative politics. In January 1994, the Zapatista Army of National Liberation (EZLN) launched an uprising in Chiapas, the southernmost state of Mexico. Ostensibly carried out in protest against the North American Free Trade Agreement (NAFTA), due to come into force at the same time, the Zapatista rebellion came to constitute a potent symbol of resistance against neoliberal globalization (Harvey 1998). Equally, after the EZLN agreed a ceasefire with the government and created a network of civil 'communities in resistance' across rural Chiapas, they initiated a series of experiments in radical democracy (Barmeyer 2008). Here, process was publicly valued over efficiency, as Zapatista communities began to construct institutions around the principle of consensus decision-making. A prefigurative approach is, therefore, evident within the Zapatista movement within Chiapas. It is also, however, prevalent among the geographically extensive movement of pro-Zapatista activist musicianship that has spread across Mexico and various parts of the world. Indeed, Graeber (2004: 103–5) cites the Zapatista movement as a key inspiration for prefigurative politics in the contemporary age.

In January 2012, Mexico City-based activist group Coordinadora Valle de Chalco (CVDC) decided to create a compilation album in support of the Zapatistas, and put out an online call for contributions which opened as follows:

> we believe that we must display all our creativity, put all our resources into the struggle and make use of all of the tools of dissemination that we have to hand to keep our peoples informed [...] we want to launch a musical project for the dissemination of the struggle of the Zapatista peoples which will consist of creating a compilation of songs of all genres [...] we call for you to join us in getting together musical material that shakes the hearts and the consciences of the people.

The group requested contributors expressing 'with different rhythms the importance of the struggle of the Zapatista peoples, their advances in education, health, culture, production, communication, justice, democracy – in other words, their autonomy'. In a step that would define the direction of the project, the organizers stated that this was 'not a call solely for dedicated musicians, but for all those that want to try it', and that contributions could be of any 'sonic and musical quality'. Finally, the idea was that the songs would be 'made available to everybody on one or several independent media [*medios libres*] websites to be downloaded, and you can spread them around [*rolar*] in your localities'. In response to this call, CVDC received almost a hundred entries, and included almost all of them in the final compilation (the collective only excluded submissions in a few cases, for example when a band sent multiple tracks). The finished album was placed online for free download in June 2012, and contained 77 tracks in total, covering a great variety of genres, such as rock, ska, hip-hop, punk, metal, cumbia, and reggae soundsystem.

As the call indicates, part of the explicit focus of this project was on a pragmatic communicative goal of 'spreading the word' to disparate audiences (cf. Green 2016). On the other hand, *Rola la Lucha Zapatista* was structured in such a way as to emphasize values inherent in the social process of music-making itself. This was seen in the inclusivity with which RLLZ was framed: as a project for amateur, as well as professional, musicians. In interviews with the organizers, value was predominantly ascribed to the 'heartfelt' nature of musicking as an activity, rather than to any features of musical sound itself. This ideal can be heard within the music it contains, some of which is professionally recorded, but much of which consists of demos, live recordings or small-scale, intimate performances recorded in a studio (sometimes fairly hastily) specifically for the project. *Rola la Lucha Zapatista* can thus be heard as a highly diverse album in process.

As an online project, RLLZ had limited reach; it was posted on several sites for free download, and after a short time placed on YouTube, where most tracks struggled to receive any more than 5,000 views. The emphasis of the project, nonetheless, changed significantly in the wake of the album's conversion into a physical compact disc (in the spring of the same year), which served as a catalyst for a series of live promotional events in public spaces. These events began to serve as a focal point for the development of an activist community, in which musicians and organizers from various parts of the country could meet together and form bonds of friendship and camaraderie, thus converting 'weak ties' to strong ones (Granovetter 1973). The disembodied and apparently 'placeless' quality of the original project, then, gave way to a more spatially grounded enterprise around which grassroots activism could be organized and face-to-face relationships formed. Indeed, the organizers of these events attempted to put into practice principles of 'horizontality, collective work, and participation of whoever wants to participate' within them. These principles were expressed in practice by, for instance, inviting participating musicians to organizers' meetings, giving musicians 'a voice and a vote', and sharing out food and drink among participants during events (interview, 24 July 2013).

Equally, in this context, music constituted the terrain on which a collective Zapatista identity could be negotiated amidst broader political differences. Zapatista sympathizers can be categorized into a variety of worldviews – such as, for instance, anarchists, feminist activists, environmentalists, hip-hop activists from the run-down outskirts of Mexico City, liberation theology Catholics and Chicano activists. This diversity has formed a central part of Zapatista ideology, summarized in the oft-cited slogan 'for a world in which many worlds fit', brought together chiefly through opposition to what the Zapatistas term the 'bad government'.

It is, therefore, interesting to note how the songs on RLLZ manage such diversity of worldview. Estado de México-based hip-hop producer Golpe El Ronin, for example, contributed a track entitled 'Nosotros' ('Us') to the compilation which produces a collective Zapatista subject that, rather than pertaining to any particular identity group, is defined by participating in 'everyday struggle'. This collective 'we' is narrated as 'those who have people spit in their face/ because of their African or indigenous accent/because of their gender, beliefs, or because they have not a peso in their pocket'; it is formed of 'victims of intolerance', 'the peasant tired of being exploited' and all kinds of 'victims of the bad government'. Here, then, the experience of marginalization – which may take a variety of forms – and the decision to resist it constitute a key entry point for affiliation with Zapatismo. Constructed around a piano sample, the beat on which this narrative is built also reflects the notion of incomplete, ongoing and perpetually shifting struggle. Eschewing any sense of resolution, it hovers around the sub-mediant, sub-dominant and dominant chords (A minor, F and G respectively), resisting any resolution to the tonic C; further, since the root of the dominant G is omitted, the song highlights an unstable augmented-fourth interval between F and B.

The notion of politics as a small-scale process, then, can be mobilized to make sense of RLLZ on several levels. Socially, it formed a locus for the cultivation of ideal social relationships built around camaraderie, friendship and egalitarianism among participants. It established ideals of authenticity and openness in the process of selecting songs for the album, in this way breaking down barriers between professional and amateur musicians. Finally, the notion of ongoing socio-political struggle may inform our interpretation of some of the music it contains at a more close-up, analytical level.

Pragmatism in music and politics: the case of Red Wedge

If the prefigurative role played by music in political activism is about embodying grassroots change, then pragmatic uses of music are very often tied to activism within electoral politics. Put like this, of course, it might be assumed that music is of peripheral significance: simply a soundtrack or servant to forces already in motion. During the 2016 US Presidential campaign, several artists – among them Adele, Queen, The Rolling Stones and Neil Young – complained about the use of their music during rallies in support of Donald Trump. Much of the attention focused on questions of whether the aggrieved artists had any recourse in law to prevent their music being used in this way – according to most readings of intellectual property law, they did not – and of what exactly motivated their sense of grievance (that is, their personal political views or their concern for their market). However, the reasons that Trump's campaign team had chosen music by these artists to begin with received far less attention. It was assumed by most, it seems, that the music was just there to ease the passage of time before the main act appeared. But while that may be part of the story, it left much out of the picture (see Trax on the Trail at http://www.traxonthetrail.com/sound-trax). The music was, we might suppose, designed to create a setting for the political speeches by putting the audience in a specific mood and to create a specific expectation of the politicians. This means that we should consider the specific reasons that Adele's song 'Rolling in the Deep' or Queen's 'We Are the Champions' were not picked at random for these events, taking into account the many tracks which were *not* chosen precisely because they were deemed inappropriate by the campaign managers.

In her book *Music in Everyday Life*, DeNora (2000) documents both how individuals use music to create an environment for intimacy or social interaction, and how retailers and others use it to engender certain kinds of human behaviour. For instance, DeNora points out that many retailers use up-tempo background music to stimulate impulse purchases, manipulating 'the aesthetic environment and, through this, the emotional conduct of consumers' (ibid.: 138). Conversely, airports buy low-tempo music specially composed to create a relaxed atmosphere for those about to fly (Treasure 2007). These cases exemplify the pragmatic deployment of music, as a means of engendering certain outcomes (for example, a romantic ambience, relaxed passengers or increased consumption), but the realization of these ends depends upon specific features of musical sound itself. The effects engendered are understood to be properties of the music as organized sound.

The same logic is deployed more or less consciously by politicians and parties to encourage voters to support them. When in 1997 the Labour Party chose D:Ream's 'Things Can Only Get Better' as the theme to their campaign, they were not just buying the sentiments expressed in the title. It was designed to achieve a particular effect, and not simply by the delivery of a specific lyrical 'message'. The same thoughts inform the use and choice of music for rallies by politicians in the US.

To explore this idea further, we focus on a rather special instance of this general phenomenon: the case of Red Wedge in 1985. Following on the example set by Live Aid and Rock Against Racism, Red Wedge was a very deliberate and self-conscious attempt to use music to boost support for the Labour Party, then languishing in the polls and trailing Margaret Thatcher's Conservative Party by some distance. This was, we suggest, a classic example of the pragmatic use of music.

Daniel Rachel (2016) has provided an oral history of Red Wedge. While Red Wedge has received occasional attention (Frith & Street 1992), Rachel's account is the first to provide a platform for all those involved, from the musicians to the politicians. His interviewees provide a rich source of material. Although the story told is somewhat rose-tinted, it is indicative of the fact that, even when music is being deployed pragmatically, it does so by aesthetic affect as much as by traditional political affect. Angela Eagle, now an MP, recalled: 'The gigs started you thinking' (Rachel 2016: 464). It was only then, after the music was over, that the Labour Party's message, documented in the Red Wedge magazine *Well Red*, had a hope of resonating.

The musicians who took part did so because of a shared commitment, but also because they recognized, albeit cautiously and with a degree of irony, that they had a measure of power. Johnny Marr, then guitarist with The Smiths, explained that Red Wedge represented 'a good opportunity for me to finally get off my butt and try and wield some of this so-called influence that popular musicians are supposed to have over their audience' (quoted in Rachel 2016: 417). The note of self-deprecation aside, Marr's thoughts are not entirely fanciful. It is evident that music can do more than entertain people in the moment. It can, as Nancy Love (2006) argues, communicate ideas and feelings. It can enable degrees of empathy and understanding that might not otherwise emerge (Street, Hague & Savigny 2013).

It would be wrong to see this simply as a story of the 'magical' power of music. These effects depended on leadership, infrastructure and money. The singer Rhoda Dakar explained: 'Paul [Weller] financed the first [Red Wedge] tour. If it hadn't been for him, it wouldn't have happened' (Rachel 2016: 410). Any account of music's role in political activism – whether pragmatic or prefigurative – depends on logistics; as Christian Lahusen (1996) notes, various forms of capital are essential to enabling music to play its role. Equally, though, it would be wrong to overlook the performative dimension; the way music, as organized sound, contributes to the political action. 'Whatever people say about the politics,' Billy Bragg (quoted in Rachel 2016: 428) argues, 'the gigs were just amazing. We all would sing "Move On Up" ...' The singer Lorna Gayle (ibid.: 428–29) reported: 'They got me to sing "Many Rivers to Cross" and everyone came on and sang it with me. That was the biggest accolade they could have given me. I felt like that song was my story. It spoke volumes to my heart and I could sing it with truth.' And Junior Giscombe (ibid.: 431) summed up what Red Wedge meant for him: 'We spoke out. We talked. We acted.'

We offer Red Wedge as a paradigmatic example of the pragmatic use of music in support of political activism. It was created for the express purpose of promoting the Labour Party among young people, achieving a political goal considered to be external to the act of participating in music. This did not imply, however, that music was not to be taken seriously. The musicians clearly found many sources of value from contributing to Red Wedge; the music both communicated more than the Party intended, and did so in different ways. Red Wedge was, then, clearly a meaningful movement for the musicians and audiences who participated in it. This project built on the potency of music to bring together diverse, otherwise stratified actors, and used this sense of togetherness to communicate pro-Labour political stances.

Music was seen, then, as key to engaging potential Labour supporters. Nonetheless, we ought to avoid echoing this stance from a scholarly perspective, perceiving musical practices as a mere tool to achieving an externally specified end. There are also ways that Red Wedge might be understood from a prefigurative standpoint; as evinced from Lorna Gayle's statement above, some musicians could be said to have experienced a kind of ideal community through their participation in these events. Yet, unlike Rock Against Racism, where the performance of black and white musicians together on stage was part of the message, and an embodiment of the ideal for which the movement strove, Red Wedge could not be understood to 'embody' the Labour Party or its principles. Indeed, it is notable how many of those who participated in Red Wedge place their greatest emphasis on the political meetings that took place during the day, prior to the evening's concerts. It was these occasions, it seems, that represented the 'real' political moments, when ideas were discussed and debated, and politicians called to account for themselves. The concerts mattered, and without them there would have been no meetings, but they were seen to matter in pragmatic rather than prefigurative ways.

Conclusion

We began this chapter by noting the ubiquity of music within political activism, and the great variety of ways that music can be understood to matter in relation to it. We also noted that, while this link is frequently observed, it is less frequently analyzed; and that when it is subject to analysis, there is a tendency to overlook the musicological and perfomative, in favour of the political. In this chapter, we have put forward one way in which this latter oversight might be addressed. We argue that we need to begin where students of political activism begin, by looking at the different roles that music may be expected to perform in political action. For this chapter, we identified a contrast between 'pragmatic' and 'prefigurative' uses of music. Using these frames, we suggest, can help us to listen carefully to the sonic dimensions of music's relationship with activism. This reveals how music affects political thought and action; how it may be understood to communicate, both intellectually and emotionally, to activists.

References

Anderson, B. (1983) *Imagined Communities*. London: Verso.

Baker, G. (2014) *El Sistema: Orchestrating Venezuela's Youth*. Oxford: Oxford University Press.

Barmeyer, N. (2008) 'Taking on the State: Resistance, Education, and Other Challenges Facing the Zapatista Autonomy Project', *Identities: Global Studies in Culture and Power*, vol. 15, no. 5, pp. 506–27.

Boggs, C. (1977) 'Marxism, Prefigurative Communism, and the Problem of Workers' Control', *Radical America*, vol. 11, no. 6, pp. 99–122.

Boucher, D. and Browning, G. (eds) (2004) *The Political Art of Bob Dylan*, Basingstoke, UK: Palgrave Macmillan

DeNora T. (2000) *Music in Everyday Life*. Cambridge: Cambridge University Press.

Eyerman, R. and Jamison, A. (1998) *Music and Social Movements: Mobilizing Traditions in the Twentieth Century*. Cambridge: Cambridge University Press.

Frith, S. and Street, J. (1992) 'Rock Against Racism and Red Wedge: From Music to Politics, From Politics to Music', in R. Garofalo (ed.) *Rockin' the Boat: Mass Music and Mass Movements*. Boston, MA: South End Press, pp. 67–80.

Goodyer, I. (2009) *Crisis Music: The Cultural Politics of Rock Against Racism*. Manchester: Manchester University Press.

Graeber, D. (2004) *Fragments of An Anarchist Anthropology*. Chicago: Prickly Paradigm Press.

Granovetter, M. (1973) 'The Strength of Weak Ties', *American Journal of Sociology*, vol. 78, no. 6, pp. 1360–80.

Green, A. (2016) 'Activist Musicianship, Sound, the "Other Campaign" and the Limits of Public Space in Mexico City', *Ethnomusicology Forum*, vol. 25, no. 3, pp. 345–66.

Harvey, N. (1998) *The Chiapas Rebellion: The Struggle for Land and Democracy*. Durham, NC: Duke University Press.

Lahusen, C. (1996) *The Rhetoric of Moral Protest: Public Campaigns, Celebrity Endorsement and Political Mobilization*. Berlin: Walter de Gruyter.

Love, N. (2006) *Musical Democracy*. New York: SUNY Press.

McDonald, K. (2006) *Global Movements: Action and Culture*. Oxford: Blackwell.

Mattern, M. (1998) *Acting in Concert: Music, Community and Political Action*. New Brunswick, NJ: Rutgers University Press.

Peddie, I. (ed.) (2012) *Music and Protest*. Farnham: Ashgate.

Rachel, D. (2016) *Walls Come Tumbling Down: The Music and Politics of Rock Against Racism, 2 Tone and Red Wedge*. Basingstoke, UK: Pan Macmillan.

Rosenthal, R. and Flacks, R. (2012) *Playing for Change: Music and Musicians in the Service of Social Movements*, Boulder, CO: Paradigm.

Saul, S. (2003) *Freedom Is, Freedom Ain't: Jazz and the Making of the Sixties*. Cambridge, MA: Harvard University Press.

Shank, B. (2014) *The Political Force of Musical Beauty*. Durham, NC: Duke University Press.

Street, J., Hague, S., and Savigny, H. (2008) 'Playing to the Crowd: The Role of Music and Musicians in Political Participation', *The British Journal of Politics and International Relations*, vol. 10, no. 2, pp. 269–85.

Street, J., Inthorn, S. and Scott, M. (2013) *From Entertainment to Citizenship: Politics and Popular Culture*. Manchester: Manchester University Press.

Tumas-Serna, J. (1992) 'The "Nueva Cancion" Movement and Its Mass-mediated Performance Context, *Latin American Music Review/Revista de Música Latinoamericana*, vol. 13, no. 2, pp. 139–57.

Turino, T. (2008) *Music as Social Life: The Politics of Participation*. Chicago: University of Chicago Press.

Treasure, J. (2007) *Sound Business*. Cirencester, UK: Management Books.

Widgery, D. (1986) *Beating Time: Riot'n'Race'n'Rock'n'Roll*. London: Chatto and Windus.

Yates, L. (2015). 'Rethinking Prefiguration: Alternatives, Micropolitics and Goals in Social Movements', *Social Movement Studies*, vol. 14, no. 1, pp. 1–21.

18

SMALL 'P' POLITICS AND MINOR GESTURES

political artists, politics and aesthetics in contemporary art

Maria Miranda and Norie Neumark

Neoliberalism strangles potential every day. But new techniques for life-living are also being invented every day, activated by minor gestures that continuously transform what it means to act.

Manning 2016: 185

Introduction

Small 'p' politics is a way of figuring practices in contemporary art where there is an animating and unresolved tension between political and aesthetic concerns, motivations and practices. For artists working in this way, neither politics nor aesthetics comes first. These are not issue-based artists, though their works do speak to political issues. Nor are they formalists, though their practices, as artists, matter. Their work and their relations to politics are diverse and often difficult to categorize. In a way which is typical of the complexities and ambiguities of small 'p' politics, these artists do not describe themselves as activist artists, even though they recognize – and, for some, embrace – the fact that their work may be experienced as political. While in other moments they may themselves be involved politically as activists, as artists they are differently engaged. And while the circumstances of their lives may be seen from the outside through the lens of the social, cultural and political, from the inside, where they are working as artists, there is also something deeply emotional and personal that they are exploring in open-ended ways.

In this chapter, we will address small 'p' politics from a big picture point of view by drawing on exemplary local works by individual and collective artists across a range of practices. We will refer to small 'p' political artists as *p*olitical artists in order to evoke the specificity of their practices as distinguished from activist political art. The artists whose work we will engage with here include: Amie Anderson, an artist whose practice is socially engaged in intimate and surprising ways; Brook Andrew, a Wiradjuri/Celtic artist whose work shifts the ground between Aboriginal and non-Aboriginal in Australian art and art history; Lyndal Jones, an artist whose latest international project is a ten-year project in regional Australia around art, place and climate change; and Soda_Jerk, a two-person collective whose sampling and remix works unsettle the 'original' and the various media they work across. In keeping with the local grounding at the heart of *politics*, we have chosen exemplary artists who are all Australians (though not all always based here); at the same time, we frame them within broader political and aesthetic concerns, debates and practices. Although this handful of artists can never *represent* a tendency that has a long history and broad and varied expressions, we hope that one exemplary work from each can speak to the importance of understanding the distinctiveness of *political* contemporary art. To think about how the bigger picture of politics and aesthetics plays out at the level of the artists making work through *political* art practices, we look to the *minor gestures* (Manning 2016) that enliven it.

As artists' minor gestures bring *politics* to life, they stir up the ground in ways that activate and make possible larger political shifts. Pragmatic rather than programmatic, minor gestures are fragile and undetermined (Manning 2016: 1–7). Artist and philosopher Erin Manning (2016: 56) proposes an 'art of participation', where minor gestures ask:

> how art can make a difference, opening up the existing fields of relation toward new forms of perception, accountability, experience, and collectivity. This aspect of the art of participation cannot be thought separately from the political, even though the work's political force is not necessarily in its content. This is not about making the form of art political. It is about asking how the field of relation activated by art can affect the complex ecologies of which it is part.

There is an uncertainty and complexity – even paradox – to Manning's minor gestures: they do not follow a major, structured Political program, yet they are deeply political in the encounters, 'co-compositions' and engagements they make possible (Manning 2016: *passim*, esp. 3, 7–8). This sort of politicalness resonates with Jacques Rancière's proposition that contemporary art is always political, because, as he puts it, art reframes common sense – what he calls the 'common sensorium'. In this sense, art is always political through the 'distribution of the sensible, or the system of divisions and boundaries that define, among other things, what is visible and audible within a particular aesthetico-political regime' (Rockhill 2004: 1). By engaging with exemplary artists and their work in this chapter, we respond to the ways that this entanglement of aesthetics and political at a regime or systemic level plays out at the everyday level of the artists who make the work – in their own process and in their relationships with audiences. For this chapter, we interviewed each of the artists, either by email or in person, between November 2016 and March 2017. We want to draw out the complexities and tensions of *political* art and of the artists' minor gestures that activate it.

Exchanges and intimate relationships: Amie Anderson's *The Soap Exchange Project*

Amie Anderson is a Melbourne-based artist whose practice is collaborative and intimate. For her *Soap Exchange Project* (2013), Anderson went around her neighborhood in Fitzroy (a mixed inner-city Melbourne neighborhood; once working class, now undergoing gentrification), knocking on doors and offering to exchange residents' used soap for her own fresh handmade organic soap. Afterwards, she wrote down anecdotes about each encounter. Living in the neighborhood at the time and aware of its two very different populations – the mainly refugee residents in the housing commission flats and the increasingly gentrifying residents in the houses – Anderson wanted to get to know her neighbours and to build a 'portrait of the neighborhood'. Soap offered a way as 'something we all have in common … [in] a daily ritual that we all share'. After the event of collecting, she experienced the soaps as molded by and materially remembering the bodies of those who had donated them. In her reflective writing and in the installation in a nearby gallery, another understanding came to the fore when Anderson displayed them on little shelves, reminiscent of the bathroom shelves from which they came, along with a handmade book of the anecdotes. She became more aware of the soaps as aesthetic objects, beautiful but often abjectly encrusted with bodily remnants such as hair.

In and through the work, Anderson saw herself and the situation of the encounters and the final work as a 'conduit' through which all, including herself, could find out about the world, rather than expecting a certain audience reaction. As with Marcel Mauss's well known understanding of the gift, Anderson explained,

> I wanted their soap and I wanted to find out more about them, in a way, so it was kind of this offering which opens up this space for a kind of sharing or exchange … and I guess that's something that might be hard for the viewer to get out of the work because it was that encounter, that personal encounter that I shared with that person at that time… There was this tension at the end … what is the work? is it the soaps or is it the encounters, those meetings? And if that's the work and you were the only one there, how do you communicate that as a piece of art? I think they're both the work.
>
> *Anderson 2016*

A decade ago, Anderson's project might have been understood as relational aesthetics in that it focused on setting up and exploring relationships between people – the social aspects of encounters and exchanges that resulted in a work. As Nicolas Bourriaud (2002a: 41) put it, relational aesthetics describes 'art … made of the same material as … social exchanges'. He understood these social exchanges as 'microclimates' where relationships with the world were rendered concrete by the art object (ibid.: 44, 48). Typical of relational aesthetics was both a conceptual approach to art and a working with performance and participation. Relational aesthetics has been subject to much debate and criticism, most notably by Claire Bishop, who decried its non-oppositional approaches leading to a loss of art's function of 'unease and discomfort' (Bishop 2004: 70; see also Bishop 2012: esp. chapter 1). We cannot rehearse this debate here, except to note that such criticism often misses the significance of Bourriaud's recognition of the particularities of the practices he described as relational aesthetics. And, from today's perspective, we sense a *political* resonance of much relational aesthetics work – and socially engaged art – with minor gestures where, as Manning (2016: 53) proposes, the process rather than the final object opens up a work's potential, inventing 'new possibilities for life-living … because of its continual investment in the question of practice'.

As a *political* artist, Anderson refuses any opposition between aesthetics, experience and politics, explaining that process and situation and personal concerns drive her practice and the work: 'My work is political in a way although I am not a political artist or activist' (Anderson 2016). She explains that the aesthetics of the project emerged in the installation – helping her engage with conceptual and political ideas – while the initial urge was to think about encounters and archives, rather than aesthetics. For us, Anderson's minor gestures evoked a vivid sense of the actual living bodies – remembered poetically in and by their soaps – that the gentrification of Fitzroy is affecting. We were conceptually, perceptually, emotionally, aesthetically and politically moved all at once by the work presented to us and the memory held in the soap of the encounters that had moved this *political* artist.

Time, narratives and Indigenous memories: Brook Andrew's *Intervening Time*

Brook Andrew is a Wiradjuri (Aboriginal)/Celtic artist whose work interrogates the colonial relationship between Wiradjuri and non-Wiradjuri global experiences. His practice connects Australia to global cultural and artistic narratives. Because, as he says, he himself shifts and his ideas change, Andrew does not fit himself into any identity-based political artistic categories. Like Anderson, Andrew is clear that he is an artist – rather than a political or an activist artist. For him, making the work is a physical experience, working from his personal cultural narrative. It is not a Political gesture, though he is well aware that for audiences the *experience* of the work he has made, the 'action on the wall', certainly can be political:

> Where the cultural stuff is personal, that action is political. So the work is both personal and political – the cultural is personal, the action on the wall is political ....Artists make stuff and people react to it. And sometimes it's seen as aesthetic sometimes seen as political. It's kind of an interesting dilemma …
>
> *Andrew 2016*

This important dilemma helps us apprehend the tensions that animate *political* art.

Andrew's work *Intervening Time* was staged in the colonial rooms at Queensland Art Gallery (QAG) in 2015 as part of APT (the 8th Asia Pacific Triennial of Contemporary Art). In an action typical of his wider practice, Andrew transformed the space in one of the rooms, which featured early colonial Australian paintings. These paintings depicted landscape and people, including Aboriginal, in ways that reflected the colonizing attitudes that ignored or hid narratives of settler colonial invasion, violence and occupation. Andrew's work involved removing the paintings from the wall and painting those same walls with black and white chevrons. The chevrons are Andrew's contemporary rendition of markings that were traditionally used at burial sites or men's ceremonial grounds, carved into trees, also known as dendroglyphs, and into shields. They have become recurring symbols for the artist that he places in various locations in ways that evoke the hidden memories those spaces hold about Aboriginal history that is hidden from dominant history. Once the chevrons covered the walls at QAG, the non-Aboriginal paintings were re-hung on top of this ground in their 'original' locations. For Andrew, this was a suggestive action that changed the narratives of the paintings and the space – transforming the space to allow for other narratives. For him the work made these other narratives possible but did not specify them. And for audiences, as we experienced, this made the space feel palpably and intensely different – making 'felt the unsayable in the said' (Manning 2016: 7). Through his minor gesture, Andrew did not suppress the paintings but rather artfully transformed them and the space, shifting the historical ground and aesthetic figure/ground – literally, acknowledging Aboriginal prior occupation as the ground upon which white settlement figures.

In *Intervening Time*, time and memory poetically intervened into the space in ways that could change narratives and change time. The experience of the work was what Anna Dezeuze has called 'poetic rupture'. As Francis Alÿs put it,

> I think the artist can intervene by provoking a situation in which you suddenly step out of everyday life and start looking at things again from a different perspective – even if it is just for an instant. That may be the artist's privilege … Sometimes doing something poetic leads to something political and sometimes something political leads to something poetic.
>
> *Dezeuze 2009: 3*

Intervening Time worked as a co-composition at a 'site of encounter that makes the cultural field tremulous' (Manning 2016: 71). A practice of co-composition involves artists, audiences, histories and the places of making and doing in an art of participation, making new connections and assemblages. To understand these, it is vital to sense the specificity of each *political* work, the different and complex ways in which politics and aesthetics play out for each, as well as within the larger assemblages as they connect. In *Intervening Time,* this assemblage was comprised of the repainted walls and the pictures re-hung on them – and the memories both held – as well as the audience's own physical sense of time, space, cultural memories and historical narratives. Being immersed in that transformed space, and experiencing the pictures hanging on the chevron walls felt disturbing, even shocking, yet uncannily it was not jarring. Experiencing *Intervening Time* was both provocative and alluring at the same time and made us sense most profoundly that 'period' rooms and the narratives of time they convey would never be the same again.

'Insistences of the ground': Lyndal Jones' *The Avoca Project*

Lyndal Jones is an artist who frequently works in projects where duration and care, rigour and generosity, waiting and attention to process are crucial. Since 2005, Jones has been making *The Avoca Project* in the small town of Avoca, in regional Victoria. Its site is Watford House, a wooden house, prefabricated in Sweden in 1850 and imported to gold rush Victoria. This project is local, regional, and international: Jones has involved local and international artists and Avoca residents in various art events housed there. The Avoca Project centres on the house as an active participant in the new materialist sense, as Jones and others respond with care for it and its gardens. Here, and in all her work, Jones abjures an 'activist' definition and generic categorizations. Her art is a grounded and open-ended way of thinking through concerns such as feminism and the environment and collaborating with others, in an approach typical of a *political* artist rather than Political activist. While Jones makes clear, 'I'm a feminist and everything I do comes from that, every public act' (Jones 2017), she also insists on both the provocativeness and the poetic in her work.

Jones engaged in a number of five- to ten-year projects before *The Avoca Project*. In these projects *waiting* – an art practice in itself for Jones – has involved an attentiveness to time and to silence, as Don Ihde's post-phenomenological understanding of silence attunes us to:

> Waiting is a "letting be" which allows that which continuously "is given" into space and time to be noted. Auditorily this is a listening to silence which surrounds sound. "Silence is the sound of time passing."
>
> *Ihde 2007: 111*

For Jones waiting's attentiveness to the materiality of place and things is a 'becoming earth', a responsiveness to the 'insistences of the ground' (Jones 2017). This plays out powerfully in an exhibition she curated in late 2016, *A Wallaby Once Sat Here … Small Acts of Celebration and Concern … Ecology and the Feminine* …. This exhibition of works by women artists of different ages and cultural backgrounds was grounded in Watford House, the exhibition's subject as well as its site. The project was a way to think through historical feminist and Aboriginal ecological understandings of land/landscape, the personal, the public and the environment. For this process, Jones invited a number of artists to engage with her in these complex, artful understandings of ecology, the feminine and the domestic.

Jones' exemplary collaborative process worked as a minor gesture to activate the exhibition, as does *The Avoca Project* itself. The process included bringing artists together at the house – to live and work there for periods of time, to get to know each other and the house – and to help their thinking-through the work they would make and install. Jones, and the house, insisted that they engage with Watford House and its grounds as a collaborator, rather than as a gallery. Some artists made work coming out of the process and for others it shaped how they installed existing work. Jones also led local women in flower arranging workshops, which in the exhibition became performances where the women responded to 'constraints' Jones had introduced – from replacing the dining room table with fish in a long tank to rendering the kitchen 'useless' by covering its surfaces with empty jars. These quiet and intense performances worked as 'small acts of celebration and concern', rather than Political community involvement – surprising and transfixing the witnessing audiences as well as the women themselves. They enlivened the rooms they worked in and opened audiences to engage with both the process and the house. Preparing the house in this, and other ways, was part of Jones' own art work for the exhibition. She also made a number of works within the rooms and on the grounds – working with netting to cover beds (indoors and outside), an entire room, and fruit trees – provoking us as audience to re-perceive and re-think the complex connections between inside and outside, between us and nature.

While her concerns are both political and personal, Jones does not make work as an activist or Political artist. Rather, she practices as an artist who 'thinks through materials' – with care and waiting, making audible and visible what is there. As Jones and the collaborating artists thought through materials for this exhibition – watching and listening – their *political* practice activated and was activated by the house and grounds. And for audiences, this collaboration with the house – rather than use of the house – vitally opened our thinking and perceptions of what was there.

Remixing time and memory: Soda_Jerk's *The Time that Remains*

Dan and Dominique Angeloro, two sisters known collectively as Soda_Jerk, are visual artists who create sampling remixes that make uncertain their 'original' sources. While remix as a practice politically refuses copyright legalities and limitations and traditional ideas of originality, Soda_Jerk do not work with this form – in videos, installations and performances – as activists. The productive tensions between politics and aesthetics in their work – and the way they embrace an uncertainty, indeterminacy and diversity of audience responses – suggests their identification as political artists is *political* rather than Political.

As Soda_Jerk describe their practice:

> We approach our use of unlicensed samples as a considered form of civil disobedience. We understand each work as a probe to test and map the contours of the legal systems in which it circulates, making visible frictions and impasses … As an illegal practice, our work is intended to unsettle systems and structures beyond those of the art world. And our projects also deal conceptually with issues relating to social politics and cultural history. But this does not mean that we want to collapse political art with activism. We believe that each has very different modes of address, spheres of action and responsibilities of articulation. Both are pivotal to our lives.
>
> *Soda_Jerk 2017*

The alluring seamlessness in Soda_Jerk's remixes belies their extreme labour-intensiveness and the diverse audience responses they provoke. This complex work is haunted by what Mark Amerika calls 'remixological inhabitations [which] are radicalized co-productions with the artists being sampled from as renewable energy sources' (Amerika 2011: 176). This resonates with Nicolas Bourriaud's idea of the contemporary art practice of *postproduction* as a form of inhabiting: 'To learn how to use forms … is above all to know how to make them one's own, to inhabit them' (Bourriaud 2002b: 18). For both postproduction and remixology, there is a shift away from 'creativity' understood as an originality of a single artist toward more of a sense of the collaborative, a relationship between an artist or media maker and previous artists and their work.

Soda_Jerk's remixes disrupt a sense of the 'normal' flow of memory and time from past to present to future, evoking what Manning has called a 'deja felt' – the 'memory' of the future which haunts the present (Manning 2016: 50–1). This is particularly exemplified in their hauntological series *Dark Matter* (2005–2012) – a 'séance fiction where encounters are staged between the past and future selves of a deceased screen star' (Soda_Jerk n.d.). One of the works in the series, *The Time that Remains* (2012), is a:

> gothic melodrama [in which] Joan Crawford and Bette Davis perpetually wake to find themselves haunted by their own apparitions and terrorized by markers of time. Isolated in their own screen space, each woman struggles to reclaim time from the gendered discourses of aging that conflates older women with a sense of expiration and invisibility.
>
> *Soda_Jerk n.d.*

The Time that Remains is an installation with two screens in conversation with each other, in looping repetition. As the video on one screen finishes, with the actor sleeping, the other begins, with its actor waking. It is as if each actor is experiencing both a waking and dreaming nightmare – as if they are not just experiencing their own nightmare but also each other's. Within each screen, time – and with it aging – moves back and forth almost as seamlessly as the editing. It is as if one screen is exploring its own memories and speaking them to the other. At the same time as visually *film noir* shadows tell of aging's dark process, sonically we hear its ineluctable force. Ticking clocks and crashing waves demand we heed their voicing of the inevitability of time rolling and roiling on. As the older Crawford faces her younger self, speaking wistfully of the time that's passed, the grain of her voice tells the same story. Crawford's gesture of grabbing the hands of a clock in hopes of stilling the voice of time's passing is vividly futile.

As with all their work, *The Time that Remains* works with the force of the original films and stunningly reinforces and disturbs them – and us – through the remix. The clocks, the thunder and wind and frantic footsteps play not just with the films Soda_Jerk has sampled but with a vast repertoire of Hollywood tropes that speak to them – voicing the stormy inevitability of aging for Hollywood screen stars. *The Time that Remains* calls out hauntingly and intensely to women, like us, who watch and wait, inhabited in our own various ways by these Hollywood memories.

Conclusion

While the works we have engaged with in this chapter are very different and come from very different places for their artists, they do share certain approaches that we understand as typical of *political* art. Process, for instance, is crucial for *political* artists and their work – an 'artful' process which is deeply personal and emotional and embedded in the workings of art as an intuitive, durational mode (Manning 2016: 13–15, 65). And for all, too, it is minor gestures that enliven that process and activate the work. These minor gestures – embodying and embodied in their work – are the very *force* that may create the condition for any major Political change:

> The minor invents new forms of existence, and with them, in them, we come to be. These temporary forms of life travel across the everyday, making untimely existing political structures, activating new modes of perception, inventing languages that speak in the interstices of major tongues.
>
> *Manning 2016: 2*

We have seen how these minor gestures – activating *political* art in complex ways – play out differently for different artists and audiences, affecting each differently. What *political* artists do share is a sense of the importance of making work *as artists*, with all that may entail. This means that an understanding of their work as *political* artists involves a recognition that theirs is a distinct and specific art practice and cannot be 'collapsed' into activism, which, as Soda_Jerk have explained with such clarity, 'has very different modes of address, spheres of action and responsibilities of articulation'. And, even though they may be motivated by their own cultural memories and the changing complexities of their personal situations (as affected by, say, race, gender or even the Political moment), for *political* artists Politics emerges in the process rather than constraining the process. While Politics and its issues matter for them, they do not seek set political effects. These *political* artists want their work to be open-ended, to leave room for audience's own complex and diverse experiences and responses, rather than being determined by any fixed or direct Political message. And, as the small 'p' politics of the *political* artists' practices reverberate through their work, we can sense the enlivening, sometimes unresolved tensions, even contradictions, that are entangled within their political and aesthetic concerns, their motivations and practices. In this way, *political* artists make works that can work forcefully, politically and even Politically, at the same time.

Acknowledgements

We pay our respects and acknowledgements to all Traditional Custodians on whose land we live, work and travel through. We would like to thank the artists for generously giving their time for interviews and offering much valuable food for thought. They each provided not just information about their work but also deeply considered understandings of the questions which brought us to this chapter.

References

Amerika, M. (2011) *remixthebook*. Minneapolis, MN: University of Minnesota Press.
Anderson, A. (2016) Interview with the authors in Melbourne, Australia, November 2016.
Andrew, B. (2016) Interview with the authors in Melbourne, Australia, November 2016.
Bishop, C. (2004) 'Antagonism and Relational Aesthetics', *October*, no. 110, pp. 51–79.
Bishop, C. (2012) *Artificial Hells: Participatory Art and the Politics of Spectatorship*. London and New York: Verso.
Bourriaud, N. (2002a) Transl. Simon Pleasance and Fronza Woods with the participation of Mathieu Copeland. *Relational Aesthetics*. Dijon: Les presses du réel.
Bourriaud, N. (2002b) Transl. Jeanine Herman, *Postproduction: Culture as Screenplay: How Art Reprograms the World*. New York: Lukas & Sternberg.
Dezeuze, A. (2009) 'Walking the Line: Francis Alÿs Interviewed by Anna Dezeuze', *Art Monthly*, no. 323, pp. 1–6.
Ihde, D. (2007) *Listening and Voice: Phenomenologies of Sound* (second edition). Albany, NY: State University of New York Press.
Jones, L. (2017) Interview with the authors in Melbourne, Australia, 2017.
Jones, L. (n.d.) *The Avoca Project: Art Place, Climate Change*. http://www.avocaproject.org, accessed 10 December 2016.
Manning, E. (2016) *Minor Gestures*. Durham, NC: Duke University Press.
Rancière, J. (2004) *The Politics of Aesthetics: The Distribution of the Sensible*. Trans. and introd. Gabriel Rockhill. London and New York: Continuum.
Rockhill, G. (2004) 'Translator's Introduction: Jacques Rancière's Politics of Perception' in Rancière, J. (2004).
Soda_Jerk. (2017) Interview with the authors in Melbourne, Australia, March 2017.
Soda_Jerk. (n.d.) http://www.sodajerk.com.au, accessed 15 December 2016.

19

I CAN HAZ RIGHTS?

Online memes as digital embodiment of craft(ivism)

Victoria Esteves

The current social media landscape boasts many features that have shaped our communication – from Facebook likes, to retweets, to Tinder swipes – most of which rely on a richness of content created by users around the world (Martens 2011: 49; Meikle & Young 2012: 56); within this quotidian digital conversation it is difficult to picture a landscape without thinking of internet memes. These pieces of online culture have found their way into our everyday lived experiences: they can be found in a myriad of online exchanges between friends and strangers; they are posted to everyone, anyone, and no one in particular, on a daily basis. Their omnipresence and versatility are such that they are inserted into casual conversations as easily as they make it onto news articles, at times appearing side by side in our news feeds, blurring the conversational line between both. As memes become further entrenched in our cultural zeitgeist, it is unsurprising to find that they have found their way into spaces beyond online communication, spilling outside the delimitations of cyberspace and manifesting in the physical world itself. Memes are showing up in posters all over cities, they are being used in billboard ads and – as I shall be addressing in this chapter – they are making their way into, among other physical embodiments, handheld placards in political protests throughout the world. I shall be exploring this contextual leap that memes have undertaken as well as delving into the consequential meanings that come with these changes.

As Graham Meikle and I have defined in previous research, internet memes are '*shared, rule-based representations of online interactions that are not only adopted but also adapted by others*' (original emphasis) (Esteves & Meikle 2015: 564). As such there is, among other aspects, an emphasis on the ability to remix memes through adaptation – this is an important aspect of internet memes since it is, after all, this easy ability to engage with and alter memes that allows for them to be passed on to others, encouraging them to do the same (i.e. you remix a meme and pass it on). As memes circulate they adapt, and with greater circulation come rising numbers of remixed versions of memes. With greater numbers of remixes, the memes also gain the possibility of becoming increasingly multi-layered in their meaning(s) (Green & Jenkins 2011: 116). As the meanings behind memes increase with their circulation, their significance increases not only for a larger number of individuals but also as cultural products of a global societal conversation that can (and does) reflect current complex events as they unfold. Our current creation of culture is reliant on our ability to remix (Lessig 2006: 16; Manovich in Meikle 2008: 375; Lankshear & Knobel 2011: 97), which in turn is also helping us make sense of our complex political climate.

These collective practices of meaning-making that we see at play in memes (particularly political ones) follow rules akin to older rationales of communal forms of making meaning (Nelson 1985: 10). It is this chain of processes – from the easiness of creating memes, to the encouragement to engage in participatory culture, to the meaning-making that arises from these collective exercises and the subsequent cultural and political significance of them – that encompasses what I am attempting to capture in this chapter.

Memes

Although there is not enough space here to discuss what memes are at length, it is useful to understand some of their basic principles and how they relate to political discourse in order to lay the foundations for this chapter. Before we begin to consider memes' interplay with explicit political affairs we must understand how memes play a role in the politics of the everyday, irrespective of what they are addressing. It can be argued that regardless of their content, all internet memes are inherently political: just by existing, memes are embodying the resistance against corporate control of ideas, as well as breaking their monopoly on entertaining content and symbols of meaning making (Greer 2008: 10; Gauntlett 2011: 56). The fact that memes require very low levels of literacy in order to be created and remixed means that memes are one of the most democratic forms of creating and communicating – the bar is set considerably low when we consider other forms of creativity and communication such as political art (Davison 2010: 121). In this sense they are political, much like DIY or craft is: memes are a form of self-made entertainment that forego the necessity for paid entertainment; for every meme (or chair, or piece of clothing, etc.) we make ourselves, our dependency on ready-made, corporate-controlled content weakens (Greer 2008: 10; Gauntlett 2011: 56), turning us instead into more independent 'produsers' (i.e. simultaneous producers and users) (Cha *et al.* 2007: 1; Bruns 2008: 240; Lussier, Raeder & Chawla 2010: 159). The act of making empowers us and makes us that little bit more self-sufficient; the act of making *together* and for each other empowers us further through the joint creation of meaning through something so simple (Broxton *et al.* 2013: 18; boyd 2012: 75; see Gauntlett 2011).

Here it is important to not get swept away by utopic ideals of the internet (and consequently its products); much like the rest of our communicative and creative outlets, these still operate within a sphere of corporate commodification. The opportunity to usurp memes for capital gains has not gone unnoticed by our consumerist society, as is evident from their circulation on advertisement-ridden videos on YouTube to the manufacture of meme-related merchandise (Beer & Burrows 2007; Lastufka & Dean 2009: 236). Nevertheless, this should not erase the possibilities afforded to us when it comes to meme usage in a global political conversation. One of the ways in which memes do this is by engaging with politics in an offline sphere; this in turn overlaps with another democratic political weapon that has been available for far longer: craftivism.

Craftivism

Simply put, craftivism (as implied by the name) is a mixture of craft and (or as) activism (Greer 2011: 175); the harnessing of various types of craft (e.g. knitting) in order to convey a political message. Craftivism can be scaled up or down to fit the needs of each context it addresses, whether it's broad issues such as racial equality or the protest against the building of tram tracks in a specific part of a city. There is something more to these knitted works than meets the eye; the pieces that are made by these non-professionals reflect not only a creative flair but also an involvement with political issues through this creativity, resulting in a craftivist piece (see Gauntlett 2011; Greer 2011).

In itself, engaging in craft is a very empowering act (Dormer 1997: 43; Greer 2008: 9; Dunbar-Hester 2014: 78). Besides having a history of subversion (Orton-Johnson 2014: 141), craft frees us from the dependency on mass-made objects that are sold to us (Greer 2008: 10; Gauntlett 2011: 56; Chidgey 2014: 104), making these craftivist objects already politicized before they even bear an explicit message; the act of making craft *is* already political (see Gauntlett 2011; Ratto & Boler 2014: 1–3). When we turn to literature on craft, the idea that 'making is both the means (…) and an end in itself' (Dormer 1997: 154) underlies this activity. Additionally, both craft objects and memes are pretty much inherently communal in their essence: both are made by anyone, for anyone. As Dunbar-Hester (2014: 77) puts it: 'activists envisioned "everyone" as a potential "maker," and thus DIY citizenship as accessible to all'. Both assign considerable weight on the value of making *with* others, placing the act of sharing and togetherness at the centre of their ethos (Gauntlett 2011: 25) – just like the social aspect that underlies the making of communal quilts (Gauntlett 2011: 70), memes were *made to be shared* (Shirky 2010: 19). This synergy between social interaction and empowerment has also been noted in the literature when it comes to memes (Broxton *et al.* 2013: 18). The emphasis on togetherness in creativity and craftivism is so strong that there have been proponents to change the 'DIY' abbreviation to 'DIT' (do-it-together) (Chidgey 2014: 103).

As with other similar offline activities (e.g. guerrilla gardening) the effects can be said to be more felt locally, as the results – whether it is an intricate piece of embroidery or sunflowers growing from sewer drains – are enjoyed first-hand by those physically present in the community (see Hargreaves & Hartley 2016). They can also be seen as physical embodiments of the issues concerning the geographic spaces where they are displayed; artistic and activist (and at times quite literally living) manifestations of societal problems that are frustratingly felt as invisible for the most part. There is also a kind of poetic beauty that underscores these activities, as many times they strive to take something ugly – whether figuratively (e.g. gross inequality) or literally (a broken fence in a public space) – and use the transformative power of remixing in order to attempt to make the world a more beautiful place in all senses. With that being said, we should not overlook the impact of these activities on a more global scale: they can (and do) inspire, engage and encourage people from all over to take up similar action, tackling causes that are important to them both on a local and global level (also referred to as 'glocally') (Orton-Johnson 2014: 149–50).

Memes in politics

In the past few years we have experienced political and social turmoil around the globe – from the Arab Spring to the Egyptian Facebook revolution. These events have been heavily played out in social media, which became not just a way of spreading the unmediated facts via citizen journalism but also a central tool for these revolutions to take place at all: social media was being used to coordinate demonstrations, keep vital information circulating beyond the grasp of State censorship and connect citizens and their resources (e.g. food and shelter) (Zuckerman 2011; Androutsopoulos 2013: 49).

As social and political unrest swept through the world, citizens took to both the physical and virtual streets in order to make their discontentment visible and audible – marked by the multitude of protests, actions and movements that arose in recent years, from the *Indignados* to the Occupy movement. As people voiced their restlessness through these phenomena, it became apparent that they also expressed it through the use of internet memes. Politically tinged memes began circulating online as quick responses to current events; at times being created while political events were not yet finished unfolding (e.g. the US presidential debates). This form of instant critique eased a form of global conversation, one which broke barriers both in speed and in reach. There is resonance between this phenomenon and Hartley's (1999: 179) notion of a DIY citizen: just like the former engage in 'semiotic self-determination' through the symbols they take from the media, DIY citizens are taking internet symbols and putting them on billboards at protests to express themselves politically. Nowadays it is almost a given that both big and small political issues will spawn memes; these will inevitably reduce complex political issues to funny one-line jokes. However, for many they may also work as entry points into political discussions – considering remixes are at times the initial exposure we have to original content – as well as working as cultural currency that can reach a much wider audience (Grinnell 2009: 593; Jenkins 2014: 68).

As the global exchange continued through the use of memes on the internet, this conversation shaped by online characteristics leapt back into the offline space, with different internet memes making regular appearances in protest signs around the world. These homemade billboards have been spotted in worldwide protests, addressing a whole variety of political issues, from corruption to unemployment. Protestors are putting their money where their mouth is: instead of sitting behind a screen making memes to complain about the status quo – a common accusation towards current generations, also known as 'slacktivism' (Christensen 2011) – they are taking to the streets with memes. This new language which is being used to confront the status quo may have the added ability of making political issues more available to the disenfranchised; it isn't just a question of making politics funnier but, more importantly, it is a question of making politics more inclusive. Political protests are now proving to be a new battleground for digital cultural literacy – regardless of how internet savvy people are, memes are finding their way to them outside the screen, demonstrating the continuity that exists between both worlds (Shirky 2010: 37; Gurney 2011: 30) – as well as a vivid reminder that online and offline barriers are no longer a useful way of thinking about our fluid, always-on lived experiences (see boyd 2012).

Arthur's Fist meme

As the craftivist movement kept on making its appearances throughout the world, it also began widening its scope; being an activist art form, it is no surprise that it is open to new ways of expressing its messages. It is here that the intersection between craftivism and memes meets, as we will see through the example of the *Arthur's Fist* meme. Although it depicts a considerably obscure piece of media that had been around for almost two decades, the *Arthur's Fist* meme first began circulating in 2016. It refers to the 1990s children's cartoon show *Arthur* and consists of an extreme close-up shot of Arthur's clenched fist, conveying a message of resentment mixed with simmering anger in a nuanced way that clashes with the show's innocent themes and colourful aesthetics. The meme that spawned featured an interchangeable caption that denotes frustrating and/or anger-inducing situations. At a first sight this meme does not appear to be particularly complex – it certainly does not require the same amount of effort of technical skill than some of its counterparts (e.g. LOLtheorists). However, this is far from a critique, as the simplicity of memes allows for further engagement and dissemination whilst also allowing for faster and easier remix and replication; its layers of meaning (and, indeed, difficulty) can be scaled up or down, subsequently opening or closing the gap of understanding to a bigger or a smaller audience.

The *Arthur's Fist* meme can also be remixed beyond the confines of cyberspace depiction, bringing it back to the offline world, as seen by recent cosplay embodiments of the meme – in an attempt to (literally) frame the meme within the desired context, a cosplayer has built a border to demarcate the meme around their fist in order to indicate the edges of the computer screen; accompanied by the fore title 'When nobody gets your cosplay'. This cosplay consists of a small part of the user's body (i.e. their hand), and thus it is irrelevant if the rest of the user's aspect (i.e. clothing, make-up, face) matches what the audience would expect the rest of Arthur to look like. In this example the meme is also self-referential: the underlying message is that the cosplayer is frustrated and annoyed by the fact that no one understands his apparently simplistic cosplay, which is enacted in physical meme form.

Here the level of meaning and effort required are both higher, as there is interplay between the online and offline meanings of the meme. In this particular use of this meme, its multi-layered message and humorous outcome are only possible due to the change in context that the meme has suffered – not only the initial change of context that makes it a meme at all (i.e. taking a screenshot from a children's show and altering its message by changing its context, which is arguably the fundamental characteristic in meme humour) but also the physical change of context, which allows the meme to develop unfolding layers of meaning and humour. By unpacking this example, we can understand how memes become political through their ability to not only allow people to take a piece of media and make it their own by injecting their personal meaning and creativity, but also to construct their own language and forms of communication – a practice that has been previously noted by Henry Jenkins, who described the process of using a fandom's language and points of reference in order to discuss issues of political transformation (Jenkins 2014: 66, 70).

The *Arthur Fist* meme is one example out of many that engages with everyday politics; however, it is also a meme that has been used offline to *explicitly* address political issues. In 2016, Hannah Hill took to craftivism in order to make a feminist statement, embroidering the *Arthur Fist* meme with the caption: 'When you remember that historically, embroidery hasn't been taken seriously as a medium because it's "women's work".' This iteration of the meme embodies a crossover between political memes and craftivism, thus being relevant to both camps. By adding explicit political layers to the piece (which already bears implicit political meanings through the choice of medium), it shines a light on the issues it addresses, elevating the act of meme making to the empowerment crafters obtain through political craft (Black & Burisch 2011: 210). Additionally, this piece engages with the creative side of political craft that is also present in the remix of memes; in the words of the authors of feminist zine *make/shift*: 'a politic that connects not just the personal to the political, but the critical to the creative' (Hoffman & Yudacufski 2009/2010: 105), also overlapping both memes and (everyday) politics. It is worth noting that this piece of embroidery took 15 hours to make, which is an impressive amount of time and work to invest in making a single iteration of a meme, making this type of investment hard to label as slacktivism. This piece is an example of the double-faceted property of an internet meme at its most basic: on the surface it appears to be an innocuous waste of time, but when we begin to unpack the power that lies in the metaphorical strands that stitched this piece together – the defiance of DIY culture, the remixed embodiment it represents, the medium itself as a political stance – it becomes clear that it holds the clout of cultural symbolism that is vital for societies (ours in particular) to make meaning (Jenkins, Li & Krauskopt 2008: 18). Like its cosplay counterpart, it is self-referential in the sense that it uses the specific medium of embroidery to make a statement about embroidery. Here McLuhan's (1964: 7) 'The medium is the message' seems to gain a fresh meaning, as the embroidery piece about embroidering speaks volumes.

It is not unusual to find craftivist works that feature feminist topics; these two concepts have a long history of mutual synergy that continues even despite craftivism's expansion into other topics and political messages (Ratto & Boler 2014: 10). It is thus, in a way, unsurprising that this cooperative trend between craftivism and feminism extends itself into the realm of internet memes: in an ever-expanding cultural reality, there is space for layers of meaning to be added upon pre-existing ideas, which (as noted above) is a key feature in internet memes. Furthermore, the flexibility and easiness of access that both memes and craftivism demonstrate make them great counterparts to be used as a form of communication that may question the status quo's formality of debate, making both optimum potential tools for resistance. The Arthur meme stitched piece echoes with Chidgey's (2014: 104) thoughts on craftivism: 'making your own culture and politics, rather than consuming those on offer, is a political mode of engagement; a strategy further politicized by being shared'. Just as works of craftivism are able to circumvent geographic – and even linguistic – limitations (Gohil 2007; Turney 2009: 205), memes are also making the most of this ability, at a considerably faster rate. Furthermore, there is a sense of community that blossoms from this shared engagement, one which cannot be contained through older notions of geographically contained citizenship (Orton-Johnson 2014: 144).

Anecdotally, memes often get dismissed as a waste of time that plagues our current culture (Shirky 2010: 18; Chen 2012: 15; Labash 2012), and have been accused of dumbing down the current generation, as well as lowering political debate into unintelligent and shallow comebacks (Marshall 2013; Larsen 2016; Milner 2016: 157) However, it is becoming clear that we should not dismiss such a considerable part of our current forms of communication and engagement with a wide range of current political issues. David Buckingham's (2000) work has explored how language is an important aspect that disenfranchises young people from political engagement; the unfamiliarity of the language employed to discuss these matters acts as a deterrent for many to attempt any kind of political participation. This is why it is important to validate a language that puts political discussion into the hands of those who feel unwelcome by its formal predecessors. Additionally, Gray (2007) demonstrates how the old perceptions of separating emotion and familiarity from the rationality and formality of political news are no longer useful or even applicable: we should bring political discussion into our own turf and terms.

With a change of context comes a change of meaning, which is evidently depicted by the transition of online memes to offline spheres of circulation. This ability to break through the confinements of the internet and make its way into our unplugged existence is of great importance (Gauntlett 2011: 8); this leap signals the significance that memes have in our daily realities, where we have made space for them in an offline place, thus creating further and more complex ways in which these pieces of culture entwine into our relationships with others and understandings of the world (Leadbeater 2009: 24; Gauntlett 2011: 8). In short, by making its way into offline spheres, we are exploring the ways in which this newly minted form of communication is shaping our communication. Lastly, by jumping back and forth between the virtual space to an offline place it is once more affirming that the rigid separation of these spaces is become increasingly unhelpful when it comes to describing our lived realities – instead, it demonstrates that it is more apt to think of these two spaces as porous (Shirky 2010: 37).

Although it is important to acknowledge that the notion of digital natives is not reflective of the reality we live in – nowadays the internet is no longer the new kids' fad and permeates most aspects of modern life, regardless of age – a large section of memes is made by (and for) what we have come to call Millennials (Curtis 2017; Urban 2017). This is a relevant aspect of meme makers since it is also this group (i.e. younger people) that is mostly ignored by politics, to the point where they are often not welcome in the conversation at all (Jenkins 2014: 70). This lack of understanding of how our current generation lives, along with its economic and moral realities – most clearly shown by media giants such as *The Economist* asking 'Why aren't millennials buying diamonds?' (Ferreras 2016) – extends to a lack of understanding regarding how this generation communicates. By using memes for political matters they are not – as sometimes is implied - reducing important issues at hand to a joke; they are instead making use of our current tools of communication and relationship development in order to engage with these problems in a manner that allows easy global and glocal conversation.

Conclusion

As memes navigate through our online social spaces, they have also found ways of circulating into offline political places; no longer used just for the lulz, memes are being mobilized for political engagement in a myriad of topics, from US election memes to issues that affect specific localities. Memes are a natural extension on the remix continuum that has been weaved for decades – from Dada, to *détournement*, to punk, and so on – and as a part of this sequence it has the ability to harness its innate popularized political power and use it for direct grassroots political action. The differentiating characteristic of memes within this framework is that they are able to be engaged with by virtually anyone: the cultural literacy necessary to enter an internet meme discussion is considerably low when compared to its previous remix counterparts.

In our current unstable political, economic and social times the internet has found a language that suits its citizens: it stands up to the status quo not only due to its message but also due to the informal and humorous format in which the message is delivered. These memes show not only that – contrary to popular critiques of political disengagement – we are a part of the political conversation. We *are* weighing in on the issues – we're just doing it on our terms and in our own cultural language.

References

Androutsopoulos, J. (2013) 'Participatory Culture and Metalinguistic Discourse: Performing and Negotiating German Dialects on Youtube', in D. Tannen and A. M. Trester (eds) *Discourse 2.0*. Washington, DC: Georgetown University Press, pp. 47–72.

Beer, D. and Burrows, R. (2007) 'Sociology and, of and in Web 2.0: Some Initial Considerations', 30 September, *Sociological Research Online*, vol. 12, no. 5, http://www.socresonline.org.uk/12/5/17.html, accessed 9 August 2017.

Black, A. and Burisch, N. (2011) 'Craft Hard Die Free: Radical Curatorial Strategies for Craftivism', in M. E. Buszek (ed.) *Extra/Ordinary*. Durham, NC: Duke University Press, pp. 204–11.

boyd, d. (2012) 'Participating in the Always-On Lifestyle', in M. Mandiberg (ed.) *The Social Media Reader*. New York: New York University Press, pp 71–6.

Broxton, T., Interian, Y., Vaver, J. and Wattenhofer, M. (2013) 'Catching a Viral Video', *Journal of Intelligent Information Systems*, vol. 40, no. 2, pp. 241–59.

Bruns, A. (2008) *Blogs, Wikipedia, Second life, and Beyond*. New York: Peter Lang.

Buckingham, D. (2000) *The Making of Citizens*. London: Routledge.

Cha, M., Kwak, H., Rodriguez, P., Ahn, Y.-Y. and Moon, S. (2007) 'I Tube, You Tube, Everybody Tubes: Analyzing the World's Largest User Generated Content Video System', *IMC'07 Proceedings of the 7th ACM SIGCOMM conference on Internet measurement*. New York: ACM, pp. 1–14.

Chen, C. (2012) 'The Creation and Meaning of Internet Memes in 4chan: Popular Internet Culture in the Age of Online Digital Reproduction', *Institutions Habitus*, no. 3 (spring), pp. 6–19.

Chidgey, R. (2014) 'Developing Communities of Resistance? Maker Pedagogies, Do-It-Yourself Feminism, and DIY Citizenship', in M. Ratto and M. Boler (eds) *DIY Citizenship*. Cambridge, MA: MIT Press, pp. 101–14.

Christensen, H. S. (2011) 'Political Activities on the Internet: Slacktivism or Political Participation by other Means?', *First Monday*, vol. 16, no. 2, http://firstmonday.org/article/view/3336/2767, accessed 9 August 2017.

Curtis, S. (2017) 'The Millennials and the Meme', *The Times*, 9 April, https://www.thetimes.co.uk/article/millennials-funny-instagram-accounts-scarlett-curtis-g0dmdtldr, accessed 1 June 2017.

Davison, P. (2012) 'The Language of Internet Memes', in M. Mandiberg (ed.) *The Social Media Reader*. New York: New York University Press, pp. 120–34.

Dormer, P. (1997) *The Culture of Craft*. Manchester: Manchester University Press.

Dunbar-Hester, C. (2014) 'Radical Inclusion? Locating Accountability in Technical DIY', in M. Ratto and M. Boler (eds) *DIY Citizenship*. Cambridge, MA: MIT Press, pp. 75–88.

Esteves, V. and Meikle, G. (2015) 'LOOK @ THIS FUKKEN DOGE': Internet Memes and Remix Cultures', in C. Atton (ed.), *The Routledge Companion to Alternative and Community Media*. London: Routledge, pp. 561–70.

Ferreras, J. (2016) 'Why Aren't Millennials Buying Diamonds, The Economist Asks', *Huffington Post*, 6 July, http://www.huffingtonpost.ca/2016/07/06/millennials-diamonds-the-economist_n_10838174.html, accessed 3 June 2017.

Gauntlett, D. (2011) *Making is Connecting*. Cambridge: Polity Press.

Gohil, N. S. (2007) 'Activists Use Knitting Needles to Make Their Point', *Columbia Journalism School News Service*, 13 March, http://jscms.jrn.columbia.edu/cns/2007-03-13/gohil-knittinginprotest.html, accessed 9 August 2017.

Gray, J. (2007) 'The News: You Gotta Love It', in J. A. Gray, C. Sandvoss and C. L. Harrington (eds) *Fandom*. New York: NYU Press, pp. 75–86.

Green, J. and Jenkins, H. (2011) 'Spreadable Media: How Audiences Create Value and Meaning in a Networked Economy', in V. Nightingale (ed.) *The Handbook of Media Audiences*. Oxford: Blackwell Publishing, pp. 109–27.

Greer, B. (2008) *Knitting for Good!* Boston: Trumpeter Books.

Greer, B. (2011) 'Craftivist History', in M. E. Buszek (ed.) *Extra/Ordinary*. Durham, NC: Duke University Press, pp. 175–83.

Grinnell, C. (2009) 'From Consumer to Prosumer to Produser: Who Keeps Shifting My Paradigm? (We Do!)', *Public Culture*, vol. 21, no. 3.

Gurney, D. (2011) '"It's Just Like a Mini-Mall": Textuality and Participatory Culture on YouTube', in M. Kackman, M. Binfield, M. Payne, A. Perlman, and B. Sebok (eds) *Flow TV*. New York: Routledge, pp. 30–45.

Hargreaves, I. and Hartley, J. (2016) *The Creative Citizen Unbound*. Bristol: Policy Press.

Hartley, J. (1999) *Uses of Television*. London: Routledge.

Hoffman, J. and Yudacufski, D. (2009/2010) 'Letters from the Editors', *make/shift*, vol. 6, no. 5.

Jenkins, H. (2014) 'Fan Activism as Participatory Politics: The Case of Harry Potter Alliance', in M. Ratto and M. Boler (eds) *DIY Citizenship*. Cambridge, MA: MIT Press, pp. 65–74.

Jenkins, H., Li, X. and Krauskopt, A. D. (2008) *Spreadability: If It Doesn't Spread, It's Dead - Creating Value in a Spreadable Marketplace*. Cambridge, MA: Convergence Culture Consortium.

Labash, M. (2012) 'The Meme Generation', *The Weekly Standard*, 4 June, http://www.weeklystandard.com/articles/meme-generation_645912.html, accessed 3 February 2017.

Lankshear, C. and Knobel, M. (2011) *New Literacies*. Maidenhead: Open University Press.

Larsen, B. (2016) 'LARSEN: Memes are dumbing-down political discourse', *The Daily Nebraskan*, 19 September, http://www.dailynebraskan.com/larsen-memes-are-dumbing-down-political-discourse/article_b2b93c14-7e05-11e6-88b5-43ec4f973ee9.html, accessed 1 May 2017.

Lastufka, A. and Dean, M. (2009) *YouTube: An Insider's Guide to Climbing the Charts*. Sebastopol, CA: O'Reilly Media.

Leadbeater, C. (2009) *We-Think*. London: Profile.

Lessig, L. (2006) '(Re)creativity: how creativity lives', in H. Porsdam (ed.) *Copyright and Other Fairy Tales*. Cheltenham: Edward Elgar Publishing Limited, pp. 15–22.

Lussier, J., Raeder, T. and Chawla, N. (2010) 'Digging up the Dirt on User Generated Content Consumption', in S. Kumar, S. Parthasarathy and S. Godbole (eds) *Proceedings of the 16th International Conference on Management of Data*. New Delhi: Allied Publishers, pp. 155–162.

McLuhan, M. (1964) *Understanding Media*. London: Routledge.

Marshall, C. (2013) 'I'm with Stupid: How the Internet Is Dumbing Down the Next Generation', *State of Digital*, http://www.stateofdigital.com/how-the-internet-is-dumbing-down-the-next-generation, accessed 16 May 2017.

Martens, M. (2011) 'Transmedia Teens: Affect, Immaterial Labor, and User-Generated Content', *Convergence*, vol. 17, no. 1, pp. 49–68.

Meikle, G. (2008) 'Whacking Bush: Tactical Media as Play', in M. Boler (ed.) *Digital Media and Democracy*. Cambridge, MA: MIT Press, pp. 367–82.

Meikle, G. and Young, S. (2012) *Media Convergence.* Basingstoke, UK: Palgrave Macmillan.

Milner, R. M. (2016) *The World Made Meme.* Cambridge, MA: MIT Press.

Nelson, K. (1985) *Making Sense.* New York: Academic Press.

Orton-Johnson, K. (2014) 'DIY Citizenship, Critical Making, and Community', in M. Ratto and M. Boler (eds) *DIY Citizenship.* Cambridge, MA: MIT Press, pp. 141–56.

Ratto, M. and Boler, M. (eds) (2014) *DIY Citizenship.* Cambridge, MA: MIT Press.

Shirky, C. (2010) *Cognitive Surplus.* London: Penguin.

Turney, J. (2009) *The Culture of Knitting.* New York: Berg.

Urban, S. (2017) 'Why Memes Are So Important for Millennials', *The Odyssey*, https://www.theodysseyonline.com/why-im-proud-to-be-part-of-the-meme-generation, accessed 1 June 2017.

Zuckerman, E. (2011) 'The First Twitter Revolution', *Foreign Policy*, 14 January, http://www.foreignpolicy.com/articles/2011/01/14/the_first_twitter_revolution, accessed 12 March 2017.

20

FEMINIST PROTEST ASSEMBLAGES AND REMIX CULTURE

Red Chidgey

Introduction

This chapter examines a set of assemblages that have become strongly attached to public feminisms in the latter half of the twentieth century and beyond: the use and modification of the historical 'We Can Do It' graphic. Introducing the concept of the 'protest assemblage', this chapter explores the creative and critical role of images, bodies, technologies and affects when imagining resistance and refusal in digital and offline contexts. Such assemblages (Deleuze & Guattari 2004) unfold within both heightened and banal settings to become hyper-visible constellations that are 'plugged into' to galvanize a sense of political affiliation, or to mobilize (or attempt to undermine) wider activist work.

Originally produced in the United States as a labour management poster during World War II, the We Can Do It! graphic is commonly known as 'Rosie the Riveter', a fictional name used within national propaganda campaigns to symbolize home front female defence workers recruited in a time of total war (Colman 1995). Illustrated by the commercial artist J. Howard Miller in 1942, the poster features a muscular but glamorous white woman in a blue shirt and red headscarf, her biceps flexed and hand curled into a fist, standing beneath a speech bubble exclaiming 'We Can Do It!'. The poster is one of the ten most requested images from the United States National Archives and Records Administration (Fried 2004) and one of the most 'over-exposed' souvenir items in the nation's capital (Kimble & Olson 2006). Curiously, the image has left its war-time context to become a ubiquitous signifier of transnational feminisms in recent decades.

Drawing on a wider research project tracking the assemblage from the 1940s to the present through archival research, visual and discourse analysis of mediated representations and interviews with producers and activists who use this graphic in their cultural work (Chidgey, forthcoming), this chapter establishes how the We Can Do It! image acts as a vibrant and creative protest assemblage. In what follows I outline how protest assemblages can be theorized through a media and cultural studies lens. I explore the critical role of remix culture – referring to a set of creative and communicative practices that modify existing cultural materials in order to create new texts – in the development and spread of highly iterative protest assemblages. As my empirical analysis, I focus on two moments within the We Can Do It! assemblage to illustrate its wider operations: Beyoncé's recreation of Miller's image on Instagram in 2014, which attracted hyperbolic praise within news commentary of being the 'ultimate feminist photo' (Greve 2014), and discursive attachments made between the Rosie the Riveter assemblage and the Russian feminist protest collective Pussy Riot.

Protest assemblages are 'sticky' and they multiply. The analytical strengths of an assemblage approach, I suggest, are that it allows us to better understand how movement images, icons and artefacts emerge, 'grip' and travel across spatial and temporal boundaries. Within such communicative repertoires, assemblages traverse bodies, discourses, technologies and social practices. Through identifying and tracking a protest assemblage (conceived here largely through its visual and communicative elements), we can analyze how protest assemblages are made of multiple, sometimes competing or contradictory elements and structures. This multiplicity sees protest assemblages transgressing a neat set of mainstream/grassroots, activist/non-activist, commodified/DIY and offline/online communicative binaries, which characterize studies of media and social movements to date (Mattoni 2013). Such an approach can also redress the lack of attention to the role of the visual within social movement research (Doerr, Mattoni & Teune 2013). Visual and communicative practices, I argue, play a vital and vitalizing role in the spread of protest assemblages, creating modal points capable of shaping wider activist discourses and practices.

Protest assemblages: a media and cultural studies perspective

Gilles Deleuze and Félix Guattari introduce the notion of the assemblage in their book *A Thousand Plateaus: Capitalism and Schizophrenia* (2004) as a means to theorize social complexity. Identifying assemblages as 'a multiplicity which is made up of many heterogeneous terms and which establishes liaisons, relations between them' (Deleuze & Parnet 2006: 52), these entities are produced through historical processes. Following the assemblage theory of Manual DeLanda (2006), assemblages cannot be reduced to their composite parts and their 'wholes' are never finalized, discrete totalities. As I develop the concept in this chapter, assemblages are constellations of *heterogeneous forces*: people, objects, expressions and practices that contingently coalesce to give certain ideas, behaviours or symbolic content prominence at any particular time and place.

Assemblages are comprised of 'circuits, conjunctions, levels and thresholds, passages and distributions of intensity' (Deleuze & Guattari 2004: 177). For Deleuze and Guattari, the horizontal axis of an assemblage is formed by content, form, action and expression as they entangle and collide with each other. Assemblages are composed of both *expressive content* (discourse and signifying systems) and *materialities* (affects, technologies, embodiment). The vertical axis of an assemblage consists of processes that stabilize or unsettle the assemblage (Deleuze & Guattari 2004: 97–98). All assemblages are subject to forces which bring cohesion and homogeneity to the assemblage (*territorialization*) and forces which dissipate the assemblage and bring new combinations and junctures (*deterritorialization*).

Assemblages have been evoked and re-worked within a broad range of disciplines, including the social sciences, anthropology, political philosophy, cinema and surveillance studies (see Hier 2003; Ong & Collier 2005; Sassen 2006; Rai 2009; Bennett 2010). Within urban geography, Colin McFarlane's (2009) conceptualization of social movements as 'translocal assemblages' usefully emphasizes how social movement actors, as well as intangible resources such as communicative and organizational practices, travel between physical and virtual sites. Here the figuration of the assemblage seeks to replace the 'network' (Castells 2004) in order to highlight issues of labour, dispersed causality and contingent becomings. First, as assemblages emphasize contingent processes of gathering, coherence and dispersion, it is necessary to attend to the *acts of labour* behind the assemblage. Who has the ability to mobilize and bring together actors/materials within social movements and protest cultures more broadly? Second, as assemblages name an uneven constellation of components that engage, cross over and self-reference each other, we can raise questions of *causality and responsibility* (McFarlane 2009: 562). How far has the We Can Do It! visual been deployed by feminists? Third, assemblages connote *emergent practices* through which power and authority are both concentrated and dispersed. To what extent have feminist identities, practices and even *imagined* histories been inscribed onto this cultural icon?

I argue that protest assemblages can be identified through their sense of *motility* and *intensity*. Within the realm of visual and communicative culture, select images, slogans or actors connected with social justice movements – be they historic or contemporary – persist or become freshly relevant again. To witness this is to see a protest assemblage at play. Notable examples include the mythology of the feminist bra-burner; the ubiquity of the Gandhian ideal 'be the change'; the afros, style politics and raised fist of the Black Power Movement; the Guy Fawkes mask of Anonymous, trademarked by Time Warner and used by activists worldwide. These symbols, practices and cultural figures are reiterated time and time again in a variety of mundane and heightened settings. Through their multiplication, modification and constitutive acts of prosumption, protest assemblages constitute a powerful, as well as frequently banal, signifying force. Both within and outside the assemblage, (human and non-human) processes and technics consolidate and unsettle the assemblage into new expressive and combinatory forms. The analytic task for the researcher, then, is 'to follow the tangled paths of the assemblage' (Bell 2007: 103) to understand its myriad productivities. With this understanding, the practice of remix culture can become key.

Remix as media activism method

Remix culture has been described as 'one of the most popular methods of media activism' today (Peverini 2015: 335; see Milner 2013; Horsti 2016). Using pre-existing texts and materials to create new content, remix practices embrace techniques such as collage, sampling, pastiche, mashups, culture jamming and détournement. Remix takes compositional elements of previous work(s) to create a new, referential piece. Through an assemblage lens, we can align this process to acts of *territorialization* (the iteration of key identifying components of the original work, maintaining a recognizable element of the source materials) and *deterritorialization* (making a fresh work, combining new elements, travelling the work in new contexts). Remix culture holds varied genealogies within arts and cultural movements of the twentieth century, and is linked to technological developments and their affordances (Meikle 2016: 61–64). Icons of political protest – whether they are drawn from the realm of activist groups or celebrity – have a particular role to play in transcultural protest work (Krieger 2015). This forging of identifiable and repeatable protest *icons* underscores how Pussy Riot and Rosie the Riveter – one actual, one fictional – can be articulated *as* assemblage formations, and can be articulated *together*.

The Russian feminist performance collective Pussy Riot created a viral Punk Prayer video (2012) of their action denouncing Vladimir Putin in Moscow's Cathedral of Christ the Saviour, earning them the label *media activist entrepreneurs* (Yaqub and Silova 2015) for successfully negotiating Russia's highly censorious mediascape. The protest led to the incarceration of two members on charges of hooliganism and inciting religious hatred. Examining the replication, modification and dissemination of images associated with Pussy Riot circulating within the Russian-language internet sphere – including user-generated videos, JPEGs, GIFs and memes – Michael Mead Yaqub and Iveta Silova position these practices as a form of polyvocal political participation, especially for young people. Emphasizing the key role that digital technologies and social media play within the 'image politics' (2015: 121) of contemporary political activism and debate, their findings demonstrate how remixed images – frequently referencing Pussy Riot's balaclavas and bright dresses as common visual elements – become gestures of political solidarity for a range of actors and constituencies. At the same time, the internet genre of *demotivationals* – a single image framed in black, accompanied with a caption written below the image in white font – is called on by other constituencies to 'ridicule and denigrate the target subject matter of the image – sometimes in vicious and vulgar ways' (2015: 124).

Tracking representations of Pussy Riot in Western media, Carrie Smith-Prei and Maria Stehle (2016: 131) question how the hypervisibility of the group as a global 'protest brand' leads to an awkward type of politics; we can turn to this analysis to tease out the implications of Pussy Riot as a protest assemblage. Describing a 2015 episode of the Netflix series *House of Cards* where Pussy Riot members Masha Alyokhina and Nadia Tolokonnikova appear as themselves, they write:

> Viewers encounter the 'real' Pussy Riot in a fictional series that features a fake protest, which, ultimately, is not all that fake since the issues at hand are real political issues (i.e. gay rights in Russia). These awkward relationships make it clear that the appearance of Pussy Riot in *House of Cards* is more than appropriation; when taken together with other 'stages' on which the group – or its two more recognizable representatives – appeared, we can see this as the moment pop and feminism fuse, though awkwardly so, for even here in the commoditized world of pay television, there is a distinct lack of ironic distance. Instead, the utter seriousness of their politics remains, but the political has slipped off screen.
>
> *Smith-Prei & Stehle 2016: 133*

This awkwardness, as well as numerous traversals and re-connections between the political and the popular, underscores how protest assemblages are unwieldy constellations populated by political actors, mediated events, sensibilities and aesthetics. When protest events and images 'move in and out of the digital realm and through different realms of culture, such as alternative culture, museum spaces, national mainstream presses, and social networking and file sharing sites' (Smith-Prei & Stehle 2016: 134), this implicitly speaks to the multiplicity of scales that a protest assemblage can galvanize and move through.

Social movement and alternative media studies would do well to see how these 'slippages' signify more than commodification (see Mukherjee & Banet-Weiser 2012; Portwood-Stacer 2013; Street, Inthorn & Scott 2013). Protest assemblages extend from their initial event to form a wider constellation of repeated iterations, modifications and circulations. While protest assemblages can be rapidly mobilized to draw attention to injustices and vulnerable bodies in the present, drawing on a multiplicity of media technologies and actors (Knudsen & Stage 2015), they also multiply through quotidian, less 'heated' exchanges, forming part of everyday, banal communicative and expressive practices. It is precisely through these range of acts that protest assemblages 'grip' and multiply. Crucially, elements of one protest assemblage (Pussy Riot) can collide and inter-mix with elements of another protest assemblage (Rosie the Riveter), underscoring the essential motility of assemblage formations.

The following suggestion of 'awesome feminist Halloween costume ideas' in a North American feminist magazine, *Bust*, demonstrates the playful invocations that protest assemblages can take as they are recomposed through everyday communicative and embodied practices, and how assemblages can come to be articulated together:

Pussy Riot: Get a couple of girlfriends together, put on some colorful ski masks, and run around causing trouble! This costume is cheap and easy to put together, would be easy to recognize, and is totally topical.

Rosie the Riveter: An oldie but a goodie, one of the most universal symbols of feminism (and a cheap and easy costume: just a blue collared shirt and a red polka dot bandana).

O'Donnell 2012: n.p.

The ubiquity of the We Can Do It!/Rosie the Riveter assemblage is captured in the expressions 'oldie but a goodie' and 'universal symbol of feminism'. This discourse gives a sense of both the common-placeness and duration of the assemblage. Indeed, Miller's We Can Do It! image has become prolific in recent decades as a symbol of feminist struggle: appearing on feminist magazine and book covers, in social media avatars, on T-shirts, to advertise political meetings. This iconography has become a key part of feminist activists' and mainstream media's visualization of feminist sentiment and identities. In its motility, the We Can Do It! artefact shares a similar cultural afterlife as the British WWII propaganda poster Keep Calm and Carry On, a poster originally produced in the event of a Nazi invasion on British soil and now a widely mobilized political and cultural meme (Hatherley 2015).

'The ultimate feminist photo': remixing feminist protest assemblages

On 22 July 2014, *Time* magazine declared that Beyoncé had just posted 'the ultimate feminist photo' on the photo-sharing site Instagram (Greve 2014). This image quickly attracted over 1.4 million likes from fans and became the star's most popular social media photo to date. The 17-time Grammy winner was poised in front of a yellow background, clad in a denim shirt with a signature red headscarf, biceps curled into a fist, with a defiant look on her face. Above her head is a speech bubble with text exclaiming 'We Can Do It!'. Cultural commentators and fans quickly made the association between this image and the iconic 'Rosie the Riveter' poster created by J. Howard Miller in 1942. Indicative of common narratives within news commentary that position this poster as a symbol of women's empowerment during WWII and as a prominent symbol within second wave feminist movements, *Cosmopolitan* labelled Beyoncé's recreation of this iconic image as a 'a short and sweet affirmation of her feminist beliefs' (Scott 2014).

There are enduring mythologies surrounding Miller's poster. In a Yahoo! news report, the original purpose of Miller's poster was described as 'boost[ing] morale for American women who had taken up jobs in factories' (Lloyd 2014). In fact, this was a labour management poster commissioned by the internal War Production Committee of Westinghouse Electric and Manufacturing Company 'to increase production, to decrease absenteeism, and to avoid strikes' within select factories (Kimble & Olson 2006: 544). A common (mainstream and alternative) media narrative is that 'second-wave feminists in the 1960s and '70s revived [the image]' in their protest actions (Sagen 2017). Such temporal assumptions are out of tune with the poster's archival and medial histories. The poster achieved public visibility in the early to mid-1980s through the actions of two key institutions: The National Archives, who created a set of note cards from WWII posters in 1982 featuring the graphic (Brennan 1982), and the National Museum of American History, who purchased copies of the original poster from J. Howard Miller in 1985 (Kurin 2013) and used these artefacts in their touring exhibitions. The image was simply not available for public consumption or activist re-use in the 1960s or 1970s.

Few reproductions and small-scale remixes occurred in US and UK feminist media productions in the 1980s (Chidgey, forthcoming). While invocations to the name 'Rosie the Riveter' did have a presence in movement media, it was not until the 2000s that the image associated with Miller's 1942 poster became publicly consolidated as a key feminist icon. There are several factors underpinning this popular resurgence. Visually, the kitsch aesthetic of war-time propaganda resonates with a larger nostalgia boom (Hatherley 2015). The generic, vaguely soli-daristic language of the 'We Can Do It!' aphorism resonates with wider neoliberal sensibilities around girl power, strength and 'can do girl' attitudes (Harris 2004). In a significant act of deter-ritorialization, a digital copy of the We Can Do It! image was uploaded to the English language site of the online user-generated encyclopedia Wikipedia in April 2007, sourced from a digitiza-tion of the original poster made by the National Archives. Alongside links to pages on WWII histories, this image frequently illustrates feminist entries internationally.

While remix practices are often embroiled in heated debates about the 'copyright wars' (Lessig 2008), Miller's We Can Do It! image has remained free from such friction. The US copy-right law in place during the 1940s was the Copyright Act of 1909, which secured copyright protection for works at the time of publication if an affixed copyright notice was attached (Joyce *et al.* 2003: 21). With no such copyright notice, Miller's We Can Do It! artwork is now available in the public domain. This copyright-free status allows Miller's image to travel, mutate and be taken up for a variety of purposes – adaptations are often made to the central figure (changing gender, even species) and the speech bubble text. This public domain status also underscores how the We Can Do It! assemblage is intensified through the transition of *images to things*.

Drawing on Scott Lash and Celia Lury's (2007) concept of 'thingification', whereby medi-ated products in contemporary consumer culture are turned into objects, Britta Timm Knudsen and Carsten Stage illustrate how 'media products are also turned into objects and things/spaces are turned into media' (Knudsen & Stage 2015: 50). Blurred boundaries exist between media-tion and materiality, as elements of protest assemblages (bodies, images, objects) move between different ontological states through the 'constant and productive intertwinement of mediation and materialisation' (*ibid*: 51). Miller's image has been reproduced through countless commodi-ties, including lunchboxes, aprons, badges, lighters, magnets, cleaning products and a Rosie the Riveter action toy. Thingification also underscores how Miller's image has become associated with feminism and how the assemblage travels. The setting of Beyoncé's Instagram photo is reportedly the National WWII Museum in New Orleans, which has a 'We Can Do It!' backdrop and Rosie the Riveter costumes. These props encourage an embodied remix strategy: partici-pants draw on key visual elements to evoke the original poster (colours, costumes, composition, pose), yet each individual, and what they do with the image (such as posting to Instagram), becomes a modality point in the wider assemblage.

Crucially, there isn't just a singular work that Beyoncé remixes through her re-staging of the iconic WWII poster – that is, this isn't just a remix of the original J. Howard Miller poster. As part of a protest assemblage (conceptualized here as the wide variety of materials, narratives and images that become 'sticky' and attached to political identities and agendas), Beyoncé remixes the *feminist assemblage*. She is calling upon the layered elements of cultural memory associated with this image (as patriotic symbol, as 'ordinary woman', as worker, as 'feminist icon') and re-works these components through her own celebrity assemblage – crucially, also remixing the whiteness of dominant mainstream feminisms and historical Rosie representations. As has been well documented and debated, Beyoncé has publically claimed a feminist identity. The singer contributed an essay entitled 'Gender Equality is a Myth!' to The Shriver Report (Knowles-Carter 2014). In the months following her Instagram post, Beyoncé performed at the MTV Video Music Awards in front of a giant screen emblazoned with the word FEMINIST. Here she was performing her hit Flawless, which samples Chimamanda Ngozi Adichie's influential TedxTalk speech, 'We Should All Be Feminists' (2013), deconstructing unfair gender expecta-tions for girls.

As a condition of their manifestation, protest assemblages sprawl across boundaries and their constitutive parts become part of wider assemblages. The Beyoncé case study is an excellent illustration of feminist, celebrity and social justice assemblages colliding and re-combining. To follow one particular line of flight: Beyoncé is a celebrity advocator for ONE, a campaigning organization taking action to end extreme poverty and preventable disease in Africa. Demonstrating the 'spreadability' (Jenkins, Ford & Green 2013) of the Rosie assemblage, and the re-embodiment aspects underpinning its remix culture, We Can Do It! iconographies became unexpectedly connected to the work of this campaigning group. As detailed in a press release promoting a remix of a previous campaign song, Strong Girl, ONE received 'hundreds of thousands of #strengthies – where people pose in the style of Rosie the Riveter' (ONE 2015). This use of embodiment (the Rosie 'pose') combined with social media practices (#strengthies – a hashtag play of strength and selfies) demonstrates aspects of the materialities and expressive content behind this protest assemblage and the ways in which the assemblage can travel. Remix practices become part of the lines of territorialization, deterritorialization and re-territorialization in which the protest assemblage moves, re-combines and consolidates.

Conclusion

This chapter has interrogated a highly mediated – and certainly banal – moment within the wider We Can Do It! assemblage: the 2014 restaging of the iconic Rosie the Riveter image on Instagram within the celebrity culture of Beyoncé. Through taking a single, hyperbolic utterance within news commentary, that Beyoncé's recreation of the iconic image was 'the ultimate feminist photo' (Greve 2014), this study has examined how protest assemblages extend from distant (and sometimes imagined) protest pasts, to co-mingle and collide with wider socio-technological assemblages, such as celebrity feminism, postfeminism and the mediated activism of Pussy Riot. Analytically, remix practices help us to understand the compositional aspects of protest assemblages. Furthermore, an assemblage lens can help us to interrogate remix practices within a wider temporal and material frame. This approach is one way in which to challenge dominant strands within remix studies, which examine remixes as 'static objects rather than creative processes that are part of public discourse surrounding an ongoing social or political concern' (Krieger 2015: 375). With an assemblage approach, remix practices can be traced through their long histories and durations, and their ontological shifts mapped across temporal and spatial boundaries.

Originally produced as a labour management poster during WWII to deter strikes and promote wartime efficiency in US defence industries, the expressive content of the 'We Can Do It!' image have been significantly reworked under the conditions of late capitalism. This has worked to deterritorialize the graphic from its strictly war-time context, and reterritorialize the image to new feminist identities and sensibilities. There is no easy consensus about the value and status of the We Can Do It! image as a suitable, and relevant, feminist icon, however. When interviewing second and third wave feminist media producers around the use and ubiquity of the We Can Do It! image (Chidgey, forthcoming), I found pockets of cynicism surrounding the over-exposed element of this fictional feminist icon, particularly when the image served to replace or obscure a more diverse appreciation of feminist iconographies and recollections of historical feminisms.

In parallel to 'originality' and 'authenticity' debates within remix studies (Lessig 2008; Gunkel 2015), commentary exists online and within my research interviews around the We Can Do It! image as a 'lazy' and 'inauthentic' visualization of feminism, remixing a fake history of feminist activism through an over-repetitive visual style which can be easily consumed. An assemblage approach involves tracking these kinds of (good and bad) affects to interrogate the kinds of cultural and political work such remixes *do*. This involves unpicking the wider cultural and political conditions through which assemblages emerge, 'grip' and spread, and under which conditions an assemblage might finally disperse and dissipate all together. In doing so, researchers and activists alike can understand how assemblages are composed and travel across mainstream/grassroots, activist/non-activist, commodified/DIY and offline/online capacities, and the co-presence of both progressive and conservative intentions, and playful and serious politics, in their articulation. Such an understanding can help us to recognize the agency of assemblages as they gather in motility and intensity, and, crucially, when such assemblages can be harnessed, and when such assemblages should be decomposed.

References

Adichie, C. N. (2013) 'We Should All Be Feminists', *TEDxTalks*, 12 April, https://www.youtube.com/watch?v=hg3umXU_qWc, accessed 15 January 2017.

Bell, V. (2007) *Culture & Performance: The Challenge of Ethics, Politics and Feminist Theory*. Oxford: Berg.

Bennett, J. (2010) *Vibrant Matter: A Political Ecology of Things*. Durham, NC: Duke University Press.

Brennan, P. (1982) 'Poster Art for Patriotism's Sake', *The Washington Post*, 23 May, https://www.washingtonpost.com/archive/lifestyle/magazine/1982/05/23/poster-art-for-patriotisms-sake/65f96528-ddcb-4507-b157-c8b2c6dc25c1/?utm_term=.c7c9db665efe, accessed 15 January 2017.

Castells, M. (ed.) (2004) *The Network Society: A Cross-Cultural Perspective*. Cheltenham, UK: Edward Elgar.

Chidgey, R. (forthcoming) *Feminist Afterlives: Assemblage Memory in Activist Times*. Basingstoke, UK: Palgrave Macmillan.

Colman, P. (1995) *Rosie the Riveter: Women Working on the Home Front in World War II*. New York: Crown.

DeLanda, M. (2006) *A New Philosophy of Society: Assemblage Theory and Social Complexity*. London: Continuum.

Deleuze, G. and Guattari, F. (2004) [1980] *A Thousand Plateaus: Capitalism and Schizophrenia*. Trans. Brian Massumi. London: Continuum.

Deleuze, G. and Parnet, C. (2006) [1977] *Dialogues II*. Trans. Hugh Tomlinson and Barbara Habberjam. London: Continuum.

Doerr, N., Mattoni, A. and Teune, S. (eds) (2013) 'Advances in the Visual Analysis of Social Movements', *Research in Social Movements, Conflicts and Change*, vol. 35. Bingley, UK: Emerald Group.

Fried, E. (2004) 'From Pearl Harbor to Elvis: Images That Endure', *Prologue Magazine*, vol. 36, no. 4, https://www.archives.gov/publications/prologue/2004/winter/top-images.html, accessed 15 January 2017.

Greve, J. (2014) 'Beyoncé Just Posted the Ultimate Feminist Photo', *Time*, 22 July, http://time.com/3018710/beyonce-rosie-the-riveter-instagram, accessed 15 January 2017.

Gunkel, D. (2015) *Of Remixology: Ethics and Aesthetics after Remix*. Cambridge, MA: The MIT Press.

Harris, A. (2004) *Future Girl: Young Women in the Twenty-First Century*. New York: Routledge.

Hatherley, O. (2015) *The Ministry of Nostalgia: Consuming Austerity*. London: Verso.

Hier, S. (2003) 'Probing the Surveillant Assemblage: On the Dialectics of Surveillance Practices as Processes of Social Control', *Surveillance & Society*, vol. 1, no. 3, pp. 399–411.

Horsti, Karina (2016) 'Communicative Memory of Irregular Migration: The Re-circulation of News Images on YouTube', *Memory Studies*, vol. 10, no. 2, pp. 112–29, http://journals.sagepub.com/doi/abs/10.1177/1750698016640614, accessed 15 January 2017.

Jenkins, H., Ford, S. and Green, J. (2013) *Spreadable Media: Creating Value and Meaning in a Networked Culture*. New York: New York University Press.

Joyce, C., Leaffer, M., Jaszi, P. and Ochoa, T. (2003) *Copyright Law: Cases and Materials*. Sixth ed. Newark, NJ: Lexis Nexis.

Kimble, J. and Olson, L. (2006) 'Visual Rhetoric Representing Rosie the Riveter: Myth and Misconception in J. Howard Miller's "We Can Do It!" Poster', *Rhetoric & Public Affairs*, vol. 9, no. 4, pp. 533–69.

Knowles-Carter, B. (2014) 'Gender Equality Is a Myth!', *The Shriver Report*, http://shriverreport.org/gender-equality-is-a-myth-beyonce/, accessed 15 January 2017.

Knudsen, B. T. and Stage, C. (2015) *Global Media, Biopolitics, and Affect: Politicizing Bodily Vulnerability*. New York: Routledge.

Krieger, J. M. (2015) 'The Politics of John Lennon's "Imagine": Contextualising the Roles of Mashups and New Media in Political Protest', in E. Navas, O. Gallagher, and x. burrough (eds) *The Routledge Companion to Remix Studies*. New York: Routledge, pp. 374–85.

Kurin, R. (2013) *The Smithsonian's History of America in 101 Objects*. New York: Penguin.

Lash, S. and Lury, C. (2007) *Global Culture Industry: The Mediation of Things*. Cambridge: Polity Press.

Lessig, L. (2008) *Remix: Making Art and Commerce Thrive in the Hybrid Economy*. London: Penguin.

Lloyd, P. (2014) 'Why Beyoncé's Recreation of the Iconic Rosie the Riveter Poster Makes Me Proud', *Yahoo! News,* 23 July, https://www.yahoo.com/news/why-beyonce-recreation-iconic-rosie-riveter-poster-makes-131700499.html, accessed 15 January 2017.

McFarlane, C. (2009) 'Translocal Assemblages: Space, Power and Social Movements', *Geoforum*, vol. 40, no. 4, pp. 561–567.

Mattoni, A. (2013) 'Repertoires of Communication in Social Movement Processes', in B. Cammaerts, A. Mattoni and P. McCurdy (eds) *Mediation and Protest Movements*. Bristol, UK: Intellect, pp. 41–56.

Meikle, G. (2016) *Social Media: Communication, Sharing and Visibility*. New York: Routledge.

Milner, R. (2013) 'Pop Polyvocality: Internet Memes, Public Participation, and the Occupy Wall Street Movement', *International Journal of Communication*, vol. 7, pp. 2357–90.

Mukherjee, R. and Banet-Weiser, S. (eds) (2012) *Commodity Activism: Cultural Resistance in Neoliberal Times*. New York: New York University Press.

O'Donnell, L. (2012) '10 Awesome Feminist Halloween Costume Ideas', *Bust*, http://bust.com/feminism/8698-10-awesome-feminist-halloween-costume-ideas.html, accessed 15 January 2017.

ONE (2015) 'Strong Girl Remix: Male and Female Artists Harmonize Together for Women's Empowerment and Justice', 28 August, https://www.one.org/us/press/strong-girl-remix-male-and-female-artists-harmonise-together-for-womens-empowerment-and-justice, accessed 15 January 2017.

Ong, A. and Collier, S. (eds) (2005) *Global Assemblages: Technology, Politics and Ethics as Anthropological Problems*. Oxford: Blackwell.

Peverini, P. (2015) 'Remix Practices and Activism: A Semiotic Analysis of Creative Dissent', in E. Navas, O. Gallagher, and x. burrough (eds) *The Routledge Companion to Remix Studies*. New York: Routledge, pp. 333–45.

Portwood-Stacer, L. (2013) *Lifestyle Politics and Radical Activism*. New York: Bloomsbury.

Pussy Riot (2012), 'Панк-молебен ""Богородица, Путина прогони"' [Punk Prayer 'Mother of God, Chase Putin Away'], 21 February, https://www.youtube.com/watch?v=GCasuaAczKY, accessed 15 January 2017.

Rai, A. (2009) *Untimely Bollywood: Globalization and India's New Media Assemblage*. Durham, NC: Duke University Press.

Sagen, E. (2017) 'What Would a Modern-Day Rosie the Riveter Look Like?', *Yes Magazine*, 1 March, http://www.yesmagazine.org/people-power/what-would-a-modern-day-rosie-the-riveter-look-like-20170301, accessed 5 March 2017.

Sassen, S. (2006) *Territory, Authority, Rights: From Medieval to Global Assemblages*. Princeton, NJ: Princeton University Press.

Scott, E. (2014) 'Beyoncé Dresses Up as Feminist Icon Rosie the Riveter, Looks ★★★Flawless', *Cosmopolitan*, 22 July, http://www.cosmopolitan.com/uk/entertainment/news/a28129/beyonce-rosie-the-riveter-feminist, accessed 15 January 2017.

Smith-Prei, C. and Stehle, M. (2016) *Awkward Politics: Technologies of Popfeminist Activism*. Montreal, Canada: McGill-Queen's University Press.

Street, J., Inthorn, S. and Scott, M. (2013) *From Entertainment to Citizenship: Politics and Popular Culture*. Manchester, UK: Manchester University Press.

Yaqub, M. M. and Silova, I. (2015) 'Remixing Riot: The Reappropriation of Pussy Riot through User-Generated Imagery across the Russian Internet', in I. Epstein (ed.) *The Whole World is Texting: Youth Protest in the Information Age*. Rotterdam, the Netherlands: Sense Publishers, pp. 115–36.

PART IV

Tactics of visibility

21

AFFECTIVE ACTIVISM AND POLITICAL SECULARISM

The unending body in the Femen movement

Camilla Møhring Reestorff

Introduction

The activist movement Femen is notorious for topless protests and the ideology 'sextremism, atheism and feminism'. The movement's manifesto reads: 'Our God is a woman! Our Mission is Protest! Our Weapon are [sic] bare breasts!' (http://www.femen.org). The references to religion are evident in phrases such as 'our God is a Woman', 'topless jihadists' (Taylor 2013), and 'godless witches' (Shevchenko 2015). In this chapter I investigate a reoccurring paradox: namely that Femen attacks religions and religious institutions, while embedding references to religion in their activist imaginary.

Christianity and Islam are often the centre of attention on Femen's official webpage – www. femen.org – making it possible to study the way in which activism, atheism and feminism are articulated in relation to the two religions. This is the background for this chapter in which I focus on three Femen protests: 1) Yana Zhdanova's grabbing of the baby Jesus doll from St Peter's Square's nativity scene on 25 December 2015, 2) the 2013 'Topless Jihad Day', and 3) the support of the imprisoned writer and activist Raif Badawi.

The chapter first suggests that in order to understand Femen's atheist disbelief (Glendinning 2012) it is necessary to expand the theoretical approach to atheism, by moving beyond traditional organizational structures and investigating atheism that emerges in networked forms of activism. Second, the concept of affective mediatized activism (Reestorff 2014) is utilized to understand how Femen produces spectacles in which icon bodies become trigger-texts for affective attunement and events. Third, the chapter investigates the relationship between Femen and the so-called 'New Atheism' and the way in which different types of atheist movements conjoin in a peculiar fight on behalf of Muslim women. This leads to the chapter's final argument: namely that Femen's atheist disbelief manifests as a specific form of political secularism (Mahmood 2016) that is simultaneously governing religion and embedded in a religious imaginary.

Atheism and activism

Women who conduct topless protests make up Femen. There are Femen groups in many countries, and an activist does not need to be part of a central organization to be recognized as a part of Femen's activist imaginary. This loose network-based structure is to some extent contradicted on Femen's official webpage, which states that Femen is 'responsible only for those acts of sextremism information of which is shared on official web resources of the movement' (http://www.femen.org). The emphasis on the 'official' Femen is indicative of a shift that appeared in the organizational structures after Femen became internationally recognized around 2011. Thus, the movement emerged as a heterogeneous assemblage formed by decentralized groups, but the increased mediatization resulted in a shift towards more centralized organizational structures (Reestorff 2014). This means that it is important to keep in mind that Femen's official communication does not necessarily encompass all Femen activists, but that it nevertheless seeks to define and centralize the movement's activist imaginary.

Atheism is, as already mentioned, a core element in Femen's ideology. Atheism is most commonly understood as the belief that there is no reason to believe that there is a god and that religion and state apparatuses must be separated. Femen's sextremist attacks on religion and religious institutions are indicative of the kind of atheism that Simon Glendinning (2012) terms atheist disbelief. Contrary to 'a-theist non-belief', which is somewhat similar to agnosticism, atheist disbelief pitches itself against religion (Glendinning 2012: 37). Femen's atheist disbelief is furthermore intertwined with notions of modernity and the modern atheist woman is positioned in opposition to religion. The aim is, Femen writes, to 'separate the church from the state and to prohibit any intervention of the religious institutions in the civic, sex and reproductive lives of modern women' (http://www.femen.org).

The intertwining of atheist disbelief and activist mobilization is interesting because atheism is often understood as individual lack of faith. Contrary to this, Femen's atheism is social, mediatized and an activist weapon. This requires a new understanding of atheism. As noted by LeDrew (2013), there is a lack of knowledge about atheism and social movements. For many years atheism was 'almost completely ignored by sociologists of religion' (LeDrew 2013: 431). But since the turn of the century the so-called New Atheism, promoted by for instance Richard Dawkins's *The God Delusion* (2006), has made atheists more visible (Smith & Cimino 2010; LeDrew 2013).

Research on the impact of media on atheist sentiments has investigated the ways in which media technologies allow individuals to seek information and engage in atheist communities. Smith and Cimino (2012: 20) write that 'as the private sphere becomes more directly constitutive of public debate, affairs, and policies, it also becomes more and more the ground for resistance, challenge, and social change'. However, atheism also needs to be understood outside the realm of the private and as a part of social movements. Stephen LeDrew notes that there have been, and still are, tensions between cultural and political dimensions of the secular movement, and between humanistic atheists whose central concerns are social justice and human welfare, New Atheists whose central concern is the ideological legitimation of authority, and atheists who focus on social justice and consider atheism an inherently political activity (LeDrew 2016: 101). Femen crisscrosses between these different atheist traditions. The movement was initially mobilized against sex tourism in Ukraine, but it also questions the legitimation of authority, in a manner similar to the New Atheists, and it considers atheism a political activity inherently tied to the female body.

Femen is difficult to categorize as a social movement because it cannot be categorized as an *organized* social movement and because atheism is not the movement's only goal. In order to understand the significance of Femen's atheism it is necessary to distinguish between atheism that emphasizes the role of organizations in structuring social conflicts and more fluid and network-based activist practices. It is certainly correct that organizations and active membership can create immediate political community (Stephan-Norris and Zeitlin 2003: 187) and that this kind of organization is prevalent in New Atheist organizations. However, activist movements,

such as Femen, often abandon traditional organizational structures in favour of 'dense but informal *networks* which allows movements to maintain a plural repertoire, testing various potential
options and combining their effects' (della Porta 2015: 161). Femen is not concerned with
organizing atheist communities, but rather relies on networkability. As such the movement
exemplifies the way in which 'networked communication technologies have allowed movements to shift from relatively centralized, hierarchical organizational structures to highly decentralized, loosely affiliated contingent networks' (Lievrouw 2011: 175). The contingent networks
are to some extent challenged by Femen's emphasis on the centralized and 'official Femen'.
Furthermore, the Femen movement does not organize atheists but mobilizes activists who are
often more concerned about matters of gender equality than of atheism. As such Femen's atheist
disbelief is neither simply everyday dissensual practices nor organized atheism. Rather, Femen
relies on revolting subjects, who mobilize their atheist disbelief and invest their bodies in public
spaces in order to document and spread the atheist activist imaginary.

Mediatized activism

Femen argues that religion is incompatible with modern women and they attack religious institutions. On 25 December 2014 activist Yana Zhdanova snatched a baby Jesus doll from St Peter's
Square's nativity scene. 'God Is Woman' was written on her bare chest. Zhdanova was chased and
detained by Vatican guards (documentation of the protest can be seen at https://www.youtube.
com/watch?v=u1jg_lHPI7M). The protest is an expression of an atheist disbelief that manifests
as 'militant feminist atheism' (Schaefer 2014). This kind of atheism focuses on 'the oppression
of women at the hands of extremist visions of religion' and 'argues for a decisive break with
religion – an obliteration – driven by the machines of reason or progress' (Schaefer 2014: 374).
Zhdanova is exactly questioning the legitimacy of religion and insisting that god is a woman.

The protest is simple. A topless activist runs to the stage and is chased and detained. But it
is not merely about the physical confrontation. Zhdanova turns her body towards the cameras
and holds up baby Jesus, expecting to be both filmed and chased. As such Zhdanova engages
in mediatized activism and the documentation of the protest becomes crucial. Mediatization is
the process in which society – or in this case activism – is increasingly dependent upon media
logics and adapted to 'symbols or mechanisms created by the media' (Hjarvard 2008: 28, 31).
Mediatized activism does not simply emerge around a stable set of media logics, but the topless
protest and the attack on recognizable icons, such as the Vatican, anticipate media coverage and
circulation.

In order to ensure documentation, the activist imaginary must engage the audience. Femen's
topless protest appropriates recognizable images of the female body, and the nativity play
becomes a place from which to generate media attention. The protest is a spectacle. It is 'a
way of making an argument, not through appeals to reason and fact', but 'through stories and
myth, imagination and fantasy' (Duncombe, in Jenkins 2007). Femen's spectacle visualizes and
animates an abstract understanding of atheism: god is a woman and she doesn't like the church.

Femen's protests are often discomforting because they expose the vulnerability of the body
(Reestorff 2014). But it is fun to observe the Vatican's guard chase a half-naked woman carrying
baby Jesus – and even after her capture Zhadonova is smiling. This humorous spectacle considers
the potential pleasure of the viewers and this is 'conceptualized in opposition to the potential
displeasure of the straightforward didactic' (Day 2011: 148). The spectacle makes the political
message lucid. It 'culture jams' the church. Culture jamming uses forms of mass culture, in this
case religion, against itself through tactics like parody and irony, and it often wages war against
commodity culture (Dery 2004). As such the protest decrypts religion, subverts the nativity

play and aims to render the seduction of religion impotent. The protest is an intrusion and reconfiguration of the religion that Femen believes is intruding on women's bodies.

Mediatized activism is intended to foster spreadability (Jenkins, Ford & Green 2013). At the protest at the Vatican, RT Ruptly, a Berlin-based video news agency owned by the Russian-based RT televised news network, which specializes in video on demand, shot and distributed footage. But footage was also produced and circulated by the visitors at the Vatican City, who used their mobile phones and cameras to document the protest. This underlines the fact that mediatized activism relies on technical resources and that the spectacle utilizes the 'attributes of media text that might appeal to a community's motivation for sharing material' (Jenkins, Ford & Green 2013: 4). Femen's protest is designed as a breeding ground for spreadability and mobilization. It is dependent on a live 'audience', who have the technical resources to document and share, and on the activists' ability to create memorable and evocative images that reach and impact a media public. This also indicates that Femen's mediatized activism is intended to generate media events. The spectacle serves to intensify media debates. It is simultaneously situated in time and space, at the Vatican City on Christmas Day, and global in the sense that its documentation makes 'those who are not physically present feel as if they were' (Rowe 2000: 2). Broadcast media and bystanders' documentation ensures that the mediatized protest becomes ingrained in the activist imaginary and that its reach is expanded as a source of activist mobilization.

Affective events and icon bodies

The protest at St Peter's Square is a media event that captures the attention of the bystanders and obtains media circulation. But the event also activates bodies and affects. According to Deleuze, an event exhibits 'the absurdity of significations' and it is 'never present, but always already in the past and yet to come' (Deleuze 1990: 136). The event is, thus, relational and never constrained to a finished object. You could argue that Femen's protest is uneventful and recognizable – another topless woman attacking an authority. But the event is also unrecognizable and 'always to come'. This is because the event is shaped in the relations between bodies.

The event is intensified in the relations between bodies and as such it concerns affective attunement. Femen's activist body is thus crucial because it becomes a trigger text not only for documentation and circulation but also for affective attunement. According to Brian Massumi, affective attunement refers to the direct capture of attention and energies by the event (in Fritsch & Thomsen 2012). The affective event can be identified in the bystanders' bodies. In the footage from the protest it is evident that bodies are directed towards the same cue, Femen's spectacle. The bodies of the bystanders are stretching to see and raising their arms to make sure that their cameras capture the events. Nevertheless, it is important to keep in mind that affect is not experienced uniformly across bodies. The affective event and attunement is differential. This means that all who encounter Femen's protest – offline or online – are, in the words of Massumi, 'taken into the event from a different angle, and move out of it following our own singular trajectories' (in Fritsch & Thomsen 2012). The activist spectacle triggers events, but participants in these events are attuned differentially. The guards, priests, visitors, staff members and people who see documentation of the protests online are all affectively attuned to the event. Yet, their attunement is differential. The affective event compiles differentially attuned bodies that energize and sustain the activist imaginary.

Femen's topless bodies become trigger-texts for affective attunement and they have come to be recognized as icons for the movement. These 'icon bodies' are used strategically to generate events, when they are introduced to challenge other – often religious – icons, e.g. Jesus, Notre Dame, the hijab, etc. Femen introduces its icon bodies in order to subvert pre-given religious meaning. But the icon bodies also enable Femen's activists to become recognizable as crowd leaders. Gustave Le Bon (2002) famously argued that people sharing a certain space are able to influence each other contagiously. Thus, a crowd is not just many people gathered in the same place, but a certain type of affectively synchronized and de-individualized gathering (Reestorff & Stage 2016) that is susceptible to leaders with a talent for suggestion, exaggeration, affirmation and repetition (Le Bon 2002: 11, 23). Femen certainly has a 'talent for suggestion, exaggeration, affirmation and repetition' and its icon bodies function as crowd facilitators because they are visual and affective suggestions that may direct the crowd into predictable rhythmic repetitions. As such Femen's mediatized activism depends on affectively informed 'power relations' (Burkitt 2014: 156). These power relations arise in patterns of relationships between objects, icons and events, and it is in these affective relations that the crowd is attuned and cued to the activist event.

Feminism and New Atheism

Femen's activists always invest and lay claim on their bodies. Yet bodies are invested in other bodies. Athena Athanasiou and Judith Butler (2013: 65–6) write that when the 'self' 'who struggles for recognition and self-recognition has been violently misrecognized' then 'the economy of recognition gets potentially and provisionally destabilized'. In this context Femen's protests can be interpreted as an attempt to destabilize recognizable discourses regarding the female body (Reestorff 2014).

However, Femen's emancipatory project is not always clear. Discrepancies often emerge in the combination of activism, feminism and atheist disbelief. At a conference on 'The Religious Right, Secularism and Civil Rights' in London in 2014, for instance, Inna Shevchenko, who often is referred to as Femen's leader, and Richard Dawkins were photographed together. In the picture shared on Twitter Shevchenko holds up her fist, as if ready for a fight, and Dawkins holds a sign saying 'Vaginal Coalition Against Bigotry'. The alleged alliance between Shevchenko and Dawkins is interesting because Dawkins on several occasions has been accused of bigotry. In 2016, for instance, he shared a highly offensive video on Twitter comparing feminism and Islamism, and his invitation to speak at the Northeast Conference on Science and Skepticism was subsequently withdrawn (Blair 2016). Most notorious is his response to Rebecca Watson, founder of the website Skepchick, who addressed misogyny in the New Atheist community. In a post entitled 'Dear Muslima', Dawkins dismissed the alleged misogyny by comparing it to Muslim women who have their 'genitals mutilated with a razor blade', indicating that Western non-Muslim women have no legitimate reason for feminist action. This appears at odds with Femen's claim that we 'live in the world of male economic, cultural and ideological occupation. In this world, a woman is a slave, she is stripped of the right to any property but above all she is stripped of ownership of her own body' (http://www.femen.org). Then how can Shevchenko and Dawkins, Femen and the New Atheists, find common ground?

They find common ground because they represent different types of atheist mobilization. New Atheism is an organizational approach to atheism and Femen is a networked and fluid movement. Furthermore, both New Atheism and Femen's atheist disbelief are pitted against religion and they believe that feminism and atheism are of special importance to Muslim women. Dawkins tweets that 'Islam needs a feminist revolution. It will be hard. What can we do to help?' And Femen requires 'immediate political deposition of all dictatorial regimes creating unbearable living conditions for women, first of all, theocratic Islamic states practising Shariah and other forms of sadism regarding women' (http://www.femen.org). Femen is not a part of the organized New Atheism, but the different types of movements – the organized New Atheists and Femen's informal networks – conjoin, not necessarily in the otherwise acclaimed scientific approach to religion, but in the 'subtle (and sometimes not so subtle) ways' they critique Islam through the '"scattergun" critique of religion in general' (Emilsen 2012: 524).

Political secularism

In 2012 Saudi Arabian writer and activist Raif Badawi was arrested on a charge of insulting Islam, and in 2014 he was sentenced with ten years in jail, a fine and 1,000 lashes. The flogging and the first 50 lashes were carried out on 9 January 2015. Femen activists, wearing red hoods referring to the torturers carrying out the flogging, protested the flogging at the Saudi Arabian embassy in Paris (documentation of the protest can be seen at https://www.youtube.com/watch?v=MJSmvEkq58c).

Femen argued that the flogging of Badawi is a part of a larger 'religious morals' and a 'cruelty of Islam' that is 'becoming a routine for our time' (http://www.femen.org). Furthermore, they connected the flogging to the shooting of 12 people at the French satirical magazine *Charlie Hebdo* and claimed the protest was 'sending a message of a sucularists's [sic] revenge, an answer to criminal nature of religious morals' (http://www.femen.org). The flogging of Badawi for expressing secularist views on Saudi Arabia's increasing violations of human rights (Amnesty International 2016) is disturbing. Nevertheless, Femen's claim that their protest is a 'secularist revenge' against 'the criminal nature of religious morals' must be scrutinized.

The claim that the flogging reflects 'the criminal nature of religious morals' is a culturalization in which religious references to morals are always already perceived as criminal. It is important to keep in mind that religious morals are called upon for many other purposes than flogging. The claim reduces non-secular life 'to something called culture at the same time that it divests liberal democratic institutions of any association with culture' (Brown 2006: 23). Secularism is often believed to be the solution to religion's controversies. This is also true in the case of Badawi, who writes that secularism is 'the practical solution to lift countries (including ours) out of the third world and into the first world' (Black 2015). Yet, the emphasis on secularism is not necessarily emancipatory. According to Saba Mahmood, 'secularism entails a form of national-political structuration organized around the problem of religious difference' (Mahmood 2016: 10). The argument is that the emphasis on secularism can reinforce the societal importance of religion because religion becomes a core-organizing element. In Femen's protest, religion becomes a key in the organization of atheist and feminist identities.

Political secularism also shaped the 2013 'International Topless Jihad Day'. At the 'International Topless Jihad Day' white non-Muslim Femen activists stood in front of the Eiffel Tower carrying banners that declared naked war and encouraged Muslim women to 'get naked'. Femen intends to create 'freedom' for Muslim women, but the intentions are corrupted by the white non-Muslim icon bodies that reinforce 'the ongoing subjugation of non-Western societies to various forms of Western domination' (Mahmood 2016: 10). The problem is that in Femen's political secularism Muslim women are inherently not free. This kind of interpellation is also present in Shevchenko's defense of the 'Topless Jihad Day'. In response to critique by a group of Muslim women Shevchenko writes:

> So, sisters, (I prefer to talk to women anyway, even knowing that behind them are bearded men with knives). You say to us that you are against Femen, but we are here

for you and for all of us, as women are the modern slaves and it's never a question of colour of skin.

Shevchenko 2013

Shevchenko simultaneously insists that her call for freedom is not a question of colour, and that Muslim women cannot be free because 'don't deny that there are million [sic] of your sisters who have been raped and killed because they are not following the wish of Allah!' (Shevchenko 2013). Certainly violence against women must be fought, but by insisting that 'there is no such thing as a feminist who supports the hijab' (Shevchenko 2016) Femen's political secularism reproduces 'the naturalization of spatial whiteness' (Agathangelou & Turcotte 2010: 54), denies Muslim women the possibility of embodying multiple subject positions and potentially limits the impact of the activist imaginary because it is 'not embedded in local culture' (Darmoni & Witschge 2015).

The body that survives and the reinvention of religion

Femen's political secularism is paradoxical because its atheist disbelief relies on religious imaginaries. Femen declares that 'god is a woman', that they are 'topless jihadists' and they wear the Ukrainian flower crown. The flower crown, they write, is 'a symbol of femininity and proud insubmission, a crown of heroism' (http://www.femen.org), but from Ukraine's early history up until the early twentieth century it has been associated with virginity and womanhood and worn at wedding ceremonies. The reference to womanhood can also be found in the many references to witches. Shevchenko writes that 'being a godless witch is fundamental to who I am' (Shevchenko 2015).

The notion of the witch is important to Femen's activist imaginary. In the early modern period witches were persecuted according to their capacity to corrupt the image of the body – witches could be persecuted for imitating or possessing bodies or for causing erections or impotence (Bliss 2017). Lauren Bliss argues that witchcraft and cinema possess a figural relation to each other in terms of their imitation of the body. This figural relation between the witch and the image can help us understand Femen's references to 'witchcraft'. Femen's mediatized activism relies on documentation, on the image, to capture and reproduce their icon bodies and affective events. It is through the interfacial relations between bodies, and between bodies and images, that bodies take shape and are attuned to the event. In that sense the affective event draws on the imaginary of witchcraft, because witchcraft was designed 'to manipulate affectations' (Kieckhefer 2012). In a similar manner, Femen's icon bodies become trigger-texts that manipulate affectations and cue bodies to the events.

Femen's utilization of religions – witchcraft, Islam and Christianity – is paradoxical because political secularism and atheist disbelief become intertwined with religious imaginaries. According to Derrida and Hägglund the common denominator for all religions is that they promote an ideal of absolute immunity beyond the condition of survival (Hägglund 2009). In prolongation of this, radical atheism is not about converting anyone, but 'about an attachment to mortal life', because only 'a mortal being requires care, since only a mortal being can be lost, injured, or violated' (ibid.: 229). In this regard it could be argued that Femen embodies radical atheism, because the vulnerable body is a crucial part of the activist imaginary. Yet their icon bodies are not only vulnerable, they are also attacking and surviving and they seek out the conflict (Reestorff 2014). Obviously a body can be hurt, but the icon body survives as the witch that modulates affect and surpasses time. In this regard the icon body becomes the religious state of immunity, because it is 'intemperately from a state of death, since nothing can happen to it' (Hägglund 2009: 228). As such Femen's icon body becomes the antithesis to radical

213

atheism: through the continuous documentation and circulation of the icon body it survives and becomes the essence of religious imaginaries.

Concluding remarks

In this chapter I have studied the intertwining of activism, atheist disbelief and feminism, and argued that in order to understand the complexity of movements such as Femen, it is necessary to investigate atheism that emerges in networked forms of activism and utilizes affective mediatized activism to produce spectacles. In Femen's activist imaginary, the topless protester has become an icon body and a trigger-text for affective attunement and events. The analysis has shown that while Femen's affective mediatized activism holds great potential in regard to activist mobilization, it also has crucial pitfalls. These pitfalls are related to questions of political secularism and Islam and to a paradoxical reinvention of religious imaginaries.

Shevchenko (2016) calls attention to the fact that she has been called both 'islamophobe and christianophobe' and argues that Femen 'would never talk about Allah or Jesus and other fantasies if those fantasies did not affect human rights'. However, Femen is not only concerned with social justice. The activist imaginary reflects a political secularism that stipulates 'what religion is or ought to be, assigning its proper content, and disseminating concomitant subjectivities' (Mahmood 2016: 3). By means of political secularism Femen's mediatized activism and atheist disbelief become a principle of governance in which secularism not so much abandons religion as employs secularism through spectacular events. These events claim to remove religion – e.g. by snatching the Jesus doll – but in fact they contribute 'to make religion more rather than less important' (ibid.: 21). Furthermore, in the intersection with political secularism Femen's icon bodies become the antithesis to radical atheism. The mediatized and circulated icon body survives; it surpasses time and becomes the essence of religious imaginaries.

References

Agathangelou, A. M. and Turcotte, H. M. (2010) 'Postcolonial Theories and Challenges to "First World-ism"', in L. J. Sheperd (ed.) *Gender Matters in Global Politics: A Feminist Introduction to International Relations*. New York: Routledge, pp. 44–58.

Amnesty International (2016) 'Saudi Arabia: A Year of Bloody Repression Since Flogging of Raif Badawi', https://www.amnesty.org/en/press-releases/2016/01/saudi-arabia-a-year-of-bloody-repression-since-flogging-of-raif-badawi, accessed 8 January 2017.

Athanasiou, A. and Butler, J. (2013) *Dispossession: The Performative in the Political*. Cambridge: Polity.

Black, I. (2015) 'A Look at the Writings of Saudi Blogger Raif Badawi – Sentenced to 1,000 Lashes', *The Guardian*, https://www.theguardian.com/world/2015/jan/14/-sp-saudi-blogger-extracts-raif-badawi, accessed 7 January 2017.

Blair, O. (2016) 'Richard Dawkins Dropped from Science Event for Tweeting Video Mocking Feminists and Islamists', *The Independent*, http://www.independent.co.uk/news/people/richard-dawkins-vdeo-twitter-necss-event-feminism-a6841161.html, accessed 29 January 2016.

Bliss, L. (2017) *The Witch and the Virgin Mary: Cinematic Reproductions of the Body* (manuscript in press).

Brown, W. (2006) *Regulating Aversion: Tolerance in the Age of Identity and Empire*. Princeton, NJ: Princeton University Press.

Burkitt, I. (2014) *Emotions and Social Relations*. Los Angeles, CA: Sage.

Darmoni, K. and Witschge, T. (2015) 'Counterpublics in the Age of Mediatisation: Local Responses to Femen in the Arab World'. *Conjunctions: Transdisciplinary Journal of Cultural Participation*, vol. 2, no. 1, pp. 118–31,.

Dawkins, R. (2006) *The God Delusion*. Boston, MA: Houghton Mifflin.

Day, A. (2011) *Satire and Dissent: Interventions in Contemporary Political Debate*. Bloomington, IN: Indiana University Press.

della Porta, D. (2015) *Social Movements in Times of Austerity*. Cambridge: Polity.

Deleuze, G. (1990) *The Logic of Sense*. London: The Athlone Press.

Emilsen, W. W. (2012) 'The New Atheism and Islam', *The Expository Times*, vol. 123, no. 11, pp. 521–28.

Fritsch, J. and Thomsen, B. M. S. (2012) 'Affective Attunement in Field of Catastrophe: A Conversation Between Erin Manning, Brian Massumi, Jonas Fritsch and Bodil Marie Stavning Thomsen', *Peripeti: Tidsskrift for Dramaturgiske Studier*, http://www.peripeti.dk/2012/06/06/affective-attunement-in-a-field-of-catastrophe/, accessed 6 June 2012.

Glendinning, S. (2012) 'Beyond Atheism', *Think*, vol. 32, no. 11, pp. 37–51,.

Hägglund, M. (2009) 'The Challenge of Radical Atheism', *The New Centennial Review*, vol. 9, no. 1, pp. 227–52.

Hjarvard, S. (2008) *En verden af medier: Medialiseringen af politik, sprog, religion og leg*. København: Samfundslitteratur.

Jenkins, H. (2007) 'Manufacturing Dissent: An Interview with Stephen Duncombe', *Confessions of an Aca-Fan*, http://henryjenkins.org/2007/07/manufacturing_dissent_an_inter.html, accessed 3 September 2015.

Jenkins, H., Ford, S. and Green, J. (2013) *Spreadable Media: Creating Value and Meaning in a Networked Culture*. New York: New York University Press.

Kieckhefer, R. (2012) *European Witch Trials*. London: Routledge.

Le Bon, G. (2002) [1895] *The Crowd: A Study of the Popular Mind*. New York: Dover Publications.

LeDrew, S. (2013) 'Discovering Atheism: Heterogeneity in Trajectories to Atheist Identity and Activism', *Sociology of Religion*, vol. 74, no. 4, pp. 431–51.

LeDrew, S. (2016) *The Evolution of Atheism: The Politics of a Modern Movement*. Oxford: Oxford Scholarship Online.

Lievrouw, L. (2011) *Alternative and Activist New Media*. Cambridge: Polity.

Mahmood, S. (2016) *Religious Difference in a Secular Age: A Minority Report*. Princeton, NJ: Princeton University Press.

Reestorff, C. M. (2014) 'Mediatised Affective Activism: The Activist Imaginary and the Topless Body in the Femen Movement', *Convergence: The International Journal of Research into New Media Technologies*, vol. 20, pp. 478–95.

Reestorff, C. M. and Stage, C. (2016) 'New Media Crowds and the Participatory Politics of Trolling in Innocence of Muslims and Happy British Muslims', in H. K. Nielsen *et al.* (eds) *The Democratic Public Sphere*. Aarhus, Denmark: Aarhus University Press.

Rowe, D. (2000) 'Gobal Media Events and the Positioning of Presence', *Media International Australia*, vol. 97, pp. 11–21.

Schaefer, D. O. (2014) 'Embodied Disbelief: Poststructural Feminist Atheism', *Hypatia*, vol. 29, no. 2, pp. 371–87.

Shevchenko, I. (2013) 'Open Letter', *Huffington Post*, http://www.huffingtonpost.co.uk/2013/04/08/inna-shevchenko-muslim-women-femens-open-letter-amina-tyler-topless-jihad_n_3035439.html, accessed 8 April 2013.

Shevchenko I. (2015) 'Godless Witch', *International Business Times*, http://www.ibtimes.co.uk/inna-shevchenko-charlie-hebdo-godless-witch-1485921, accessed 30 January 2015.

Shevchenko, I. (2016) 'There's No Such Thing as a Feminist Who Supports the Hijab', *International Business Times*, http://www.ibtimes.co.uk/hijab-day-theres-no-such-thing-feminist-who-supports-hijab-1556252, accessed 22 April 2016.

Smith, C. and Cimino, R. (2010) 'The New Atheism and the Empowerment of American Freethinkers', in A. Amarasingam (ed.) *Religion and the New Atheism: A Critical Appraisal*. Leiden, the Netherlands: Brill, pp. 139–58.

Smith, C. and Cimino, R. (2012) 'Atheisms Unbound: The Role of the New Media in the Formation of a Secularist Identity', *Secularism and Nonreligion*, vol. 1, pp. 17–31.

Stephan-Norris, J. and Zeitlin, M. (2003) *Left Out: Reds and America's Industrial Unions*. New York: Cambridge University Press.

Taylor, J. (2013) *Topless Jihadis: Inside Femen, the World's Most Provocative Activist Group*. London: Atlantic Books.

22

THE PURCHASE OF WITNESSING IN HUMAN RIGHTS ACTIVISM

Sandra Ristovska

Witnessing is a communicative practice that facilitates the relay of information about previously indeterminate events. As such, it is closely associated with notions about truth telling, and it is thought of in relation to an audience as the ultimate addressee that partakes in the production of knowledge (e.g. Laub 1992; Frosh & Pinchevski 2009). Witnessing, therefore, signals not only the sensory experience of an event but also 'the discursive act of stating one's experience for the benefit of an audience that was not present at the event and yet must make some kind of judgment about it' (Peters 2001: 709). Borrowing from its origin in religious and legal discourses, witnessing by now has become a cultural form of communication (Thomas 2009) that is inextricably linked to some form of suffering and operates within the matrix of knowledge, responsibility and action. In this context, to bear witness constitutes an act through which an audience assumes responsibility for the suffering of others (e.g. Zelizer 1998; Tait 2011) as a first step towards moral, political or legal action.

Witnessing has long formed the backbone of human rights work. Sliwinski (2006: 335) insists that 'human rights discourse serves principally as a response to the witnessing of traumatic violence'. According to her, the photographs of colonial atrocities in Congo at the turn of the twentieth century not only summoned witnessing publics in the UK and the US, but they also helped introduce a new way of thinking about human responsibility in political discourse. In this sense, Sliwinski (2006: 334) argues that 'the conception of rights did not emerge from the articulation of an inalienable human dignity, but from a particular visual encounter with atrocity'. Concerned with systematic experiences with abuse and suffering, humanitarian and human rights activism has since drawn from witnessing as a particular mode of seeing that helps legitimize activist claims.

The entanglement of witnessing with a language of seeing, for example, lingers in popular conceptions of human rights work: human rights violations happen in the dark; they need to be exposed or uncovered; we need to watch the perpetrators of violence, so their deeds do not remain hidden. Underlying them is the deep-rooted relationship between visuality and power in Western cultures, such as the idea that looking is a practice through which power dynamics are asserted or challenged (e.g. Foucault 1979; Scott 1998), so claiming *the right to look* (Mirzoeff 2011) empowers activists to expose states' wrongdoings. The human rights activist right to look, then, is assumed to imply commitment to truth telling, justice and accountability. In other words, the right to look is implicated in the responsibility to bear witness as a strategy for social change that turns witnessing into a political practice.

As images materialize the right to look, they provide signposts for how to bear witness to human rights abuses. Various types of visuals have thus been central to how human rights activists have operationalized witnessing as a political practice in instances as wide-ranging as the campaign to bring relief to the survivors of the Armenian genocide in the early 1900s (e.g. Torchin 2012), the anti-fascist posters of *Taller de Gráfica Popular* in the 1940s in Mexico (e.g. García de Germenos & Oles 2008), the eyewitness images of the Yugoslav wars in the 1990s (e.g. Ristovska 2017) and the unfolding video advocacy work of global human rights organizations (e.g. Gregory 2010). Even in the context of testimonial accounts, the function of witnessing through audiovisual media has been to attend to the gestures, silences and distortions that exceed the semantic content of the survivors' testimonies but are visible to the camera's eye and central to understanding the magnitude of the experienced trauma (e.g. Pinchevski 2012; Delage 2014). These instances illustrate the inextricable link between witnessing and seeing that has long been assumed to provide access to meaning that is irreducible to words alone, lending human rights activism its persuasive power.

This chapter documents how witnessing as a mode of seeing has become a political practice by which human rights activists legitimize their claims. Tackling its purchase historically and today, the chapter distinguishes between two approaches to witnessing that characterize human rights activism: witnessing of an event – where bearing witness to an occurrence so that publics can attend to the human rights violation is imperative both morally and historically – and witnessing for a purpose – where rendering witnessing legible to specific audiences who can take a concrete action is of key political importance (Ristovska 2016a). Mapping the shift away from *witnessing of* to *witnessing for* in human rights activism, this chapter argues that the power of witnessing as a mechanism for social change draws from its entanglement with images, which navigate the evidentiary and emotional terrains simultaneously. Witnessing thus designates a particular mode of seeing where seeing is felt and feeling is seen.

Witnessing of an event

Witnessing helps generate knowledge about an event. And 'in the legal, philosophical and epistemological tradition of the Western world, witnessing is based on, and formally defined by first-hand seeing' (Felman 1992: 217). Witnessing, then, also designates the performance of the act of seeing through which facts about an event can be established. It indicates an 'utterly unique and irreplaceable topographical position with respect to an occurrence' (ibid.: 206). What is worthy of attention in the context of human rights work is the personal experience with suffering as a way of establishing the occurrence of a human rights violation and comprehending the magnitude of the crime.

The development of various visual technologies over the last two centuries has raised the role of the camera in providing evidence about human rights violations that extends the experience of first-hand seeing beyond the initial scene. Photographs of the catastrophic famine in southern India between 1876 and 1878, for example, introduced the practice of showing images of suffering as truth claims that could prompt humanitarian action (Twomey 2012: 258). Mark Twain characterized the Kodak camera as incorruptible in the context of the Congo reform movement, 'the only witness I couldn't bribe' (in Sliwinski 2006: 346), cementing the long-standing assumption that the camera could transport the viewer to the atrocious scene, enabling one to bear witness to the otherwise irretrievable moment of trauma and suffering. Both examples indicate the supposed importance of witnessing facilitated by visual technology as a mechanism through which a human rights violation is being interpreted and rendered meaningful for a larger public. It is in this sense that Zelizer (1998: 10) writes that bearing witness with photography's assistance 'implies … that the very fact of paying heed collectively is crucial'. The event is so significant that it merits critical attention and moral engagement.

Bearing witness has long called for the use of images. Beyond photography, the interlinking of visual imagery with human rights concerns is evident in the work of *Taller de Gráfica Popular* (TGP) – People's Graphic Workshop – a print art collective in Mexico led by Pablo O'Higgins, Leopoldo Méndez and Luis Arenal. Developed in the aftermath of the Mexican Revolution of 1910, TGP's work bridged visual arts and activism, using flyers and posters to empower the silenced voices of the Mexican workers and peasants and to engage local communities in conversations about global politics. As early as 1938, TGP produced multiple posters and held public lecture series at the Palacio de Bellas Artes in Mexico City that supported the anti-Nazi League. In 1943, TGP produced a series called *Libro negro del terror nazi en Europa* (The black book of Nazi terror in Europe), which included 'the first known image outside of Europe of the Holocaust' (Craven 2002: 67). This was Méndez's renowned *Deportación a la muerte* (Deportation to death), a linocut that depicts the horrific moment of deportation to the concentration camps (in the foreground two Nazi soldiers are depicted as they are about to close a train wagon crowded with people). Some of the posters also warned against Francisco Franco's infiltrators in Mexico (Ricker 2002). What is significant about TGP's work is how witnessing is deeply engraved in the articulation of activist impulses. The visual here sustains witnessing although it goes beyond the indexical relationship with the depicted reality emblematic of photographic technologies. Through printmaking, TGP implicitly insists on the importance of bearing witness to events that have destroyed a common sense of human dignity, sanctioning interpretations of them as politically relevant and worthy of attention.

Witnessing is not only shaped by evolving technologies, but also, by now, it has become common to speak of media witnessing as an inseparable concept. Frosh and Pinchevski (2009) identify two paradigm cases of media witnessing: the Holocaust and 9/11. The first testifies to the impossibility of bearing witness – the traumatic event is so profound, it has affected the survivors' abilities to reflect on it because they have witnessed it all too well. It is therefore of utmost importance to break away from the silence that trauma imposes to start a process of personal recovery and collective remembrance. As the emphasis is on understanding the traumatic event, media witnessing, for Frosh and Pinchevski (2009: 7), can be thought of as 'the continuation of Holocaust witnessing by other means, bearing out the imperative of speaking against evil and misfortune wherever and whenever they might occur'. A civilian video of the shelling of the Markale Market in Sarajevo during the Yugoslav wars of the 1990s is illustrative of this point. As survivors of the attack try to move dead and injured bodies away from the streets, a voice can be heard addressing the person with the camera: 'Please record the woman over there, please.' The plea is to document the emotional and physical suffering that has unfolded so that there is a historical video record to assist others in bearing witness to a horrific human rights violation.

In contrast to the crisis of witnessing epitomized by the Holocaust, Frosh and Pinchevski (2009: 11) argue that 9/11 marks the ubiquity of witnessing – the deliberate interpellation of audiences as the ultimate witnesses by modern media, 'putting society permanently on view to itself for its own sake'. Here, witnessing becomes constitutive of the (traumatic) world. The impulse to record both extraordinary and mundane events from the scenes of their unfolding facilitated by the proliferation of digital technologies and platforms has turned media witnessing into an integral part of experiencing the world. It is not surprising, then, that McLagan (2003: 606) writes, 'human rights activists make ethical claims through media, and these media operate by making ethical claims on us'. The assumption is that witnessing orients the viewer in how to understand suffering both distant and near. Hinegardner (2009), on the other hand, goes a step further. Implicit in her analysis of human rights filmmaking in Mexico is the conceptualization of media witnessing as a vehicle for becoming a political actor when the legal channels provided by formal institutions are closed. The imperative to bear witness to injustice is what transforms citizens from bystanders into active participants and what fuels activist energy.

This brief overview – though by no means exhaustive or representative of the wide-ranging human rights activist work around the world – points to the lingering importance of creating a visual field for witnessing as a basis for activist claims. Centred on a deeply felt need to expose and work through trauma, witnessing is assumed to operate as a moral compass for understanding human rights crimes, echoing the visual underpinnings of the emergence of human rights as culturally, politically and legally meaningful framework for social justice. The last decade, though, has seen new forms of media witnessing that characterize the current work of human rights groups to which I turn next.

Witnessing for a purpose

Unfolding developments in the global human rights community have also shaped the tenor of media witnessing. Leading human rights groups like Amnesty International (hereafter Amnesty), Human Rights Watch (HRW) and WITNESS have incorporated and sought to professionalize the practices long associated with video activism as a central component of their advocacy work (Ristovska 2016b). The prevailing notion is that 'video is becoming more and more the medium in … which [human rights] issues are raised and discussed' (B. Wille, pers. comm., 25 June 2015). This turn to video by global human rights groups – some of which also train citizens and other activists how to utilize it efficiently and safely – has contributed to an increasing specialization and diversification of tactics in leveraging the power of media witnessing for social change.

On the most fundamental level, video is assumed to create a space for witnessing that provides a platform for the testimony of human rights survivors. Human rights groups, therefore, seek to both give voice to these personal stories and to bring them to relevant stakeholders who could potentially do something to alleviate the suffering and end the abuse. Priscila Neri (pers. comm., 6 August 2015), Senior Program Manager at WITNESS, iterates that video 'has an unparalleled power to bring the voice of the person who's directly affected into crucial spaces'. Her group, for example, produced the video *Rightful Place: Endorois' Struggle for Justice* in collaboration with the Center for Minority Rights Development in Kenya that was screened as evidence in front of the African Commission on Human and Peoples Rights. Through personal testimonies and title cards that show passages from relevant human rights laws and legislations, the video documented four decades of forced evictions of the Endorois community from their lands by the Kenyan government. It facilitated the transmission of the testimonies of some community members in court whose ruling found the expulsion illegal.

This example highlights how human rights groups operationalize witnessing not necessarily through the moral and historical imperative to understand an event, but through the strategic purpose of presenting evidence in a form appropriate for the targeted audience. In other words, there is a move away from the kind of unbounded testimonies seen and heard at the Eichmann trial and transmitted around the world via video – as the vital case for the role of human rights testimonies in the facilitation of justice (e.g. Felman 2002) – to a deliberate recording and editing of survivors' stories so that the resulting videos can be presented in relevant institutional spaces, such as courts, global, national and local governing bodies. In the case of *Rightful Place*, the testimonial excerpts provided sufficient personal touch to the depicted human rights violation, accentuating the legal breach illustrated by the accompanying title cards for the court case in front of the African Commission on Human and Peoples Rights.

Video is an important tool for witnessing not only because it serves as a vehicle for testimony, but also because it can document human rights violations as they unfold. It 'provides people who aren't there the opportunity [to see and hear] what the individuals who were collecting and producing the content were witnessing and seeing' (R. Althaibani, pers. comm., 7 August 2015). Human rights groups tap into this potential of video both by utilizing it strategically in their own advocacy work and by training others.

Amnesty, for example, produced *The Gaza Platform Findings* in partnership with the Forensic Architecture team at Goldsmiths University of London. It urged international governments to support the work of the International Criminal Court so that it could investigate the war crimes committed by Israel during the Gaza conflict of 2014. The legal purposes for this video defined its production parameters. Prime Minister Benjamin Netanyahu's statement to the United Nations that his government has done 'everything possible to minimize Palestinian casualties' is contrasted with interviews with forensic experts and Amnesty's researchers alongside graphic eyewitness footage of the attacks and the immediate aftermath. The eyewitness footage, though, is presented through a visual filter (sepia tones), and a short segment demonstrates the authentication process of audio-visual records. There are also title cards featured against a satellite map of the region with numbers indicating the civilian deaths and the different locations of the attacks. Together, these editing techniques reinforce a sense that forensic rigour has shaped Amnesty's findings and the subsequent call for action. The strategic shaping of human rights witnessing through this video, then, underscores the perceived importance to sanction an interpretation of the crime in a form legible to the legal forum.

WITNESS, on the other hand, is a human rights group that has gradually shifted its focus from producing original content to training others how to work with video. It has organized on-site and online video activism workshops, produced training guides and developed various technologies of witnessing to help human rights activists and interested citizens utilize video strategically. The Video as Evidence Field Guide, for example, discusses both filmmaking techniques and legal principals about evidentiary standards in regards to reliability and relevance as well as procedures for proving crimes. These lessons are intended to teach activists how to document various human rights violations in ways that increase the likelihood that the videos could be legally useful. A series of smart phone-based applications, such as Proofmode, supplement the training efforts by providing a tool for taking and sharing videos with securely encrypted metadata so that journalists, human rights investigators and courts could use verifiable videos in their work. Underlying these efforts are normative assumptions about witnessing potential for social change when the activist claims are shaped according to the modalities of the institutional venues where the videos are presented.

The unfolding video work of Amnesty, HRW and WITNESS illustrates how audience differentiation has become a defining feature of current forms of media witnessing that insist on rendering activist claims according to a clear purpose and legible to relevant stakeholders. In other words, witnessing now signals a strategic position in regards to an audience. In this process, the act of bearing witness is becoming an authoring mode of political involvement through which activists seek to make truth claims about human rights violations via the institutional channels through which human rights receive fuller recognition and restitution. And while numerous human rights activists, social art groups and media collectives have utilized visuals to bear witness so that the public understands traumatic occurrences, human rights groups today highlight the purpose for doing so, turning witnessing into material suitable for policymaking. Witnessing thus becomes a socially embedded mechanism for change, indicating that pragmatic positions might be overtaking other parameters in considering what human rights violations are covered, in what manner and to what ends.

The purchase of witnessing

This chapter has surveyed the purchase of witnessing to human rights activism. In doing so, it has highlighted the shift away from witnessing of an event to witnessing for a purpose as a strategy for political involvement. Central to the configuration of witnessing as a political practice has been its entanglement with wide-ranging images that materialize the activist right to look, seeking to expose and end human rights violations. Witnessing, then, is a pathway to visual meaning-making. This is significant because images facilitate processes of knowledge formation that navigate the evidentiary and emotional levels of signification simultaneously. They appeal to reason, imagination and emotion at once. As such, they are tools for witnessing that help relay key information about the occurrence of human rights crimes while also capturing the marks of trauma that seemingly exceed representation.

Witnessing with the aid of visual technologies has long provided human rights activists with an emotionally charged epistemological foundation from which to articulate ethical, historical and political claims. It is in this sense that witnessing signals a mode of seeing entangled with feeling that enables visual records to serve as both forensic evidence and persuasive device in human rights work. In other words, witnessing suggests a kind of seeing that is assumed to surpass meaning provided by other measures because images enable seeing that is felt and feeling that is seen.

The ability of images to sustain witnessing as an entry point to an immersive engagement with human rights crimes in their complex historical and emotional dimensions is at the heart of their use in diverse human rights activist endeavours. Both forms of witnessing tackled in this chapter – witnessing of an event and witnessing for a purpose – rest on the interplay of factual, visual and emotional relays of information that can kindle the persuasive power of human rights activism. The former generates knowledge about an occurrence via various visual media, rendering the human rights violation worthy of critical attention. The latter emphasizes the kinds of rhetorical and aesthetic video strategies that might best appeal to the envisioned specialized audience. It is important to look at both to shed light on how, under which circumstances and to what ends witnessing has become a metaphor for the empirical and political purchase of seeing in the work of human rights activists.

References

Craven, D. (2002) *Art and Revolution in Latin America, 1910–1990.* New Haven, CT: Yale University Press.

Delage, C. (2014) *Caught on Camera: Film in the Courtroom from the Nuremberg Trials to the Trials of Khmer Rouge.* Philadelphia, PA: University of Pennsylvania Press.

Felman, S. (1992) 'The Return of the Voice: Claude Lanzmann's *Shoah*', in S. Felman and D. Laub (eds) *Testimony: Crises of Witnessing in History, Literature and Psychoanalysis.* New York: Routledge, pp. 204–83.

Felman, S. (2002) 'Theaters of Justice: Arendt in Jerusalem, the Eichmann Trial, and the Redefinition of Legal Meaning in the Wake of the Holocaust', *Theoretical Inquiries in Law*, vol. 1, no. 2, pp. 1–43.

Foucault, M. (1979) *Discipline and Punish: The Birth of the Prison.* New York: Vintage Books.

Frosh, P. and Pinchevski, A. (2009) 'Introduction: Why Media Witnessing? Why Now?', in P. Frosh and A. Pinchevski (eds) *Media Witnessing: Testimony in the Age of Mass Communication.* New York: Palgrave Macmillan, pp. 1–19.

García de Germenos, P. and Oles, J. (2008) *Gritos Desde el Archivo: Grabado Político del Taller de Gráfica Popular.* Mexico, D. F.: Universidad Nacional Autónoma de México.

Gregory, S. (2010) 'Cameras Everywhere: Ubiquitous Video Documentation of Human Rights, New Forms of Video Advocacy, and Consideration of Safety, Security, Dignity and Consent', *Journal of Human Rights Practice*, vol. 2, no. 2, pp. 191–207.

Hinegardner, L. (2009) 'Action, Organization and Documentary Film: Beyond a Communications Model of Human Rights Videos', *Visual Anthropology Review*, vol. 2, no. 25, pp. 172–85.

Laub, D. (1992) 'Bearing Witness or the Vicissitudes of Listening', in S. Felman and D. Laub (eds) *Testimony: Crises of Witnessing in History, Literature and Psychoanalysis*. New York: Routledge, pp. 57–74.

McLagan, M. (2003) 'Principles, Publicity, and Politics: Notes on Human Rights Media', *American Anthropologist*, vol. 105, no. 3, pp. 605–12.

Mirzoeff, N. (2011) *The Right to Look: A Counterhistory of Visuality*. Durham, NC: Duke University Press.

Peters, J. D. (2001) 'Witnessing', *Media, Culture and Society*, vol. 23, no. 6, pp. 707–23.

Pinchevski, A. (2012) 'The Audiovisual Unconscious: Media and Trauma in the Video Archive for Holocaust Testimonies', *Critical Inquiry*, vol. 39, no. 1, pp. 142–66.

Ricker, M. (2002) 'El Taller de Gráfica Popular', *Graphic Witness*, http://graphicwitness.org/group/tgpricker2.htm, accessed 14 November 2016.

Ristovska, S. (2016a) 'Strategic Witnessing in an Age of Video Activism', *Media, Culture and Society*, vol. 38, no. 7, pp. 1034–47.

Ristovska, S. (2016b) Human Rights Through the Lens: The Institutionalization and Professionalization of Video Activism. Unpublished doctoral dissertation. Philadelphia, PA: University of Pennsylvania.

Ristovska, S. (2017) 'Video and Witnessing at the International Criminal Tribunal for the Former Yugoslavia', in H. Tumber and S. Waisbord (eds) *The Routledge Companion to Media and Human Rights*. New York: Routledge, pp. 357–65.

Scott, J. C. (1998) *Seeing Like a State: How Certain Schemes to Improve the Human Condition Have Failed*. New Haven, CT: Yale University Press.

Sliwinski, S. (2006) 'The Childhood of Human Rights: The Kodak on the Congo', *Journal of Visual Culture*, vol. 5, no. 3, pp. 333–63.

Tait, S. (2011) 'Bearing Witness, Journalism and Moral Responsibility', *Media, Culture and Society*, vol. 33, no. 8, pp. 1220–35.

Thomas, G. (2009) 'Witness as a Cultural Form of Communication: Historical Roots, Structural Dynamics and Current Appearances', in P. Frosh and A. Pinchevski (eds) *Media Witnessing: Testimony in the Age of Mass Communication*. New York: Palgrave Macmillan, pp. 89–111.

Torchin, L. (2012) *Creating the Witness: Documenting Genocide on Film, Video, and the Internet*. Minneapolis, MN: University of Minnesota Press.

Twomey, C. (2012) 'Framing Atrocity: Photography and Humanitarianism', *History of Photography*, vol. 36, no. 3, pp. 255–64.

Zelizer, B. (1998) *Remembering to Forget: Holocaust Memory Through the Camera's Eye*. Chicago, IL: The University of Chicago Press.

23

PALESTINE ONLINE

Occupation and liberation in the digital age

Miriyam Aouragh

> The kind of connectivity from social media made it harder for Israel to hide what they are committing in Palestine. They can't hide a big ship coming to help Gaza, a child being killed, hospitals bombed. It is harder for them to counter, even if they push really hard, the two forces: social media and our grassroots work.
>
> *Amani, Ramallah, August 2015*

Between 1947 and 1949 Palestinians underwent an exodus evolving into what the UN termed 'one of the longest-lasting cases of forced migration in modern history' (UNRWA 2015). Whole communities dispersed; families spread across neighbouring countries in a region at war were unable to reach each other (either physically or by post or telephone) or re-establish contact with those left behind. Palestinians – whether uprooted inside Palestine or forced into exile across the world – continue to nurture a tight connection to the land and a strong sense of a shared political cause. Violent dispossession and military occupation meant that an important lifeline of Palestinian communication was broken.

The development of the internet allowed Palestinians to overcome part of their immobile isolation, recover lost memories and begin dispelling the persistent trauma of the *Nakba*. After six decades, people were reunited through websites, chat-rooms and email. Extraordinary scenes of Palestinians in different refugee camps being connected through webcams on big screens connected to an internet-enabled computer can still be found via earlier website links. This was made possible by the Across Borders Project (Aouragh 2011: 133). As is to be expected, cultural preservation and political resistance play an important role in the discursive and practical framework of online resistance and solidarity.

The all-pervasiveness of resistance necessitates an analysis of the relationship between digital activism and political change carried out through the local political landscape. Both of these forms of activity already have an indirect interdependency with global power relations. Despite the semantic connotations of the term 'virtual space', this chapter therefore explicitly frames Palestinian internet use as *already* grounded in offline reality. Ever since its inception, Palestinian online politics conformed to a form of participation that has to be at core offline, constantly geared to the major power forces at play and ultimately centred on a collectively shared aim for decolonization.

In order to contextualize this chapter appropriately, I briefly outline the context of Palestinian resistance. Then I delve into a number of instances played out against the background of Palestinian digital activism and offer a critical review of digital media as a site of contestation. This exploration continues in the second half of the chapter. I proceed to draw insights from fieldwork in different places across (historic) Palestine during the spring and summer of 2015 as part of a larger project during which I talked with and joined people in their activities to understand how online technologies affect their activism. All the interviews in this chapter are anonymized. Because of the danger of being identified and the risks Palestinian activists face from the Israeli military and security apparatus, their locations are altered as well.

These activists can help us understand how digital infrastructures affect the basic algorithms of Palestinian politics, such as the aesthetic and vernacular possibilities of expression. I propose three main areas of online politics – witnessing, documenting and protesting – and discuss all three in reference to other available literature about the internet in Palestine. But first we will zoom out of the focus on digital technology and sketch out the broader context of Palestinian communications, outside of which Palestinian internet use cannot be fully understood.

Palestine's media ecology

Ten years ago only government and rich people had access to internet media, this shifted and now social media is accessible to anyone. It's not only limited to those who can afford it. It is fertile ground for social and personal expression and actually very cheap. To make a video and upload it on YouTube; Tweet it with a hashtag so that millions of Twitter users will see it trending; you can put a petition online … these tools, which hardly cost a thing, are more accessible to social movements. This wasn't the case before. It's huge; there is no denying that. But I don't think it's only the evolution of media. I don't think Israel would witness this backlash without for instance the BDS movement.

Bahiya, Be'er Sheva, August 2015

The history of resistance is embedded in digitally mediated recollections. Not only symbolically so, for the establishment of an independent media and technology sector has, itself, been a part of the resistance process. The conditions for the existence of such a sector – independence, self-determination, border autonomy, infrastructure and defence – were repeatedly postponed. Israel did not want to concede these conditions and delayed the process of the internet being made available to Palestinians. The Palestinian media environment developed more independently from the late 1980s into the 1990s after decades without its own broadcasting and with most of its press censored by Israel. This long history of absence and reliance on other forms of communication and mobilization meant that new media and broadcasting, once allowed after the Oslo peace process, were not necessarily used actively for political organizing, and when they were, were often oriented towards outside audiences (Bishara 2010: 78).

However, even after a semi-independent media sector, problems of access and censorship did not disappear. This became very clear after the Arab uprisings. The Palestinian leadership feared that the protests might fuse the already present sparks and erupt in mass movements with demands being presented to the Palestinian political elite. This was reflected in 2011 by the forceful entrance of *Hiraak* onto the stage. New collaborations between young activists and more experienced organizers initiated the first big protests in March, but anger about ongoing colonial subjugation and the complicity of Palestinian leaderships really culminated in May and exploded on the annual Nakba commemoration protests on 15 May. The 2011 Nakba Day was an international coordinated event whereby, in a Million Man march, thousands streamed towards the borders of Palestine, many youths were killed (mostly refugees) and the need for a united front against the occupying power was a dominant sentiment brought to the surface by the inspiration of the protests rocking the region in the spring of 2011 (Pace 2013: 48).

Similar paradoxes have structured the Information and Communication Technology (ICT) sector, exaggerated by a persistent promotion of e-commerce and enthusiasm for start-up entrepreneurs despite the colonial realities. The investment in a digital economy has been harnessed by the USAID and the World Bank. And the ways in which social media analysts promote the benefits of the internet provide fascinating examples of how reality and fantasy coalesce in the world of policy making. Some experts propose that scanning documents for minimum wage will soon allow unemployed Palestinian youths to forget their national subjugation (Mualem 2015). Most Palestinians treat these pretensions with cynicism and humour. Such was the irony as social media activism turned into an opportunity for Palestinian activists. This is not a surprise, for Palestinian consciousness is marked by a history of resistance.

The historic uprising of 1987–1991 (the First Intifada) ended with the secret Madrid negotiations and was followed by the Oslo peace process, which led to a semi-autonomous entity, a small part of the 1967 territories headed by Yasser Arafat. In early 2000, when grassroots pressure was increasing, a new stratum of youth politics emerged, shaped by a generation that had lived through the deceptions of the Peace Process. The internet was available by this point, albeit only on a very piecemeal basis. Nevertheless, much of the visual content published since then has revolved around photo and video collages of the second Intifada. Since the very first public experimentations with the internet, a recurring focus has been the dream of reunification. For Lina Alsaafin (2013): 'It is a surreal feeling and a minor victory that we owe to our utilization of social media to rebuild these splintered connections with each other.'

Internet use is not a *neutral* (blind) technological issue. Social media statements calling for peace have been cheered. But, as Nabulsi put it with regard to 'youth' Facebook initiative 'Gaza Breaks Out', this discourse 'caters to western tastes and desires, especially to the fantasy of a digitally connected youth emerging from cyberspace as agents of transformative change in the real world'. It is important to stress the complex political dynamics that determine the potentials of technology. It is not as if the internet is not a 'real' phenomenon. The statistics speak for themselves, with three-quarters of the Palestinian population in the occupied Palestinian territories (oPt) on the internet (ITU 2016). What is more, internet access in the Palestinian territories is relatively open and, compared with most regional regimes, almost unfiltered (Open Internet Initiative 2009). Digital mediation even validates other media forms. Israeli anxieties on the matter make sense, but can this become a decolonizing force?

Online resistance … as decolonization?

> I believe that what's going on online now is an extension to the real world, it's not detached from it. A lot of these battles then also happen on Facebook, on Twitter, on Tumblr, on blogs. It is a manifestation of what happens in real life, we need to acknowledge that. Also because it's not only that, what happens online is just the tip of the iceberg of what is happening in real life.
>
> *Cherif, Ramallah, July 2015*

As tactics and styles are part of specific experiences, forms of resistance are constantly adapted. Palestinian political agency began to transcend into virtual reality when Palestinians in the diaspora began eagerly engaging with online political activism in order to fill important gaps offline. In due course, this would alter the traditional tactics of activists. It evoked a new type of media activism discussed elsewhere as claiming the 'permission to narrate', to push against stereotyped portrayals of Palestinians as either 'terrorists' or 'victims'. The convergence of online mobilization and political participation formed a new amalgam termed *Cyber Intifada* (Aouragh 2008). This label suggests that politics and technology are inseparable. This is in line with social movement theories, where 'repertoires' of contemporary activism do not exist outside historical and cultural frameworks.

One of the first internet examples, the *Electronic Intifada* diary project 'Live From Palestine', was set up during the siege of 2002, a very violent phase of the Intifada. It is a good example of 'eye-witness' reports that began to emerge when Israel systematically denied access to journalists to report from the occupied territories. This genre began to play a dominant role in online politics, and as the infrastructure evolved, this blend of testimonial and reportage script spread from websites and mailing lists to social networking. The internet also inspired activism of a creative/collaborative nature. An instance of this is the collaborative Wiki project *Wiki Project Gaza* during the war on Gaza in 2009. This improved the quality of geographic mapping and, thereby, humanitarian relief efforts. A similar example is that of online tools mapping Israeli attacks. The *Gaza Platform*, for instance, made it possible to piece together a vast number of attacks and the enormous scale of destruction to reveal patterns and thus expose the systematic nature of the violations.

Many feared that Israel's panic about the 2011 Arab uprisings might spin out of control, in the face of the mounting pressures from grassroots groups like *Hiraak* that erupted during the uprisings. This whirlwind revived in 2012 during the so-called *Pillar of Clouds* military campaign and the even more fatal *Operation Protective Edge* in 2014. Outrage was unprecedented. Social media was flooded with expressions of solidarity. Embedded in Palestine's larger decolonial project, we saw this form of activism used in two ways: to strengthen internal collective resistance and to galvanize international solidarity. Mobilization in and of itself was the major function of Palestinian internet use. Moreover, translocal networks are a fairly common social reality and cultural infrastructure for fragmented, expelled, dispersed communities. This stands as part of a much longer tradition and is similar to the experiences of other oppressed groups.

Social media allows oppressed and forcibly displaced peoples to make themselves be heard. Palestinian attempts to recall the Nakba are partly a reminder to the world of the millions of refugees still waiting in desolate camps to return to their homes. Thus, while many of the issues are shared with minorities elsewhere, dynamics of solidarity grow to become a major factor, from specific cases of police violence to general debates about ways to best conceptualize settler-colonialism. The enthusiastic adoption of online tools and spaces into everyday tactics makes sense since oppositional voices are increasingly banned from 'mainstream' media. Furthermore, the phenomenon of *Black Twitter* is a clear example of reclaiming part of an online space to congregate and speak out. Initiatives such as *#NotYourAsianSideKick* have been set up as vehicles for critique by Arab and Asian women, and form what Kuo (2016) terms 'racial digital enclaves'. Her examination of 'hashtag discursivity' identifies how Twitter's form, its users and its interface connect with underlying ideologies.

These examples all rouse a pro-active and energetic engagement, and this is not surprising, for, as Norman (2009) argues, Palestinian youth media is best understood as a form of *participatory media*. We can also think of Palestinian hip-hop, which is creatively rich and forms a part of the overall context of a youth culture we encounter with online activists as well (Stein & Swedenburg 2007). But over the years, the style, the level and the scope of digital (online and offline) activism changed. In part, this was due to a greater awareness of Israel's access to and use of sophisticated digital technologies and military strategies via its cyber warfare and online surveillance. Equally, the extreme restrictions of everyday life (such as curfews and roadblocks which prevent people from visiting relatives and friends or attending work and school) have continued to severely stifle Palestinian society. This has made it hard to garner enthusiasm for digital activism. But as we will see next, physical offline collective resistance and online activism are not mutually exclusive.

Palestinian digital politics

When I was 17 I joined Facebook. For the PA it is more an issue to be active online and for the Israelis it's more dangerous to be an activist on the ground, in fact Israel tries to keep us busy online, to prevent people from doing politics in real life. The PA bans criticism online because they feel threatened. The Israelis have more sophisticated networks, they study us, they really analyse the sociology of the Palestinians, know every move we make. When I was arrested by the PA they kept insisting and for days tried to extract my Facebook password. When I was arrested by the Israelis they didn't care about my Facebook password because they can get whatever they want anyway in cooperation from Facebook admins.

Emile, Ramallah, August 2015

The complex context of Palestine I laid out above calls for a scholarship that goes beyond quantitative assessments and challenges top-down policies. In recent years an interesting body of literature has offered a framework for understanding the politics of the internet where online engagements have allowed Palestinians to reimagine liberation struggles, to salvage their own narrative or to build solidarity. Such subversive interventions provided experimental spaces for participatory politics. Sometimes this served as a turning point for radical politics, either resulting in new activists being enlisted or (sometimes equally important) rejuvenating former activists. It certainly helps lower the threshold of what might be considered activism, as the general commentary goes. But taking this argument at face value can be problematic.

Digital technologies were a key tool for solidarity groups across the world during the 2009 Operation Cast Lead. But in the aftermath Palestinian grassroots participation reached a historical low-point, and the hopes projected onto digital activism evaporated. The 2011 uprisings made a radical change, partly due to new priorities and unique practices, but even more so perhaps due to the broad solidarity expressed with the widely shared international Prisoners Campaign. The fact that these campaigns were carried out by various networks of activists across the world who organized strikes and sit-ins was crucial. As Emile commented in addition to the above quote: 'You know what made the difference, all capitals all over the world protested in solidarity with Palestine; if you are strong online and weak offline, you are weak *overall*.'

The case of Palestine requires particular caution. Here, geopolitical dynamics directly shape the policies and infrastructures of the internet. A good example is Facebook itself. Although forgotten by now, its own rules and regulations and supposed neutrality, built into its algorithms, sparked debate, illustrating that the site's definition of what constitutes a *country* is deeply flawed. The main setup for one's identification is geographic-state affiliation, and the option 'Palestine' was on the original listing. But merely a few months into use, it was removed after Israeli pressure. It required a massive petition and many personal pleas towards Mark Zuckerberg to get the option reinstated. One of the main petitions was entitled 'Against delisting Palestine from Facebook' (Jacobs 2007). This story is a reminder that the assumed participatory potentials of digital technology are conditioned. The controversies with Facebook have not ended, as Palestinian editors and activists have found their accounts disabled as a result of Israeli agreement with Facebook to coordinate against what it deems 'incitement' by Palestinians (Abunimah 2016). The colonial context is prevalent on *all* technological levels in this ethnographic equation.

Those aiming to visit Palestinians (especially journalists, activists and critical researchers) must cross Israeli-controlled borders where soldiers demand to see Facebook or Twitter accounts or even confiscate laptops and phones.

Interestingly, this did not significantly deter solidarity work. The December to January military siege on Gaza in 2009 had already begun to transform public political opinions. Cast Lead in particular was seen as brutal because Gaza was already under siege and in lock-down and therefore, without question, politicized many across the world. Rather than disengagement, what occurred among many Palestinians was a sentiment of 'if only we could document and show the world', and as such a key area of digital Palestinian politics is *witnessing*. Providing an 'alternative' narrative became a common objective of online activism. The fact that this was manifested in the form of 'citizen media' is not a coincidence but historically rooted in progressive regional internet politics. Such a politics first emerged around 2003 (amidst the invasion of Iraq) and developed the 2006 Israeli war on Lebanon. In these cases the combination of unofficial videos on blogs inspired excited debates. There has always been an underlying assumption that unrecorded abuse will go unpunished and thus that the reverse is true too (Menassat 2008). In 2009 the culture of blogging took a leap in Palestine.

It happened that at the time I had myself begun following the Palestinian blogosphere as part of an ethnographic experimentation to record how offline events correlate with online productions. I devised a written timeline to identify the (overarching) categories. From these observations on Palestinian blogs I unearthed three spheres: the need to archive and bear witness; the necessity to offer alternative or 'citizen' media; the urge to express unity or organize solidarity. As a matter of fact, the three domains turned out to be a useful conceptual categorization that consequently illustrates the main approaches of digital activism.

To witness, to prove, to protest

Israel is flipping. At a session in the Knesset, Netanyahu mentioned the examples about BDS and social media campaigns numerous times; they realized what's happening is global and how it's bringing those believing in the Palestinian cause together. This is unique, that's why they feel threatened now, I think that's the power of new media.

Amani, Ramallah, August 2015

Internet infrastructures have important consequences for Palestinian media use. *Firstly*, the need to archive cannot be ignored and remains a very serious way to engage and bear witness, partly with the implicit hope to construct ideological legitimacy for the collective struggle. While social media activates, strengthens and helps support the bond between publics, the basic need to *record* still plays a role in combatting dehumanization. Palestinian internet activism is about re-propositioning new discourses against what is dogmatically absorbed by the international community (Solombrino 2016: 128). Thus, there is a recovery of a humanity at stake, and the disavowal of Palestinian subjectivity in the process in order to 'regain the right for Palestinians to tell their own history and stories, memory and memories' (ibid.: 134). We can expand on this and think about a somewhat individual experience in the digital realm, e.g. when a re-propositioning of physical reality is *played out* via video games. On the one hand, Palestinian players re-live their own realities, and on the other, the game functions as a mediator. This current within the study of digital politics illuminates how Palestinian politics is re-envisioned through gaming. The procedural forms structure the understanding of complex realities (Šisler 2009) by the players or help them to re-enact experiences (Tawil-Souri 2007). There is a fine line between fiction and reality when games reference actual cities, such as Jenin (*Road of Heroes*), Hebron (*Under Siege*), Jerusalem (*Under the Ashes*) or Gaza (*Raid Gaza!*). Conversely, many games produced in the US and Europe use Palestine as negative props, construed in an orientalist manner. This means they garner very different and particularly politicized 'terrorist' interpretations (Šisler 2009: 277).

Witnessing also facilitates expression and information sharing that liberate individual and collective imaginations. Whereas the previous section illustrated that a different emphasis is applied in political contexts of oppressed groups, it is clear that communities are held together through deep feelings of engagement as well as through material, structural conditions. As Khalili (2004) described earlier with reference to Palestinian grassroots commemoration politics in Lebanon, it is especially the *oppositional* dimension that is aided by the internet. This echoes the suggestion that affective politics links to the ways digital politics often nurtures counter-hegemonic 'alternative' discourses (Karatzogianni & Kuntsman 2012).

Thus, *secondly*, Palestinian internet illuminates the notional difference between 'media' and 'alternative media'. The proliferation of Palestinian spaces like *I am Palestinian I am not a terrorist* rewrite the flow of information so that websites turn into a kind of 'networked archipelago' (Solombrino 2016: 139). This has certainly been the case with blogging as a platform which has further opened up terrains of activism. I point to a style that connotes Palestinian use of the internet as a means to document injustice and oppression (Shalhoub-Kevorkian 2012: 57). Compared to media journalism, blogging has a more honest and personal tendency. For Alsaafin, who does both, '[in my blogs] I can comfortably rant against the PA and use "strong language", such as describing them as collaborators led by a quisling without worrying about getting censored or for the post to be deemed "inappropriate".' Both websites and blogging have been sustained but their growth has stalled. There have been suggestions that Palestinian blogging weakened with the eruption of the Arab Spring. The timing suggested a decline in the Palestinian blogosphere as all attention moved from Palestinians to other Arab youths. Yet Palestinian rebellion was not *replaced* with, but *joined* by, a regional intifada including youths in Egypt, Syria, Yemen, Bahrain and Morocco. But the overall decline of Arab blogging has much more to do with the rise of a different type of online engagement, especially as social networking has become more common (al-Ghoul 2013).

As Karatzogianni (2006) has argued, internet politics governed by decentralized networks (which she calls 'rhizomatic structures') allow for new forms of mobilization. So, *thirdly*, the expression of solidarity is one of the most powerful qualities of online politics. In *Tweeting #Palestine*, Siapera (2013) gives an interesting analysis of just how widespread the use of #Palestine is across the world. This clearly points to a collective and distributed mediation. She also frames it as a struggle for power over representation by activist experience-based affective news mediated on social media vis-à-vis mainstream media and its focus on 'hard' news. The content and emerging narrative of #Palestine are the result of a collective authorship in which producers contribute from their own vantage point or to which they contribute through retweeting or information dissemination. This narrative is co-constructed (Siapera 2013: 14). Palestinian activists avoid engaging with pro-Israeli content, suggesting that Palestinian tweeting is aimed at internal community-building and at mobilizing international supporters. This strategy is partly a response to Israeli digital propaganda campaigns geared towards distraction and *casting doubt* (Aouragh 2016). Thus, the above description by Amani of Israel 'flipping' is mainly about the successes of the BDS campaigns in recent years. Instead of wasting time on their opponents, activists invest in building solidarity, and the fact that this process is the focus of high-level Knesset gatherings confirms that it does pay off. What all these different areas demonstrate is that the relationship between occupation and liberation is extremely ambivalent.

Conclusion

Every time they do something, I write about it. When we were kids we used to play in some ways knowing we might get a broken arm or leg, but that didn't stop us from playing. For Palestine, I won't stop writing and exposing online even if I got beaten, playing as a kid isn't more valuable than my homeland Palestine.

Emile, Ramallah, August 2015

Emile, quoted here, knows very well the risks involved in activism both online and offline. But this is, in its way, not dissimilar to regular life under military occupation. A little later, towards the end of our long talk, he said, 'The Israelis bombed our house, once they broke in and started shooting; when I was kid they broke in at least seven or eight times; during the Intifada my father was hunted and didn't live with us most of the time, so I'm used to all this type of stories'. This is why it was important in this chapter to not only illustrate but also contextualize how different ICTs enabled the construction of dissident tools and spaces for grassroots activism. The internet has been a counter-public space for Palestinian liberation politics for almost two decades. As this chapter shows, the development of digital media has been ground-breaking. Few could have envisioned that (free) video applications on smartphones and the spaces to upload and distribute the footage uncensored could one day show the extreme violence of Israeli soldiers or settlers. Biased media coverage has long plagued Palestinians, hence uncensored visual media becomes a real 'alternative' news source. Palestinians are, above all, (re)claiming dignity on digital spaces.

While Palestinians are tirelessly overcoming media bias through alternative reporting and improving their protests by strengthening the movement, many of the potential opportunities presented are themselves severely limited by settler-colonial diktats. But these diktats are rejected across the world. As Sam told me:

I see it as an attempt to frame a very unconvincing reality in order to avoid international focus on pressuring to change this reality. You can call it public relations, public diplomacy, propaganda, but the bottom line is that it's a framing exercise. During the war on Gaza they prepared whole packages and whole social media campaigns, over something that was, in the end, indefensible.

Meanwhile, settler-colonialism continues to force upon grassroots activists a constant political manoeuvring aimed at capturing the blessings of the internet whilst avoiding its curses. Local activists have learned to cope with the contradictory impact of technology. The insights from Amani, Bahia, Cherif, Emile and Sam help foreground the dilemmas of locally rooted grassroots activism. The strategy is collective rather than individual, and is one of *opposition* (to colonialism, imperialism and free-market dogma) rather than *compromise*.

References

Aouragh, M. (2008) 'Everyday Resistance on the Internet: The Palestinian Context', *Journal of Arab and Muslim Media Research*, vol. 1, no. 2, pp. 109–30.

Aouragh, M. (2011) *Palestine Online: Transnationalism, the Internet and the Construction of Identity*. London: I. B. Taurus.

Aouragh, M. (2016) 'Hasbara 2.0: Israel's Public Diplomacy in the Digital Age', *Middle East Critique*, vol. 25, no. 3, pp. 271–97.

Aouragh, M. and Tawil-Souri, H. (2014) 'Intifada 3.0? Cyber Colonialism and Palestinian Resistance', *Arab Studies Journal*, vol. 23, no. 1, pp. 102–33.

DeVries, M., Simry, A., and Maoz, I. (2015) 'Like a Bridge over Troubled Water: Using Facebook to Mobilize Solidarity among East Jerusalem Palestinians during the 2014 War in Gaza', *International Journal of Communication,* vol. 9, pp. 2622–49, http://ijoc.org/index.php/ijoc/article/view/3581/1445, accessed March 2017.

ITU (2016) 'Palestine Territory (Gaza and West Bank) Internet Usage, Broadband and Telecommunications Reports', *ITU,* http://www.internetworldstats.com/me/ps.htm, accessed March 2017.

Jacobs, M. (2007) 'Facebook Sparks Palestine Debate', *Jerusalem Post*, 9 October, http://www.jpost.com/International/Facebook-sparks-Palestine-debate, accessed March 2017.

Karatzogianni, A. (2006) *The Politics of Cyberconflict*. London: Routledge.

Lunat, Z. (2009) 'The Palestinian Hidden Transcript: Domination, Resistance and the Role of ICT's in Achieving Freedoms', *Electronic Journal on Information Systems in Developing Countries*, vol. 37, no. 1, pp. 1–22.

Menassat (2008) 'Video Nation', *Menassat*, 25 July, http://www.menassat.com/?q=en/print/4282, accessed August 2015.

Mualem, M. (2015) 'Will Social Media Spark a Third Intifada?' *Al-Monitor.* 12 October, http://www.al-monitor.com/pulse/originals/2015/10/jordan-prince-orit-perlov-social-media-gaza-facebook-stab.html.

Open Internet Initiative (2009) *Gaza and the West Bank*. 10 August, https://opennet.net/research/profiles/gazawestbank, accessed March 2017.

PCBS (2015) 'Indicators', http://www.pcbs.gov.ps/site/lang__en/881/default.aspx#InformationSociety, accessed March 2017.

Shalhoub-Kevorkian, N. (2012) 'E-Resistance and Technological In/security in Everyday Life: The Palestinian Case,' *British Journal of Criminology*, vol. 52, no. 1, pp. 55–72.

Siapera, E. (2013) 'Tweeting #Palestine: Twitter and the Mediation of Palestine', *International Journal of Cultural Studies*, vol. 17, no. 6, pp. 539–55.

Šisler, V. (2009) 'Palestine in Pixels: The Holy Land, Arab-Israeli Conflict, and Reality Construction in Video Games', *Middle East Journal of Culture and Communication*, vol. 2, no. 2, pp. 275–92.

Solombrino, O. (2016) '"Permission to Narrate" and the Palestinian Politics of Representation through Digital Media', in B. Baybars-Hawks (ed.) *Framing Violence: Conflicting Images, Identities, and Discourses*. Newcastle, UK: Cambridge Scholars Publishing, pp. 127–44.

Stein, R. L., and Swedenburg, T. (2005) *Palestine, Israel, and the Politics of Popular Culture*. Durham, NC: Duke University Press.

Tawil-Souri, H. (2007) 'The Political Battlefield of Pro-Arab Video Games on Palestinian Screens', *Comparative Studies of South Asia, Africa and the Middle East*, vol. 27, no. 3, pp. 536–51.

UNRWA. (2015) 'The Long Journey of Palestine Refugees: A Chronology of Palestinian Displacement and Dispossession', https://www.unrwa.org/newsroom/photos/%E2%80%98-long-journey-palestine-refugees-chronology-palestinian-displacement-and, accessed March 2017.

24

TURNING MURDERS INTO PUBLIC EXECUTIONS

'Beheading videos' as alternative media

Joe F. Khalil

Alternative media are one of the central features animating investigations of sociopolitical movements (Couldry & Curran 2003; Castells 2012). These movements are often counter-hegemonic, appealing to a form of insurrectionary resistance, and operating in the underground to challenge the status quo. They are accompanied by a massive explosion of alternative media uses and supported by the spread of internet and other digital technologies – from the phone camera to cyber security (Bailey, Cammaert & Carpentier 2008; Downing 2011). In the process, these sociopolitical movements redefine and exploit these technologies for their 'different' purposes.

While technologies offer opportunities to produce and distribute alternative media content, this massive explosion also represents a global discontent and resistance to hegemonic sociopolitical, economic and media forces. Operating under a different mandate than the profit motive, these media offer perspectives absent from commercial and state-owned outlets. They particularly serve to provide a platform for these movements and their supporters. The goals of these movements and the content of their media reflect a wide spectrum from the democratic to the autocratic, from the peaceful to the violent, and from the tolerant to the myopic.

The relationship of alternative media to sociopolitical movements is no longer an issue only for those interested in the practices of marginalized groups who might explicitly envision their 'artistic' or 'creative' activities as having political outcomes, media commentators who are trying to explain the rise of radical movements, or the variety of mainstream media that exploit these groups by routinely publishing or broadcasting their messages. This chapter addresses 'the typical divorce [that] persists unabated between media studies research and theory and research by sociologists, political scientists, and historians' (Downing 2008: 41). For anyone wanting to make sense of the roles and functions of media in society and in sociopolitical processes, it has become particularly important to understand this relationship.

This chapter is concerned with a specific form of alternative media associated with the rise of extremist violent groups in the Arab world. The circulation of videos produced by kidnappers is a common feature of certain news media, dedicated websites, Twitter feeds, YouTube channels and Facebook accounts. These videos range from an individual reading a list of demands to more complex edited sequences, some even featuring the decapitation of the kidnapped person. Since their emergence in Iraq in the 2000s, these media-labelled 'beheading videos' have raised questions about their religious justification, mainstream media's role in their distribution, their psychological significance and other issues (Nacos 2014; Friis 2015; Rand Corporation 2015; Weiss & Hassan 2016; Redmond 2017; Spiesel 2017). Less commented upon, though no less significant, is the use of these videos as alternative media tools by various extremist organizations addressing both their communities and their enemies.

While videos work in tandem with alternative media forms ranging from the oratory to the symbolic, and including traditional forms (magazines) to non-traditional (graffiti), this chapter focuses on videos associated with the execution of hostages in the Middle East. These videos are part of a long list of media messages, practices and platforms that these groups use to influence mainstream media or target their communities and the public at large. If we learnt anything from Marxist cultural criticism, it is that creative and cultural activities have political and ideo-logical content of necessity (Lukacs 1997). Beheading videos are politics, both at the levels and spheres of local and transnational groups, and as a display of power to order and organize society. These videos embody different expressions of power through physical force and through the production and management of a population's consent to the existing shape and form of rule. And just like these groups' ideologies, their media practices, including the production of these videos, have been re-embedded in various communities across the Middle East and beyond.

Drawing on the longer history of public fascination with filmed beheadings, this chapter examines three phases of hostage videos in the Arab world: the Beirut hostage videos of the 1980s, the Iraqi videos of the 2000s, and the videos produced by the Islamic State in Iraq and Syria (ISIS) in 2014 through 2017. Many of these hostage videos include forms of assassination such as hanging, beheading, shooting and immolation. Given their circulation via television, the internet and social media, these videos reveal a complex array of readings, editorial decisions and audiences. Understanding these videos, situating them in a historical context, describing their development and relating their ability to combine religious radicalization with contemporary media tropes require studying them from different angles.

The practice

For the purposes of this chapter, beheading is defined as a social, religious or judicial sentence carried out in public. As a punishment, all ancient civilizations practiced it, using swords or axes against condemned criminals. The Romans beheaded citizens but crucified non-citizens. The French revolutionaries of 1789 used the guillotine, a notorious instrument for decapitation, to carry out public executions with efficiency. In the Middle East, beheading is still practiced in Saudi Arabia and Iran as a judicial verdict and a theologically recommended, publically accepted capital punishment. In the past twenty years, various forms of beheadings appeared in various parts of the world, including Chechnya, the Philippines, Algeria and Afghanistan.

Beheading videos that focus on the act of beheading may also include a list of demands, a reading of a verdict and/or a confession statement or 'last word' read by the hostage, and the beheading scene may be followed by sequences of jubilance edited to music or chants. As we will discuss, these videos evolved from amateur/militant witness productions to more profes-sionally executed videos that are part of a media message. The early videos were characterized by a raw look and feel: shaky camera, low light, in-camera editing, natural sound. The camera operator seemed to follow the action, documenting the beheading as it unfolded. In contrast, recent videos reveal a professional approach that may include highly specialized skills: multiple cameras (including a jib arm and wide-angle lenses), special video effects editing, multiple audio tracks and graphics. The various actions seem to be choreographed for the camera.

A quick look at the development of these productions shows an increase in aesthetic sophis-tication and storytelling using cutting-edge techniques. The content reveals attention to political message construction, 'marketing' savviness and an ability to react and adapt to counter-messaging. It has been established that 'the beheadings are part of ... IS (Islamic State) media products ... created and communicated according to a consistent strategy' (Lombardi 2015: 98). The strategy guides a 'media jihad' (Lombardi 2015: 98) or war, targeting both local and international audiences. It complements an on-the-ground, battlefield-based 'offensive jihad' (Baghdadi, cited in Bunzel 2016: 10). Bypassing mainstream media, these video messages are also alternative representations of the group. They are no longer framed as a loosely trained paramilitary group, but as a strong army with clear political demands. The videos allow the groups full control over message construction, production and distribution.

Mainstream media, particularly television, were used to disseminate images of the behead-ings. The choice ranged between news agencies (such as Associated Press) and international tel-evision channels (such as al Jazeera Arabic channel). Such platforms guaranteed an expanded and global audience reach. Benefiting from media convergence, producers of these videos extended their distribution to include extremist websites and social media (such as Twitter, Facebook and Instagram). Combining mainstream media and alternative platforms, these producers ensured a relatively uncensored and uncontrolled circulation of their videos.

Over time, three identifiable patterns of distribution and circulation of these videos emerged. First, witnesses or collaborators would record and 'smuggle' a video with the purpose of coun-tering or confirming a narrative – consider videos of ousted Iraqi dictator Saddam Hussein. Second, the executing group might 'leak' a carefully produced video and public statement to mainstream media, providing evidence of and explanation for the execution – consider Al Qaeda videos. Third, the group might self-publish various versions of the video to selected websites with the intention of controlling the timing, the message and the target audience – consider the videos of ISIS. As with most alternative media, these approaches to distribution have evolved and overlapped over time. Digital and internet capabilities provide increased control over the distri-bution process. In addition to constructing unconventional content, these patterns reveal alter-native methods to either use mainstream media or create alternate pathways for the distribution and circulation of these videos.

Commenting on the current strategies of video dissemination, Bolt (2012: 41) argues that:

> there is a tendency in the West to assume messages, such as those emanating from Islamic political groups, target either a single Western mass audience or a partisan, domestic pop-ulation. But they identify and segment audiences for whom they cater messages. These are branded and delivered to diverse markets, sometimes locally, sometimes globally.

Yet it is almost impossible to engage in an empirical reception study of beheading videos. Most methods of gauging audience reception fail to capture what happens once these videos are disseminated. As mainstream media censor or completely ignore these videos, the viewing and interpretation of them is increasingly left to audiences of alternative platforms. While coun-terterrorism agencies are able to trace who uploads these videos and how they are shared, it is increasingly difficult to monitor the multitude of 'platforms' where these videos are reproduced, reedited, explained or discussed. Herein lies the challenge as these beheading videos end up with a faceless yet assumed audience.

The development

There is a long and interesting history surrounding beheading videos. In 1939, the secret film-ing of Eugen Weidmann's beheading prompted a decision to cease *public* beheading in France

(Edwards 2014). In 2002, Al Qaeda's execution of US journalist Daniel Pearl in Pakistan ushered a new wave of beheading videos produced and distributed globally (Martin & Kushner 2011). As media production tools (cameras, smartphones, editing software) become cheaper and easier to master, beheading videos are increasingly 'produced' as political, social and aesthetic objects. The following are three cases or waves associated with the rise and widespread distribution of hostage videos and the inclusion of various forms of execution, including beheading. What seems to be a linear trajectory that emerges in the discussion should be considered as revealing overlapping temporalities, and the typology of videos presented is illustrative of a spectrum, rather than a genre.

Between 1982 and 1992, during what is known as Lebanon's Western hostage crisis, there were 104 kidnappings with at least eight killed or dead in captivity (Jaber 1997: 113). While a number of organizations claimed responsibility for these kidnappings, it is believed that they were related to the Iranian-backed group Hezbollah ('Party of God') (Norton 2007). The kidnappers often released hostage videos, but rarely videos of the killing. The videos were offered anonymously to local or international media organizations. One significant video featured US Colonel William Higgins, who headed the UN peacekeeping mission in Southern Lebanon and was kidnapped in February 1988 by a radical group called the Organization of the Oppressed on Earth who accused him of being a CIA operative. The colour videotape appeared 18 months after his capture. The 30-second tape included a close-up of Higgins's face, apparently beaten up and hanging from a rope. The tape was accompanied with a one-page, typewritten statement detailing the circumstances of the execution and the organization's demands. These *evidence videos* were constructed to demonstrate why and how a hostage was kidnapped, and to offer proof of his death. They included various familiar tropes: an establishment of the taping date, usually through holding a newspaper, an off-camera interrogation, a 'voluntary' confession and a list of demands. These videos appeared to be oriented for intra-organizational use as well as for a coordinated media message.

Between 2004 and 2006, ransom and beheading videos reached a peak. With Iraq as their primary scene, there were a total of ten beheading videos in 2004. Nicholas Berg's beheading video emerged on the blogosphere in 2004, two days after his body was found (Brisard & Martinez 2005). For the first time, these videos were fully *mediated*, making use of both traditional broadcast channels and the internet. The execution sequences in these videos account for a small percentage of the videos' total length, in comparison with the reading of the verdict and the post-execution clip. Against conventional religious doctrine, which recommends a swift decapitation, the videos reveal a torturous, slow slashing of the victim's neck using a knife. Emulating court martials, the verdict is read by a militia leader surrounded and protected by a group with full military gear. The verdict includes Qur'anic verses, a list of charges and a threatening statement to the victim's country of citizenship or its leaders. The post-execution clip includes a range of images and sounds to boost the morale of partisans and scare non-partisans; it can include military training stunts cut to a beat or lyrics, or a range of paramilitary activities. These videos are complete with captions and graphic elements. Seen in the Iraqi context, these videos were the product of competing groups with similar ideological beliefs. The videos were used to assert these groups' territorial control and to demonstrate their might. In spite of Al Qaeda's stance against beheading videos, Abu Musab al-Zarqawi, the leader of Al Qaeda in Iraq, aggressively pursued the production and distribution of these videos. More generally, the videos were used as a tool to render the execution public by circulating the videos via mass media and targeted websites. As an internal and external communication tool, these *mediated* videos have increased the producers' ability to control their dissemination, using the internet as a primary tool.

Between 2015 and 2017, the Islamic State inherited Zarqawi's interest in controlling both the production and distribution of the message. They developed their beheading videos into a spectacle of individual beheadings of Westerners and Japanese, or mass beheadings of Syrian and Iraqi nationals belonging to security services, and Christian Ethiopians and Egyptians (Weiss & Hassan 2016). Far from an amateur production, these *choreographed* videos are developed as an audiovisual performance using tropes from traditional media (production design, sound effects, blocking, etc.). The execution is no longer restricted to a quick beheading act but has been extended to an unhurried, ceremonial, sadistic display of terror. These producers of a 'theater of cruelty' make calculated use of 'soft focus, slow fades, colour saturation, superimpositions and carefully layered soundtracks' (Ibish 2015). The videos are constructed using storytelling structures complete with hook, cliffhanger and climax. They also use the confession technique from reality TV. These choreographed videos are circulated with the intention of consolidating followers, attracting recruits and scaring opponents. Although the videos have become more professional, they have also become less numerous.

From user-generated content to professionally generated content

The beheading videos have been transformed from user-generated content (UGC) to professionally generated content (PGC). The former videos are produced by the kidnappers themselves, who have no apparent interest in aesthetic and technical qualities. Often distributed to mainstream media, these videos are often censored, framed and constrained in circulation. In contrast, the professionally generated content imitates the aesthetic and production qualities of mainstream film and television. It also develops digital distribution networks that allow users more flexibility in controlling the message and targeting its receivers. At the same time, this emerging content imitates the rules of the old form, including a constructed message, a clearly targeted audience and a deliberate release time. Also, both users and professionals are political actors in their own right – those who produce, film, edit, upload or distribute.

The revolutionary dimensions of UGC have revealed the evolutionary affordances of PGC. In other words, the UGC videos may have lost their emancipatory, liberating potential and become part of the media milieu, perhaps on par with other competing political discourses (Peer & Ksiazek 2011; Kim 2012). The ability of these groups to develop and distribute an alternative message has been transformed into a message that conforms to mainstream media. So instead of the amateurish raw message, the current messaging compounds radical messages with professional 'Hollywood' packaging. In illustrating the development from user-generated to professionally generated content, the following three instances reveal multiple dynamics of publicness and temporality.

In the first example, the video circulated by Hezbollah appeared a year and a half after the hanging that it documented had occurred. The timing of the video release coincided with a political message the radical group wanted to emphasize: that the assassination or murder of its leaders would be revenged. By releasing the video to international news agencies in Beirut, Hezbollah enlisted local and regional channels to publicize its content. As a second case, the videos released by Zarqawi's group share similar ideological and aesthetic characteristics with Al Qaeda's videos, but represent several noteworthy differences. First, Zarqawi's beheading videos escape the politically controlled media: they are released on the internet and rarely made available to television networks. Benefiting from online marketing opportunities, the Zarqawi group made the internet their central platform for video distribution. Finally, the execution and beheading videos released by ISIS have demonstrated technical and aesthetical professionalism often compared with that of professional movie industries. Symbolic values aside, the videos revealed a targeted distribution through social media networks to a niche audience comprised of sympathizers. Taking the lead from hackers, ISIS injects execution videos into mainstream media's news cycle, causing significant interruptions.

These three instances reveal change and continuity in the production and distribution of these videos. The development of an alternative self-expressive narrative and the ability to reach local and global audiences has continued to obsess radical groups from Hezbollah to ISIS. The technologies of production and distribution have adapted to the mechanics of censorship and control while simultaneously adopting mainstream media's content and aesthetic practices.

The contexts of production, distribution and reception are clearly intertwined with the political interpretations and implications of these videos. These three contexts transform these videos from audiovisual objects to sociopolitical instruments of power.

Discipline, control, publicness and temporality

After considering the practice and development of beheading videos, it is important to ask what the significance of their production and circulation might be (among other significant issues). These videos provide frameworks and themselves are framed; they construct a vision, and are constructed within and by that vision. At the core of this questioning are three interconnected areas that offer vistas into future inquiries about these videos.

The acts of beheading reflect Foucault's disciplinary society, where techniques of power are organized around the control of individual bodies. According to Foucault (2003: 242), the disciplinary society is a 'whole system of surveillance, hierarchies, inspections, bookkeeping, and reports'. As we detailed, beheadings are practised in such disciplinary societies consisting of states, pseudo-states or radical groups with specific visions or sociopolitical identities. In the wake of disciplinary societies, Deleuze (1995) suggests that 'societies of control' emerge. While the beheadings represent closures of disciplinary societies, the production and circulation of the beheading videos reveal a disseminated, disembodied and discontinuous space of marketing – a society of control. Through their production aesthetics and their networks of circulation, these videos codify power as free-floating, anonymous and autonomous. Deleuze (ibid.: 174) offers an apt and helpful remark: 'We are moving toward control societies that no longer operate by confining people but through continuous control and instant communication.' If beheadings are intended to discipline ruled societies, the beheading videos are intended to maintain control and extend it to the to-be-conquered societies.

These videos are animated by radical politics intended to 'supplement, and gradually extend, transform and displace the traditional forms of publicness' (Thompson 1995: 126). Before videos, beheadings were executed on military sites or in public squares, restricting the publicness to the plurality of individuals physically present at the time of the execution – a case of 'traditional publicness of co-presence' (ibid.: 125). Consider the regular attraction for Saudis and foreigners during the 1970s and 1980s of public beheadings in what was called 'head-chopper square'. The beheading videos offer a fundamental break in spreading images and sounds of beheadings across digital and broadcast networks, converting the physical witnessing into an audiovisual experience, and relocating publicness from spatio-physical to the symbolic – a form of 'mediated publicness' (ibid.: 127). Instead of the mob or rabble that often characterizes public execution, these videos reveal rational social actors who mobilize significant power resources – both creative and technological – at their disposal to develop and circulate these videos as media messages.

The emergence and re-emergence of these videos reveal multiple temporalities. They expose how competing groups revisit historical time to draw temporal structuring of individual and global existence. They aim to bring back a time when Muslim society was pure and uncontaminated by modernity. At the same time, these videos show how other temporalities persist and subsist as marginal practices poised for resurgence under specific conditions. While the practice of witnessing beheadings existed through oral histories, paintings and other forms of storytelling, the production and dissemination of videos can be seen as capturing a similar temporal structure. As an understanding and a lived experience of time, these videos are embedded in postmodern temporality's sense of nihilism. After the failure of modernity's grand narratives of reason and progress, the videos reveal a plurality of interacting temporal flows (Islamic, Arab, Colonial, Post-colonial, etc.).

While each video's time of release, duration and content are all manipulations of time, the producer/consumer time is yet another subjective factor integral to interpretation itself. From the ordering of video sequences to the use of slow-motion editing, producers manipulate time. And, once released, the video's life cycle is extended beyond the 24-hour news cycle to exist permanently on the internet as shared links, mash-up videos, compilation videos, and so on.

The beheadings and their videos make it necessary to use both the Foucauldian disciplinary-society thesis as well as the society-of-control concept to be able to account for the practice itself, as well as the ensuing media messages. At one crucial and substantive level, beheading videos are implicated in mediated publicness, for providing a framework for the publication of these private executions, the expansion of public debate and the creation of degree of fear. These are indeed strange times in which the overlapping of temporalities, the old and new, make it difficult to grasp the magnitude and the implications of these videos.

Conclusion

Beheading videos are a significant but repugnant instance of alternative media associated with radical groups or movements. Though media and social commentators have been shocked by the violence of radical organizations in the past decade or so, it is the aesthetic appeal, production standards, dissemination networks and audience appeal of these videos that are new – not their actions or political message. These sociopolitical movements have in significant degrees been defined by progressive, self-expressive media intrusions into the sociopolitical world, of which the most significant have arguably been the beheading videos. Relying on mainstream media, and now on social media, these videos have become central to the ways in which radical groups communicate with their sympathizers and the world. At the same time, these videos have become central to the way the public and experts create a framework for understanding, explaining and reacting to these groups. These videos provide the symbolic resources and tools for making sense of the complexities of these groups' ideologies. These communication processes and constructed meanings are instances of the development and circulation of alternative media. Using media technologies, political messaging and religious tropes, these videos have extended the sociopolitical role of beheadings, no longer requiring co-presence, to circulate their symbols in social life. By blending mainstream production and circulation practices with alternative/underground practices, these beheading videos should be evaluated as integral to processes of sociopolitical change and as a bridge to link local, trans-local and transnational manifestations of politics.

If we pursue the discussion into the realms of alternative media, and from the perspective of those who (for the most part) are mostly, or most significantly still, on the producing end of beheading videos, I argue that there are profound moral and ethical issues to be addressed in confronting the role of beheading videos and that these issues revolve around questions of action and responsibility. What kinds of claims do these 'producers' make on their audiences, and what kind of claims can, or should, audiences be making on these videos and their 'producers'? What kinds of actions related to the beheadings or their audio-visual documentation are morally (or even religiously) possible in a world in which practices, images and narratives are trans-local? What kind of responsibility can or should be taken by audiences for actions they only see as glorified and glamorized, and for the 'producers' who provide those images and stories? These videos provide an alternative platform characterized by 'an innovative, open-source, interactive, participatory operation' (Farwell 2010: 128). But in providing alternative content and organization, these videos are shaping interpretive frameworks for seeing, being, acting in power and control.

In a world of changing global power dynamics, these videos appear to be part of a process of sociopolitical change characterized by the reinstitution of presumably Islamic political and social arrangements. But the production, circulation and reception of beheading videos are closely linked to ideological transformations, as well as to the emergence of multiple communication outlets, from global broadcasters to unrestricted social media platforms. While, as this chapter demonstrates, beheading videos are not recent phenomena, their production and reception are a reflection of a postmodernist ethos. The development of these videos might be described in paradoxical terms: it is a reaction against postmodernity that draws on postmodernity's features. First, the politics of culture features prominently, as this obsession with fetishized Islamic styles and techniques is reshaped and reintegrated in these videos. Second, these videos are constructed to appeal to a multicultural yet incoherent community of fearful 'apostates' and faithful followers. Third, the social identity of the 'beheaders' is constructed by these videos' carefully composed sequences of images, captions and music. Fourth, the videos are not attributed to individuals but to a collective, declaring the death of the author and distributor as producers blend into audiences. Yet in many ways, this reaction repeats the resistance to modernity that existed throughout the twentieth century.

References

Bailey, O. G., Cammaert, B. and Carpentier, N. (2008) *Understanding Alternative Media*. Maidenhead, UK: Open University Press.

Bolt, N. (2012) *The Violent Image: Insurgent Propaganda and the New Revolutionaries*. London: Hurst.

Brisard, J.-C. and Martinez, D. (2005) *Zarqawi: The New Face of Al-Qaeda*. New York: Other Press.

Bunzel, C. (2015) 'From Paper State to Caliphate: The Ideology of the Islamic State'. *Brookings Project on US Relations with the Islamic World*, Analysis Paper No. 19, http://www.brookings.edu/~/media/research/files/papers/2015/03/ideology-of-islamic-state-bunzel/the-ideology-of-the-islamic-state.pdf, accessed 25 July 2017.

Castells, M. (2012) *Networks of Outrage and Hope: Social Movements in the Internet Age*. Cambridge: Polity Press.

Couldry, N. and Curran, J. (eds) (2003) *Contesting Media Power: Alternative Media in a Networked World*. Lanham, MD: Rowman & Littlefield.

Deleuze, G. (1995) *Negotiations, 1972–1990*. New York: Columbia University Press.

Downing, J. (2008) 'Social Movement Theories and Alternative Media: An Evaluation and Critique', *CCCR Communication, Culture & Critique*, vol. 1, no. 1, pp. 40–50.

Downing, J. (2011) *Encyclopedia of Social Movement Media*. Thousand Oaks, CA: Sage.

Edwards, S. (2014) 'Photographing the Guillotine', *The Appendix*, vol. 2, no. 4, http://theappendix.net/issues/2014/10/photographing-the-guillotine, accessed 25 July 2017.

Farwell, J. P. (2010) 'Jihadi Video in the "War of Ideas"', *Survival*, vol. 52, no. 6, pp. 127–50.

Foucault, M. (2003) *Society Must Be Defended*. London: Penguin.

Friis, S. M. (2015) 'Beyond Anything We Have Ever Seen: Beheading Videos and the Visibility of Violence in the War Against ISIS', *INTA International Affairs*, vol. 91, no. 4, pp. 725–46.

Ibish, H. (2015) 'The ISIS Theater of Cruelty', *New York Times*, 18 February, http://www.nytimes.com/2015/02/19/opinion/the-isis-theater-of-cruelty.html, accessed 25 July 2017.

Jaber, H. (1997) *Hezbollah: Born with a Vengeance*. New York: Columbia University Press.

Kim, J. (2012) 'The Institutionalization of YouTube: From User-Generated Content to Professionally Generated Content', *Media, Culture & Society*, vol. 34, no. 1, pp. 53–67.

Lombardi, M. (2015) 'IS 2.0 and Beyond: The Caliphate's Communication Project', in M. Maggioni, P. Magri and M. Lombardi (eds) *Twitter and Jihad: The Communication Strategy of ISIS*. Milan: Italian Institute for International Political Studies (ISPI), pp. 83–122.

Lukacs, G. (1997) *History and Class Consciousness: Studies in Marxist Dialectics* (L. Rodney, trans.). Cambridge, MA: MIT Press.

Martin, G. and Kushner, H. W. (2011) *The Sage Encyclopedia of Terrorism*. Thousand Oaks, CA: Sage.

Nacos, B. L. (2014) 'Tactics of Terrorism', in M. Eid (ed.) *Exchanging Terrorism Oxygen for Media Airwaves: The Age of Terroredia*. Hershey, PA: IGI Global, pp. 110–23.

Norton, A. R. (2007) *Hezbollah: A Short History*. Princeton, NJ: Princeton University Press.

Peer, L. and Ksiazek, T. B. (2011) 'YouTube and the Challenge to Journalism', *Journalism Studies*, vol. 12, no, 1, pp. 45–63.

Rand Corporation (2015) 'Experts React to ISIS's Gruesome Execution of Jordanian Pilot', http://www.rand.org/blog/2015/02/experts-react-to-isiss-gruesome-execution-of-jordanian.html, accessed 25 July 2017.

Redmond, S. A. (2017) Who Views Graphic Media and Why? A Mixed-Methods Study of the ISIS Beheading Videos. MA thesis, University of California, Irvine, http://escholarship.org/uc/item/7x37b4j6, accessed 25 July 2017.

Spiesel, C. (2017) 'Gruesome Evidence: The Use of Beheading Videos and Other Disturbing Pictures in Terrorism Trials', in D. Tait and J. Goodman-Delahunty (eds) *Juries, Science and Popular Culture in the Age of Terror: The Case of the Sydney Bomber*. Basingstoke, UK: Palgrave Macmillan, pp. 67–85.

Thompson, J. B. (1995) *The Media and Modernity: A Social Theory of the Media*. Stanford, CA: Stanford University Press.

Weiss, M. and Hassan, H. (2016) *ISIS: Inside the Army of Terror*. New York: Regan Arts.

25

URBAN GRAFFITI, POLITICAL ACTIVISM AND RESISTANCE

Noureddine Miladi

Graffiti writings and political slogans painted on street walls, doors and sometimes on pavements and grounds of public spaces have become significant means of effective communication. This chapter analyzes the development of graffiti art from mere self-expression into a tool for political activism and resistance. It also discusses how far graffiti is about a struggle over the definition of space and the claims to the ownership of that space. It looks at the extent to which such works of art have been employed as means for political activism and can work as counter flows of information against hegemonic power structures.

This work further probes, on the one hand, how far the new façade of this urban environment has been flourishing thanks to many gifted activists who do not hide their identities any more, and on the other, the power of graffiti to bypass the immediacy which characterizes Twitter feeds and Facebook messages, for instance. Its potentials of resisting the limitations of time and space are viewed as having a more lasting effect in reaching out to a wider local and even international public.

In this chapter, graffiti is partly understood as a struggle between order and disorder. But most importantly I discuss its potential as a tool for communication through which certain messages get disseminated. I look at how activists produce public space and the extent to which graffiti writers pose a challenge to the established order and power structures in society.

Graffiti artists and the struggle for recognition

Graffiti is not a new phenomenon but as ancient as human civilization. Artistic manifestations in the form of written words, scratches, drawings, paintings, symbols and signs on walls date from Ancient Egypt, Greece and the Roman Empire. The modern origin of the term graffiti can be traced back to the Italian word *graffiare*, which means to 'scratch'. As an artistic genre, graffiti developed from the reproduction of stenciled images into sophisticated aesthetic pieces of art. Namely in the 1970s, graffiti had started to appear in New York City, Toronto, Barcelona, Paris, London and other world cities. Stenciled graffiti as an artistic genre was associated mainly with social activism, social injustices, war, freedom and human dignity.

In contemporary times, graffiti started in marginalized US suburbs among black youth. The late 1960s witnessed the emergence of writings on walls as part of youth expression: young people tagging street walls to grab the attention of the opposite sex or express certain feelings in order to make them public. By the late 1980s, graffiti art leaped from dark streets and subways to art galleries. This embrace by the art industry is a recognition of this art practice, which has led to a transformation of the role of graffiti art in society.

In the Arab world and Middle East, graffiti is much related to the more historically rooted art of calligraphy. The Arabic calligraphy stands for artistic fine handwriting using the Arabic alphabet and mainly about reproducing the Qur'an. Verses from the scripture written in endless shapes and fonts tend to decorate Mosques, courts, palaces, universities and other public places. Arabic, Ottoman and Persian calligraphy remained during the last millennium a significant artistic expression of the Islamic civilization. Calligraphy is also a blending of religion and culture in which the interface of the language symbolizes the artistic beauty of the written word. Cordoba, Istanbul, Baghdad, Cairo and other cities under the Islamic civilization thrived as cultural hubs in which the art of calligraphy blossomed and these cities remained grand displays of artistic illustrations.

However, around the world it took graffiti artists decades to be recognized and graffiti to be considered a legitimate art practice. Graffiti writers were initially criminalized and Anti-Graffiti Task Forces were set up in New York and London, for instance. From its emergence until the late 1980s, debates around street arts revolved around two extremes: art practice and juvenile criminal activity (McAuliffe & Iveson 2011).

Artist Doze Green from New York used to be among the youth who employed the streets of New York as their canvas. His graffiti drawings decorated tens of the city streets. Nowadays, he is one of the successful artists whose works are appreciated by millions in international galleries. A New York graffiti activist expresses this transformation by arguing that as a marginalized youth, originally graffiti:

> got me on a more positive direction towards expressing myself instead of smashing a window or smashing a head … What I'm doing, it's a new vocabulary … new ways of looking at the same thing … Whether it's accepted by the elite or the guy in the street, what's important to me is people in general feel my work.
>
> *CNN.com 2005*

Nowadays, his works compete with great artists, attract big corporations and adorn galleries in various capitals.

Scholarship around the study of graffiti art is not new either, but in modern times it goes back at least to the 1970s. It has attracted scholarly interest from varied disciplines such as communication, linguistics, history, geography, cultural studies and psychology. But academic perceptions to this social phenomenon were diverse. Subway graffiti, for instance, was seen as a space where the power of the state is not present, an 'uncontrolled' space as perceived by Glazer (1979). Others such as McAuliffe and Iveson (2011) have a conflicting response to graffiti as they consider it both artistic representation and a criminal offence that spoils public properties.

Others perceive graffiti as a sign of social transformations of the modern era. Modernity and postmodernity are partly characterized by the emergence of subcultural identities, which tend to break away from the mainstream and develop various tools for resistance and survival. Being pushed away from political influence and censored from expressing their view freely, youth tend to capitalize on graffiti. Such works are not only artistic manifestations of gifted citizens, but a cry for recognition by marginalized groups in society. This trend has been known over the last few decades as subcultures or subcultural identities.

Graffiti and subcultural identities

In the late 1960s and early 1970s, graffiti grew in the subway system of New York City. The vast outreach of underground trains across the suburbs made it easier for graffiti writers to connect and spread their works (Abel & Buckley 1977). That decade also witnessed the growth of graffiti as part of a subculture which maintains territorial mentality and gang culture.

Graffiti artists can be drawn to graffiti art because through it they can form friendships and have a sense of community. Also, graffiti becomes a form of self-expression for those disenfranchised by the wider society that is free from any form of restraints and control. Artists escape all sorts of inhibitions like state censorship and police vigilance. Themes which surface in graffiti arts differ around the world. In Western liberal democracies they may be associated with unemployment, equality, civil rights, racism, etc. However, in other parts of the world such as China, Russia, Brazil and the Arab world among others, graffiti may be essentially about freedom, democracy, equal opportunities and human rights.

Among the above activist communities thrive subcultural identities brought together through graffiti art. For instance, one of the components of defining rappers as a music group is often related to disenfranchised youth in modern society. The urban space of the street is a place for talk, given over as much to the exchange of words and signs as it is to the exchange of things. Also, graffiti appears in places where young people can hide from the surveillance of society and say what they cannot express in public. Such slogans can be found in the most private places when people are in total seclusion like toilets, prison cells or under bridges.

Subcultural groups in this case build their *raison d'être* through controlling space via graffiti and cement their subcultural bond through its various expressions. Ferrell (1996) and Macdonald (2001) associate graffiti with the emergence of subcultural groups in society such as the 'hip-hop graffiti' or the hip-hop movement which capitalized on graffiti as one of the constituents of its identity. Others, such as Mitchell (2003), suggest that graffiti signifies contested terrains of power struggle which he calls 'counterpublics', as in the business of claiming back public space from the dominant publics.

The counter-information flow in the subcultural terrain

Beyond the aesthetic consideration in street graffiti and murals in modern urban environments, street art can be looked at as a communicative tool, a channel through which language is coded and deciphered between activists and the public. As Min Sook Lee (2000) argues, graffiti can be defined as 'an alternative system of public communication'. In countries where the media is monopolized by the state, street art may serve as an alternative communication channel. It provides contentious readings on events, people and place. Graffiti activists see themselves in this process involved in creating a new discourse contrasting that of the official apparatus.

During the Tunisian and Egyptian revolutions, for instance, to many activists, writing on walls served as a substitute for TV, radio, newspapers and magazines. Before 2011, at times when the regimes of Ben Ali in Tunisia or Hosni Mubarak in Egypt censored mass media outlets from any form of critical speech, street walls served as the alternative media. Like social media networks, writings on walls all over the capital Tunis and the streets of Cairo functioned as channels for expressing thoughts, sharing information, sending coded instructions among political activists and organizing public protests. This form of protest art remained for years a tool of dissent and proof of agency in disturbing the regimes' control of the visual sphere, especially public spaces.

Beyond the Arab Spring countries, today all over the world graffiti has become an artistic genre in its own right, a form of artistic expression and statement of selfhood. In various countries, artists capitalize on street graffiti nowadays to decorate ugly city walls, bring communities together or spread awareness about certain causes.

Among the various initiatives to internationalize the culture of street graffiti as a continuous artistic performance and social expression is 'Living Walls, The City Speaks'. The annual conference which is part of this community project started in 2010 in the US and facilitated the exchange of dialogue about urban space. Its organizers write that Living Walls 'seeks to promote, educate and change perspectives about public space in our communities via street art' (Living Walls, n.d.). However, what started as a one-off annual event has expanded into a year-long community engagement programme. Well-known artists got immersed with the city citizens in an intimate experience of producing artistic murals. This process of bringing together celebrities in the art world with the common people has changed the community's perception of public spaces and their role in shaping it.

Another example from Baton Rouge, Louisiana emerged in 2012 as 'The Walls Project', a community initiative funded by various entrepreneurs. The raison d'être of this citywide venture was '… to bridge the gap between the artistic and business communities in order to accomplish not only city beautification but also economic development in order to serve a greater social good' (The Walls Project, n.d., a). The result of this work went beyond the 'mural walls' as suggested by the organizers:

> By adding our voice to the global public art movement we have seen a transformation beyond the mural walls. Communities are coming together around the art to contribute to the re-imagining of their city artistically and socially. World-class artists are painting alongside children from local neighborhoods and inspiring future generations of artists.
>
> *The Walls Project n.d., b*

The above initiatives have transformed the perception of public spaces in modern urban environments and the role of the citizen in shaping them. Urban architecture, in most cases, is imposed by state planners and most of the time without the consultation of citizens. Minorities, namely the marginalized in society, do not have a say in the design of their neighborhoods, the placement of shopping malls, state buildings and any other entertainment infrastructure. All of these urban apparatuses tend to be enforced on inhabitants by hegemonic authorities, especially in countries under non-democratic rule. To this end, it can be argued that graffiti has transformed streets and public spaces into spaces of dialogue and communication between citizens in the city: something Lefebvre (2003) alluded to by observing that public spaces have been transformed to places of conversation and talk exchange as much as they are places of exchanging 'things'.

Building on Henri Lefebvre's thesis, engagement with society through 'The Walls Project' may serve as an alternative space for marginal views to emerge and brought to the attention of the establishment. One's creative powers are brought to bear through repeating such persistence of keeping graffiti slogans visible, an assertion of a strong will to the positive act of revered activism. This desire to be recognized as qualified human beings with agency for change and positive contribution is the very *raison d'être* for subcultural groups which yearn for recognition by the mainstream culture. This urge is reflected in Fanon's statement: 'As soon as I desire I am asking to be considered. I am not merely here-and-now sealed into thingness. I am for somewhere else and for something else' (1967: 218). Fanon refused to be 'an object in the midst of other objects' (1967: 109) and asserted his existence to challenge hegemony: a power struggle that recurrently manifests itself in his works and resistance.

Strategic tools for mobilization and resistance

Graffiti is about a struggle over the definition of space and claims to the ownership of that space. In this case, graffiti artists have understood their potential in the power matrix. They negotiate their positions and manage to partake in society's power struggle. Street graffiti, as argued by Keesee-Clancy (2014: 29), 'is one such practice of resistance that articulates where power's trajectory is interrupted'.

As alluded to above, during the 2011 uprisings in Tunisia and Egypt graffiti served as a counter-hegemonic discourse to the dictatorial regimes of Ben Ali and Hosni Mubarak. In Tunisia, for instance, a single word written on street walls and public spaces of the capital became emblematic of the public's insistence for Ben Ali's regime to step down and leave power. *Irhal*, which stands for a strong urge to vacate authority, reverberated across Tunisia from north to south and went viral across the region to Libya, Egypt, Yemen and Syria. Publics in the Arab Spring countries became empowered with such mottos as *Irhal, Alshaab yureedu isqaat alnidham* (the public want to topple the regime) which got painted on banners, T-shirts, street walls and even lampposts.

Similarly, in Egypt art painted on walls and public buildings served as a tool for political expression. This is predicated by various studies which analyzed the use of graffiti by political activists before and after the revolution of 25 January 2011. Campbell (2011), Rane and Salem (2012), Hamdy (2013) and Miladi (2015), among many others, spoke about graffiti during that time as a form of political mobilization. Like social media, street art deployed by activists in the streets of Cairo and in public spaces enthused protesters with a will power to challenge police brutality and the regime's attempt to monopolize the use of public spaces.

The interplay of power in any society is complex when understood in its sociopolitical context. Considering that graffiti is one of its manifestations, its impact can be studied in various stages of development. On the one hand, graffiti writings can be seen as a form of disruption to the status quo enforced by any regime. This interruption is partly visual and partly intellectual. By placing their artistic writings on murals, street walls and public buildings, graffiti activists deliberately challenge the visual look of urban cities maintained by ruling regimes. This reality is ostensibly supposed to show control, organization and civility. In the regime's eyes, any attempt to disrupt this status quo is antisocial and a sign of lawlessness and disorder. On the other hand, through painting graffiti slogans activists attempt to demonstrate a deliberate affirmation of their being in terms of their political beliefs as opposed to a regime's establishment holding power in society. In fact, these sites decorated with all sorts of anti-regime catchphrases serve as sites of challenging the state hegemony. They slowly develop according to the social consciousness into spaces where the hegemonic discourse is confronted and contested.

One of the enduring examples of the above political struggle in modern history is the Palestinians' resistance against the Israeli occupation. Graffiti works on the Separation Wall in Palestine enforced by the Israeli occupation are a manifestation of the Palestinian outrage towards the occupiers. The Wall, which is reminiscent of the Berlin Wall, has been turned in part into a permanent exhibition which documents the Palestinian Nakba, Israeli day-to-day occupation of the Palestinian land and the ordeal of separation that Palestinians go through daily in the West Bank.

Usually, centres of power consider graffiti activists as illegitimate actors, sometimes trouble makers, and dangerous in that they threaten the stability of the established order. During the 23 years of the Ben Ali regime in Tunisia, which ended in the revolution of 14 January 2011, street writings were considered a form of vandalism severely punishable by law. People caught or thought to be responsible for writing political slogans on street walls or in public spaces got relentlessly detained by the police. Visibility of anti-regime slogans used to be considered highly offensive to the system and a form of defiance to the power centre. That is why, up until the fall of the regime in 2011, the regime employed special units among council workers used to be employed in every town and city to be in charge of removing or defacing writings on walls.

In various countries, graffiti served as a tool of democratic resistance through which demands for democratic rights were recorded and transmitted to the world. In this terrain, activists claim this public sphere as a space for self-expression since they are denied access to influential media outlets like TV, radio and newspapers. Especially youth and student activists who cannot invest in advertising find in these spaces publicity outlets for their ideal society, ideal rule and hope for a just system.

Graffiti and power struggles

In political and social activism, graffiti writing carrying subversive political slogans can be partly understood as an arm-twisting contest interfering with any established regime's power and visually reordering the balance of power in favour of marginalized people. Further analysis of the Tunisian revolution in 2011 shows that powerful slogans on walls in the capital Tunis such as 'Let the people's torturer fall', 'Down with the regime', and 'Ben Ali you are coward' served to interrupt the regime's pervasive claim to power and strong command. Also, the longevity of these slogans visually demarcated where power was actually held.

In December 2016, while Aleppo inhabitants were forced by the Syrian regime to leave their city, they marked their love and strong will to return and challenge the oppressor on city walls. While leaving their city, residents of Aleppo decorated its walls with graffiti scribbles expressing their love for the place they had been forced to evacuate. One mural reads 'under every destroyed building there are families buried along with their dreams', 'love me away from the country of humiliation, away from my city which is filled with death scenes ... Besieged Aleppo this is the last day, 15 December 2016'. Another mural inspired by the singer Fairouz who dreamt of return: 'We will be returning oh my love'. Another mural reads 'to the one who shared my siege I love you' (Al Jazeera Arabic TV 2016).

By raising slogans, highlighting problems and bringing awareness to the public, protest art can be understood as a preliminary phase for public mobilization. The Tunisian revolution's graffiti slogans such as '*Yaskut jalladu ashaab*' (death to the torturer of the people), or '*Lan narkaa*' (we will not bow down in submission), served as sources of challenge to the regime and empowerment of the public. For the first time, people felt that the dictatorial regime was waning, as slogans painted on walls had remained for days without being defaced by the police or regime vigilantes.

In this sense, graffiti operates outside the realm of prohibitive order that governs public space. It does not recognize the overwhelming power placed by the state on public spaces. Such slogans scribbled on walls and public buildings symbolize illustrations of power struggle in society. This struggle is, on the one hand, between order and disorder: order embodied in the system, or the establishment, and disorder embodied in graffiti artists. On the other hand, graffiti can be viewed through the lens of power and resistance to that power. In this sense, power is every representation of the government apparatus. Resistance is every citizen who attempts to challenge that power.

Beyond the immediacy of social media

Analysis of the potential of social media networks in political activism, particularly during the Arab Spring revolutions, has been thoroughly studied. Surging interest by researchers on new media and social activism has proven the effectiveness of platforms like Facebook, YouTube and Twitter for collective action in Tunisia and Egypt, for instance (Papaioannou & Olivos 2013; El-Nawawy & Khamis 2014; Miladi 2016). However, the proliferation of social media networks has also served another dimension of social activism – that is, the wide dissemination of graffiti messages across space and time. Graffiti artists express their opinions via artworks on street walls and murals at the same time they run social media sites in which they can further their real-life graffiti arts. This sharing of mural images creates an interlink between graffiti and social media platforms where these works of art become permanent sites of resistance on virtual internet spaces. This becomes even more important when such murals and graffiti writings keep getting defaced or removed from their original places on street walls and public spaces while they remain alive on social media spaces. In sum, the power of graffiti serves to bypass the immediacy which characterizes Twitter feeds and Facebook messages. Graffiti has the potential of resisting the limitations of time and space in that it has a more lasting effect in reaching out to a wider local and even international public.

Conclusion

Although it is not a new form of artistic expression, graffiti art is still popular in various parts of the world. Street art is an informal unregulated practice often, in the past, considered a form of delinquency and a disorder that is punishable. To some, such as former mayor of New York Ed Koch, graffiti is 'garbage'. To others, it is high art and an aesthetic expression of the self. But as discussed earlier in this chapter, before it was embraced by museum galleries it had made a transition from subways to more visible arenas, i.e. streets and public spaces/buildings. It was in the 1980s that graffiti witnessed a breakthrough in terms of how activists and graffiti itself were perceived by mainstream societies. This is when graffiti artists became appreciated as talented people and their works as fascinating artistic manifestations of an era.

A few decades after the growth of this phenomenon across the world, and despite the increasing embrace of social media networks globally, this feature of public activism has not dissipated, either in countries where there are well-established democracies or others which undergo dramatic political and social changes. It is worth noting that over the last few years, street walls have remained spaces of free expression, although youth and activists across the world have found in social media networks great outlets to freely express their views and sometimes frustrations. Also, graffiti art is becoming increasingly globalized in terms of its outreach and appeal due to the circulation of images of murals and street graffiti on Google Images, Facebook, Twitter, Instagram, Snapchat, WhatsApp and personal homepages/blogs. Artwork decorating urban spaces in local neighborhoods is not local any more, but graffiti art expressed by artists in the neighbourhoods has become a phenomenon of the global village; and its audience is not local any more, but of a global nature.

In sum, across various parts of the world, street art remains mainly a yearning for attention. It is created mainly by youth who are not able to otherwise express their voices freely or have been denied certain opportunities in society. In the absence of free speech and free media, in some parts of the world, street art serves as a platform through which people's opinions get expressed. To this end, graffiti is partly understood as a way to analyze/understand social or political issues in society. Sometimes such expression of opinion does not find free platforms where they can be articulated, though the mass media such as radio and TV are expected to be where such ideas find their way.

In the contour of murals rests the manifestation of a power struggle between the state and marginalized civilians, and in those realms excluded voices tend to extend and demonstrate their agency. Although they exist on public walls, graffiti writings demarcate, on the one hand, space ownership between regime apparatuses and the protesters as public; and on the other hand, they delineate symbols which are meant to stay and challenge the state's authority. They eventually signify a form of communication that is 'both personal and free of the everyday social strains that normally prevent people from giving uninhibited reign to their thoughts' (Abel & Buckley 1977: 3).

References

Abaza, M. (2013) 'Walls, Segregating Downtown Cairo and the Mohammed Mahmud Street Graffiti', *Theory, Culture & Society*, vol. 30, no. 1, pp. 122–39.

Abel, L. and Buckley, E. (1977) *The Handwriting on the Wall: Toward a Sociology and Psychology of Graffiti*, Westport, CT: Greenwood.

Al Jazeera Arabic TV (2016) *This Morning*, 17 December.

Austin, J. (2002) *Taking the Train: How Graffiti Art Becomes an Urban Crisis in New York*. New York: Columbia University Press.

Bauder, H. (2003) *Work on the West Side: Urban Neighborhoods and the Cultural Exclusion of Youths*, Lanham, MD: Lexington Books.

Boraie, S. (ed.) (2012) *Wall Talk: Graffiti of the Egyptian Revolution*, Cairo: Zeitouna.

Campbell, D. (2011) *Egypt Unshackled: Using Social Media to @#:) the System*, Carmarthenshire, UK: Cambria Books.

Carrington, V. (2009) 'I Write, Therefore I Am: Texts in the City', *Visual Communication*, vol. 8, no. 4, pp. 409–25.

Chalfant, H. & Prigoff, J. (1987) *Spraycan Art*, New York: Thames & Hudson.

CNN (2005) 'From Graffiti to Galleries', 4 November, http://edition.cnn.com/2005/US/03/21/otr.green/index.html, accessed 10 December 2016.

El-Nawawy, M. and Khamis, S. (2014). 'Governmental Corruption Through the Egyptian Bloggers' Lens: A Qualitative Study of Four Egyptian Political Blogs', *Journal of Arab & Muslim Media Research*, vol. 7, no. 1, pp. 39–58.

Everhart, K. (2012) 'Cultura-Identidad: The Use of Art in the University of Puerto Rico Student Movement', *Humanity & Society*, vol. 36, no. 3, pp. 198–219.

Ferrell, J. (1996). *Crimes of Style: Urban Graffiti and the Politics of Criminality*. Boston: Northeastern University Press.

Glazer, N. (1979) 'On Subway Graffiti in New York', *Public Interest*, no. 54 (Winter), pp. 3–11.

Green, J. (2003) 'The Writing on the Stall: Gender and Graffiti', *Journal of Language and Social Psychology*, vol. 22, no. 3, pp. 282–96.

Hamdy, B. and Stone, D. (eds) (2013) *Walls of Freedom: Street Art of the Egyptian Revolution*. Berlin: From Here to Fame Publishing.

Hassan, B. A. (2013) 'The Pragmatics of Humor: January 25th Revolution and Occupy Wall Street', *Mediterranean Journal of Social Sciences*, vol. 4, no. 2, pp. 551–62.

Islam, G. (2010) 'Backstage Discourse and the Emergence of Organizational Voices: Exploring Graffiti and Organization', *Journal of Management Inquiry*, vol. 19, no. 3, pp. 246–60.

Keesee-Clancy, K. (2014) 'Graffiti and Street Art Resistance in the Middle East', *Research Discourse*, vol. 5, no. 2, pp. 29–45.

Lee, M. S. (2000) 'Anandan's Wall', *Bad Subjects*, no. 52 (November), http://bad.eserver.org/issues/2000/52/lee.html, accessed 18 May 2013.

Lefebvre, H. (2003) *The Urban Revolution* (R. Bononno, trans.), Minneapolis, MN: University of Minnesota Press.

Living Walls (n.d.) 'Mission Statement', http://livingwallsatl.com/about/mission, accessed 27 December 2016.

McAuliffe, C., and Iveson, K. (2011) 'Art and Crime: Conceptualising Graffiti in the City', *Geography Compass*, vol. 5, no. 3, pp. 128–43.

Macdonald, N. (2001) *The Graffiti Subculture: Youth, Masculinity, and Identity in London and New York*, New York: Palgrave.

Manco, T. (2002) *Stencil Graffiti*, New York: Thames & Hudson.

Miladi, N. (2016), 'Social Media and Social Change', *Digest of the Middle East Studies*, vol. 25, no. 1, pp. 36–51.

Mitchell, D. (2003) *The Right to the City: Social Justice and the Fight for Public Space*, London: The Guilford Press.

Papaioannou, T. and Olivos H. E. (2013) 'Cultural Identity and Social Media in the Arab Spring: Collective Goals in the Use of Facebook in the Libyan Context', *Journal of Arab & Muslim Media Research*, vol. 6, no. 2, pp. 99–144.

Parry, W. (2011) *Against the Wall: The Art of Resistance in Palestine*. Chicago: Laurence Hill Books.

Rane, H. and Salem, S. (2012) 'Social Media, Social Movement and the Diffusion of Ideas in the Arab Uprisings', *Journal of International Communication*, vol. 18, no. 1, pp. 97–111.

Sorensen, M. L. (2008) 'Humor as a Serious Strategy of Nonviolent Resistance to Oppression', *Peace & Change*, vol. 33, no. 2, pp. 167–90.

Tripp, C. (2013) *The Power and the People, Paths of Resistance in the Middle East*, Cambridge: Cambridge University Press.

Walls Project (n.d., a) 'Who We Are', http://thewallsproject.org/about, accessed 27 December 2016.

Walls Project (n.d., b) 'Events', http://thewallsproject.org/events-2, accessed 27 December 2016.

26

LEAKTIVISM AND ITS DISCONTENTS

Athina Karatzogianni

Introduction

With the appearance of Anonymous and WikiLeaks from 2006 onwards, the past decade has witnessed the unstoppable acceleration and proliferation of what has been as a form of whistle-blowing plugged straight into twenty-first century, information-age global politics: what Micah White (2016) dubbed 'leaktivism' and Gabriella Coleman (2017) called 'the public interest hack (PIH)'. Between 2015 and 2017, the DNC Leaks, DCLeaks, and the Panama Leaks follow the trend set by WikiLeaks (Brevini *et al.* 2017) to global prominence in 2010, and Edward Snowden (2013) as significant examples of what is fast becoming the decade of 'leaktivism'. In normative terms, the 'internet' is used to obtain, leak and spread confidential documents with political ram-ifications, with the aim to expose corruption, wrongdoing and inequality, potentially enhancing accountability in the democratic process, through greater transparency. Coleman provides a typology and then an excellent brief genealogy of this in 'The Public Interest Hack' (2017) in the *Hacks, Leaks and Breaches* issue she co-edited with Christopher Kelty for the journal *LIMN*, exploring 'how are hacks, leaks and breaches transforming our world, creating new collectives, and changing our understanding of security and politics' (Coleman & Kelty 2017).

The purpose of this chapter is certainly in the spirit of that exploration, but in this case focus-ing on the politics of specific instances of leaktivism. Providing typology, overall history and in-depth empirical cases is not in the scope of the discussion here. They are sure to be analyzed and published in the extensive academic scholarship of the future. Here I want to point to central issues and themes in leaktivism, which emerged in the examination of cases in my own scholar-ship (Karatzogianni 2015), in order to cut through the fog of vast amounts of knowledge gener-ated by information from large volumes of empirical data. This approach could zoom directly into the core themes and debates they bring to the fore, or are likely to dominate the politics of digital media, and in turn, the impact of digital media on global politics.

Transparency versus secrecy, openness versus control

Data leaks bring out new information in an accelerated hybrid media environment; however, the ethical and ideological debates, tactics and targets of leaktivism are, by all accounts, not new at all. The demands, tactics and politics of whistleblowers, leaktivists or public interest hackers are as old and modernist as politics back in the twentieth century, if not before: transparency, participation, power, democracy, equality, anti-corruption, reform, revolution, insurgency, propaganda, information warfare, espionage and so on. Nevertheless, these actors are operating in a highly hybrid media environment, which is unprecedentedly vast, voluminous, networked, global and moreover corporatized and controlled by global trusted networks (Karatzogianni & Gak 2015). A case in point, the biggest leak so far: Panama Papers, or, as was later adopted after protests from the Panamanian government, the Mossack Fonseca Papers (released 2015), belonging to the law firm and corporate service provider Mossack Fonseca, involves 11.5 million leaked documents and 214,488 offshore entities. An activist calling themselves 'John Doe' leaked the papers to Bastian Obermayer from *Süddeutsche Zeitung* (SZ) and explained his motivation was inequality and the injustices their contents described. SZ requested the help of the International Consortium of Investigative Journalists (ICIJ), and eventually 107 media organizations from 80 countries collaborated to bring stories out starting from spring 2016. In terms of size at 2.6 terabytes, this is the biggest leak historically. It is also yet another example (with the WikiLeaks and Snowden affairs) of the transformations that journalism is undergoing in terms of extensive use of data software tools and the transnational collaboration involved. One needs to read a minimum of 100 pages before grasping only a very basic understanding of actors, relationships and elites in the countries involved in the truly vast amount of documentation leaked (https://panamapapers.icij.org).

Although the Mossack Fonseca is, in terms of size, the biggest leak in history, implicating elites around the globe, to my analysis undoubtedly the most visible and continuous impact in the arena of cyber conflict and global politics is from WikiLeaks, especially starting from the 'Collateral Damage' video in the summer of 2010 (on WikiLeaks's ideological and organization conflicts and the politics of emotion, see Karatzogianni 2012). We found in examining scholarship between 2010 and 2012 (Karatzogianni & Robinson 2014) that in international relations (IR) and related disciplines, including diplomacy studies, the main focus is on *transparency* versus *secrecy*: the ethics of whistleblowing versus national security, the impact of leaks on the 'war on terror' and American foreign policy. In disciplines more closely aligned to the social such as culture, media, communication studies and sociology, the major debate is between *openness* versus *control*: here, issues include the relationship between WikiLeaks and the hacker ethic, the constraint of overwhelming state power, the emergence of a global digital public sphere, the changing relationships between old and new media, and the emergence of shifts in social relationships marked by the current wave of social movements and their use of ICTs. These differences emerge for a particular reason: the framing of the state–network conflict through the gaze of the state – or from an interpretive standpoint framed by the attempt to understand the social: the people's standpoint.

The two debates, transparency versus secrecy and openness versus control, tend to dominate discussions on leaktivism throughout the WikiLeaks saga and polarize transnational publics, even providing one of the first examples of affective politics and the polarization of global public opinion over both the organization, and particularly the radically opposite significations and outpour of emotion surrounding Julian Assange as hero or traitor, in mobilizations and petitions in support of his release by a wide network of actors, and even in products of popular culture such as films, books and documentaries (Karatzogianni 2012).

The following section illustrates how these two core debates (secrecy versus transparency and openness versus closure) influence the framing of ethics and tactics, and produce unintended consequences for actors and relationships surrounding leaktivism. To illustrate my argument, I refer to DCLeaks, and WikiLeaks' DNCLeaks and CIALeaks. These specific empirical examples are chosen because there is a consistent thematic on intelligence, secrecy and transparency, democratic accountability, propaganda and sabotage in global politics involving prominent actors in the United States and Russia, as well as proxy countries across the East–West Cold War axis.

Key leaks 2016–2017

DCLeaks

DCLeaks broke out in June 2016 with leaks of military and government emails in the United States, which the American intelligence community and private security firms attributed to Russian intelligence undermining the 2016 US elections. DCLeaks' purpose as stated on their site is 'to find out and tell you the truth about US decision-making process as well as about the key elements of American political life', while they describe themselves as 'the American hacktivists who respect and appreciate freedom of speech, human rights and government of the people' (dcleaks.com).

The leaks involved 300 emails from Republican targets and information about 200 Democratic party targets. Portfolios included Bill and Hillary Clinton, DNC official William Rinehart, former NATO commander General Philip Breedlove and a Democratic Party-linked PR professional called Sarah Hamilton. US Gen. Philip Breedlove had already retired and was formerly the top military commander of the North Atlantic Treaty Organization; emails from his personal account show him complaining that the Obama administration wasn't paying enough attention to European security, particularly in relation to Ukraine. Breedlove told CNN that the emails were stolen as part of a state-sponsored intelligence operation.

Self-defined on their website as 'a new level project aimed to analyze and publish a large amount of emails from top-ranking officials and their influence agents all over the world' (twitter.com/DCLeaks), initially it was thought to be a right-wing political-opposition researcher outlet and not hackers/hacktivists, because of how the site and its digital structure were set up. However, in subsequent analysis what dominated global media discourse is that it was another front being used by Russian intelligence. Analysis from cybersecurity firms linked DCLeaks to both 'Guccifer 2.0' (a hacker calling himself Guccifer 2.0 and purporting to be Romanian initially took credit for the DNC hack; that claim was viewed sceptically, in part because the hacker didn't appear to speak Romanian) and Fancy Bear (a Kremlin-affiliated hacking group subsequently thought to be connected to the DNC Leaks). WikiLeaks founder Julian Assange said at the time that there's 'no proof whatsoever' that Moscow was involved. DCLeaks.com was registered in April 2016, and many of the documents were posted in early June. A DCLeaks administrator, who identified himself by email as Steve Wanders, didn't respond to written questions, including why much of the material focuses on Russia or Russian foreign-policy interests. Cyberintelligence firms have linked that hacking group to the GRU, Russia's military intelligence service, whose Moscow headquarters is nicknamed the Aquarium. Three private security groups have linked the DNC incursion to that group and another Russian hacking group associated with the FSB, the country's civilian intelligence agency.

According to domain records, the dcleaks.com address was registered in mid-April via a small web hosting company in Romania. The site itself traces back to an IP address in Kuala Lumpur, Malaysia. DCLeaks corresponded with *The Smoking Gun* (*TSG*) via a Gmail account in the name of 'Steve Wanders'. Since being provided a password by 'Guccifer 2.0', *TSG* has monitored DCLeaks for further evidence that the site is being used as a cut-out for the cabal behind the DNC hacking and the 'spear phishing' directed at Clinton campaign workers (we will return to this DNC and DC problem of connection below).

The same summer of 2016, DCLeaks released 2,576 files from George Soros's Open Society Foundations, laying out strategies, plans and internal communication from the foundation's international activities. The most prominent leak from Soros's Open Society Foundations included internal files that totalled a significant 1.51 GB in size with funding reports, contracts and confidential briefing memos. The foundation defines itself as working 'to build vibrant and tolerant democracies whose governments are accountable and open to the participation of all people' (www.opensocietyfoundations.org/about/mission-values). The information appears to date back to somewhere between the 2008 and 2009 timeframe, and has more current documentation up to 2016 as well. The leak contains internal memos, end of year reports, grants, contracts, agenda details and biographies of all staff and board members. In the case of Soros's Open Society, hackers stole a trove of documents after accessing the foundation's internal intranet, a system called Karl, according to a person familiar with its internal investigation. On 3 August 2016, the DCLeaks. com Twitter account tweeted 'Check George Soros's OSF plans to counter Russian policy and traditional values', attaching a screenshot of a $500,000 budget request for an Open Society pro-gramme designed to counter Russian influence among European democracies.

DCLeaks offered nothing about Hillary Clinton, Bernie Sanders or Donald Trump, con-sidering reports that Soros has donated or committed more than $25 million to boost Hillary Clinton and other Democratic candidates and causes, according to Federal Election Commission records. DCLeaks notes that Soros is 'named as the architect and sponsor of almost every revo-lution and coup around the world for the last 25 years'. In a Facebook post, the site reported that the hacked documents revealed Soros's plans to support opposition movements in Ukraine, Russia, Georgia, Armenia and other countries 'where the United States desire to promote their interests' (Bastone 2017).

WikiLeaks and DNCLeaks

In July 2016, WikiLeaks released the DNCLeaks with two publications of 44,053 emails and 17,761 attachments (wikileaks.org/dnc-emails) covering the period between January 2015 and May 2016 from the accounts of seven key figures in the Democratic National Convention: Communications Director Luis Miranda (10,520 emails), National Finance Director Jordon Kaplan (3,799 emails), Finance Chief of Staff Scott Comer (3,095 emails), Finance Director of Data & Strategic Initiatives Daniel Parrish (1,742 emails), Finance Director Allen Zachary (1,611 emails), Senior Advisor Andrew Wright (938 emails) and Northern California Finance Director Robert (Erik) Stowe (751 emails).

Several security vendors, including CrowdStrike, ThreatConnect and Fidelis, have looked at both the Democratic Party (DNC) breach and the Democratic Congressional Campaign Committee (DCCC) breach, and said that the same Russian group was behind both attacks. The timing of the DCCC and the Soros data published on DCLeaks is causing speculation about the connection of Guccifer 2.0 with DCLeaks, although it has been denied by DCLeaks and WikiLeaks. Several security groups have theorized that 'Guccifer 2.0' is a Russian inven-tion, a hype man tasked with publicizing criminal acts that were actually committed by skilled government hacking groups. While he has described himself in emails as an 'unknown hacker with a laptop' and a foe of 'all the illuminati and rich clans which try to rule the governments', Guccifer 2.0 has acted more like a press flack, promising 'exclusives' and pushing journalists to do stories based on stolen documents carrying little news value. Guccifer 2.0 told *The Smoking Gun* that the material would be available through DCLeaks, a web site he described as a 'sub project' of WikiLeaks. Assange denied any connection with DCLeaks.

WikiLeaks and CIA leaks

In March 2017, WikiLeaks released CIA Vault 7 and continued with steady releases of what they claimed was only 1 per cent of the CIA material it had available, saying that the CIA had 'lost control' of an archive of hacking methods circulated 'among former US government hackers and contractors in an unauthorized manner, one of whom has provided WikiLeaks with portions of the archive' (see 'Year Zero', wikileaks.org/ciav7p1/cms/index.html).

The first part of the WikiLeaks Vault 7 series of 8,761 documents allege how CIA's malware targets iOS and Android, Windows, OSX and Linux routers using USB sticks, software on CDs, and turning the Samsung F8000 Smart TV into a listening device by putting the TV into 'fake-off' mode. Two stand out: 'Fine Dining', a questionnaire identifying which tools can be used for which operation, and 'Hive', a customized malware suite of implants for Windows, Solaris and MikroTik used in internet routers and Linux platforms, and a Listening Post (LP)/Command and Control (C2) infrastructure to communicate with these implants. This explosive development means that the US government is now well into leaking-like-a-paper-bag territory. The impact of the historically continuous competition between the CIA, the NSA and FBI, and the exploitation of the internal feuds in the intelligence community in the US by the Trump administration means that many more leaks are yet to come. The fact that US intelligence agencies formally accused Russia of intervening in the US elections to help Trump get elected (after the 2,000 emails hacked from the Clinton campaign which WikiLeaks released) and the war between Trump and the so-called 'deep state' are symptoms of stark divisions and polarization in the US government, and exacerbated by the political conflicts, well inside the intelligence communities.

The sacrifice of legal and ethical principles to the madness of internal intelligence and political wars is crystal clear, as well as how impossible it is to safeguard against leaks in such an environment. The first problem is CIA's Remote Devices Branch's (wikileaks.org/ciav7p1/cms/page_20251151.html) UMBRAGE group (wikileaks.org/ciav7p1/cms/page_2621751.html), where the CIA maintains a library of stolen malware produced in other countries. This malware can be used to disguise and misdirect attribution of where attacks have originated from in 'false flag' operations. This is feeding into theories that US intelligence services might have engineered such an operation to point to Russia as the culprit of the meddling with the elections, as it falls into the hands of the Trump administration, which denies vehemently collaboration with WikiLeaks or Russia during the US elections. According to WikiLeaks, Tradecraft DO's and DON'Ts (wikileaks.org/ciav7p1/cms/page_14587109.html) contains CIA rules on how its malware should be written to avoid fingerprints implicating the 'CIA, US government, or its witting partner companies' in 'forensic review'.

A secondary complication revolves around the commitment of the US government to the Vulnerabilities Equities Process. Tech companies lobbied for and won the disclosure of all pervasive vulnerabilities after 2010. The CIA keeping knowledge of these exploits to itself means that tech companies will not fix them and systems can be open to hacking by other governments, non-state actors and cybercriminals. This puts tech companies yet again, as with the Snowden revelations, in a place of mistrust against the US government at a sensitive point in the country's history of fake news and accusations of bugs in the Trump Tower against the Obama administration. It does not matter if vulnerabilities have been fixed, as tech giants were too quick to reassure: the fact they were kept in the dark and were left exposed continuously is a significant break of any trust left in their own government. It also means that any cyberweapons used by the CIA at any point in time can be exploited by third parties everywhere and anywhere. Cyberweapons infecting machines in the wild are no longer classified.

The impact of internal intelligence wars and their exploitation by the Trump administration is a great big mess for the US and its relationships with other intelligence agencies. MI5 faced leaks that it allegedly devised 'Weeping Angel', which transforms a Samsung TV model F8000 into a listening device when it appears to be switched off and sends the recording to a CIA server. CIA also uses the US consulate in Frankfurt as a covert base for its hackers covering Europe, the Middle East and Africa, and the whole world knows.

Leaktivism's discontents

Leaktivism puts intelligence agencies in an impossible position of forced transparency, which has transformed business as usual in the spy business, ever since the first WikiLeaks documents on Iraq and Afghanistan, with Snowden's death nail documenting the pervasive complete structural metadata acquisition by the NSA. Ultimately, the US has been unable to protect its secrets since 2010, and this puts the intelligence communities and US allies in a world where secrecy is now impossible, even when devices are switched off. It places individual citizens in a world where privacy is a victim of longstanding political domestic and international conflicts and intelligence predatory cyberwar tactics with no accountability or oversight, no effective action to get a grip on leaks and where tech companies are the last to know about vulnerabilities on their systems, like the cheated husband. It is a world of hack or be hacked.

The political economy of the digital environments involved is significant here. This is a particular problem in the articulation of digital politics: the process of political disenfranchisement brought about by corporations looking to profit, governments looking to regulate information flows and co-opted groups in civil society looking to appropriate the legitimate concerns of users for their own political and financial subsistence. The distinct features of this quasi-totalitarianism include: the monopoly of digital planning on surveillance that rests on back-channel and secret communication between government, tech corporate elites and, sometimes, NGOs; the use of civil society NGOs as mechanisms for circumventing democratic processes; 'enterprise association' politics, aimed at ensuring that the dual goal of state (security) and capital (profit) continues unabated and with little unaccountability; the unprecedented scope offered by total structural data acquisition on the part of western intelligence matrixes; the persecution and prosecution of journalists, whistle-blowers and transparency actors outside the scope of civil society groups; and the significant if insufficient contestation by members of the public concerning the infringement on civil liberties (see Karatzogianni & Gak 2015).

This *ménage à trois* of 'trusted' global networks – governments, corporations and NGOs – are holding a de facto mandate, and effective planning power, in the digital field. They clothe themselves in a bastardized version of publicness, and in this guise usurp the political agency of individual members of society. In fact, these three supposedly trusted networks constitute an oligopoly that dominates the space in which governance is negotiated. They relegate the individual to a place of marginality, from where they are only able to address the threat of surveilling agents to their privacy from a position of acute precariousness. It is the individual who has to pay for digital equipment, access and their own necessary digital literacy, thereby funding the processes of purchase, connectivity and training; and it is also the individual who has to acquire the necessary skills and software to protect their privacy in the digital homes that are built by tech elites and surveilled by governments (in the name of security) and corporations (for the sake of profit). The individual citizen is put in a rather impossible situation, in which they must simultaneously procure the tools for the enforcement of the legal guarantees presumably held by the state to protect their rights, and at the same time develop tools to enforce them. In this environment – in which the state undermines privacy in the name of security, commercial interests collude with the state while offering false shelter, and civil society groups hijack the very voice of political engagement – the individual has only one choice: hack or be hacked.

It is the precarious state of rights in the face of these developments that is a particularly thorny problem when individuals and groups engage in leaktivism or public interest hacks to create awareness about a particular ethical problem in the digital political economy, security, intelligence gathering or digital policing.

A case in point: Edward Snowden's leaks of hundreds of thousands of National Security Agency documents. Notwithstanding the conspiratorial tone, the response by the group Anonymous to Snowden's attempt to put surveillance under public scrutiny shows quite poignantly the reaction to the revelations by movements instinctively opposed to quasi-totalitarian models of the digital public sphere:

> Your privacy and freedoms are slowly being taken from you, in closed door meetings, in laws buried in bills, and by people who are supposed to be protecting you … Download these documents, share them, mirror them, don't allow them to make them disappear. Spread them wide and far. Let these people know, that we will not be silenced, that we will not be taken advantage of, and that we are not happy about this unwarranted, unnecessary, unethical spying of our private lives, for the monetary gain of the 1%.
>
> *www.facebook.com/anonymouslv/posts/521076614608161*

In its communiqués, Anonymous often portrays itself as a bearer of the values of civil association, as protector of the fellowship of civility. Understandably, the articulation of this un-trusted network's commitment is advanced in moral terms, and more often than not they present themselves as a new surreptitious actor who engages in global political vigilantism in order to mount resistance against surveillance, censorship, perceived injustice and corruption, and in solidarity with movements fighting repressive and authoritarian governments. Anonymous and Snowden serve to demarcate the space of resistance to the hidden mechanics of thoroughgoing political penetration of the social, and in so doing reveal the totalitarian mechanisms which they each claim to resist.

As I wrote with Martin Gak in 'Hack or be Hacked' (2015), leaktivism is a tactic resisting state and corporate actors' influence; that influence, however, can be also co-opted by those same actors. NGOs are perhaps one of the most interesting cases concerning the usurpation and concealment of corporate and government interests under the cloak of civil association. The explicit argument here is that the corporate funding of NGOs has an impact on leaktivist ideological directions and impact of leaks. Certainly the leaktivism wars do not just impact governments and intelligence, but target or involve in one way or another corporate-funded civil-society actors. Besides the leaks which set out to harm Soros, which were mentioned above, to illustrate my argumentation we can turn to eBay founder Pierre Omidyar, who eventually set up *The Intercept*, which published unredacted Snowden documents. Having begun his philanthropic activities in the late 1990s, by early 2014 Omidyar had given out $1 billion to all sorts of organizations and projects. In 2013 alone, his organizations gave out grants of $225 million. As well as personal donations, its funding is organized through three organizations: the Omidyar Network Fund, HopeLabs and Humanity United. Michael Gentilucci of Inside Philanthropy has argued that: 'We're dealing with an archipelago here, not a solid land mass, and the overarching entity is The Omidyar Group.' NGOs funded by Omidyar include Change. org; Center on Democracy, Development, and the Rule of Law; Global Integrity; Fundación Ciudadano Inteligente; Global Voices; Media Development Investment Fund; The Open Data Institute; Open Government Partnership; Project on Government Oversight (POGO); Sunlight Foundation; The Transparency and Accountability Initiative; The Foundation for Ecological Security; the Endeavor Foundation; and Ashoka. Omidyar's American record includes contributions to the presidential campaign of Wesley Clark, and he is a co-investor with the CIA's venture capital firm IN-Q-TEL and Booz Allen Hamilton (an NSA subcontractor and former employer of Edward Snowden). Omidyar was the man who eventually became the guardian of the Snowden papers. In 2013, with a pledge of $250 million dollars, Omidyar had started a media network under the name First Look Media. His first three hires were Glenn Greenwald, Laura Poitras and Jeremy Scahill. In February 2014 First Look Media spun off a second media structure under the name of *The Intercept*. This online publication was devised in order to publish the unredacted Snowden documents and to 'produce fearless, adversarial journalism across a wide range of issues'.

To be explicit, the main discontent with leaktivism is that corporate-funded leaktivist organizations of various descriptions tend to be involved in aspects of disrupting government intelligence, as well as other civil society organizations funded by either corporate or government actors.

Conclusion

In synopsis, leaktivist individuals and/or organizations present themselves as new surreptitious actors who engage in global political vigilantism, in order to mount resistance against surveillance, censorship, perceived injustice and corruption, and in solidarity with movements fighting repressive and authoritarian governments. Anonymous and Snowden serve to demarcate the space of resistance to the hidden mechanics of thoroughgoing political penetration of the social, and in so doing reveal the totalitarian mechanisms which they each claim to resist. Furthermore, leaktivism can have devastating timing and can partially influence elections, to the extent that in the public discourse leaktivism is seen as both enhancing democracy by holding governments and corporations accountable and enforcing transparency, and at the same time disrupting the democratic process, when the leaks are manipulated to influence public opinion and voting behaviour, as witnessed with the phenomenon of election-timed leaks occurring in the US, and subsequently in France and the UK during 2017. Lastly, to use a metaphor, the two faces of leaktivism – enhancing versus disrupting democracy – are historically continuous with debates observed from the very start of WikiLeaks in 2010: the openness versus closure, stemming from social and communication fields, and transparency versus control debates, stemming from international relations and security fields, continue to characterize the controversies and discontents surrounding the phenomenon.

References

Bastone, W. (2017) 'Tracking the Hackers Who Hit DNC, Clinton', *The Smoking Gun*, 12 August, http://www.thesmokinggun.com/documents/investigation/tracking-russian-hackers-638295, accessed 11 September 2017.

Brevini, B., Hintz, A. and McCurdy, P. (eds) (2013) *Beyond WikiLeaks: Implications for the Future of Communications, Journalism and Society*. New York: Palgrave Macmillan.

Coleman, G. (2017) 'The Public Interest Hack', in G. Coleman and C. Kelty (eds) *Hacks, Leaks, and Breaches*, *LIMN*, no. 8 http://limn.it/the-public-interest-hack, accessed 11 September 2017.

Coleman, G. and Kelty, C. (eds) (2017) *Hacks, Leaks, and Breaches*, *LIMN*, no. 8, http://limn.it/issue/08, accessed 11 September 2017.

Karatzogianni, A. (2010) 'Blame It on the Russians: Tracking the Portrayal of Russians during Cyber Conflict Incidents', *Digital Icons: Studies in Russian, Eurasian and Central European New Media*, vol. 4, pp. 127–50.

Karatzogianni, A. (2012) 'WikiLeaks Affects: Ideology, Conflict and the Revolutionary Virtual', in A. Karatzogianni and A. Kuntsman (eds) *Digital Cultures and the Politics of Emotion: Feelings, Affect and Technological Change*. Basingstoke, UK: Palgrave Macmillan, pp. 52–73.

Karatzogianni, A. (2015) *Firebrand Waves of Digital Activism 1994–2014: The Rise and Spread of Hacktivism and Cyberconflict*. Basingstoke, UK: Palgrave Macmillan.

Karatzogianni, A. and Robinson, A. (2014) 'Digital Prometheus: WikiLeaks, the State-Network Dichotomy and the Antinomies of Academic Reason', *International Journal of Communication*, vol. 8, Feature 1–20, pp. 2704–17, http://ijoc.org/index.php/ijoc/issue/view/10#more4, accessed 11 September 2017.

Karatzogianni, A. and Gak, M. (2015) 'Hack or Be Hacked: The Quasi-Totalitarianism of Global Trusted Networks', *New Formations: A Journal of Culture, Theory, Politics*, no. 84/85, pp. 130–147, http://www.lwbooks.co.uk/journals/newformations/issue/nf8485.html.

White, M. (2016) 'The Panama Papers: Leaktivism's Coming of Age', *The Guardian*, 5 April, https://www.theguardian.com/news/commentisfree/2016/apr/05/panama-papers-leak-activism-leaktivism, accessed 11 September 2017.

27

COUNTER-CARTOGRAPHY

Mapping power as collective practice

André Mesquita (translated by Victoria Esteves)

How can collective mapping practices help artists and social movements to build broader communal and popular collaboration, to produce autonomous knowledge? Subverted by use, cartography as a purely specialized, academic and scientific activity, turned solely inwards towards its own discipline's issues and problems, has been radically changed in the last decades through the actions of artist-activists who have dedicated themselves to mapping out conflicts, power networks and invisible geographies. Maps became potential tools of resistance and free distribution of images, methodologies, critical reflections and concepts.

Traditionally speaking, a map is an instrument of power that has been used for centuries by governments, empires, armies, churches, intelligence agencies, think tanks and companies as a way of administering territories, populations and knowledge. Naturalizing a map as a 'mirror' of the world implies affirming it as true and impartial, as if its image were an exact representation of reality (Harley 2001: 35). If maps are reproduced and affirmed in such a way, it is only because there are institutions that have worked for centuries to make it so – specialists, political and academic elites. In general, the maps created by such institutions and agents defend values that are directly linked to surveillance, authoritative and governmental interests.

The myth of scientific naturalization of maps leads us to believe and accept that their images depict the world exactly as it is, when in reality these are cultural or even individual creations that incorporate rhetorical manipulations (persuasion, induction, seduction or deception), distortions, errors, points of view and values (Lippard 1997: 78; Jacob 2006: 6). By using text, lines, colours and iconography as a way of indicating empirical observations, geographic accidents, lived experiences, itineraries and social, historical and economic data, maps appear to be neutral in order to hide their underlying interests. Behind a map lies a mesh of power relations with specifications that are imposed by a particular individual, by the market and/or by State bureaucracy. The powers at play are not always clear. Projection and scale manipulation, intentional distortion of contents, or territorial absences are conducted with diverse goals – from state secrets to blank spots that conceal strategic places (military bases, airports, laboratories, prisons, etc.). Maps involve presences and absences; they build knowledge over a territory in order to dominate it (Harley 2001: 63). Maps *lie*, even with all the 'transparency' and 'exactness' that new location tools supposedly offer (GPS, Google Maps, etc.), but which nevertheless reveal a great opacity of interests and limitations that legitimize a logistic and militaristic view over the entire planet.

If the state uses cartography to occupy, destroy or control, then why not use the cartographic tools towards social struggles, subsequently valuing an autonomous and collaborative process? Instead of simply accepting the authority of imperial and military maps, why not make cartography a collective and communal practice capable of mapping systems of oppression, whilst also making critical knowledge accessible to all? It is necessary to decode the capitalist machine in order to intervene, and thus situate our procedures and operations. Cartography must leave its academic field and its positivist readings; it must go beyond the idea of representation itself. Art must leave its self-reflective and isolated field in order to gain strength and competence. It is fundamental to combine cartography, activist and artistic practices in order to produce tools of analysis, research and action.

Counter-cartography

Mappings made by artistic activist collectives and social movements engender experiences of production of knowledge. They also multiply different views of the world and help in the guidance, observation and intervention in disputes, conflicts and power relations. To resist capital's grip on culture, the instrumentation of the forms of expression, and the regulation of the forces of cooperation that tend to be absorbed, captured and neutralized by business, military and commercial mechanisms, requires both the production of new imagined radicals and possibilities of political autonomy and shared invention, such as the creation of conceptual and analytical tools that allow to visualize the ever sophisticated capitalist structures, causing new oppositions and engagements.

The artistic and activist appropriation of cartographies can transform them into 'political machines that work on power relations' (Institute for Applied Autonomy 2007: 30), thus supplying alternative interpretations of history and spaces, as pointed out by the collective Institute for Applied Autonomy (IAA). For IAA, the emergence of such political machines may be understood as 'tactical cartographies': 'spatial representations that confront power, promote social justice and are intended to have operational value (as an example of operational value, think of maps used by military planners)' (Institute for Applied Autonomy 2007: 29). This idea is linked to the use of new DIY technologies regarding social issues, named in the 1990s as 'tactical media' (Garcia & Lovink 1997). This term was inspired by Michel de Certeau's definition of 'tactic' featured in his book *The Practice of Everyday Life* (1980):

> A tactic is a calculated action, determined by the absence of a proper locus. No delimitation of an exteriority, then, provides it with the condition necessary for autonomy. The space of a tactic is the space of the other. Thus it must play on and with a terrain imposed on it and organized by the law of a foreign power.
>
> *De Certeau 1984: 36–37*

Tactical media, according to David Garcia and Geert Lovink, have allowed individuals and groups that have been oppressed or excluded from the wider culture to produce a new dissenting aesthetic, employing temporary and open situations with a wide variety of goals. In 'The ABC of Tactical Media' (1997), Garcia and Lovink reassure that the producer or consumer may obtain potential by using texts and artefacts that surround us through even more creative and rebellious methods. For these authors,

> [De Certeau] described the process of consumption as a set of tactics by which the weak make use of the strong. He characterized the rebellious user (a term he preferred

to consumer) as tactical and the presumptuous producer (in which he included authors, educators, curators and revolutionaries) as strategic. Setting up this dichotomy allowed him to produce a vocabulary of tactics rich and complex enough to amount to a distinctive and recognizable aesthetic. An existential aesthetic. An aesthetic of Poaching, tricking, reading, speaking, strolling, shopping, desiring. Clever tricks, the hunter's cunning, manoeuvres, polymorphic situations, joyful discoveries, poetic as well as warlike.

Garcia & Lovink 1997

I consider that the mapping practices exercised by artistic activist collectives, such as Counter-Cartographies Collective (US – www.countercartographies.org), Bureau d'Études (France – bureaudetudes.org) and Iconoclasistas (Argentina – www.iconoclasistas.net), re-appropriate in a poetic and skilful manner dynamics, concepts, images and techniques commonly used by the military, academics and governments. Defying the interests of cartographic domination is an act that reconfigures the articulations between political action and forms of intervention in multiple scales (spatial, semiotic, social, etc.), considering here the concept of *intervention*, according to Critical Art Ensemble, as 'the appropriation of material, knowledge, and territory for the purpose of undermining or revealing the authoritative and repressive structures and vectors that produce and manage a given territory' (in Thompson & Sholette 2004: 117). In practice, the tactical appropriation of the means of production and the means of circulation of maps from such collectives occur in a form that is free and independent from official institutions. Iconoclasistas, Bureau d'Études and Counter-Cartographies Collective rely on the user-friendly aspect of graphic design *software* to create lines, symbols, pictograms, texts and map keys, as well as the benefit of internet access in order to finesse their research. The political potential of networks is explored by these collectives in the electronic distribution of their projects in websites, blogs and digital communities. Printed versions may be paid for through art show budgets or be self-funded, allowing the maps to circulate in autonomous spaces, schools, workshops, open classes, protests and activist meetings, handed out for free or passed on among people. This allows immediate public access, open and unlimited to these works. Within a political and anticapitalist leaning, the maps from these collectives invert the sovereignty of a cartography of control in order to create *counter-cartographies*.

Counter-cartographies are understood here as maps and practices that challenge the normative maps and break with the scientific, military and specialized tradition of cartography. Thus counter-cartographies question the conventional models of maps provided by states and elites, and seek to highlight their power relations. These practices may act tactically over the time of action and strategically over the analysis of networks and spaces, in order to generate bottom-up social change. Deconstructing the political and economic logic of mechanisms, organizations and social hierarchies to reveal contradictions and invisibilities is one of its primordial tasks. It is that kind of experiment that also turns art political: not through its approach of a 'political matter', but because its sensitive and intuitive expression is able to make explicit the violence and conflicts that are often hidden, whilst also confronting the influence of official know-how. A counter-cartography is less of a visual object that accumulates information and more of an opportunity of going beyond the representation in traditional maps in order to create dialogues and discoveries. It is as much a critique of how maps work as it is a means of generating new ways of researching, collaborating and organizing (Stallmann 2012: 5). Counter-cartography is a key element in the repertoire of the artistic and activist forms of struggle; it is a tool within multiple tactical actions and artistic interventions performed in public spaces, available to use according to specific situations and confrontations. The counter-cartographies featured in this chapter value the social and political organization of life inserted between limits and demarcations, through analysis, experiences and accounts about physical and subjective borders, both visible and invisible. They reflect the strength of cooperation between collectives, artists, communities, movements and temporary coalitions, originating a joint work of research and methodologies of creation, exhibition and construction of critical narratives.

Beyond the border, biopoetics

When we begin to form our own mental maps about capitalism, we ask ourselves if these same maps may or may not correspond to reality and if they are capable of incorporating even more complex, invisible and abstract relations. How may a global society that is networked, militarized and efficient in commercially capturing our bodies and desires be visualized? If social mobilizations reappear as places of indignation, confrontation and change, in what ways can counter-cartography lead to an active participation of individuals, spacing actions that allow the reconfiguration of the world and imagining an alternative future? According to Mezzadra and Neilson (2013: vii):

> As many scholars have noted, the border has inscribed itself at the center of contemporary experience. We are confronted not only with a multiplication of different types of borders but also with the reemergence of the deep heterogeneity of the semantic field of the border. Symbolic, linguistic, cultural, and urban boundaries are no longer articulated in fixed ways by the geopolitical border.

Boundaries and limits may be understood when we cross the imaginary line of power materially represented by the police force present at a demonstration, or when details are revealed in our bodies, documents, belongings forcefully x-rayed, inspected, conferred and registered by the taxing security control in airport immigration areas. For Mezzadra and Neilson (2013: 3), borders are 'complex social institutions, which are marked by tensions between practices of border reinforcement and border crossing'.

Maps like the ones produced by Counter-Cartographies Collective (3Cs), formed by Maribel Casas-Cortés, Sebastian Cobarrubias, Craig Dalton, Liz Mason-Deese, John Pickles, Tim Stallmann, Nathan Swanson and Lan Tu, work with perspectives of analysis over the different crossings of official and institutional borders. Although sustained as a research project within a university, it is in the intersection between academic production, militant research and extra-disciplinary activity that their members act. In interviews with students and during workshops, 3Cs produced a *DisOrientation Guide* (www.countercartographies.org/category/disorientation-guides) in 2006 and 2009 apropos its North Carolina University campus, located in the 'Research Triangle' formed by the cities of Durham, Raleigh and Chapel Hill. The guides show diverse maps and diagrams connecting their student struggles in their own institution with demonstrations happening in other countries.

Certainly, it is worth asking what is the impact of those 3Cs maps on an academic community. They are an attempt at introducing the techniques of counter-cartography as activist tools: helping to reformulate the understanding over a territory where people live, study, work and occupy; opening up to a communal space where the insurgent knowledges and individual experiences of intellectual, social and administrative activities can be disseminated; radically politicizing relations and productive forces. Universities are not privileged bubbles, isolated spaces or ivory towers separated from the world: they are instead factories that concentrate flexible work markets, economies of knowledge, corporate research, financial capitalism and gentrification. To intervene and re-symbolize such factories may intensify the potential of a collective engagement, rewriting the limits and boundaries of their struggles.

In May 2010, 3Cs collaborated with the postgraduate students of Queen Mary University in London in order to do a mapping workshop related to governmental politics, the working conditions within campus, immigration cases and resistance movements in England. Collaborators worked together in the processes of research, collection of data and design of *Counter\mapping QMary: finding (y)our way through borders and filters* (www.countercartographies.org/countermapping-queen-mary-university). This resulted in a map that shows the university not only as a factory of knowledge, but also as a border that regulates the entries and exits of bodies and money.

On the *Counter\mapping QMary,* trajectories indicate the arrival of Asian, African and North American students at London's international airports. 3Cs' map is populated by points of protest, occupations and strikes. Lines with information connecting the flux of capital between the English government, banks, universities and economic markets illustrate how the freedom of networks of the centres of power facilitates the circulation of money in a world of financial operations without borders – an antithesis to bottom-up solidary globalization, defended by autonomous movements such as the right to the freedom of movement and the destitution of all migratory control laws. The *Counter\mapping QMary* outlines and texts articulate combinations between map and route, retaking the richness of cartographies with its itineraries. Drawings of airplanes landing in airports are received by sieves, regulating the arrival of students and by grids that denounce the Immigration Removal Centres, built close to English airports. These invisible and apparently neutral operations may now be noted and narrated. *Counter\mapping QMary* questions traditional geopolitical boundaries, which are now submersed by the waters of international bureaucracy, administering a total control over transiting citizens throughout continents. Overleaf the map features a game that invites people to participate in the long way travelled in order to enter academic life. In this way, 3Cs' investigation of academic territory is not separated from action.

What can happen when a multiplicity of artistic and activist machines of expression and resymbolization is converged towards direct action on one of Europe's most powerful borders? In July 2002, the internationally coordinated work among anticapitalist groups, independent media centres and the *noborder* international network (noborder.org/strasbourg) promoted a 'camp without borders' in Strasbourg with discussions, protests and parties over the course of ten days and with the participation of close to three thousand people. The choice of place for the camp was absolutely strategic. Strasbourg is located on the border between France and Germany, and it is where one can find a database with all the details of movements and residences of immigrants throughout Europe, the Schengen Information System (SIS). This database is used by the signatories of the Schengen Agreement – the convention among countries that allows circulation within its territories. SIS controls the security space of these 'open-bordered' countries; however, it collects information of a private nature regarding thousands of individuals for their respective governments. Invisible or diluted, external borders have become virtual and originate a hidden landscape, full of multiplied internal limits and a rigidity of exclusions (Raunig 2007: 245, 256).

With the slogan *no border, no nation,* the camp was organized to make SIS' functions publicly known, undertaking a critical approach regarding the form in which the system's data is used in a discriminatory way in order to reinforce policies of migration control, surveillance and racist laws, and how that information could be redistributed and opened to the general public. The Bureau d'Études collective participated in the *noborder camp* by setting up an infoshop for research and mapping workshops; it also did an en masse distribution of part of an edition of seven thousand copies of a map made especially for the gathering. With the aid of a collaborative group, Bureau d'Études produced *Refuse the Biopolice* (archive.org/details/pdfy-3iAX3hkSno2zKCvX), in order to show 'how an increasingly interconnected network of data gathering systems has been developed and implemented by collusion between specific individuals, transnational corporations, governments, interstate agencies and "civil society" groups', as underlined by the text written by Brian Holmes that featured in the introduction of the counter-map.

The map as a two-dimensional representation of the topographical surface of the earth does not feature in *Refuse the Biopolice* or in most cartographic projects of Bureau d'Études, formed by the conceptual artist duo Léonore Bonaccini and Xavier Fourt. The guidance is cognitive and subjective. To navigate the coordinates of an abstract and uncommon place that is this administered planet, conventional compasses are not compatible or sufficient. Bureau d'Études' organizational maps (or organograms) help the reader to navigate (and to get lost too) over a social and symbolic complexity that expresses a reflective and denouncing content, represented by pictograms identifying states, corporations, agencies, families and individuals. For Bureau d'Études, the organogram is a 'figurative rendering of social space, with its actors (institutional, economic, social, religious, personal) and its constitutive relations and interactions (administrative, strategic, friendly, financial, religious, political, etc.)' (Bureau d'Études 2003).

Bureau d'Études maps and analyzes exactly the social, jurisdictional, economic and institutional webs of contemporary capitalism, elaborating counter-cartographies of these powers, and distributing them freely to social movements. Thus, you may read *Refuse the Biopolice* by imagining your three maps overlapping in order to understand how networks of influence connect to systems of identification and surveillance and the prison-industrial complex. Alternatively, you may decipher it as a small atlas divided into three maps that accumulate the history of a global police, invisible to most citizens around the world, in a diagrammatic form. The networks of influence map is dominated by pictograms of families and individuals that are connected to secret networks or societies composed by the political elite, governments, international public organizations, industrial companies, think tanks and banks connected through administrative, financial and technical lines. European nations are interlinked to immigration detention centres, situated mostly in Britain. A powerful group of tourist services is directly associated to a detention centre in France. As shown on the map, two hotel floors belonging to them have been used by the French government with the intent to detain foreigners. English security companies also finance such centres through governmental aid. A list informs the reader of the places and addresses of detention centres in Europe, and there are partial accounts of political detainees in France, Britain and Italy. This kind of content can be used to identify illegal prisons and centres, as well as to aid local protests and anti-deportation actions.

The most exceptional part of *Refuse the Biopolice* lies on its third page. Naturally, the member countries of the Schengen Agreement are interconnected to SIS and the secret service agencies and national security. However, the United States Department of Defense is associated to the 'Biometric Consortium' – a project created by the National Security Agency (NSA) and the National Institute of Standards and Technology (NIST) in the 1990s for research, development, testing and employment of personal authentication technology based on biometrics. At the present time, the reading of this map's organograms proves that the world has veered into total surveillance, where *smartphones* use fingerprints in order to authenticate user access and North American corporations are involved in biometric technologies capable of mapping our faces and DNA strands, allowing this information to be sent to intelligence databases. It is also relevant to see in this map the French government connected to databases of fugitives, prisoners, immigrants and terrorists. There are also lines connecting corporations that make data collection and surveillance equipment connected to computers in London.

'But the limits to surveillance are in our own lives: open minds, open hearts, open eyes. Beyond the biopolice is a biopoetics. Move beyond the spectacle of party politics as we know it: throw a party on all sides of the borders!' This description, which closes the introductory text of *Refuse the Biopolice*, seems to have been captured in the air by the activist actions of the camp in Strasbourg. The limits of surveillance hid and reappeared with the new forms of social, physical and virtual control, increasingly stronger, increasingly fluid, increasingly more integrated and internalized in our lives. The illegal detention of immigrants in European countries – as exposed by the counter-cartography of Bureau d'Études – is a reality funded by governmental institutions and technological security corporations. The current visibility of these authoritarian regimes of control serves to feed an extraordinary chance of seeing a multiplication of social movements that denounce naturalized forms of repression as well as their rhetoric based on threats and fear.

Tensions over borders are becoming bigger and more constant in an unstable cartography of the world; 'biopoetics' wishes to transgress its limits – both Bureau d'Études and Counter-Cartographies Collective are constantly reminding us of these issues. Boundaries exist to be challenged, to bring to light what is being excluded by them. The Iconoclasistas' *mapeo colectivo* practice is one of the movements that helps us to illuminate the permeability of borders, where the dispersion of exploration and the economic domain over an ever-changing territory is confronted with countless ways of counter-powers acting upon it.

According to two Iconoclasistas members, the communicator Julia Risler and the graphic artist Pablo Ares, the *mapeo colectivo* is 'a process of creation that subverts the place of enunciation in order to challenge the dominating accounts of territories, through the knowledge and everyday experiences of the participants' (Iconoclasistas 2013: 12). The group's mapping workshops are collaborative practices that articulate visual production and alternative pedagogies on different levels. They re-appropriate cartography's resources to build their own methodologies, work dynamics and socialization of knowledge together with university groups, neighbourhood associations, social, student and artistic movements. Instead of tracing a genealogy of these mappings, I would like to cite the workshop held by Iconoclasistas in May 2010 in Lima, in a meeting named *Taller de diálogo entre movimientos sociales*. Organized with the presence of representatives from diverse Latin-American movements – LGBT, feminists, afro-descendants, farmers, indigenous people, populations affected by mega-mining and researchers – Iconoclasistas' mapping workshop assured the integration of these militants in a mutual space of creation.

As usual, Julia Risler and Pablo Ares began the workshops by presenting a PowerPoint in order to comment on how maps can be used as tools of control and capitalist domination over a territory. This is an important part of the process. As the geographer Denis Wood says, once we accept a map as it is, recognizing its historical contingency and liberating it of its pretence of objectivity reduced to the passivity of its viewing, its interests can no longer remain hidden. The interests that serve maps may be ours (Wood 1992: 182, 183). The mapping workshop turns to the creation of collective reports, and all of the contributions are essential. Statements, dates, fragments of conversations and personal accounts are registered. Some people may experiment with telling their stories by hand-drawing maps, signalling the cartography of the spaces through icons and collages, in order to point out the problems that affect the regions and cities where they live.

It has always come to my attention with the work of Iconoclasistas that some of their maps reproduce the hegemonic cartographic representations of territories. At times I would ask: why not engage in distortion, remaking or inverting of traditional cartographies as a symbolic gesture of criticism to the dominant order of global capitalism? The map produced as a 'photograph' of the meeting in Lima with the social movements, *América Latina Rebelde* (www.iconoclasistas. net/peru-y-latinoamerica-rebelde), managed to provoke this restlessness in me. Over the known territory of South America, icons are distributed throughout the image. On many borders we see military and paramilitary groups represented. Along the coast of the continent, there are areas of deforestation and open-pit mining, from Argentina to Mexico. Close to those same areas, resistances, popular rebellions and communities affected by these extractions are occupying these same regions. Would the re-symbolization of a territory through these icons, words or accounts be able to transform it? A bell hooks text on language and power has helped me to problematize these questions:

> Like desire, language disrupts, refuses to be contained within boundaries. It speaks itself against our will, in words and thoughts that intrude, even violate the most private spaces of mind and body. It was in my first year of college that I read Adrienne Rich's poem, "The Burning of Paper Instead of Children." That poem, speaking against domination, against racism and class oppression, attempts to illustrate graphically that stopping the political persecution and torture of living beings is a more vital issue than censorship, than burning books. One line of this poem that moved and disturbed something within me: "This is the oppressor's language yet I need it to talk to you." I've never forgotten it. Perhaps I could not have forgotten it even if I tried to erase it from memory. Words impose themselves, take root in our memory against our will. The words of this poem begat a life in my memory that I could not abort or change.
>
> *hooks 1994: 167*

Even if provisionally, I could deduce from hooks that the language of hegemonic maps is still rooted in our memories; if we are able to recover the collective experiences of that language, we will be able to change it in order to create new accounts. For Iconoclasistas:

> retaking an official map is a key question, for example, in situations of re-territorialization fulfilled with the original communities, where the need to signal with precision, from official borders, becomes urgent when returning to that information as part of a demand of territorial recognition presented to the national government.
>
> *Iconoclasistas 2015*

Remembering hooks (1994: 175) again, let us take the language of the oppressor and turn it against itself: 'We make our words a counter-hegemonic speech, liberating ourselves in language'.

Everyday narratives distributed and mapped in these meetings defy the conformity of languages and official speeches. The moments when the workshops take place are stages that are just as important as the need of having a map obligatorily concluded at the end. All the working processes and forms of public circulation of these maps are thought and defined by their collaborators, so their actions may come from a specific place and reach other people. The map that will be redesigned, edited, printed or distributed as electronic archive is the conceptual edition of a working method. That map helps us distribute a politically understood reality in order to act together.

Map = use value and commonplace knowledge

The maps from Counter-Cartographies Collective, Bureau d'Études and Iconoclasistas open themselves up to the commons when they are shared among people that are interested in the reading of its information as a piece of property that belongs to no one and possesses no market value. The readers do not own these maps – they are *users*. Counter-cartographies are not mere practices of opposition that question a technical and specialized field. They are also politicized forms of tactical and activist appropriation of map making. To deconstruct and rebuild a map, widening its critical territory, refusing the established conventions and proposing new uses and contents, are stages of an action that leads to the disclosure of social, political and economic conditions that we wish to understand, make evident and transform. As political machines, counter-cartographies are the equivalents of open source coding programs that 'can be modified, amended and improved by anyone with the appropriate programming skills' (Barbrook 1998), and which are in continuous development by their users.

A new meaning is attributed to cartography through these counter-maps: no longer as a particularized activity or restricted knowledge, but instead as a possible project that disseminates to the maximum a kind of information circumscribed to specific publics and sources. These maps are instant portrayals of the effort of collective intelligences, offering free knowledge to anyone interested in researching in order to commence their own inquiries. Counter-cartography work may not only reveal systems of power, but it may also modify the statement that claims 'maps produce territory'. May that territory be the place where maps are built – with their stories, accounts and traces – until they may be accessed and distributed. The tools for a radical cartography are already open. It is up to us to use them.

References

Barbrook, R. (1998) 'The Hi-Tech Gift Economy', *Nettime* http://www.nettime.org/Lists-Archives/nettime-l-9810/msg00122.html, accessed 14 April 2017.

Bureau d'Études (2003) 'Mapping Contemporary Capitalism: Assumptions, Methods, Open Questions', *Drift*, https://chtodelat.org/b8-newspapers/12-68/bureau-detudes-mapping-contemporary-capitalism-assumptions-methods-open-questions, accessed 14 April 2017.

De Certeau, M. (1984) *The Practice of Everyday Life*. Berkeley, CA: University of California Press.

Garcia, D. and Lovink, G. (1997) 'The ABC of Tactical Media', *Nettime*, <http://www.nettime.org/Lists-Archives/nettime-l-9705/msg00096.html>, accessed 14 April 2017.

Harley, J. (2001) *The New Nature of Maps: Essays in the History of Cartography*. London: The Johns Hopkins University Press.

hooks, b. (1994) *Teaching to Transgress: Education as the Practice of Freedom*. New York: Routledge.

Iconoclasistas (2013) *Manual de mapeo colectivo. Recursos cartográficos críticos para procesos territoriales de creación colaborativa*. Buenos Aires: Tinta Limón.

Iconoclasistas (2015) 'Talleres de mapeo. Recursos lúdicos y visuales para la construcción de conocimiento colectivo', Ecología Política, http://www.ecologiapolitica.info/wp-content/uploads/2015/02/048_Risleretal_2015.pdf, accessed 14 April 2017.

Institute for Applied Autonomy (2007) 'Tactical Cartographies', in L. Mogel and A. Bhagat (eds) *An Atlas of Radical Cartography*. Los Angeles, CA: Journal of Aesthetics and Protest Press, pp. 29–37.

Jacob, C. (2006) *The Sovereign Map: Theoretical Approaches in Cartography throughout History*. Chicago, IL: The University of Chicago Press.

Lippard, L. (1997) *The Lure of the Local: Senses of Place in a Multicentered Society*. New York: New Press.

Mezzadra, S. and Neilson, B. (2013) *Border as Method: Or the Multiplication of Labor*. Durham, NC: Duke University Press.

Raunig, G. (2007) *Art and Revolution. Transversal Activism in the Long Twentieth Century*. Los Angeles, CA: Semiotext(e).

Stallmann, T. (2012) Alternative Cartographies: Building Collective Power. Master's thesis. Chapel Hill, NC: University of North Carolina.

Thompson, N. and Sholette, G. (eds) (2004) *The Interventionists: Users' Manual for the Creative Disruption of Everyday Life*. Cambridge, MA: MIT Press.

Wood, D. (1992) *The Power of Maps*. New York: Guilford Press.

PART V

Contesting narratives

28

CLIMATE JUSTICE, HACKTIVIST SENSIBILITIES, PROTOTYPES OF CHANGE

Adrienne Russell

During the 2015 United Nations Climate Summit in Paris (COP21), one the most widely reported and visually compelling protests featured a group of indigenous men and women from around the world paddling canoes down the Seine. The point was to prod world leaders to include indigenous rights protections in the pact they had gathered to negotiate. The action organized by the Indigenous Environmental Network and Amazon Watch made an intentional and powerful juxtaposition, setting the protestors in traditional garb with handmade banners reading 'leave fossil fuels in the ground' and 'protect sacred water' against the opulently materialist Paris cityscape.

Images from the action captured by journalists, activists and passersby circulated widely though connective media networks. They appeared at news outlets, on NGO and other activist sites and throughout social media feeds —quickly becoming part of the larger coverage of the summit. The event and related speeches and press conferences centred on the broad cause of climate justice but also drew attention to the ways local issues depend for resolution on global action – issues such as the deforestation of the Amazon and the polluting and pipelining of native territories. The protest action at the summit also highlighted the sophisticated coordination and media strategies practiced by the grassroots groups assembled there and intent on influencing meanings attached to the summit, building alliances and mobilizing publics in support of their cause.

The Canoes on the Seine event, like climate activism more generally, brought local struggles to a global stage and traversed both online and offline space. It was an example of what makes the annual UN Climate summits rich sites to study the changing media environment. By bringing together international political actors and journalists, the summits create a sort of microcosm of global politics, where power dynamics are played out in real-time at the sites where official and unofficial delegates gather in the summit host cities as well as in the larger global mediated networked stage. As climate journalism scholars Eide and Kunelius (2010: 12) have pointed out, the summits offer a unique opportunity to study emergent transnational public spheres:

> As a global problem calling for coordinated action, [climate change] is the paradigmatic case to look for to encourage the emergence of transnational or global public spheres – or spaces or moments in which networks of communication flows enable and force global and national civil society.

Studies of past summits demonstrate that while traditional journalists covering the summits tend to adhere to norms of professionalism that privilege the status quo, national political perspectives, and frames that reinforce traditional power relations (Eide *et al.* 2010), alternative and activist media expand the voices and themes included in the coverage (Russell 2013; Painter *et al.* 2016). During the 2015 Paris summit, together with NGO and alternative media outlets and activists on the street, coverage by new media players such as *Vice, Buzzfeed* and *Huffington Post* helped expand the themes and voices included in the coverage, and the forms the coverage takes (Painter *et al.* 2016).

The 2015 Paris COP took place in the shadow of a series of coordinated terrorist attacks that hit the city and Saint-Denis on 13 November 2015. The attacks heightened security concerns and prompted crackdowns on activists and a ban on protest. The tension was palpable in the city and in and around the Bourget, where the summit was being held: known activists were placed under house arrest, security checkpoints were erected all over the city and sharp shooters perched above the lines of people waiting to get into the conference venue. The anti-terrorist measures threatened to reduce the negotiations to a conversation between bureaucrats and specialists. Activists and NGO staffers and supporters nevertheless poured into the city from all over the world, setting up alternative media centres, carrying out acts of civil disobedience, holding alternative conferences – their aim being to disrupt bureaucratic control of the event. The work of activists at the summit points to the ways climate justice advocates have long worked to build their movement through media, by creating media spaces, content and strategies teamed with real-world events that spur real-time citizen and activist-generated coverage of the summit through social media.

The summit took place within a changing media environment, in which the role of social media as a source of news gained increased traction. It was the era when the tremendous growth in smartphones as a way of accessing news and the growing importance of video underpinned the rise of popular 'digital-born media brands' or 'new players', also known as 'second wave' digital companies that produce their own news content (Digital News Report 2016). Of these, the leading outlets in terms of profit and circulation numbers are the *Huffington Post, Vice* and *Buzzfeed*, all of which have built up a strong presence in several countries and languages and give editorial priority to environmental issues. According to the 2016 Digital News Report by the Reuters Institute for the Study of Journalism, in the US, the *Huffington Post* is the single most widely used source among people 'highly interested' in environmental news. In the US and the UK, *Buzzfeed* and *Vice* are also very popular with the same demographic. So, an enormous audience was receiving its news on the Paris summit from outlets that either did not exist or were just coming to life when previous climate summits were being held. It is against this social, political and technological backdrop, and the increasingly intense and visible impact of climate change, that the Paris summit took place.

This chapter explores the material and symbolic elements of strategies used by climate justice activists at the summit. It highlights three examples of media activism that disrupt the top-down power dynamics of the summit and climate politics more generally in distinct and sophisticated ways that reshape narratives, cartographies, meanings and modes of accountability. The activist-organized 'PlacetoB' alternative media centre, the Climate Games coordinated media action and the Exxon Mock Trial event all draw on old and new tactics and tools, flexible and distributed networks, and are driven by a hacktivist sensibility that marries technological skills with critical thinking and that generally mistrusts authority and aims to promote human rights, freedom of information and decentralized media skills and production (Levy 2001; Russell 2016). As philosopher Peter Ludlow explained to *New York Times* readers in 2013, dedication to furthering the public interest threads throughout: 'Hacking is fundamentally about refusing to be intimidated or cowed into submission by any technology, about understanding the technology and acquiring the power to repurpose it to our individual needs, and for the good of the many', he wrote. '[W]hat is critical is that the technologies be in our hands rather than out of our control. This ideal, theoretically, should extend beyond computer use, to technologies for food production, shelter and clothing, and of course, to all the means we use to communicate with one another' (Ludlow 2013). By highlighting the practices of media activists, the chapter demonstrates some of the ways hacktivist sensibilities are leading them to exploit the malleability of mainstream and alternative or niche technologies, and in the process, build prototypes of alternative forms of media and social organization.

Media and social change

Recent scholarship makes clear the ways contemporary social movements rely on a combination of on- and off-line tools and strategies, creating a hybrid space, and in the case of COPs of official or 'blue-zone' activity and unofficial action meant to not only protest but also build alliances, solutions and alternatives 'official' and activist activities, ideas and narratives (Juris 2012; Treré 2012; Bennett & Segerberg 2013). Bennett and Segerberg (2013) identify what they call 'the logic of connective action', born of the availability of open technologies and an approach to communication that prioritizes individualism, distrust of authority and inclusivity, arguing that contemporary publics contribute to movements through personalized expression, rather than through group actions tied to traditional institutions or through ideologies that foster collective identities. Papacharissi (2015: 117) notes that publics networked through social media are 'feeling their way into' news issues and events, and she explores the forms those publics take. She applies influential cultural studies theorist Raymond Williams' notion of *structures of feelings* to collaborative discourses organized through hashtags and other virally circulating cultural content like memes and videos or artefacts of engagement (Clark 2016), challenging those who discount their significance by pointing out the ways they reflect and lend agency to the 'culture, mood and feel' of our particular historical moment. In doing so, she reminds us that culture is a central vein of power.

The notion of spectacular environmentalisms, the mediated spaces through which we collectively come to understand climate change and related environmental issues, is useful when considering the ways activists are exerting influence on climate politics. Goodman *et al.* (2016) argue that spectacular environmentalism operates through visual grammars and registers, perhaps even more than through verbal messaging. In Paris, the indigenous activists canoeing down the Seine; digital projects of pro-environment messages on the Eiffel Tower (100% renewable, For the Planet, Action Now, No Plan B); the subverts calling out corporate polluters; the ubiquitous images of polar bears on posters, Facebook feeds and as mascots, for example Aurora Greenpeace's giant mechanized polar bear; and the infographics explaining climate change in numbers all exemplified the ways spectacular environmentalisms shows as much as tells the story of climate change. The importance of visuals puts an emphasis not only on facts but also on particular values and affective triggers. They write:

> We see, but most vitally, feel the determination of activists sitting in trees, the green celebrity's anger that rapidly turns to tears and shouting as that last tree is cut down to make way for 'progress', the joy and hope in the announcer's over-dubbed voice commentating about a new elephant/tiger/orangutan sanctuary.
>
> *Goodman et al. 2016*

Or as Papacharissi (2015) would put it, we are feeling our way into the issue of climate change.

The idea of spectacular environmentalism builds on Situationist Guy Debord's key text *The Society of the Spectacle* (1967), in which he argues that under capitalism, life is reduced to an immense accumulation of mere appearances where 'all that once was directly lived has become mere representation'. To undermine the spectacle, the Situationists used *détournement*, or what they described as 'the excision of an item of culture (whether image, text, or object) from its normative context and its subsequent juxtaposition with another fragment in order to establish and analogical relationship between the two' (McDonough 2007: 5). Activists, according to this way of thinking, entered the spectacle only to disrupt it and thus inhabited a permanently marginal role – reacting to dominant discourse rather than shaping it. This way of thinking about activists in relation to the spectacle fails 'to consider politics beyond the immediate protest, to consider the complex ways people use media to connect and disconnect, or to account for how the balance of power can change through media and its manipulations' (Goodman *et al.* 2016: 2).

In order to update the concept of the spectacle in light of the contemporary media environment we need to consider the context of what Michela Ardizzoni (2016) calls matrix activism, or resistance that exists within the market logic of contemporary societies, 'between production and consumption, activism and commercialism, centre(s) and margin(s), the local and the transnational'. This allows us to distinguish between the spectacle driven by commercial interests and amounting to fake representations of reality and what Duncombe (2007) calls the ethical spectacle: spectacular interventions that are ethical and emancipatory, and that amount to a sort of propaganda of truth. Unlike the Situationists who saw the spectacle as something to be disrupted, both the ideas of matrix activism and ethical spectacle suggest that in order to be effective, activists ought to enter into the realm of the spectacle.

This chapter considers how the spectacle plays out in the contemporary media context, arguing that in a media environment that trades on user contribution, the fact that activists can work existing platforms to broaden the range of voices and provide representation helps expand the meaning of the summit. Through examples, the chapter demonstrates how alternative journalists and media activists can now create new forms of media and spaces of exchange, a feat that was nearly impossible previously in an era defined by scarcity of broadcast channels, high cost and tight regulation. Here I turn to three examples to demonstrate that, in the hybrid media environment, the spectacle is no longer the exclusive terrain of forces erosive to public life.

New narratives

One of the most vibrant summit-related hubs during the duration of COP21 was the alternative media centre PlacetoB, housed in a youth hostel St Christopher Inn and Belushi bar in central Paris. The space welcomed media makers from 50 different countries who were in Paris to cover the negotiations, including artists, alternative journalists, NGO media staff, bloggers and researchers. It provided them on and offline space to meet and collaborate away from the negotiations, where the climate was about more than the political deals being brokered. Anne-Sophie Novel, founder of the space, says she created it in response to the 2009 UN climate summit in Copenhagen, where she went in 2009 as a blogger and spent much of her time in the Fresh Air Center, a space funded by the UN, Google and organized by 350.org and TckTckTck for online activists and NGO staff to work and mingle. Novel says she was inspired by that space but wanted to create one that was more inclusive of unaffiliated activists, educators, designers, developers, bloggers and so on. The goal, she says, was 'to create a new narrative' around climate change, one that expands beyond the perspectives of the bureaucratic élites involved in the negotiations to a narrative that has science and justice at its core and includes a much wider collection of voices and formats than more mainstream coverage (Russell 2015).

During the summit, each afternoon PlacetoB held a live broadcast briefing where scientists, activists, celebrity authors – most of whom had access to the inside of the negotiation venue – reported an overview of what went on that day. The broadcasts were streamed on the PlacetoB website and excerpts were often broadcast by the television network TF1, and posted on France 3 and Ushuaia TV websites. PlacetoB also had a 'creative factory' where they workshopped climate change-related problems. Every two days a new problem was presented and participants would make a plan of action to address it. For example, representatives from the Marshall Islands presented to the group the issue of preserving their culture – the stories that weave together their communities – as they carry out relocation because their island is becoming uninhabitable. Film makers, journalists, poets, activists and developers all brainstormed for two days and came away with a plan to document and preserve the stories and an online funding campaign to support these efforts.

Novel and her collaborators are exhibiting hacktivist sensibility in their reinvention of climate narratives and reimagining the newsroom to include a much broader set of professionals and members of the public. PlacetoB is a sort of prototype, or what Andrew Boyd calls prefigurative intervention, for an engaged newsroom – one that advocates for climate solutions. They are creating alternatives to show what is possible by, as Andrew Boyd (2012: 82) describes it: 'direct[ing] action at the point of assumption – where beliefs are made and unmade and the limits of the possible can be stretched.' In 1999, the Seattle Independent Media Center (IMC), a collective of independent media organizations and hundreds of journalists used the internet to support and coordinate protests against World Trade Organization meetings held there that year. The IMC site featured constantly updated multimedia reports on the protests and the protesters' clashes with police, reports uploaded mostly by amateur or what came to be known as 'citizen journalists'. IMC spurred centres in cities throughout the world and became the prototype for varied experimental participatory news projects (Halleck 2002). Seventeen years later Novel and her colleagues have created an independent media space specifically for the issue of climate change and that combines, professional and novice participation, and more directly engages and indeed contributes to shaping the spectacle.

Cartography of resistance

During the summit, Paris became the site of Climate Games, dubbed 'the world's largest disobedient action adventure game', and an example of coordinated media activism that garnered media attention and promoted public engagement. The games were organized by The Laboratory of Insurrectionary Imagination, a collective based in Southern France, first rolled out by the Dutch group GroenFront in 2014, and further developed through a series of hackathons.

The COP21 Climate Games were a real time and real space cartography of resistance. Teams of players collaborated to carry out acts of civil disobedience, racking up points for creative, non-violent action. All of this was mapped in real-time using the app created for the games. All elements of the city landscape were integrated into games: police and other security were 'team blue', tasked with making it as difficult as possible to score points. Those seen as sabotaging the summit (green washing businesses, lobbyists and so on) were 'team grey'. Organizer John Jordan describes how the games reference and are part of a long tradition of resistance in Paris:

> Paris has shaped our ideas of revolution for centuries. … It was on its medieval streets in the spontaneity of resistance that the rebel architecture of the barricade was invented. It was the first capital city of the modern era to experience a system of 'real

democracy' and be run by its citizens independently of the state (the Commune). It was in its bars and cafes that the divisions between art and revolution were abolished (Dada, Surrealism, Situationism).

As quoted in Hickey 2015

Perhaps the most visible Climate Game team, Brandalism, plastered 600 spoof ads in public spaces around Paris using the Climate Games app to avoid being caught. The ads critique corporate sponsors of the summit, a counter to the green washing happening all over town in exhibits and sponsorships that falsely promoted the world's biggest polluters as earth friendly. This was a sort of fact checking on the city streets and a 'revolt against corporate control of the visual realm', by practicing a contemporary form of *détournement*, reusing elements of well-known media to create a new work with a different message, often one opposed to the original, to undermine or disrupt the spectacle. The messages conveyed in the subvertisements went far beyond the Paris streets where they were plastered, through social media feeds and news stories in outlets all over the globe.

Using a map app to coordinate and to lend alternative meaning to the city is a strategy that proved to effectively spur direct action and engagement. As Solnit (2010: 8) puts it: 'Maps are always invitations in a way that texts are not; you can enter a map, alter it, plan with it'. ClimateGames used hacktivist sensibility to overcome challenges to claim civic space. It helped facilitate 140 different direct actions during the two weeks of the summit – clowns mocking politicians, IPCC report printed on rolls of toilet paper, blockades erected, redlines drawn – all confronting power dynamics directly in attempt to change them.

New modes of accountability

In Montreuil, the site of the 'alternative village' set up at COP21, Bill McKibben and Naomi Klein were prosecutors in a court case against ExxonMobil. The 'trial' was organized by climate change activist organization 350.org in a community centre and occasional concert hall packed with a crowd of a few hundred. For two hours, witnesses from around the world – a reindeer herder from the artic, an activist from Nigeria, scientists from the US, among others – testified to the havoc already wrought by carbon-based energy economies dominated by Exxon and other fossil fuel companies. They spoke of the deleterious effects on the climate that oil and gas produce and the great success such companies have enjoyed in pushing climate change-denial science.

The trial was based on reporting by the Pulitzer Prize–winning website *Inside Climate News*, and the *Los Angeles Times* (with the help of the Columbia Journalism School), confirming that ExxonMobil discovered the role played by fossil fuels in speeding up global warming in the mid-1980s and then spent the next few decades systematically funding climate denial and lying about their own and other scientific findings. The trial transformed a news story into a public event, spurring real-time citizen and activist-generated coverage using the hashtag #ExxonKnew, tweets, videos, blogs, photo essays, Facebook 'open letters' and reports of the event delivered news of the event – both informational and affective – to international publics. More than an informational event, the trial was a performance, fraught with emotional and fact-based testimony delivered to those beyond Montreuil through video, articles and social media posts connected together with the hashtag #ExxonKnew.

So-called 'hashtag activism' is a strategy to bring attention to issues being ignored or mis-represented by mainstream media and usually works like this: a hashtag is created that aggre-gates tweets and Facebook posts around an issue; it circulates among a small group; with luck it gains circulation among a wider group of Twitter users; and then the mainstream press and politicians take notice and respond. In the case of #ExxonKnew, it serves as an outlet for the story, a sort of multimedia crowd-authored 'special issue' on the intersection of climate denial and corporate malfeasance that features regularly posted new material from around the world by what Papacharissi (2015) calls the 'storytelling public'. The affect that characterizes much of the material is raw and powerful and fuels reaction. Tweets elicit more tweets, routinely turning local incidents of ExxonMobil and other fossil fuel industry related green washing into national news, connecting incidents that might otherwise seem isolated, pointing to the systemic nature of the problem, spurring mainstream media coverage and shaping larger public understanding on the issue. Roughly a year after the trial in Montreuil, #ExxonKnew became a rallying cry for those seeking to block the appointment of ExxonMobil CEO Rex Tillerson as US secretary of state, continuing its role in raising awareness and making connections between corrupt fossil fuel industry practices and climate change.

Hacking the media landscape: beyond disruption

These are just a few examples that suggest ways hacktivist sensibilities are influencing the strategies and tools media activists are developing to disrupt the power dynamics of the negotiations. They also demonstrate the creation of the ethical spectacle delivered through an alternative newsroom that generated community and alternative narratives to global publics; through public performance broadcast to the networks around the world by the live spectators in attendance; and through a civil disobedience game that merges offline and online components.

The question of the nature of the spectacle – whether it is dominated by commercial interests and against the interests of the public or that provides for the possibility of ethical and emancipatory interventions – relates to what Todd Gitlin (1980) has described as a fundamental and inescapable dilemma of protest movements. The dilemma he describes sees activists on the one hand 'standing outside' the realm of dominant discourse and thus 'consigned to marginality and political irrelevance' and on the other hand working within conventional rules and facing tactical constraint or being confined working within the existing system rather than establishing a new one.

In recent years, key protest-movement media strategies have been reinvented, reflecting larger shifts in media technologies and practices, and overcoming this dilemma between marginalization versus tactical constraint. It is true that media power has been consolidated in the networked era, that media monopolies have grown, that the industry has been deregulated (Bagdikian 1987; McChesney & Nichols 2009) and that new types of digital-age control have taken hold (Freedman 2014; Gillespie 2014). But it also true that more media outlets and platforms exist every day, and media makers now routinely go beyond attempts to attract mainstream media attention. They are hacking media content, practices and architectures, refusing to be subject to a media environment beyond their control, vying to channel media power directly. They are motivated by the new-level of consciousness, some of it surely instinctual in the networked mediated age, that greater access to media power alters larger power dynamics in society. Today, as has been illustrated in this chapter, protest-movement approaches to garnering attention and establishing legitimacy are more diffuse. Participants make their own media. They tailor their mediated messages to 'go viral' and relatively unfiltered over networks that can reach people in every country in the world and that can work to broaden the range of voices, themes, tactics, spaces in the larger communication environment and bring new narratives into the mainstream.

They are also introducing experimental communication genres that inform and engage the public and policy makers on different levels than straight news coverage does – on emotional and metaphorical and creative levels. These are genres that see greater public involvement in reporting. Results include community building and activation, where publics may be moved beyond the passivity of the spectacle and media consumption. These new meanings and genres of news-related media are key to shaping the cultural politics of climate change or people's understanding of climate-related issues as these issues move from formal climate science and policy through the media and into the realm of public discourse and action.

They can also challenge and influence the norms and practices of traditional news-media makers not only by providing them with events to cover, sources to quote, and content to run, but also by modelling new styles and genres of coverage. New digital players like *Vice* and the *Huffington Post*, for example, recognized the dynamic climate justice work being done in Paris and, through their more immersive and opinionated styles, focused on the voices of activists and NGOs, bringing the theme of climate justice to the centre of their coverage of COP21 (Painter *et al.* 2016).

In the contemporary media environment, activist media power goes beyond disrupting or attracting the mainstream media; it seeks to develop new strategies and tactics, practices and tools that expand the issues and voices in the public sphere and also the forms public discourse takes. Despite restrictions placed on civil society, Paris was the site of what Nico Carpentier (2017) calls maximalist participation, in which participation is multidirectional and includes but also goes beyond institutionalized politics to include the media and cultural spheres. Media activists in Paris focused their attention on democratizing not just the official negotiations but also the environmental spectacle that both became and helped define the summit.

References

Ardizzoni, M. (2015) 'Matrix Activism: Media, Neoliberalism, and Social Action in Italy', *International Journal of Communication*, vol. 9, pp. 1072–89.

Bagdikian, B. (1997) *The Media Monopoly*. New York: Beacon Press.

Bennett, W. L. and Segerberg, A. (2013) *The Logic of Connective Action: Digital Media and the Personalization of Contentious Politics*. Cambridge: Cambridge University Press.

Boyd, A. (2012) *Beautiful Trouble: A Toolbox for Revolution*, New York: OR Books.

Carpentier, N. (2017) 'The Concept of Participation: If They Have Access and Interact, Do They Really Participate?', in L. Iannelli and P. Musarò (eds) *Performative Citizenship Public Art, Urban Design, and Political Participation*. Mimesis International.

Clark, L. S. (2016) 'Participants on the Margins: #BlackLivesMatter and the Role That Shared Artifacts of Engagement Played among Minoritized Political Newcomers on Snapchat, Facebook, and Twitter', *International Journal of Communication*, vol. 10, pp. 235–53.

Debord, G. (1967) *Society of the Spectacle*. Detroit, MI: Black and Red.

Duncombe, S. (2007) *Dream: Re-imagining Progressive Politics in an Age of Fantasy*. New York: The New Press.

Eide, E. and Kunelius, R. (2010) 'Preface', in E. Eide, R. Kunelius and V. Kumpu (eds) *Global Climate – Local Journalisms: A Transnational Study of How Media Make Sense of Climate Summits*. Göteborg: Nordicom, pp. 7–8.

Eide, E., Kunelius R. and Kumpu. V (2010) *Global Climate – Local Journalisms: A Transnational Study of How Media Make Sense of Climate Summits*. Göteborg: Nordicom.

Freedman, D. (2014) *The Contradictions of Media Power*. London: Bloomsbury Academic.

Gillespie, T. (2014) 'The Relevance of Algorithms', in T. Gillespie, P. Boczkowski and K. Foot (eds) *Media Technologies: Essays on Communication, Materiality, and Society*. Cambridge, MA: MIT Press, pp. 167–94.

Gitlin, T. (1980) *The Whole World Is Watching*. Berkeley, CA: University of California Press.

Goodman, M. K., Littler, J., Brockington, D. and Boykoff, M. T. (2016) 'Spectacular Environmentalisms: Media, Knowledge and the Framing of Ecological Politics'. Introduction to Littler, J., Goodman, M. K., Brockington, D. and Boykoff, M. T. (eds) *Environmental Communications: A Journal of Nature and Culture*, Special Issue on Spectacular Environmentalisms, vol. 10, no. 6, pp. 677–88

Halleck, D. (2002) 'Indymedia: Building an International Activist Internet Network', paper presented at International Association of Media and Communication, July, http://newmedia.yeditepe.edu.tr/pdfs/isimd_04/12.pdf, accessed 3 May 2017.

Hickey, A. (2015) 'Winning Back the Climate', Center For Creative Ecologies, 2 November, https://crea-tiveecologies.ucsc.edu/hickey-cop21, accessed 3 May 2017.

Juris, J. (2012) 'Reflections on #Occupy Everywhere: Social Media, Public Space, and Emerging Logics of Aggregation', *American Ethnologist,* vol. 39, no. 2, pp. 259–79.

Levy, S. (2001) *Hackers.* New York: Penguin.

Ludlow, P. (2013) 'What Is a Hacktivist?', *New York Times*, 13 January, https://opinionator.blogs.nytimes.com/2013/01/13/what-is-a-hacktivist/, accessed 15 January 2013.

McChesney, R. and Nichols, J. (2009) 'The Life and Death of the Great American Newspaper', *Nation*, 18 March, https://www.thenation.com/article/death-and-life-great-american-newspapers/, accessed 1 August 2011.

McDonough, T. (2007) *The Beautiful Language of My Century.* Cambridge, MA: MIT Press.

Novel, A. S. (2015) Unpublished interview with author, Paris, 8 December.

Painter, J., Erviti, M. C., Fletcher, R., Howarth, C., Kristiansen, S., León, B., Ouakrat, A., Russell, A. and Schäfer, M. S. (2016) *Something Old, Something New: Digital Media and the Coverage of Climate Change.* Oxford: Reuters Institute/I.B. Tauris Press.

Papacharissi, Z. (2015) *Affective Publics: Sentiment, Technology and Politics.* Oxford: Oxford University Press.

Reuters Institute for the Study of Journalism (2016) *Digital News Report 2016*, 14 June, http://www.digi-talnewsreport.org, accessed 15 December 2016.

Russell, A. (2013) 'Innovation in Hybrid Spaces: 2011 UN Climate Summit and the Changing Journalism Field', *Journalism*, vol. 14, no. 7, pp. 904–20.

Russell, A. (2016) *Journalism as Activism: Recoding Media Power.* Cambridge: Polity.

Solnit, R. (2010) *Infinite City.* Berkeley, CA: University of California Press.

Treré, E. (2012) 'Social Movements as Information Ecologies: Exploring the Coevolution of Multiple Internet Technologies for Activism', *International Journal of Communication*, vol. 6, pp. 2359–77.

29

THE BRITISH NATIONAL PARTY

Digital discourse and power

Chris Atton

This chapter draws upon research previously published in 2004 and 2006 (Atton 2004: chapter 3, 2006), which examines the BNP's website as a form of activist, alternative media. I go on to reconsider my findings in the light of subsequent political developments in the UK. In particular it is possible that we might find traces of the BNP's discourse in UKIP's promotion of the 'Leave' position in the 2016 EU Referendum in the UK, which saw a majority of voters in favour of leaving the EU. However, in the second half of the chapter I warn against an easy transference of findings from one activist site to another and indeed to large sections of the mainstream media, particularly in an academic environment where British media scholars appear to be overwhelmingly sympathetic to a leftist bloc of 'progressive' media activism and amongst whom, it appears, there is little support for the outcome of the EU Referendum.

The original research focused on how the website involved members and supporters in its discursive construction of racism. I found that the discourses and identities produced were played out through a radical reformation of the concepts of power, culture and oppression. Drawing on the post-colonial notion of the Other, the BNP sought to present itself, its activities and its members as responses to racism and oppression that, it argued, are practised by the Other. While this discourse is constructed through the everyday experiences and attitudes of its members, the hierarchically determined nature of the site prevented those members from sustained, active involvement in the construction of their own identities. For this reason, the study concluded, the BNP's site was far from the more open, non-hierarchical practices of 'progressive' alternative media.

In the ten years since the research was undertaken, the BNP's significance as a right-wing party in the UK has diminished, though aspects of its political programme (specifically, immigration and the UK's relationship with the EU) have been taken up and transformed (some might say made palatable) by the UKIP, founded in the early 1990s, but growing in popularity throughout the 2000s.

The discourse of far-right media

The 1990s saw a dramatic movement of the European far right towards the centre of national politics. Parties with policies based primarily on nationalism and immigration (such as Jörg Haider's Austrian Freedom Party and Jean Marie Le Pen's Front National in France) resonated with publics increasingly disillusioned with what they saw as centralist policies of the EU, of a liberalism that to them appeared to favour the rights of immigrants above native-born citizens, and a globalization that seemed to ignore domestic issues such as law and order, housing and employment. Such parties sought, with some success, to normalize a racial nationalism based on 'whiteness as an essentialized social identity which they say is under threat' (Back 2002a), a strategy also followed by the BNP.

Little attention has been paid to right-wing media as alternative, activist media. At the first international meeting for alternative media scholars ('Our Media, Not Theirs', Washington, DC, May 2001) there was much debate over the morality of studying such media. Even amongst those who recognize the area as being of interest, there was concern that the extremely hierarchical methods of organization and production within the groups promoting such media work against consideration of far-right media as 'alternative'. Here 'alternative' is employed to denote media practices that 'strengthen democratic culture' (Downing *et al.* 2001: 95). The desideratum of 'self-governing media is simply not imaginable' (ibid.: 94) for what Downing *et al.* term the 'repressive radical media' of the far right. Nick Couldry (2000: 140) emphasizes the place of alternative media in creating and sustaining a 'community without closure'. Central to such a community is dialogue; independent control over symbolic resources is crucial to enable the 'exchange [of] representations of such "reality" as we share' (Couldry 2002). For Couldry, 'one of the central values of, say, neo-Nazi media is to *close off* certain others' abilities to speak of their experience, as part of constructing or sustaining a community *with* closure' (ibid., original emphases). One objection to this argument is that, however compelling it might be from an ethical perspective, it assumes an idealized, 'pure' form of alternative media practices that apparently operate without such closure. There is, for instance, evidence to suggest that there is a distinct ideological framework within which certain of Indymedia's media practices operate. In Indymedia's coverage of 9/11 and its aftermath, a distinctive version of events is significantly privileged, leaving little room for other, even sympathetic counter-discourses (Atton 2003). A hierarchical control over symbolic resources is apparent even in this highly democratized communication process. We need to consider the extent to which organizations such as Indymedia and the Occupy movement present 'free spaces' for media activists, and the extent to which they function as communities that themselves are, if not 'closed' in the same way that Couldry finds neo-Nazi media, are nevertheless exclusive.

Les Back has found that far-right media in the UK has recently assimilated the language of multiculturalist discourse through its adoption of terms such as 'equality', 'fairness' and 'rights' – significantly he notes that the BNP's 'house publication' has been relaunched as 'Identity': 'their dominant motif is that whites are now the victims' (Back 2002a). He has also noted the attempts on a White Power website to co-opt the writings of Adorno on the culture industry into the canon of extreme racist literature: 'Adorno's work is *used* to criticize the involvement of cultural entrepreneurs and then organized into a conspiratorial anti-Semitic view' (Back 2002b: 637, original emphasis).

To examine how such discourses are generated, we need to identify the historical resources upon and through which discourses are constructed, and how those discourses are mobilized to construct new social formations and identities. In their study of Pakeha ('White') racism in New Zealand, Wetherell and Potter (1992: 86) argue for a 'double movement' of discourse analysis which comprises of an interplay between the 'established' aspect of discourse and a 'genealogical' or constitutive aspect. Following Foucault (1980), they argue that discourse is not only constituted by existing social formations and historical accounts, but is itself constitutive of social groups, subject positions and identities. Discourse is not only produced, it is productive: productive of agents and subjects, of material interests. To consider it as little more than reflecting existing class positions or material interests is to ignore the role of discourse in producing power. For Foucault, power is not merely played out or exhibited in discourse; it is produced through discourse. Knowledge is constituted through discursive formations and through that knowledge is constituted power. This generation of power is capable of forming agents and subjects. In contrast with the 'established' approach, a constitutive understanding of discursive formations emphasizes how discourse can produce forms of social action, not merely reflect them ideologically. We might consider these discursive formations as 'rituals of power' and look for the effects such rituals have on agents and subjects. Power becomes the central term, and it is through discourse (knowledge production) that power is created and dispersed.

The policies of the BNP

Under its first leader and founder, John Tyndall, the BNP had been notorious for promoting forced repatriation and racial violence. In 1995, party activist Nick Griffin wrote in the extremist publication, *The Rune*, that the defence of 'rights for whites' could only come from 'well-directed boots and fists. When the crunch comes, power is the product of force and will, not of rational debate' (cited in *Searchlight* 1999). Since becoming chairman of the party in 1999 Griffin sought to distance himself from such rhetoric and to reposition the BNP as a party of 'racial nationalism and social justice' and to build a 'responsible' movement that 'becomes the focus of the hopes not just of the neglected and oppressed white working class, but also of the frustrated and disorientated traditional middle class' (ibid.). Despite this shift in rhetoric (and some dilution of its earlier policies) towards a 'new nationalism', the BNP's policies appear to remain founded on racism. Its primary policy is that of immigration, and from this all its other policies proceed:

> On current demographic trends, we, the native British people, will be an ethnic minority in our own country within sixty years. To ensure that this does not happen, and that the British people retain their homeland and identity, we call for an immediate halt to all further immigration, the immediate deportation of criminal and illegal immigrants, and the introduction of a system of voluntary resettlement whereby those immigrants who are legally here will be afforded the opportunity to return to their lands of ethnic origin assisted by generous financial incentives both for individuals and for the countries in question. We will abolish the 'positive discrimination' schemes that have made white Britons second-class citizens. We will also clamp down on the flood of 'asylum seekers', all of whom are either bogus or can find refuge much nearer their home countries.
>
> *'Immigration – Time to say NO!', www.bnp.org.uk/policies.html#immigration*

Its other policies – on Europe (the BNP seeks 'independence from the EU'), on the economy and employment ('British workers first!'), on education (the party is against 'politically incorrect indoctrination' and for 'knowledge of and pride in the history, cultures and heritage of the native peoples of Britain') – all assume a White racism based implicitly on a racially pure, historically embedded notion of 'British' culture. Nevertheless, the party is emphatic that it is not racist, only interested in the preservation of British culture:

> Q: The politicians and the media call the BNP 'racist'? Is this true? A: No. 'Racism' is when you 'hate' another ethnic group. We don't 'hate' black people, we don't 'hate' Asians, we don't oppose any ethnic group for what God made them, they have a right

to their own identity as much as we do, all we want to do is to preserve the ethnic and cultural identity of the British people. We want the same human rights as everyone else, a right to a homeland, security, identity, democracy and freedom. We are not against immigrants as *individuals*. We are against a *system* which imports cheap labour regardless of the wishes of the host population. The British people were never asked if they wanted a multi-cultural society, immigration was forced on us undemocratically and against the clear wishes of the majority.

www.bnp.org.uk/faq.html, original emphases

Constructing cultural history

The BNP's plea is not for the alienation, repatriation or (as in much supremacist discourse) the destruction of immigrant populations and communities, nor even for the defence of Whites against an immigration 'onslaught'. It is much simpler than either of these. The 'Heritage and Culture' section of the BNP's website seeks to isolate the defining characteristics of British culture, the better to 'preserve all the positive aspects of our culture' (www.bnp.org.uk/culture/poetry/2003_apr.htm). This culture is emphatically pan-British, emphasizing Celtic and Anglo-Saxon influences. It draws both on myth and on the literary canon for its explanatory power – an explanatory power, though, that is left unstated, as if already understood.

The works of Shakespeare (voted '5th Greatest Briton' by BNP members in a 2003 poll) are prominent here, available online (with a link to MIT's Shakespeare site) as a corrective to the 'onslaught of "politically correct" reworkings' of his plays. Each month a poem by a British writer is presented in this section, along with a brief critical appraisal of its significance. Poets are chosen from across the British Isles and are generally in the canon: G. K. Chesterton, Sir Walter Scott, W. B. Yeats. A poem from Scott's novel *Ivanhoe* is made to represent both the ancient roots of Britain and the present necessity to fight against Britain's 'disappearance' into the EU. The reasons for choosing Auden's 'Night Mail' are less clear, unless it is to stand for the security that might come from nostalgia, as might the emphatically non-canonical choice of 'Albert and the Lion'. Similarly, the anonymous folk lyric 'John Barleycorn' celebrates a timeless past through its depiction of brewing ('a very key aspect of British society'). The selection points to a past of innocent pride – even Scott's martial poem is set in myth – there is no engagement here with an actual history of power. The culture portrayed is benign and worthy of preservation; by implication, 'our' British present is likewise benign and in need of defence, for it is under cultural attack. The Other, it is suggested, might not only be the 'immigrant'; it might easily be other 'British' people – most obviously 'liberals' and 'the left'. The Other is constructed as the threat of multiculturalism, against which the BNP's discursive construction of its cultural heritage presents itself paradoxically as a monoculture that draws on a variety of cultural histories.

At the same time these discursive resources construct White identity as othered (seen as repressed and in need of defence) and as under threat by cultures which themselves are subject to othering. The imaginary of White cultural history is here presented as immutable; a collective history that produces identity to the degree that its fixity assures and asserts its normalization. This imaginary is confronted, according to the BNP, by a colonizing power that seeks to speak for 'us' and to reduce 'our' capacity for self-determination. This is sophistry of a particularly pernicious type – we need only to look at the continuing struggles in the UK for the human rights of asylum seekers, the identification of institutional racism in the police force and other public services, the persistence of racial discrimination in employment and education. For the historical colonizers – the oppressors – to construct themselves as the Other, as both repressed and silenced, appears shocking.

This ensuing 'powerlessness' is not, to use Stuart Hall's phrase, the historical outcome of 'the old, the imperialising, the hegemonising, form of "ethnicity"' (Hall 1990: 235). The cultural discourse of the BNP suggests a choice – they have chosen to place power in the hands of the Other; this is not a structured, historical condition. Of course, there is no actual transfer of power here – the objects of the BNP's racism are hardly empowered by this 'transfer' – it is a purely rhetorical act that seeks to represent the BNP itself as repressed, as Other. The rhetoric of ceded power is deployed as evidence for an actual ceding of power.

Just as the BNP's discourse of cultural heritage seeks to normalize what we might term a 'positive racism' through a set of cultural-historical symbols that are (obscurely) intended to fully explain and establish White British identity, so the 'new nationalism' of the BNP entails a normalization of the individuals who constitute it and who must therefore be similarly constructed as othered by the Other. It is to the discourse surrounding these individuals – that both constitutes them and is constituted by them – to which we now turn. In particular, we shall examine the extent to which the BNP's promotion of White cultural identity has usurped the 'old racism' and how social and cultural relations are presented by and through the rank and file members of the BNP through their letters and personal profiles on the website, 'the ways in which Whiteness is brought into being as a normative structure, a discourse of power, and a form of identity' (Ware & Back 2002: 13).

Racism and the everyday

As part of its Resources section, the site features 'Meet the Real BNP', which profiles four 'ordinary people just like you' who have joined the BNP to 'stand-up [sic] and do something positive to change this country for the better'. Beneath a photograph, each member has contributed a couple of sentences summarizing their reasons for joining the party. Below each text is a longer paragraph written by, we can assume, a BNP press officer or other party official, arguing the reasons for joining the party. Though brief, the contributions by the four 'ordinary' members emphasize unspecific statements of problems ('the changes in this country which are threatening our way of life'; 'I want to help make Britain great again'), the maintenance of value systems ('traditional and Christian') and the hope for a 'British future for my children'. The only explicit mentions of racialized actions are attributed to non-Whites. It is 'asylum seekers' who inflict 'racial abuse'; the implicit racism of the BNP is born out of suffering and repression, not hatred. This 'strong current of victimology in far-right discourse' (Ware & Back, 2002: 50) is played out in the everyday lives of the BNP members depicted here – and what could be more everyday than a 'retired vet', a 'businessman' and a 'customer services adviser and mother' (we have only a name for the fourth)?

If a triumphalist, imperialist history (from which the discourse of a multicultural history is entirely absent) is the cultural bedrock of the BNP's policies, its social imperative for the future rests on a racist construction of White children and young people. In the same year, the headline banner on the BNP site advertised 'Camp Excalibur: The Young BNP Event of the Year'. Here an appeal to a mythical history is conjoined with the everyday: an 'annual activity-packed getaway' for BNP families. Activities include 'paintballing, five-a-side football, archery, water-sports, Saturday night social and a full English breakfast'.

The photo galleries that document the BNP's Red, White and Blue festival of 2003 similarly demonstrate the normalization of racist politics as harmless social activities (www.bnp. org.uk/rwb2003/gallery1.htm). Whilst we do find there displays of the Union Jack, pictures of BNP leafleters and a portrait of a distinguished visitor, an unnamed representative of the 'FN'

(Front National), there is an abundance of photographs showing the banalities of an out-door, family festival: a bouncy castle (captioned 'Safe Fun'), people wandering around the site ('Finding Family and Friends') and buying ice-cream ('Keeping One's Cool'). A shot of children is captioned 'Our Bright Future'. It was at this festival in 2001 that Nick Griffin, the BNP's chairman, declared that 'his party was not the mouthpiece of racial hatred. On the contrary, the BNP, he said, was "the party of love"' (Back 2002a). If the visual discourse of the 2003 festival does not explicitly espouse 'love', it certainly seeks to annul the notion of the BNP as a racist party, even as its very appeal to ordinariness, reasonableness and respectability is founded on prejudice, separatism and oppression.

The EU referendum and academic activism

My choice of the BNP as an object of research was prompted by the visibility of the party in the British media at the time. Arguably this peaked in October 2009, when the BBC's political discussion programme *Question Time* invited Nick Griffin as one of five panellists. Earlier in that year Griffin had been elected as a member of the European Parliament. Uniquely for the programme, all the questions given to the panel explicitly addressed one political party: the BNP. Griffin was expelled from the party in 2014, after which the visibility of the BNP has waned. In one sense we might find its ideology persisting in the English Defence League, which enjoyed a modest presence in the mainstream media, though with an agenda on immigration and multiculturalism that owed more to the National Front than the BNP. In another sense, we might consider the BNP's agenda 'mainstreamed' by UKIP. The two parties are in broad agreement about immigration controls and sovereignty. One week after the UK voted to leave the EU on 23 June 2016, an article published on the BNP's website claimed that the party 'created the road to Brexit' (Edwards 2016) by raising awareness of the issue long before UKIP came to prominence.

This is not to suggest that the BNP and UKIP share a discursive identity of the type analyzed in this chapter. Research remains to be done on the discourse of UKIP to compare its discourse with that of the BNP. This is not to say that we might find in the UKIP's Euroscepticism a strain of xenophobia alongside more reasonable calls for controls on immigration. Ford, Goodwin and Cutts (2012) have argued that support for UKIP draws less on the explicit racism found in the BNP and in what they term 'polite' xenophobia, allied to anti-immigration and a distrust of dominant political leadership.

As I noted in my introduction, some media scholars do not consider activist media of the far right worthy of examination. The bulk of research into activist media overwhelmingly focuses on the mobilization of 'progressive', 'emancipatory' and even revolutionary politics. There is in activist media research an emphasis on social movement media, where slippery concepts such as 'neoliberalism' (against which activist media must struggle) and 'community' (always a good thing) are routinely deployed in the service of leftist strategizing. To study the BNP is to examine how 'community' might be deployed otherwise, for repressive and exclusionary reasons, though a more critical assessment of left-leaning activist media might ask deeper questions about how 'progressive' activists view community, from positions arguably equally exclusionary (leadership, for example, is rarely discussed in studies of social movement media, being displaced by appeals to anti-hierarchical and horizontal forms of communication). It should be obvious that here I am not equating the media of racial exclusion with media that promote, say, racial and sexual diversity, class struggle and multiculturalism. Instead, I am thinking of the alignment we find amongst alternative media scholars with causes espoused by the subjects of their research (except in those rare cases where those subjects represent an ideological enemy). Which perhaps explains why we do not find the distinctions made by Ford, Goodwin and Cutts between the BNP and UKIP in the work of

British media scholars. Instead, we seem to find the seeds of an eliding of ideologies, a collapse of all right-wing discourse into a single discursive enemy. We can see this taking place in texts by media scholars where research appears in the service of a political position.

I am writing only six months after the UK voted to leave the EU. It is too early to expect any detailed research into the discourses employed by both sides in the referendum (Leave and Remain), but we already have strong signals from British media and communication scholars about what to expect. The result of the UK's EU referendum seems to have provided opportunities for many media scholars to connect their personal political positions with their professional roles and to present themselves as media activists.

Bethany Usher (2016) of Teesside University proposes that media academics 'fight the rise of the right'. For her, the right includes UKIP, the BNP, Britain First and 'other right-wing groups'. She shows little interest in exploring the differences between these groups, preferring instead to encourage her colleagues to convince 'working class people' that they need not vote for or support the right: 'surely we are capable of being better communicators than the likes of Nigel Farage and Britain First?'. This is a troubling position to take. Usher seems to suggest that academics use their skills not to understand but to condemn and to propagandize. Moreover, she is keen to educate the next generation in her ways: 'On the morning after Brexit I watched with pride as one graduate picked apart Nigel Farage's statement using ideas discussed in seminars'. There is no place here, it seems, for discourse analysis that is not ideologically wedded to the politics of the left.

Also in the wake of the EU Referendum, Natalie Fenton, Professor of Media and Communications at Goldsmiths College, London, casts Leave voters as part of a recent history of 'public manifestations of dissent':

> the tag line for the Leave campaign – 'Let's Take Back Control' – speaks to a very real disaffection that this democracy doesn't work for the vast majority of its members.
>
> *Fenton 2016: unpaginated*

Yet for Fenton the success of the Leave campaign is due not to public engagement in political activism, but to voters convinced by

> a convenient xenophobic and often racist rhetoric that was spewed out by the three white men of [Boris] Johnson, [Michael] Gove and [Nigel] Farage all too willing to feed a tabloid frenzy.
>
> *ibid.*

Fenton is careful not to stereotype those who voted to leave the EU as dupes or racists themselves. She finesses her argument by avoiding any simplistic appeal to media effects: 'the media's influence resides in telling us what to think *about* rather than telling us what to think' (original emphasis). She goes on: 'we also know that people consume news from sources that largely reinforce their views'. Fenton, though, is far from subtle when she concludes that the British newspapers that supported the Leave campaign provided 'incitement to racial hatred'. There is little room here for an understanding of the motivation of voters or for an examination of discourse – indeed for anything but an absolutist and hyperbolic presentation of politicians and the mass media.

We might argue that Usher and Fenton are not presenting research in these opinion pieces, but they both elide the personal with the scholarly in very powerful ways. Moreover, Fenton's piece for the Open Democracy website also appears in a collection which, though published within ten days of the referendum, is described by its editors as providing 'authoritative analysis of the campaign' (Jackson, Thorsen & Wring 2016: 8). Where contributors indicate where their sympathies lie (and many do), it is clear that they cleave to the Remain side. What passes for discourse analysis in the collection is thin. Rowinski (2016: 52) claims that

> initial linguistic analysis has established a discursive construction, prevalent in the mainstream mainly right-of-centre national newspapers [that shows how] never before in living memory have some newspapers fed the public's hopes, fears and yes prejudice [sic] against Europe (and Europeans) [and] have damaged our democracy and played a pivotal role in creating the crisis we now face.

Bold claims indeed to derive from an editorial in the *Sun* and one in the *Daily Mail*, without any mention of how such discourse converts into voting behaviour. I worry that these hasty, yet unequivocal assessments might colour subsequent research, as well as the application and interpretation of the work of others (perhaps including the research presented in this chapter). Following the EU referendum, a febrile research environment has appeared, an environment populated by media scholars seemingly determined to find racism, separatism and prejudice throughout the British media. Such an attitude is able to feed on research into the discourses of the far right, to easily and unreflexively transfer the analysis of those discourses to mainstream media organizations. Our work should try to understand media cultures, not to support (nor to live inside) those cultures with which we happen to agree politically, and to dismiss and vilify those with which we disagree. In such a methodologically diverse field as ours, it is significant that amongst media studies scholars it appears *de rigueur* to be seen to support 'progressive' initiatives and movements. Or else the field itself attracts scholars already sympathetic to these causes – perhaps they are already activists themselves. It would be ironic for a section of the liberal intelligentsia to close off, rather than encourage, research into right-wing activism simply to serve its own political ends.

References

Atton, C. (2003) 'Indymedia and "Enduring Freedom": An Exploration of Sources, Perspectives and News in an Alternative Internet Project', in N. Chitty, R. R. Rush and M. Semati (eds) *Studies in Terrorism: Media Scholarship and the Enigma of Terror*. Penang: Southbound Press, pp. 147–64.

Atton, C. (2004) *An Alternative Internet: Radical Media, Politics and Creativity*. Edinburgh: Edinburgh University Press and New York: Columbia University Press.

Atton, C. (2006) 'Far-Right Media on the Internet: Culture, Discourse and Power', *New Media and Society*, vol. 8, no. 4, pp. 573–87.

Back, L. (2002a) 'When Hate Speaks the Language of Love'. Paper Presented at Social Movement Studies Conference, London School of Economics, April. Unpaginated.

Back, L. (2002b) 'Aryans Reading Adorno: Cyber-Culture and Twenty-First Century Racism', *Ethnic and Racial Studies*, vol. 25, no. 4, pp. 628–51.

Couldry, N. (2000) *Inside Culture*. London: Sage.

Couldry, N. (2002) 'Alternative Media and Mediated Community'. Paper Presented at the International Association for Media and Communication Research, Barcelona, 23 July. Unpaginated.

Downing, J. with Ford, T., Villarreal, G. and Stein, L. (2001) *Radical Media: Rebellious Communication and Social Movements*. Thousand Oaks, CA: Sage.

Edwards, P. (2016) 'How the BNP Created the Road to Brexit', British National Party, 13 August, http://www.bnp.org.uk, accessed 3 August 2016.

Fenton, N. (2016) 'Brexit: Inequality, the Media and the Democratic Deficit', openDemocracyUK, 30 June, https://www.opendemocracy.net/uk/austerity-media/natalie-fenton/brexit-inequality-media-and-democratic-deficit, accessed 22 July 2016.

Ford, R., Goodwin, M. J. and Cutts, D. (2012) 'Strategic Eurosceptics and Polite Xenophobes: Support for the United Kingdom Independence Party (UKIP) in the 2009 European Parliament Elections', *European Journal of Political Research*, vol. 51, no. 2, pp. 204–34.

Foucault, M. (1980) *Power/Knowledge: Selected Interviews and Other Writings, 1972–1977.* C. Gordon (ed.). New York: Pantheon.

Hall, S. (1990) 'Cultural Identity and Diaspora', in J. Rutherford (ed.) *Identity: Community, Culture, Difference.* London: Lawrence and Wishart, pp. 222–37.

Jackson, D., Thorsen, E. and Wring, D. (eds) (2016) *EU Referendum Analysis: Media, Voters and the Campaign.* Poole: Bournemouth University, Centre for the Study of Journalism, Culture and Community.

Rowinski, P. (2016) 'Mind the Gap: The Language of Prejudice and the Press Omissions That Led a People to the Precipice', in D. Jackson, E. Thorsen and D. Wring (eds) *EU Referendum Analysis: Media, Voters and the Campaign.* Poole: Bournemouth University, Centre for the Study of Journalism, Culture and Community, p. 52.

Searchlight (1999) 'Griffin Heads for Victory', *Searchlight,* October, http://www.searchlightmagazine.com/stories/GriffinVictory.htm, accessed 12 January 2003.

Usher, B. (2016) 'How Can Media Academics Fight the Rise of the Right?', *Three: D – The Newsletter of MeCCSA, the Media, Communication and Cultural Studies Association,* no. 26, p. 12.

Ware, V. and Back, L. (2002) *Out of Whiteness: Color, Politics and Culture.* Chicago, IL: University of Chicago Press.

Wetherell, M. and Potter, J. (1992) *Mapping the Language of Racism: Discourse and the Legitimation of Exploitation.* New York and London: Harvester Wheatsheaf.

30

MAPPING SOCIAL MEDIA TRAJECTORIES IN ZIMBABWE

Bruce Mutsvairo

Introduction

In today's globalized world, the growth of digital media is bringing about fundamental changes in the way people in sub-Saharan Africa think and act (Mutsvairo 2016). The availability of online movements provides a firsthand opportunity to critically examine current digital engagements among citizens and activists seeking political reform in Zimbabwe. The chapter argues that while social media is leading to a great deal of virtual awareness, very little action is taken to end the plight of citizens, thereby weakening the real impact of social media activism. ICTs, and more specifically the digital media, have radically changed the way cultures, economies, governments and human beings interact with each other. Similarly, the development of global information and communication infrastructures has radically transformed ways in which knowledge and content are created, produced and distributed. Conceptualizing activism in an African context requires a cross-disciplinary examination of factors facilitating and inhibiting its growth across the continent. This chapter, therefore, attempts to look at opportunities and challenges facing online protests in the wake of growing social media prevalence in Zimbabwe.

It is being assumed that with protests movements such as the Arab Spring, Occupy Movement, #BlackLivesMatter and #BringBackOurGirls taking centre stage, social media is playing an instrumental role in driving the popularity of socio-political movements throughout the world. Online civic campaigns are also gathering momentum in Zimbabwe with netizens using social media platform to demand political change. For example, social media outrage was prompting civil society organizations and opposition parties to turn out in huge numbers countrywide during the 2016 anti-government demonstrations and rallies, which they hoped would force former President Robert Mugabe's government to resign, giving many a renewed hope for political change.

This chapter uses data collected from face-to-face discussions with members of the Zimbabwean communities in the North East of the UK to determine ways through which digital participation among expatriate Zimbabweans is contributing to both online and offline activism in the Southern African nation. Focus group discussions with ten participants were bolstered by further in-depth interviews with 15 other Zimbabweans, along with a case study analysis of current digital protest movements in the country, which are gaining ground on Twitter, Facebook and YouTube. All interviews were conducted between January and April 2016. To this end, the study investigates how local Zimbabwean activists utilize digital and social media, identifying tactical similarities and differences to the use of these platforms in other regions of the world.

The chapter also explores the apparent advantages and disadvantages of using such platforms. Indeed, the suggestion by Dalton (2007: 143) that a Chinese student at the 1989 Tiananmen Square democracy rally held a poster that read, 'I don't know what democracy means, but I know we need more of it', potentially provides a powerful picture of the extent to which the notion of democracy is perceived and comprehended across the world, including in Africa. For that reason, findings from this chapter will seek to demonstrate the real potential of cyberactivism insofar as strengthening or weakening increased online and offline democratic participation of Zimbabwean citizens is concerned. The chapter further questions whether online protests are indeed 'liberation technologies' as suggested by Diamond (2010: 70) and if so, the extent to which they are. The main research question for this chapter is: to what extent is social media aiding and strengthening citizen participation in politics in Zimbabwe?

As political leaders in Africa, including long-time Kenyan opposition leader Raila Odinga, utilize digital technologies to communicate, reach out and debate their political agendas with citizens, the role played by platforms such as Twitter and Facebook cannot be underestimated, given social media's ability to virtually mediatize information and connect people. Content sharing and online debating is making citizens active participants in political decisions that affect them. This has led to the inevitable introduction of 'electronic democracy' on the world scene (Tsagaraousianou *et al.* 1998). These scholars claim electronic democracy best describes the intermediary role of digital technologies in augmenting citizen participation in the political stratum. The flourishing usage of the internet has, for example, helped a string of blogs and websites establish themselves as leading providers of Zimbabwe-focused digital news, drawing readers from the country's diaspora communities both in the West, Africa and beyond.

Zimbabwean context

The open space provided by social media platforms is not only allowing some Zimbabweans to freely comment and critique news from an array of sources, but citizens are now sharing content with family and friends, helping spread news and information about events and issues that affect them. The possibility to provide comments to each published article has led to the creation of a new form of interaction as readers share comments and opinions with each other. These people have become the 'new journalists' of the modern day, gathering news and distributing them on social media forums. Those living in Zimbabwe are also able to access these platforms, a development which has challenged state media's monopolization of news. For example, the 2015 disappearance of human rights activist Itai Dzamara, allegedly at the hands of state agents, has confirmed social media's status as a venue for dissent, activism and political campaigning, as citizens turn to Facebook and other social networks to criticize the government for allegedly engineering the activist's abduction. Government denials of involvement in Dzamara's disappearance have been met by revolts on social media, particularly on Facebook and WhatsApp. Ex-president Mugabe had declared his interest in extending his 37-year reign before a military coup ousted his government in November 2017. While Mugabe, now 94, made sure media laws prohibiting 'insults' to his presidency stayed intact, activists turned to social media networks and the Zimbabwean blogosphere, which they flooded with debates on political reform, rising polarities and increasing interest in human rights activism.

While not every Zimbabwean citizen has access to the internet or social media in particular, online debates dominating the cyber-space point to a paradigm shift in terms of the gathering and sharing of new media content. Zimbabweans living in the North East of the UK and elsewhere across the world have used their own access to social media and other digital platforms to spearhead campaigns that potentially have helped shape events at home, even though evidence on the ground still showed that Mugabe, their long-serving president, was not giving up. But recent online protests are taking a cue from recent developments in the Middle East and elsewhere across the world where citizens have taken to new technologies to demand political reform. Uprisings in Tunisia (Lotan *et al.* 2011), Egypt (Tufekci & Wilson 2012) and China (Yang 2012) were spearheaded and coordinated on various social media platforms.

Ahead of Mugabe's resignation, previously unknown clergyman Evan Mawarire had managed to harness social media for political engagement by using Facebook, Twitter and YouTube in search of government accountability. He became a household name among Zimbabweans, who followed his message to take the country's flag everywhere they go, demanding government accountability. The viral sharing of Mawarire's videos on social media platforms was by no doubt rapidly stimulating online political activity and community activism. What made Mawarire stand out though was his ability to engage officials both online and offline. When the country's reserve bank chief announced plans to introduce 'bond notes' to ease out the pending financial constraints, Mawarire used social media networks to oppose the move. Even better, he organized a meeting with the governor, with anti-government activists in attendance, to demonstrate his group's opposition to the idea. There is still no evidence as to what role social media played towards Mugabe's departure, but signs of Mawarire's ability to turn online interactions into offline realities made the clergyman and his supporters believe the online platform was giving them a unique voice.

Interestingly, protest music is emerging as a dominant form of civil and mass political participation movement in Zimbabwe. Thanks to a long and sustained relationship with political reform in Africa, the movement is using social media platforms to reinvigorate political songs as strategic tools for political and human rights activism. Zimbabwe's best-known musician, Thomas Mapfumo, has played a leading role through his music in the promotion of human rights, freedom and transparency, both in pre- and post-independence Zimbabwe. Mapfumo, who tirelessly sang against colonialism in Africa, maintained his celebrity status on social media by posting anti-Mugabe clips on YouTube accusing the former president's government of committing gross human rights violations, including its purported failure to guarantee citizens with freedom of assembly.

Freedom of speech and assembly, and the right to dissent, have all long been sensitive topics both in colonial and post-colonial Zimbabwe. Zimbabwe cannot be put in the same league as North Korea when it comes to totalitarianism. While anti-government journalists have in the past been targeted, the country's laws guarantee freedom of speech and association. Newspapers critical of Mugabe including the *Daily News, The Standard, The Independent* and *Newsday* have traditionally been allowed to publish, even though it is perhaps fair to say many journalists and indeed social media users, as confirmed by focus-group interviews with Zimbabweans living in the east of England, self-censor for fear of reprisals. Mugabe had maintained that no one could lecture him on human rights because he has fought for universal suffrage, leading to the country's independence in 1980.

Methodology

Focus group interviews with Zimbabweans living in the UK were used as a principal methodology in this chapter. As part of Empathy & Trust In Communicating Online (EMoTICON) – a sponsored research project on social media and democracy in Zimbabwe, in which I was the principal investigator – a very small sample size was originally used for this research.

This was deliberate, as the intention was to pursue frank and deep-seated discussions in a face-to-face setting with individuals involved in online participation. In pursuance of this objective, participants were invited to a workshop at Northumbria University in March 2016, with one Zimbabwean currently studying at the university acting as a key go-between between the project and the Zimbabwean community. The workshop, which lasted for close to seven hours, included presentations from members of the research team, along with open discussions with the participants who were asked to share their experiences and views regarding diasporic influences towards democracy in the country. A blogging workshop, involving learning and sharing blogging skills, also featured on the programme. Apart from the student who facilitated the meeting along with another member of the Zimbabwean community in the region, none of my research team members had previously met any of these participants.

Following the initial results from the workshop, 15 more interviews were conducted with Zimbabwean activists and journalists. Two of the 15 had participated in the workshop. These interviews were not only aimed at ascertaining the level of online participation that the interviewees were engaged in, but also examining whether they thought sharing information online was contributing to the enhancement of democracy in the country. The majority of those interviewed individually had originally wanted to participate in the workshop but had either pulled out or had shown preference to be interviewed individually. A trip to Zimbabwe in April 2016 completed a series of interviews as part of this project. In Zimbabwe, eight journalists were asked to share their thoughts on increased online participation and practices among Zimbabweans. They were also asked to share their opinions on whether they thought citizen journalism was crippling or boosting their work. Furthermore, they also had to share their perspectives on social media and its potential to free societies such as Zimbabwe's. Interviews were chosen as the primary methodology because I wanted to interact with the people who are using these technologies. Besides, interviews are widely used in qualitative research for various reasons (see Trochim 2000; O'Leary, 2004). In my case, I wanted to find out more about why people are engaging in online practices with the hope of making political changes, their worries, their predictions and their biases. I emphasized the participatory nature of data gathering, focusing on the people who participate in online deliberations in order to find out what they do and why they do it. The pilot study in Newcastle Upon Tyne also gave me an opportunity to mingle and socialize with members of the Zimbabwean diasporic community, all of whom confirmed their active use of social media to participate in social and political issues within their own communities and beyond. Data was processed and analyzed inductively in pursuit of what Marshall and Rossman (1999: 154) describe as identifying 'salient themes, recurring ideas or language, and patterns of belief'.

Findings and discussion

Digital activism in Zimbabwe remains in an evolving stage even though it is precipitously spreading. Social media's transformative ability to appeal to multiple audiences is driving new forms of social interaction, exchange, dialogue and online collaboration, unquestionably helping transform lives by giving hope to the politically marginalized. Zimbabwe, in spite of its political quagmires, has 6 million internet users, which is half of the population (POTRAZ 2016). While clearly not all of these users are digital activists, ten of the 15 interviewees confirmed that they believed easy access was enabling the participation of citizens in online political engagements. Results further showed that even though the majority of Zimbabweans see the potential route towards political change in the country as a direct result of the mass use of social media, issues such as the use of law to cripple online dissent are still a major concern. A government minister under Mugabe's regime stated in 2017 that the government was looking at legal ways to ensure that social media users would be 'responsible' for what they say online. The introduction of such a law could have led to increased self-censorship, all ten participants in the workshop agreed. This did not stop Mugabe from appointing what perhaps was the world's first cabinet minister in charge of 'cyber security'; a ministry that was discontinued by his replacement, Emmerson Mnangagwa.

It, however, must be noted that when it comes to the laws that govern the media, contemporary Zimbabwean media owes a lot to the pre-independence, White-led governments. If African natives did not have civil, political or social rights under colonial rule and the post-independence government has failed to meaningfully allow the flourishing of views opposed to the state, then one can understand why the media has been at the centre of state political control and manipulation of the masses both before and after independence in 1980. In the same vein, *The Rhodesia Herald* (renamed *The Herald* at independence), along with the Bulawayo-based *Chronicle* and their sister weeklies the *Sunday Mail* and the *Sunday News,* represented elitist White interests in Rhodesia. Repressive laws were used to protect these interests. Participants in the workshop tended to agree that the current government had used colonial era laws to punish dissent. In the same way Mukasa (2003) concludes: 'The journalistic ethos of the times was to promote European cultural standards while denigrating African culture and political agitation as the nemesis of Western civilization and Christianity.' Participants agreed the current government had used state media to target and ridicule opponents.

Several challenges stand in the way of social media activism. The generational gap is visibly one of them, results showed, as interviewees were able to highlight this as a major challenge facing digital activism in Zimbabwe. While youths around the country have been early adopters of social media, recognizing the profound opportunities that platforms such as Twitter and Facebook are offering, Mugabe's generation does not understand social media. This may sound like an advantage to activists, but the problem is when it comes to engaging politicians online, very few are willing to take part because not all of them understand the dynamics of social media. Besides, there simply is no defined policy on how to react to social media insults. Aside from the generational issue, not everyone understands social media, young or old. Even when they do, they may not know how to use it for the purposes of activism. A comment by one of the interviewees sums up this dilemma: 'I may know how to use social media but my grandmother in rural Chibi has never heard of it. I don't know how to educate her about it and besides what is the point of doing that?' Indeed, it may not be in the interest of an 80-year-old struggling to feed herself to know how to use social media for the purposes of activism. What it comes down to is the fact that it is a matter of priorities. Those starving will first seek food. Joining Facebook, therefore, becomes a luxury.

Events in the past were forcing those interviewed in Newcastle to self-censor their participation online. Some said they had two Facebook accounts: a 'real one and a fake one. When I use a fake account, I say whatever I want, when I use my real name, I have to censor what I write on Facebook'. It is widely reported that Mark Chavunduka and Ray Choto, senior journalists from the weekly *Standard* newspaper, were arrested and tortured by state security agents in 1999 following publication of a story in which they alleged – citing military sources – that some senior army officers had been detained in connection with a coup attempt on Mugabe's government. Chavunduka died in 2012 while Choto has since relocated to Washington, DC, where he worked for Voice of America. While incidents like this were forcing some to self-censor their content, all eight journalists interviewed in Zimbabwe confirmed that safety was not a major worry among them. Instead they were more critical of the government's desire to curtail freedom of speech, especially on social media platforms. Apart from the skirmishes involving

Chavunduka and Choto, as well as inestimable threats and possible arrests against some of his journalists, Trevor Ncube's *Standard* and *Independent* weeklies, as well as the *Newsday* daily, have been publishing in the country for years, despite their fierce and formidable anti-Mugabe stance. Social media, journalists agreed, was making it difficult for the government to target its critics as several activists make anonymous contributions.

AIPPA, or the Access to Information and Protection of Privacy law, which was introduced in 2002 and gave the Media minister authority to determine who could work as a journalist, was proving difficult to enforce because in the digital age: 'everyone can be a journalist', a freelance journalist told me. Signed to become law by ex-President Mugabe on 22 May 2013, the new constitution, in unprecedented fashion, includes a bill of rights, which stipulates freedom of expression. In a departure from the past, artistic expression and academic freedom are also recognized in the new constitution. While participants in the initial workshop welcomed the new constitution, they still were sceptical about the government's commitment to respecting freedom of expression. They pointed to the fact that the current situation had been better compared to the past when journalists were targeted dubiously through the use of AIPPA. In the year of its inception, at least seven journalists including the *Guardian*'s American-born correspondent Andrew Meldrum were arrested for violating the law's provisions. Other victims of the law in 2002 included local journalists Dumisani Muleya, Chris Gande, Farai Mutsaka, Bornwell Chakaodza, Geoff Nyarota and Fungayi Kanyuchi. The availability of social media was making it difficult for government to target specific people.

Again, to suggest social media platforms provide a potential to facilitate political and social changes provides a falsely alarming assumption that despotic regimes are not seeking to regulate and restrain these supposedly liberating spaces. African governments, especially those with a history of stifling freedom of association and assembly, will certainly be watching who is saying what on Facebook, which without doubt has been widely adopted as a mobile communicative tool across Africa. For example, Ugandan President Yoweri Museveni's government forcefully reacted against social media-coordinated political protests in April and October 2011, banning protests, arresting organizers and blocking access to social networking sites. In Zimbabwe, an activist was arrested in the second city of Bulawayo in March 2011, accused of attempting to use Facebook as a platform for dethroning Mugabe's government. The activist had posted a message on what was believed to be opposition leader Morgan Tsvangirai's Facebook wall, saying Zimbabweans should replicate the Arab Spring protests in Egypt. The legitimacy of social media-led political activism has not just attracted debate in Africa.

Yet Mugabe has never been the one to lightly take criticism. Criticizing Mugabe had long been a taboo. However, in the social media age, protesters attack the president willy-nilly. While he still retained power, the opportunity to pass a negative comment against the feared leader was something many illustriously accept as a positive shift in circumstances. For this reason, many consider social media as a democratizing space, given its ability to give them an opportunity to anonymously voice their concerns against Mugabe and his government. From sharing social media memes of his dramatic fall at the airport in 2015, to peacefully confronting his government on the streets, Mugabe became a subject of constant ridicule; his stranglehold on power appeared to wane in the wake of spirited protests, most of which were coordinated online.

It seems as if the most difficult challenge facing social media's potential to transform societies like Zimbabwe politically is the issue of coordinating people online. With people freely saying what they want as they wish, it is difficult to tell people what to do, because in many instances you are dealing with people you do not know. As noted by one interviewee: 'there is indeed democracy online. People say what they want but I don't think Mugabe cares what is being said online because the people who vote him into power are not even online.' Remarkably, this comment demonstrates the fundamental problems associated with using social media for political purposes. What the interviewee was alluding to is the fact that most of the ruling party's supporters live in rural areas where they hardly access social media; and if they do, having access to the internet is not their main priority as they are faced with various other challenges. These are the people that Mugabe and his party were concerned with. They do not have, in most cases, digital literacy skills. Their main priority is to get food on the table instead of 'liking' or signing an online petition.

'With mobile phone penetration in Zimbabwe almost hundred percent, there is great scope for successful citizenship journalism initiatives,' a veteran journalist said. 'More and more Zimbabweans are seeking cheap alternative sources of news and mobile phones, through social media platforms, have become instant hits. Citizen journalists have grabbed the momentum and find it easy to circulate news on social media.' This view is shared by several journalists who were adamant that citizen journalists are not a threat to their profession. They see the diversity of news sources and platforms as a healthy sign of a democracy. Still, it is very easy to underestimate the importance of internet literacy when assessing the real impact that technology, and particularly citizen journalism, could have in Zimbabwe and elsewhere in Africa. Many people use the internet for a purpose that they are familiar with. Not everyone is aware of the internet's multi-purpose functions. Moreover, not everyone with access to the internet understands what it is, or is keen to invest in trying to find out – something that confirms why the digital divide is still a real threat to progress. Worse still, in the case of Zimbabwe, unless you access the internet using free wireless networks, the costs involved are too high: meaning unless you are an activist, accessing the internet for political purposes does not become your immediate main priority.

Conclusion

While it certainly would be wrong to underestimate the kind of potential that social media could have in enhancing democracy in Zimbabwe, it is quite clear more ground needs to be covered in terms of accessibility and education. It may seem easy for those living in the Diaspora to see the remarkable potential that social media carries, but the reality on the ground begs to differ. There is widespread hunger in the country and many people are surviving on selling fruit or vegetables, which means that unless the quality of life among Zimbabweans changes, it is very difficult to conclude that social media will bring more democracy to the country, since access to it is a mere luxury. Opportunistic social media campaigns, such as Mawarire's, do not always lead to real reform.

The sizeable number of people following Mawarire on Twitter does not point to any success in transforming his online initiative into a radical street movement. However, other copycat protest groups such as #Tajamuka or 'We have said No' have risen in the aftermath of Mawarire's campaign bearing the brunt on state's resolve to crackdown on protesters. Protest musicians are also providing an alternative medium of critique to the regime, but interviewees believed musicians such as Mapfumo would have a real impact if they were criticizing Mugabe from within the country, because not every one of their supporters is active on social media. Hashtag activism, they argued, was new to Africa and carried with it a form of elitism, which citizens from low income areas were not keen to quickly identify themselves with. Besides, they were adamant the number of followers online or their determination to seek change should not measure the level of success for these groups, which means that their ability to force change or to influence

Mugabe to rethink his policies would be seen as a major victory because the authoritarian rarely accepts defeat. The low level of activism attributed to self-censorship by the interviewees also stands in the way of the successes of online engagements. Even those living in England are still very careful about the language they use in criticizing Mugabe for fear of unknown consequences. Thus, while it's true to say social media is impacting the lives of Zimbabweans, it will take more time for it to actually have meaningful contributions towards political and social change given the country's public sphere is still very much constrained.

References

Bastos, M. T., Mercea, D. and Charpentier, A. (2015) 'Tents, Tweets, and Events: The Interplay Between Ongoing Protests and Social Media', *Journal of Communication*, vol. 65, issue 2, pp. 320–50.

Benkler, Y. (2006) *The Wealth of Networks*. New Haven, CT: Yale University Press.

Bond, P. (2008) 'Lessons of Zimbabwe: An Exchange Between Patrick Bond and Mahmood Mamdani', *Links: International Journal of Socialist Renewal*, http://www.links. org.au/node/815, accessed 16 June 2016.

Coleman, S. and Blumler, J. G. (2009) *The Internet and Democratic Citizenship*. Cambridge: Cambridge University Press.

Dalton, R. J. (2008) *Citizen Politics: Public Opinion and Political Parties in Advanced Industrial Democracies* (fifth edition). Washington, DC: CQ Staff Directories.

Fuchs, C. (2011) *Foundations of Critical Media and Information Studies*. New York: Routledge.

Fuchs, C. (2014) *Social Media: A Critical Introduction*. London: Sage.

Habermas, J. (1962) *The Structural Transformation of the Public Sphere: An Inquiry into a Category of Bourgeois Society*. Cambridge, MA: MIT Press.

Joyce, M. (2010) *Digital Activism Decoded: The New Mechanics of Change*. New York: International Debate Education Association.

Kedzie, C. (1997) Communication and Democracy: Coincident Revolutions and the Emergent Dictator's Dilemma. Unpublished PhD dissertation. Santa Monica, CA: RAND Graduate School.

Kirkpatrick, G. (2008) *Technology and Social Power*. Basingstoke, UK: Palgrave Macmillan.

Larrauri, H. P. (2014) 'Digital Activism in Sudan', in E. Zuckerman and L. LeJeune (eds) *Global Dimensions of Digital Activism*. MIT Center for Civic Media, http://book.globaldigitalactivism.org/chapter/digital-activism-in-sudan, accessed 2 May 2017.

Lerner, D. (1958) *The Passing of Traditional Society*. New York: The Free Press.

Lotan, G., Graeff, E., Ananny, M., Gaffney, D., Pearce I. and boyd, d. (2011) 'The Revolutions were Tweeted: Information Flows During the 2011 Tunisian and Egyptian Revolutions', *International Journal of Communication*, vol. 5, pp. 1375–405.

McChesney, R. (1999) *Rich Media, Poor Democracy*. Urbana and Chicago, IL: University of Illinois Press.

Marshall, C. and Rossman, G. B. (1999) *Designing Qualitative Research*, third edition. Thousand Oaks, CA: Sage.

Meikle, G. (2016) *Social Media: Communication, Sharing and Visibility*. New York: Routledge.

Meyer, B. and Moors, A. (2006) *Religion, Media and the Public Sphere*. Bloomington, IN: Indiana University Press.

Morozov, E. (2010) 'Think Again: The Internet', *Foreign Policy*, 26 April, http://foreignpolicy.com/2010/04/26/think-again-the-internet, accessed 2 May 2017.

Morozov, E. (2011) *The Net Delusion: How Not to Liberate the World*. New York: Public Affairs.

Mukasa, S. (2003) 'Press and Politics in Zimbabwe', *African Studies Quarterly*, vol. 7, issues 2 and 3, https://asq.africa.ufl.edu/files/Mukasa-Vol-7-Issues-23.pdf, accessed 2 May 2017.

Mutsvairo, B. (2013) *Power and Participatory Politics in the Digital Age: Appraising the Role of New Media Technologies in Railroading Political Changes in Zimbabwe*. PhD Thesis. Leiden University: the Netherlands.

Mutsvairo, B. (2016) 'Dovetailing Desires for Democracy with New ICTS' Potentiality as Potent Platform for Online Activism', in B. Mutsvairo (ed.) *Digital Activism in the Social Media Era: Critical Reflections on Emerging Trends in Sub-Saharan Africa*. Basingstoke, UK: Palgrave Macmillan, pp. 1–20.

Norris, P. (2001) *Digital Divide*. New York: Cambridge University Press.

O'Leary, Z. (2004) *The Essential Guide to Doing Research*. London: Sage.

POTRAZ [Postal and Telecommunications Regulatory Authority of Zimbabwe] (2015) *Abridged Sector Performance Report 1st Quarter: Zimbabwe*, https://www.potraz.gov.zw/images/stats/First_Quarter_2015.pdf, accessed 16 June 2016.

Trochim, W. (2000) *The Research Methods Knowledge Base*, second edition. Cincinnati, OH: Atomic Dog Publishing.

Tsagaraousianou, R., Tambini, D. and Bryan, C. (eds) (1998) *Cyberdemocracy: Technology, Cities and Civic Networks*. London: Routledge

Tufecki, Z. and Wilson, C. (2012) 'Social Media and the Decision to Participate in Political Protest: Observations from Tahrir Square', *Journal of Communication*, vol. 62, no. 2, pp. 363–79.

UNDP [United Nations Development Program] (2010) 'Zimbabwe has Highest Literacy Rate in Africa', *The Southern Times*, 16 July.

White, G. (1998) 'Constructing a Democratic Developmental State', in M. Robinson and G. White (eds) *The Democratic Developmental State: Political and Institutional Design*. Oxford: Oxford University Press.

White, M. (2010) 'Clicktivism is Ruining Leftist Activism', *Guardian*, 12 August, http://www.guardian.co.uk/commentisfree/2010/aug/12/clicktivism-ruining-leftist-activism, accessed 29 March 2017.

Yang, G. (2012) 'A Chinese Internet? History, Practice, and Globalization', *Chinese Journal of Communication*, vol. 5, no. 1, pp. 49–54.

31

THE CASE OF THE DESTROYED PLAQUE

Social media, collective memory and activism in Cartagena, Colombia

Anamaria Tamayo-Duque and Toby Miller

Cartagena de Indias in Colombia is a World Heritage City, well known for its beautiful colonial architecture, imposing international colloquia, racialized social inequality and child-sex tourism; not so much for online activism. In November 2014 an event involving the British royal family changed that; or did it?

A remarkable mobilization of Twitter and *bourgeois*-press activism was triggered by the unveiling of what turned out to be a very controversial plaque. It commemorated the failure of British and American troops under the command of Admiral Edward Vernon to seize the city in 1741 in the face of resistance led by the Spanish Admiral Don Blas de Lezo. The troops included Lawrence Washington, George's older brother, who named their property Mount Vernon after the Admiral.

The plaque represents the collision of two histories. One is about Colombian nationalism prior to nineteenth-century independence; the other, twenty-first-century tourism planning. One is to do with repelling the British; the other with attracting them. One celebrates dispatching the British military; the other welcomes British visitors. One centres around sustaining a blockade; the other opening a city.

This research draws in part on work on tourism done by Olga Lucia Sorzano and help from Aaron Eduardo Espinosa. Drawing on participant observation, textual analysis and political economy, we examine this case from several perspectives, teasing out its value as an instance where popular history gained a certain expression through activist media – but in a partial way.

The city

Cartagena exists in a nation bedevilled by violence. Both Human Rights Watch (2015) and the Colombian government (BBC News 2015) estimate that over 200,000 people have been killed and almost 7 million displaced in a national conflict that has coloured the country's daily life over the last half-century (also see https://www.hrw.org/americas/colombia). Beginning as a *guerrilla* strategy to bring about rural land reform, the conflict has seen the splintering of leftist groups, their ethical disintegration into kidnapping, murder and drugs, and a brutal response from the government and *paramilitares*. And Colombia remains as unequal as it was when the conflict began: Oxfam

(2016: 5–6)estimates that 'over 67 percent of productive land is concentrated in 0.4 percent of agricultural landholdings'. This is despite significant economic growth and virtually zero inflation (Organización para la Cooperación y el Desarrollo Económico 2015: 8).

Cartagena was founded in 1533 by the Spanish, from whom it declared its independence in 1811, and was named the Distrito Turístico y Cultural de Cartagena de Indias in 1991. Cartagena's World Heritage status derives from its material place in the annals of military and religious history – the fortifications are the largest in South America, at almost 200 hectares, and one of the most intact colonial examples. The city's monuments represent remarkable testimony to faith and craft alike, and zones within the Old Town correspond to areas once occupied by slaves, merchants, artisans and the colonial élite. UNESCO sees these as of great import, both because they illuminate the history of maritime trade routes and because they are imperilled by tourism's impact on the natural and built environments (http://whc.unesco.org/en/list/285). A fortified history and a contemporary dependence on tourism based in colonial architecture characterize a racially-divided city in a fractured nation, torn apart by conflict.

The 2005 Census suggests that Cartagena's population is close to a million. The Census defined approximately 63 per cent of its residents as what we would call *mestizos* (with mixed heritage from native peoples, Spaniards and the Arab world) and 36 per cent as Afro-Colombian descendants of enslaved Africans. There are small numbers of indigenous people (http://www.dane.gov.co/files/censo2005/PERFIL_PDF_CG2005/13001T7T000.PDF). (Such surveys classically regard indigenous or native peoples as those whose heritage is genetically and linguistically distinct.) Lighter-skinned *mestizo* oligarchs dominate finance, business, education and politics. The decades-long conflict in Colombia has seen many internal exiles flee the centre of the country for the Caribbean, where the *guerrilla* rarely focused their efforts, but where death still comes easily due to the violence of the state's proxies, the *paramilitares*.

The image of Cartagena internationally is not so much an exile's sanctuary, a site of light-skinned privilege, or an endangered ecology, but a tourist's paradise. It offers spectacular views of the Caribbean from the old town, fortified architecture, narrow streets, horse-drawn transportation, luxury hotels, street life and a cornucopia of music and dance. That hides the realities of massive child sexual exploitation, extreme Afro-Colombian poverty and the awful history of the left being assassinated by the *paramilitares*. How does tourism articulate to the plaque in question?

By the early 1950s, Cartagena was regarded as Colombia's major tourist destination. Its remarkable heritage of architecture, history and myth made it a 'ciudad turística con un ambiente alegre y múltiples diversiones' [a tourist city with a relaxed environment and many enjoyable activities] (PCNT 1952: 20). Two decades later, the World Bank proposed a strategy for diversifying the Colombian economy and generating foreign exchange. It suggested that the 11 kilometres of beach between Venezuela and Panama become an economic-development zone, drawing on the comparative advantage ascribed to the Caribbean: proximity to the US, reverse climatic seasons and a long expanse of beach (World Bank 1972: 4). Cartagena would convert itself into a paradise of 'sol y playa' [sun and sand], a playground for North Americans, in keeping with the four S's sought by US visitors: sea, sand, sun and sex (Boyer 2002).

The Centro de Investigación Económica y Social argued that tourism needed 'exenciones e incentivos claros y atractivos' [clear and attractive tax exemptions and incentives]. It acknowledged the risk of 'una distorsión social de consecuencias imprevisibles' [social disruption of a kind that cannot be precisely predicted] and expressed anxiety that a service class of workers, poor and poorly treated, would arise in order to meet the needs created by an influx of tourists (Fedesarrollo 1972: 140).

That prediction was prescient. The sector's growth has been accompanied by unemployment, underemployment, social clearances and sex tourism – and all done in the dual names of economic growth and international relations. Numerous studies conducted by the third sector, academia and the Instituto Colombiano de Bienestar Familiar [Colombian Institute of Family Welfare] attest to these outcomes (Mosquera & Bozzi 2005; Bernal-Camargo *et al.* 2013; Londoño *et al.* 2014).

The gradual lessening of tensions in Colombia has stimulated a visitor revival. Local tourism's official slogan 'realismo mágico' [magical realism] emphasizes the coterminous appeal to spectacular ecology, 'beautiful women' and a Nobel Laureate novelist in Gabriel García Márquez (http://www.procolombia.co/noticias/colombia-realismo-magico; http://colombia.travel/realismomagico). Many lighter-skinned oligarchs remain in denial of the structure and causes of racial inequality (Valle 2017).

While the US figures most centrally in the Colombian national imaginary of wealthy outsiders, daily flights from London to Bogotá began right at the time of the controversy that is the centre of our chapter, and since 2015, the UK has been the fastest-growing source of visitors to the region, thanks to their wealth, their taste for travel to warm climes and, ironically, their desire to avoid terrorism (Maslen 2014; Boletín Mensual, December 2015).

Historical context

A complex history ties the region to the British and their short-lived plaque. Cartagena de Indias was a key site in the struggle between Spain and Britain for economic control of the Caribbean during the eighteenth century, because it was a slave port and outpost of Spain's naval power and trade. Vernon's despicable – and ultimately failed – blockade attempted to starve the local population into submission, position the British empire to seize Spanish gold and territory and support the exchange of cross-imperial contraband. The siege also incarnated Britain's desire to assert its treaty right to deploy slaves in Spanish territory and engage in the 'free' trade of goods (and people). Part of what was once known as the War of Jenkins' Ear/*La Guerra de Asiento* is now categorized as a battle in the War of Austrian Succession.

The attack on the port city took place between 13 March and 20 May 1741. Vernon oversaw an immense fleet: 186 ships, 2,620 pieces of artillery and more than 27,000 men. By contrast, the Spanish defence of Cartagena was composed of six ships, 4,000 soldiers and 600 archers (the historical literature varies in its estimates). The latter were a mix of regular Spanish troops, militia comprised of creoles (as *mestizos* were then known), native peoples, Africans and their descendants (Robertson 1919; Lemaitre 1998; 'Vista' 2014; Mazzotti 2016).

Bizarrely, illegal British supply chains provisioned the Spanish *guarda costa* [coast guard], which helped ensure the blockade's ultimate failure, along with chronic illness from tropical diseases (Earle 1996; Schmitt 2015). The chaos brought on by fever and insect-borne death produced both the expression 'Mosquito Empire' (McNeill 2010) and a nation of beef eaters, because that became the key ration for the Colombian military, prisoners and slaves from the time of the siege (Van Ausdal 2008). Just four decades after Vernon's assault, a similarly unsuccessful attempt by the Spanish to undo independence movements in Cartagena marked the nation's freedom from empire. The city, therefore, incarnates high points of history for all Colombians. It is laden with symbolism: independence, but equally a site of Spanish colonialists and their subalterns vying with British invaders.

Ironically, London has a statue in Belgrave Square of South America's official independence hero, Simón Bolívar, who celebrated Britain as a beacon of freedom in the struggle against imperialism. The plaque quotes him as saying: 'I am convinced that England alone is capable of protecting the world's precious rights as she is great, glorious and wise.' That contradiction continues.

The offending plaque

This triumph over the British quickly became, and has remained, a point of pride in Cartagena's collective memory. But if we fast forward to today, the city's oligarchs seemed to take a different view when they elected to construct a plaque celebrating the gallant British and their heroic siege. They invited the Prince of Wales and the Duchess of Cornwall to unveil the following tribute:

> Esta placa fue develada por sus altezas reales el Príncipe de Gales y la Duquesa de Cornualles en memoria al valor y sufrimiento de todos los que murieron en combate intentando tomar la ciudad y el fuerte de San Felipe, bajo el mando del almirante Edward Vernon en Cartagena de Indias en 1741 [This plaque was unveiled by their Royal Highnesses the Prince of Wales and the Duchess of Cornwall in memory of the valor and suffering of those who, under Admiral Vernon, died in combat attempting to take the city and fort of San Felipe in Cartagena de Indias in 1741].

The event was timed by the Corporación Centro Histórico Cartagena De Indias [Historical Centre Corporation of Cartagena De Indias] (a private institution with ties to élite politics and corporate business) to coincide with Charles and Camilla's 2014 visit to Colombia. The somewhat opaque, if not mysterious, corporation argued that the commemoration would increase service-sector revenues from British tourists cathected onto their warrior past. Sabas Pretel de la Vega, a corrupt politician banned from holding public office for a decade, and a member of the Corporation, not only approved the text of the plaque, but planned a cross in Tierrabomba to honour the British battlefield dead, in the hope of luring additional tourists ('Cambiar el texto' 2014). He also believed that the chosen text on the plaque was sacrosanct, because 'it was approved by the British'. Any changes might give offence (El Tiempo 2014b).

From the day after the ceremony unveiling this unfortunate object, there was a massive Twitter campaign and unfavourable media coverage in Cartagena and the rest of the country over the plaque's celebration of inhumane cruelty. The voices of protest began with the upper-middle class on social media and editorials and op-eds by well-known journalists, politicians and even the capital Bogotá's mayor. The governor likened the idea to London commemorating German pilots who had bombed it during the Blitz (El Tiempo 2014c; El Tiempo 2014b). There was collective outrage at violating the country's historical memory, honouring the perfidious British Empire and betraying those who fought and died to defend their city.

Journalist Daniel Coronell tweeted 'Placa que debe avergonzar a Cartagena. Por la lagartería de unos cuantos terminamos homenajeando a un verdugo' [The plaque should embarrass Cartagena. To satisfy the oleaginous self-interest of a few, we are paying homage to a killer]. Governor Juan Carlos Gossain stated:

> No quiero causar molestias incómodas por este tema, pero soy cartagenero y amo profundamente la historia de la ciudad. La batalla contra los ingleses fue el combate más importante de los que ha librado el país en su historia, y poner una placa en honor a los ingleses es como si un banco pusiera una placa en honor a los ladrones que se lo robaron. Lo que vino Vernon fue a robar, a saquear a Cartagena, pero no pudo [I don't want to cause discomfort on this subject, but I am from Cartagena and love its history very deeply. The battle against the English was the most important conflict in our nation's history. Creating a plaque to honour them is like a bank erecting a plaque to honour thieves who stole from it. Vernon came to rob and plunder Cartagena, but was unable to do so].
>
> *El Tiempo 2014a*

Chastened, the then-mayor of Cartagena, Dionisio Vélez Trujillo, undertook to have the offending item removed. But before his apparatchiks could so, Jaime Rendón, an engineer originally from Medellín but a long-term resident of Cartagena, defaced the plaque and publicized his action. Within 24 hours, the offending item was officially excised.

It had all been just a matter of days from the old boy and his consort landing in Cartagena to remove the veil and the removal of what lay beneath it (Hernández-Mora 2014). The mayor left office some time afterwards, amidst spiralling scandals about his love life and financial affairs that culminated with exposure in the *Panama Papers* (El Universal 2016). It was not a highlight of British–Colombian cultural relations.

Interpretation

The incident can be read in various ways. Superficially, it marks the protection of popular historiography against a crude, reactionary élite revisionism driven by craven desires to promote Anglo tourism. Whilst no one could argue for the Spanish Empire as a beacon of human endeavour or human rights by contrast with its similarly venal British equivalent, the fact is that the *Cartageneros'* defence, in both the eighteenth and twenty-first centuries, represents a storied moment in local and national mythology – participating in, and then commemorating, Blas de Lezo's victory. As an ironic note, in the same year as the action against the plaque in Cartagena, Catalan nationalists in Spain militated for the removal of a statue of Blas de Lezo in Madrid, because he, too, had run a starvation blockade (of Barcelona) (Medialdea 2014).

And the event can be said to illustrate the power that the so-called social media (SBS and the CBC are anti-social?) are conventionally said to wield (Castells 2012; Lago Martínez 2012). We appreciate that the grandiloquent rhetoric of citizen empowerment, gatekeeper-free expression and social-movement triumphalism, supposedly enabled by new technologies, is largely overblown (Passy & Monsch 2014). But it is important to scrutinize instances where power-hungry forms of surveillance capitalism (*vide* Twitter) also provide a sphere for effective action by ordinary people – counter-power against hegemonic governments, whether embodied in small-minded mayors or small-minded heirs (Puyosa 2015).

That said, it is worth noting that in this instance, some Tweeters had more influence than others. For example, Rendón, the citizen who destroyed the plaque, was inspired to do so by a Tweet from Senator Navarro Wolff, who threatened to deface it, and other commentaries on the issue in social media ('Me les adelanté' 2014). This was not a voice to the voiceless, so much as a conduit expressing splits within the oligarchy over celebrating colonial conquerors versus recruiting jingoistic tourists.

This protest was no Twitter campaign from below. Even though the technology gap in Cartagena is not immense – most citizens have access to cell phones and many participate in social media – barriers of race and class in everyday life translate into virtual conduct. For example, people marginalized from power who have access to instant messaging do not regard it as a route to political influence; they view their marginalization as immune to mitigation through democratic processes. They use communications technologies to meet one another or express feelings rather than engage in political action. After centuries of slavery, decades of conflict and fruitless attempts to make their case, this is hardly surprising.

In explaining this reality, our community informants – local intellectuals and artists working with and/or from under-privileged groups – insisted that the social media cannot be seen as routes to political participation. Minorities experience a fundamentally unequal, segregated society. Their attempts at civic engagement have produced few successes, and they remain systematically denied access to power, policies and programs. Trying to influence such things via social media seems as pointless as any other form of communication (Barrios 2016; Salcedo 2016).

This issue relates to Cartagena's status as a place that is designated and managed more for tourists than its own people. The city is called 'the Heroic one' because it withstood attacks throughout its history, the two most prominent being against the British and Spanish Empires. It is filled with streets, statues and neighbourhoods that have been named to celebrate and commemorate Spanish *conquistadores* [conquerors] and rulers. Pedro de Heredia, who 'founded' the city, and Blas de Lezo are among the most prominent. Along with the case of the 2014 plaque, Dionisio Trujillo's administration sought to legitimize Cartagena's colonial past by returning the city's logo (a celebration of the eradication of slavery and independence from Spain) to the old emblem of the Spanish colony (Abello 2016). Commenting on the unveiling of the plaque and the return to this 'colonialist' emblem, Alberto Salcedo Ramos tweeted 'El alcalde de Cartagena es, tristemente, de esos cartageneros que presumen de virreinales y tienen nostaligia del látigo' [The mayor of Cartagena is, regrettably, one of those *Cartageneros* who love royalty and are nostalgic for the lash] (2014). Aberrant moments in this history are erased from it. Consider the case of General José Prudencio Padilla. A fierce leader of the independence movement, he was falsely declared a traitor, executed by Bolívar, and airbrushed from the record until very recently (Helg 2012).

It's significant that few Tweets protested the plaque's commemoration of the British Empire, or its exclusion of the indigenous, Afro-descended and Creole fighters who died in battle. Rather, most Tweets highlighted the need to celebrate the Spanish armada in the new world, embodied by Blas de Lezo. The perceived betrayal was not of the Colombian nation as a tri-ethnic mosaic, but a Colombian nation that still imagines itself as part of the Spanish Crown, albeit brokered through latter-day oligarchic nationalism (Arcieri 2014).

Neither side in the debate engaged a truly revisionist popular history, which would focus on indigenous peoples' resistance to the *conquista*, the roles of women and Afro-Caribbeans, and challenges to the longstanding corrupt traditions of the city's ruling élite, incarnated in figures such as Benkos Bioho, a slave who led a rebellion in the sixteenth century (Urbina Joiro 2006). Today, leading Afro-Caribbeans are routinely deployed to justify neoliberalism as supposed signs that anyone with talent can succeed (Sierra Becerra 2017). Instead, the incident became one more moment of forgetting native and Afro-descendant struggle against all imperialism.

But the Twitter campaign achieved something beyond our headline story. Its discussion threads opened what has become an ongoing debate about what a revisionist history might comprise – how it could engage groups hitherto hidden from history and criticize the historiographic power of local authorities.

And perhaps the national conversation is opening up. The world of popular art, notably murals, is a key site for the expression of resistance to racism and inequality. That non-virtual world of expression may be a more important venue for liberation than the social media (Rolston & Ospina, 2017). And there has been some official progress: the 2016 Bicentennial Law declared 6 December a civic celebration commemorating defeat of the Spanish siege of 1815. It acknowledged the efforts and central role of *Cartageneros* during the struggle for independence. In addition, Padilla and Benkos Bioho are slowly gaining a presence in the imaginary of the city; but it remains to be seen whether that will open doors for all *Cartageneros* to experience their home fully, and participate satisfyingly in political processes through both actual and virtual worlds.

Tension over collective memory and history is prevalent throughout Colombia, where there is a schizophrenic identification with a lost past of order, and even a certain grandeur, associated with European domination; and a pride in having thrown it over. This bizarre contradiction is animated by racial difference and inequality and a sense of the country constantly being re-forged through horrific violence and a struggle over the definition and curation of national narratives.

But it is hardly surprising that the social media do not provide a utopic place where democracy and political participation are accessible by all, and each person has a voice. Race and class determine whose voice is heard in the virtual world. Marginalized people in Cartagena are all too aware of the fact that no amount of texting or posting gives them real access to power. The struggle for the meaning of Cartagena – what it is and who defines it – is ongoing. Twitter played its part in starting a debate in popular historiography, but largely among élites.

References

Abello, A. (2016) Personal interview, 7 December.

Arcieri, V. (2014) "'Estaba Indignado por el Irrespeto a los Héroes de Cartagena y po Reso le di con una Mona": Ingeniero Rendón', *El Heraldo*, 5 November, https://www.elheraldo.co/bolivar/ingeniero-partio-la-polemica-placa-en-cartagena-en-homenaje-los-ingleses-caidos-172770, accessed 4 May 2017.

Barrios, W. (2016) Personal interview, 8 December.

BBC News (2014) 'Plaque Unveiled by Prince Charles in Colombia Is Removed', 8 November, http://www.bbc.com/news/world-latin-america-29963392, accessed 4 May 2017.

BBC News (2015) 'Colombia's Santos "in Serious Difficulty" if Farc Deal Fails', 18 November, http://www.bbc.com/news/world-latin-america-34864194, accessed 4 May 2017.

Bernal-Camargo, D. R., Varón-Mejía, A., Becerra-Barbosa, A., Chaib-De Mares, K., Seco-Martín, E. and Archila-Delgado, L. (2013) 'Explotación Sexual de Niños, Niñas y Adolescentes: Modelo de Intervención', *Revista Latinoamericana de Ciencias Sociales, Niñez y Juventud*, vol. 11, no. 2, pp. 617–32.

Boyer, M. (2002) 'El Turismo en Europa, de la Edad Moderna al Siglo XX', trans. Carlos Larrinaga Rodríguez, *Historia Contemporánea*, vol. 25, pp. 1331.

Canchila García, A. (2014) 'Cambiar el Texto de la Placa Seria una Ofensa a los Ingleses', *El Universal*, 4 November, http://www.eluniversal.com.co/cartagena/cambiar-el-texto-de-la-placa-seria-una-agresion-los-ingleses-sabas-pretelt-175903, accessed 4 May 2017.

El País (2014) 'Visita Real: Detalles de la legada del Príncipe Carlos a Colombia', 27 October, http://www.elpais.com.co/elpais/entretenimiento/noticias/visita-real-detalles-llegada-principe-carlos-colombia, accessed 4 May 2017.

El Tiempo (2014a) 'Citan a Alcaldía de Cartagena para Responder por Polémica Placa', 4 November, http://www.eltiempo.com/colombia/otras-ciudades/placa-principe-carlos-en-cartagena-citan-a-secretario-general/14787676, accessed 4 May 2017.

El Tiempo (2014b) 'Gobernador de Bolívar Critica Placa que Descubrió Príncipe Carlos', 4 November, http://www.eltiempo.com/colombia/otras-ciudades/gobernador-de-bolivar-critica-placa-que-descubrio-principe-carlos/14786136, accessed 4 May 2017.

El Tiempo (2014c) 'Me les Adelanté a los Politicos', 5 November, http://www.eltiempo.com/colombia/otras-ciudades/un-hombre-rompen-placa-de-cartagena/14796760, accessed 4 May 2017.

El Universal (2016) 'Se Investiga Relación de Préstamo de Exalcalde Vélez con los "Papeles de Panamá"', 17 June, http://www.eluniversal.com.co/politica/se-investiga-relacion-de-prestamo-de-exalcalde-velez-con-los-papeles-de-panama-228487, accessed 4 May 2017.

Castells, M. (2012) *Redes de Indignación y Esperanza: Los Movimientos Sociales en la Era de Internet*. Madrid: Alianza Editorial.

Clarke, N. (2007) 'The Night Camilla Lost Her Virginity—And Changed the History of the Royals', *Daily Mail*, 3 June, http://www.dailymail.co.uk/femail/article-459315/The-night-Camilla-lost-virginity--changed-history-royals.html, accessed 4 May 2017.

Colombia (2015) Oficina de Estudios Económicos, Ministerio de Industria y Comercio. *Boletín Mensual, Sección Turismo*. Bogotá, December, http://www.mincit.gov.co/loader.php?lServicio=Documentos&lFuncion=verPdf&id=77374&name=OEE_DO_WA_Turismo_Diciembre_05-02-2015.pdf&prefijo=file, accessed 4 May 2017.

Coronell, D. (2014) 'Placa que Debe Avergonzar a Cartagena. Por la Lagartería de Unos Cuantos Terminamos Homenajeando a un Verdugo', *Twitter*, 2 November, https://twitter.com/DCoronell/status/529021931995922432, accessed 4 May 2017.

Diaz, J. C. and Montaño, J. (2014) 'La Fallida Toma de Cartagena que Desató Debate 273 Años Después', *El Tiempo*, 5 November, http://www.eltiempo.com/colombia/otras-ciudades/debate-por-placa-puesta-en-el-castillo-de-san-felipe-/1479065, accessed 4 May 2017.

Earle, R. (1996) '"A Grave for Europeans"? Disease, Death, and the Spanish-American Revolutions', *War in History*, vol. 3, no. 4, pp. 371–83.

Fedesarrollo. (1972) 'Turismo', *Coyuntura Económica,* http://hdl.handle.net/11445/2846, accessed 4 May 2017.

Helg, A. (2012) 'Simón Bolívar's Republic: A Bulwark Against the "Tyranny" of the Majority', *Revista de Sociologia e Política*, vol. 20, pp. 21–37.

Hernández-Mora, S. (2014) 'Colombia: El Ridículo Histórico del Príncipe Carlos de Inglaterra y del Alcalde de Cartagena a Cuenta de una Placa Homenaje al Admirante que Intentó Conquistar la Ciudad', *Radio Tierra Viva,* 6 November, http://radiotierraviva.blogspot.com.co/2014/11/colombia-el-ridiculo-historico-del.html, accessed 4 May 2017.

Human Rights Watch (2015) *World Report 2015: Events of 2014*, https://www.hrw.org/sites/default/files/wr2015_web.pdf, accessed 4 May 2017.

Lago Martínez, S. (ed.) (2012) *Ciberespacio y Resistencias: Exploración en la Cultura Digital*. Buenos Aires: Hekht Libros.

Lemaitre, E. (1998) *Breve Historia de Cartagena*. Medellín: Editorial Colina.

Londoño, N. H., Valencia, D., García, M. and Restrepo, C. (2014) 'Factores Causales de la Explotación Sexual Infantile en Niños, Niñas y Adolescentes en Colombia', *El Ágora USB Medellín-Colombia*, vol. 15, no. 1, pp. 241–54.

McNeill, J. R. (2010) *Mosquito Empires: Ecology and War in the Greater Caribbean, 1620–1914*. New York: Cambridge University Press.

Maslen, R. (2014) 'Avianca to Return to London Market in July 2014', *Routes,* 4 February, http://www.routesonline.com/news/29/breaking-news/238576/avianca-to-return-to-london-market-in-july-2014, accessed 4 May 2017.

Mazzotti, J. A. (2016) 'Criollismo, Creole, and Créolité', in Y. Martínez-San Miguel, B. Sifuentes-Jáuregui and M. Belausteguigoitia (eds) *Critical Terms in Caribbean and Latin American Thought*. Basingstoke, UK: Palgrave Macmillan, pp. 87–99.

Medialdea, S. (2014) 'Madrid no Retirará la Estatua a Blas de Lezo y afea a Barcelona la Reedición Interesada de la Historia', *ABC,* 20 November, http://www.abc.es/madrid/20141120/abci-madrid-blas-lezo-barcelona-201411201433.html, accessed 4 May 2017.

Mosquera, M. V. and Bozzi, C. O. (2005) 'El Abordaje de la Problemática de Explotación Sexual Infantil en Cartagena', *Palabra*, no. 6, pp. 137–53.

Organización para la Cooperación y el Desarrollo Económico (2015) *Estudios económicos de la OCDE: COLOMBIA,* http://www.oecd.org/eco/surveys/Overview_Colombia_ESP.pdf, accessed 4 May 2017.

Oxfam (2016) *Unearthed: Land, Power, and Inequality in Latin America,* https://www.oxfam.org/sites/www.oxfam.org/files/file_attachments/unearthed-executive-en-29nov-web.pdf, accessed 4 May 2017.

Passy, F. and Monsch, G. A. (2014) 'Do Social Networks Really Matter in Contentious Politics?', *Social Movement Studies*, vol. 13, no. 1, pp. 22–47.

Puyosa, I. (2015) 'Los Movimientos Sociales en Red: Del Arranque Emocional a la Propagación e Ideas de Cambio Politico', *Chasqui: Revista Latinoamericana de Comunicación*, no. 128, pp. 197–214.

Robertson, J. A. (1919) 'The English Attack on Cartagena in 1741; And Plans for an Attack on Panama', *Hispanic American Historical Review*, vol. 2, no. 1, pp. 62–71.

Rolston, B. and Ospina, S. (2017) 'Picturing Peace: Murals and Memory in Colombia', *Race & Class*, vol. 58, no. 3, pp. 23–45.

Salcedo Ramos, A. (2014) 'El Alcalde de Cartagena es, Tristemente, de Esos Cartageneros que Presumen de Virreinales y Tienen Nostalgia del Látigo', *Twitter,* 2 November, https://twitter.com/SalcedoRamos/status/529081837818482688, accessed 4 May 2017.

Salcedo, E. (2016) Personal interview, 10 December.

Schmitt, C. S. (2015) 'Virtue in Corruption: Privateers, Smugglers, and the Shape of Empire in the Eighteenth-Century Caribbean', *Early American Studies: An Interdisciplinary Journal*, vol. 13, no. 1, pp. 80–110.

Sierra Becerra, D. C. (2017) 'The First Black Miss Colombia and the Limits of Multiculturalism', *Latin American and Caribbean Studies*, vol. 12, no. 1, pp. 71–90.

Soloudre-La France, R. (2015) 'Sailing Through the Sacraments: Ethnic and Cultural Geographies of a Port and its Churches–Cartagena de Indias', *Slavery & Abolition: A Journal of Slave and Post-Slave Studies*, vol. 36, no. 3, pp. 460–77.

Urbina Joiro, H. (2006) *Entre las Huellas de la India Catalina*. Sevilla: Academia de la Historia de Cartagena de Indias.

Valle, M. M. (2017)'The Discursive Detachment of Race from Gentrification in Cartagena de Indias, Colombia', *Latin American and Caribbean Studies*, pp. 1–20.

Van Ausdal, S. (2008) 'When Beef Was King. Or Why Do Colombians Eat So Little Pork?', *Revista de Estudios Sociales*, no. 29, http://www.scielo.org.co/scielo.php?script=sci_arttext&pid=S0123-885X20 08000100006, accessed 4 May 2017.

World Bank (1972) *Economic Growth of Colombia: Problems and Prospects: Report of a Mission Sent to Colombia in 1970 by the World Bank*. Chief of mission and co-ordinating author Dragoslav Avramovic. Baltimore, MD: The Johns Hopkins University Press.

32

THE MEDIA STRATEGY OF THE ABORIGINAL BLACK POWER, LAND RIGHTS AND SELF-DETERMINATION MOVEMENT

Gary Foley and Edwina Howell

Although this chapter is co-authored, we have chosen to write in the first person and to refer to Gary Foley using the pronoun 'I' for clarity, simplicity and to clearly articulate Professor Foley's place within the activist movement we are writing about.

Introduction

Aboriginal activists involved in the Black Power, Land Rights and Self-determination Movement in the late 1960s and 1970s in Australia sought to create the conditions under which Aboriginal people could determine their own futures. This meant the upending of almost 200 years of colonial oppression as well as breaking through a culture of White supremacy, a culture conditioned by what the anthropologist William Stanner (1969) famously coined as 'the Great Australian Silence', yet regarded by many Aboriginal people as a systematic process of conscious and violent forgetting (Foley 2013: 19).

Referred to interchangeably as the Land Rights, Self-determination or Black Power Movement, the force of Aboriginal activism emerging in the late 1960s and early 1970s in Australia was the response mainly of a collective of young Aboriginal men and women who were dissatisfied with the federal government's insipid uptake of the will of the populace as expressed in the 1967 Referendum, as well as with the tactics and strategies of the campaigners and activists of the older generation. The 1967 Referendum campaign (which proposed the inclusion of Aboriginal people in the census and the granting of constitutional power to the Commonwealth to make laws for Aboriginal people) effectively put the question to the Australian public, 'Do you believe in justice for Aboriginal people or not?' The result had been an overwhelming YES with over 90 per cent of votes in the affirmative. Yet in the years immediately following the referendum Aboriginal people experienced little, if no, improvement.

In fact, after the referendum the material conditions of Aboriginal people living in the state of New South Wales (NSW) became worse. In response to the referendum the NSW Aboriginal Protection Board arbitrarily ceased to support Aboriginal missions and reserves, closing down the last vestiges of the Australian apartheid system. Although the end of the Protection Board days was welcomed, the arbitrary and sudden nature of the closures meant that Aboriginal people previously confined to the reserves by law, who had not been allowed to seek employment off reserves and were not eligible for social welfare that other non-Aboriginal people were entitled to, struggled to find a means of subsistence. The rural recession that coincided with the closures created conditions that forced Aboriginal people into the cities in their thousands to seek employment.

It was within the context of the growth of the Aboriginal population of the inner-city Sydney suburbs of Redfern, Alexandria and Newtown, where Aboriginal people from rural NSW ended up due to the accessibility of cheap housing and the diaspora pull of a Black urban community, that the Black Caucus, a small group of young Aboriginal activists, emerged. Led by Paul Coe, with the mentorship of Chicka Dixon, the group included myself, Gary Williams, Billy Craigie, Tony Coorey, John Newfong, Alana and Samantha Doolan, Lynn (*née* Craigie) and husband Peter Thompson, Bob and Kaye Bellear, Naomi Mayers, Norma Williams and Pam Hunter (Goodall 1988: 338; Foley 2009: 14). These activists had come together motivated by their common experience of police brutality and their desire to do something to alleviate the conditions of poverty that they witnessed all around them.

In seeking to determine the best methods of social transformation, the Black Caucus members trained themselves in revolutionary philosophy and investigated the decolonization strategies of other oppressed Black peoples of the world. They had read George Jackson's prison letters, Eldridge Cleaver's *Soul on Ice*, Malcolm X's autobiography and Franz Fanon's treaties on decolonization, and were inspired by the likes of Che Guevara, Patrice Lumumba, Ho Chi Min and Mao Tse-tung, as well as the leaders of the American Indian Movement and the Black Panthers of Oakland, California.

At the same time that the Black Caucus was emerging in Sydney, similar developments were taking place in Brisbane with the emergence of a youth movement led by Denis Walker, Sam Watson and Pastor Don Brady, The Brisbane Black Panthers, and in Melbourne with a push for Aboriginal control of the Aboriginal Advancement League and the adoption of Black Power by Bruce McGuinness and Bob Maza.

Events in 1970, in particular the Black Power push to ensure Aboriginal control of the only national Aboriginal organization, the Federal Council for the Advancement of Aboriginal and Torres Strait Islanders (FCAATSI), and the ensuing establishment of the National Tribal Council in response to its failure, brought key members of these activist groupings into contact with each other. The resulting loose collective of activists congregating around the political goal of self-determination to be achieved by demanding Aboriginal control of Aboriginal affairs is what I am referring to when I refer to the Black Power, Land Rights or Self-determination Movement.

The Black Power Movement regarded Aboriginal land rights as the necessary precondition for achieving economic independence. Activists had concluded that economic independence, in the social context of a hegemonic culture that worshipped money, was absolutely vital if Aboriginal people were to achieve their primary goal of self-determination.

In assessing the practical realities of our situation when compared to other recently decolonized nations, in light of the number of Aboriginal people compared to colonial occupiers as well as the military might of the Australian colonial state, armed resistance was dismissed by the majority of activists in the Black Power movement as a viable route to self-determination (Howell 2013: 160–1). Instead the objectives of:

- raising Black people's political consciousness and self-confidence, undoing the psychological damage that decades of colonial rule had wrought;
- transforming the hearts and minds of the broader Anglo-Australian public regarding the history of colonial oppression and solutions for change;

- and putting international pressure on the federal government to force political change

were set out as revolutionary strategies (Howell 2014).

The first objective, activists determined, required letting actions speak for themselves, in that community controlled organizations such as the Aboriginal Legal Service (ALS) and Aboriginal Medical Service in Redfern, and Victorian Aboriginal Health service in Fitzroy, Melbourne, set up by Aboriginal activists engaging the Aboriginal community, were solving the problems faced by Aboriginal communities. It was Aboriginal people's experience of this community self-confidence and agency that was at the heart of positive social change. A revolution in the arts, in particular the birth of the National Black Theatre, also played a vital role in this self and community, psychological and social transformation. The documentary *The Redfern Story* (ABC TV 2014) directed by Darlene Johnson is an excellent depiction of the evolution of Black consciousness and the arts.

The second and third objectives, bringing the general Australian public onside regarding Aboriginal land rights and self-determination and putting international pressure on the Federal government to achieve these goals, required the transformation of the 'other', or at the very least an opening in the armour of the colonial machinery. In pursuit of both of these objectives Black Power activists set about a full-scale public relations war. The remainder of this chapter investigates the history of that public relations war. The translation of Black political consciousness through the arts, in particular through the National Black Theatre, was certainly an aspect of the media strategy of the Black Power movement and thus a component of the same 'public relations war'. However, this chapter focuses on two other vital components of the strategy: firstly, the creation and uptake of the Aboriginal flag as a unifying symbol for the emerging Land Rights and Self-determination Movement and secondly, the news-media strategy of the Black Power activists in the lead-up to and during the ultimate success of the Aboriginal Embassy, a six-month-long protest from January–July 1972 on the lawns of Parliament House in response to the then-Prime Minister William McMahon's rejection of Aboriginal demands for Land Rights.

Birth of the Aboriginal flag

In 1971 I was involved in an exercise that, at the time, did not seem all that significant to me, but which is today regarded as a part of history: the development and design of the internationally known emblem of the Black Power era, the red, black and yellow Aboriginal flag. My involvement came about because of a request in 1971 from the Nunga community in Adelaide to the Redfern Aboriginal Legal Service to send someone to Adelaide to advise and assist in the creation of an ALS in South Australia.

During my first visit to Adelaide I had met, and been interrogated and tested by, the legendary South Australian activist matriarch Gladys Elphick, and over the next week I met and worked with other leaders including Vince Copley, Ruby Hammond and others associated with the Aboriginal Community Centre in Adelaide.

It was during that visit to Adelaide that I met a young artist from the Northern Territory named Harold Thomas, who was then working at the South Australia Museum, and we struck up an immediate friendship. Harold and I were on the same wavelength politically, but he was much more knowledgeable about the South Australian and Northern Territory scene than I and we spent many hours discussing the state of the world. I would return to Adelaide frequently over the next twelve months, organizing demonstrations and assisting where I could with the development of the new legal aid organization. Before one particular demonstration I found myself in intense discussion with Harold Thomas over a case of Victoria Bitter (VB) beer. The discussion was one of lament that we Australian Aboriginal people did not have a symbol that both represented our struggle and that could serve as a unifying emblem.

After a certain number of cans of VB and the consequent bravado that they bring, as well as a very lively discussion, it was decided between us that we would sit down and design one. Harold, being the artist, pulled out some pencils and a sketchbook and we began discussing a range of ideas. To cut a long story (not to mention drinking session) short, many cans later Harold had in front of him the now familiar red, black and yellow design, along with our interpretation of what it meant.

We both thought it was a great design, but that was pointless unless others felt the same way and would embrace it. We had a couple of flags made up to our specifications and we were aware a demonstration was being planned in Adelaide for late January 1972 (just three days before the Aboriginal Embassy was erected in Canberra). We knew this because I was one of the organizers of the demonstration, which was in support of a Western Australian Aboriginal prison escapee Lionel Brockman who had gone on the run with his entire family, and the entire Western Australian police force was unable to find them in the outback for six months. In the process, he became a minor folk hero and Bobbi Sykes had started a campaign in support of Brockman. The other organizers of the rally were local Nunga woman Ruby Hammond and the White State Secretary of the Amalgamated Engineering Union, Mr John Scott. I was scheduled to speak at the demonstration in support of Brockman, and Harold and I decided it would be a good occasion to introduce his proposed Aboriginal flag to the world.

Rather than seek support of the trade unions that were co-sponsoring the rally, and because we knew we could depend on the support of Ruby Hammond, we decided we would unfurl the flag 'spontaneously' during the march. We knew our trade union 'brothers' were in reality still a politically tame lot when it came to questions such as 'Black Power' and were sure it was better to spring the flag on their members who marched with us than to alert them in advance and create unnecessary aggravation.

Thus, on the 22 January 1972, the Aboriginal flag had its first public display and generated a minor flurry of interest, but otherwise remained unknown until a month later when in Sydney on 22 February, a tabloid newspaper named the *Daily Mirror* published a profile of me written by journalist Guy De Brito, along with the design that I had called 'a flag for Aboriginal Australia'. This was the first major public and media appearance of the Aboriginal flag (Foley 2012: 177–80).

On reflection, I believe one of the reasons I put the flag in the *Daily Mirror* article was that I was trying to manoeuvre the design into a position where the Black Power Movement couldn't ignore it. The Black Power collective was a fairly unwieldy sort of animal. Politically most of us in the Black Power Movement were basically anarchists. The Australian Security Intelligence Organization and everybody else thought we were Communists but essentially, we were a bunch of mad anarchists. We developed an extremely effective cohesive group where decisions ultimately were made by consensus. We were trying to do things in what we regarded as traditional Aboriginal ways of decision-making, we believed consensus was our way of doing things, we didn't have majority rule; if you had an idea you had to sit there and argue it through with a group until everybody in the group had fused whatever the original idea was into something that everybody agreed with.

In order to get anything decided in the Black Power Movement you had to convince a lot of people and get them to go along with you. In terms of the *Daily Mirror* article, I believe I saw that as a good means of at least focusing the broader group's attention on the design and making ones amongst us who may not have even known about it at that time aware that it was out there. Perhaps I figured that by getting the flag into a high-profile mainstream newspaper they would at least have to take notice of it. I suppose I was hoping also to present them with a *fait accompli*: bang, here's your flag, whether you like it or not.

Somehow or other in the course of the Aboriginal Embassy, by the time the Embassy was knocked down six months later, the flag was established. It took off like a rocket all over Australia, which in itself is a testament to the genius of it as a piece of graphic design; it's one of the most successful pieces of graphic design in Australian history (Foley 2012: 180).

The Aboriginal flag thus became a weapon of power in a war of positions. It was a war in which the government would come to use 'any means necessary' to undermine the growing popularity and strength of Aboriginal demands for land rights as the basis of their program of control over their own destinies (Howell 2014: 67).

Black Power news media strategy

I had been taught the art of media engagement as a teenager during the final years of the successful decade long FCAATSI constitutional referendum campaign by two legends of the Aboriginal movement, Faith Bandler and John Newfong. It was the Aboriginal journalist John Newfong who was the media mastermind behind the Aboriginal Tent Embassy and its Minister for Communications, and it was he who taught me how to work the 'media machine'. John Newfong was the Australian equivalent of a cross between James Baldwin and Oscar Wilde. He was singularly the most brilliant Aboriginal writer there has ever been to this day. He was the first Aboriginal professional journalist in Australia, writing for *The Australian*, for *The Bulletin*, *The Age, the Sydney Morning Herald*; he was one of the best journalists in Australia.

Through John Newfong, I came to understand the importance of keeping up to date with the latest technology as well as the importance of cultivating relationships with journalists. He taught me the need to ensure that media releases are delivered to the press as quickly as possible and the targeting of journalists who would be most favourable to the position of the story as well as the importance of manifesting a presence in the media through stories that would satisfy the media's preference for drama, spectacle and tumult.

The introduction of the technology of the telex machine had been revolutionary for the Black Power public relations campaign. Prior to the telex the best available technology was the print and stencil machine. This would require the operator to cut out the stencil and wind the reel to print out copies one at a time, which would then need to be placed in envelopes and posted to individual media outlets. The telex allowed the collective to distribute ten media releases at once and each could be directed straight to the preferred journalist. The impact of this quick-fire distribution method was enormous. In addition to learning the practical aspects of how to run a media campaign through activists such as Faith Bandler and John Newfong, Black Power activists also learnt to cultivate the skills of gaining and sustaining media attention.

We were aware that the news media would be drawn to report on events that were dramatic and visually striking. In this context, Black Power drew power from the image of Black Power that the African American movement in the US had created. As a result of news media, coverage of the Black Power movement in the US in particular coverage of the Black Panthers, Black Power had come to represent Black militancy and Black violence in the minds of the majority of Australian Aboriginal activists involved in the Black Power movement in Australia. They utilized this fear of the other to position themselves on the precipice of possibility, engaging colonial fear to invoke a sense of the imminence of change. Drawing on the Black Power aesthetic, Aboriginal Black Power activists took on the 'Afro', black leather jackets, dark sunglasses, black berets and clenched fists, as an assertion that 'black is beautiful' and in acknowledgement of the shared oppression they faced as coloured peoples of the world (Lothian 2007: 23). However, the Black Power image also operated to bolster the movement as spectacle, and thus as newsworthy.

On 5 December 1971 Rupert Murdoch's *Sunday Australian* published a double page article with the headline 'BLACK POWER COMES TO AUSTRALIA'. It carried the subtitle:

'We only have a small supply of explosives left at present and thought we'd save it for something important'. A prominent photo of four 'Black Power field marshals' with their fists raised in the well-recognized Black Power salute covered half a page. Journalist Simon Townsend reported the emergence of the Australian Black Panther Party, which he declared was 'Dedicated to Violence', promoted violence as 'the only means left to force change', and was committed to violence as a means of focusing both national and international attention on the plight of Aboriginal people. The article claimed that the party was responsible for 'smashing the front window of the Foundation for Aboriginal Affairs in Sydney and for daubing a statute of Captain Cook in Hyde Park, Sydney, in land rights slogans' and reported one Black Panther as having said:

> The only reason we didn't blow old Captain Cook up was that we only have a small supply of explosives at present and we thought we'd save it for something more important. With planned strategic violence, bombing if necessary, assassination if necessary – we'll get land rights 20 years faster.

Townsend also reported that the group planned to train a select group of activists in urban guerrilla tactics and the use of explosives as well as their intention to be 'ready to move in a month' at which point 'all hell will break loose'.

In February 1972 a special news broadcast, *Black Mood*, aired on the ABC. It focused on the rising Black consciousness in Australia and described Black Power activists as 'rather aggressive'. As an interviewee in the broadcast, I was asked to explain what was meant by Black Power, and responded, 'If we have to go about violent means of getting the power to control our own destinies then we will; we're quite prepared to.' 'But is it realistic for such a small minority as Aborigines are to talk about violence?' the presenter asked. 'Realistic or not, I think you've got to face up to the fact that if the Aboriginal situation does not change very rapidly in this country what we're going to see is more or less a spontaneous violence coming out,' I replied. The news feature concluded with the host's summation that 'on the evidence … black militancy is not likely to go away. If anything it will increase'.

There was perhaps a tension between the approaches of different Black Power activists, but there is also a tension between fact and fiction, between present and possibility, a predictive and performative element that was strategically harnessed to be a force for motivating social change. Members of the Black Power Movement utilized this possibility, this moment in time, to illuminate the urgency of their calls. There may very well have been the tremor of violence afoot, frustrations that had built up over centuries of subjugation, but even if there was no such seismic trembling, the Black Power activists knew that a big Black community made the White fellas nervous and they had decided to exploit that wave of hysteria.

A key method advanced in media discourse and by government to discredit the Black Power movement was to portray the activists involved as urban militants. Explicitly such representations of Black Power stated that as urban militants Black Power activists were just a small group of Aboriginal people and were therefore unrepresentative of Aboriginal opinion generally (Goodall 2008: 402). Yet implicitly, the classification of Black Power as urban and militant attempted to represent Black Power as fraudulent. This operated at two levels: firstly, militancy was considered by the colonizer as a characteristic foreign to 'the Aborigine', and secondly their position as 'urban' was evidence for the colonizer that they were assimilated and therefore not really Aboriginal at all. In the communist party newspaper *Tribune* 1–7 February 1972, Bruce McGuinness aimed to counter such representations of Black Power as both unrepresentative and as fraudulent, announcing to the reporter that militancy, as an 'aggressively political' strategy of 'defence and not offence', existed well beyond the Brisbane Black Panthers:

We have seen areas like Wattie Creek, Roper River (where they threw all the whites off), Cunnamulla ... and the Purfleet reserve near Tareet in New South Wales where Aboriginal people have bluntly said they would take up guns if necessary to prevent people touching their land.

Yet the Aboriginal Tent Embassy protest, a six-month-long protest on the lawns of Parliament House in Canberra that began as a media stunt, was about to disrupt this representation of the Black Power movement once and for all. The Aboriginal Embassy was to become the most disarming event yet in the Black Power movement's media strategy and in their war of positions demonstrating to the nation and to the world that Aboriginal people from all over Australia supported demands for Aboriginal land rights and self-determination.

The Aboriginal Tent Embassy

1971 witnessed the escalation in frequency and numbers attending Aboriginal land rights demonstrations. Black Power activists had joined the Gurindji in street demonstrations in Sydney. Anti-apartheid demonstrators challenged by Black Power activists to look at the situation in their own backyard had taken up the call, and Justice Blackburn's decision in the Gove Land Rights case, handed down in April 1971, had resulted in public outcry motivating even more people to takes to the streets demanding Aboriginal land rights.

Then Prime Minister, William ('Billy') McMahon, compelled by the growing prominence of Aboriginal demands for land, decided to make a major government statement on Aboriginal land rights. Provocatively the McMahon government chose 26 January 1971 to announce its new policy. Known to most Australians as Australia Day, 26 January celebrates the arrival of the First Fleet in Australia. It is a particularly controversial date in the Australian calendar since for Aboriginal people and their allies, national celebration of this date represents celebration of the invasion of Aboriginal lands and the attempted genocide of Aboriginal people by the British and Australian Governments.

The McMahon Government, rather than making a progressive statement on Aboriginal land rights, offered a new type of lease to some Aboriginal people based on a series of restrictive conditions. Essentially the McMahon Government had announced that it would never grant land rights to Aboriginal people. The statement was considered by Aboriginal activists in the Black Power Movement as particularly provocative considering the decision to make such a statement on 26 January.

Members of the Sydney Black Power collective, the Black Caucus, decided to respond to the statement by sending a deputation of four Aboriginal activists to Parliament house to protest. The aim was to get a photo of the protest in the paper the following day so that people would be aware that the Black Power movement rejected the Government's position absolutely. What ensued was a six-month long occupation by Aboriginal activists of the lawns of Parliament house by the Aboriginal Embassy. The story of the Aboriginal Embassy is told in detail elsewhere, in particular in *The Aboriginal Tent Embassy: Sovereignty, Black Power, Land Rights and the State,* G. Foley, Schaap and Howell eds (Routledge 2014) and in my PhD, *An Autobiographical history of the Aboriginal Embassy and the Black Power Movement* (Foley 2013). What is important for this retelling is that in setting up an Embassy, the Aboriginal activists illuminated that the McMahon Government's policy made Aboriginal people aliens in their own land. As a camp, a series of tents, the Aboriginal Embassy also highlighted the poverty in which Aboriginal people were forced to live as well as the provisional nature of land leases rather than Land Rights. It was the perfect media spectacle.

Importantly, the protest was non-violent. It had struck a chord with the rebel sensibility that Australians call *a larrikin streak* in many people, and the public seemed to be amused by the inability of the authorities to do anything about it. Aboriginal Embassy's Minister of Communication, John Newfong, ran the Embassy's media campaign. Newfong, along with journalists such as Stewart Harris and Michelle Grattan, ensured that the analysis and critique of Government policy by Aboriginal activists of the Embassy continued to be heard in mainstream news-media. The Aboriginal Embassy protest featured in news media coverage in over 70 countries, bringing both the conditions under which Aboriginal people were forced to live and the demands of Aboriginal people for Land Rights and self-determination to an international audience.

Embarrassed and humiliated, the McMahon Government sought to remove the Aboriginal Embassy by the only means it could. It rapidly passed new laws in the middle of the night making it illegal to camp on the lawns of Parliament House. These laws then legalized police removal of the protest.

Police then attempted to dismantle the Embassy on both 20 July and 23 July. On the first occasion, police took protestors by surprise and a strategic decision was made to protect the office tent. Demonstrators decided that if police tried to take the office tent they would resist. Media coverage of the melee that followed caused large numbers of Aboriginal people and their supporters from all over the country to converge on Canberra in the days that followed so that by the time the police tried to dismantle the tents for the second time there were over 3,000 people there to defend them.

On both occasions, news media coverage of the Aboriginal activists' struggle to maintain a legitimate protest against enormous numbers of Federal and NSW police troops, in particular footage of the police violence used against demonstrators to remove what had previously been a legal non-violent protest, made ordinary Australians aware of the nature and extent of the violence the state considered legitimate to use against Aboriginal people (Robinson 1994: 58; Dexter 2015: 236).

As police were set to remove the protest site for a third time on 30 July, key organizers came together and, rather than risk the lives of the many young and old who had gathered from all over Australia in support of demands for Land Rights, decided that they would let police remove the tent but that they would claim the moral victory. They knew that the event of the Embassy had turned the tide of public opinion absolutely in their favour and that in orchestrating a theatrical dismantling of the tents by police and claiming the moral victory would only further cement public opinion.

Six months later the Whitlam Labor Government came to power on a policy platform that promised 'Land Rights for Aborigines'.

Conclusion – who won the war?

The media strategy of the Black Power movement, particularly at the Aboriginal Embassy, had achieved a revolution. It had made the world aware of the injustices Aboriginal people were suffering. It had brought an end to 23 consecutive years of conservative rule, ended the bi-partisan policy of assimilation and had thus officially ended the policy of genocide. Moreover, in playing a significant role in the demise of the McMahon government and in causing the Labor party to change its policy on Aboriginal land rights, it achieved Government commitment to Aboriginal land rights as well as the promise of Aboriginal rights to minerals on and under Aboriginal land, and it had made the way possible for a new era of self-determination.

The public relations battle over Aboriginal Land Rights was, however, eventually won by mining and pastoral industry lobby groups with a multi-million-dollar propaganda campaign against Aboriginal Land Rights. Decades later, we are still witnessing the dire backlash against Aboriginal people which that campaign wrought.

In a recent interview, I was asked if we had won the battle but lost the war and I tentatively answered yes.

We changed the world, but we took our eye off the ball and the world changed back … But of course, the war isn't over yet.

References

Dexter, B. (2015) G. Foley and E. Howell (eds) *Pandora's Box: The Council for Aboriginal Affairs 1967–1976.* Southport, Queensland: Keeaira Press.

Foley, G. (2009) 'Black Power in Redfern 1968–1972', in K. De Souza and Z. Begg (eds) *There Goes the Neighbourhood: Redfern and The Politics of Urban Space.* Sydney: Breakout, pp.12–21.

Foley, G. (2013) *An Autobiography of the Black Power Movement and the 1972 Aboriginal Embassy.* Doctorate of Philosophy, History, University of Melbourne.

Goodall, H. (1988) 'Crying Out for Land Rights', in V. Burgmann and J. Lee (eds) *Staining the Wattle: A People's History of Australia since 1788.* Fitzroy, Victoria: McPhee Gribble, pp.181–97.

Howell, E. (2013) *Tangled Up in Black: A Study of the Activist Strategies of the Black Power Movement Through the Life of Gary Foley.* Doctorate of Philosophy, Anthropology, Monash University, Melbourne.

Howell, E. (2014) 'Black Power – By Any Means Necessary', in G. Foley, A. Schaap and E. Howell (eds) *The Aboriginal Tent Embassy: Sovereignty, Black Power, Land Rights and the State.* London: Routledge, pp. 67–83.

Lothian, K. (2007) 'Moving Blackwards: Black Power and the Aboriginal Tent Embassy', in I. Macfarlane and M. Hannah (eds) *Transgressions: Critical Australian Indigenous Histories.* Acton: ANU E-Press.

Robinson, S. (1994) 'The Aboriginal Embassy: An Account of the Protests of 1972', *Aboriginal History*, vol. 18. no.1., pp. 49–63.

Stanner, W. (1969) *After the Dreaming. Black and White Australians: An Anthropologist's View.* Sydney: Australian Broadcasting Commission.

PART VI

Changing the media

33

POLICY ACTIVISM

Advocating, protesting and hacking media regulation

Arne Hintz

> Urgent reform is needed to reclaim the media in the interest of the public.
> *Media Reform Coalition, http://www.mediareform.org.uk*

Introduction

Media technologies and platforms offer many possibilities for people to become active citizens and make their voices heard. From pirate radios to the alternative press, from social media activism to fan culture and from local wireless networks to global citizen journalism, activists have both used available communication channels and created new infrastructure. However, these activities are conditioned – sometimes enabled, sometimes constrained – by the legal and regulatory context. Censorship laws (and/or practices) may prevent critical journalism, unlicensed radios may be shut down, internet surveillance may hinder free online expression, social media companies may restrict the use of their platforms and a lack of media pluralism may limit the representation of the wider public. For that reason, some media activists and advocacy organizations have focused on the legal and regulatory conditions of media production. They have intervened in the processes, debates and institutions that regulate, enable or obstruct media practices and communications infrastructure. These interventions will be explored in this chapter.

Policy activism has addressed a wide range of agendas, from the legalization of community radio to the principles of internet governance. Traditionally, much of it has been advanced by larger networks and advocacy organizations, such as the World Association of Community Broadcasters (AMARC), the Association for Progressive Communications (APC), digital rights organizations such as the Electronic Frontier Foundation (EFF) and professional associations such as the International Federation of Journalists (IFJ). However, as we will see, a broader range of grassroots networks and diverse coalitions has emerged around policy issues and has intervened into policy debates at national and international levels. Some of these have focused on lobbying and advocacy, others on protesting and raising public pressure in order to draw policymakers' attention to critical issues. Some have applied the practices of self-organization, creativity and DIY (do-it-yourself) development, which are prominent in media activism, to experiment with new forms of policy-making and with self-guided policy responses outside the sphere of classic regulatory institutions and debates. This chapter will review a range of different approaches to policy activism and will consider, particularly, those that draw from the principles of technological development and media activism to generate characteristic forms of policy interventions into media policy.

The chapter will begin with a review of key concepts and research findings from the fields of policy studies, social movement studies and media and communication studies regarding the contexts, conditions and strategies of policy activists. It will identify four distinct practices and address each of those with examples and case studies from different countries and media sectors. Some of these will be informed by primary research on policy initiatives, others will draw from existing literature. Finally, the chapter will draw a set of conclusions from the case studies regarding the opportunities and challenges of media policy activism. While policy activism exists across different areas of social justice, the media field points us to action repertoires that transcend both classic advocacy and protest, and it broadens our perspective on what policy intervention means in the contemporary political environment.

Policy interventions, media reform and global governance

Policy activism is an intervention into the regulatory environment of media and communications, and into the rules and norms that shape the media landscape. To understand its practices and challenges, we need to take a closer look at how such rules and norms are created, based on which values and interests, and by whom. In the contemporary context of global governance, this is no straightforward matter. While governments, parliamentary law-makers and national regulatory institutions continue to play a key role in policy development, the regulatory landscape has expanded into 'a complex ecology of interdependent structures' with 'a vast array of formal and informal mechanisms working across a multiplicity of sites' (Raboy 2002: 6–7). This means that policy is being developed at 'different and sometimes overlapping levels—from the local to the supra-national and global' (Raboy & Padovani 2010: 16). Norms elaborated at global summits or by regional institutions constrain national policies, and laws in one country affect policy development in another. It also means that governmental and institutional policymaking is increasingly influenced – and sometimes even replaced – by non-state actors. Global forums for policy development, such as the World Summit on the Information Society (WSIS) and the Internet Governance Forum (IGF), and regulatory bodies such as the Internet Corporation for Assigned Names and Numbers (ICANN), have experimented with new forms of multi-stakeholder collaboration that incorporate civil society and the business sector (Hintz 2009; Mueller 2010). This reflects the history of the development of communications infrastructure, in which non-state actors have traditionally played a large role. Businesses were already involved with telecommunications policy-making in the nineteenth century (Hamelink 1994), and technologists, civil society and internet companies have been the leading forces in the institutions that create the standards and protocols for the internet (DeNardis 2009). Further, in the era of 'platform capitalism' (Srnicek 2016), the policies set by social media and 'sharing economy' websites overlap with national laws and regulations and lead to a 'shift of the responsibility for monitoring and policing Internet conduct onto strategically positioned private sector intermediaries' (Mueller 2010: 146). So, while national law remains an anchor point for media policy, it is affected by a variety of processes outside the governmental realm.

Scholars of communication policy have investigated the sites and shifts of the regulatory landscape, the process of policy-making, the interactions between different social forces, and societal norms and ideologies that underpin policy trends (Freedman 2008). This interest is often shared by scholars applying a political–economic approach to understanding communications structures and incorporating the objectives and capacities of social forces in shaping the global media environment (Mosco 1996; McChesney 2007; Chakravartty & Yuezhi 2008;

Pickard 2014) and by science and technology studies (STS), which highlight the politics of technical architecture and the networked interactions of human and nonhuman forces (Musiani 2014). Social movement studies offer particularly helpful conceptual approaches and empirical evidence regarding policy interventions by civil society actors – from grassroots activist groups to large non-governmental organizations (NGOs) (Tilly & Tarrow 2006). Scholars have investigated their repertoires of action, types of contention and necessary conditions for intervention. They have demonstrated how civil society groups define problems, set agendas, prescribe solutions and hold institutions accountable to previously stated policies and principles, and thereby shape and alter the norms that underpin policymaking. Key strategies for success have included the creation of conceptual frames, which articulate the characteristics of an issue to policymakers; securing powerful allies both within and outside an institutional arena where policy is made; and the creation of networks and collaborations across movements, both domestically and transnationally (Keck & Sikkink 1998; Khagram, Riker & Sikkink 2002). These interventions have often required favourable 'policy windows', i.e. temporary openings and institutional settings that affect policy change. A crisis (or cracks) in a social, political, economic or ideological system may create a dynamic in which established social orders become receptive to change and new actors can enter the field and advance their agendas (Kingdon 1984). Policy interventions have also benefitted from, or been constrained by, broader normative and ideological trends, such as the predominant model of industry self-regulation in the late twentieth century and the return of stricter state interventions in the new millennium. While the former was conducive to the self-regulatory models of internet governance, the latter has underpinned increased content restrictions and surveillance and a more restrictive approach to internet policy (Goldsmith & Wu 2006; Zittrain 2008).

In conceptualizing the strategic practices of policy activists, social movement theorists typically distinguish between 'insider' and 'outsider' strategies. 'Insiders' interact directly and cooperatively with power-holders through advocacy, lobbying and participation in multi-stakeholder fora, whereas 'outsiders' question the legitimacy of power-holders and address them through protest and disruptive action (Tarrow 2005). While the two approaches are often politically and ideologically opposed to each other, research suggests that a combination of grassroots mobilization 'outside' with lobbying 'inside' may yield the most promising results of policy interventions as it complements advocacy with public pressure (McChesney 2004; Hackett & Carroll 2006; Pickard 2015). However, the binary model of inside-outside activities may not cover the full range of media policy activism. It often focuses on the activities of classic forms of civil society (particularly, large professionalized NGOs) and neglects informal networks and loose collaborations amongst engaged individuals – including forms of 'connective' rather than 'collective action' (Bennett & Segerberg 2012). More importantly, it does not capture repertoires of prefigurative action that are widespread in media activism and technological development.

Technical communities have long engaged in latent and invisible policy-making by setting technical standards and developing new protocols and infrastructure that allow some actions and disallow others (e.g. Braman 2006; DeNardis 2009). Media activists have often focused on the creation of alternative infrastructure that bypasses regulatory obstacles, rather than lobbying for, for example, digital rights. This prefigurative approach points to interactions with the policy environment that take place neither 'inside' nor 'outside' institutional or governmental processes, as they do not directly address power-holders, but 'beyond' those processes by creating alternatives to hegemonic structures and procedures and by adopting a tactical repertoire of circumvention (Hintz & Milan 2013; Milan 2013). Moreover, civil society initiatives have also applied prefigurative action as part of a close engagement with 'inside' processes. Rather than advocating and lobbying for change, they have developed regulatory proposals, formulated legal texts and created model laws. Taking law-making into their own hands, they have broken up the classic division between, on the one hand, those that develop policy (typically governmental institutions) and, on the other hand, those that provide normative input and public pressure (typically civil society). As these initiatives often re-assemble components from other policies and tinker with the law, their practice has been called 'policy hacking' (Hintz 2016). The use of digital tools to open up the policy process and crowdsource policy constitutions is a prominent feature of this approach and situates it in the wider context of crowdsourced policymaking (Aitamurto & Chen 2017).

A rich literature has emerged that investigates interventions into a wide range of local, national and international policy frameworks. Studies have addressed, among many other issues, historic policy debates (McChesney 1990; Pickard 2014), campaigns against media ownership concentration and for media reform (McChesney 2004; Gangadharan 2013), transnational communication rights movements (Calabrese 2004), advocacy for the legalization of community and non-profit broadcasting (Coyer & Hintz 2010), campaigns against the strengthening of intellectual property regimes (Sell 2013) and internet surveillance (Hintz & Brown 2017), and analyses of the diverse strategies applied by policy activists and media reform initiatives (Freedman *et al.* 2016). In the rest of this chapter, I will discuss some of these examples, organized around the four strategic approaches mentioned above.

Inside: advocating for change

Advocating for policy change in direct interaction with policymakers is at the core of civil society-based policy activism. Organizations and initiatives submit statements to, and engage in conversations with, power-holders in order to affect norms and advertise alternative routes for policy development. A wide variety of lobby groups and coalitions have emerged that address different concerns on both national and international levels. For example, digital rights such as online freedom of expression and privacy are advocated by organizations such as the Open Rights Group (ORG) at the national (in this case, UK) level and European Digital Rights (EDRI) at the European level, and community broadcasting is supported by the Community Media Association (CMA) in the UK and the Community Media Forum Europe (CMFE) in Europe. The CMFE, for example, has facilitated meetings between community media practitioners and representatives of the European Parliament, has participated in ministerial conferences on media policy by the Council of Europe (CoE) and has been a member of regular CoE committees and other policy-related networks. Its awareness-raising efforts have led to several declarations by European institutions that advise national policymakers to legalize and support community media. For example, the European Parliament (EP) issued a report in 2008 in which it '[a]dvises Member States [...] to give legal recognition to community media as a distinct group alongside commercial and public media' (European Parliament 2008). The success of advocacy initiatives varies, however. In 2016, a broad coalition of digital rights organizations, businesses and technological experts lobbied the UK government as the latter developed a new surveillance law, the Investigatory Powers Act, and submitted numerous statements and detailed proposals for the restriction of state surveillance and the protection of privacy. Yet the prominence of intelligence interests inside government and a public discourse dominated by security concerns led to a law that expanded, rather than limited, surveillance (Hintz & Brown 2017).

Sometimes 'inside' actually means inside government institutions and policy fora. As the government of Uruguay developed new media laws to legalize, support and regulate community radios in the mid-2000s, it enlisted the services of community media expert and AMARC member Gustavo Gomez. As National Director of Telecommunication, he oversaw the implementation of the new laws, developed appropriate regulations and allocated licences to a large number of citizen-based non-profit radio stations (Light 2011). Multi-stakeholder processes such as the two World Summits on the Information Society (WSIS) in 2003 and 2005 and their numerous preparatory conferences have offered promising opportunities for civil society groups to contribute directly to policy development. A vast range of them created thematic caucuses, developed statements and fed them into the negotiation process. They spoke at plenary events, were included in working groups that would normally be reserved to government officials and engaged in corridor lobbying. They developed a common declaration – 'Shaping Information Societies for Human Needs' – and they organized numerous side-events and thematic conferences around the summit and thereby intervened into the discourses on information society that span around the summit's core. The final summit documents did not reflect all of civil society's concerns, many of which were eliminated during governmental negotiations, but civil society groups left their mark on how information society came to be understood and the policy catalogues that emerged from the summit (Raboy & Landry 2005; Hintz 2009).

Outside: protesting injustice

While 'insiders' engage with policy forums cooperatively and constructively, 'outsiders' typically seek to exert public pressure to affect policy reform. The most straightforward application of pressure are public protests, rallies and demonstrations that express public dissatisfaction and demand change. While the theme of media and communication (in contrast to, for example, racism and the environment) has not been a classic rallying point for public protest, occasional protest actions have underlined other forms of advocacy. Efforts to legalize community media, for example, have sometimes included street protests and creative actions outside of policy venues. The campaign for changing broadcast laws in Argentina was supported by a demonstration of 20,000 people that brought a proposed new law to parliament where it was later adopted (Hintz 2014). Demonstrations and protests against internet surveillance have brought tens of thousands of people to the streets of European capitals since 2007. Initially triggered by the EU Data Retention Directive, annual protests like the 'Freedom not Fear' demonstrations in Berlin criticized the mass data collection that the Directive required. Combining street protest with a variety of other repertoires of action, including legal cases, the campaigners were successful: several countries suspended or abandoned data retention laws, and in 2014 the Court of Justice of the EU declared the Directive invalid.

In the era of online communication, street protests are often complemented by creative forms of digital protest. The mobilizations against the SOPA/PIPA copyright enforcement bills in the US included an online action day on 18 January 2012, when thousands of websites, including major platforms such as Google, Wikipedia and Reddit, blacked out parts of their homepages to demonstrate the potential effects of the bills for online content, and pasted black 'Stop Censorship' banners on their sites. They also encouraged site visitors to call Congress and express their opposition to the legislation. The hacktivist network Anonymous organized denial-of-service actions against major copyright holders and published embarrassing information on companies supporting the bills after hacking into their databases. Mass boycotts targeted, particularly, the domain registration service GoDaddy that had supported the bills, leading to the company dropping its support for the proposed legislation. The mobilizations benefitted from a broad coalition of actors that included digital rights and civil liberties organizations, and a wide range of activists, bloggers and scholars, but also technology firms such as Google and Amazon, social media companies such as Facebook and Twitter and political actors such as Green Parties and Pirate Parties in several countries. It managed to develop a common frame by focusing on the claim that the proposed rigid definitions and prosecution of copyright infringement would restrict freedom of expression. Despite participation by some of the heavyweights of online business, the protests were seen as 'a David and Goliath story in which relatively weak activists were able to achieve surprising success against the strong' (Sell 2013: 68). As with the community media and anti-surveillance protests, 'outside' actions were embedded in, or connected with, 'inside' initiatives and this combination proved to be a powerful force for change. Shortly after the main day of action, the bills were shelved.

Beyond: bypassing policy challenges

A combination of inside–outside repertoires accompanied the above-mentioned WSIS, too. While NGO advocates tried to affect the negotiations inside the summit venue and during the preparatory process, media activists organized a series of events outside the WSIS summit under the title *WSIS? WeSeize!* Sceptical about government-led institutional processes, *WSIS? WeSeize!* explored ways of 'intervening without participating'. However, it did so without resorting to classic protest actions. Partly, it served as an alternative summit in which tech activists, members of grassroots alternative media groups and advocates of free software and free culture discussed themes such as the privatization of ideas through intellectual property rights, infowar and media misinformation, hacking and ICT activism. Partly, it was a space for experimentation with technology in a collaborative, grassroots and non-commercial way, and for the development of alternative technological infrastructures. *WSIS? WeSeize!* thus offered a reference point for alternative discourses on 'information society'; a thematic vision, which went beyond the themes laid out in both the official summit results and the alternative declaration of the civil society groups operating inside the summit process; the relevance of self-organized communication systems; and the feasibility of extra-institutional tactics (Hintz 2009). It was situated outside the summit, yet it did not aim at protesting the summit but rather at bypassing it altogether and developing alternatives. As a policy-related action that did not intervene into policy negotiations through neither lobbying nor protest, it demonstrated a different repertoire of action that takes place 'beyond' immediate policy debate.

This repertoire is applied also by activist groups like Riseup.net that develop alternative communications infrastructure, such as mailing lists, web space and collaborative tools that protect user privacy and online freedoms at the level of technology. The sector encompasses non-profit social network platforms such as Lorea and Diaspora; open-publishing content-sharing sites, such as Indymedia; and tools for encrypted chats, such as Signal, and anonymous web browsing, such as TOR. These initiatives address the consequences of laws and regulations, such as content regulations, media access and surveillance, and they thus engage with policy. However, they do so through neither advocacy nor protest, but prefigurative action. By envisioning and creating a different communications system, they by-pass regulatory challenges and develop policy at the level of code rather than law. As the design of technology pre-determines what information and communication technology systems can and cannot do, designers and developers become 'policy-makers' at a less visible but not less effective level. They do not advocate or demand but create change. In the words of an Indymedia activist:

> I don't think we need to focus on "asking" or "having a voice". I think we have "to do", "keep doing" and keep building working structures and alternatives that are diametrically opposed to the ways capitalism forces us to function in our everyday lives. Our job, as activists, is to create self-managed infrastructures that work regardless of "their" regulation, laws or any other form of governance.
>
> *Hintz & Milan 2013*

Policy hacking: writing law

If the 'beyond' approach demonstrates a type of prefigurative action that takes place mostly outside policy venues and without any collaborative interaction with them, 'policy hacking' takes the strategy of self-organized development back to the 'inside' realm. The previously-mentioned campaigns to change broadcast laws in Uruguay and Argentina may serve as examples. The Argentinian 'Coalition for Democratic Broadcasting' – a civil society network of unions, universities, human rights groups and community media – developed the core elements of a new policy framework, and a coalition member drafted a law based on this framework. The draft was discussed at open hearings, comments by a variety of organizations, activists and experts were included in the document, and thus a legal text was produced by civil society which later became law (Hintz 2014). This approach of DIY policymaking has been applied across local and national jurisdictions, and by transnational mobilizations. On the local level, for example, the 'Hamburg Transparency Law Initiative' in the German city of Hamburg developed an open data law in 2010 and convinced the local parliament to adopt it in 2012. Rather than starting a classic advocacy campaign to put pressure on the city council to create and pass policy, the initiative decided to write the law themselves. They drafted a legal proposal, published it on a wiki page and collected input from other civil society organizations and members of the public. Key to the initiative's self-organized development of a law was a review of best practices in other German states ('Laender') and other European countries, and the re-assemblage of these components towards a new policy package. This practice was applied also by the Icelandic Modern Media Initiative (IMMI), which created a bundle of legal and regulatory proposals for strengthening freedom of expression in a digital age, in the wake of the financial collapse of 2008. IMMI cherry-picked laws and regulations from other jurisdictions and created a jigsaw puzzle of tried-and-tested components. In both Hamburg and Iceland, the policy proposals were adopted by parliament and partly implemented, but were affected by changing political environments and policy windows (Hintz 2016).

These initiatives relate to practices of hacking rather figuratively by tinkering with the law in DIY fashion, similar to technological hackers tinkering with soft- and hardware. Policy hackathons, on the other hand, have applied the concept of hacking literally. The annual EU Hackathons, for example, bring together interested people (often, but not always, with technological skills) to analyze and, ideally, improve policies. Events such as 'Hack4YourRights' and 'Hack4Participation' have served to develop apps to understand the state of government surveillance tools and to enhance citizen participation in European policy debates. Their organizers seek to widen citizen participation in policy processes and understand their initiative as 'closing the gap' (Hintz 2016) between people and the policy level. By facilitating the development of technical tools to both enable and analyze the inclusion of citizen voices, they aim at expanding and thereby institutionalizing the role of citizens in policy-making.

Conclusion: opportunities and challenges for policy change

The policy initiatives that were outlined here offer a rich pool of experiences that can help us understand the diversity of strategies that policy activists apply, but also the conditions and constraints of their interventions. To start with, we have seen a creative mix of approaches, from advocacy 'inside' to public pressure 'outside', to technology-oriented practices 'beyond' immediate policy interventions, to 'policy hacking' and the creation of model laws and regulatory proposals. While these different approaches are often based on different cultural backgrounds, ideological values and strategic assessments of policy engagement, the examples discussed here also demonstrate collaborative efforts in which different strategies interact with and complement each other. Second, the cases presented here highlight the importance of a policy window. In Iceland and Argentina, an economic crisis led to public criticism of established practices and a (temporary) retreat of traditional political forces. In Hamburg, a local construction scandal led to a political climate for change. In the EU and at WSIS, a legitimacy crisis led to the need for policymakers and institutions to open up to civil society groups. Third, the initiatives portrayed here have applied strategies such as framing and alliance-building that have been highlighted in the social movement literature. IMMI emphasized that its proposal would create an international reputation for Iceland as a transparency haven; in Latin America, policy initiatives referred to widespread concerns regarding the democratization of communication; in Europe they tapped into current debates on social cohesion and media literacy; and in the US, they referred to the Constitution and the highly-valued right to free expression. Most initiatives were based on strong alliances amongst civil society and public-interest groups, sometimes including partners from the state and commercial sectors, and they benefitted from the presence of sympathetic individuals inside the institutional or political space where relevant decisions were made. In some cases, movement members came to occupy strategic positions and facilitated the process from inside state institutions.

While these observations confirm core findings of social movement literature, the examples presented here also point us to distinct practices of media policy activism that are based in characteristic features of media activism, and of the media and communications sphere more generally. 'Inside' actors – as demonstrated by WSIS and internet governance institutions – often move beyond lobbying and get involved more directly in policy development. 'Outsiders' and 'beyonders' – like those assembled at *WSIS? WeSeize!* or those that run alternative ISPs – often focus on creating alternative infrastructure that safeguards users' communication rights and disregards or bypasses regulatory obstacles, rather than protesting the latter. They aspire to social change not primarily through advocacy or public pressure but by creating a new (both material and normative) framework. If 'code is law' (Lessig 2006), their practice partly complements, partly determines formal policy processes, and constitutes a latent form of policy intervention. Their DIY approach of creating, rather than demanding, change is applied by the 'policy hackers', too. Focusing on legal text rather than technological infrastructure, they engage more directly with the policymakers who adopt and implement laws and regulations, and their actions are often embedded in, or closely related to, other forms of advocacy. Yet they share a focus on prefigurative action.

The approaches to policy activism that are highlighted here as characteristic for the media field share a claim about the prominence of civil society groups, technological developers and other non-state actors (including, in some cases, the private sector) in policy development and reject the exclusive role of the state. They move beyond the normative role that has traditionally been assigned to civil society. This shift is significant but not without risk or criticism. Multistakeholder participation may lead civil society to be incorporated into (and thus legitimize) the agendas of far more powerful actors from the state and business sectors (Hintz & Milan 2013). Practices of hacking and tech development are often based in strategies of improving, fixing and solving discrete problems, rather than addressing power imbalances in policy development, and may therefore tend towards a reductionist 'solutionism' (Morozov 2013). All these practices question (and, potentially, weaken) established rules of public and democratically-legitimated policymaking. However, they open up previously closed policy spaces for public participation, they assume a far more central role for civil society, public interest groups and social movements in the policy process, and they thereby expand our understanding of civil society-based policy reform initiatives.

References

Aitamurto, T. and Chen, K. (2017) 'The Value of Crowdsourcing in Public Policymaking: Epistemic, Democratic and Economic Value', *The Theory and Practice of Legislation*, vol. 1, no. 1, pp. 55–72.

Bennett, W. L. and Segerberg, A. (2012) 'The Logic of Connective Action', *Information, Communication and Society*, vol. 15, no. 5, pp. 739–68.

Braman, S. (2006) *Change of State: Information, Policy, and Power*. Cambridge, MA: MIT Press.

Calabrese, A. (2004) 'The Promise of Civil Society: A Global Movement for Communication Rights', *Continuum: Journal of Media & Cultural Studies*, vol. 18, no. 3, pp. 317–29.

Chakravartty, P. and Yuezhi, Z. (2008) *Global Communications: Towards a Transcultural Political Economy*. Lanham, MD: Rowman & Littlefield.

Coyer, K. and Hintz, A. (2010) 'Developing the "Third Sector": Community Media Policies in Europe', in B. Klimkiewicz (ed.) *Media Freedom and Pluralism: Media Policy Challenges in the Enlarged Europe*. Budapest, Hungary: Central European University Press, pp. 275–98.

DeNardis, L. (2009) *Protocol Politics: The Globalization of Internet Governance*. Cambridge, MA: MIT Press.

European Parliament (2008) *Report on Community Media in Europe, 2008/2011, (INI)* (Approved September 25, 2008), <http://www.europarl.europa.eu/sides/getDoc.do?language=EN&referenc e=A6-0263/2008>, accessed 20 June 2017.

Freedman, D. (2008) *The Politics of Media Policy*. Cambridge: Polity.

Freedman, D., Obar, J., Martens, C. and McChesney, R. (2016) *Strategies for Media Reform: International Perspectives*. New York: Fordham University Press.

Gangadharan, S. P. (2013) 'Translation in the Media Ownership Debate: The Work of Civil Society Groups and the Federal Communications Commission, 2002–2007', *Communication, Culture & Critique*, no. 6, pp 550–67.

Goldsmith, J. and Wu, T. (2006) *Who Controls the Internet? Illusions of a Borderless World*. Oxford: Oxford University Press.

Hackett, R. A. and Carroll, W. K. (2006) *Remaking Media: The Struggle to Democratize Public Communication*. London: Routledge.

Hamelink, C. (1994) *The Politics of World Communication: A Human Rights Perspective*. London: Sage.

Hintz, A. (2009) *Civil Society Media and Global Governance: Intervening into the World Summit on the Information Society*. Münster, Germany: LIT.

Hintz, A. (2014) 'Towards Community and Non-Profit Media Legislation in South America: Challenging Media Power Through Citizen Participation', in C. Martens, R. W. McChesney and E. Vivaraes (eds) *The International Political Economy of Communication: Media and Power in South America*. Basingstoke, UK: Palgrave Macmillan, pp. 46–62.

Hintz, A. (2016) 'Policy Hacking: Citizen-based Policy-Making and Media Reform', in D. Freedman, J. Obar, C. Martens and R. McChesney (eds) *Strategies for Media Reform*. New York: Fordham University Press.

Hintz, A. and Brown, I. (2017) 'Enabling Digital Citizenship? The Reshaping of Surveillance Policy After Snowden', *International Journal of Communication*, vol. 11, pp. 782–801.

Hintz, A. and Milan, S. (2013) 'Networked Collective Action and the Institutionalized Policy Debate: Bringing Cyberactivism to the Policy Arena?', *Policy & Internet*, vol. 5, no. 1, pp. 7–26.

Keck, M. E. and Sikkink, K. (1998) *Activists Beyond Borders. Advocacy Networks in International Politics*. Ithaca, NY: Cornell University Press.

Khagram, S., Riker, J. V. and Sikkink, K. (2002) 'From Santiago to Seattle: Transnational Advocacy Groups Restructuring World Politics', in S. Khagram, J. V. Riker and K. Sikkink (eds), *Restructuring World Politics: Transnational Social Movements, Networks, and Norms*. Minneapolis, MN: University of Minnesota Press, pp. 3–23.

Kingdon, J. W. (1984) *Agendas, Alternatives, and Public Policy*. Boston, MA: Little, Brown.

Lessig, L. (2006) *Code Version 2.0*. New York: Basic Books.

Light, E. (2011) 'From Pirates to Partners: The Legalization of Community Radio in Uruguay', *Canadian Journal of Communication*, vol. 36, no. 1, pp. 51–67.

McChesney, R. W. (1990) 'The Battle for the US Airwaves, 1928–1935', *Journal of Communication*, vol. 40, no. 4, pp. 29–57.

McChesney, R. W. (2004) 'Media Policy Goes to Main Street: The Uprising of 2003', *The Communication Review*, vol. 7, no. 3, pp. 223–58.

McChesney, R. W. (2007) *Communication Revolution: Critical Junctures and the Future of Media*. New York: The New Press.

Milan, S. (2013) *Social Movements and Their Technologies: Wiring Social Change*. Basingstoke, UK: Palgrave Macmillan.

Morozov, E. (2013) *To Save Everything, Click Here: The Folly of Technological Solutionism*. New York: Public Affairs.

Mosco, V. (1996) *The Political Economy of Communication: Rethinking and Renewal*. London: Sage.

Mueller, M. (2010) *Networks and States: The Global Politics of Internet Governance*. Cambridge, MA: MIT Press.

Musiani, F. (2015) 'Practice, Plurality, Performativity, and Plumbing: Internet Governance Research Meets Science and Technology Studies', *Science, Technology & Human Values*, vol. 40, no. 2, pp. 272–86.

Pickard, V. (2014) *America's Battle for Media Democracy: The Triumph of Corporate Libertarianism and the Future of Media Reform*. Cambridge: Cambridge University Press.

Pickard, V. (2015) 'Media Activism from Above and Below', *Journal of Information Policy*, no. 5, pp. 109–28.

Raboy, M. (2002) *Global Media Policy in the New Millennium*. Luton, UK: University of Luton Press.

Raboy, M. and Landry, N. (2005) *Civil Society, Communication and Global Governance: Issues from the World Summit on the Information Society*. New York: Peter Lang.

Raboy, M. and Padovani, C. (2010) *Mapping Global Media Policy: Concepts, Frameworks, Methods* (Working paper), http:www.globalmediapolicy.net, accessed 20 June 2017.

Sell, S. K. (2013) 'Revenge of the "Nerds": Collective Action Against Intellectual Property Maximalism in the Global Information Age', *International Studies Review*, no. 5, pp. 67–85.

Srnicek, N. (2016) *Platform Capitalism*. Cambridge: Polity Press.

Tarrow, S. (2005) *The New Transnational Activism*. New York: Cambridge University Press.

Tilly, C. and Tarrow, S. (2006) *Contentious Politics*. New York: Oxford University Press.

Zittrain, J. (2008) *The Future of the Internet—And How to Stop it*. New Haven, CT: Yale University Press.

34

MEDIA ACTIVISM

Media change?

Natalie Fenton

Every once in a while, something happens that causes such outrage and public consternation that it makes it impossible for politicians to avoid acting. Such events rarely occur in isolation but speak to a history that has been accumulating over time – rubbish that has been gathering in the streets until finally the stench is too overbearing to ignore and something has to be done to clean up the yard and make it habitable once more. The phone hacking scandal in the UK was one such event (Davies 2014).

In the summer of 2011 the national Sunday newspaper, *News of the World*, owned by Rupert Murdoch's News International, stood accused of illegal, unethical behaviour through the systematic phone hacking of politicians, members of the royal family, celebrities and murder victims and their families. Murdoch subsequently closed down the *News of the World* and several ex-editors and journalists found themselves under criminal investigation. The Prime Minister, David Cameron, publicly embarrassed by his employment of Andy Coulson, a former editor of *News of the World*, as his director of communications (Coulson was arrested by the Metropolitan Police Service in July 2011 for allegations of corruption and phone hacking), called for a public inquiry chaired by Lord Justice Leveson to investigate the issues involved. This very public shaming of certain sections of the media, combined with political circumstances, brought about a very public response from the prime minister, and sparked a reinvigorated approach to media reform in the UK led by two campaign groups: Hacked Off and the Media Reform Coalition (MRC). This chapter reflects on the author's involvement in the Hacked Off Campaign (as vice-chair of the Board of Directors) and the MRC (as a founding member), and considers what we can learn from them practically as media activists and how they can inform our thinking theoretically as media scholars.

The birth of a movement

Hacked Off began in 2011 as a campaign that was initially part of the Media Standards Trust that first called for a public inquiry into press practices. In the summer of 2012 it became a separate campaign group by the same name and registered as a not-for-profit company. The then-director of the Campaign, Professor Brian Cathcart, a former journalist, published a book *Everybody's Hacked Off: Why We Don't Have the Press We Deserve and What to Do about It* (Cathcart 2012), and Hacked Off set about helping victims of press abuse tell their stories about the experience of phone hacking, stalking, bullying and harassment, and campaigning to ensure that independent and effective regulatory mechanisms for dealing with such transgressions were put in place. It began as a group of people who through their work had reached the conclusion that the current system of press self-regulation was failing desperately: we were three media academics who had researched news and journalism over many years; media lawyers engaged in privacy and libel cases; representatives of civil society who were constantly trying to flush out errors in reporting and improve press standards; as well as a celebrity victim of press abuse, and a former Member of Parliament. The ambition of Hacked Off was (and remains) tightly focused on processes of accountability. Its aim is to bring about an independent and effective mechanism of press regulation that holds the press accountable for unethical and illegal behaviour. The means to achieve this was directed largely towards the formal democratic processes in Parliament. In other words, a form of regulation that had independence from industry and government at its core but was underpinned by statute.

The Media Reform Coalition was set up in September 2011 to coordinate the most effective contribution by civil society groups, academics and media campaigners to debates over media regulation, ownership and democracy in the context of the phone hacking crisis and proposed communications legislation. It took advice from the media reform movement in the US and Canada and set about building an alliance of partner organizations and supporting individuals to produce research and to organize campaigning activities aimed at creating a media system that is more plural, more accountable and could better support investigative and local journalism in particular (issues deemed to be suffering the most in the struggling economic context of newspapers in the UK).

The work of the MRC began with three main strands of activity: plurality, ethics and funding. But after the Leveson Inquiry its main focus became plurality in terms of both media ownership and media content. This was partly because Hacked Off was focusing heavily on systems to underpin journalism ethics and standards but also because the research that became the Coalition's main focus saw the constitution of media power as located in the concentration of media ownership (MRC 2014). It is important to recognize that each campaign enabled and sustained the other: the sordid tales of abuses of media power that wreaked havoc in the lives of ordinary people and distorted the democratic process (Dean 2011) allowed the constitution of media power – a more fundamental critique about capitalism and the distribution of cultural resources – to become a matter of public concern (Baker 2007; Winseck 2008; Curran 2011).

Addressing the symptoms of the problem in two contrasting ways also enabled different organizations and individuals with diverse interests and politics to take part. As such, a focus on plurality better suited one of the key players in the coalition – the National Union of Journalists – more at ease with a critique of corporate media power than one that criticized the practices of journalism per se (albeit in a corporate context). The ability to speak to a range of organizations with differing political values and appeal to cross-party politics was key to the longevity of the campaign and its parliamentary and public purchase.

After part one of the inquiry lasting nearly a year and a half, Lord Justice Leveson delivered his recommendations in November 2012. The report discussed in detail how the newspaper industry had become too powerful and that meaningful reform was needed to restore public confidence in the press. Leveson also needed to convince the industry that his recommendations had taken account of their concerns – that this was about enshrining press freedom and ensuring that any subsequent regulatory system was independent from government. He also had to satisfy the many victims of press abuse that his recommendations would bring about an independent regulatory system with teeth, which could hold the industry to account when necessary. And he needed the recommendations to be politically palatable so that the Prime Minister would not be pressurized by the press into brushing it off as unsustainable and fatally flawed.

Leveson did this in two ways: first by focusing largely on journalism and developing a system for complaints against transgressions in journalistic practice. This was a response to the immediate concerns of the victims of press abuse but one which lacked any systematic attempt to redress more structural inequalities in influence and power through tackling issues of ownership concentration and media plurality (House of Lords Select Committee on Communications 2008). Second, Leveson located his recommended system in independent self-regulation underpinned by statute thereby responding to the industry's concerns over governmental interference in press freedom yet still ensuring that the press could not, as was popularly remarked, mark their own homework (Eberwein *et al*. 2011; Fielden 2012).

Thus, the framework for reform was clearly established around a narrower set of issues than previous academic analyses had assessed as vital for substantive change to take place (McChesney 2008; Curran *et al*. 2012). Notably, media plurality was sidelined and the funding of news all but ignored in favour of a rather more modest focus on a mechanism for complaints (albeit an effective and independent mechanism that had never before existed). Instead Leveson called for further development of a new system for measuring and tackling media concentration of ownership (Leveson 2012: 1461–76) that included online publications, acknowledging that unchecked media concentration over several decades had allowed some media groups to accumulate vast amounts of revenues and influence with adverse consequences for media and democracy. He noted that one such consequence had been the development of intimate relationships between political and media elites in a way which 'has not been in the public interest' (Leveson 2012: 1956). Although the Leveson Report (2012: 1470) suggested certain approaches for dealing with concentration of ownership (e.g. that triggers for intervention should be 'considerably lower' than those appropriate to ordinary competition concerns and address organic growth within media markets), the exclusion of explicit recommendations for addressing media plurality was seen to be a missed opportunity. This was either too complex for the inquiry to deal with or they took a political decision that the press may be more inclined to come on board if the market were left well alone.

Nonetheless, the focus of the Leveson report spoke directly to the concerns of both media reform groups and most forcefully to the work of Hacked Off who then set about campaigning in support of the Leveson recommendations. This involved making the case for the implementation of Leveson's proposals amongst the wider public as well as within parliament by ensuring that key politicians understood the issues, were aware of strong public feeling and had the means and tools to implement Leveson. This work involved a combination of parliamentary drafting, public polling and then highlighting public opinion, lobbying and persuading politicians and parliamentarians, media monitoring and rebutting, mobilizing supporters and supporting victims of press abuse, persuading and debating with journalists and the public, and then briefing and reporting on all aspects of this work. They worked closely throughout with victims of press abuse in the face of relentless and often bitterly hostile resistance from leading national newspaper groups who initially appeared to be sympathetic to at least some of Leveson's recommendations but over time repudiated most of them.

The scandal of phone hacking allowed media reform to suddenly become a big political issue. The job of the activists for media change was to keep the issue alive, research and identify possibilities for reform and then campaign for them. The core strength of the campaigns was firmly lodged in the public support behind them with constant polling over a period of five years showing high levels of support for media reform and a firm rejection of press manoeuvring. A poll undertaken by YouGov for Hacked Off in January 2017, after an onslaught of anti-press regulation coverage across all news media, still showed that 73 per cent of the public thought press behaviour had either got worse or not changed since the Leveson enquiry.

Consistent surveys (e.g. Park *et al.* 2013; Media Intelligence Service 2016) also revealed that the public did not trust the press.

'Freedom of the press': freedom of the powerful over the powerless

Yet still the press industry objected with a simplistic response to so-called government interference in the workings of the press. This prompted the prime minister, David Cameron, who had initially said he would implement the Leveson recommendations unless they were 'bonkers', to state that even statutory underpinning – a law to enact the costs and incentives of a new system with no interference whatsoever in the actual running of, or decision making of the new self-regulatory body – would be 'crossing the Rubicon'. In other words, the sacrosanct position of a free press in a free society would be irreparably undermined and there would be no going back.

Invoking the language of free speech became the default position of the press lobby (Fenton 2014). Of course, nobody would dispute the freedom of the press to hold power to account, but this does not put the press themselves beyond accountability. Freedom without accountability is simply the freedom of the powerful over the powerless which, arguably, is precisely what the press were trying to preserve: freedom to run roughshod over people's lives causing harm and distress for the sake of increased newspaper sales. Furthermore, freedom has always been enshrined in law. The press, for example, is protected by the right of freedom of expression under Article 10 of the European Convention of Human Rights. Article 10, however, is not absolute but conditional and qualified by article 10.ii:

> The exercise of these freedoms, since it carries with it duties and responsibilities, may be subject to such formalities, conditions, restrictions of penalties as are prescribed by law and are necessary in a democratic society, in the interests of national security, territorial integrity or public safety, for the prevention of disorder or crime, for the protection of health or morals, for the protection of the reputation or rights of others, for preventing the disclosure of information received in confidence, or for maintaining the authority and impartiality of the judiciary.
>
> *ECHR n.d.: 11*

Article 10 is also subject to Article 8 of the Convention, which covers the right to privacy.

Media reformers hit back, arguing that freedom works both ways and that freedom of the press had to be balanced by freedom of the public to assess and challenge the nature of that communication: freedom shared not power abused. In other words, they argued that democratic practice requires protective and enabling legislation and that is why it exists in other areas of public life. But with a general election creeping ever closer, Cameron bowed to the rhetoric of 'press freedom' and opted for setting up a new press self-regulatory body not by statutory underpinning but by Royal Charter – a process that nobody seemed to fully understand. This created a political dilemma. A Royal Charter could deliver a new system of self-regulation that was independent and effective, in other words Leveson-compliant, but it was via a circuitous route that appeared less democratic. At a point when it seemed like this was the only offer on the table and it looked like the press lobby were willing to accept it (after all, it had been devised in response to their concerns), Hacked Off decided to support the Charter that was sealed on the 30 October 2013. This was a major concession. Powerful press interests soon backtracked and found excuses to repudiate this mechanism, making it quite clear that they had no intention of ever agreeing to a system that they were not able fully to control.

It is worth reflecting on the history of failed press regulation (Curran 2011) in the UK. The first Royal Commission on the Press (1947–1949) led to the press industry creating the General Council of the Press (1953). Dissatisfaction with its practice led to the second Royal Commission on the Press and to the General Council being replaced by the Press Council in 1962. In 1972 the Younger Committee report on Privacy was critical of the Press Council who rejected their concerns. In 1974 a third Royal Commission on the Press looked into editorial standards and freedom of choice for consumers. It suggested a new written Code of Practice. The Press Council again rejected the Commission's suggestions. In 1990 the Calcutt Committee was established to look into press intrusion. Calcutt recommended replacing the Press Council with a new Press Complaints Commission (PCC) and a new Code of Practice. In 1993 Calcutt reported on the progress of the PCC. He determined that sufficient progress had not been made and recommended the introduction of a Statutory Press Complaints Tribunal. Once more the press industry objected and the government failed to act on the recommendation. In 1995 the National Heritage Select Committee published a report on privacy and press intrusion and made recommendations on a new Statutory Press Ombudsman. The press objected and yet again the government yielded and rejected the recommendations. In 2009 the PCC published a report in response to the Guardian phone hacking investigation *Phone Message Tapping Allegations* (that was subsequently withdrawn on 6 July 2011). In July 2011 the Leveson Inquiry was announced. The discredited PCC was replaced by the Independent Press Standards Organisation (IPSO) and the majority of the mainstream press signed up to it. A cross-party agreement resulted in a Royal Charter designed to bring about independent and effective self-regulation of the press. However, IPSO refused to be part of the system of press regulation under the Royal Charter.

What this history tells us is that the press has consistently promised to self-regulate adequately and consistently failed to do so. The government, keen to maintain good relations with the press, has consistently bowed down to industry pressure.

The Royal Charter sets out a mechanism for independent self-regulation of the press overseen by an independent body called the Press Recognition Panel (PRP). The job of the PRP is to ensure that any organization that regulates the press and seeks recognition is independent, properly funded and able to protect the public. Any recognized regulator must meet the 29 criteria listed in the Charter. These criteria were designed to secure press freedom and protect the public interest. In order to respond to criticisms of government interference in press regulation it was agreed that the Charter can only be amended by a two-thirds majority of each of the House of Commons, the House of Lords and the Scottish Parliament and with unanimous agreement of the PRP Board. IPSO has so far refused to seek recognition and only meets 12 of the 29 criteria (Media Standards Trust 2013). But another press regulator IMPRESS, set up by a free speech campaigner Jonathan Heawood, was recognized as an approved regulator on 25 October 2016. Finally, five years after the Leveson enquiry, a new system was in place … well, almost.

A crucial part of this new system relied on persuading the press to join a recognized regulator. Leveson knew this would not be easy and so devised a system hinged on costs and incentives that sought to balance two key objectives: providing access to justice for ordinary people wronged by the press without the risk of huge legal costs and protecting news publishers from wealthy litigants threatening them with financially ruinous court proceedings. Section 40 of the Crime and Courts Act does this through a system of carrots and sticks – if a news publisher joins a recognized regulator then access to low cost arbitration becomes mandatory. This removes the threat of potentially huge losses for both ordinary citizens who may be the victims of illegal journalistic behaviour and for publishers who may be threatened by a wealthy litigant who does not like what they have printed. Only claimants with a genuine legal case can be offered arbitration thereby avoiding trivial and malicious claims being brought. In reverse, if a newspaper decides not to join a recognized regulator and thereby refuses to offer affordable access to justice, then they will be liable to pay all costs of court action against them. The new system of regulation also includes protection for local and regional publishers to prevent causing them financial hardship.

Section 40 is integral to the success of the Royal Charter framework of press regulation and the press knew it. Why would anyone choose to join a recognized regulator and subject themselves to independent scrutiny if it was not financially beneficial to do so? Consequently, even after Section 40 had become law (but had not yet been commenced) they went on a propaganda offensive to try to ensure it never saw the light of day. Karen Bradley, the new secretary of state for Culture, Media and Sport, came under increasing pressure from both sides of the debate and capitulated by putting the commencement of Section 40 out to public consultation (giving herself powers of decision over the terms of press regulation that had already been agreed by Parliament and immediately flouting the principle of no government interference).

Herman and Chomsky (1988) evoke the idea of 'manufacturing consent', whereby propaganda is used to naturalize ideas of the most powerful groups in society and to marginalize dissent. Their propaganda model depends on five 'filters' working on the media that ensure a structural bias in favour of dominant frames: concentrated private ownership, the power of advertising, the domination of elite sources, the use of 'flak' (sustained attacks on oppositional voices) and the construction of an enemy, here – so-called liberal leftie luvvies/élites. Mainstream media perform an ideological role – none more so than the 'liberal' media who foster the greatest illusions precisely because their liberalism produces a deceptive picture of a pluralistic media system when, in reality, there is none (Fenton & Freedman 2014). All media, whether 'liberal' or 'conservative', are tied to current relations of power and are involved in distorting, suppressing and silencing alternative narratives to capitalist power – in this case represented by themselves. During the period of public consultation, the press engaged in an industrial shutdown of debate over media reform. This was not a struggle for organizations whose fundamental mission is to hold power to account. Far from it. This was about hanging on to power without accountability.

Understanding the role of the news as an industry and news organizations as corporate entities is crucial to our understanding of how 'freedom' can be more easily claimed by some to the detriment of others. 'Freedom of the press' as an ethical practice does not somehow magically transcend the market or render invisible the power base to which it is connected. Rather, 'freedom of the press' is embroiled in a particular political–economic system. This is a system that tells us that productivity is increased and innovation unleashed if the state stays out of the picture and lets businesses get on with it (Fenton 2015). This is particularly important for multinational corporations who do not want to be stymied by trifling national policies that threaten to scupper their growth. Productivity in the market and hence news as a commodity takes precedence over the social and political concerns of news as a mechanism of democratic process. In other words, the less 'interference' in the form of regulation, the more liberalized the market, the better the outcome (Jessop 2002). The form of press freedom we are left with is what Victor Pickard calls corporate libertarianism – a market ontology that says anything less than complete deregulation is the 'end of 300 years of press freedom'.

'Freedom' in this sense becomes a narrative device to sidestep the deeper, systemic problems of the newspaper industry of which these ethical misdemeanours are but one symptom. Freedom of the press stands in for *all* activities of the press regardless of whether they have democratic intent or not. This kind of short-cut libertarian defence, which aligns freedom with established and vested power interests' ability to do whatever they like within the law, means that any form of regulation that may encourage news organizations to behave in particular ways is assumed to be detrimental to democracy and involvement of the state in any form whatsoever in relation to the press becomes nothing more than state censorship.

Understanding the role of the news as an industry and news organizations as corporate entities in these relations is crucial to our understanding of how 'freedom' can be more easily claimed by some to the detriment of others. The industry response to the hacking scandal in the UK largely conformed to this neo-liberal premise. Freedom of the press expressed purely as the need to get the state to butt out and give commercial practice free rein is about nothing more than enabling market dominance to take priority over all other concerns. Freedom of the press expressed in this way is not a precondition or even a consequence of democracy so much as a substitute for it.

Conclusion

It would be easy to surmise that the fledgling campaign for media reform in the UK has failed – after all, there are still no major publishers signed up to a Leveson-compliant regulator. But this would be misplaced and play into the hands of those who would like to squash this movement once and for all. Rather, we can point to four crucial achievements:

1. It has made media policy a political issue that has made its way into the election manifestoes of some political parties and is a frequent subject of parliamentary debate. In the process the wily entanglement between media and political elites has been exposed such that it is much harder to insulate media reform from political reform because of the lack of autonomy of the media 'field' from the actions of the state and the market (Hackett & Carroll 2006). I have no doubt that were the media reform movement to dissipate, then media policy would also fall off the agenda and this is precisely what corporate media want.

2. It has reinvigorated the link between media and democracy putting citizens and the public interest back at the heart of the relationship (Barnett 2012). At a time when market rationality has overtaken all others, this is no mean feat. In his work on media reform movements, McChesney (2008) argues that the contemporary US media reform movement was triggered by the anti-globalization struggles that took place from the late 1990s and which raised serious questions about the incorporation of the right to communicate within neoliberal frames and policies. Bringing the citizen back into a frame that has been dominated by a consumer rhetoric may well have repercussions beyond the objective of media reform.

3. The media reform movement has suggested to new players on the news scene that it can be done differently. By challenging the agendas of mainstream corporate press, other start-ups and local/hyper-local ventures have found renewed justification in pursuing alternative models of ownership, from local media co-operatives like Bristol Cable (created and owned by over 1480 people in the city) to slow journalism projects such as 'Delayed Gratification' (a printed, non-partisan independent magazine free from the influence of search engine algorithms and advertisers' agenda that works to counter kneejerk, cut-and-paste journalism). Such ventures put an increased emphasis on shared meaning-making, participation and equality, and seek to transform the dominant machinery of representation in the media.

4. And we have shown that despite its tentacles of power that reach far and wide, the media industry can be challenged and we should never let its power go unaccounted. The ordinary citizen has begun to talk back to media power.

Media activism faces a particular challenge as no meaningful campaign for media reform is likely to be supported by the media itself or, indeed, by any people in positions of power. We need to create the conditions not simply in which we frame modest demands in the hope of them being accepted, but to campaign hard for a shift in the public's attitude to these issues precisely in order to apply pressure on the politicians and regulators who have the formal power to act. Confining reform demands to very modest and narrow proposals is unlikely to stave off opposition by the media or politicians. Indeed, the primary audience for media reform is not simply politicians and policymakers but publics: ordinary citizens whose needs are not being met and whose communicative rights are being undermined.

References

Baker, C. E. (2007) *Media Concentration and Democracy*. Cambridge: Cambridge University Press.

Barnett, S. (2012) 'Public Interest: The Public Decides', *British Journalism Review*, vol. 23, no. 2, pp. 15–23.

Cathcart, B. (2012) *Everybody's Hacked Off: Why We Don't Have the Press We Deserve and What to Do about It*. London: Penguin.

Curran, J. (2011) *Media and Democracy*. London: Routledge.

Curran, J., Fenton, N. and Freedman, D. (2012) *Misunderstanding the Internet*. London: Routledge.

Davies, N. (2014) *Hack Attack: How the Truth Caught up with Rupert Murdoch*. London: Chatto & Windus.

Dean, M. (2011) *Democracy under Attack: How the Media Distort Policy and Politics*. Bristol: The Policy Press.

Eberwein, T., Fengler, S., Lauk, E. and Leppik-Bork, T. (eds.) (2011) *Mapping Media Accountability – in Europe and Beyond*, Herbert Von Halem Verlag, http://www.mediaact.eu/81.html, accessed 13 December 2017.

Fenton, N. (2014) 'Defending Whose Democracy? Media Freedom and Media Power', *Nordicom Review*, vol. 35, 31–43.

Fenton, N. (2015) 'Post-democracy, Press, Politics and Power', *Political Quarterly*, vol. 87, no. 1, pp. 81–5.

Fenton, N. and Freedman, D. (2014) 'The Politics and Possibilities of Media Reform: Lessons from the UK', in T. Miller (ed.) *Routledge Companion to Global Popular Culture*. London: Routledge, pp. 458–70.

Fielden, L. (2012) *Regulating the Press: A Comparative Study of International Press Councils*. Oxford: Reuters Institute.

Hackett, R. and Carroll, W. (2006) *Remaking Media: The Struggle to Democratize Public Communication*. London: Routledge.

Herman, E. and Chomsky, N. (1988) *Manufacturing Consent: The Political Economy of the Mass Media*. New York: Pantheon.

House of Lords Select Committee on Communications (2008) *The Ownership of the News Report*. Vol I and Vol. II: Norwich: The Stationery Office Limited, http://www.publications.parliament.uk/pa/ld200708/ldselect/ldcomuni/122/122i.pdf, accessed 13 December 2017.

Jessop, B. (2002) *The Future of the Capitalist State*. Cambridge: Polity Press.

Leveson (2012) *The Leveson Inquiry: The Report into the Culture, Practices and Ethics of the Press*. London: The Stationery Office.

McChesney, R. (2008) 'The U.S. Media Reform Movement: Going Forward', *Monthly Review*, vol. 60, no. 4, pp. 51–59.

Media Intelligence Service (2016) *Trust in Media 2016*. European Broadcasting Union, www3.ebu/ch/publications, accessed 13 December 2017.

Media Reform Coalition (2014) *The Elephant in the Room: A Survey of Media Ownership and Plurality in the United Kingdom*. London: MRC.

Media Standards Trust (2013) *The Independent Press Standards Organisation (IPSO)*. London: Media Standards Trust.

Park *et al.* (2013) *British Social Attitudes: The 30th Report*. London: NatCen Social Research.

Winseck, D. (2008) The State of Media Ownership and Media Markets: Competition or Concentration and Why Should We Care? *Sociology Compass*, vol. 2, pp. 34–47.

35

FAN ACTIVISM

Samantha Close

Introduction

In the contemporary age in which old and new media systems, technologies and cultures are converging together, long-established but also long-underground media fan cultures are coming to greater mainstream prominence. Media fans are people who engage deeply with particular media, be they a television show, sports team, video game franchise or even the works of a classic author (Coppa 2006; Gray, Sandvoss & Harrington 2007; Duffett 2013). While people can certainly be fannish on their own, 'groups of individuals constitute a fandom through interest-driven affiliations, forming a sense of collective or subcultural identity around shared tastes' (Brough & Shresthova 2011: para. 2.1; Jenkins 1992). Organized fandoms nurtured grassroots practices of media production and theoretical critique which have proved impressively resilient in their queer, feminist and anti-commercial practices despite their transition out of subcultural safety in obscurity and into viral popularity, the halls of academia and even mainstream publication.

It might seem odd to think about fan activism as a characteristic way of approaching politics, or even about fans as activists at all. But societies of shared interests like fandoms hold out clear political potential in their ability to bring people together across divides in identity, politics and location (Putnam 2001; Fiske 2011; Swartz & Driscoll 2014). In areas of heated conflict such as the Kashmiri province of India, fans coming together to watch and discuss *Indian Idol 3* in public 'created the possibility and the space for the renewal of everyday forms of interaction across ethnic, religious, spatial and linguistic boundaries that had been subdued and rendered difficult, if not impossible, over the decades' (Punathambekar 2011: para. 3.1). Fans are often divided or ambivalent about applying terms like 'activism' or 'political' to their engagement, even as actions like lobbying corporations, writing social critique, organizing marches and holding debates seem unmistakably political to an outside view. Fannish activism thrives on populist ideas of 'just giving a shit' or 'making a difference where it matters to us', largely bypassing an official political system (including traditional activism) often seen as elitist, overly partisan or simply ineffective and out of touch (Buckingham 2000; Brough & Shresthova 2011; Coleman 2013; Jenkins, Shresthova, Gamber-Thompson, Kligler-Vilenchik & Arely Zimmerman 2016).

Study of fan activism provides essential insight into the power of self-organized, bottom-up, passion-driven activism and the unique communication tactics by which fans exercise this power. They also highlight common problems with this type of political work, particularly as fandom's diversity means there remain deep ideological divisions, competing campaigns and many different spokespeople who claim to represent fans as a whole. This makes fan activism an ideal place in which to observe how activists with very different opinions still come together – or not – in the same cultural sphere.

'Save Our Show' activism

The kind of activism most associated with fans are 'Save Our Show' campaigns, which seek to convince power brokers in the entertainment industry not to cancel their beloved programs. American and Canadian fans of the Japanese animated series *Sailor Moon*, for instance, organized via the early internet to apply strategic pressure to advertisers, television stations and production companies in an eventually successful effort to bring the Japanese show back on the air in North America (Close 2017). Such ends are less obviously political in an institutional sense, but they are crucial because of their attention to the politics of representation and everyday life (Jenkins & Carpentier 2013).

Fans have also historically advocated for studios to make projects deemed risky for mainstream audiences and to feature people of marginalized identities in a more central way. Gaylaxians, for instance, pushed for the inclusion and more complex depiction of gay, lesbian and bisexual people within the utopian future universe of the *Star Trek* science fiction franchise (Jenkins & Campbell 2006). Such groups share many aims with organizations like GLAAD, created by LGBTQ people as a media watchdog and advocate for queer politics in the entertainment industry. But fans like the Gaylaxians come from a differently inflected speaking position – rather than outside interest groups perceived as bringing politics to texts or agitators looking to police political correctness, activist fans present themselves 'as vitally involved with the life of the series and firmly committed to its survival' and excellence (Jenkins & Campbell 2006: 93).

Fan actions have become much more visible in the age of networked communication. And in a system where new and old technologies and corporate organizational systems are merging, networks sometimes find themselves looking to fans for guidance in how to navigate, for example, Twitter promotion (Guerrero-Pico 2017). Fans, as well as scholars within and without fandom, have raised important concerns about corporate exploitation of freely performed fan labour in these developing relationships (Andrejevic 2008; De Kosnik 2013; Stanfill & Condis 2014). More critical views argue that corporations unjustly benefit from 'the collective effort of viewers … to take on the work of finding ways to make a show more interesting', and such work should be compensated (Andrejevic 2008: 28). Others see more political potential in building on the gift economy practices which govern non-monetary exchanges between fans (De Kosnik 2013; Turk 2013).

Struggles between vocal, influential fans on social media and networks used to being the only ones with the microphone are redefining the power dynamics of popular media industries. *Once Upon a Time*, a family drama with fantasy themes that began airing on the US ABC network in 2011, is an excellent example of the struggle over cultural representational power between fans and networks. The *Once* series begins when the ten-year-old Henry unexpectedly shows up at the door of Emma Swan, the biological mother who gave him up for adoption as a teenager. Henry is convinced that Emma must return with him to Storybrooke in order to break a curse which transported all of the town's inhabitants from the realm of classic fairy tales, erasing their memories of life in the fantasy world. Emma soon meets Henry's adopted mother, Regina Mills, the mayor of Storybrooke and revealed to the audience as the Evil Queen of the fairy tale world who cast the curse on the town.

Once attracted a loyal fanbase not only through its fantasy plot but for its two central, complex female characters' struggles to 'navigate what it means to be co-parents to Henry, a negotiation similar to that of divorced or separated parents' (Vanderhoof 2015). Many fans of the series read Emma and Regina as a homosexual couple working through a complicated and realistic parenting dynamic, referring to both the pair and their fan affiliation as 'SwanQueen'. Gay, lesbian and bisexual representation is still fairly rare on mainstream, prime-time television. Series like *Once* arguably benefit a great deal from loyal viewing, social media posting, personal recommendations and other word of mouth by queer and queer-reading fans – and producers are aware of it. Fans have popularized the term 'queer baiting', however, to critique series which they see as cynically hinting at gay and lesbian relationships in order to gain viewers but with no intention of actually depicting such a relationship (Romano 2014; Vanderhoof 2015; Fanlore Editors 2017).

As *Once* more firmly established itself, writers, producers and some of the cast began to publicly distance themselves from the SwanQueen reading, even criticizing fans who advocate for the series to confirm Emma and Regina as a couple (Romano 2014). Fans spoke back, both through algorithmic and more traditional means. *Once* attempted to engage its fandom with a poll on the ABC website asking which character was the best romantic partner for Emma Swan. Although only male characters were named options, the poll contained an 'Other' button – which won handily, with many comments indicating 'Other is for Regina'. SwanQueen fans propelled the pairing to the top of popular LGBT website AfterEllen's 'femslash tournament' for two years in a row, forcing the show's creators to publicly defend their dismissal of the relationship in a queer-friendly forum or forego the free press (Piccoli 2015). Many fans publicly quit the show, with one prominent podcasting team writing, 'we mostly don't feel comfortable promoting and supporting a show whose cast and actors can't treat a f/f ship as just one of many options' (Romano 2014).

Many of the skills – and organizations – fans develop conducting these media property-focused campaigns are applicable in traditional political action. For example, fans of the *Avatar: The Last Airbender* cartoon came together in the outrage about the racial politics of the series' translation to live-action film. While *Avatar: The Last Airbender* is set in a fantasy world inspired by different Asian cultures and most of the characters are of colour, the live action film version of the cartoon initially cast white actors and actresses in all of the central roles. Although the fans were not able to achieve their goal of pressuring the studio to cast actors and actresses of Asian descent in all of the central roles, mirroring the original source, the organization they created in their campaigns, *Racebending.com*, is proving a long-lasting and active forum for political organizing and discussion around issues of race and mass culture (Lopez 2012). Similarly, the Harry Potter Alliance and associated 'Imagine Better' campaign have proved remarkably active and resilient organizations even years after the end of the official *Harry Potter* book and film series releases. These fans continue to use the narratives and values of the series to advocate for change, for instance pointing to the importance of libraries in the wizarding universe as motivation to oppose Trump-era federal defunding of public libraries in the US. Fandoms very often outlive the official publications of their beloved texts, particularly those for franchises such as *Harry Potter* and *Star Wars*. The HPA's political actions build on that continuing love for and interest in a fictional world, connecting it to political action.

Imagining different worlds

Fans do not limit themselves to influencing professional media producers and outlets. Building off the shared bodies and narratives of popular media, they themselves remix official content to create the stories they want to consume in forms such as fiction, videos, art and commentary.

Such 'transformational' fandoms are often female dominated, and there are strong sub-genres of explicitly feminist work (Coppa 2008; Jenkins 2008). The non-commercial circulation of these fannish texts creates powerful alternative discourses and media structures.

Perhaps the most well-known of these fannish discourses is the genre of 'slash'. Slash fandoms envision same-sex relationships between characters who usually do not have such a relationship inside a canonical media text (Jenkins 1992; Penley 1992; Busse & Lothian 2009). SwanQueen, as discussed earlier, is a slash fandom. But while many SwanQueen fans campaigned for changes in the official series, they envisioned the relationship themselves in a vast plethora of different ways. The majority of slash works are created by women and focus, perhaps surprisingly, on relationships between men (Jenkins 1992; Green, Jenkins & Jenkins 1998; porluciernagas 2014). In the West, slash is generally traced back to writing that romantically linked *Star Trek* characters Kirk and Spock, indicating their content as 'K/S'. But it is by no means a strictly American or even Western phenomenon – Japan has a strong, independent tradition of such fan creations, termed *yaoi* (Levi, McHarry & Pagliassotti 2008; Mizoguchi 2003; Suzuki 1998). Japanese commercial publishers of manga and literature have been more open to this genre, which they publish professionally under the term 'boys' love'. While the sexually explicit nature of slash and concerns about censorship are one argument against its professional publication, reader support of translated boys' love manga, animation and literature helped keep the Japanese publishing industry viable in America through the shaky years of the recession (Brienza 2016).

But rather than any one significant generic direction or particular fan-created textual world, the powerful political force of fan production is its continual re-working and re-thinking of common ground. It enacts polyvocality and pluralism without the need for democratic, but distancing, representation or the authoritarian collapse of communal imagining into one master vision – creating what Duncombe (2007) calls an ethical spectacle. There is a great deal of power in creating a living 'alternative' world through which people can directly experience and understand what a better world could be like. In this, fans precede and mirror much of the vision that animated Occupy's collectivist ethics and dedication to direct action (Castells 2015). Fans recognize and advocate for the value of this way of thinking about and acting in the world through sentiments such as 'I'm a fan of fandom' or 'Vidding is my fandom'.

An essential part of this vision-in-action is a quietly radical revision of copyright and for-profit media culture. Fan texts overwhelmingly circulate in a gift economy, rather than for profit (Jenkins 1992; Leonard 2005; Busse & Lothian 2009; Hellekson 2009; Turk 2013). In a world where more and more of life is conducted over privately owned internet platforms, however, this can be problematic. Fans resisted an early attempt by non-fans to commercialize fan fiction via the platform FanLib, in large part because of the way it diverted legal ownership, copyright and profits away from fans and back to professional media producers and FanLib's administrators (De Kosnik 2009; Jenkins 2008). But communities have also discovered that depending on any outside platform can be problematic (Lothian 2010; De Kosnik 2016; Fanlore Editors 2016a). When blogging and video hosting services go out of business, they can take your work with them by deleting their archives. Even when stable, such companies yield easily to copyright challenges by media corporations and obscenity reports by moral crusaders, even when fans are protected by law.

In response to these challenges, fans created the Organization for Transformative Works (OTW). As a non-profit volunteer group, the OTW works to preserve fandom's existing archives and to protect fans and fan practices moving forward into the future. The OTW provides legal advocacy for fans who find themselves the targets of copyright or obscenity charges. In 2012, it partnered with the Electronic Frontier Foundation to successfully achieve exemptions for fan video creators from the Digital Millennium Copyright Act (OTW Admin 2012).

The OTW also supports the Archive of Our Own (AO3), a non-profit archive run 'by fans, for fans' as a stable, friendly archive for fan works as well as an interface by which to comment on and curate these works (Lothian 2010; De Kosnik 2016). These efforts are not without flaw. For instance, the focus on transformation and production can create a de facto 'right way' to be a fan, protecting only some at the expense of others and distorting the balance between love and critique on which fandom thrives (Zubernis & Larsen 2012; Close 2014). But they demonstrate the dimension of fan activism which looks directly to structural change, taking the initiative to protect and support fan practices of doing culture differently.

Contesting common ground

Fans' activism is not confined to struggles between fans and professional media producers. Structural inequalities of racism, sexism and homophobia do not stop at the boundaries of fandom. For example, one common fan practice is cosplay, or 'costume play', in which fans create costumes of popular media characters and wear them to conventions and other fan gatherings. Unfortunately, rape culture also shows up at these conventions – both women and men in costume have problems such as other fans touching them inappropriately or photographing them without their knowledge. The Cosplay Is Not Consent campaign seeks to change this culture through petitions pressuring conventions to create and enforce sexual harassment policies, educating cosplayers and photographers on what to do if they witness or experience harassment, and creating an evocative archive of photographs and statements of both support for the campaign and personal experiences of harassment (Close 2016).

Science fiction and fantasy literature fandom is an illustrative crucible for activist debate within fandom. 'RaceFail '09' is the name given to a massive and months-long conversation about race and ethnicity within the science fiction and fantasy genres, particularly around issues of cultural appropriation and privilege, which eventually included thousands of fans and a great many professional writers (Jemisin 2010; Fanlore Editors 2016c). The debate was not always civil, to put it mildly. Fan historians and scholars point to a continuing cycle whereby many fans and even some fan scholars implicitly define themselves and fannish communities as white spaces, such that fans of colour are compelled to continually defend their legitimacy as fans and their right to speak as such (Jenkins 2014; Wanzo 2015; Flourish Klink *et al.* 2016). As its name indicates, RaceFail '09 demonstrated problems with how many fans understood race and ethnicity as well as how fan practices could replicate, rather than resist, structural privilege. But it could also be said to draw its vibrancy from the hopes of many participants for a more just and progressive world of science fiction and fantasy, and for some it initiated powerful experiences of connection with other fans of colour (Jemisin 2010). Activist fans compiled lists of suggested reading materials, both of fictional works by authors of colour or featuring non-white characters and of academic material explaining critical race studies.

Coming from the other side of the political spectrum, the annual Hugo Awards in 2013 saw the first (metaphorical) shots of backlash from highly conservative writers and fans. The Hugo Awards are science fiction and fantasy literature's longest-running and most prestigious awards. Their nomination process is grassroots-based, wherein fans who attend or purchase 'supporting memberships' for the WorldCon convention nominate works, authors and fans for awards. The 'Sad Puppies' campaign in 2013 organized conservative fans to buy supporting memberships in large numbers and to nominate a particular slate of works and writers with limited diversity of identity whom they perceived as right-wing. The Sad Puppies argue that a small elite concerned with liberal politics, political correctness and valuing social importance over good storytelling have hijacked the Hugo Awards, and they are attempting to take it back via controlling the nominating process – a strategy similar to the Tea Party's approach to the mainstream American Republican party (Skocpol & Williamson 2012). The 'Rabid Puppies' campaign, with actively misogynist and racist political leanings, copied many of the Sad Puppies' tactics but with the goal of destroying the Hugo Awards as a prestigious shared space for literature and fandom, rather than reclaiming them (Marks 2015). The two campaigns' successes at both the nomination and awards stage have been notable, shocking many in the science fiction and fantasy world (VanDerWerff 2015; Fanlore Editors 2016b). Counter-campaigns urged fans to vote 'No Award' for many categories in which there were Sad or Rabid Puppy nominees, so as to indicate resistance to the campaigns through their visible refusal to participate – mirroring the 'conscientious non-voter' approach of many Young Libertarians to general elections (Jenkins *et al.* 2016). Their success has also been notable, and in 2015 the Hugo Awards gave out as many 'No Award' results in one night as they had in their entire previous history (Standlee 2015).

As this case study of recent history in science fiction and fantasy fandom suggests, change is messy and difficult. But in order to persist through painful setbacks and to unite groups of diverse people, activists need a vision of a better world (Duncombe 2007; Brough & Shresthova 2011; Jenkins *et al.* 2016). Some fan organizations have found theirs in the cultural logics and ethical principles of their favourite media worlds and are mobilizing them to create 'real world' change (Hinck 2011; Jenkins 2011). Andrew Slack (2010), leader of the Harry Potter Alliance, explains this as 'cultural acupuncture … finding where the psychological energy is in the culture, and moving that energy towards creating a healthier world'. As previously discussed, the Save Our Sailors campaign sought to bring the Japanese animated series back onto the air in North America. They took their signature approach of positivity and change through forming alliances in the existing system of media power, rather than through boycotts and overt critique, from the way *Sailor Moon*'s heroines fight with the power of love and friendship in opposition to 'Negaverse' villains intent on draining positive energy out of the world (Save Our Sailors 2003). Such activism also draws parallels between the stories of fictional characters beloved by mainstream society and those of marginalized social groups. Undocumented American youth advocating for access to higher education and paths to citizenship, for example, point out that Superman himself is an undocumented immigrant – he was brought from the planet Krypton at a young age without formal paperwork and yet becomes an extremely valuable member of American society (Jenkins *et al.* 2016).

Conclusion

Throughout this chapter, I have analyzed fannish engagement as political in its own right as well as an opportunity to develop evergreen organizing skills applicable to many different causes and situations. Fannish activism, as a self-aware and growing force, gives people, particularly young people, a language through which to engage with politics even in a society that is growing more and more divided, under institutional political systems many of them believe to be corrupt or beyond their ability to affect.

Fan efforts to impact their beloved media help to shape the everyday politics of the world in which we live, particularly around questions of representation and marginalization. Fannish media production puts a vision of a more pluralistic, directly democratic society into actual practice, just as Occupiers did in their camps. The organizations fans create to help them do both of these things have life and longevity far beyond the original impetus for their creation. Fan activists come from different ideological points of view, and the struggles going on within fannish spaces indicate both the vitality of common interests in bringing diverse people together and how difficult it is to keep them that way.

The stories of fan activism do not always have happy endings. But the tactics and principles they have developed, such as drawing from shared media to create models for change, directly creating what they want to see rather than ceding that power to professional producers, building their own commonly owned infrastructure and leveraging existing technological and social systems to pursue their ends, are powerful tools.

References

Andrejevic, M. (2008) 'Watching Television without Pity: The Productivity of Online Fans', *Television & New Media*, vol. 9, no. 1, pp. 24–46.

Brienza, C. (2016) *Manga in America: Transnational Book Publishing and the Domestication of Japanese Comics*. London: Bloomsbury Academic.

Brough, M. M. and Shresthova, S. (2011) 'Fandom Meets Activism: Rethinking Civic and Political Participation', *Transformative Works and Cultures*, vol. 10, http://journal.transformativeworks.org/index.php/twc/article/view/303/265, accessed 11 March 2017.

Buckingham, D. (2000) *The Making of Citizens: Young People, News and Politics*. London: Routledge.

Busse, K. and Lothian, A. (2009) 'Bending Gender: Feminist and (Trans)Gender Discourses in the Changing Bodies of Slash Fanfiction', in I. Hotz-Davies, A. Kirchhofer and S. Leppänen (eds) *Internet Fiction(s)*. Cambridge: Cambridge Scholars, pp. 105–27.

Castells, M. (2015) *Networks of Outrage and Hope: Social Movements in the Internet Age* (second edition). Cambridge: Polity Press.

Close, S. (2014) 'Popular Culture through the Eyes, Ears, and Fingertips of Fans: Vidders, Anime Music Video Editors, and Their Sources', in D. Laderman & L. Westrup (eds) *Sampling Media*. Oxford: Oxford University Press, pp. 199-211.

Close, S. (2016) 'Fannish Masculinities in Transition in Anime Music Video Fandom', *Transformative Works and Cultures*, vol. 22, http://journal.transformativeworks.org/index.php/twc/article/view/713, accessed 11 March 2017.

Close, S. (2017) 'Moon Prism Power!: Censorship as adaptation in the case of Sailor Moon', *Participations: Journal of Audience & Reception Studies*, vol. 14, no. 1, pp. 264–281.

Coleman, S. (2013) *How Voters Feel*. Cambridge: Cambridge University Press.

Coppa, F. (2006) 'A Brief History of Media Fandom', in K. Hellekson and K. Busse (eds) *Fan Fiction and Fan Communities in the Age of the Internet: New Essays*. Jefferson, NC: McFarland & Co, pp. 41–59.

Coppa, F. (2008) 'Women, "Star Trek," and the Early Development of Fannish Vidding', *Transformative Works and Cultures*, vol. 1, http://journal.transformativeworks.org/index.php/twc/article/view/44, accessed 11 March 2017.

De Kosnik, A. (2009) 'Should Fan Fiction Be Free?', *Cinema Journal*, vol. 48, no. 4, pp. 118–124.

De Kosnik, A. (2013) 'Interrogating "Free" Fan Labor', *Spreadable Media*, http://spreadablemedia.org/essays/kosnik, accessed 11 March 2017.

De Kosnik, A. (2016) *Rogue Archives: Digital Cultural Memory and Media Fandom*. Cambridge, MA: MIT Press.

Duffett, M. (2013) *Understanding Fandom: An Introduction to the Study of Media Fan Culture*. New York: Bloomsbury.

Duncombe, S. (2007) *Dream: Re-imagining Progressive Politics in an Age of Fantasy*. New York: New Press.

Fanlore Editors (2016a) 'Archive of Our Own' [Wiki], http://fanlore.org/wiki/Archive_of_Our_Own, accessed 7 October 2016.

Fanlore Editors (2016b) 'Puppygate' [Wiki], http://fanlore.org/wiki/Puppygate, accessed 3 May 2017.

Fanlore Editors (2016c) 'RaceFail '09' [Wiki], http://fanlore.org/wiki/RaceFail_%2709#cite_note-44, accessed 1 February 2017.

Fanlore Editors (2017) 'Queer Baiting' [Wiki], http://fanlore.org/wiki/Queer_Baiting, accessed 1 February 2017.

Fiske, J. (2011) *Reading the Popular* (second edition). London: Routledge.

Flourish Klink, Minkel, E., Quinn, H., Pande, R., Shadowkeeper, Clio and Punla, P. (2016) Transcript: Episode 22A: Race and Fandom Part 1 [Podcast, 23 May], http://fansplaining.com/post/144813752418/transcript-episode-22a-race-and-fandom-part-1, accessed 1 February 2017

Gray, J., Sandvoss, C. and Harrington, C. L. (eds) (2007) *Fandom: Identities and Communities in a Mediated World*. New York: New York University Press.

Green, S., Jenkins, C. and Jenkins, H. (1998) '"Normal Female Interest in Men Bonking": Selections from the Terra Nostra Underground and Strange Bedfellows', in C. Harris and A. Alexander (eds) *Theorizing Fandom: Fans, Subcultures, and Identity*. Caskill, NJ: Hampton Press, pp. 9–38.

Guerrero-Pico, M. (2017) '#Fingre, Audiences and Fan Labor: Twitter Activism to Save a TV Show From Cancellation', *International Journal of Communication*, vol. 11, pp. 2071–2092.

Hellekson, K. (2009) 'A Fannish Field of Value: Online Fan Gift Culture', *Cinema Journal*, vol. 48, no. 4, pp. 113–18.

Hinck, A. (2011) 'Theorizing a Public Engagement Keystone: Seeing Fandom's Integral Connection to Civic Engagement through the Case of the Harry Potter Alliance', *Transformative Works and Cultures*, vol. 10, http://journal.transformativeworks.org/index.php/twc/article/view/311, accessed 11 March 2017.

Jemisin, N. (2010) 'Why I Think RaceFail Was the Bestest Thing Evar for SFF', *N. K. Jemsin*, 18 January, http://nkjemisin.com/2010/01/why-i-think-racefail-was-the-bestest-thing-evar-for-sff, accessed 1 February 2017.

Jenkins, H. (1992) *Textual Poachers: Television Fans & Participatory Culture*. New York: Routledge.

Jenkins, H. (2008) *Convergence Culture: Where Old and New Media Collide*. New York: New York University Press.

Jenkins, H. (2011) '"Cultural Acupuncture": Fan Activism and the Harry Potter Alliance', *Transformative Works and Cultures*, vol. 10, http://journal.transformativeworks.org/index.php/twc/article/view/305, accessed 11 March 2017.

Jenkins, H. (2014) 'Fandom Studies as I See It', *Journal of Fandom Studies*, vol. 2, no. 2, pp. 89–109.

Jenkins, H. and Campbell, J. (2006) '"Out of the Closet and into the Universe": Queers and Star Trek', in *Fans, Bloggers, and Gamers: Exploring Participatory Culture*. New York: New York University Press, pp. 89–114.

Jenkins, H. and Carpentier, N. (2013) 'Theorizing Participatory Intensities: A Conversation about Participation and Politics', *Convergence*, vol. 19, no. 3, pp. 265–86.

Jenkins, H., Shresthova, S., Gamber-Thompson, L., Kligler-Vilenchik, N. and Zimmerman, A. (2016). *By any Media Necessary: The New Youth Activism*. New York: New York University Press.

Leonard, S. (2005) 'Celebrating Two Decades of Unlawful Progress: Fan Distribution, Proselytization Commons, and the Explosive Growth of Japanese Animation', *Entertainment Law Review*, vol. 12, no. 2, pp. 189–265.

Levi, A., McHarry, M. and Pagliassotti, D. (eds) (2008) *Boys' Love Manga: Essays on the Sexual Ambiguity and Cross-Cultural Fandom of the Genre*. Jefferson, NC: McFarland & Co.

Lopez, L. K. (2012) 'Fan Activists and the Politics of Race in *The Last Airbender*', *International Journal of Cultural Studies*, vol. 15, no. 5, pp. 431–45.

Lothian, A. (2010) 'An Archive of One's Own: Subcultural Creativity and the Politics of Conservation', *Transformative Works and Cultures*, vol. 6, http://journal.transformativeworks.org/index.php/twc/article/view/267, accessed 11 March 2017.

Marks, R. (2015) 'The Night Science Fiction's Biggest Awards Burned', *The Escapist*, 2 September, http://www.escapistmagazine.com/articles/view/video-games/columns/garwulfs-corner/14559-The-Night-The-Hugos-Burned-The-Sad-and-Rabid-Puppies-Explained, accessed 29 April 2017.

Mizoguchi, A. (2003) 'Male-Male Romance by and for Women in Japan: A History and the Subgenres of "Yaoi" Fictions', *U.S.-Japan Women's Journal*, vol. 25, pp. 49–75.

OTW Admin. (2012) 'OTW Secures DMCA Exemption from U.S. Copyright Office', *Organization for Transformative Works*, 27 October, http://www.transformativeworks.org/otw-secures-dmca-exemption-us-copyright-office, accessed 11 March 2017.

Penley, C. (1992) 'Feminism, Psychoanalysis, and the Study of Popular Culture' in L. Grossberg, C. Nelson and P. A. Treichler (eds) *Cultural Studies*. New York: Routledge, pp. 479–500.

Piccoli, D. (2015) 'SwanQueen Is the Winner of the 2015 AfterEllen Ultimate Femslash Tournament', *After Ellen*, 24 November, http://www.afterellen.com/tv/463621-swanqueen-winner-2015-afterellen-ultimate-femslash-tournament, accessed 11 March 2017.

porluciernagas. (2014) 'Sexualized Saturdays: Femslash and Fandom', *Lady Geek Girl and Friends*, 18 January, https://ladygeekgirl.wordpress.com/2014/01/18/sexualized-saturdays-femslash-and-fandom, accessed 11 March 2017.

Punathambekar, A. (2011) 'On the Ordinariness of Participatory Culture', *Transformative Works and Cultures*, vol. 10, http://journal.transformativeworks.org/index.php/twc/article/view/378/267, accessed 11 March 2017.

Putnam, R. D. (2001) *Bowling Alone: The Collapse and Revival of American Community*. New York: Simon & Schuster.

Romano, A. (2014) 'How to Kill your Slash Fandom in 5 Steps', *The Daily Dot*, 21 July, http://www.daily-dot.com/parsec/how-to-kill-your-fandom-sterek-queerbaiting, accessed 31 January 2017.

Save Our Sailors (2003) 'The Official SOS FAQ v0.05.1.1', 12 December, https://web.archive.org/web/20031212180739/http://pei.physics.sunysb.edu/~ming/dau/sos/sosfaq, accessed 1 May 2016.

Skocpol, T. and Williamson, V. (2012) *The Tea Party and the Remaking of Republican Conservatism*. New York: Oxford University Press.

Slack, A. (2010) 'Cultural Acupuncture and a Future for Social Change', *Huffington Post,* 2 July, http://www.huffingtonpost.com/andrew-slack/cultural-acupuncture-and_b_633824.html, accessed 11 March 2017.

Standlee, K. (2015) '2015 Hugo Award Winners Announced', *The Hugo Awards,* 23 August, http://www.thehugoawards.org/2015/08/2014-hugo-award-winners-announced, accessed 11 March 2017.

Stanfill, M. and Condis, M. (2014) 'Fandom and/as Labor', *Transformative Works and Cultures*, vol. 15, http://journal.transformativeworks.org/index.php/twc/article/view/593/421, accessed 11 March 2017.

Suzuki, K. (1998) 'Pornography or Therapy? Japanese Girls Creating the Yaoi Phenomenon', in S. A. Inness (ed.) *Millennium Girls: Today's Girls around the World*. Lanham, MD: Rowman & Littlefield, pp. 243–67.

Swartz, L. and Driscoll, K. (2014) '"I Hate Your Politics but I Love Your Diamonds": Citizenship and the Off-Topic Message Board Subforum', in M. Ratto and M. Boler (eds) *DIY citizenship: critical making and social media*. Cambridge, MA: MIT Press, pp. 295–307.

Turk, T. (2013) 'Fan Work: Labor, Worth, and Participation in Fandom's Gift Economy', *Transformative Works and Cultures*, vol. 15, http://journal.transformativeworks.org/index.php/twc/article/view/518, accessed 11 March 2017.

Vanderhoof, B. (2015) 'Swan Queen Shippers and the Need for Lesbian Representation on TV', *In Media Res,* 24 June, http://mediacommons.futureofthebook.org/imr/2015/06/24/swan-queen-shippers-and-need-lesbian-representation-tv, accessed 1 February 2017.

VanDerWerff, T. (2015) 'How Conservatives Took Over Sci-Fi's Most Prestigious Award', *Vox*, 26 April, http://www.vox.com/2015/4/26/8495415/hugos-sad-puppies-controversy, accessed 1 February 2017.

Wanzo, R. (2015) 'African American Acafandom and Other Strangers: New Genealogies of Fan Studies', *Transformative Works and Cultures*, vol. 20, http://journal.transformativeworks.org/index.php/twc/article/view/699, accessed 11 March 2017.

Zubernis, L. and Larsen, K. (2012) *Fandom at the Crossroads: Celebration, Shame and Fan/Producer Relationships*. Newcastle upon Tyne, UK: Cambridge Scholars.

36

ACTING OUT

Resisting copyright monopolies

Steve Collins

Introduction

How should citizens respond when copyright laws appear out of touch with how media are used, and only exist to shore up business models that seem absurd in a digital networked environment? What kind of actions can citizens take when copyright overreaches and impinges on creativity and free expression? This chapter explores methods for resisting exclusionary monopolies that form from copyrights. The first two examples look at fair use and Creative Commons, both of which use the law to resist an 'all rights reserved' approach to copyright. The third example looks at how purposeful infringement such as file-sharing can act as a form of civil disobedience against copyright monopolies.

Copyright law grants authors a bundle of exclusive rights (that may be individually or collectively assigned to other parties such as a record company or book publisher) concerning copying, publication, distribution, performance and the creation of derivatives for a limited amount of time. Copyright is a temporary monopoly intended 'to provide an incentive to create works that would inform and advance society' (Young 2015: 47). Seventy years after its author's death, the copyrighted work loses its protection and falls into the public domain, from where it can plucked and freely used by anyone. The law protects a vast range of creative works, including books, films and television shows, music and games, and as such, copyright occupies a 'special place in ordering a nation's culture' (Goldstein 1994: 35).

Background to copyright

Copyright finds its origins in eighteenth-century England, where an enlightened Parliament sought to break the monopoly over literature that had become concentrated in the Stationers' Company, a Crown-chartered cabal of London-based publishers. Up until the early 1700s, publishers purchased manuscripts from authors, taking them as their own property in perpetuity. The Statute of Anne (1710), the world's first copyright law, challenged established trade practices by granting authors exclusive rights for a limited duration.

The first copyrights under the Statute of Anne expired in 1731, leaving commercially important works by Shakespeare, Milton, Bunyan, Locke and Burnet in the public domain bereft of protection. Fearing financial ruin as cheap reprints made their way into the country from

Scotland and Holland, the Stationers petitioned Parliament for further protection, but legislative attempts to curb imports proved ineffectual (Feather 1988: 378). Supplying books to the north of England proved challenging for the London-based Stationers and the territory had all but been ceded to the Scottish publishing trade.

The next three decades saw much legal action concerning literary property. Publishers of cheap reprints claimed they were drawing from the public domain, a repository of books no longer protected by copyright under the Statute of Anne. The Stationers, however, argued that statutory copyright was merely supplementary to their common law property rights in perpetuity. This conflict climaxed when the House of Lords heard the case of Donaldson v. Becket (1774). A Scottish publisher who specialized in inexpensive reprints of public domain works, Alexander Donaldson was a provocateur and possibly the first copyright activist. He opened a store in London, the heartland of the Stationers' Company, and sold reprints undercutting his reluctant neighbours by 30–50 per cent (Rose 1993: 93). Successfully defending himself against a flurry of lawsuits, Donaldson accused the Stationers of using their market dominance to terrorize provincial publishers (Feather 1994: 87) and used the legal system to push back against their assertions of exclusivity and monopoly. Favouring Donaldson, the House of Lords ruled that copyright was entirely contingent on statute and dismissed the Stationers' claims for a natural right in literary property. The prospect of literary property lasting forever was untenable, placing too much cultural determinism in the hands of publishers, 'who will set what price upon it their avarice chooses to demand, till the public becomes as much their slaves, as their own hackney compilers are' (17 Cobbett, Parliamentary History, col. 1000).

The problem with copyright

While the Stationers lost that particular battle, they ultimately won the war for future rights holders. Contingency on statute means that broader rights can be secured by changing the law, and that is exactly what happened. Multiple iterations of copyright laws expanded rights to govern a range of uses. Contemporary copyright law – especially in the US – has been heavily critiqued as its emphasis on exclusion has become a way of financially exploiting intellectual properties with the concomitant effects of stifling creativity and free expression (Lessig 2001, 2004; Vaidhyanathan 2003; McLeod 2005a). Copyright owners have enjoyed successive boons: multiple extensions to the copyright duration (Ou 2000: 31), new legislation such as the US's Digital Millennium Copyright Act 1998 and a supporting policy that reinforces a property-oriented view of copyright (Easterbrook 1990: 112, 118; Netanel 1996: 306–35; Collins 2006).

For its critics, copyright allows the formation of untenable monopolies that restrict access to, use of and participation in culture. As Patry (2008) laments:

> We are well past the healthy dose stage and into the serious illness stage … things are getting worse, not better. Copyright law has abandoned its reason for being: to encourage learning and the creation of new works. Instead, its principal functions now are to preserve existing failed business models, to suppress new business models and technologies, and to obtain, if possible, enormous windfall profits from activity that not only causes no harm, but which is beneficial to copyright owners.

Contemporary copyright extends beyond merely providing an initial incentive to create and actually 'serves as a vehicle for directing investment in existing works' (Netanel 1996: 286). Intellectual properties are commodified and any use(s) must be licensed in order to exploit the financial potential of the work. This characterizes a 'permission culture' in which previously unregulated zones of activity are no longer disregarded by the law (Lessig 2004: 8). There is less and less an acknowledgement that *use of the work* and *use of the copyright* are two different things (Patterson & Lindberg 1991: 6).

Fair use

Copyright confers a bundle of exclusive rights, but the extent of those rights is qualified. As previously noted, the protection term is limited (albeit to the rather lengthy author's life plus 70 years), but the exclusivity is also held in check by the doctrine of fair use. In the North American copyright system, fair use acts as a safety valve on monopolies that form out of copyrights and ensures that works can still be freely used for a range of transformative purposes such as review, criticism, parody and news reporting. It is a necessary component to ensure that copyright does not 'stifle the very creativity which that law is designed to foster' (Campbell v. Acuff-Rose Music, Inc. 1994: 577). The contours around fair use are necessarily fuzzy – it is difficult to draw bright lines around 'how much is too much?' when it comes to copying. Whilst this allows fair use to be flexible and adapt to new scenarios, it can lead to unpredictability and unreliability. Heins and Beckles (2005: 15–22) document a series of anecdotes from discussion groups comprised of members from PEN American Center, Women Make Movies, the College Art Association and Location One Gallery. They note that the participants often found it difficult to find accurate information on fair use and a clear lack of consistency across their experiences. One author stated:

> I find the whole copyright thing enormously arbitrary. Some people charge you $350 for five lines. Some charge you nothing for several pages. There are no rules, so you're always in a rather stupid, mendicant position as a permission seeker.
>
> *Heins & Beckles 2005: 17*

Relying on a fair use defence can be a huge risk, not just financially, but to the integrity of a work if copyrighted portions need to be removed. Inequality in bargaining power between authors and rights holders is often enough to prevent a claim of fair use. As Lessig states:

> [t]he fuzzy lines of the law, tied to the extraordinary liability if lines are crossed, means that the effective fair use for many types of creators is slight. The law has the right aim; practice has defeated the aim.
>
> *Lessig 2004: 99*

While fair use has become marginalized in the face of aggressive assertions of copyright, it remains a powerful means of resistance against encroaching private rights.

Fair use is frequently considered an affirmative defence, i.e. where copyright infringement occurs but liability is mitigated by being an acceptable or *fair* use. Recently, however, the Court of Appeals for the Ninth Circuit was explicitly clear that fair use is a *right* (Lenz v. Universal Music, 2015: 13–14). Constructing fair use as a right represents an important and positive shift in preserving free expression from the subjugation of a 'permission culture'. For example, in February 2007 Stephanie Lenz uploaded to YouTube a 29-second video of her toddler dancing (www.youtube.com/watch?v=N1KfJHFWlhQ). The audio quality is poor but captures 20 seconds of Prince's 'Let's Go Crazy' playing on the radio in Lenz's Philadelphian kitchen. By June, the video had been viewed just 28 times before YouTube removed it in compliance with a Digital Millennium Copyright Act 1998 (DMCA) take-down notice from copyright owner,

Universal Music. That same month, Lenz responded with a successful counter-notification claiming fair use and YouTube reinstated the video six weeks later. Not content to leave the matter there, Lenz (aided by the Electronic Frontiers Foundation) pursued an action for misrepresentation against Universal Music and also sought a declaratory judgment that her use of 'Let's Go Crazy' was fair.

Under section 512(c)(3)(a)(v) of the DMCA, copyright owners need to have 'a good faith belief that use of the material in the manner complained of is not authorized by the copyright owner, its agent, or the law'. Lenz v. Universal Music (2015) hinged on the technical point of whether Lenz was duly authorized by the law to make a copy of Universal's intellectual property. Universal argued that fair use is not 'authorized by … the law' because as an affirmative defence it excuses otherwise infringing actions. The court disagreed, clearly articulating that fair use is a right and as such amounted to authorization.

Stephanie Lenz's case against Universal Music is just one among similar stories collected by the EFF for a series of studies conducted by the US Copyright Office. (The stories are viewable as part of the EFF's 'Takedown Hall of Shame' at www.eff.org/takedowns.) The flexing of fair use rights provides a vital resistance to monopolies and abuses of copyright law. A healthy public dimension of copyright requires that 'Copyright holders should be held accountable when they undermine non-infringing fair uses' (EFF 2016). Historically, personal uses of copyrighted materials fell outside the scope of the law. Copyright was designed to protect rights holders against competing with unauthorized copies of their own works in the market, but as Netanel notes, 'with the advent of online dissemination of authors' works, the distinction between mass market infringement and personal use appears to be breaking down' (1996: 371). This is especially so when copyright enforcement is handed over to technological systems like YouTube's 'Content ID' (Collins 2014: 97–103) or SoundCloud's audio-fingerprinting. According to EFF Attorney Marcia Hoffman, the result is the privileging of copyrights over free expression: 'Copyright abuse can shut down online artists, political analysts or -- as in this case -- ordinary families who simply want to share snippets of their day-to-day lives' (EFF 2016). Despite the fact that it took nearly nine years of litigation to resolve a case involving less than 30 seconds of poor-quality but copyrighted music, the EFF and Stephanie Lenz clearly believe that there are principles worth protecting. As of July 2016, the video has in excess of 1.8 million views and many comments expressing solidarity and support. YouTube user redlol123 says, 'thank you for helping creators and artists around the internet by fighting Universal's bullshit. You're a god damn hero.' Another user, Ken Chen, echoes the sentiment: 'I think many people on this website owe you a "thank you".'

Fair use can certainly be a powerful tool in protecting free expression against copyright monopolies, but as noted, its application is far from perfect. Copyright is a complex area of law and while the last two decades have seen it cross into public awareness, many – perhaps naturally – still stumble over questions of how and when it is permissible to re-use something. When even the courts can arrive at different conclusions in similar cases, it is no small wonder that non-legal professionals experience difficulty in understanding the boundaries of acceptable copying (Collins 2014: 96). It does not help the situation that digital technologies make it increasingly easy to copy and share, just as the law increasingly regulates against such behaviour (Lessig 2004: 13). Disenchantment with these characteristics of copyright led to the creation of a new licensing platform for creative works, Creative Commons.

Creative Commons

In the wake of an unsuccessful challenge to the Copyright Term Extension Act 1998, Lawrence Lessig, Hal Abelson and Eric Eldred felt that copyright had reached a point where it was no longer promoting free expression; rather, it was achieving the opposite. The Copyright Term Extension Act (also known as the Sonny Bono Copyright Term Extension Act and the Mickey Mouse Act) was responsible for extending the duration of copyright in the United States by another 20 years. As its other names suggest, the Act was intimately connected to Sonny Bono, an advocate of extending the protection term (to forever) who died nine months prior. More drastically, the Act prevented a number of copyrighted works from entering the public domain, the most notable being Disney's Mickey Mouse. Eric Eldred and a number of small publishers had prepared a number of works for publication in expectation of those works losing copyright protection and entering the public domain. Eldred (represented by Lessig) challenged the extension on constitutional grounds, arguing that Congress is only authorized to protect intellectual property rights for 'limited times' (US Constitution. Art./Amend. I, Sec. 8.). If Congress could just keep extending copyright terms, then it was implementing, as Jaszi (1999) put it, a 'perpetual copyright on the installment plan'. The Supreme Court rejected Eldred's arguments, finding that as long as extended copyright terms are finite, then Congress is acting within the bounds of the Constitution. In practical terms, works could continuously remain under protection freezing growth of the public domain. The response was to establish the Creative Commons licensing platform in 2001 with the view to making 'access and the exchange of ideas easier through reducing costs and resisting regulation' (Barker 2012: 370). Although established in symbiosis with the US copyright system, Creative Commons has been ported to 56 jurisdictions, with another 20 slated as planned or currently in development.

According to Elkin-Koren (2006: 327), 'Creative Commons perceives the current copyright regime as the major obstacle for creative activity' and so aims to promote creativity and free expression by giving authors a language through which they can explicitly indicate how their works can be used rather than defaulting to 'all rights reserved'. All works carry the compulsory attribution licence accompanied by a set of mix-and-match options for adaptation, sharing or commercial use. The suite of human-readable freedoms and restrictions is far more legible, certain and cheaper than licensing arrangements that are often prohibitively costly and difficult to negotiate (Lessig 2004: 81–83; Collins 2005; Bloemsaat & Kleve 2009: 237–8). Creative Commons licences layer on top of copyright rather than providing an alternative; they co-opt the law to promote a vibrant public domain economy modelled on 'free culture' – low transactional costs in time, expertise and deployment. As Elkin-Koren states, 'The normative framework assumes that it is possible to replace existing practices of producing and distributing informational works by relying on the existing proprietary regime' (2006: 325).

Popular criticisms of Creative Commons focus on its enforceability and opt-in nature. Although licences are intended to unequivocally clarify freedoms and restrictions, disputes do arise and must be resolved by regular copyright law (Bloemsaat & Kleve 2009: 244). Access to the courts, however, may be compromised by the costs involved, leaving an author unable to enforce their rights. Creative Commons is a movement based on ideals about content and culture that is reacting to a greater copyright hegemony. As an opt-in scheme, it is only ever as good as the works that use it. Prominent examples include Wikimedia, Flickr, two Nine Inch Nails albums, Cards Against Humanity, Open Courseware and a number of books (mostly on topics related to 'free culture'). Whilst over a billion works use Creative Commons licences, the majority of people might be pushed to name one. This criticism aside, Creative Commons makes important statements about content, ownership and control by focusing on creativity and sharing that is not intrinsically focused on commercial exploitation. It allows authors to signal a rejection of the 'all rights reserved' model for distributing creative works. Elkin-Koren asserts that 'Creative Commons is a form of political activism and is best understood as a social movement seeking to bring about a social change' (2006: 332). She identifies libertarian sentiments that promise authors choice over how their works are used – '*What if we can take the law into our own hands? What if we can make our own rules?*' (2006: 333). It is a reminder that 'the world is not is, but is made' (Gitlin, as cited in Cammaerts 2007: 217). Creative Commons seeks social change by acting as 'a countervailing discourse to the growing propertization of knowledge' in an effort to puncture and replace ideas of scarcity with those of abundance (Haunss 2013: 213). The aim of a vibrant and accessible sphere of creative works at the heart of Creative Commons echoes the House of Lords' *raison d'être* for copyright: 'Why did we enter into society at all, but to enlighten one another's minds, and improve our faculties, for the common welfare of the species' (17 Cobbett, Parliamentary History, col. 999).

Creative Commons licensing and assertions of fair use rights are cooperative forms of resistance that use the existing law to defend free creativity and use against increasingly stringent copyrights. For others, however, the blunt tool of out-and-out purposeful infringement is used to protest monopolies that control access to cultural works.

Torrenting as civil disobedience

Entertainment media are sites for frequent battles concerning copyright. *Grey Album* (DJ Dangermouse's unauthorized mashup of The Beatles' *White Album* with Jay-Z's *Black Album*) pitted the freedom to create against EMI's rights to exclude unlicensed use of The Beatles' material. An online protest – 'Grey Tuesday' – was organized to support the album's distribution and at least 170 websites offered *Grey Album* for download in defiance of cease and desist orders and at risk of legal action from EMI, copyright owners of *White Album* (McLeod 2005b: 80). In addition to being an act of civil disobedience, 'Grey Tuesday' also highlighted the challenges for copyright enforcement where online digital media are concerned (Rimmer 2007: 133–4). As Jessica Litman (2001: 195) argues, large numbers of people will fail to comply with laws that they do not believe in: 'the less the law's choices strike the people it affects as legitimate, the less they will feel as if breaking that law is doing anything wrong.' There is no doubt that file-sharing has impacted on the entertainment industries and that many individuals are simply motivated in getting something for nothing, but for some it is an act of protest against business models that seem increasingly absurd in a digitally networked world (Lunny 2001). In this context, downloading is an act of 'civil disobedience designed to protest the excessive scope of copyright protections and attendant limits on distribution and price gouging' (Easley 2005: 166). Australia's relationship with television provides a prime example, but parallels also exist with other media, for example academic texts (see Young 2008; Rosenwald 2016).

In 2007, Alex Malik, a Sydney-based lawyer, conducted a survey of television shows broadcast in Australia. He observed that on average it took 17 months for a program first broadcast in the US or UK to make its way to Australian free-to-air viewers (Malik 2007). Further, he complained of reading about television shows online, but not to being able to actually access and watch them:

> what do you mean I can't watch Survivor Fiji on free-to-air on Australia. Oh I don't live in America. But I can read about it. I can view the photos. I can read the weblog. I can probably buy the T-shirts and coffee mug too. But I can't watch it. Even on the internet … where it is being promoted.
>
> *Malik 2007*

The following year, Leaver (2008) wrote about how Australian fans of *Battlestar Galactica* were geo-blocked from accessing online inter-season webisodes and forced to resort to torrenting. Even after the introduction of legitimate streaming platforms such as Netflix,

Stan and Presto, access and availability remain issues; in 2015 'just *four* TV shows – out of 47 that were surveyed– were available in Australia on TV *and* online within a day of their international premiere' (Spencer 2015). Pricing is also a major problem. During the annual run of *Game of Thrones*, tens of thousands of Australian fans torrent, download and stream episodes in response to Foxtel's exclusive distribution monopoly of the show. The cheapest package that includes *Game of Thrones* costs $30 per month for 480p low-resolution viewing on Play, Foxtel's streaming service.

Many Australians feel that the costs involved in legitimately accessing *Game of Thrones* are unfair and there are no other real-time, legal alternatives. In light of his own experiences with Foxtel Play, Mark Serrels, editor of gaming website *Kotaku*, wrote 'I Refuse to Feel Guilty for Torrenting Game of Thrones', arguing that 'it's actually insane to expect consumers to subscribe a $30 a month service just to watch one single show. It's bordering on anti-consumer to tell Australians that this is their only avenue to watch that show' (Serrels 2016). Not alone in publicly voicing his objections, a post on HBO's Facebook wall colourfully explains that:

> using Foxtel is like hitting up an all you can eat banquet at a cheap Indian restaurant. It costs you $30 to get in when all you really wanted was the butter chicken … Their services are well below industry standards and incredibly overpriced.
>
> *Hyslop 2016*

So, along with tens of thousands of other fans unwilling to subscribe to Foxtel, Serrels turns to alternative means. As Lunny (2001: 870) argues, this form of civil disobedience 'may offer the only effective means for ordinary consumers to express their political discontent with copyright's excessive scope'. While any demonstrative impact on HBO's choice of Australian licencing partners is yet to manifest, purposeful copyright infringement as an expression of discontent undermines the exclusive distribution rights tendered to Foxtel as file-sharing communities circumvent 'a whole industry designed to profit from the distribution of creative work' (Kurtz 2007: 515).

Conclusion

Copyright is an arbiter of culture, deciding who can access and use works, and to what extent. It is small wonder that it is a site for struggles over cultural determinism. In the eyes of its critics, contemporary copyright is more focused on securing private rights than promoting a free culture. Monopolies form off the back of copyrights when the balance is lost between these private and public interests (Aufderheide & Jaszi 2011: 16–17). This is risky because decisions about copyright involve 'not pure economic regulation, but regulation of expression, and what may count as rational where economic regulation is at issue is not necessarily rational where we focus on expression' (Eldred v. Ashcroft, 2003: 3). The protection offered by copyright is supposed to stimulate creativity, and while it is certainly important to foster and protect investment in creativity, 'sufficient incentive' is less than 'perfect control' (Lessig 1999: 133). In 1774, Lord Camden warned that 'If the [copyright] monopoly is sanctified … exorbitant price will be the consequence' (17 Cobbett, Parliamentary History, col. 1000). That price is not simply financial; creativity and free expression suffer. The broad cultural effects are well documented (Lessig 2001, 2004; Vaidhyanathan 2003; McLeod 2005a; Patry 2008). There are limited ways in which copyright policy can be challenged; lobbying for change is outside the logistical scope for the majority of private individuals and remains the privilege of those rights holders with the most at stake. This chapter demonstrates that the legitimacy of copyright is important and that methods exist for resisting overreaching monopolies. Creative Commons licencing and assertions of fair use ensure that limits, however fuzzy, are set for copyright. Further, file-sharing as an aggressive form of resisting copyright monopolies highlights that people simply will not obey a law that they consider unfair.

References

Aufderheide, P and Jaszi, P. (2011) *Reclaiming Fair Use: How to Put Balance Back in Copyright*. Chicago, IL: University of Chicago Press.

Barker, C. (2014) *Cultural Studies Theory and Practice* (fourth edition). London: Sage.

Bloemsaat, B. and Kleve, P. (2009) 'Creative Commons: A Business Model for Products Nobody Wants to Buy', *International Review of Law, Computers and Technology*, vol. 23, no. 3, pp. 237–49.

Cammaerts, B. (2007) 'Activism and Media', in N. Carpentier and B. Cammaerts (eds) *Reclaiming the Media: Communication Rights and Democratic Media Roles*. Bristol, UK: Intellect, pp. 217–24.

Campbell v. Acuff-Rose Music, Inc., 510 U.S. 569 (1994).

Collins, S. (2005) 'Good Copy, Bad Copy: Covers, Sampling and Copyright', *M/C Journal*, vol. 8, no. 3.

Collins, S. (2006) '"Property Talk" and the Revival of Blackstonian Copyright', *M/C Journal* vol. 9, no. 4.

Collins, S. (2014) 'YouTube and Limitations of Fair Use in Remix Videos', *Journal of Media Practice*, vol. 15, no. 2, pp. 92–106.

Easley, R. (2005) 'Ethical Issues in the Music Industry Response to Innovation and Piracy', *Journal of Business Ethics*, no. 62, pp. 163–8.

Easterbrook, F. H. (1990) 'Intellectual Property Is Still Property', *Harvard Journal of Law & Public Policy*, no. 13, pp. 108–18.

EFF (2016) 'Lenz v. Universal', *Electronic Frontier Foundation*, no date, https://www.eff.org/cases/lenz-v-universal, accessed 16 January 2017.

Eldred v. Ashcroft [2003] 537 US 186; Justice Breyer dissenting.

Elkin-Koren, N. (2006) 'Exploring Creative Commons: A Sceptical View of a Worthy Pursuit', in L. Guibault and P. B. Hugenholtz (eds.) *The Future of the Public Domain: Identifying the Commons in Information Law*. Maryland, MD: Kluwer Law International, pp. 325–44.

Farrand, B. (2014) *Networks of Power in Digital Copyright and Policy*. New York: Routledge.

Feather, J. (1988) 'Authors, Publishers and Politicians: The History of Copyright and the Book Trade', *European Intellectual Property Review*, vol. 10, no. 12, pp. 377–80.

Feather, J. (1994) *Publishing, Piracy and Politics: An Historical Study of Copyright in Britain*. London: Mansell.

Fogerty v. Fantasy Inc. 510 US 517 (1994).

Gitlin. T. (2003) *Letters to a Young Activist*. New York: Basic Books.

Goldstein, P. (1994) *Copyright's Highway: The Law and Lore of Copyrights from Gutenberg to the Celestial Jukebox*. New York: Hill and Wang.

Haunss, S. (2013) *Conflicts in the Knowledge Society: The Contentious Politics of Intellectual Property*. Cambridge; New York: Cambridge University Press.

Heins, M, and Beckles, T. (2005) *Will Fair Use Survive?: Free Expression in the Age of Copyright Control: A Public Policy Report*. New York: Brennan Center for Justice at NYU School of Law.

Hyslop, J. (2016). Post on HBO's Facebook page. *Facebook*, 11 May, https://www.facebook.com/HBO/posts/10153695248045208, accessed 21 August 2016.

Jaszi, P. (1999) H.R. 354, 106th Cong., 1st Sess.

Kurtz, A. (2007) 'Electronic Democracy', in G. Anderson and K. Herr (eds.) *Encyclopedia of Activism and Social Justice* Volume 1. London: Sage, pp. 513–15.

Leaver, T. (2008) 'Watching Battlestar Galactica in Australia and the Tyranny of Digital Distance', *Media International Australia*, no. 126, pp. 145–54.

Lenz v. Universal Music Corp., 801 F.3d 1126 (2015).

Lessig, L. (1999) *Code and Other Laws of Cyberspace*. New York: Basic Books.

Lessig, L. (2001) *The Future of Ideas*. New York: Random House.

Lessig, L. (2002) 'Free Culture' Keynote at OSCON 2002, *O'Reilly*, http://archive.oreilly.com/pub/a/policy/2002/08/15/lessig.html, accessed 23 July 2016.

Lessig, L. (2004) *Free Culture*. New York: The Penguin Press.

Litman, J. (2001) *Digital Copyright*. New York: Prometheus Books.

Litman, J. (2003) 'Ethical Disobedience', *Ethics and Information Technology*, vol. 5, no. 4, pp. 217–33.

Lunny, G. (2001) 'The Death of Copyright: Digital Technology, Private Copying, and the Digital Millennium Copyright Act', *Virginia Law Review*, vol. 87, no. 5, pp. 813–920.

McLeod, K. (2005a) *Freedom of Expression: Overzealous Copyright Bozos and Other Enemies of Creativity*. New York: Doubleday.

McLeod, K. (2005b) 'Confessions of an Intellectual (Property): Danger Mouse, Mickey Mouse, Sonny Bono, and My Long and Winding Path as a Copyright Activist-Academic', *Popular Music and Society*, vol. 28, no. 1, pp. 79–93.

Malik, A. (2007) 'TV Show Delays … An Engine for Piracy?', *Malik's Law*, 21 February, https://web.archive.org/web/20070717101343/http://alexmalik.blogspot.com/2007/02/tv-show-delays-engine-for-piracy.html, accessed 16 August 2016.

Netanel, N. (1996), 'Copyright in a Democratic Civil Society', *Yale Law Journal*, no. 106, pp. 283–388.

Ou, T. (2000) 'From Wheaton v. Peters to Eldred v. Reno: An Originalist Interpretation of the Copyright Clause', *Berkman Center for Internet & Society*, http://cyber.law.harvard.edu/eldredvreno/OuEldred.pdf, accessed 21 April 2016.

Patry, W. (2008) 'End of the Blog', *The Patry Copyright Blog*, 1 August, http://williampatry.blogspot.com/2008/08/end-of-blog.html, accessed 23 May 2016.

Patterson, L. R. and Lindberg, S. (1991) *The Nature of Copyright: A Law of Users' Rights*. Athens, GA: University of Georgia Press.

Rimmer, M. (2007) *Digital Copyright and the Consumer Revolution: Hands off My iPod*. Cheltenham, UK; Northampton, USA: Edward Elgar Publishing.

Rose, M. (1993) *Authors and Owners: The Invention of Copyright*. Cambridge, MA; London: Harvard University Press.

Rosenwald, M. S. (2016) 'Meet the Woman Who Put 50 Million Stolen Articles Online So You Can Read Them for Free', 2 April, http://www.independent.co.uk/news/world/americas/meet-the-woman-who-put-50-million-stolen-articles-online-so-you-can-read-them-for-free-a6964176.html, accessed 29 April 2016.

Serrels, M. (2016) 'I Refuse to Feel Guilty for Torrenting Game Of Thrones', *Kotaku*, 27 April, http://www.kotaku.com.au/2016/04/i-refuse-to-feel-guilty-for-downloading-game-of-thrones/, accessed 28 April 2016.

Spencer, G. (2015) 'The Great Australian TV Delay: 2015 Edition', *Reckoner*, 24 July, http://reckoner.com.au/2015/07/the-great-australian-tv-delay-2015-edition/, accessed 3 August 2016.

Vaidhyanathan, S. (2003) *Copyrights and Copywrongs: The Rise of Intellectual Property and How It Threatens Creativity*. New York and London: New York University Press.

Young, S. (2015) 'A Hack for the Encouragement of Learning', in P. McGuinness (ed.) *Copyfight*. Sydney: University of New South Wales Press, pp. 35–48.

Young, T. (2008) 'Founder of Textbook-Download Site Says Offering Free Copyrighted Textbooks Is Act of "Civil Disobedience"', *The Chronicle of Higher Education*, 2 July, http://www.chronicle.com/blogs/wiredcampus/founder-of-textbook-download-site-says-offering-free-copyrighted-textbooks-is-act-of-civil-disobedience/4064, accessed 4 November 2016.

37

DISABILITY AND MEDIA ACTIVISM

Katie Ellis and Gerard Goggin

Introduction

With over a billion people in the world estimated to experience a significant disability, people with disabilities represent an increasingly activated, creative, forceful and diverse group of media activists. Because of their unique relationships with social life, technology and media, people with disabilities constitute an extremely interesting and significant new domain of activism, especially when it comes to emergent media forms, formats, cultures of use and politics. In this chapter, we provide an overview and introduction to disability and media activism.

First, we provide a brief introduction to understanding disability and associated categories, such as impairment, as socially shaped and culturally located phenomena that are as much subject to power relations as they are bodily and materially constituted. This has implications for how we understand activism in the first place – so it is important to appreciate that disability challenges conventional notions of activism, as indeed disability fundamentally unsettles our taken-for-granted ideas of what media and communications are.

Second, we discuss the emergence of media activism, especially in the mid-twentieth century, across a number of key countries. We trace the histories of disability activism as they involve and engage media, then in the following decades as they take shape as a world-wide, and ultimately globally referenced, if not coordinated, set of movements.

Third, we focus on the transformations in disability media activism, associated with waves of digitally enabled and inflected activism from the 1990s onwards, through email, web culture and blogging, but especially gathering momentum with the advent of mobile and social media. We consider the different affordances of various social media platforms, including Twitter, Facebook, video platforms and visual cultures.

Finally, we look at the debates among disability activism concerning the politics and implications of different kinds of media.

Disability challenges for activism

Activism has been enormously important to the emergence of disability as a rich, significant and accepted part of society and human life. This transformation in disability, while still uneven and contested, has been an unfinished accomplishment by a wide range of disability and allied movements globally.

With particular reference to the US and Britain, Denise Nepveux notes that disability activism 'arose in the late nineteenth and early twentieth centuries as some people with disabilities began to organize to resist restrictions on their freedoms and demand economic opportunities within industrial economies' (Nepveux 2015: 22), and form their own associations. In the intervening century of struggle, disability activists have fought for social, economic, political and cultural rights, across a wide range of terrains and settings. Drawing on the work of the US disability historian and scholar Paul Longmore (2003), Nepveux (2015: 21–2) draws attention to 'shared goals and stances' across diverse disability movements and struggles, including the 'framing of "disability" as a social and political, rather than simply a medical and rehabilitative, problem'.

Suffice to say that such common elements can scarcely contain the rich variety of disability activist efforts, including oft celebrated movements such as those of: disabled war veterans; the independent living movement in the US; the UK's Union of the Physically Impaired against Segregation (UPIAS); Deaf activist groups; feminist disability collectives and organizations; queer, crip, feminist movements (Kafer 2013); many different kinds of particular struggles focusing on how people are treated at the beginnings and ends of life (debates on abortion or euthanasia), as well as in health and social support systems throughout the life course; mental health, illness and madness; autism or neurodiversity; and so on. There is now an extensive literature on disability activism, protest and struggle (Shapiro 1993; Barnartt & Scotch 2001; Block *et al.* 2016) although there is much more to be added, especially across the many countries where visibility and resources have been lacking to document, debate and research activism (Ghosh 2016; Grech & Soldatic 2016). Activists and scholars have reflected upon the engagement of disability activists with a range of other social, political and cultural movements, including anti-apartheid struggles in South Africa and internationally (Watermeyer *et al.* 2006), African American and other civil rights movements in the US, HIV/AIDs activism, indigenous peoples' struggles, environmentalism, animal activism, disability arts, and museums.

Many movements of disability activism have involved drawing attention to neglected areas of mistreatment, injustice, equality and oppression, and challenging these, making public trouble of what has often been regarded as a private matter (Newell 2006; Prince 2009). Disability activism often involves 'micro-political' contexts of everyday life and other settings (Roets & Braidotti 2012). As disability has become an increasingly visible and legible force among other social, political and cultural movements, it has also challenged key assumptions of what activism is, looks like and does, and what public spheres and publics are (Garland-Thomson 2004; Clifford 2012), something that has caused consternation, division and debate within and across activism, disability activism included (Hughes 2009). Much of this activism has drawn upon, adapted, invented and relied upon media, yet these innovations, and their basis in collective, 'protest identities' (Gerbaudo & Treré 2015) have not received much acknowledgement in broader discussions of activism – let alone in research.

Histories of disability media activism

Like many other areas, disability media activism involves two potentially distinct areas, that often productively cross over – but are still worth distinguishing between (Couldry *et al.* 2018). First, there is disability activism that uses media as a key focus or tool for social change. Second, there is disability activism that focuses upon the media as a key site in social justice, rights, democracy and other struggles. In relation to both of these areas, dedicated histories of disability media activism are still to be written – but we will briefly indicate key examples and coordinates here.

First, it is striking, when viewed from the lens of media activism, how much disability activism, especially from the 1960s onwards, engages media. These efforts have focused on images, access and the struggle to be heard. An important stage of the development of disability media activism is represented by the various protests against the power of 'disabling' images of disability in the 1980s and 1990s (Gartner & Joe 1987; Barnes 1992). While such images were widespread across many societies, these were particularly pronounced in relation to the still powerful charity models of disability, used for fundraising campaigns. An important moment in such activism is represented in the work of British activist and photographer David Hevey in using photography to create alternative kinds of disability imagery to critique charitable stereotypes (Hevey *et al.* 1992). Activists and scholars also protested against the 'despicable' portrayal of people with disabilities in the regular Telethons, especially those hosted by the comedian Jerry Lewis (Charlton 1998: 35; Longmore 2016). Telethons, a uniquely televisual genre, offered activists an opportunity to highlight the problematic ways in which people with disabilities are denied a voice in their own experiences.

People with disabilities continue to protest media content, protests often picked up by the mainstream media. In the last 15 years, two films in particular have garnered the attention of disability activists for devaluing the lives of people with disabilities – the 2004 *Million Dollar Baby* (for instance, see Dolmage & DeGenaro 2005; Haller 2010; McRuer 2010) and, more recently, the 2016 *Me Before You*. Both films address the issue of euthanasia as a response to acquired disability and saw people with disabilities physically protesting cinema screenings, writing op-eds in the mainstream media, engaging in furious debate on blogs, and, in the case of *Me Before You*, coordinating global social media protests (Crippled Scholar 2016).

When we turn to the second area of disability activism, focused on media themselves as key sites of struggle, we find even further material to expand conceptions of activism. The starting point here is the longstanding exclusion of many people with disabilities from successive media systems. The advent of various systems for writing, followed by the printing press and the important print media (books, journals and magazines, newspapers) of successive centuries, extended media and their sensory systems, but also created new forms of exclusion for those for whom print was not accessible, not only those with vision impairments or blindness, but those with various forms of print disabilities (Ellis & Goggin 2015). Radio was a highly influential medium in the twentieth century, and has proven flexible and enduring (even in the digital age), as has television; but both have also been associated with exclusions for people with disabilities, as well as offering new forms of access for others.

People with disabilities access audio–visual and print media in several different ways depending on the effects of their impairments, contexts of access and use and affordances of technologies. A significant example is provided by the case of disability activism for television access and fair and inclusive design. Television remains a key medium and most recently has been deeply involved in the digital transformations of contemporary media. Yet it has long been inaccessible for many audiences and users with disabilities. For example, people who are D/deaf or hard of hearing may require captions and people who are blind or vision impaired use audio descriptions to fully enjoy television. It has taken significant activist organizing and activities to make closed captions and audio description progressively more available. Key figures in these activist efforts include official organizations for people with disabilities, ordinary people engaging in campaigns and increasingly, celebrities. Marlee Matlin, a Deaf American actor, has been particularly active in this area and provides an example of the changing approach to disability media activism in the changing media context.

In the late 1980s and early 1990s the National Association for the Deaf in the US campaigned aggressively for legislation that required captions on television culminating in the passing of the *Television Decoder Circuitry* Act, requiring that any television with a screen larger than 13 inches sold in the US be fitted with a decoder chip (Peltz Strauss 2006; Downey 2008). In Matlin's testimony at the hearing for the Act, she reflected on the ways a lack of access to television limited her sense of social inclusion and her imaginings about the life she would have (United States Government 1990). The requirements outlined in this legislation impacted the worldwide provision of captions as a number of countries implemented similar regulations (Ellis 2015). Matlin again reflected on her experience of social isolation when Netflix streamed an uncaptioned version of *The Wizard of Oz* (Fisher 2014). Taking to Twitter to share her frustration and call for change, Matlin was again instrumental in the implementation of both commercial commitments to include captions online and legislative requirements mandated via the *21st Century Communications and Video Accessibility Act* (CVAA) (Federal Communications Commission [FCC] 2010) (Ellis & Kent 2015).

Digital disability activism

From the 1990s onwards, disability media activism has been influenced by waves of digitally enabled and inflected activism such as email, web culture and blogging, but especially has been gathering momentum with the advent of mobile and social media. Thus, while in 2009 Matlin and members of the NAD wrote letters and emails to Netflix to call for the international video on demand provider to introduce captions on their platform (see Ellcessor 2012; Ellis 2015), she has more recently embraced an online disability media activist identity to participate in and support Twitter activist efforts and hashtags such as #CaptionTHIS (Ellcessor 2016).

Social media offer significant opportunities for people with disabilities to participate in public life and particularly activist activity (Haller 2010). Platforms such as Facebook and Twitter are suited to advocacy efforts due to their accessibility, connectedness and the fact people are already using them in their everyday lives (Ellis & Kent 2016). Social media activism facilitates a 'third space' of activism, felt by some to be 'non-political', whereby personal narratives can be shared in such a way that enables the participation of disenfranchised citizens who otherwise would not become involved in disability activism (Trevisan 2017).

One of the most potent examples of the ways people with disabilities participate in social media activism is the 2010–2012 welfare cuts in Britain (Ellis, Goggin & Kent 2016; Trevisan 2017). Filippo Trevisan's study of the diversity of online platforms and the technical know-how of the disabled citizens making use of them reveal three distinct groups of disability advocates using social media to resist these cuts. Each made use of social media platforms in different ways and for different purposes. First, the formal and more established organizations such as existing self-advocacy groups who made use of platforms for specific campaigns. The second group identified by Trevisan consisted of experienced disabled self-advocates with strong roots in the social model of disability or independent living activist efforts of the 1980s and 1990s. This group typically met at protest rallies and then set up a web presence afterwards. Finally, a new group of online-only activists of digitally connected millennials emerged to protest the welfare cuts. Trevisan describes this group as geographically dispersed 'digital action networks' who would never have met if not for these online spaces (Trevisan 2017: 83–4).

When it comes to disability activism, the interconnection of what Manuel Castells has termed the 'space of place' and 'space of flows' (involving digital networks, technologies and data) are richly significant (Castells 2010, 2012). Online activism offers an opportunity to participate for people unable to leave the house due to the effects of their impairments or the inaccessibility of public space (Burke & Crow 2016). Liz Crow's 2012–2013 art installation *Bedding Out* (Crow 2013) illustrates the ways social media activism offers a way to reclaim public spaces. The live durational performance performed across forty-eight hours saw Crow take to bed in a public space. Designed in response to the language used by politicians and the media during the 2010–2012 welfare cuts, *Bedding Out* revealed the contradictions Crow experienced as a disabled person in her public and private life. Crow used online activism in this durational performance to complement her reclamation of public spaces. People experiencing their own 'bed lives' and unable to come to the performances in the public space were able to have their experiences heard and amplified via social media (Burke & Crow 2016).

As we consider such important cases, it is also important to be aware that scholarship has noted a paradox when it comes to disability and social media activism. While it affords social inclusion by amplifying the voices of people with disabilities, it can likewise further disable if the platforms are not made accessible (Ellis & Goggin 2014). The inaccessibility of social media has itself prompted further activist activities. For example, only four months after the launch of Facebook, a petition was created using the platform's functionality calling on Facebook to improve its accessibility (Ellis & Kent 2011). Inaccessible design is also being overcome by tech savvy people with disabilities who share their workarounds of inaccessible platforms online (Hollier 2012; Trevisan 2017). However, focusing exclusively on these crucial issues of access via narrow, static conceptions of accessibility or via simplistic accounts of the so-called 'disability digital divide' (for critiques, see Ellis & Kent 2011; Foley & Ferri 2012; Jaeger 2012; Dobransky & Hargittai 2016) can have the consequence of neglecting the ways people are using digital media, often for activism (Trevisan 2017). For example, online communities offer a diversity-friendly activist space for neurodiverse people as the individual has much more control over the experience of interpersonal interaction (Boundy 2008). Sarah Parsloe's work explores the ways online spaces facilitate the communicative construction of autistic identity. Taking the online community Aspie Central as her case study, she finds that members engage with online disability discourses to reclaim, subvert and position themselves within discourses of normality and moral value. These online communities offer a site for coalition building amongst members to reclaim a common identity and cultural experience whereby autism can be reframed as a political identity (Parsloe 2015). Parsloe's subsequent work has considered the relationship between 'cyberactivism' and disability advocacy via an analysis of the #boycottautismspeaks hashtag (Parsloe & Holton 2017). Parsloe and Holton argue that the various actors involved in the #boycottautismspeaks movement managed to bring together logics of 'connective action' (Bennett 2013) with logics of collective action and social identities. Especially interesting is Parsloe and Holton's finding that such movements bridge and develop 'affective publics' (Parsloe & Holton 2017: 11), picking up Zizi Papacharissi's influential notion (Papacharissi 2014, 2016) apt for indicating this crucial element of contemporary disability media activism – and how it moves beyond traditional kinds of activism and publics.

While a critical approach to disability has historically straddled intellectual pursuit with activism (Longmore 2003), the discipline is increasingly paying attention to the importance of disability media activism with several recent publications addressing various aspects of disability media activism (Kuppers 2014; Ellis & Goggin 2015; Ellis & Kent 2016; Hampton 2016; Trevisan 2017). For example, Ellis and Kent's (2016) *Disability and Social Media: Global Perspectives* begins with a section on 'Advocacy', and includes various other papers addressing activist activities (e.g. Parent & Veilleux 2016). Many of these studies draw attention to several common features of disability online activism.

First, activists celebrate the usability of the social media platform, not least because usability as a subset of accessibility is important for online participation. Second, activists cross geographical boundaries to effect change both locally and globally. Finally, groups select their own leaders.

The importance of people with disabilities in leadership positions within disability activist groups is a longstanding theme (cf. UPIAS 1976) vital to progressing disability activism beyond the interests of traditional charities, who have been criticized by disabled people for perpetuating disempowering stereotypes and excluding people with disabilities from positions of leadership (Shakespeare 1993; Trevisan 2014). However, such optimist approaches to online activism have also been contested, with key debates among disability activism concerning the politics and implications of different kinds of emergent media – as we shall briefly explore.

Debates in media and disability activism

The new digitally inflected wave of disability media activism has fomented significant and often instructive debate. Central questions are: is Twitter-based disability activism just a 'bubble' that attenuates or misrepresents the collective activism of people with disabilities? Or do people with disabilities congregate in genuinely new and aggregative ways, as publics, communities, movements and activists, around hashtags, and other tools of social media struggle?

Two issues raised by Shakespeare (2013) relating to shared identity and leadership positions within activist movements are key to why social media activism has an important place within disability activism, and why also the complex dynamics of collective identities are crucial to placing digital disability activism. A shared identity is a crucial first step on the path to demanding political and social change (Shakespeare 1993). Shakespeare discusses the formation of identity and group consciousness as 'about the subversion of stigma: taking a negative appellation and converting it into a badge of pride' (Shakespeare 1993: 253). He discusses the parallels between activists reclaiming the word 'queer' and reclaiming the word 'cripple' or 'crip' (Shakespeare 1993: 253). Drawing on Shakespeare's account, we can appreciate the way in which a reclamation of such words via hashtags and digital action networks asserts a group identity emerging through political and cultural struggles. For example, the #cripplepunk movement is an interesting case of people subverting expectations and constructions of themselves based on their disabilities (conelykk 2016). Another illustrative example is #cripthevote, an instance of a more mainstream, government-focused activism in the 2016 US election (Pulrang 2016). Such cases underscore the ways in which online environments facilitate opportunities for the formation of self-constructed communities of people with disabilities.

In *Studying Disability Arts and Culture* Petra Kuppers offers instructions about how students can participate in online activism, for example by participating in the #occupy disability blog carnival or by writing or challenging Wikipedia pages. Through a series of short activities Kuppers shows how disability media activism complements and extends the activities of protests occurring in public spaces. She further encourages students to assist organizers to think through access issues so that people with disabilities can participate in activism. While sections of the wider digital activism literature assert that online activism is deeply connected to these physical spaces of protest (Gerbaudo 2012; Croeser & Highfield 2014), these spaces cannot necessarily be separated for people with disabilities who do not participate in public spaces in the same way.

Conclusion

In this chapter, we aimed to introduce key features of disability media activism, to put this vibrant area into the mix with other kinds of media activism.

First and foremost, as we have suggested, disability media activism requires us to rethink media and communications themselves. While media environments, affordances, economies and costs are changing, the threshold for people with disabilities and their allies to engage in activism is typically accessibility. Much media, even taken-for-granted online, mobile, locative, social, computational and data media and infrastructures remain inaccessible; so disability activism is often a struggle for social justice in media. Such activism provides the opportunity to broaden understandings of access to, use and control of and governance in, media. Disability media activism necessitates imaginative work across the full range of media modes and engaging all senses, because many people with disabilities do not have traditional written text and print media, for instance, as their preferred media choice.

Second, disability media activism encourages us, once again, to enlarge our understanding of what activism is, who might participate, and what its constituencies and publics are. Because people with disabilities have been excluded from, or not 'fitted' into, existing templates, rituals, space and notions of media and other activism, new approaches have been devised.

Third, disability media activism requires us to take seriously the disability as a legitimate, pressing and often central site of activist struggles, especially using the crucial tools of media.

References

Barnartt, S. and Scotch, R. (2001) *Disability Protests: Contentious Politics, 1970–1999*. Washington, DC: Gaulladet Press.

Barnes, C. (1992) *Disabling Imagery and the Media: An Exploration of the Principles for Media Representations of Disabled People*. Halifax, UK: British Council of Organisations of Disabled People and Ryburn Publishing, http://www.leeds.ac.uk/disability-studies/archiveuk/Barnes/disabling%20imagery.pdf, accessed 14 December 2017.

Barnes, C. and Mercer, C. (2010) *Exploring Disability: A Sociological Introduction*. Cambridge: Polity Press.

Bennett, W. L. and Segerberg, A. (2013) *The Logic of Connective Action: Digital Media and the Personalization of Contentious Politics*. Cambridge: Cambridge University Press.

Block, P., Kasnitz, D., Nishida, A. and Pollard, N. (eds) (2016) *Occupying Disability: Critical Approaches to Community, Justice, and Decolonizing Disability*. Dordrecht: Springer.

Burke, L. and Crow, L. (2016) 'Bedding Out: Art, Activism and Twitter', in K. Ellis and M. Kent (eds) *Disability and Social Media: Global Perspectives*. London: Routledge, pp. 57–74.

Castells, M. (2010) *The Rise of the Network Society*, 2nd edition. New York: Wiley.

Castells, M. (2012) *Networks of Outrage and Hope: Social Movements in the Internet Age*. Cambridge: Polity Press.

Charlton, J. I. (1998) *Nothing About Us Without Us: Disability Oppression and Empowerment*. Berkeley, CA: University of California Press.

Clifford, S. (2012) 'Making Disability Public in Deliberative Democracy', *Contemporary Political Theory*, vol. 11, no. 2, pp. 211–18.

conelykk (2016) 'Cripple Punk', 3 March, https://andafewbricks.wordpress.com/tag/cripple-punk, accessed 20 June 2017.

Couldry, N., Rodriguez, C., Bolin, G., Cohen, J., Goggin, G., Kraidy, M., Iwabuchi, K., Kwang-Suk, L., Qiu, J., Volkmer, I., Wasserman, H. and Zhao, Z. (2018) 'Media and Communications', Chapter 13, *Report of the International Panel on Social Progress*. 3 vols. Cambridge: Cambridge University Press.

Crippled Scholar (2016) 'Media Roundup of *Me Before You* Criticism', 28 May, https://crippledscholar.com/2016/05/28/media-roundup-of-me-before-you-criticism/, accessed 14 December 2017.

Croeser, S. and Highfield, T. (2014) 'Occupy Oakland and #oo: Uses of Twitter within the Occupy Movement', *First Monday*, vol. 19, no. 3, http://firstmonday.org/article/view/4827/3846, accessed 14 December 2017.

Crow, L. (2013) Bedding Out. [video]. http://www.roaring-girl.com/work/bedding-out/, accessed 14 December 2017.

Dobransky, K. and Hargittai, E. (2016) 'Unrealized Potential: Exploring the Digital Disability Divide', *Poetics*, vol. 58, pp. 18–28.

Dokumaci, A. (2016) 'Micro-Activist Affordances of Disability: Transformative Potential of Participation', in M. Denecke, A. Ganzert, I. Otto and R. Stock (eds) *ReClaiming Participation: Technology, Mediation, Collectivity*. Bielefeld: Transcript, pp. 67–83.

Dolmage, J. and DeGenaro, W. (2005) '"I Cannot Be Like This Frankie": Disability, Social Class, and Gender in *Million Dollar Baby*', *Disability Studies Quarterly*, vol. 25, no. 2, http://www.dsq-sds.org/article/view/555/732, accessed 14 December 2017.

Downey, G. J. (2008) *Closed Captioning: Subtitling, Stenography, and the Digital Convergence of Text with Television*. Baltimore, MA: Johns Hopkins University Press.

Ellcessor, E. (2012) 'Captions On, Off on TV, Online: Accessibility and Search Engine Optimization in Online Closed Captioning', *Television & New Media*, vol. 13, no. 4, pp. 329–52.

Ellcessor, E. (2016) '"One Tweet to Make So Much Noise": Connected Celebrity Activism in the Case of Marlee Matlin', *New Media & Society*, published online, 10 August, https://doi.org/10.1177/146144481 6661551, accessed 14 December 2017.

Ellis, K. (2015) 'Netflix Closed Captions Offer an Accessible Model for the Streaming Video Industry, But What about Audio Description?', *Communication, Politics & Culture*, vol. 47, no. 3, pp. 3–20.

Ellis, K. and Goggin, G. (2014) 'Disability and Social Media', in J. Hunsinger and T. Senft (eds) *The Social Media Handbook*. New York: Routledge, pp. 126–43.

Ellis, K. and Goggin, G. (2015) *Disability and the Media*. New York: Palgrave Macmillan.

Ellis, K., Goggin, G. and Kent, M. (2015) 'FCJ–188 Disability's Digital Frictions: Activism, Technology, and Politics', *The Fibreculture Journal*, vol. 26, pp. 7–30, http://twentysix.fibreculturejournal.org/fcj-188-disabilitys-digital-frictions-activism-technology-and-politics/, accessed 14 December 2017.

Ellis, K. and Kent, M. (2011) *Disability and New Media*. New York: Routledge.

Ellis, K. and Kent, M. (2015) 'Accessible Television: The New Frontier in Disability Media Studies Brings Together Industry Innovation, Government Legislation and Online Activism', *First Monday*, vol. 20, http://firstmonday.org/ojs/index.php/fm/article/view/6170, accessed 14 December 2017.

Ellis, K. and Kent, M. (eds) (2016) *Disability and Social Media: Global Perspectives*. London: Routledge.

Federal Communications Commission (FCC) (2010) *21st Century Communications and Video Accessibility Act (CVAA)*, https://www.fcc.gov/consumers/guides/21st-century-communications-and-video-accessibility-act-cvaa, accessed 27 May 2016.

Fisher, L. (2014) 'How Marlee Matlin Helped Force Streaming Video Closed Captions Into Digital Age', *ABC News*, 29 April, http://abcnews.go.com/Entertainment/marlee-matlin-helped-force-streaming-video-closed-captions/story?id=23503281, accessed 14 December 2017.

Foley, A. and Ferri, B. A. (2012) 'Technology for People, Not Disabilities: Ensuring Access and Inclusion', *Journal of Research in Special Educational Needs*, vol. 12, no. 4, pp. 192–200.

Garland-Thomson, R. (2004) 'Integrating Disability, Transforming Feminist Theory', in B. G. Smith and B. Hutchinson (eds) *Gendering Disability*. New Brunswick, NJ: Rutgers University Press, pp. 73–104.

Gartner, A. and Joe, T. (eds) (1987) *Images of the Disabled, Disabled Images*. New York: Praeger.

Gerbaudo, P. (2012) *Tweets and the Streets: Social Media and Contemporary Activism*. New York, London: Pluto.

Gerbaudo, P. and Treré, T. (2015) 'In Search of the "We" of Social Media Activism: Introduction to the Special Issue on Social Media and Protest Identities', *Information, Communication & Society*, vol. 18, no. 8, pp. 865–71.

Ghosh, N. (ed.) (2016) *Interrogating Disability in India: Theory and Practice*. New Delhi: Springer.

Goggin, G. and C. Newell (2003) *Digital Disability: The Social Construction of Disability in New Media*. Lanham, MD: Rowman and Littlefield.

Grech, S. and Soldatic, K. (eds) (2016) *Disability in the Global South: The Critical Handbook*. Cham, Switzerland: Springer.

Haller, B. (2010) *Representing Disability in an Ableist World: Essays on Mass Media*. Louisville, KY: Advocado Press.

Hampton, J. (2016) *Disability and the Welfare State in Britain: Changes in Perception and Policy 1948–1979*. Bristol: Policy Press.

Hevey, D. with Spence, J. and Evans, J. (1992) *The Creatures Time Forgot: Photography and Disability Imagery*. London: Routledge.

Highfield, T. (2016) *Social Media and Everyday Politics*. Cambridge: Polity Press.

Hirschmann, N. J. (2015) 'Invisible Disability: Seeing, Being, Power', in N. J. Hirschmann and B. Linker (eds) *Civil Disabilities: Citizenship, Membership, and Belonging*. Philadelphia, PA: University of Pennsylvania Press, pp. 204–22.

Hirschmann, N. J. and Linker, B. (eds) *Civil Disabilities: Citizenship, Membership, and Belonging*. Philadelphia, PA: University of Pennsylvania Press, pp. 204–22.

Hollier, S. (2012) *Sociability: Social Media for People with a Disability*. Sydney: Media Access Australia and ACCAN, pp. 1–36, https://accan.org.au/files/Reports/Sociability%20Report.pdf, accessed 14 December 2017.

Hughes, B. (2009) 'Disability Activisms: Social Model Stalwarts and Biological Citizens', *Disability & Society*, vol. 24, pp. 677–88.

Jaeger, P. (2012) *Disability and the Internet: Confronting a Digital Divide*. Boulder, CO: Lynne Rienner.

Kafer, A. (2013) *Feminist, Queer, Crip*. Bloomington, IN: Indiana University Press.

Kelly, C. and Orsini, M. (eds) (2016) *Mobilizing Metaphor: Art, Culture, and Disability Activism in Canada*. Vancouver and Toronto: UBC Press.

Kuppers, P. (2014) *Studying Disability Arts and Culture*. New York: Palgrave Macmillan.

Longmore, P. K. (2003) *Why I Burned My Book and Other Essays on Disability*. Philadelphia, PA: Temple University Press.

Longmore, P. K. (2016) *Telethons: Spectacle, Disability, and the Business of Charity*. New York: Oxford University Press.

McRuer, R. (2010) 'Neoliberal Risks: *Million Dollar Baby, Murderball*, and Anti-National Sexual Positions', in S. Chivers and N. Markotič (eds) *The Problem Body: Projecting Disability on Film*. Columbus, OH: Ohio State University Press, pp. 159–77.

Merry, S. (2016) '*Me Before You* Has a Disabled Main Character – But Activists Are Angry. Here's Why', *Washington Post*, 3 June, https://www.washingtonpost.com/news/arts-and-entertainment/wp/2016/06/03/me-before-you-has-a-disabled-main-character-but-activists-are-angry-heres-why/?utm_term=.673e7136a703, accessed 14 December 2017.

Nepveux, D. M. (2015) 'Activism', in R. Adams, B. Reiss and D. Serlin (eds) *Keywords for Disability Studies*. New York: NYU Press, pp. 21–5.

Newell, C. (2006) 'Disability, Ethics, and Rejected Knowledge', *Journal of Medicine and Philosophy*, vol. 31, no. 3, pp. 269–83.

Papacharissi, Z. (2014) *Affective Publics: Sentiment, Technology, and Politics*. New York: Oxford University Press.

Papacharissi, Z. (2016) 'Affective Publics and Structures of Storytelling: Sentiment, Events and Mediality', *Information, Communication, & Society*, vol. 19, pp. 307–24.

Parent, L. and Veilleux, M.-E. (2016) 'Transport Mésadapté: Exploring Online Disability Activism in Montréal', in K. Ellis and M. Kent (eds) *Disability and Social Media: Global Perspectives*. London: Routledge, pp. 89–100.

Parsloe, S. M. (2015) 'Discourses of Disability, Narratives of Community: Reclaiming an Autistic Identity Online', *Journal of Applied Communication* Research, vol. 43, no. 3, pp. 336–56.

Parsloe, S. M. and Holton, A. E. (2017) '#Boycottautismspeaks: Communicating a Counternarrative through Cyberactivism and Connective Action', *Information, Communication & Society*, published online 17 March, http://dx.doi.org/10.1080/1369118X.2017.1301514, accessed 14 December 2017.

Peltz Strauss, K. (2006) *A New Civil Right: Telecommunications Equality for Deaf and Hard of Hearing Americans*. Washington, DC: Gaulladet University Press.

Prince, M. (2009) *Absent Citizens: Disability Politics and Policy in Canada*. Toronto: University of Toronto Press.

Pulrang, A. (2016) 'What Is #CripTheVote?', 30 June, https://storify.com/AndrewPulrang/what-is-cripthevote, accessed 26 April 2017.

Roets, G. and Braidotti, R. (2012) 'Nomadology and Subjectivity: Deleuze, Guattari and Critical Disability Studies', in D. Goodley, B. Hughes and Lennard Davis (eds) *Disability and Social Theory: New Developments and Directions*. Houndsmills, UK: Palgrave Macmillan, pp. 161–78.

Sandell, R., Dodd, J. and Garland-Thomson, R. (eds) (2010) *Re-presenting Disability: Activism and Agency in the Museum*. London: Routledge.

Shakespeare, T. (1993) 'Disabled People's Self-Organisation: A New Social Movement?', *Disability, Handicap & Society*, vol. 8, no. 3, pp. 249–64.

Shapiro, J. P. (1993) *No Pity: People with Disabilities Forging a New Civil Rights Movement*. New York: Times Books.

Trevisan, F. (2014) 'Scottish Disability Organizations and Online Media: A Path to Empowerment or "Business as Usual?"', *Disability Studies Quarterly*, vol. 34, no. 3, http://dsq-sds.org/article/view/3359/3648, accessed 14 December 2017.

Trevisan, F. (2017) *Disability Rights Advocacy Online*. New York: Routledge.

Union Of The Physically Impaired Against Segregation (UPIAS) (1976) 'Mission Statement', amended version, 9 August, http://disability-studies.leeds.ac.uk/files/library/UPIAS-UPIAS.pdf, accessed 20 June 2017.

United States Government (1990) *Television Decoder Circuitry Act of 1990: Report of* Senate *Committee on Commerce, Science, and Transportation.* Washington, DC: US Government Printing Office, pp. 1–11, https://transition.fcc.gov/Bureaus/OSEC/library/legislative_histories/1397.pdf, accessed 20 June 2017.

Vromen, A. (2017) *Digital Citizenship and Political Engagement: The Challenge from Online Campaigning and Advocacy Organisations.* Basingstoke, UK: Palgrave Macmillan.

Watermeyer, B., Swartz, L., Lorenzo, T., Schneider, M. and Priestly, M. (eds) (2006) *Disability and Social Change: A South African Agenda.* Cape Town: Human Sciences Research Council.

PART VII

Beyond social media

.

38

FROM DIGITAL ACTIVISM TO ALGORITHMIC RESISTANCE

Emiliano Treré

Introduction and outline

Discourses on algorithms are increasingly populating the media and pervading public conversations. Newspapers are filled with stories on how algorithmic power is impacting our choices in the realms of politics, journalism, music, sport, research and healthcare. The recent inclusion of the term in the influential *Digital Keywords* volume (Peters 2016) also signals a growing interest in the concept and its consequences within various fields and strands of research in the academia, and especially within media studies. As Gillespie (2016) has pointed out, the term appears in recent scholarship not only as a noun but also increasingly as an adjective, in relation to issues of identity, culture, ideology, accountability, governance, imaginary and regulation. In this chapter, I focus on the changes that algorithmic power is bringing to the realm of politics and the transformations of digital activism. The chapter begins with a brief outline of the significance of algorithms in digital politics. Then, it focuses on two diverse conceptions and manifestations of algorithmic power in politics (algorithm as propaganda/repression and algorithm as appropriation/resistance) that emerge from the explorations of two case studies.

The first case study is an examination of the contemporary Mexican scenario where institutions and parties have massively deployed algorithmic strategies for propagandistic and repressive purposes. The second case is an investigation of the digital media practices of the *Indignados* that reveals how Spanish activists used their knowledge of the Twitter algorithm to maximize their visibility, drive the protest narratives and infiltrate the mainstream media agenda. Lessons on the achievements and challenges of algorithmic power in digital politics are outlined in the conclusion, along with suggestions for future lines of research.

The reflections on the practices of algorithmic resistance and appropriation of the Spanish *Indignados* are based on 20 semi-structured interviews carried out with a range of social movement organizations: from well-established radical activist groups to informal groups of newly politicized individuals; from traditional hierarchical social movement organizations to horizontal, social movement groups such as anarchist, free culture or hacker collectives; from non-activist social media users to very experienced tech activists; and from inexperienced citizen journalists to unemployed professional journalists contributing to alternative media. This research was supported by an Insight Development Grant from the Social Sciences and Humanities Research Council of Canada [file number 430-2014-00181] held by Dr Sandra Jeppesen at Lakehead University Orillia, Canada.

Algorithms as ecologies

Before addressing the role of algorithms in political practice, an assessment of what constitutes an algorithm is needed. As Gillespie (2014: 167) notes, algorithms 'are encoded procedures for transforming input data into a desired output, based on specified calculations'. According to Willson (2016: 4), 'algorithms make things happen – they are designed to be executed and to bring about particular outcomes according to certain desires, needs and possibilities.' The metaphor of the recipe is often evoked to define them, since it identifies an endpoint (a meal), provides a list of ingredients and includes a step-by-step description of a process that describes in a detailed order what needs to be done and at which exact point in time.

If we are to understand the social and political implications of algorithms, we have to take into account that they do not exist in isolation, as separate technical entities, but are instead embedded in multi-faceted ecologies of social, cultural and political interactions, and therefore reflect particular ways of conceiving the world (Postigo 2014). Ignoring this 'complex assemblage of people, machines and procedures' (Gillespie 2016: 26) may also result in the obscuration of the agency of the people behind algorithms. It may also conceal the fact that we need to look at algorithms in connection to broader global socio-technical shifts such as the process of *datafication*, i.e. the transformation of social action into online quantified data.

This process, along with the possibilities provided by big data, initially eulogized for its ground-breaking possibilities, has now entered a critical phase with scholars pointing out that the process of datafication and the big data phenomenon are controversial mythologies that have to be critically engaged with (boyd & Crawford 2012; Mosco 2014), since they bring with them new regimes of control and discrimination, and generate issues in relation to privacy, surveillance and inequality (van Dijck 2014; Lyon 2014). Furthermore, algorithms' roles should be appraised within the increasingly complex junctions among the process of automation, and the upward diffusion of the internet of things (Howard 2015).

Algorithms and politics

Algorithms are deeply affecting the realm of the political. The rapid diffusion of networked devices, paired with the increasing generation of data over multiple platforms, coupled with the massive adoption of social media as tools for political engagement constitute a landscape within which new algorithmic agents proliferate. Most of the studies on algorithms in politics have highlighted the negative consequences of new forms of *computational propaganda* in relation to *political bots* (Shorey & Howard 2016; Woolley 2016; Woolley & Howard 2016).

Political bots are defined as 'the algorithms that operate over social media, written to learn from and mimic real people so as to manipulate public opinion across a diverse range of social media and device networks' (Woolley & Howard 2016: 4885). Over the last few years, political bots have been deployed in numerous countries, from Europe to Latin America, from the US to North Africa and Asia (for a comprehensive charting of the phenomenon, see Woolley 2016) to manipulate public opinion, spread propaganda, create an illusion of popularity and undermine digital dissent (Treré 2016). As Woolley and Howard (2016: 4886) put it: 'computational propaganda is among the latest, and most ubiquitous, technical strategies to be deployed by those who wish to use information technology for social control.'

Mostly scholars appear to be concerned in showing how automated technologies as Twitter trolls and political bots, part of a new kind of *robopolitics* (Tambini 2016), are hurting democracy by discouraging social media's democratic potential and forcing politicians to limit their digital presence, or abandon online environments altogether (Theocaris *et al.* 2016). The last electoral campaign in the US has provided a clear example of the deployment of this kind of techniques, with political bots massively spreading erroneous information and fake news to potential voters, often to the benefit of Donald Trump (Resnick 2016). Indeed, these studies are able to account for the new ramifications of the dark side of digital politics, but there is often a sense of hopelessness within this strand of research, as if social actors were completely deprived of their agency in front of these new forms of algorithmic manipulation.

While it is key to examine the depths of the dark side of the algorithm, it is also pivotal to explore the ways through which, in specific socio-political contexts, algorithmic power redefines activists' practices, and to investigate the conditions under which social movement actors are able to repurpose the power of big data to pursue social justice (Milan 2015; Dencik *et al.* 2016). Indeed, in the current scenario we are also experiencing unpredicted forms of algorithmic resistance that acquire a variety of shapes: activists, civil society organizations and radical tech groups are proving to be increasingly more skilful in unmasking algorithmic propaganda on social media, showing through data visualizations how governments use bots to undermine dissent, and exploiting the power of the Twitter algorithm to boost a protest movement's popularity. In the following sections, we will then look at both sides of algorithmic political power. Drawing on the case of contemporary Mexico, we will shed light on algorithms used as propaganda and repression; then, based on the experience of the *Indignados* in Spain, we will instead look at manifestations of algorithms as appropriation and resistance.

Algorithms as propaganda

Before the 2012 general elections, Mexican politicians had never considered politics through digital platforms a priority, relying instead on the powerful media propaganda system provided by television as their main channel for campaigning. This is not to say that during the 2012 elections the mainstream media were not important: the role of the so-called Mexican *telecracy* – the media television duopoly Televisa y TV Azteca, which controls 99 per cent of the market (Huerta-Wong and Gómez 2013) was indeed pivotal, since – as documented by numerous investigative journalists (Villamil 2010; Tuckman 2012) – for six years the Mexican media titan Televisa shaped the candidacy of Enrique Peña Nieto (EPN) of the PRI party (the current Mexican president), while simultaneously delegitimizing his left-wing opponent Manuel López Obrador. But the 2012 elections also witnessed what some saw as an explosion of digital politics, with politicians conquering social media to engage in dialogue with citizens.

However, what was perceived by a superficial look as an embrace of the digital sphere for fostering citizen engagement, revealed to more analytical eyes that these politicians mostly considered online spaces as sites for both the premeditated construction of consensus and the algorithmic construction of consent, rather than environments for reinforcing democracy through genuine dialogue and participation. Mexican scholar Octavio Islas has framed this behaviour as 'authoritarian engineering' (Islas 2015:1), a concept similar to 'computational propaganda' that indicates the adoption by Mexican politicians of opaque online strategies to boost popularity and undermine oppositional voices.

Studies of the social media strategies of Mexican politicians during the 2012 campaign underline that an intensified use of digital technologies did not correspond to an increase in democratic participation between candidates and voters, but was instead constituted by a massive deployment of strategies including: the creation of false universes of followers; the use of political bots to automatically generate tweets; the hiring of trolls (people who tweet in favour of a candidate, and against their opponent); and ghost followers (empty accounts aimed at boosting a candidate's followers). By employing these strategies, Mexican politicians discarded the possibility of using digital platforms to include voters' feedback into their decisions and incorporate democratic visions into their ways of doing politics (Ricaurte Quijano 2013).

These algorithmic strategies were paired by the activities of an army of so-called PRI *@ctivistas* ('electronic activists'), dedicated to tweeting according to the instructions of EPN's campaign leaders, and trying to counteract, isolate or sabotage criticisms of PRI from civil society actors. This network was formed in December 2009, and its leaders have always claimed to be nothing more than a network of independent young volunteers and PRI supporters. But, as other researchers have recognized (Figueiras 2012), the organization of an estimated 100,000 *@ctivists* (Islas 2015) was used systematically during the PRI campaign to successfully spread and situate Peña Nieto's image on digital media. In particular, this network was 'activated' when Peña Nieto's public image suffered: for instance, after his speech at the Guadalajara International Book Fair, when he was unable to accurately name three books that had influenced his life, and when the student movement #YoSoy132 emerged in May 2012, condemning the dangerous interconnections between media and politics that the PRI candidate impersonated.

Although one of Peña Nieto's campaign managers (who later became Secretary of Education) acknowledged in May 2012 that 20,000 *@ctivists* were tweeting without receiving any monetary compensation, the issue is controversial, with other sources showing that thousands of these activists were actually hired to perform their activities. The Mexican case study clearly shows the possibilities for impacting, distorting and manufacturing public opinion within digital environments that institutional parties with immense financial resources like the PRI have at their disposal.

Algorithms as repression

In the Mexican scenario, the use of algorithms for propaganda goes together with its use for repressive purposes. Since 2012, political activists and civil society organizations have denounced the dangers algorithmic attacks have on social media, arguing that they criminalize protest and segregate dissident voices, and underlining the need to act immediately to prevent their intensification. Political strategies that rely on digital technologies to undermine dissent through the use of political bots have been enhanced in the years since the 2012 election, up to the point where they have become an essential component of the government's *modus operandi*, used repeatedly during 2013.

For instance, EPN critics mobilizing for the #MarchaAntiEPN (March against Peña Nieto) on Twitter were systematically attacked and blocked online, and dissident voices were 'drowned' on various occasions by orchestrated bot attacks (Verkamp & Gupta 2013). A study, commissioned by the news programme of a liberal Mexican journalist and carried out by the data-mining agency *Mesura,* exposed the massive use of bots to build an illusion of online support for a controversial energy reform (Aristegui Noticias 2015). Mesura documented the systematic deployment of bots to tweet and re-tweet in support of the reform, discovering that the time gap between the sending of a supportive original message and its re-tweeting was too short to be accomplished by a human being. The report's pessimistic conclusions warned about the risks to which citizens are exposed in an era when the importance of digital politics is growing day by day, and when those in power have no ethical problems with manipulating public perception, creating new forms of authoritarianism enabled by digital technology (Soto 2013).

On 26 September 2014, a group of students departed the Ayotzinapa Rural Teachers' College for a protest in the city of Iguala (about 130 km away) but they never arrived. At least three students were killed and another 43 remain missing. The Mexican government's official version is that the students were killed after being handed over to the *Guerreros Unidos* cartel on the orders of the mayor of Iguala, but investigations conducted by various media outlets, such as the Mexican critical magazine *Proceso* and the US publication *The Intercept* portrayed a darker picture of government complacency. After the event, several activists started to protest on social media, and the Twitter hashtag #YaMeCanse (I am tired) – which expressed the feeling of not being able to tolerate any more violence in the country – soon became the core for mobilizing and spreading information.

Journalist Erin Gallagher, who covers political mobilizations for the online magazine *Revolution News,* soon noticed something atypical in the search results for the #YaMeCanse hashtags: that they were flooded with tweets including the hashtag but no other content apart from random punctuation marks. The accounts tweeting this kind of empty content were in fact bots that lacked followers, and were tweeting automatically. The noise they created made it difficult for citizens to share information using #YaMeCanse, and thus the hashtag dropped out of Twitter's trending topics.

Mexican blogger and data-mining analyst Alberto Escorcia has discovered a reliable way of detecting bot accounts by examining the number of connections a Twitter account has with other users, and has been documenting the use of bots in Mexico to sabotage protests by preventing information from spreading, and to send death threats to specific activists in a wide array of political campaigns in the last few years. For instance, since February 2015, professor, activist and blogger Rossana Reguillo has received regular death threats on various social media platforms (Saucedo Añez 2015). Particularly harsh attacks via Twitter lasted more than two months, and data-mining analysis of the Twitter campaign revealed that bots and trolls were responsible for most of the attacks. As these cases show, algorithmic propaganda and repression are particularly virulent in the Mexican scenario, where the propagandistic *modus operandi* of mainstream media have infiltrated the digital sphere. But the scenario is not entirely dark, as the previous examples attest, various bloggers, journalists and tech activists are developing diverse tactics of algorithmic resistance through which they are able to expose and sometimes counteract the dirty digital strategies of institutions and parties.

Algorithms as appropriation and resistance

The 15M or *Indignados* movement that emerged in 2011 in Spain developed extremely sophisticated forms of digital political action (Candón Mena 2011; Gerbaudo 2012) and it is thus considered a powerful laboratory for experimentation and innovation in practices of political communication that is contributing to the reconfiguration of democracy (Feenstra *et al.* 2016). This movement refined and perfected the repertoires of contention and communication of previous Spanish mobilizations (such as the 13M demonstration in 2004 and the 'Movement for the Right to Housing' that emerged in 2006), leading to the development of sophisticated practices of hybrid synchronization between online and offline activism, and to the appropriation of multiple digital media platforms to create and spread content, organize, mobilize and document protest.

The digital activism of the *Indignados* has been described by both scholars and activists themselves as *technopolitics*, a multi-faceted form of communicative action that is a complex blend of technological knowledge and digital expertise used for radical political purposes with the technology itself envisaged as a site of struggle (Alcazan *et al.* 2012; Monterde 2015; Toret *et al.* 2015; Treré *et al.* 2017). The origins of technopolitics are deeply rooted in the non-hierarchical, collaborative and open spirit of the Free Culture Movement (Fuster Morell 2012; Postill 2016), and in the principles of positive meritocracy and the remix *ethos* of hacker ethics (Himanen 2001). *Open Source* culture has shaped the agenda of the movement in relation to information and knowledge policies and practices, and has situated the digital commons as a pivotal topic and a crucial site of contention for the *Indignados* (Fuster Morell & Subirats 2012). Moreover, it has moulded the movement's organizational logic through horizontal, decentralized coordination that massively relied on digital media.

The technopolitical practices of the *Indignados* covered a wide and diverse ecology of platforms used for collective action. On one side, activists produced their own radical media, such as the N–1 alternative social media platform, the *¡Democracia Real YA!* website, and various media projects such as *Sol TV*, *Ágora Sol Radio*, *Toma La Tele* and the printed newspaper *Madrid15M*. Furthermore, they also heavily relied on free and open-source software, advocating for technological infrastructure sovereignty and self-determination where viable.

But what has been a fundamental character of technopolitics is the tactical and massive appropriation (that Spanish media activists qualified as 'hacking social media') of corporate social platforms such as Twitter and Facebook in order to 'transform them into real weapons of massive information diffusion' (SuNotissima *et al.* 2012: 18). Through the strategic appropriation of social media, the *Indignados* were capable not only of launching calls for action and organizing mobilizations, but also of influencing journalistic coverage and situating their claims in the media agenda. Through social media appropriation, Spanish activists were able to achieve that their 15 May call for action was mentioned 37 times by printed press (Candón Mena 2013), and in many other occasions they obtained international press coverage on newspapers such as *The Washington Post* and *The New York Times*, making it impossible for Spanish media outlets to ignore their claims (Toret *et al.* 2015).

One of the most effective strategies adopted by 15M activists consisted in the systematic creation of *trending topics* on Twitter, which was carefully planned using a combination of internal communication technologies and social media platforms. Internal communication tools such as *pads* (digital notepads for collective writing such as *Titanpad*) were used to collectively select possibly successful hashtags and build the narrative of the protest, while external social media platforms such as Twitter were deployed to massively spread the information and obtain the desired outcome. Inside the pads, activists first brainstormed diverse possible hashtags in order to reach an agreement over the most effective one for the specific political campaign that was tackled. Once a hashtag was chosen, an array of potential tweets was created accordingly and sent to other activist collectives through other internal communication tools such as direct messaging services (*WhatsApp* and *Telegram*) and mailing lists.

This type of sophisticated digital action is based on the collective synchronization of thousands of accounts that tweet at the same time selecting among the already provided tweets. To reach this aim, it is fundamental to rely on an already established network of activists' profiles that can be activated at any time. This kind of technopolitical practice represents a clear form of resistance and appropriation of the Twitter algorithm. Interviewees themselves admitted that this tactic originates precisely from trying to understand how the Twitter algorithm worked and how it could be exploited for boosting the movement popularity and influence the mainstream media agenda. Through daily practices of self-reflexivity on the potential of social media, activists saw that general trending topics had a short cycle of 24 hours maximum, and that in order to create them all the accounts had to tweet with the same hashtag simultaneously, and that the hashtag had to be a previously unused one. The *Indignados'* capacity to create trending topics and master this new kind of viral politics is unmatched within contemporary movements. It is based on the fundamental role that hackers and techies played within the movement, acting as a tech-vanguard that applied their tech expertise not only for the creation of radical alternative media, but above all for the appropriation and *cyber-material détournement* (Galis & Neumayer 2016) of corporate social media.

This tech expertise manifests itself also as 'radical media education' (Barbas 2015), since basically every political action and campaign of the last seven years in the Spanish scenario has been accompanied by a flow of online tutorials, manuals and skill-share workshops about how to increase the effectiveness of social media campaigns by exploiting corporate social media's algorithms (Feenstra *et al.* 2016).

These new forms of algorithmic resistance are dissimilar from the spontaneous 'smart mobs' that had characterized the Spanish scenario ten years before the *Indignados* (Sampedro *et al.* 2005). They signal a new level of technological awareness and finesse in the realm of digital activism, and also sharply contrast enthusiastic claims about the complete spontaneity of digital protests, because they constitute carefully envisioned and planned political actions.

Conclusions: contextualizing algorithmic power

Throughout this chapter, we have begun to appraise the relevance of algorithmic power within contemporary politics and digital activism. The two case studies I have examined display the ambivalences inherent in this kind of power. While in the Mexican scenario conventional politics and institutions have used algorithmic power for propagandistic and repressive purposes, in Spain social movements have been able to repurpose this power in order to pursue social change. What are the main lessons we can learn from this brief journey into algorithmic power? First of all, the importance of looking at the agency involved in this kind of power. If we conceive of algorithms as ecologies of humans, machines and procedures, in order to evaluate their role, we have to learn how to disentangle and make sense of their complex interrelations. This means also contextualizing algorithmic power in order to assess which actors are using these mechanisms, for which purposes and with which level of expertise. The Mexican case illustrates that civil society has been slower than institutional politics in 'catching up' with the power of the algorithm in politics, while the Spanish case shows exactly the contrary. These two contextual analyses demonstrate that understanding contemporary digital politics increasingly means understanding how algorithmic power works.

This power is reorienting the new practices of digital activism within movements and civil society organizations. In this evolving scenario, digital media literacy is increasingly relevant, as social actors have to learn not only how to unmask and denounce new authoritarian digital strategies carried out by governments and parties, but also, at the same time, they need to develop sophisticated techniques and tactics to 'bend the algorithm' according to their sociopolitical needs, in order to pursue social justice and political change.

References

Alcazan, A. *et al.* (2012) *Tecnopolítica Internet y R-evoluciones. Sobre la Centralidad de las Redes Digitales en el #15M.* Barcelona: Icaria.

Aristegui Noticias (2012) 'La Cargada de Funcionarios en Twitter a Favor de #reformaenergética', http://aristeguinoticias.com/2609/mexico/la-cargada-de-funcionarios-en-twitter-a-favor-de-reformaenergetica, accessed 25 January 2017.

Barbas, Á. (2015) 'Comunicación Educativa y Cultura Política en el Movimiento 15–M. Aproximación Teórica y Reflexiones Preliminares en Torno a un Estudio Etnográfico', *Kultur*, vol. 2, no. 4, pp. 179–92.

boyd, d. and Crawford, K. (2012) 'Critical Questions for Big Data: Provocations for a Cultural, Technological, and Scholarly Phenomenon', *Information, Communication and Society,* vol. 15, no. 5, pp. 662–79.

Candón Mena, J. (2013) *Toma la Calle, Toma las Redes: El Movimiento 15M en Internet.* Sevilla: Atrapasueños.

Dencik, L., Hintz, A. and Cable, J. (2016) 'Towards Data Justice? The Ambiguity of Anti-surveillance Resistance in Political Activism', *Big Data & Society,* vol. 3, no. 2, pp. 1–12.

Feenstra, R., Tormey, S., Casero-Ripollés, A. and Keane, J. (2016) *La Reconfiguración de la Democracia: El Laboratorio Político Español*. Granada: Comares.

Figueiras, L. (2012) 'El Movimiento Estudiantil en el Proceso Electoral 2012', in L. Figueiras (ed.) *Del 131 al #YoSoy132. Elección 2012*. Mexico: Comunicación y Política Editores.

Fuster Morell, M. (2012) 'The Free Culture and 15M Movements in Spain: Composition, Social Networks and Synergies', *Social Movement Studies*, vol. 11, nos. 3–4, pp. 386–92.

Galis, V. and Neumayer, C. (2016) 'Laying Claim to Social Media by Activists: A Cyber-Material Détournement', *Social Media + Society*, vol. 2, no. 3, pp. 1–14.

Gerbaudo, P. (2012) *Tweets and the Streets. Social media and Contemporary Activism*. London: Pluto.

Gillespie, T. (2014) 'The Relevance of Algorithms', in T. Gillespie, P. J. Boczkowski and K. Foot (eds) *Media Technologies: Essays on Communication, Materiality, and Society*. Cambridge, MA: MIT Press, pp. 167–94.

Himanen, P. (2001) *The Hacker Ethic and the Spirit of the Information Age*. New York: Random House.

Huerta, W. E. and Gómez, R. (2013) 'Concentración y Diversidad de los Medios de Comunicacion y las Telecomunicaciones en México', *Comunicación y Sociedad*, no. 19, pp. 113–52.

Islas, O. (2015) 'Los Neoectivistas: El Recurso contra la Participación Ciudadana', http://www.etcetera. com.mx/articulo/los_neoectivistas_el_recurso_contra_ la_participacion_ciudadana./35375, accessed 22 January 2017.

Lyon, D. (2014) 'Surveillance, Snowden, and Big Data: Capacities, Consequences, Critique', *Big Data & Society*, vol. 1, no. 2, pp. 1–13.

Milan, S. (2015) 'When Algorithms Shape Collective Action: Social Media and the Dynamics of Cloud Protesting', *Social Media + Society* vol. 1, no. 2, pp. 1–10.

Monterde, A. (2015) *Emergencia, Evolución y Efectos del Movimiento-red 15M (2011–2015). Una Aproximación Tecnopolítica*. Barcelona: UOC–IN3.

Mosco, V. (2014) *To the Cloud: Big Data in a Turbulent World*. Boulder, CO: Paradigm

Peters, B. (ed.) (2016) *Digital Keywords: A Vocabulary of Information Society and Culture*. Princeton, NJ: Princeton University Press.

Postigo, H. (2014) 'Capture, Fixation and Conversation: How the Matrix Has You and Will Sell You, Part 3/3', *Culture Digitally*, 10 April, http://culturedigitally.org/2014/04/capture-fixation-and-conversation-how-the-matrix-has-you-and-will-sell-you-part-33/#sthash.6sGBTcmy.mXWelSyy. dpuf, accessed 8 January 2017.

Postill, J. (2016) 'Freedom Technologists and the Future of Global Justice', *Transnational Institute*, https:// www.tni.org/en/publication/freedom-technologists-and-the-future-of-global-justice, accessed 19 January 2017.

Resnick, G. (2016) 'How Pro-Trump Twitter Bots Spread Fake News', *The Daily Beast*, 17 November, http://www.thedailybeast.com/articles/2016/11/17/how-pro-trump-twitter-bots-spread-fake-news. html, accessed 18 January 2017.

Ricaurte Quijano, P. (2013) 'Tan Cerca de Twitter y tan Lejos de Los Votantes: Las Estrategias de los Candidatos Presidenciales Mexicanos Durante la Campaña Electoral de 2012', *Versión 31*, pp. 118–32.

Sampedro, V. F. (ed.) (2005) *13–M: Multitudes on Line*. Madrid: Catarata.

Saucedo Añez, P. C. (2015) 'Amenazas de Muerte en la Red Contra Investigadora y Activista Mexicana Rossana Reguillo', *GlobalVoices*, https://es.globalvoices.org/2015/03/04/amenazas-de-muerte-en-la-red-contra-investigadora-y-activista-mexicana-rossana-reguillo, accessed 3 February 2017.

Shorey, S. and Howard, P. N. (2016) 'Automation, Algorithms, and Politics| Automation, Big Data and Politics: A Research Review', *International Journal of Communication*, vol. 10, p. 24, http://ijoc.org/index. php/ijoc/article/view/6233, accessed 8 May 2017.

Soto, J. C. (2013) 'Tecnoautoritarismo', *Desmesura*, http://desmesura.org/firmas/tecno-autoritarismo, accessed 4 January 2017.

Tambini, D. (2016) 'In the New Robopolitics, Social Media has Left Newspapers for Dead', *Guardian*, 18 November, https://www.theguardian.com/commentisfree/2016/nov/18/robopolitics-social-media-traditional-media-dead-brexit-trump, accessed 15 January 2017.

Theocaris, Y. *et al.* (2016) 'Twitter Trolls are Actually Hurting Democracy', *Washington Post*, 4 November, https://www.washingtonpost.com/news/monkey-cage/wp/2016/11/04/twitter-trolls-hurt-democracy-more-than-you-realize-heres-how, accessed 12 January 2017.

Toret, J. (ed.) (2015) *Tecnopolítica y 15M: La Potencia de las Multitudes Conectadas*. Barcelona: UOC.

Treré, E. (2016) 'The Dark Side of Digital Politics: Understanding the Algorithmic Manufacturing of Consent and the Hindering of Online Dissidence', *IDS Bulletin*, vol. 47, no. 1.

Treré, E., Jeppesen, S. and Mattoni, A. (2017) 'Comparing Digital Protest Media Imaginaries: Anti-Austerity Movements in Spain, Italy & Greece', *TripleC*.

Tuckman, J. (2012) 'Mexican Media Scandal: Secretive Televisa Unit Promoted PRI Candidate', *Guardian*, 26 June, http://www.theguardian.com/world/2012/jun/26/mexican-media-scandal-televisa-pri-nieto, accessed 8 May 2017.

van Dijck, J. (2014) 'Datafication, Dataism and Dataveillance: Big Data Between Scientific Paradigm and Ideology', *Surveillance and Society*, vol. 12, no. 3, pp. 197–208.

Verkamp, J–P. and Gupta, M. (2013) 'Five Incidents, One Theme: Twitter Spam as a Weapon to Drown Voices of Protest', Unpublished Presentation from 3rd USENIX Workshop on Free and Open Communications on the Internet, Berkeley, CA.

Villamil, J. (2010) *El Sexenio de Televisa: Conjuras del Poder Media'tico*, México DF: Grijalbo.

Willson, M. (2017) 'Algorithms (and the) Everyday', *Information, Communication & Society*, vol. 20, no. 1, pp. 137–50.

Woolley, S. (2016) Automating Power: Social Bot Interference in Global Politics. *First Monday*, vol. 21, no. 4, http://firstmonday.org/ojs/index.php/fm/article/view/6161/5300, accessed 8 May 2017.

Woolley, S. C. and Howard, P. N. (2016) 'Automation, Algorithms, and Politics| Political Communication, Computational Propaganda, and Autonomous Agents – Introduction', *International Journal of Communication*, vol. 10, p. 9, http://ijoc.org/index.php/ijoc/article/view/6298, accessed 8 May 2017.

39

ON THE QUESTION OF BLOCKCHAIN ACTIVISM

Oliver Leistert

Let's Build a New Internet.

ConsenSys Media 2017

Recent developments in finance announce a new killer application: the blockchain has become a key technological innovation strategy. Initially received only as the 'layer' for the crypto-currency Bitcoin, blockchains have skyrocketed to the fore of so-called fintechs (startups in the finance industry), and are being tested by a wide spectrum of companies beyond finance, such as logistics, health care or real estate. The potentials for massive rationalizations within corporate and industrial processes are immense, announcing a new machinic paradigm to take over administration and management tasks that vertically integrates into production, distribution and consumption processes.

Blockchains as an additional layer of the internet are in a testing and early application phase all around. This new layer or functional addition to the internet is commonly about value, ledgers, rights, transactions, security and most of all: control. In this sense, blockchain technologies can be understood as a major technological breakthrough for an emerging machinic control order that introduces a new integration for commodification processes to the net: a transfer of micro – and macro-economic and – societal processes in very large numbers from human administration towards machine-to-machine communications. Blockchain technologies offer a shortcut between transfers of values and rights that excludes human interaction by setting up cryptological trust between machines for value and rights administration.

From a media activism point of view, blockchain technologies offer a variety of perspectives that may illuminate what vectors of media activism need to be rethought to remain contemporary: their conceptual functionality as implicitly coded governmental trajectories is as important as their security features and distributed architecture, described as trustworthy communication technologies. Like protocols for the web browser, the blockchain is a networked layer technology governed by protocols, which structure processes and thus governs immanently (Galloway 2004). Its protocological design inherits, on a conceptual level, socio-cultural imaginaries. These point towards a new regime of automated rights control and value administration before anything else.

Because blockchain technologies are about to establish a new way to govern ownership and use regimes of digital and non-digital objects, one part of this text starts a discussion on digitally mediated property, ownership and use regimes, since media activism needs to find new grounds within this emerging regime too. Since blockchain technologies can be applied to various ends, some classical use cases for media activism, such as censorship resilience or secured communication tools, are being developed too. But these I touch on only briefly, as these are mostly coding projects that take the blockchain as a tool to solve established problems better in a pure technical sense.

'Native' blockchain media activism is developing too. In the current main development area of blockchains – finance – some media activism has emerged that utilizes the blockchain to introduce new paradigms of value, inspired by early techno-ecological thinkers such as Félix Guattari. A brief discussion of the Economic Space Agency will serve as an example of media activism that embraces the new layer of the net in order to extend it and get beyond it.

Finally, on a more philosophical tune, blockchain technologies can be understood as a sedimented hedge against the possible and the event, two core concepts for political change. Here, blockchains are supplementing other political technologies of pre-emption that calculate the future in order to close its possibilities. For media activism, such machine capture of history becomes more and more of a central theme to resonate with, as claims for social justice have been on its political agenda from the start.

I begin with an introduction into basic technical concepts and processes of the blockchain, its different historical types, followed by a problematization of its central features like decentralization or transparency.

The core concepts of blockchain technologies

At the core of blockchain technologies are two technical developments: distributed computing and asymmetric encryption. Both are not new and can be traced back to the 1970s. A first discussion of privacy in online payments dates back to 1982 (Chaum 1982), but the integration of these technical elements on the level of one protocol only happened recently with Bitcoin in 2008 (Nakamoto 2008). To understand blockchain technologies, the metaphor of a decentralized ledger is helpful and often used, but has its limits, as we will see.

A block in the blockchain contains a bundle of transactions, like records in a ledger, and each block is linked sequentially so that the blockchain has a chronological order that expresses a sovereign time-stamping regime. The size of each block determines the blockchain's capacities: large blocks containing many transactions make each transaction cheaper, since the computational work to mine a block is being incentivized by the fees each transaction costs. These early design decisions have severe consequences for the later operationality of the blockchain concerned. For instance, Bitcoin's initial design now shows that it implemented blocks too small for the many transactions waiting to be computed. Blockchains like Bitcoin are called permissionless, because no agent taking part in mining (i.e. solving the cryptographic puzzle to add a new block to the last one of the chain) can exclude anyone else from doing the same. These blockchains are transparently distributed ledgers based on asymmetric cryptography, whose puzzle solving is based on the principle 'the winner takes it all'. Such a principle is highly competitive and only agents with huge resources in specialized computation powers have a considerable chance to win the race. This leads to a recentralization of the blockchain to computationally powerful parties. It must be noted that not all blockchains follow this line. Litecoin, for instance, was designed to prevent this hashrate race to some extent (https://litecoin.com).

Once the ledger is updated with a new block containing current transactions, agents (full nodes in the network) holding a copy of the blockchain either verify or falsify computationally this addition. A block that is verified by a protocologically designated number of agents becomes a permanent item in the chain, impossible to be removed or tampered with, since this would falsify all past computations of the blockchain, including the necessity to tamper with the majority of the distributed copies of the ledger. This is seen as one of the blockchain's main security features from which all kind of imaginaries are expressed, such as the end of corruption or tampering in general.

The ecosystem of blockchains is growing tremendously fast. First generation blockchains, like Bitcoin, remain an important proof of concept for future developments, and its existing mining infrastructure offers various possibilities for experimentation. Bitcoin's function as a currency is what is commonly only known about it. Its mysterious libertarian inventor, going under the pseudonym Satoshi Nakamoto, aimed at a currency that is not linked to identification (although it is not anonymous) and that is beyond third-party, intermediary control, as it works peer to peer (Nakamoto 2008). This has paved the way for Bitcoin's reception as a drug market and money laundering currency with considerable effects on these trades.

While these first generation blockchains remain to be fully explored, a second generation has emerged, and is already operational, that adds another layer of functionality: 'smart contracts'. Smart contracts, for instance in the Ethereum network (https://www.ethereum.org/), are in their most basic conception the automated execution of one or many transactions from one party to another in a blockchain, defined by rules and conditions to apply that translate the (imagined) contract into Turing complete programming terms. A simple way to look at it is the programming routine, if then, a condition is met, triggering the execution of a difference. A loan is taken and has to be paid back on conditions that are defined in a 'contract' stating such decision trees. Under the blockchain regime, this can be fully automated, securing the profits for the loan giver.

There is no practical limit to nesting such contracts within other contracts. It is reasonable to expect the emergence of a very complex contract execution system, comparable with finance products like derivatives, albeit fully automated and immune to external factors. The chaining or bundling of smart contracts today is usually called a Distributed Autonomous Organisation (DAO), but it remains to be seen if this will have been a mere proposal and if other names and concepts evolve (Jaya Klara Brekke provides a good resource on blockchains from a less technical perspective: http://distributingchains.info).

Since the execution of a smart contract is guaranteed, the future after the contract becomes a calculable present and thus executable, paving the way for a new contract working on the present future captured. Smart contracts, in other words, naturally trigger more smart contracts by setting up in the present executable loops from a captured future. From this perspective, they are an immunization strategy against risks inherent in a society based on contracts.

Smart contracts, at least conceptually, are of pure immanence, since all relevant conditions need to be defined within the code before its execution. As such, they run the risk of becoming detached from the chaotic unfoldings of the real. But since they are automatically executed, they nonetheless operate in this real they know nothing about, having considerable impact on this unknown real. This grants them *ontopowers*, to borrow a term from Brian Massumi (2015).

Decentralization, transparency and smart contracts as ideological concepts

All blockchain talk is highly induced with ideologies of decentralization and transparency, and packed with promises of a new distribution of powers and integrity. Bitcoin's imaginative powers rest on these vectors to large extents. I will problematize these ideologies briefly.

The couple centralization–decentralization almost automatically invokes a long history of struggles of different kinds: for instance, the centralized state and its centralized administration as a loss of agency for individuals. Neoliberalism was highly successful in using the phantom of a monstrous state administration to call, in the name of the free entrepreneur, for a lean state (Foucault 2008), to let the 'natural' play of the market regulate a society. Thus, decentralization as a concept without context carries like a crystal over time this fragment of neoliberalism untouched with it. The now highly centralized powers to mine Bitcoins provide a good example of how decentralization of a technology alone does not alter power relations in favour of a just distribution of powers, but brings agents to power that, following McKenzie Wark (2004), belong to the vectoralist class. This class owns the vectors of communication and designs the way wealth is being distributed in the digital realm, and now, with the blockchain, more and more in the real:

> Their power lies in monopolizing intellectual property – patents, copyrights and trademarks – and the means of reproducing their value – the vectors of communication. The privatization of information becomes the dominant, rather than a subsidiary, aspect of commodified life.
>
> *Wark 2004: 32*

Transparency is another heavily burdened concept whose literal counterpart, opaqueness, almost automatically produces a defensive reaction. But here again, it is crucial to see the wider societal implications of transparency: while state and companies should be as transparent as possible to citizens and customers, the latter two should not. Blockchain technologies, like Bitcoin, are absolutely transparent and it is possible to follow each and every single transaction ever transmitted on the network. To benefit from this transparency, accumulated knowledge of different specialized fields needs to be brought together, while for common people the blockchain remains garbled non-information. The benefits of transparency are reserved for members of the vectoralist class, those who have the knowledge and capacities to analyze the blockchain and operationalize this knowledge in their favour.

In the case of smart contracts, the fog gets much thicker. First of all, a contract hinges on the contracting parties trusting each other to the degree that the terms of the contract can be effective. To establish contracts as code executed by machines does not bring contracts to this new level, but brings executed code to the level of contracts, and hereby the very nature of the contracting media changes (for a comparison of governance in blockchain technologies and social contract theories, see Reijers *et al.* 2016; for a preliminary legal discussion of smart contracts, see Kõlvart *et al.* 2016 and Künnapas *et al.* 2016).

To engage with the notion of 'smart contracts', I propose an ontological angle. The two components of smart contracts, the blockchain and the scripts executing on conditions stated therein, make a difference in the real on an ontological level. Since the blockchain administrates value and rights by way of a digital anchor of real world processes that in the last instance hinge on finite human time, it interferes beyond the symbolic with what is called reality. The blockchain integrates and translates physical real world (micro) entities and processes into computable problems. It closes the gap between the symbolic and the real. A smart contract then is a machinic execution for the modulation of, for instance, ownership – whether ownership over digital goods or real-world entities, a distinction that becomes blurred by the blockchain. Smart contracts, executed by machines, are, in the end, governing human bodies as they tap their time and regulate their agency.

These wider implications of smart contracts can be made intelligible in the case of emerging regimes of modulated ownership and use regimes of commodities. What is at stake for media and technology activism can be demonstrated drastically through these scenarios.

Modulation of ownership and use regimes in the era of blockchains

Blockchains answer a problem that transforms all individual addressability from the ground, or better, they for the first time unfold it to the level of a permanent control. But it is important to give some historical background about the establishment of our liberal society and what tricks were used to divide it into different classes.

Michel Foucault, in his 1972–1973 lectures on the punitive society, analyzed the establishment of the bourgeois morality as a modulation of laws in the fields of ownership and property. He identified a betrayal at work, as property owners and owners of the means of production, once they had violently established their property regimes via a theft (such as the theft of the commons and their transformation into private property), instrumentalized theft as a core element of their penalty system. Thus, he brings together the bourgeois betrayal on the possibility of theft as a method to govern the labour force that owned nothing but their labour time (Foucault 2015).

Today, the triad *property, betrayal* and *theft* extends its problematic beyond the physical distribution of goods into an area that until recently kept the quality of ownership and use in a permanent state of artificiality. The digital realm requires a quasi-counter-intuitive mental operation of insight into the problem of theft, because the question of ownership and use here decouples itself from the concrete good. A digital good, whose exemplary identity is not related to production or consumption, challenges a moral modulating law system, which differentiates its own operations of betrayal positively, as Foucault (2015: 175–200) remarked, by modulating theft negatively. The relation between an excess of goods here and their lack somewhere else, had up until now found its most pressing problematic in the digital realm, where the political concept of scarcity is unknown: whereas rights violations have been a catalyst for the dissemination of the internet within large parts of the populations by way of illegal downloading, and as such has been a welcomed aspect in the establishment of a networked society, in the long run they are too problematic and care intensive for the current order of property and ownership. Digital goods lack exemplary identity and thus digital stolen goods require a different set of identity operations; otherwise they are not stolen, because stealing conceptually includes loss for the previous owner. Digital commodities in data formats can be called ontologically queer, neither here nor there, but dissolved in distribution. As such, they are damaged commodities, but not compromised as a product. Until now, the anonymous mass practice of unlawful (re-)distribution of digital goods profited from the fact that digital products are non-identifiable. The non-identity of the commodity as a produced single item and its unlimited distribution did not match the criteria established prior to the physical commodity.

The blockchain reworks these mismatches on the level of the condition of the commodity itself. Digital artefacts that have been made discriminable and identifiable by a cryptographic time-stamp of existence in a blockchain re-adjust the bourgeois order of betrayal and theft in favour of the bourgeois betrayal. By discriminating formerly non-discriminable data, a registration of digital objects is introduced that at the same establishes a new regime of control. With the introduction of the concept of digital existence a new parametric modulation of its ontological and epistemological status has become operative. For instance, in this set-up stolen digital goods would lose their functionality since their legal status is negative.

Within this trajectory, the use or consumption of a commodity is bound to conditions that do not have to be defined outside of the commodity, in a contract stating the acquisition and with it, the rights to use it, but they move, so to say, into the interior of a commodity through control over its functionality. The blockchain is the trusted ledger from which the conditions of use are defined and unlocked. With its *object orientation*, the blockchain can lock a stolen good from a distance and render it (data) trash. 'Smart' in this context signifies an encroachment of exterior control beyond the acquisition of the commodity – into the time of its use. This resonates with the so-called 'sharing economy', which is aiming exclusively at a regime of use values – a substitution of use value with abstract value in Marxian terms.

Such an 'acquisition until revocation' or 'acquisition under limited conditions' establishes an operational extension of the initial bourgeois betrayal on property, as described by Foucault, into the time of consumption and eliminates the possibility of theft by non-legally acquiring parties.

It is this basic operation of use-control that renders (digital) objects insusceptible to theft and illegal uses. By way of a historical entanglement of two fundamental axioms of the bourgeois order – negatively the impossibility of distinguishing instances of digital objects and positively the masking of their historicity through the commodity form – that the question of ownership 'retreats' into the object itself via its hashed anchors in the blockchain and reveals an ontological status. Up until now it was an attribute of things ('my car'), which in case of doubt had to be settled legally (proven by documents exterior to it, like a receipt). *Blockchain technologies transfer proof of ownership and rights into a quality of the object itself.* We can expect modulated use regimes controlling how, when, by whom, how often, where, etc. objects are usable.

This described evolutionary path of a technologically controlled rights regime for objects, as the blockchain signals it, and which has its physical technological counterpart in the so-called internet of things, contains management and logistics strategies which aim at an automated administration of things by distance. The profit potentials are enormous. Think tanks and policy bodies are about to adjust the bourgeois operating system to these new captures of profit. The blockchain, from this perspective, reterritorializes a thrust of the digital that before contained some deviant and subversive trajectories. It secures the order of bourgeois property and ownership, and at the same time enhances it with new modulations of control.

The relation of betrayal and theft, once forcefully established by the bourgeois classes to invent and sustain ownership over means of production against the labour force, 'objectifies' as it materializes in the commodity itself. This happens parallel to a ubiquitous, individual addressability and individual surveillance through mobile networked devices as the default condition of sociality that offer the blockchain's existential modulations a ubiquitous interface.

Royalty payments, for instance, could be executed automatically via the blockchain. There is nothing wrong with royalty payments, only that they mutated into a capture mechanism for the music and film industry. And there is no reason to believe that blockchain technology will change that. Thus, blockchains should be expected to become enforcers of the existing highly problematic and unjust ownership regimes instead of grand power relations shifters.

Technically, as mentioned above, most of this is to do with hashes. Hashes are mappings of data objects. They themselves do not tell anything about the object. They are used in this context as the digital anchor of this property and rights regime to modulate access and use. Hashes of objects, ownership and terms of use in a blockchain identify uniquely each copy or instance of an object. By reproducing the hash via access to the hashed object, and checking it against the time-stamped hash in the blockchain, a proof of existence and identity is established. This is the basic mechanism referred to as 'proof of existence' in the blockchain idiom. It can be applied to all sorts of data, objects or processes. It must be noted that such blockchain applications are still in very early development and includes permissioned systems, excluding third parties from access to the complete blockchain, as it is mostly commerce and industry investing in it.

Possible classic media activism use cases

This detailed introduction into the scenarios and expectable realities of what blockchain technologies are aiming at within current societies was meant to show that blockchain technology is a powerful functional shortcut between legal regimes, bourgeois morality and physical and digital objects. For media activism interested in social justice, these programmes of self-governed objects pose complex new problems. For instance, in the field of so-called media and software piracy: what is left, once non-legal downloads of media items cannot bring the objects to display (in case of films) because no equivalent hash can be produced to unlock it? For the huge majority of the global population, this equates to an exclusion from access to culture.

Media activism in the age of the blockchain is confronted with old problems anew. This time, the commodities themselves pose them, not rather abstract moral and law regimes, whose enforcement was hindered by the dangers of an excess of costs. One can only speculate that media activism in the age of the blockchain will have to find new vectors and agency. Maybe this will be the advent of the hegemony of licenses like the creative commons, or viral licenses like the GNU software license, because once access to blockchain enforced objects is controlled in detail on the base of each access, the property regime might itself mutate into something else. In its current incarnation, it hinges on the impossibility of its enforcement down to each use case.

Finally, the blockchain depends on complex networks, on electricity and on a ubiquitous distribution of networked devices. This makes it, like the old internet, susceptible to attacks and outages. The blockchain thus adds a layer to objects that is very much dependent on remote control. Governing from a distance, as Foucault called it, acquires a new meaning when it extends into self-governing objects.

Media activism from within the blockchain: the ECSA

Since blockchain technologies are about to become a key technology for the government of a large variety of societal processes and objects, media activism might have to embrace it to some extent in order to make it history. Beyond the foreseeable 'applications for the good', like censorship resistance (tempering with contents changes hashes of the documents, causing a mismatch with the equivalent hashes registered in the blockchain), media activism after the introduction of the 'internet of value' might have to change its perspective and become a value operation itself, embracing a slogan by Johan Sjerpstra that the best way to rob a bank is to design a currency.

Such an outstanding example of blockchain activism is the Economic Space Agency (ECSA), whose project attacks the vectors of money from within. The ECSA has studied the problem of financial products, most importantly derivatives, and came to the conclusion that abstraction, the main operation inherent to derivative finance products, can and should be exploited for the social good. 'Abstraction without exploitation' is the motto, as one of their collaborators, Érik Bordeleau, explained to me in a personal talk.

Inspired by Félix Guattari's discussion of different value systems in his *Three Ecologies*, the ECSA is interested in all kinds of value systems beyond money and to integrate them within an ecology of blockchain based entities. Guattari in 1989 already argued that:

> the question becomes one of how to encourage the organization of individual and collective ventures, and how to direct them towards an ecology of resingularization. ... On this basis we must if not oppose, at least superimpose instruments of valorization founded on existential productions that cannot be determined simply in terms of abstract labor-time or by an expected capitalist profit.

Guattari 2014: 44; and see Massumi 2017

The attack vector of the ECSA aims at an integration of heterogeneous, qualitative values next to the general equivalence dictate, by producing an economic ecology that enables relations between entities whose interests go far beyond the general equivalence axiom. The ECSA has identified the question of tokens as one of the fields of experiments for media activism after the blockchain: as 'programmable money', tokens define the nature and governance of economic spaces, in addition to defining stakeholdership. But beyond the renewal of venture forms, the ECSA is about 'creating emergent relational fields that provide us protection from the barbarity of neoliberal economy. New disjunctive collectivities that allow for the production of surplus value of life away from the non-necessary neo-Darwinist jungle' (Bordeleau). To capture all kinds of values on all kinds of terms, to use economic spaces for different social self-expressions and discourses: 're-inventing finance as a collective practice of crafting futures at the end of the economy as we used to know it,' as Bordeleau explains in a personal conversation.

Since the ECSA's programmatic is fuelled by a diversity of speculative philosophical thought, such as relationality and affect, but at the same time by a true investment in coding the final generation of blockchain technology as an ecology of abstractions for the social good, the matter is much more complex than this little description I can give here can cover. Blockchain technologies and the question of value need to be rethought and brought into new resonances in order to not lose track of one of the primary current developments in finance and banking. Econauts, the personae that navigate such futuristic borderspaces of finance, will have to embark in large numbers and bring back intensive images of their findings to make this ecology of economic spaces a reality.

Code execution against the possible and the open

The ECSA is considering abstractions from the real inherent in derivatives and their execution in blockchains as a prospect for social justice. Within less inspired approaches, the emerging control regime of a digital modulation of the real entails further important aspects for media activism: just as smart contracts capture the future into programmable instructions, the blockchain's inherent time regime is flat and prescriptive. Its control capacities extend into the future, which in turn becomes a mere parameter of computational operations.

Media activism, on the other hand, has had its best moments when it managed to effect real world processes, such as political uprisings, street protests and, in more abstract terms, when it contained and delivered seeds of the possible, or at least amplified those seeds in the minds and actions of people.

In political terms, the possible is the other of the predicted. The possible is, as Louise Amoore (2013) has convincingly shown, what poses a risk to the established orders such that considerable efforts and energies are mobilized to turn it into the predicted. A basic example of this is the policing of activists or the containment of masses. The translation of the possible into the predictable today has remained a key concern of governmental programmes, extending into the minds of the people to work on their subjectivities, as Foucault (2007, 2008) has analyzed in his lectures on governmentality.

What the blockchain adds to this translation of the possible into the predictable is its sedimentation into technologies of government on a day-to-day basis in micro scales. The powers of a multitude of blockchains are not only performative and prescriptive on the level of single objects and subjects, but at the same time on a time regime that contains and structures these objects and to some extents, subjects. By prescribing a chronicle time line against an open future of possibilities, blockchains aim at becoming a technology of structuration against events, a hedging technology against risks.

Concluding remarks: governing from a distance as techno-environmentality

The emerging techno-environmental control regimes, of which blockchains, the internet of things and ubiquitous networking are technical elements that bring governing from a distance to a new evolutionary step, need to find fallouts in media activism. While hacking and DIY techno-cultures have increased and are playful grounds for digital literacy, on policy and institutional levels, not much resistance against this new form of value capture can be expected. The prevailing neoliberal dogma to let the market decide on the fate of societies embraces new ways of capture and control in order to expand the profit regime further and tap into new sources of wealth. Media activism aiming at social justice will have to study and analyze these new paradigms in order to transverse them. Blockchain technologies are closing important leaks that before could be used for tactical media activism, like the re-distribution of music and films, to name just the boldest one. The industries' interests in closed value capture systems have come considerably closer to reality with blockchain based value and rights management. To quote, once again, Bordeleau, one of the Econauts of the Economic Space Agency: 'we have to jump in, in order to jump out.' I agree that now there is still time to fiddle with the control order yet to come. Today, media activism, this goes almost without saying, is technology activism.

References

Amoore, L. (2013) *The Politics of Possibility: Risk and Security beyond Probability*. Durham, NC: Duke University Press.

Chaum, D. (1982) 'Blind Signatures for Untraceable Payments', *Advances in Cryptology Proceedings of Crypto*, vol. 82, no. 3, pp. 199–203.

ConsenSys Media (2017) 'Let's Build a New Internet', https://media.consensys.net/lets-build-a-new-internet-4d897def3f66, accessed 29 May 2017.

Foucault, M. (2007) *Security, Territory, Population: Lectures at the Collège de France, 1977–78*. Basingstoke, UK: Palgrave Macmillan.

Foucault, M. (2008) *The Birth of Biopolitics: Lectures at the Collège de France, 1978–79*. Basingstoke, UK: Palgrave Macmillan.

Foucault, M. (2015) *The Punitive Society: Lectures at the Collège de France 1972–1973*. Basingstoke, UK: Palgrave Macmillan.

Galloway, A. R. (2004) *Protocol: How Control Exists after Decentralization*. Cambridge, MA: MIT Press.

Guattari, F. (2014) *The Three Ecologies*. London: Bloomsbury Academic.

Kõlvart, M., Poola, M. and Rull, A. (2016) 'Smart Contracts', in T. Kerikmäe and A. Rull (eds) *The Future of Law and eTechnologies*. Cham, Switzerland: Springer International Publishing, pp. 133–47.

Künnapas, T. (2016) 'From Bitcoin to Smart Contracts: Legal Revolution or Evolution from the Perspective of de Lege Ferenda?', in T. Kerikmäe and A. Rull (eds) *The Future of Law and eTechnologies*. Cham, Switzerland: Springer International Publishing, pp. 111–31.

Massumi, B. (2015) *Ontopower: War, Powers, and the State of Perception*. Durham, NC: Duke University Press.

Massumi, B. (2017) 'Virtual Ecology and the Question of Value', in E. Hörl and J. Burton (eds) *General Ecology: The New Ecological Paradigm*. London: Bloomsbury Academic, pp. 345–73.

Nakamoto, S. (2008) 'Bitcoin: A Peer-to-Peer Electronic Cash System', http://bitcoin.org/bitcoin.pdf, accessed 14 January 2017.

Reijers, W., O'Brolcháin, F. and Haynes, P. (2016) 'Governance in Blockchain Technologies & Social Contract Theories', *Ledger*, vol. 1, no. 1, pp. 134–51.

Wark, M. (2004) *A Hacker Manifesto*. Cambridge, MA: Harvard University Press.

40

'DEAR MR. NEO-NAZI, CAN YOU PLEASE GIVE ME YOUR INFORMED CONSENT SO THAT I CAN QUOTE YOUR FASCIST TWEET?'

Questions of social media research ethics in online ideology critique

Christian Fuchs

1 Introduction

Consider the following tweets posted on 9 November 2016, one day after Donald Trump won the US presidential election:

> "President Trump wants to know if you have any last words Mr Soros?" #RevengeWillBeSweet #WhiteGenocide #RapeJIhad #RWDS #Trump #Trump16 [+ image of a Nazi shooting a Jewish person]
>
> #Trump 卐 The end of #WhiteGenocide in America. #Nazi #SiegHeil
>
> We won! This is a BIG win for the white race as a whole. And we won't stop. We will take back what is ours! #MAGA #WhitePride #14words
>
> Anti-Whites are shitting themselves right now. They do not like whites taking back their country!! #WhitePride #Trump2016
>
> Gonna go kill some niggers, mexicans, and muslims tommorow trump will just pardon me lol cant wait wooo #MAGA

The examples indicate the prevalence of fascist, racist, nationalist ideology in public discussions of Trump's victory. Given that the world economic crisis of 2008 has turned into a political crisis that has brought about the intensification of nationalism, xenophobia, racism and fascism, it is an important task for critical research to study how and why these phenomena exist. Social media is a kind of mirror of what is happening in society. Studying social media content is therefore a good way of studying society. But whenever we conduct social research, ethical issues regarding anonymity, informed consent, and privacy may arise.

Research ethics is a key aspect of social science. Not only is there a general etiquette of publishing, but also ethical questions that arise in the collection of data. The emergence of what some call 'social media' and 'big data' has complicated research ethics. In this contribution, I reflect on research ethics in respect to the study of online ideologies, especially in the context of 'negative' social movements and forms of online expression that are fascist, racist, nationalist, anti-socialist, and anti-Semitic in character.

Doing online research complicates research ethics. So when for example conducting a Critical Discourse Analysis (CDA) of White supremacist content, the question arises whether you have to obtain informed consent for including and analyzing a fascist tweet. Writing an email asking 'Dear Mr. Neo-Nazi, can you please give me your informed consent so that I can quote your fascist tweet?' may not just result in rejection, it could also draw the attention of fascists towards you as a critical researcher and put you in danger.

This chapter deals with the question of how to deal with research ethics in qualitative online research. First, the chapter discusses the limits of established research ethics guidelines (Section 2). Second, it outlines foundations of critical-realist internet research ethics (Section 3). Third, it provides some examples of how to use such a framework (Section 4). Finally, some conclusions are drawn (Section 5).

2 Established research ethics guidelines

An obvious approach of how to deal with questions of research ethics in qualitative online research is to look at established research ethics guidelines provided by academic associations.

The Association of Internet Researchers' ethical recommendations (2012: 6–7) contains a list of questions that one can ask when conducting online research and points out ethical problems that may arise:

> People may operate in public spaces but maintain strong perceptions or expectations of privacy. Or, they may acknowledge that the substance of their communication is public, but that the specific context in which it appears implies restrictions on how that information is – or ought to be – used by other parties. Data aggregators or search tools make information accessible to a wider public than what might have been originally intended. … Social, academic, or regulatory delineations of public and private as a clearly recognizable binary no longer holds in everyday practice. … Yet there is considerable evidence that even 'anonymised' datasets that contain enough personal information can result in individuals being identifiable. Scholars and technologists continue to wrestle with how to adequately protect individuals when analysing such datasets. … These are important considerations because they link to the fundamental ethical principle of minimizing harm.

We can find two important points here:

1   In the online world, the boundary between the private and the public realm is messy. The question therefore arises if all Twitter content can be considered public content, as in a newspaper, or if there may also be content that is more private and intended for a limited audience.
2   Anonymization becomes difficult online because data is stored on servers and is searchable. In the case of Twitter, search engines such as backtweets (http://backtweets.com) allows us to search for archived tweets. Anonymity of cited content therefore becomes difficult to ascertain.

But does this mean that any qualitative analysis and quoting from Twitter violates research ethics? Or does one have to attain informed consent for each tweet one uses from others? The AoIR-document points out the complexity of online research ethics, but it does not provide any guidelines on how to actually deal with such questions.

The British Sociological Association (2002: §41) recommends in its *Statement of Ethical Practice* that researchers studying the internet should keep themselves updated on relevant issues:

> Members should take special care when carrying out research via the Internet. Ethical standards for internet research are not well developed as yet. Eliciting informed consent, negotiating access agreements, assessing the boundaries between the public and the private, and ensuring the security of data transmissions are all problematic in Internet research. Members who carry out research online should ensure that they are familiar with ongoing debates on the ethics of Internet research, and might wish to consider erring on the side of caution in making judgements affecting the well-being of online research participants.

This short paragraph certainly does not help an internet researcher in any particular situation in which s/he deals with ethical issues. The International Sociological Association's 2001 *Code of Ethics* argues in respect to informed consent:

> The security, anonymity and privacy of research subjects and informants should be respected rigourously, in both quantitative and qualitative research. The sources of personal information obtained by researchers should be kept confidential, unless the informants have asked or agreed to be cited. Should informants be easily identifiable, researchers should remind them explicitly of the consequences that may follow from the publication of the research data and outcomes. ... The consent of research subjects and informants should be obtained in advance.

The ISA code does not mention the specificities of online research. Anonymity often does not exist online. Obtaining informed content when working with a large online dataset is for the most part practically impossible due to time restrictions. In the online world, the private and the public spheres do not uphold clear boundaries.

The American Sociological Association's (1999) *Code of Ethics* says the following about anonymity and informed consent:

> *11.06 Anonymity of Sources* (a) Sociologists do not disclose in their writings, lectures, or other public media confidential, personally identifiable information concerning their research participants, students, individual or organizational clients, or other recipients of their service which is obtained during the course of their work, unless consent from individuals or their legal representatives has been obtained. (b) When confidential information is used in scientific and professional presentations, sociologists disguise the identity of research participants, students, individual or organizational clients, or other recipients of their service. ... *12.01 Scope of Informed Consent* (a) Sociologists conducting research obtain consent from research participants or their legally authorized representatives (1) when data are collected from research participants through any form of communication, interaction, or intervention; or (2) when behavior of research participants occurs in a private context where an individual can reasonably expect that no observation or reporting is taking place. ... (c) Sociologists may conduct research in

public places or use publicly-available information about individuals (e.g., naturalistic observations in public places, analysis of public records, or archival research) without obtaining consent.

The ASA code does not specifically mention online research. It does not recognize that in online research it is not straightforward to keep cited content anonymous. However, it does makes a good point in remarking that there is a difference in obtaining informed consent in respect to the question of whether communication, interaction and behaviour take place in a private context or in a public place. In relation to social media, this means that one needs to ask which communications are private and which ones are public.

Overall, the discussion shows that established ethics guidelines do not direct much attention to the particularities of online research ethics.

3 Towards critical-realist internet research ethics

There are two extremes in internet research ethics. The one extreme argues that one must obtain informed consent for every piece of data one gathers online. The other argues that what is online is out there and can and should be analyzed without regard to ethical considerations.

Zimmer (2010) discusses the question of whether or not it is ethical to harvest Twitter data without informed consent:

> Yes, setting one's Twitter stream to public does mean that anyone can search for you, follow you, and view your activity. However, there is a reasonable expectation that one's tweet stream will be "practically obscure" within the thousands (if not millions) of tweets similarly publicly viewable. Yes, the subject has consented to making her tweets visible to those who take the time and energy to seek her out, those who have a genuine interest to connect and view her activity through this social network. But she did *not* automatically consent, I argue, to having her tweet stream systematically followed, harvested, archived, and mined by researchers (no matter the positive intent of such research). That is not what is expected when making a Twitter account public, and it is my opinion that researchers should seek consent prior to capturing and using this data.

Some of the people commenting on this blog post heavily disagreed with Zimmer's (2010) perspective:

> It's like a blog. (Originally, Twitter was called "the microblogging service".) You can quote and attribute from blogs, but you can't pretend it's your work … As for someone deciding to analyse me from my tweets and publish the results – well, not much i can do about the analysis
>
> The web is not an environment that supports a reasonable expectation of privacy in public. Unmistakeably not. Nor does twitter as a subculture gesture toward such an expectation. *Once tweeted, a birdsong is gone forever. No deleting or taking back what's been broadcast to the world. If someone seeks privacy, they should seek another method of communication.* TWITTER IS PUBLIC – NO QUESTION ABOUT IT. Tweets (from the public stream) are like to be treated like blogs (microblogs) and webpages – PUBLIC. No consent required for analyzing them, unless of course they are DMs (which are like emails – confidential) or sent to your "followers only". … You tweet because you want to get your message out, and not only to our friends (ever heard of retweets?). This is

VERY different from discussion boards, chat rooms, or even Facebook. … I simply dispute that ANYBODY who tweets (regardless of whether he has read the privacy policy or not) does so under the expectation of privacy or having a "limited" audience (if they want to do that, there is a privacy setting for that). Anybody who tweets sees on a daily basis that others are retweeting their tweets or quoting from their tweets also appear in search engines and on the twitter homepage itself.

The discussion shows that there is a conflict between research ethics fundamentalists and big data positivist. Research ethics fundamentalists tend to say:

You have to attain informed consent for every piece of social media data you gather because we cannot assume automatic consent. Users tend not to read a platform's privacy policies – they may assume that some of their data is private, and they may not agree to their data being used in research. Even if you anonymize the users you quote, many might still be identified in the networked online environment.

There are limits of informed consent. It can censor critical research and cause harm for a researcher conducting critical online research if s/he contacts a user, asking: 'Dear Mr. Misogynist/Nazi/Right-Wing Extremist etc.! I am a social researcher gathering data from Twitter. Can you please give me your informed consent for quoting your violent threat against X?' The researcher may be next in line for being harassed or threatened.

A solution would be to only use aggregated data. But such an approach is biased towards quantitative methods and computational social science. Critical discourse analysis and critical interpretative research thereby become impossible.

Big data positivists tend to say: 'Most social media data is public data. It is like data in a newspaper. I can therefore gather big data without limits. Those talking about privacy want to limit the progress of social science.' This position disregards any engagement with ethics and is biased towards quantification (meaning big data positivism, digital positivism). Zimmer and Proferes (2014) conducted a meta-study of 382 works focusing on Twitter research. Only 4 per cent of the works discussed any ethical aspects. While privacy fetishism is one extreme, another extreme is the complete ignorance of research ethics, a kind of 'anything-goes' attitude towards the question what researchers are allowed to do.

Privacy fetishism holds the danger of censoring and disabling critical research. It can endanger the critical researcher and result in violence directed against him/her by fascists, racists, nationalists, etc. Downright ignoring research ethics is often associated with a positivist approach to online research that focuses on the digital Lasswell formula: who says what online, who do they say it to, how many likes, followers, re-tweets, comments, and friends do they have? The problem of this formula is that it leaves out questions such as the following: how are meanings expressed? What power structures condition the communication? What are the communicator's motivations, interests and experiences? What contradictions does the communication involve?

We need critical-realist digital media research guidelines that go beyond research ethics fundamentalism and big data positivism. The approach needs to be realist in the sense that it avoids the two extremes of fundamentalism and positivism. The approach has to both engage with research ethics and enable the conduction of actual online research. The approach is critical in that it takes care to formulate guidelines in such a way as to enable and foster critical online research. By critical online research, we can understand any study that investigates digital media in the context of power structures (Fuchs 2017b).

In February 2016, I was part of a group of 16 scholars that met for a workshop funded by the Economic and Social Research Council (ESRC) at the University of Aberdeen. The task was that we create social media research ethics guidelines. The group consisted of a diverse range of scholars taking different perspectives on research ethics. Overall, the group managed to formulate some guidelines for a critical-realist research ethics framework (Townsend *et al.* 2016).

As one of the starting points for a realist perspective, we found a recommendation in the British Psychological Society's 2009 *Code of Ethics and Conduct* helpful: 'Unless informed consent has been obtained, restrict research based upon observations of public behaviour to those situations in which persons being studied would reasonably expect to be observed by strangers' (BPS 2009: 13). The British Psychological Society's 2013 *Ethics Guidelines for Internet-Mediated Research* applies this principle to online research:

> Where it is reasonable to argue that there is likely no perception and/or expectation of privacy (or where scientific/social value and/or research validity considerations are deemed to justify undisclosed observation), use of research data without gaining valid consent may be justifiable.
>
> *BPS 2013: 7*

Based on this insight, we formulated the following general guideline in the framework *Social Media Research: A Guide to Ethics*:

> The question as to whether to consider social media data as private or public comes down, to some extent, to whether or not the social media user can reasonably expect to be observed by strangers (British Psychological Society 2013; Fuchs forthcoming). Things to consider here are: is the data you wish to access on an open forum or platform (such as on Twitter), or is it located within a closed or private group (e.g. within Facebook) or a closed discussion forum? Is the group or forum password protected? Would platform users expect other visitors to have similar interests or issues to themselves? Does the group have a gatekeeper (or admin) that you could turn to for approval and advice? How have users set up their security settings? Data accessed from open and public online locations such as Twitter present less ethical issues than data which are found in closed or private online spaces. Similarly, data posted by public figures such as politicians, musicians and sportspeople on their public social media pages is less likely to be problematic because this data is intended to reach as wide an audience as possible. If the data you wish to access is held within a group for which you would need to gain membership approval, or if the group is password protected, there are more ethical issues to take into consideration.
>
> *Townsend et al. 2016: 10*

Practically speaking, this means that analyzing private messages and conversations in a closed group of recipients on Twitter requires informed consent. Most tweets, especially those using hashtags, aim at public visibility and therefore do not require informed consent in online research. How should one deal with Twitter users' identifiability? As good practice, one should not mention usernames, except for well-known public persons and institutions. One can instead use a pseudonym. It may still be possible to identify who posted a particular text that the researcher uses, but as this requires additional effort on the part of the person who wants to find out, the researcher does not directly identify the user.

Here is a specific example of how to apply these guidelines:

Context: A researcher conducts a critical discourse analysis of a dataset of tweets using the hashtags #DonaldTrump; #TrumpTrain; #VoteTrump2016; #AlwaysTrump; #MakeAmericaGreatAgain or #Trump2016. These are analysed in order to find out how Trump supporters argue for their candidate on Twitter. Concerns: Can we consider this data public? Are there any issues of sensitivity or risk of harm? Do we need to seek informed consent before quoting these tweets directly?

Solution: Trump supporters use these hashtags in order to reach a broad public and convince other people to vote for Trump. It is therefore reasonable to assume that such tweets have public character: the authors expect and want to be observed by strangers in order to make a political point that they want others to read. The researcher can therefore directly quote such tweets without having to obtain informed consent. It is, however, good practice to delete the user IDs of everyday users, who are not themselves public figures.

Townsend et al. 2016: 15

4 Example cases of critical-realist internet research ethics

I want to outline an example of how I have dealt with research ethics in qualitative online studies that used critical discourse analysis. I will here deliberately abstract from the actual research results and merely focus on the ethical questions.

The study 'Fascism 2.0: Twitter Users' Social Media Memories of Hitler on his 127th Birthday' (Fuchs 2017a) analyzed how Twitter users communicated about Hitler on his 127th birthday. It utilized empirical ideology critique as its method. I used the tool Texifter to obtain all tweets from 20 April 2016 that mentioned any of the following hashtags: #hitler OR #adolfhitler OR #hitlerday OR #1488 OR #AdolfHitlerDay OR #HeilHitler OR #SiegHeil OR #HappyBirthdayAdolf OR #HitlerNation OR #HappyBirthdayHitler OR #HitlersBirthday OR #MakeGermanyGreatAgain OR #WeMissYouHitler. The search resulted in 4,193 tweets that were automatically imported into Discovertext, from where I exported them along with meta-data into a csv file. Using such hashtags on Hitler's birthday clearly aims at creating public attention. We can therefore say that the use of these hashtags in the context of Hitler's birthday constitutes a public space. Informed consent for analyzing such postings is therefore not needed.

The study 'Red Scare 2.0: User-Generated Ideology in the Age of Jeremy Corbyn and Social Media' (Fuchs 2016b) asked: how has Jeremy Corbyn during the Labour Leadership Election been framed in an ideological manner in discourses on Twitter and how have such ideological discourses been challenged? The study stands in the context of the negative framing of Corbyn during and following his run for the Labour Party leadership. With the help of Discovertext, I gathered 32,298 tweets based on the following search query: Corbyn AND anti-Semite OR anti-Semitic OR chaos OR clown OR commy OR communism OR communist OR loony OR Marx OR Marxist OR pinko OR red OR reds OR socialism OR socialist OR Stalin OR Stalinist OR terrorist OR violent OR violence. The data gathering was active for 23 days, from 22 August 2015 (23:25 BST) until 13 September 2015 (12:35 BST). Corbyn was announced as the winner on 12 September 2015 (11:45 BST). It is reasonable to assume that users who tweet about Jeremy Corbyn during times when he is subject to increased public attention are directing their communication at the public. Also in this case, informed consent is therefore not required.

The study entailed a focus on the ten most active and most mentioned pro- and anti-Corbyn users (see Table 40.1). In the analysis, I anonymized individual users who are not well-known public figures and did not anonymize public figures (such as Glenn Greenwald, Rupert Murdoch, David Schneider) and institutions (such as the *Daily Telegraph, Russia Today, The Independent*).

Table 40.1 Most active and most mentioned users in the Corbyn dataset

Users with largest no. of tweets	Frequency	Most mentioned users	Frequency
Redscarebot	322	anonymous2 (UKIP supporter)	723
Mywoodthorpe	241	ggreenwald	689
Ncolewilliams	237	independent	552
houseoftwits	51	davidschneider	324
houseoftwitscon	43	rupertmurdoch	323
gcinews	38	jeremycorbyn	311
anotao_news, anotao_nouvelle	37	Telegraph	284
sunnyherring1	34	RT_com	221
anonymous1 (Corbyn-supporter)	32	edsbrown	215
friedrichhayek	32	uklabour	212

The most active users were Twitter bots (redscarebot, mywoodthorpe). A bot based on an algorithm conducts certain online behaviour. Given that technologies do not maintain ethics, they likewise do not have expectations about privacy. They therefore do not need to be anonymized.

The study 'Racism, Nationalism and Right-Wing Extremism Online: The Austrian Presidential Election 2016 on Facebook' (Fuchs 2016a) stands in the context of the Austrian presidential election 2016 that saw a run-off between the Green party candidate Alexander Van der Bellen and the Freedom Party of Austria's (FPÖ) far-right candidate Norbert Hofer. The paper asks: how did voters of Hofer express their support on Facebook? The FPÖ is the prototype of a European far-right party that bases its ideology on nationalism and xenophobia. Under the leadership of Jörg Haider (1986–2000), it was expanding and growing in popularity. Its current leader is Heinz Christian Strache.

I used Netvizz in order to collect comments on postings related to Hofer's presidential candidacy. I accessed Norbert Hofer and Heinz Christian Strache's Facebook pages on 30 May 2016, and used Netvizz for extracting comments to postings made between 25 and 30 May. Given that the collected comments were posted in the days after the presidential election's second round, it is likely that the dataset contains data that refers to the political differences between Hofer and Van der Bellen. I selected postings by Hofer and Strache that were particularly polarizing. This selection resulted in a total of 15 postings: ten by Strache, five by Hofer. There were a total of 6,755 comments posted as responses to these 15 Facebook postings. So the analyzed dataset consisted of 6,755 items.

The Facebook pages of Norbert Hofer and Heinz Christian Strache are public pages. All postings and comments on these pages are visible to everyone visiting them, not just to those who 'like' them. One does not have to have a Facebook profile to access the two pages, as they can also be viewed without logging into Facebook. All postings and comments are thus visible in public. Furthermore, politicians are public figures. Citizens expect them to be present in the public. This includes that they post in public on social media and offer possibilities for public communication on their profiles. Given the public character of Strache and Hofer's Facebook pages, it is reasonable to assume that someone posting a comment on such a page can expect to be observed by strangers. In such a case, a researcher does not have to obtain informed consent for analyzing and quoting comments. Given that the users are not public figures themselves, but only make public comments when posting on a politician's public Facebook page, I do not mention the usernames in the analysis. Netvizz does not save the usernames and so the collected dataset does not contain any identifiers.

5 Conclusion

Objectively speaking, the far right is fairly effective when it comes to utilizing social media for political communication. Yet if one looks at the body of works published in social movement media studies, one gets the impression that political communication in the internet age is by far dominated by politically progressive, left-wing, social movements. There are comparatively few studies that focus on the internet and far-right politics (Caiani & Kröll 2015). The far right's use of the internet has hardly been studied and is a blind spot in social movement media studies. W. Lance Bennett and Alexandra Segerberg's book *The Logic of Connective Action* (2013) mentions Occupy 70 times, but the Golden Dawn, Jobbik, the National Front, UKIP, Svoboda, Farage, or Le Pen not a single time. The *Encyclopedia of Social Movement Media* (Downing 2011) presents 600 pages of analyses of 'alternative media, citizens' media, community media, counterinformation media, grassroots media, independent media, nano-media, participatory media, social movement media, and underground media' (Downing 2011: xxv). The focus here is on all sorts of progressive and left-wing media, from the likes of the Adbusters Media Foundation to Zapatista media. The editor John Downing (2011: xxvi) admits that 'much less examination of media of extreme right movements occurs in this volume than there might be', but he does not explain why this is the case, why it is problematic, and how it could be changed.

Most social movement researchers like to do feel-good research. They study progressive left-wing movements that they like and are sympathetic towards, consider such studies as a form of solidarity, and tend to simply celebrate how these groups organize and communicate. Such studies make the researchers feel good and politically engaged. But celebratory studies of these movements hardly help us to understand the difficult contradictions that left-wing activism faces in the capitalist world. They neglect analyzing right-wing movements and groups that pose a threat to democracy. And thus this is the blind spot of social movement media studies.

One might now be tempted to argue that far-right groups are not part of social movement studies because they tend to be hierarchic, have a populist leader, and aim at a society that is governed from the top in an authoritarian or even fascist manner. However, such a definitional exclusion overlooks that also left-wing progressive movements often develop certain hierarchies and forms of leadership. Left-wing movements too attempt to define the social as a progressive political concept by arguing that the far right has anti-social political goals. The 'social' in social movements means nothing more than the circumstance that social movements are groups that act collectively in order to change society and move it in a certain direction. It tells us nothing about these groups' political content. The point is that in a contradictory world, social movements are contradictory. They contest how society is developing. Two options that are today possible are the democratic socialist option of participatory democracy and the authoritarian option of fascist barbarism. Social movement studies should focus on studying the diverse range of political movements.

Studying online politics poses ethical challenges in respect to privacy/the public, anonymity and informed consent. Conventional research ethics guidelines often ignore qualitative online research or have little to say on the topic. Conducting studies of online nationalism, racism, xenophobia and fascism poses additional challenges because these phenomena are inherently violent. Debates on internet research ethics face two extremes. On the one side, research ethics fundamentalism obstructs qualitative online research. On the other, big data positivism lacks a critical focus on qualitative dimensions of analysis. The alternative is a critical-realist online research ethics that informs critical studies of digital media.   •

References

American Sociological Association (1999) Code of Ethics and Policies and Procedures of the ASA Committee on Professional Ethics, http://www.asanet.org/sites/default/files/code_of_ethics.pdf, accessed 18 April 2017.

Association of Internet Researchers (2012) Ethical Decision-Making and Internet Research, http://aoir.org/reports/ethics2.pdf, accessed 18 April 2017.

Bennett, W. L. and Segerberg, A. (2013) *The Logic of Connective Action. Digital Media and the Personalization of Contentious Politics.* Cambridge: Cambridge University Press.

British Psychological Society (2009) Code of Ethics and Conduct, http://www.bps.org.uk/system/files/documents/code_of_ethics_and_conduct.pdf, accessed 18 April 2017.

British Psychological Society (2013) Ethics Guidelines for Internet-Mediated Research, http://www.bps.org.uk/system/files/Public%20files/inf206-guidelines-for-internet-mediated-research.pdf, accessed 18 April 2017.

British Sociological Association (2002) Statement of Ethical Practice, https://www.britsoc.co.uk/equality-diversity/statement-of-ethical-practice, accessed 18 April 2017.

Caiani, M. and Kröll, P. (2015) 'The Transnationalization of the Extreme Right and the Use of the Internet', *International Journal of Comparative and Applied Criminal Justice*, vol. 39, no. 4, pp. 331–51.

Downing, J. D. H. (ed.) (2011) *Encyclopedia of Social Movement Media.* Thousand Oaks, CA: Sage.

International Sociological Association (2001) Code of Ethics, http://isa-sociology.org/en/about-isa/code-of-ethics, accessed 18 April 2017.

Fuchs, C. (2016a) 'Racism, Nationalism and Right-Wing Extremism Online: The Austrian Presidential Election 2016 on Facebook', *Momentum Quarterly – Zeitschrift für Sozialen Fortschritt (Journal for Societal Progress)*, vol. 5, no. 3, pp. 172–96.

Fuchs, C. (2016b) 'Red Scare 2.0: User-generated Ideology in the Age of Jeremy Corbyn and Social Media', *Journal of Language and Politics*, vol. 15, no. 4, pp. 369–98.

Fuchs, C. (2017a) 'Fascism 2.0: Twitter users' social media memories of Hitler on his 127th birthday', *Fascism: Journal of Comparative Fascist Studies*, no. 6.

Fuchs, C. (2017b) *Social Media: A Critical Introduction* (second edition). London: Sage.

Townsend, L. *et al.* (2016) Social Media Research: A Guide to Ethics, http://www.gla.ac.uk/media/media_487729_en.pdf, accessed 18 April 2017.

Zimmer, M. (2010) 'Is It Ethical to Harvest Public Twitter Accounts without Consent?', http://www.michaelzimmer.org/2010/02/12/is-it-ethical-to-harvest-public-twitter-accounts-without-consent, accessed 18 April 2017.

Zimmer, M. and Proferes, N. J. (2014) 'A Topology of Twitter Research: Disciplines, Methods, and Ethics', *Aslib Journal of Information Management* vol. 66, no. 3, pp. 250–61.

41

BEYOND 'REPORT, BLOCK, IGNORE'

Informal responses to trolling and harassment on social media

Frances Shaw

Introduction

People experiencing trolling and harassment have limited governance tools available to them (Crawford & Gillespie 2014; Sanfilippo *et al.* 2017: 1809). However, there are also unofficial or informal strategies for combatting trolling and harassment (Jane 2016). This chapter focuses on discourses surrounding tools to combat trolling and harassment on Twitter, drawing on and extending previous work on discursive tactics against harassment in feminist blogs (Shaw 2013) and on the use of screenshots in response to harassment on dating apps and sites (Shaw 2016), as well as other forms of 'feminist digilantism' (Jane 2016).

Platform governance for social networking sites has yet to catch up with the scale of tactics used by harassers (particularly organized groups of harassers) in places like Twitter and Reddit (Gillespie, forthcoming). Twitter in particular has been widely and increasingly criticized for failing to create adequate protections for the safety of users and the facilitation of free and civil discussion (Warzel 2016), despite moves to change this (Benner 2016).

However, rather than the ongoing problems of platform governance, this chapter is primarily concerned with the informal and *ad hoc* strategies used by participants in particular platforms and discussions to deter or respond to trolling and harassment. I focus on a case study of an alternative mode of response – the block list, and the arguments mobilized around these tools, both for and against. This chapter sits in the context of broader research by the author on constructions of speech, political responsibility, listening and safety in digital spaces. In this chapter I will limit my analysis to blocklists as a strategy, and how opponents and proponents discursively support or undermine the legitimacy of these practices.

I consider the practice of developing algorithms to create responsive and dynamic blocklists, as well as the practice of sharing blocklists between people on Twitter as a method for deterring or preventing harassment (see Geiger 2016 for a comprehensive breakdown of broader tactics and views on trolls and trolling, as well as bot-based blocklists in particular). In this piece, I analyze Reddit.com conversations about the use of these tools to draw out what discourses are used to legitimize or delegitimize the use of these tools. It is not within the scope of the chapter to attempt to measure the effectiveness of bot-based or list-sharing blocklisting strategies. Instead, this chapter contributes to research examining *ad hoc* strategies (Jane 2016; Sanfilippo *et al.* 2017) that are developed to handle harassment and trolling in digital spaces, and considers these strategies as in themselves activism and as responses to particular workings of power and governance in digital spaces. It draws out the political claims that are being made through, with, and against these tools and strategies.

Methodology

In providing an account of these tactics and strategies for responding to harassment, I use a feminist approach to event analysis, paying attention to feminist events and *techne*. This mode of analysis is exemplified by the work of Carrie Rentschler (Rentschler & Thrift 2015), Elizabeth Groeneveld (2015) and Samantha Thrift (2012, 2014). Techne refers to 'the technical practices and practical knowledge feminists come to embody as they do feminism with media', and includes 'technological, affective and cultural infrastructures' (Rentschler & Thrift 2015). My approach relies on the analysis of conversations around particular feminist (and other activist) practices and the discourses that circulate around and against these techniques. My analysis assumes that the techniques deployed to deter or cope with harassment are not only technical solutions in response to an identified problem, but also can be understood as activist techniques that in themselves make or enact claims about what is politically acceptable in particular spaces, and on the basis of legitimating claims. However, although I argue that blocklists are activism in themselves, they also have implications for existing discussions of digital ethics, algorithmic accountability and social media speech norms in ways that need further unpacking.

The chapter involves the analysis both of the strategies in their contexts and the legitimizing and delegitimizing discourses that occur around them. First, I briefly describe the use of blocklists. Then I provide some discussion of the contexts of these strategies in their cultural and temporal settings, particularly how they have been responded to in technology media. However, the methodological centrepiece of the chapter is a thematic analysis of selected legitimizing and delegitimizing discussions about these strategies.

Because consent has not been sought to quote participants in this chapter, and participants in comments would be readily re-identifiable from quote searching, I provide a thematic analysis and overview rather than one based on quotes. This piece is not intended to be an ethnographic study of a community, rather an analysis of media texts surrounding an issue, and their responses. A small number of illustrative quotes have been fabricated to prevent re-identification and targeting of individuals (Markham 2012). However, I have chosen to make a distinction between the original post or article (discussed in specific terms, and quoted) and the comments on that post (discussed in aggregate with quotes fabricated if used). This is for two reasons: comments can easily be taken out of context, and spotlighting individual responses may result in consequences for the participants, and second, the original post provides the context and stands alone, and citing these texts makes the threads easily accessible for further analysis and verification of findings.

The movement that blocks together stays together? The discursive contestation of technological solutions to trolling and harassment

This part of the chapter is composed of a thematic analysis of threads discussing the technological response to targeted and organized harassment: unofficial Twitter blocklists (via tools and sites such as BlockTogether [Long 2015] and theblocklist.com) and then the more recent official launch of the feature enabling users to distribute lists to collectively block particular people

(Assar 2015). More recently Twitter has also added additional tools including the capacity to block tweets containing particular keywords or hashtags from view; however, the conversations discussed here occurred prior to the introduction of these new tools. The analysis considers debates among networks of stakeholders in these issues, including on the one hand feminist activist networks and individuals seeking ways to prevent and avoid harassment, and on the other hand groups who perceive themselves as being targeted on ideological grounds through such tools.

In this chapter, these discourses are explored in relation to people involved in conversations surrounding GamerGate. The term 'GamerGate' refers to an ongoing controversy and Twitter hashtag loosely associated with gaming subcultures and gendered politics within them (Burgess & Matamoros-Fernández 2017). GamerGate evolved out of a series of incidents in 2014 that related to the shaming and doxing of game developer Zoe Quinn by a range of people, instigated by her former boyfriend Eron Gjoni, and then subsequently a range of other campaigns, mainly against women who participated in gaming culture and cultural commentary, as well as their supporters (Todd 2015). GamerGate developed through the extensive use of the hashtag by supporters on Twitter. Associated discussion spaces such as /r/KotakuInAction, and /r/AgainstGamerGate were then established as subreddits (topic-based forums) on Reddit.com, and the analysis in this chapter focuses on these.

Recent research has extensively documented the scale and impacts of more or less organized harassment and abuse campaigns (Massanari 2015; Salter 2017). After an intensification of gender-based harassment in 2014–2015, at least partly associated with proponents of GamerGate, a number of lobbying and support organizations were set up by feminist networks, including the Crash Override Network against abuse and harassment, and Randi Lee Harper founded an initiative called Online Abuse Prevention Initiative (OAPI) (Cotton 2015). OAPI aims to create anti-harassment tools for users.

There are a number of tools and apps that have been developed and shared for the purposes of blocking *en masse*. These tools prevent people from 'seeing your tweets and appearing in your notifications, [and] have become an increasingly popular tool to screen out noise, idiocy, and outright harassment' (Auerbach 2015). Many of these tools, and certainly many of the blocklists themselves, have been generated by activists, such as the previously mentioned anti-harassment activist Randi Harper. Harper's tool (GGautoblocker) has been particularly controversial, in part because it functions differently to other blocklists. Rather than collectively generated, user-reported lists, the GGautoblocker script built a list using an algorithm to predict people's affiliations with key figures associated with GamerGate. This meant that rather than responding to specific instances of harassment, it attempted to predict its likelihood based on association. In an interview with OSCON (Open Source Conference), Randi Lee Harper (in Cotton 2015) explained:

> I'm a DevOps engineer at heart, and I tend to think of most things in the terms used in my field. Much of harassment I was receiving that had a detrimental affect on my daily life had to do with volume. When dealing with social interactions, especially those that are negative, humans don't scale. One night, I wrote a script, ggautoblocker, that would help filter out the people that I knew I didn't want to talk to: Gamergate supporters. A lot of people expressed interest in this script, so I posted it online and it became a pretty big success.

The Block Bot was a tool created by Twitter user @oolon. The criteria for inclusion on the list is 'anyone that a blocker defines as block list worthy' (Nolan Brown 2015). *Block Together* is a crowdsourced solution created by Jacob Hoffman-Andrews of the Electronic Frontier

Foundation, responding to strong demand resulting from daily and exhausting experiences of harassment by some Twitter users (Long 2015). It is a web app that people can log in to using Twitter log-in details, which then connects to their Twitter account and blocks users on their behalf. It enables the sharing of blocklists between Twitter users but does not create or maintain its own lists (Auerbach 2015). *Block Together* therefore provides support for other lists.

In June 2015, Twitter likewise enabled a similar tool as a native feature of the site. Users are able to import and export lists of accounts to block (Raymundo 2015). This action was taken as part of a series of actions to increase security and privacy protections on the platform. *Bustle* magazine covered the feature (Siese 2015) and said that it could be used to 'combat the trolls' cooperatively. However, *Wired* magazine (Assar 2015) described the implementation of this feature as 'bafflingly underwhelming', due to the fact that the blocklists can be imported and exported to and from a file but cannot actually be directly shared, in-platform, with other users. Third-party apps and tools like Dropbox, email and USB drives have to be used for the actual transfer (Assar 2015). Assar (2015) asserts that the third-party apps and programs mentioned above remain more robust than Twitter's native function.

Each of these tools has attempted to create effective responses to some of Twitter's most galling issues with targeted and generalized harassment, and each works on a principle of bulk blocking. Beyond the mechanics of the tools themselves, and their potential uses, there have been a number of critical responses in the technological and other digital press (see e.g. Auerbach 2015, Long 2015).

Discourses about blocklists in politically charged discussion settings

The analysis in this section is based on two threads taken from the aforementioned subreddits on Reddit.com, /r/KotakuInAction and /r/AgainstGamerGate. These are spaces that are either associated with harassment and subsequent blocklisting, or as oppositional spaces are associated with the use of blocklisting as a tool against harassment. The threads were chosen by searching for the term *blocklist* on the site Reddit.com as a whole, and then within commonly occurring smaller subreddits in order to have multiple viewpoints represented.

I have chosen to focus on the GamerGate controversy and discourses within the KotakuInAction subreddit (loosely pro-GamerGate) and the AgainstGamerGate subreddit (loosely in opposition to it) because GamerGate – to the extent that affiliation is identifiable – has been the focus of block-listing practices, and the opposition to it has been associated with the use of blocklists. Reddit.com has been chosen because it is one of the sites for contestations and controversies to do with these networks, and is a site for organization and discussion in relation to the phenomenon (Massanari 2015), and also because it provides a source for bounded conversations about these issues.

I should note however that this chapter confines itself to discussing the discursive positional-ity of arguments for and against blocklists within these threads rather than the political analy-sis of GamerGate or its opposition. That is for another paper, and has been comprehensively explored by other scholars immersed in the ambivalences at play in gaming culture (see Foxman & Nieborg 2016 for one such discussion).

However, the politics of the conversations occurring within these two subreddits necessar-ily impacts on and also reflects the way that discursive positions for or against blocklists unfold, although some of these positions will be specific to these forums. I also provide the caveat that the conversations currently available and represented on these threads may not necessarily rep-resent the way the conversation unfolded, because of the possibility of later deletion by modera-tors or participants, as well as the later deletion of accounts. In particular, /r/AgainstGamerGate appears to be carefully moderated, with several deletions apparent in that thread with reasons given (often abusive language).

As well, there is a limitation to this research, in that positions cannot be easily attributed based on participation in particular subreddits. In other words, participants in both groups may not necessarily position themselves as supporters of or opponents of blocklists, and participants in these conversations may not always position themselves truthfully as on one or another side of the argument (to the limited extent that these positions can be neatly described as for or against (a) GamerGate and (b) blocklisting as a practice). See discussions of concern trolls and false flag participation in digital settings (Bishop 2014) for further explication on the issues with assuming online conversations to be representative of the views of a particular group. For example, in my analysis it became apparent that participants with views apparently sympathetic to GamerGate (to the extent that it can be defined as a concrete political position) are more likely to participate in AgainstGamerGate than apparent opponents are to participate in /r/KotakuInAction, the subreddit closely associated with GamerGate. Participation in AgainstGamerGate is therefore more heterogeneous, in spite of the smaller membership, leading to increased levels of debate and exchange. However, the use of 'concern trolling' (feigning concern in order to mount an argument, for example by using the construction 'I support *x*, but am concerned about *y* as a consequence of *x*') and other tactics and strategies are also difficult to uncover in such a shallow analysis, where the political identity, position and sincerity of individual participants cannot often be inferred or assumed.

With those limitations aside, the analysis of these threads serves the purpose of exposing claims in particular about political ethics in relation to tools against harassment. What are the problems discussed in these settings? How are particular tools and actions legitimized through political claims-making, and how are they delegitimized? Discussion will be based on a face-value analysis of the following threads:

Thread 1, from subreddit /r/KotakuInAction. Thread: 'For anyone thinking that ggautoblocker and theblockbot are separate things, READ THIS' (Yurilica 2015). Analysis of original post and 54 comments

The original post points out the differences and similarities between different *ad hoc* blocking tools and resources, stating that GGautoblocker compiled a list based on common follows between prominent GamerGate figures and other accounts, and that it was developed using this or a similar algorithm. TheBlockBot was a separate resource that existed before GamerGate that made use of the GGautoblocker list. The post then explained the reason for GamerGate's concern about the use of blocklists and tools, citing the case of Chris Mancil as an example. 'Chris Mancil, an EA [Games] employee, instantly lost 2500 followers for a simple retweet' (Yurilica 2015). The thread that followed discussed problems with blocking tools from the perspective of participants, and discussed ways to potentially break or beat different blocking tools.

Thread 2, from subreddit /r/AgainstGamerGate. Thread: 'GamerGate and the BlockBot' (SHOW_ME_YOUR_GOATS 2015). Analysis of original post and 206 comments

In this initial post, the OP writes that KotakuInAction is currently discussing 'the blockbot on Twitter'. The OP positions themselves as agnostic on the question of blockbots and blocklists, but says that 'If people don't want to see GG spamming a frequently used hashtag I don't see any issue with blocking them', asking others to explain the argument against their use.

Themes emerging in discussion

Censorship and free speech: A common claim against blocklists is that they constitute censorship. For example, in Thread 1, the original post argues that blocklists create an 'artificial, censoring, blacklisting' environment. They argued that blocklists silence and segregate people along ideological lines. One participant mentioned they were afraid that the tool might be taken up in an official capacity or commercialized for use by companies, leading to widespread silencing. More commonly, opponents to blocklists (particularly those in the US) considered blocklists a potentially illegal attack on freedom of speech.

Libel or abuse in itself: There was speculation in Thread 1 as to whether the inclusion of a particular person on a blocklist constitutes libel, since it may be understood to make a claim that the person has engaged in harassing behaviour, whether or not that is true. One participant argued that blocklists contravene Twitter rules and constitute targeted harassment of people on the list themselves. Related to the worry in the previous theme that the blocklists would be distributed commercially, some worried that a person's inclusion on a blocklist might result in societal discrimination (e.g. for employment).

Dogmatism or epistemic closure: Related to the above, some anti-blocklist participants saw the use of blocklists as evidence of ideological dogmatism or of what they call 'epistemic closure'. Epistemic closure is a concept from epistemology, referring to the way in which a person's capacity to know something is limited by the knowledge they already have. However, in informal (particularly conservative) vernacular it has erroneously come to refer to ideological closed-mindedness (Cohen 2016).

You can't handle the truth: Related to 'epistemic closure', this is an idea that users of blocklists cannot handle dissent, or face up to any challenge of their beliefs. However, it is slightly different from the above in that it is less about ideology than about the belief that the people blocking others are weak or cowardly or unable to defend their ideas.

Too much power: In the original post in Thread 1, the writer claims that 'The BlockBot is the final boss on Twitter'. Implicit in this is the idea that the people who run or facilitate blocking tools have too much power. One participant said that the owner of GGautoblocker deciding who the leaders of GamerGate are is exercising too much power.

No accountability: In relation to GGautoblocker, one interesting claim was that the algorithm was making decisions about who to block, and that therefore no one could be held responsible for those decisions.

Misrepresentations: A handful of participants argued that the claims of blocklist tool creators that the tools are anti-harassment are false, and that blocklists would be more legitimate if they did not misrepresent either their capacity to meaningfully prevent harassment, or that all Twitter users on the blocklist are potential or actual harassers.

Blocklists are capturing innocent people: Some criticisms against blockbots by participants in these threads argue that the blocklists are problematic because they are capturing people who are not engaged in harassment. They argue this is either due to poor management (below), crude algorithms, motivated by censorship, or caused by co-option (below).

Vulnerability to co-option: Ironically, this prospect was raised in Thread 1 as something to aspire to rather than an argument against blocklists, through the discussion of potential ways to co-opt or disrupt blocklists in order to use it against the people who created them. Blocklists may be more or less vulnerable to co-option depending on how they are managed.

Poor algorithms/programming: In Thread 1, referring to GGautoblocker, participants first questioned how it worked, and then argued that it did not work, or worked badly. Criticisms were made of Randi Harper's coding skills.

Non-transparency: Related to above, participants complained that the functioning of blockbots was non-transparent.

Using blocklists is a choice: It is up to an individual to make a decision about whether to use a blocklist or not, and whether to take on any attendant risks of blocking friends or potential allies. This argument frames critics of blocklists as either insulting the intelligence of particular blocklist users, or as aiming to prevent others from making that choice. Some saw the use of blocklists as representing the choice to close oneself off to new ideas, while others saw it as a necessary evil for those experiencing ongoing abuse.

It causes no harm: In multiple threads, commenters argued that it causes a person no actual substantive harm not to be seen by others. However, it does cause a person harm to be exposed to harassment and hate speech.

Not censorship/No right to be heard: Related to the above, participants argued that autoblockers are not censorship, because they do not remove anyone's right to speak, they only make it easier for others not to listen. By the same token, people do not have the right to be heard.

Critics are disingenuous: Questioners argued that critics claim to be against blocklists because they have concerns about ethics, power and responsibility, as well as poor management, but in fact the real reason that they are against blocklists is that they wish to be able to harass others with impunity. One commenter parodied the alarmist positions of blocklist opponents (regarding libel, discrimination, censorship, the potential for false positives) and then suggested they had other reasons to oppose blocklists: 'It's almost like they're motivated by something else!'

Changing the channel: Several media consumption metaphors were used to justify the use of blocklists. Proponents argued that just as they have no obligation to give equal time to all channels available on their television, they have no obligation to listen to a particular set of voices, and therefore the use of blocklists to prevent intrusive discourses and harassment was entirely justified.

Digital private space: In a related metaphor, participants described their Twitter feed as a domestic or private space, and that repeated intrusion into that space through the use of @ replies to troll and harass people is not something that they are obligated to tolerate.

Harassment as preventing participation: This was an argument for blocklists with considerable force, seen as justifying minor issues. These participants said that harassment prevented people from participating in digital life fully, and that therefore the use of blocklists were important in order to make participation manageable. Without blocklists, particular individual or group targets found themselves inundated by threats and spam. Blocklists remove the often intolerable costs of participation for some people. People talked about blocklists enabling them to maintain their sanity, or enabling them to continue participating in discussions on Twitter.

Blocklists are imperfect but necessary for some: Several pro-blocklist participants in Thread 2 argued that blocklists are imperfect tools that have many issues, but help in stemming the tide of abuse and harassment.

Platforms should do more: Both an argument for the use of blocklists in the absence of better governance, and an argument against their existence, participants in Thread 2 argued that blocklists fill a vacuum left by the lack of governance on the part of Twitter.

Conclusion

Ethics loom large in the discussion in multiple ways, particularly in terms of power and responsibility, transparency, risk and harm. However, notably absent is a discussion around the ethical responsibility to prevent harm to those on the receiving end of harassment and violent speech.

This includes the capacity of highly targeted but numerically strong activist groups to use social media to converse without being harassed, but also of marginalized people who may not have the resources and the allies to develop and use tools to prevent that harm. This speaks once more to the broader responsibility of platform developers and for the empowerment of individual users within platform governance. Like Jane (2017) in her recent article on the ethics of feminist digilantism, I argue that blocklisting tools remain necessary where platform governance is not meeting the challenge. The recent capacity to individually filter keywords and phrases is a beginning. Many of the above critiques and responses to blocklisting leave out differences in people's everyday experiences, and therefore their capacity to participate in political discourse without recourse to imperfect tools that allow them to do so relatively unbothered.

Salter (2017) argues that the gendering of technology creates the conditions for the types of abuse seen in these cases, and that 'the particular logics and values instantiated within technology [...] can promote the instrumental attitudes and exploitative relations that naturalise gendered inequalities and drive mass campaigns of online abuse'. The ambivalence (even among potential users) towards technological tools against technological problems is likely to rest on the recognition that the amelioration of abuse requires 'cultural, technological *and* industry responses' (Salter 2017: 2, emphasis mine). These tools are perhaps seen as methods for making the best of a bad situation, and as justified only by the extremity of the problem and the difficulty of acting politically within that reality. Beyond this, I argue for the understanding of blocklisting tools not only as practical activism against targeted harassment and hate speech, but also as technology that speaks. These feminist tools carry with them discursive claims about what is necessary and what is possible in digital culture. While imperfect, blocklists in themselves constitute an argument for full and equal participation, and a challenge to the expectation and experience among the relatively privileged that all people are able to participate fully and equally in digital culture.

References

Assar, V. (2015) 'The Glaring Hole in Twitter's New Shared Blocking Feature', *Wired*, 16 June, https://www.wired.com/2015/06/glaring-hole-twitters-new-shared-blocking-feature, accessed 26 January 2017.

Auerbach, D. (2015) 'Beware the Blocklists', *Slate*, 11 August, http://www.slate.com/articles/technology/bitwise/2015/08/twitter_blocklists_they_can_stop_harassment_and_they_can_create_entirely.html?wpsrc=sh_all_dt_tw_top, accessed 26 January 2017.

Benner, K. (2016) 'Twitter Adds New Ways to Curb Abuse and Hate Speech', *The New York Times*, 15 November, https://www.nytimes.com/2016/11/16/technology/twitter-adds-new-ways-to-curb-abuse-and-hate-speech.html, accessed 26 January 2017.

Bishop, J. (2014) 'Trolling for the Lulz? Using Media Theory to Understand Transgressive Humour and Other Internet Trolling in Online Communities', in J. Bishop (ed.) *Transforming Politics and Policy in the Digital Age.* Hershey, PA: IGI Global, pp. 155–72.

Braithwaite, A. (2016) 'It's About Ethics in Games Journalism? Gamergaters and Geek Masculinity', *Social Media + Society*, vol. 2, no. 4, pp. 1–10.

Burgess, J. and Matamoros-Fernández, A. (2016) 'Mapping Sociocultural Controversies Across Digital Media Platforms: One Week of #gamergate on Twitter, YouTube, and Tumblr', *Communication Research and Practice*, vol. 2, no. 1, pp. 79–96.

Cohen, P. (2016) '"Epistemic Closure?" Those are Fighting Words for Conservatives', *The New York Times*, 3 January, http://www.nytimes.com/2010/04/28/books/28conserv.html, accessed 4 February 2017.

Cotton, P. (2015) 'Troll Repellent: Fighting Online Harassment with Open Source', *Open Source*, 2 July, https://opensource.com/life/15/7/interview-randi-harper-online-abuse-prevention-initiative, accessed 9 January 2017.

Crawford, K. and Gillespie, T. (2016) 'What Is a Flag for? Social Media Reporting Tools and the Vocabulary of Complaint', *New Media & Society*, vol. 18, no. 3, pp. 410–28.

Foxman, M. and Nieborg, D. B. (2016) 'Between a Rock and a Hard Place', *Journal of Games Criticism*, vol. 3, no. 1, pp. 1–27, http://gamescriticism.org/articles/foxmannieborg-3-1, accessed 9 January 2017.

Geiger, R. S. (2016) 'Bot-based Collective Blocklists in Twitter: The Counterpublic Moderation of Harassment in a Networked Public Space', *Information, Communication & Society*, vol. 19, no. 6, pp. 787–803.

Gillespie, T. (2018) 'Governance of and by Platforms', in J. Burgess, A. E. Marwick and T. Poell (eds) *Sage Handbook of Social Media*, London: Sage, pp. 254–78.

Jane, E. A. (2016) 'Online Misogyny and Feminist Digilantism', *Continuum*, vol. 30, no. 3, pp. 284–97.

Jane, E. A. (2017) 'Feminist Digilante Responses to a Slut-shaming on Facebook', *Social Media + Society*, vol. 3, no. 2.

Long, M. (2015) 'Block Together: Why a Tool Built to Stop Harassment is Now Used by ISIS', *Make Use Of*, http://www.makeuseof.com/tag/blocktogether-tool-built-stop-harassment-now-used-isis, accessed 9 January 2017.

Luper, S. (2016) 'Epistemic Closure', in E. N. Zalta (ed.) *The Stanford Encyclopedia of Philosophy* (Spring 2016 editon), https://plato.stanford.edu/archives/spr2016/entries/closure-epistemic, accessed 12 February 2017.

Markham, A. (2012) 'Fabrication as Ethical Practice: Qualitative Inquiry in Ambiguous Internet Contexts', *Information, Communication & Society*, vol. 15, no. 3, pp. 334–53.

Massanari, A. (2015) '#Gamergate and The Fappening: How Reddit's Algorithm, Governance, and Culture Support Toxic Technocultures', *New Media & Society*, vol. 19, no. 3, pp. 329–46.

Nolan Brown, E. (2015) 'Block Bots Automate Epistemic Closure on Twitter. Are You Blocked?', *Reason.com*, 10 April, https://reason.com/blog/2015/04/10/areyoublocked/print, accessed 26 January 2017.

Raymundo, O. (2015) 'Twitter Now Lets You Share Your Block List to get Rid of Multiple Trolls at Once', *Macworld*, 10 June, http://www.macworld.com/article/2933346/twitter-now-lets-you-share-your-block-list-to-get-rid-of-multiple-trolls-at-once.html, accessed 16 January 2017.

Salter, M. (2017) *Crime, Justice and Social Media*. London: Routledge.

Sanfilippo, M. R., Yang, S. and Fichman, P. (2017) 'Managing Online Trolling: From Deviant to Social and Political Trolls', in *Proceedings of the 50th Hawaii International Conference on System Sciences*, Hawaii, pp. 1802–11.

Shaw, F. (2013) 'Still "Searching for Safety Online": Collective Strategies and Discursive Resistance to Trolling and Harassment in a Feminist Network', *Fibreculture Journal*, no. 22, http://twentytwo.fibreculturejournal.org/fcj-157-still-searching-for-safety-online-collective-strategies-and-discursive-resistance-to-trolling-and-harassment-in-a-feminist-network, accessed 14 February 2017.

Shaw, F. (2016) '"Bitch I Said Hi": The Bye Felipe Campaign and Discursive Activism in Mobile Dating Apps', *Social Media + Society*, vol. 2, no. 4, pp. 1–19.

SHOW_ME_YOUR_GOATS (2015) 'GamerGate and the BlockBot', *Reddit.com*, 17 March, https://www.reddit.com/r/AgainstGamerGate/comments/2zeh2m/gamergate_and_the_blockbot, accessed 9 December 2016.

Siese, A. (2015) 'How to Use Twitter's Block List Feature to Combat the Trolls & Help Your Friends Fight Them, Too', *Bustle*, 11 June, https://www.bustle.com/articles/89490-how-to-use-twitters-block-list-feature-to-combat-the-trolls-help-your-friends-fight, accessed 14 December 2016.

Thrift, S. C. (2012) 'Feminist Eventfulness, Boredom and the 1984 Canadian Leadership Debate on Women's Issues', *Feminist Media Studies*, vol. 12, no. 3, pp. 406–21.

Todd, C. (2015) 'COMMENTARY: GamerGate and Resistance to the Diversification of Gaming Culture', *Women's Studies Journal*, vol. 29, no. 1, p. 64.

Wagner, K. (2016) 'Twitter Will Let You Block Tweets with Nasty Words in its Latest Attempt to Combat Abuse', *Recode*, 15 November, http://www.recode.net/2016/11/15/13634504/twitter-safety-abuse-features-block-keywords, accessed 9 December 2017.

Warzel, C. (2016) '"A Honeypot for Assholes": Inside Twitter's 10-Year Failure to Stop Harassment', *Buzzfeed*, 11 August, https://www.buzzfeed.com/charliewarzel/a-honeypot-for-assholes-inside-twitters-10-year-failure-to-s, accessed 9 December 2017.

Yurilica (2015) 'For Anyone Thinking That GGautoblocker and Theblockbot are Separate Things, READ THIS', *Reddit.com*, 16 March, https://www.reddit.com/r/KotakuInAction/comments/2z9l6n/for_anyone_thinking_that_ggautoblocker_and/, accessed 9 December 2017.

42

ORGANIZED NETWORKS IN THE AGE OF PLATFORM CAPITALISM

Geert Lovink and Ned Rossiter

All revolutions are impossible until they happen. Then they become inevitable.

Albie Sachs

Caught in the real-time regime all we can do is speculate about the future value of concepts. Over the past decade we've worked together on many texts producing one concept: organized networks. Prior to examining the challenge of organization, let's examine the ups and downs of the network paradigm. Organizing presupposes a Will to Act. So, before we regress into the 'interpassivity' that dominates our conspiracy age, it's important to address the status of the online self: how can we prevent portraying ourselves as victims of fake news? How will we recover from the Big Data regression? If refusal of social media is no longer an option, how do we master the fear of missing out and take matters into our own hands?

It was in the year 2016 that networks were pushed aside by the overarching term 'platform'. This unnoticed shift, not just in the literature but also in the common language, was reflected in two rather different publications: Benjamin Bratton's grand design theory, *The Stack: On Software and Sovereignty*, and Nick Srnicek's critical essay, *Platform Capitalism*. Both use the network term frequently but no longer give it much significance. (If there's something like Dark Deleuze [Andrew Culp], how long should we wait for Critical Castells?). In the age of Uber, Airbnb, Google, Amazon and Facebook, networks have been downgraded to a secondary organization level, a (local) ecology, only significant for user experience. It no longer matters whether the network as a (visualized) set of correlations has any meaning. Networks can be big or small, distributed or scale-free. As long as their data and potential surplus value can be exploited, everything runs smoothly.

What can we hold up against the nihilist reality, assuming we want to 'come together'? One proposal would be to de-historicize and re-design the media–network–platform triangle into layers – or stacks, if you like. But platforms are not our destiny. Let's sabotage Kevin Kelly's notion of 'the inevitable'. In the same way as media are not merely about communication, networks are more than social media. How can we upset the Hegelian synthesis that is presented to us as the best of all possible worlds? How can we undermine the logic of prediction and pre-emption? What does it take to disrupt the correlation machines?

The much desired 'commons' will not be offered up to us on a plate. We need to get our hands dirty by collectively building up old-school independent infrastructures before we can begin a detox programme that cleaves us from our dependency on 'free' services. How can we collectively design 'commoning' as if it were a popular sport? To develop cooperative alternatives to the data centre logic of Silicon Valley and East Asia's 'smart cities' is not a mystery. What could be today's equivalent of the 'temporary autonomous zone'? If once there was a fear of appropriation, these days there is simply no more time and space where subversion can unfold. What's needed is a new form of shadow, since we can no longer hide in the light of consumer culture and pop aesthetics (Hebdige 1989). Once the 'meme' has been designed, there are enough real-time amplification channels available to spread the message.

Looking back at network cultures

The historical question we need to ask here is why networking became such a big topic in the first place – and what this could teach us, decades later. The trouble may all have started with the introduction of the 'scale-free network'. With the dramatic drop in the prices of hardware, software and connectivity in the early 2000s, it no longer mattered if an ICT start-up catered for a thousand, million or billion users. This 'infra-relativism' led to a culture of global indifference. The question no longer was whether or not these services could be delivered, but who got there first to secure the 'lock-in' in order to establish the necessary monopoly. This is what platforms do: they do not create but eliminate markets. One of the first authors to describe this dotcom logic is Michael Wolff (1998). Wolff describes the venture capital logic as an aristocracy principle: it's all about land, not trade. The start-ups depend on the capital market rather than customer-based income. 'We're an industry without income'. Twenty years later this logic is still in place.

Let's go back in time and ask ourselves how we got here. Take S. Alexander Reed's *Assimilate* (2013), which presents itself as 'a critical history of industrial music'. Reed's account can be used as a mirror, an inspiration to tell the story of the 1990s 'short summer' of network counter-culture, an avant-garde that was all too aware of its own post-1989 inability to make larger claims, let alone be utopian. Reed traces the 'pure darkness' of industrial music back to Italian futurism, Artaud's Theatre of Cruelty and William Burroughs' cut-up techniques. The sound of the squats coming out of the rust belts and deserted inner cities not only expressed the existential anger of a lost post-punk generation, it also produced early digital culture. This self-destructive Reagan/Thatcher era also transfigures into the first generation of personal computers that were used to produce zines and sound samples. Reed tells the story of isolated, self-producing small units. These 'UFOs', as Patrick Codenys of Front 242 calls them, were autonomous nodes with a strong desire to communicate. According to Reed (2013: 110) the isolation in this pre-internet period was

> merely a geographic one: a vital connection exists between early industrial music and the global network established through the Fluxus art movement, its outgrowth of mail art, and the cassette and small press cultures that arose in the late 1970s.

It is this cultural ecology, defined by weak ties of like-minded producers, that would be the ideal context in which the early internet could spread like a wild fire.

Surrounded by the doom and gloom of the neo-liberal order with its permanent austerity, factory closures, the take-over of global finance, environmental disasters (from acid rain to Chernobyl) and mass unemployment, it was both tempting and subversive to embrace 'the new' that the baby-boomer, post-war generation and the powers-to-be had no clue about. Reed (2013: 41) refers to musician La Monte Young's preference of the new over the good:

'The new is a non-directional, non-teleological one, thus differing from the traditionalist and reactionary preconceptions of "progress", which were synonymous with "good".' 'Good' was the realm of priests and politicians, academics, critics and curators, and their conservative judgement had been predictable for years. Chaos and mess was not their preferred structure of feeling. According to the discourse police, the DIY aesthetics of the 'ingenious dilettantes' was neither 'professional' nor 'pop' and was thus ignored. Networks were not good; for certain they were new, and yet invisible for authorities.

Much like the industrial music scene, early cyber-culture was ambivalent about its own democratic imperative. Networking was first and foremost networks-for-us. The claim to provide 'access for all' (the infamous name of the Dutch hackers ISP that would be sold in 1998 to the former national telecom firm KPN) only came later and was an explicit counter-historical anomaly in an era when public utilities were being carved up and privatized. Autonomy became synonymous with an inward-looking worldview one step away from total narcissism. Network tools had to be democratized. The concepts and software were easy to copy and install. The networks themselves were not necessarily open to all. If you got the groove, it was easy to find your way in.

Reed (2011: 40) sums up this position accurately under the term 'techno-ambivalence'.

> In his 1992 collaboration with the band Ministry, Burroughs orders us to "Cut word lines. Cut music lines. Smash the control images. Smash the control machines". This cutting and smashing is by no means a rejection outright of the viral agents of mind control—words, technology and belief—but instead it's a reversal of these agent's powers upon themselves. As both the fragmented recordings to be cut up and as the recording device, machines are necessary to smash the machine, just as the vaccination is achieved through viral exposure.

The ambivalence between technophobe elements (computer as the 1984 control machine) and technophile (liberating production) promises remains unsolved. Take SPK's song *Metal Dance*, in which, according to Reed, the band attempts to have its revolution and dance to it too (in comparison to the now lame and politically correct warning that merely demobilizes collective desire: 'If I Can't Dance, I Don't Want To Be Part of Your Revolution').

In the cultural context of the 1990s, networks were neither inhabited by individuals (users with a 'profile') nor by institutions. They created light and fluid swarms, not homogeneous masses. Consider networks as connectors between pockets of initiatives. Networks were not NGOs, neither did they have much resemblance with the emerging hipster start-ups. If any philosophy could come close in describing them, it would be the rhizomatic dreamscapes of Gilles Deleuze and Félix Guattari (ecstasy), combined with the leather jacket power politics of Michel Foucault (speed). Without exception the 'new media' collectives were products of previous social movements (squatting, feminism, ecology, anti-racism) and cannot be understood outside of that context. Following Adilkno's (1994: 16) definition of 'the movement as the memory of the event', there's a task here to reconstruct the origins of network initiatives. What was their event in the past and what's the event today? It's too easy to say it ought to be located in the offline world. Certainly the social element is key, but not the question of whether the magic moment happened in real life or was mediated through machines. There was no need to make a distinction between the two.

Post-Facebook, the question is no longer about scale. No matter how much we all wish to have our fair share of exposure, networks can only scale down from here. That's when organized networks (or orgnets) come into play. Orgnets are an organizational model that addresses institutional, technical and political realities of the present. Global connectivity reached its moment of entropy sometime in the period after September 11, the ongoing wars in the Middle East, the ubiquity of so-called Web 2.0 and the general consensus that humanity and capitalism have destroyed the planet. Tactics have now shifted to 'meme design' inside a protected environment. Orgnets is an 'out of season' concept because its time has either not yet come, already passed, or never materialized. In retrospect, we could claim that underground cultural networks dealing with industrial music, raves, zines, squatting and independent publishing during the late 1980s and early 1990s had 'orgnet' characteristics: the actors developed strong ties, despite the fact that they did not know each other and had to work across large distances. As today's social media platforms systematically neglect (read: ban) collective networking tools, local and regional organizations still have unknown revolutionary potentials, beyond the existing organizational forms such as the political party and event-based occupations and other forms of protest. For some, their decisive moment will be an image burnout. For others it will be war, permanent stagnation (or permanent vacation, as it was once called). What some fear as 'balkanization' of the net, many will celebrate as a true cultural, organizational and eventually economic empowerment.

After the party

Ultimately, network theory didn't go anywhere. Its normative approach in favour of the distributed network model rendered an entire field-in-the-making irrelevant once rhizomes were replaced by scale-free platforms for the billions. Who still creates networks? Computers are supposed to do that for us. Companies and other authorities visualize and utilize our real existing networks for their purposes. We merely swipe, click and like. What's left are network visualizations that no one seems to be able to read, not even the machines. Maps of network topologies are essentially eye candy, generated for the few networks in need of aesthetic affirmation. From an organizational perspective the network has not delivered either. It may be promising that one-day vagueness and non-commitment might transform into firm, long-term engagement. But who's honestly going to wait for all these hyper-informed social media users that have no clue anymore about the basics of self-organization?

Dean's critique of the network form is interesting in this context. Her plea to return to the (communist) party reads like a Hegelian proposal to overcome dispersed short-term commitment. In *Crowds and Party* she asks how mass protests become an organized activist collective. 'How can acts remain intelligible as acts of a collective subject? How do people prevent their acts from being absorbed back into communicative capitalism?' (Dean 2016: 218). Social media architectures actively prevent autonomous organization (not to mention the obvious techniques of surveillance and aspects of social control). The 'leaderless' Occupy approach was only able to orchestrate one-off protests and failed to set up sustainable grass-roots initiatives. Following in the footsteps of Elias Canetti she states that the 'the crowd wants to endure', and pushes this desire in a particular direction by stating that 'the party provides an apparatus for this endurance' (ibid.: 217).

According to Dean (2016: 218), what's missing in our current understanding is the 'affective infrastructure of the party, its reconfiguration of the crowd unconsciousness into a political form'. The party is presented as 'the bearer of the lessons of the uprising' (ibid.: 155). For Dean (ibid.), 'the party, especially the communist party, operates as a transferential object—a symbol and combination of rituals and processes—for the collective action of the many.' It is all about reconfigurations and reverberations, or overtone. 'The party is tasked with transmitting the event's overtone'. Regrettably this is a stillborn academic exercise as it presumes that Lenin is going to be a role model for the social media masses. Some might adopt his goatee beard as they guzzle down another latte, but that's about the extent of it. Why this self-defeating proposition to return to the party form celebrated by Marxist-Leninism is made, remains unclear. The historical culmination of such an organizational form manifests as a socialist state that is structurally tied to capitalism. So really what's the substantive difference going on here for Dean and her intellectual inspirations and fellow-travellers such as Slavoj Žižek and Alain Badiou? There are no reports included in their various tracts, manifestos and books of attempts to start such a party, or how to join one. This makes the enterprise rather hollow, despite Dean and her cadre advocating the founding of the communist party for a number of years.

We see the challenge elsewhere, earlier in the process. A progressive meme design will have to start from scratch, developed and promoted in a protected yet participatory culture with the aim to beat the alt-right imaginary. Whether these motives, images and role models will be used later on by a party remains to be seen. What also needs to be addressed is Dean's proposed transformative act of becoming a member as a way to ferment desire, to capture the energy of a collective event. Is it true that we all long to sign up and feel nostalgic about 'membership'? There might be regression everywhere today, yet there are no signs for a 'return' to membership organizations. We've all read the statistics of membership decline in unions, sports clubs and religious organizations in the West. The social media ideology does not address us as committed members; we're merely users with a profile. How can we alter and differentiate this dominant form of digital subjectivity?

As Dean rightly observes, the party form is no longer recognized as an affective infrastructure that can address problems. The twenty-first-century political party is precisely not a form of concentration and endurance. The question shouldn't be party or no party. What's on the table is the strategic question regarding what the institutional form of this era will look like (presumably we want to reverse the current social entropy). The problem of Dean's approach is not one of analysis or urgency but one of over-determination. The question 'what is to be done?' should be an open-ended one. Agreed, we need synchronous political socialization, one that can overcome the feeling of being stuck in the lonely social media crowd. Let's see it as a start. The key to the problem lies elsewhere. It is 'social networking' (as it is still called in Italy, rather than social media) that should be transformed. Let's not repeat the mistakes of the 1990s cyber-generation who were utterly unprepared for the take-over by intermediaries such as Google, Amazon and Facebook or, for that matter, Alibaba, Renren and Weibo. We need contradictory platforms that break through the unconscious numbness of smooth interfaces. Let's build a toolkit and hack the attention economy. It should be easy to smash the online self and its boring cult of narcissism. These are the post-network challenges.

New institutional forms as vehicles of transition

If there is a legacy of the twentieth century that might be worth looking into, it will be neither communism or the Party but 'commoning' as a new form of organization. How can we shape the elements that we have in common into an organized form? Attempts initiated by the group around Michel Bauwens and the Peer-to-Peer Foundation or the 'platform cooperativism' of Trebor Scholz and others demonstrate that sustainable networks are viable as long as you stick to the topic and build a movement together with a dedicated group.

We consider the question of organizational form as central to a politics unhinged from the monopoly effects of platform capitalism. How to organize is always a question of media and mediation. Dean shows us the difficulty of supposing that political forms – whether as a party or otherwise – might somehow be distinct from media forms. The practice and concept of the 'people's mic' suggests that even in the seemingly all too human moment of the general assembly, the capacity to amplify and relay sound across space is predicated on the repetition of bodies in machinic ways.

Political subjectivities are conditioned by media of operation. The possibility of digital media technologies and infrastructures constituting new social-political forms is not without its own challenges. British media scholar Couldry (2012: 92–3) asks:

> What are the chances of creating new political *institutions* with sufficient authority to transform regimes of evaluation and challenge the framing of political space? I suggest they are small: if well-established political institutions' possibilities of "sustained performance across events and issues" becomes more difficult, how much more difficult is it to establish new political institutions with the authority required for sustained programmes of radical policy action?

Where Couldry's focus is on how political space is framed and evaluated in ways that command and sustain authority, we find the emphasis on chance here as one beholden to a particular political mindset, however latent that may be.

Chance is the foundation of technocratic game theory. What, for instance, were the chances of the internet in the mid-eighties? Such a question belies a form of neo-conservatism, hidden in statistics. What was the chance of a revolution in Russia, early 1917? Systems implode, and Couldry is obviously not ready for that. Markets crash. As do ruling political institutions. The question is, who's ready to take over? Baudrillard was right: we long for an explosion, and all we got is a lousy implosion, a never-ending stagnation, Japanese style (1980s predictions were correct, Japan is the twenty-first-century role model, but a rather different one from what was predicted).

Who's got a plan? Over the past decade the geopolitical shift to global markets and centres in East Asia has impacted enormously on the economic and social fabric enjoyed in North America and Europe for a few decades following World War II. With new technologies of automation now impacting employment prospects across the world, what happens when 20, 40, 60 per cent of the population is written off, without a job, and sliding into a life of destitution below the poverty line? Democracy as an orchestrated ensemble of the élites falls apart. Even the seeming stability of authoritarian capitalism in countries like China will rapidly struggle to govern populations in conditions of mass crisis.

The creation of new institutions will only happen once the old ones have gone. Foucault's (1972: 59) criticism of revolution was that inevitably the new guard simply end up occupying the warmed-up seats of the old guard:

> In order to be able to fight a State which is more than just a government, the revolutionary movement must possess equivalent politico-military forces and hence must constitute itself as a party, organised internally in the same way as a State apparatus with the same mechanisms of hierarchies and organisation of powers. This consequence is heavy with significance.

While an element of structural determinism lurks within Foucault's response to his Marxist interlocutors, his statement nonetheless invites the question: what is the difference between revolution (as a reproduction of the same) and taking control of the infrastructures of those in power? Neither result in an invention of new institutional forms. When movements organize as a party, the possibility of alternatives is extinguished. This is the brilliance of Foucault's analysis, and a position that Dean reproduces in her valorization of the party as the primary vehicle for political articulation. In both cases, however, there is nowhere left for radical politics within organizational apparatuses of equivalence.

There's a legitimacy crisis for new institutions. The New can reach a crisis status as well, well before it has come to the level of full implementation. The imaginary and real power of existing institutional frameworks so often works against the possibility of new institutional forms arising with the capacity to displace existing powers. In this regard, it is more strategic to consider orgnets as transitional vehicles. They are not the solution, but not the problem either. That much is clear. The proposal and push by ex-minister of finance in Greece's Syriza government, Yanis Varoufakis, to create a pan-European network, DiEM25, is similarly caught within the trap of solutionism. DiEM is not an 'alternative for the European Commission'. That's nonsense. DiEM is neither a pan-European think tank, nor an NGO. If anything it is a networked movement. It creates European, national and local networks. DiEM prepares people, but in the event of an EU collapse DiEM is not going to be less ugly because of it. With 'a view to conjuring up a democratic surge across Europe, a common European identity, an authentic European sovereignty, an internationalist bulwark against both submission to Brussels and hyper-nationalist reaction', the utopianism of DiEM transfers the core tenets of liberal democracy from the sovereign power of nation-states to the populist delusion of networks able to govern populations in scale-free ways. Any organizational entity founded on the values espoused by DiEM is necessarily an entity that traffics in the politics of exclusion, which, like Weber's concept of the modern state, is predicated on a 'monopoly of violence'. DiEM is not in any rush to point out the histories of colonialism that in so many ways condition the world of migration and lifestyles of contemporary Europe. DiEM's common Europe of transparent decision making is not open to barbarians beyond its borders and instead focuses on inner-European inequalities. Varoufakis is not prepared to reconcile this logical endpoint of a post-EU world with networks that function as *de facto* states.

Needless to say, DiEM can be conceived as a transitional vehicle or messenger that might support radical policy reforms within the Brussels lobby scene. But such a status can often enough precipitate an identity crisis, and this is exactly what has happened with DiEM (no matter that it's unwilling to acknowledge this, at least in public). DiEM claims to be a network of movements from below while also functioning much like a political party where meet-ups all too often are assumed as equivalent to (representational) membership. We recall a meeting between DiEM and political party Die Linke (The Left) in September 2016 held at Astra-Kulturhaus, an indie rock venue in Berlin's hip district of Friedrichshain. In between a rush of other appointments, Varoufakis took to the stage with all of the ease and frothy eroticism expected of political rock stars these days (Corbyn and Sanders aside). In his message to comrades, Varoufakis made a point of highlighting a White Paper recently prepared by the DiEM executive (or 'coordinating collective') for tabling in Brussels. Stunning here was the assumption that a document as deadening as the genre of policy recommendations might somehow do the magical work of galvanizing movements into action, let alone sustain political passions. Maybe that can happen inside political party headquarters, but it's highly unlikely amongst social movements. Nor, for that matter, was anyone in Brussels about to lend credibility to a report coming from DiEM.

So, is DiEM25 a movement or party? Or perhaps a new entity altogether? Reporting in *Il Manifesto* on an earlier meeting in Berlin in February 2016 for the launch of the DiEM 2025 manifesto, Marco Bascetta and Sandro Mezzadra (2016) signal the inherent contradiction when an embryonic movement traffics generic notions of democracy that also have to scale to the supra-state level of the EU. As many political theorists and philosophers are wont to say, democracy is an indefinite project, always to be deferred. As an aspiration of a society to come, perhaps the key problem facing DiEM is the confusion it has at the level of organizational form. DiEM is either a movement or a party, yet it cannot help but try and act as both.

This predicament is one shared with Dean, who also imagines a continuum can be stretched from the assemblies to the party form. Podemos and the earlier incarnation of Syriza have perhaps more than others been able to straddle the tension of populist politics caught between the party and the street. But in both cases the movements eventually drift away, returning to their former fragmented sects. The impasse of democracy as an imaginary and desire around which politics is organized might better be put aside for a politics of struggle that focuses instead on other names.

Organizing Next Nature

Let's forget about organized platforms (that's a monstrous contradiction) and bet on a necessary renaissance of the network mode. What role might orgnets play in the core debates around environmental catastrophe that define the increasingly rapid decimation of planetary life as we know it? Can a social-technical mode of doing things in collective ways in the world have any correlation with techno-ecologies populated by robots, automated systems (AI, machine learning, enterprise resource planning software) and extractive machines? The question of organization will never go away. The social can be calculated, mapped, simulated and ultimately eliminated, but the act of organizing itself can never fully be outsourced. No matter how much economy, labour and life are defined by automation and repetition, the machine needs constant maintenance, resources, upgrades, supervision and care. The substrate from which organization emerges – whether this is human, machine, environment or thing – is first and foremost a relation of transformation underscored by material, affective, social and kinetic propensities.

For German media philosopher Erich Hörl, the 'general ecology' of the techno-sphere analyzes the contemporary condition of governance and cybernetic control in a technical world. Hörl (2017: 9) maintains we are in an:

> environmental culture of control that, thanks to the radical environmental distribution of agency by environmental media technologies, ranging from sensorial to algorithmic environments, from bio- to nano- and geotechnologies, renders environmentality visible and prioritizes it like never before.

Yet environmentality understood as a new idiom of control is only visible inasmuch as it manifests on a scale of perceptible transformation. The infrastructural and technical components of environmental media are more often highly secluded and inaccessible data facilities, or computational systems operating in the background of routine transactions, processes and practices. The political question of power goes beyond a philosophical politics of sense, theory and concepts (see Hörl 2017: 5, 14). To attribute a politics to such struggles of thought we would need to identify the institutional and geo-cultural terrains in which conceptual dispute is materialized.

We agree with Hörl that a techno-environmentality paradigm succeeds and displaces the primacy of human agency and bind of reason. There's an embarrassing juvenility that attends the human pretence of control. Though we would sideline the question of politics as a problem for theory ('decision design') and instead ask how environmental media relates to the organization and politics of movements. In terms of a program for orgnets operating within these sort of parameters, one critical question concerns how to organize in ways that are responsive to new infrastructures of distribution and new agents of power? A techno-ecology of robots and automation receives a steady stream of reporting in the mainstream press and tech-magazines. The eradication of jobs is the common narrative across these reports. The displacement of the human as the primary agent of change in the world is thus coincident with the increasing extension of technical environments that manage social and economic life. Why don't we switch our attention instead to architectures of inoperability? One tiny (unknown) disruption and the robot falls silent – that's the new certainty of our age, where 'the "assembly life" [has] replaced the assembly line' (Lotringer 2003: 194).

Another case could be the Next Nature Network, an Amsterdam cultural organization aka non-profit design collective that sets out to draw up scenarios in which the society of adaptation is amplified in ways that suggest new species-beings will unsettle the established order of things. Such a program resonates with Hörl's general ecology. Inquiring into the techno-environments that condition the adaptation of life in an epoch of mass distinction is at the core of the project by the Next Nature Network. Their question of organization is, unlike Hörl, also a social-political one. Among the many 'unlikely futures' that Next Nature conceptualizes in its blog postings, presentations, books and exhibitions, it is their proposal for a radical remake of the (Dutch) ecology movement that interests us most here. How can green activism shed its out-dated, romantic, nineteenth-century version of nature and develop a new understanding of politics that integrates human interventions into a version of nature as a radical design? 'Virtual worlds, printed food, living cities and wild robots; we're so surrounded by technology that it's becoming our next nature. Next Nature Network is *the* international network for anyone interested to join the debate on our future—in which nature and technology are fusing' (https://www.nextnature.net/welcome). Their slogan is: Forward to Nature! Heritage and conservation are deconstructed from a post-human perspective, becoming legacy architectures and systems that condition contemporary transformations. But what's even more interesting about this 'prototyping' of protest is the demand that the 'general ecology' itself should be included in the design of future forms of organizing. The aim of NNN is topical: how to transform a (cultural) organization into a movement, using the network as a vehicle?

What do orgnets mean within such a context? Welcome to the social stack. How can we think of orgnets as the contemporary expression of collective human activity? Can they operate as a transitionary vehicle in this period of techno-ecological consolidation? Should orgnets be seen as organizational forms that facilitate alternative futures, producing unforeseen mixtures of critique and innovation, or are they better placed to help realize the seeming inevitability of a world ruled by machines? The latter is the accelerationist option that celebrates the nihilism of capital accumulation and an anticipatory delirium of the revolutionary event. The former suggests a reformist agenda – a position for us that holds minimal appeal and is all too often beholden to a moral code of progressive politics predicated on identity and exclusion.

In our times of economic stagnation and ideological austerity, orgnets are a model for the hyper-efficient distribution of poverty. Stop sharing, start organizing. The orgnets question is first and foremost a media question regarding the organizational logic of technological forms and instituent practices. This means it lends itself to a critique of control, which at the current conjuncture is emerging and indeed consolidating in the form of platform capitalism. If we focus on the organizational logic of instituent practices, then we need to address the social dimension that creates alternatives to the monopoly effects of platform capitalism. To live a life outside the partitioned walls of platform capitalism and social media we really do have to accept the fact that no one will hand out better solutions on a plate. There is no technological fix. We have become deeply enamoured with the so-called 'free services' of platform capitalism and all too willing to open our data-generating selves to inspection and extraction economies. Sure, one option is to sit it out and wait for the demise of platform capitalism. That will happen. But meanwhile life passes by and models of organizing society and economy remain in the hands of the few (and they usually are nasty by default).

How to instigate a federated culture of networks combined with user-friendly secure communication is, for us, key to the collective design of a general ecology of our techno-spheres. This is not the fantasy of interoperability espoused by logistical media industries and operators jostling like platform capitalists for market control, but rather a loose alliance of strong ties that comes together out of collective desires for autonomous production. Inspiring on this front is the transit-organization work of the Barcelona Initiative of Technological Sovereignty (BITS). Drawing on the history and experience of organizing local councils in southern Europe (particularly in Italy and Spain), BITS brings activists from the movements together with academics and policy makers to reorganize the distribution of services and support within urban settings. Such initiatives actively produce autonomous infrastructures of distribution and have no interest in passively adopting the free solutions dished out by Silicon Valley. Connected to the spread of Right to the City and Rebel City movements (Lefebvre, Harvey), but drawn from much longer histories of self-determination and localized critiques of urban renewal, the strategic question to draw from these meso-political networks is how to design scalability into these local efforts in order to address the politics of distribution. We are not thinking here of scale as in scale-free networks, but rather scale as a technique through which social and political relations are forged to address particular problems that are often very local.

Organization is inseparable from experimentation and design. Platform capitalism demonstrates loud and clear that neither of these are bundled into the 'free' software of service providers. The regressive propositions for a revived party politics are also not going to do the job. Movements are made when passions are not only ignited, but also organized in ways that respond to our media situation.

References

Adilkno (1998) *Media Archive*. Brooklyn, NY: Autonomedia.

Barcelona Initiative for Technological Sovereignty (BITS) (n.d.), https://bits.city, accessed 28 January 2018.

Bascetta, M. and Mezzadra, S. (2016) 'La Costituente di Varoufakis Sociale e non Sovranista', *Il Manifesto*, 9 February. Rough English translation at: https://global.ilmanifesto.it/varoufakis-appeals-for-demo-cratic-awakening, accessed 26 May 2017.

Bratton, B. (2016) *The Stack: On Software and Sovereignty*. Cambridge, MA: MIT Press.

Couldry, N. (2012) *Media, Society, World: Social Theory and Digital Media Practice*. Cambridge: Polity Press.

Culp, A. (2016) *Dark Deleuze*. Minneapolis, MN: University of Minnesota Press.

Dean, J. (2016) *Crowds and Party*. New York: Verso.

Deleuze, G. and Guattari, F. (1987) *A Thousand Plateaus: Capitalism and Schizophrenia*. Trans. B. Massumi. Minneapolis, MN: University of Minnesota Press.

DiEM (2017) DiEM25 Manifesto, https://diem25.org/manifesto-long, accessed 29 May 2017.

Foucault, M. (1972) 'Body/Power', in *Power/Knowledge: Selected Interviews and Other Writings 1972–1977*. Ed. C. Gordon, trans. C. Gordon, L. Marshall, J. Mepham and K. Soper. New York: Pantheon Books.

Harvey, D. (2012) *Rebel Cities: From the Right to the City to the Urban Revolution*. London: Verso.

Hebdige, D. (1989) *Hiding in the Light: On Images and Things*. London: Routledge.

Hörl, E. (2017) 'Introduction to General Ecology', in E. Hörl with J. Burton (eds) *General Ecology: A New Ecological Paradigm*. London: Bloomsbury Academic.

Kelly, K. (2016) *The Inevitable: Understanding the 12 Technological Forces that Will Shape Our Future*. New York: Viking.

Lefebvre, H. (1996) 'The Right to the City', in *Writings on Cities*. Eds. and trans. E. Kofman and E. Lebas. Cambridge, MA: Blackwell Publishers, pp. 147–59.

Lotringer, S. (2003) 'Better than Life', *Artforum International* 41 (April): 194–97, 252–53.

Next Nature Network (n.d.) https://www.nextnature.net, accessed 14 December 2017.

P2P Foundation (n.d.) https://p2pfoundation.net, accessed 14 December 2017.

Reed, S. A. (2013) *Assimilate: A Critical History of Industrial Music*. Oxford: Oxford University Press.

Scholz, T. (2017) *Uberworked and Underpaid: How Workers are Disrupting the Digital Economy*. Cambridge: Polity Press.

Srnicek, N. (2017) *Platform Capitalism*. Cambridge: Polity Press.

Varoufakis, Y. (2016) 'Why We Must Save the EU', *The Guardian*, 5 April 2016, https://www.theguardian.com/world/2016/apr/05/yanis-varoufakis-why-we-must-save-the-eu, accessed 1 May 2016.

Weber, M. (2008) 'Politics as Vocation', in M. Weber, *Complete Writings on Academic and Political Vocations*. Ed. John Dreijmanis, trans. Gordon C. Wells. New York: Agora Publishing, pp. 155–207.

Wolff, M. (1998) *Burn Rate: How I Survived the Gold Rush Years on the Internet*. New York: Simon & Schuster.

INDEX

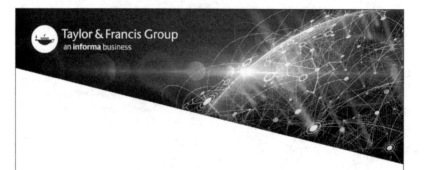